Inuit
Koyukon
Ingalik
Tanana
Kutchin
Hare
Aleut
Tutchone
Dogrib
Inuit
Tlingit
Nahane
Haida
Tsimshian
Slave
Chipewyan
Beaver
Kwakiutl
Shuswap
Sarsi
Nootka
Blackfoot
Cree
Quinault
Kutenai
Assiniboin
Kalapuya
Yakima
Crow
Mandan
Ojibwa
Hupa
Nez Perce
Pomo
Shoshoni
Dakota
Sauk
Miwok
Pawnee
Iowa
Fox
Yokuts
Paiute
Arapaho
Ute
Cheyenne
Illinois
Kiowa
Hopi
Papago
Navajo
Pueblo
Osage
Chickasaw
Tipai-Ipai
Pima
Zuñi
Creek
Choctaw
Comanche
Natchez
Apache
Tonkawa
Timucua

Inuit
Nascapi
Montagnais
Beothuk
Micmac
Algonquin
Abnaki
Huron
Pequot
Mahican
Iroquois
Delaware
Miami
Shawnee
Powhatan
Cherokee

Culture Areas

A CONCISE DICTIONARY OF
INDIAN TRIBES
OF NORTH AMERICA

Culture Areas
SHOWING TRIBAL GROUPS

Arctic
Sub-Arctic
Northwest Coast
Plateau
Plains
Eastern Woodlands
Southeast
Southwest
Great Basin
California

A Concise Dictionary of
Indian Tribes
of North America

A Concise Dictionary of
Indian Tribes
of North America

BARBARA A. LEITCH

REFERENCE PUBLICATIONS, INC.

Published 1979

Library of Congress Cataloging in Publication Data

Leitch, Barbara A.

  A concise dictionary of Indian tribes of North America.

  Includes bibliographies and index.

  1. Indians of North America—Dictionaries and encyclopedias. LePoer, Kendall T. II. Title.

E76.2.L44 970'.004'97 78-21347

ISBN 0-917256-09-3

Library of Congress Catalog Card Number: 78-21347
International Standard Book Number: 0-917256-09-3

Reference Publications, Inc.
218 St. Clair River Drive
Algonac, Michigan 48001

Prefatory Note

The *Concise Dictionary of Indian Tribes of North America* represents the realization of another step in the planned program of Reference Publications to present knowledge on specific ethnic groups in a systematic and accessible form. Too often, in ethnic studies as in other subject areas, over-specialization and specialists' jargon have presented a barrier to the general diffusion of useful knowledge. By the publication of works such as this, we seek to eliminate this barrier.

Research having identified the need for a one-volume work on this subject, a list of Indian tribes was prepared, a standard article format established, and Barbara Leitch engaged, on a "work for hire" basis, to write some of the articles, or all if she wished, within a specified time. At her request, her husband, Kendall T. LePoer, was assigned to do the initial editing.

We wish to thank Joyce Weston for preparing the maps on Language Groups, Culture Groups, and Indian Lands and Communities in the United States, as well as Douglas Holdaway, Tiena Stone-Pfimister, and Pamela Long, who were in varying degrees responsible for the preparation of the regional maps.

The index, prepared by the General Editor, contains about 8,500 entries, and has been made as comprehensive as possible. The intention here is that the index will not only fulfill the usual function of rendering the material accessible, but will also be seminal in character by further arousing the reader's curiosity about the contents, and by stimulating ideas.

We are most gratified to present this publication, and wish to thank all those who have contributed to this result.

KEITH IRVINE
General Editor

JOHN SOMERS
Business Manager

Acknowledgements

Acknowledgements are made to the following for their help:
Dr. Herman J. Viola and the staff of the Smithsonian Institution National Anthropological Archives; the staff of the Prints and Photographs Division of the National Archives; the staff of the Prints and Photographs Division of the Library of Congress; the staff of the Audio-Visual Archives Division of the National Archives; Tom Oxendine and the staff of the Public Information Office of the Bureau of Indian Affairs; Amber Eustus of the Economic Development Administration; Carolyn Maddox of the U.S. Travel Service; the photo library staff of the National Park Service; Robert B. Dickerson, Jr., for help with the Index; and last but not least the reference staff of the Library of Congress.

Special acknowledgements are made to Claudia Faherty, for typing the manuscript.

Contents

CONTENTS

CONTENTS

MAPS

VINE DELORIA, Jr., the distinguished American Indian spokesman, is a member of the Standing Rock Sioux tribe. Currently a professor at the University of Arizona, Tucson, he is the author of several books, including **Custer Died For Your Sins** *(1969),* **God is Red** *(1973), and* **Behind the Trail of Broken Treaties** *(1974). A graduate of Iowa State University, the Lutheran School of Theology in Chicago, and the University of Colorado School of Law in Boulder, Colorado, he has received numerous honors and awards for his work.*

Introduction

Reference works must be accurate and easy to use. In the wealth of materials which represent the fields of human knowledge we need maps if we are to cover the terrain successfully. Scholars often lose sight of this objective and present us with such precise and heavy materials that attempting to discover basic facts becomes a tedious and time-consuming task more suited to the drone than to the active mind.

Indian affairs in all its aspects represents one of the more exotic fields of human knowledge. For several centuries scholars and laypeople have been compiling data on the tribes inhabiting North America and the secondary, tertiary and quaternary sources are now legion. Unless one is well versed in the materials it is almost impossible to find an accurate source that can be used in a variety of situations.

One must plow through hundreds of pages of irrelevant materials in order to piece together simple chronologies and overviews of the subject under consideration. And, for all the data available, mistakes of a fundamental nature are still the order of the day.

In the early 1970s a controversy arose on the Blackfeet Reservation in Montana. Under consideration was the question whether the tribal court had jurisdiction over certain subjects or whether the state court was the proper forum for resolution of the conflicts. The case came before a federal court and both sides presented their arguments. The judge ruled in favor of the Blackfeet on the basis of their treaty which he compared to a Navajo treaty signed in the same year. Experts in the field were puzzled with the decision. The Blackfeet signed a treaty in 1868 but it was never ratified by the United States and it was not the treaty cited by the court as the basis for the decision. The treaty mentioned by the judge was that of the Sioux and Arapaho and among the Sioux *bands* who signed that document were the Blackfeet, a group now comfortably living on the Standing Rock reservation in North Dakota, and occasional enemies of the Montana Blackfeet.

The 1970 census was the first major effort by the United States to achieve an accurate count of tribal membership. On the forms were places for Indians to designate their tribal affiliations and census takers were encouraged to spend an inordinate amount of time with the Indiana data to ensure accuracy. Yet as the preliminary figures on tribal enrollment were compiled, the census showed an amazing number of Twana, a small tribe in western Washington state, living on the east coast, particularly in Maine. The uninitiated would have assumed that this tribe was the only group in American history to be transported east instead of west. A mis-indentification of tribal names had dramatically shifted population figures and had the census takers not stumbled over a concerned scholar they might have made one of the classic mistakes in reporting.

One could multiply these examples ad infinitum. Indian affairs are simply too complex and bulky to fit easily into the layperson's head and it is a gargantuan task to keep thousands of facts on hand which may not be used but once in a decade. Yet there must be a way to preserve, in a form that is easy to reach and use, the basic facts and character-istics of North American Indians.

We believe that this *Concise Dictionary of Indian Tribes of North America* answers a multitude of needs admirably and will prove to be important to readers and users of widely varying backgrounds including federal judges and census takers. Its major value is in its concise descriptions of tribal profiles. The entries are accurate but concise and the reader need not wade through endless pages of description to find embedded there an important fact. The history of each tribe is given briefly so that the reader is not lost in the sequence of events but quickly learns the major events that influenced the lives of the people. Sufficient reference to the religion of the tribe is made so that serious scholars can quickly survey the entries and understand both similarities and differences in tribal religious traditions without becoming overburdened with descriptions of ceremonial detail.

References to language are brief but important for they give an overview of linguistic relationships without confusing the reader about the complexities of language changes and theoretical constructs used by the more specialized scholar. As important in many respects is the inclusion of the geographic locations of the tribes both today and in historical periods. This aspect alone will prove invaluable to people wishing to learn about Indians and to people entering the field professionally who need a quick introduction to Indians in North America.

While each entry is designed to give in capsule form a sketch of the tribe it treats, the net effect of the dictionary is to present an intelligible overview of what we do know about Indians of North America, what their collective history has been, where they are and have been located, and some of the general characteristics which they have mantained as distinct human communities. Any work which gives sufficient data so that readers can devise for themselves in memorable fashion such an overview is critically important. It enables us to understand Indians as people and to see their communities as clusterings of individuals not radically different from those of our own home towns and favorite regions. This human dimension is missing in other works which become so involved in articulating the divergent or exotic aspects of Indian life as to make Indians seem creatures apart—impossible to understand and mysterious to behold.

Although the dictionary is designed to provide a maximum profile of each Indian tribe for the layperson, I suspect it will find its way onto the shelves of people working professionally in the field of Indian affairs. There it will become the secret bible that enables them to speak with authority on a variety of topics and to gain knowledge about the most obscure things. But we should not project that only people professionally involved in Indian matters will use the book. As professional people in other fields come into contact with the expanding area of Indian concerns, the book will provide a welcome source of information that will enable them quickly to orient themselves to the subject at hand. In short, the book promises to provide a service and source of information not presently available and to do it well.

A final word can be added. Short bibliographical references have been added to most entries. These do not, of course, pretend to be definitive. They are designed for the intelligent layperson who seeks further information in a particular tribe. The paucity of references may be seen by some reviewers as a deficiency but I think it is a positive contribution to the field. Too often we find exhaustive bibliographies presenting us with such a choice as to further confuse us. By keeping the bibliographical references short and authoritative, the dictionary enables the reader to enter the world of his favorite choice step by step for he will surely find in the sources cited additional references which can be tracked down. In restricting the bibliography to a few citations, then, we invite the reader to explore the world of the American Indians and do not attempt to impress him with the magnitude of the field or with our scholarly training.

I trust that readers and users of this book will find it a reliable guide to the field of Indian affairs; a guide they will use continually and one which will inspire them to drink more deeply at the well of human knowledge.

ABNAKI: a group of linguistically related tribes located along the major rivers of Maine, New Hampshire, Vermont and adjacent areas of Massachusetts and Quebec, numbering together perhaps 8,000 in the early 17th century. In the late 1970s, there were about 2,000 Abnaki descendants connected with reservations in Maine and Quebec, plus an unknown number scattered throughout New England and Quebec.

The Abnaki (more properly spelled Abenaki), spoke dialects of the same Algonquian family language, and called themselves Wabanaki, meaning "dawn land people." There were two major geographical divisions, eastern and western. The eastern Abnaki, located mostly in Maine, included the Abenaki, Pigwacket, Arosaguntacook, Kennebec and Penobscot as major subdivisions. The western Abnaki, located in Vermont, New Hampshire, Massachusetts and Quebec, included the Sokoki, Cowasuck, Winnipesaukee and Pennacook.

In historic times, the term Abnaki (or Wabnaki) was applso applied to a confederacy formed in the mid-18th century, which included various Abnaki groups, as well as the Malecite, Passamaquoddy and Micmac. Originally allied with the French and opposed to the English and the Iroquois Confederacy, the Abnaki confederacy faded out in the late 19th century.

Traditional leadership among the eastern Abnaki was informal and based on personal appeal and strength of personality. There was also a tendency for leadership to be hereditary in the male line. After European contact, leaders of the various eastern subdivisions were known as sagamores. Each of the western groups had a civil chief and a war chief, both of whom held office for life. Each group also had a tribal council, composed of the two chiefs and elders of the various households.

The basic western Abnaki social unit was the household, composed of several related nuclear families living together in a bark longhouse. Descent was in the male line, and newly-married couples usually lived with the groom's family. Marriage, which was usually formalized with gifts to the bride's family, was an occasion for feasting and dancing. Eastern Abnaki sagamores occasionally practiced polygamy.

The Abnaki relied on their knowledge of medicinal plants to cure most illnesses, resorting to shamans for persistent or mysterious maladies. They had a rich·mythology, including the culture hero Gluskabi, the trickster figure Raccoon, the seven Thunderers, dreaded flying creatures and an assortment of underwater people and creatures. The western Abnaki believed it was Tabaldak, the Owner, who created all living things, including Our Grandmother, the earth.

Many Abnaki ceremonies were an acknowledgement of their dependence on game animals and a good harvest. Dancing and singing accompanied most occasions, including marriages, the first corn harvest, the presence of visitors, and funerals. The Abnaki buried their dead with

An Abnaki birchbark lodge (1899).

weapons, tools, food and other personal items for their use in the afterlife. The western Abnaki enclosed the body of the deceased in a roll of bark and covered the grave with a tent-shaped structure. Widows wore a hood during their year of mourning.

Abnaki villages were usually located on navigable streams, and were composed of birchbark houses of various styles. The western Abnaki built longhouses, and the eastern Abnaki made both dome-shaped houses and square houses with a pyramid roof. Most villages also had a small dome-shaped sweat lodge.

Subsistence activities differed somewhat between the eastern and western Abnaki, even varying within each division, according to the environment. In the spring, the eastern Abnaki fished along the coast for salmon, shad, eels, sturgeon, alewives and smelt, using hooks, leisters (three-pronged spears), nets, weirs and spears. Shellfish, crabs and lobsters were also gathered from the sea, and berries, grapes, cherries, ground nuts and maple sap for syrup were collected to supplement the diet. Seal, porpoise and waterfowl were also hunted along the coast. Winters were spent hunting land game, including moose, deer, bear, caribou, beaver, muskrat and otter.

The western Abnaki spring subsistence activities of fishing, plant gathering and maple sap collecting were similar, with the addition of the planting of gardens of corn, beans, squash and tobacco. In late summer, they harvested their crops, picked berries and collected medicinal plants. Fall was spent gathering butternuts and chestnuts and hunting migrating birds. In winter they hunted game similar to that of the eastern Abnaki. Birchbark canoes were the main means of transportation, with snowshoes used in winter. Birchbark was also used to make an assortment of containers and trays. Some groups made wooden spoons and dishes, as well as pottery vessels. The Abnaki had clothing of finely-tanned skins, including breechclouts, moccasins, leggings, moose skin coats, fur robes and caps.

In the late 16th century, the eastern Abnaki were visited by European explorers, and the French explorer Samuel de Champlain wrote about various eastern Abnaki groups encountered in his 1603-05 explorations. Both eastern and western Abnaki were quickly caught up in the fur trade with both the French and English. French missionaries were active among them, and there was considerable intermarriage between the French and Indians. The English, however, who were more active as colonizers, pushed the Abnaki groups continually northward. In the 17th and 18th centuries, the Abnaki became involved in the numerous wars between the French and English and between the English and themselves. Both eastern and western Abnaki groups gradually fled to Quebec, settling mostly at Saint Francis and Bécancour. The Penobscot were the only Abnaki group to remain in the United States after the American Revolution. They also were the leading Abnaki group in the Wabnaki confederacy, from which they withdrew in about 1862.

In the late 1970s, there were about 1,000 Penobscot descendants in the area of the Penobscot Reservation on Indian Island at Old Town, Maine. Perhaps 1,000 eastern and western Abnaki descendants lived in Quebec, with about 250 at Saint Francis village at Odanak. There were a few remaining speakers of both eastern and western Abnaki dialects.

BIBLIOGRAPHY: Speck, Frank G. *Penobscot Man: The Life History of a Forest Tribe in Maine.* Philadelphia: University of Pennsylvania Press, 1940; Trigger, Bruce G., and Sturtevant, William C., (eds). *Handbook of North American Indians.* vol. 15. Washington: Smithsonian Institution, 1978.

ACHOMAWI: a Hokan people of northeastern California, numbering about 3,000 at the time of European contact. In the late 1970s, there were about 1,000 Achomawi living mostly in California. Achomawi (or Achumawi) is a term meaning "river people." They were also known as the Pit River Indians, and together with the Atsugewi, they made up the Palaihnihan branch of the Hokan language family.

The Achomawi were composed of about nine politically autonomous tribelets or bands, connected by language, culture and inter-marriage. Chiefs of the various tribelets were chosen for their popularity, ability and personal possession of supernatural powers.

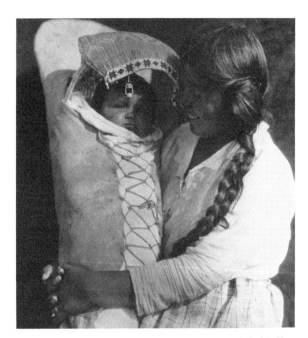

An Achomawi
woman with a
baby in a
cradle board
—a photograph
taken by
Edward S. Curtis.

Smithsonian Institution National Anthropological Archives

Upon reaching adolescence, boys went to lonely mountain retreats in search of a *tinihowi,* or guardian spirit, who would give them super-natural powers. Shamans, or doctors, provided the Achomawi with both religious leadership and medical care. They had considerable knowledge of medicinal plants, and often used wild tobacco in curing rituals.

When an Achomawi died, his body was cremated and all of his posses-sions buried. Mourners cut their hair, covered their heads with pitch, and did not pronounce the name of the deceased again.

The Achomawi built conical summer houses of a light pole framework covered with tule mats. Their semi-subterranean winter houses were of a wood frame covered with grass, tule or bark and a layer of earth. The houses were about 15 feet square, with entrance by a ladder through the central smoke hole in the roof.

Achomawi territory varied from high mountains to lowland swamps, providing variety in food supply. Salmon, bass, catfish, pike, trout and other fish were netted in the many streams and lakes. Ducks, geese and other waterfowl were caught with nets, and their eggs were gathered. Swampy areas provided tule sprouts, which were eaten in spring, as well as tule stalks for houses and mattresses.

From the meadows and grasslands they gathered various seeds, roots and bulbs as well as insects and larvae. The forest areas provided berries, acorns and pine nuts, as well as deer, bear, beaver, badger and many types of small game. The deer were often taken by means of pitfalls dug along their usual trails. Early settlers named the Pit River people for this practice.

The Achomawi made bows of yew or juniper and arrow points, spear points and knives of obsidian. They made tools of stone, antler and obsidian, as well as fine basketry of grasses and willow, decorated with designs made with vegetable dyes. Their clothing was made of deerskin and shredded juniper bark.

Around 1828, trappers began entering Achomawi territory with little repercussion. Later, however, the flood of miners and settlers that followed the discovery of gold in California led to outbreaks of Achomawi hostility, which were put down by volunteers and army regulars. By the late 19th century, several hundred Achomawi had been forced onto the Round Valley Reservation and small rancherias. In 1938, the 9,000 acre XL Ranch was established for some Achomawi families.

By the late 1970s, probably less than ten percent of the 1,000 or so Achomawi were located on trust lands. Attempts to organize themselves had been unsuccessful, and the rich cultural heritage of the Achomawi was slipping away.

BIBLIOGRAPHY: Wheeler-Voegelin, Erminie. *Pitt River Indians of California.* New York: Garland Publishing, Inc., 1974.

ACOMA: a Pueblo tribe of the Keresan language family, located in west-central New Mexico. Acoma Pubelo, located on a 350-foot-high mesa is one of the oldest continuously inhabited villages in the United States, having been established in about 1200 AD. At the time of the first encounters with the Spanish in the 1500s, their population was estimated at about 3,000. In the 1970s, they numbered about 2,700, still living in their historic mesa-top homesite.

Other Keresan tribes included the Zia, Santa Ana, Santo Domingo, San Felipe, Cochiti, and Laguna. The Acoma and Laguna together comprise the western division of the Keresan. In the late 1970s, the language was still spoken, but was being largely replaced by English among the young. The name Acoma was derived from their name for themselves, Akome, meaning "people of the white rock."

The Acoma were divided into about 20 matrilineal clans. Marriage was forbidden within the mother's clan, while allowed but disapproved of within the father's clan. Leadership of the pueblo was provided by the cacique, assisted by a war captain, or *hocheni.* Both were chosen for life by certain clan-associated priesthoods. The cacique was aided by ten *principales,* who helped control land distributions. Under the Spanish, this leadership was supplemented by a governor, two lieutenant

The view from the pueblo (village) of Acoma, New Mexico, in 1899. Acoma, situated on top of a 350-foot high mesa, is one of the oldest continuously inhabited villages in the United States, having been in existence since about 1200 AD.

governors and a council, who served as a liaison between the outside world and the religious leadership of the pueblo.

The Acoma religion was very complex, largely revolving around various traditions concerning their origin. Their greatest deities were Sky Father and Earth Mother, with numerous other deities and folk heroes. Dances and ceremonies were held in semi-subterranean chambers called *kivas.* Leadership was provided by the cacique and a number of religious fraternities or priesthoods. Numerous ceremonies and festivals held annually included the Rain Dance and the Corn Dance. After the Spanish introduction of Christianity, the fiesta of San Estevan, the patron saint of the Franciscan mission at Acoma, became an important celebration.

When a person died, the soul was believed to hover around its earthly home for four days, before traveling to Shipapu, the traditional place of origin of the Keresan people. Within 24 hours of death, the body was wrapped in a blanket and buried, with the head toward the east, in a graveyard next to the San Estevan church.

The village of Acoma was composed of three rows of terraced, three-story adobe houses, each 1,000 feet long. Like modern apartment buildings, the first adobe houses were divided into separate, single family units. The first, or lower, level had no doors or windows and consisted mainly of storage rooms and the ceremonial *kivas.* Ladders led to the upper two levels which served as dwelling places. Each unit typically contained an open hearth for cooking and three corn grinding troughs at one end. Baking ovens were located outside. Prominent in the village after 1699 was the huge church of San Estevan, 150 feet long, 60 feet high, and with 10 foot thick walls. To the north of the village were two natural cisterns, where rain water collected, which supplied a large part of the village water requirements. Acomita and Pueblo, smaller farming villages, occupied during the summer, were located on the plain, some 15 miles distant.

The Acoma were primarily agriculturists, using their land on the plains below for growing corn, beans and squash. Wheat, melons, peaches and chilies were introduced by the Spanish. Corn was the staple food, often being baked into a thin bread, *mut-tze-nee*, on special flat rocks used only for this purpose. They also raised considerable herds of sheep, goats, horses and donkeys, introduced by the Spanish, and in earlier times, turkeys. Hunting of rabbits and deer, was also important, as well as gathering of wild foods such as pine nuts, gooseberries, soapweed pods and prickly pear cactus fruit.

The Acoma women were excellent potters, producing some of the best pottery in North America. Some weaving was also done, mostly by the men. They also produced silver necklaces and other ornaments, which they used for adornment.

The traditional place of origin of the Acoma was Si-pa-pu, or Shipapu, a mythical place somewhere in the north. By about 1100, they probably lived along the Rio de los Frijoles (Bean River) in northern New Mexico. They moved successively to a series of villages, the last of which was probably on Katzimo, the Enchanted Mesa, before settling, probably in about 1200, on the mesa where Acoma is presently located.

Their first European contact was with Spanish explorers, having been visited in about 1540 by Hernando de Lavarado. Vicente Zaldivar, to avenge his brother's death, destroyed half the population in 1599, decreasing the population to around 1,500. Decades of Spanish domination followed. In 1629, Franciscan father Juan Ramirez founded the first lasting mission, building a huge church. Rebuilt in 1699, the church still stood in the late 1970s. In 1680, the Acoma participated in the general Pueblo Revolt, forcing the Spanish to flee the region. However, by 1699, the Spanish had reconquered the area. Smallpox and other diseases took their toll during the 18th century, and by 1800 the population had dwindled to 800.

In about 1821, Mexico won independence from Spain, and took over control of Acoma. The United States then took over control in 1846. Subsequent years were marked by land disputes with the U.S. and with adjacent Laguna Pueblo. In 1858, the U.S. Congress confirmed the land grant made by Spain in 1689. The completion of the Santa Fe Railroad in 1881 brought Acoma into closer touch with the outside world.

Acoma women drawing water —a photograph taken in about 1910 by Edward S. Curtis.
Library of Congress

In modern times, the Acoma, compared with most tribes, have been relatively unaffected by white culture. In the 1970s, many of the old ways were still practiced, with the addition of some modern schooling and income sources. Economically they had shifted from sheep raising to cattle, with a community herd started in 1940. Tourism was a source of income, including the selling of pottery, silverwork, leatherwork and beadwork. Clay, obsidian and coal were being mined on the reservation.

In the late 1970s the population of the Acoma was on the rise, with 2,700 Indians living on 245,346 tribally owned and 320 allotted acres of land. The tribal government was, administratively, in the hands of a governor, one or two lieutenant governors, and a tribal council. The old ways were still valued, but the Acoma sought closer ties with the rest of the world.

BIBLIOGRAPHY: Minge, Ward Alan. *Acoma, Pueblo in the Sky.* Albuquerque: University of New Mexico Press, 1976; Sedgewick, Mrs. William T. *Acoma, The Sky City: A Study in Pueblo-Indian History and Civilization.* Cambridge: Harvard University Press, 1927.

ADAI: *See* CADDO.

AHTENA: a small tribe living in Alaska on the Copper River and its tributaries, numbering about 500 in the 18th century. In the 1970s, there were about 300 Ahtena, living in their traditional area.

They spoke a language of the Athapascan language family, which was still spoken by some in the 1970s. In their language, Ahtena meant "ice people." They were also known as the Copper River Indians.

The Ahtena were divided into three geographic groups, speaking three dialects of the language: the Ahtna'ht'aene, nearest the river mouth, the

Dan'ehwt'aene, and the Tate'ahwt'aene, from the uppermost part of the river. The three groups were closely related by culture and by inter-marriage, and spoke only slightly different dialects. They were further divided into a number of villages, each containing one to several families and ruled by its own chief, or *tyone*. In addition, there were lesser officials called *skillies*, as well as shamans, commoners and a servant class, in a complex social structure. Some polygamy was practiced, and women were generally subservient to the men. Ahtena ceremonial life centered around the potlatch, a ritualized gift distribution and feast, lasting several days.

Ahtena villages were composed of semisubterranean family homes from 8 feet by 10 feet to 24 feet by 36 feet in size, each housing one family. The houses were constructed of pole and wood-slab framework covered with spruce bark, and often had a second room used as a sweat bath. Rectangular temporary summer homes were constructed of poles and boughs of spruce or cottonwood. The two sides were enclosed while the ends were covered by skins.

Fur trading, hunting, fishing and gathering were all important to the economy. The Ahtena also controlled the copper for which their river is named. Salmon was the primary food, caught in streams near their villages, with traps, weirs, dip nets and spears. In summer they hunted moose, mountain sheep, bear, caribou, and especially rabbits, at the stream headwaters. Berries, a fruit called *tomba*, and a parsnip-like root called *chass* were gathered to supplement the diet. Trading was engaged in three times a year at Nuchek on Prince William Sound. They traveled there by moosehide boats, which they abandoned there, returning upstream by inland routes, sometimes using snowshoes.

Ahtena history prior to the 18th century is largely unrecorded. Their first encounters with Europeans were with Russian traders in the 18th century. Numerous early Russian attempts to explore the Copper River were repulsed. A combined Russian-American trading post, established in 1819 at the confluence of the Copper and Chitina rivers, was short lived, being forced to withdraw by Indian attacks. In 1843, the last Russian attempt, by Serebrannikov, failed when he was killed. Except for a few American explorers, the Ahtena were then left alone until gold was discovered in about 1899. Subsequently, civilization (railroads, stern-wheelers, etc.) encroached on the area. The construction of the Alaskan Highway during World War II and the paving over the Glenn and Richardson Highways in the 1950s also had impact on the tribe.

In the 1970s, they were organized into Ahtna, Incorporated, to become eligible for the benefits of the Alaskan Native Claims Settlement Act of 1971. At that time, about 300 Ahtena remained, living in seven villages in their traditional territory. Much of the hunting and fishing

Walter Charley, of Ahtna Inc., Copper Center, Alaska.

Economic Development Administration

culture remained, although game was getting scarce. The tribe was feeling the impact of the Alaskan Oil Pipe line, which went through the area, providing a number of jobs. Potlatches were still given, and classes in the traditional Ahtena language and culture were being taught.

BIBLIOGRAPHY: Hanable, William S. and Workman, Karen W. *Lower Copper and Chitina River: An Historic Resources Study.* Alaskan Division of Parks, Dept. of Natural Resources, 1974; Allen, Henry T. "Atnatanas: Natives of Copper River, Alaska." *Annual Report of the Board of Regents of the Smithsonian Institution.* Part 1, 1886 (Published 1889).

ALABAMA: a tribe of the Creek Confederacy, formerly located in southern Alabama, and living, in the late 1970s, on a state reservation on the Trinity River in Polk County, Texas.

The Alabama spoke a language of the Muskogean linguistic family. Sometimes spelled Alibamu, the tribal name may mean "medicine gatherers" or "thicket clearers."

Customs of the Alabama were similar to those of other tribes of the Creek Confederacy, a loose confederation of tribes located in Alabama and Georgia. Towns of the Alabama were defended by a wooden stockade sealed with mud. A typical town had a ceremonial center which included a covered circular meeting place roofed with bark, an open air plaza used for outdoor meetings and ceremonies, and a yard for playing chunkey. This popular game was played by rolling a stone disc and throwing a pole after it. Points were scored by hitting the rolling stone or coming closest to its stopping place.

The Eagle Dance
being performed
at the Alabama-
Coushatta Indian
Reservation,
near Livingston,
Texas.

Economic Development Administration

The early Alabama traditionally buried their dead with their heads toward the east, sometimes placing a knife in their hand with which to fight an eagle they might encounter along the spirit trail. Most Alabama today are Protestant with some revival of interest of old beliefs.

According to ancient traditions, the Alabama and other tribes of the Creek Confederacy migrated from the northwest, somewhere beyond the Mississippi River. The Alabama were encountered in central Mississippi by the Spanish explorer Hernando DeSoto in 1541. By the late 17th century, however, they were established along the banks of the lower Alabama River and were encountered by the French who established themselves on Mobile Bay in 1702. Population estimates for this period range from 700 to 1,000.

After the surrender of that region to the British in 1763, the Alabama began to break up. Some went to Florida and joined the Seminole; some moved to the Mississippi River 60 miles above New Orleans, and others went to Indian Territory in Oklahoma. The largest number, about 200, settled in Polk County in eastern Texas, where the new Republic of Texas granted them two leagues of land.

Losing this land to white settlers, the Alabama were given 1,280 acres by the State of Texas at the recommendation of Gen. Sam Houston. This was shared by the Coushatta Indians, who were also of the Creek Confederacy and had migrated from Alabama. Another 3,071 acres was added to the reservation by the U.S. government in 1928. Federal control was terminated in 1954 and the reservation came under the trusteeship of the state of Texas. In the 1970s the tribe requested an end to state aid as well.

The number of Indians, including Alabama and Coushatta, living on or near the reservation in the 1970s was estimated at about 500, with virtually no unemployment. Tourism was a major factor in the tribal economy, with camping and picnicking facilities open to the public. A museum focused on Alabama and Coushatta history, while Indian dances, pow-wows, and craft work helped preserve cultural traditions.

BIBLIOGRAPHY: Folsom-Dickerson, W.E.S. *The White Path.* San Antonio: The Naylor Company, 1965.

ALEUT: a group occupying the Aleutian Islands and western Alaska, numbering 20-25,000 in the early 18th century, prior to European contact. In the late 1970s, there were about 5,000 Aleut, living in the same area. They spoke three dialects of the Aleut language of the Inuit-Aleut language family, and were closely related to the Inuit (Eskimo). The name Aleut was probably derived from an Inuit term meaning "island," whereas they referred to themselves as Unangan.

During precontact days, most of the 69 islands of the Aleutian chain were inhabited by Aleut. Villages or groups of villages were led by chiefs, sometimes hereditary, who acted mainly as advisors.

They lived in underground houses up to 240 feet long by 40 feet wide, and housing as many as 150 people. The earth-covered dwellings had a framework of driftwood and whale bone, and were entered through an opening on the roof above a notched log ladder. In later times, they built semisubterranean, single-family, sod dwellings called *barabara*.

The Aleut harpooned seals, sea lions, sea otters and walrus from single or double hatch kayaks, or *bidarkas*. Whales were occasionally hunted using poison tipped lances. Spears, hooks and nets were used to take salmon, cod, flounder, herring and trout. Ducks, ptarmigan, geese, cormorant and puffin were brought down with bolas or bird darts hurled with a throwing board. Fox, caribou and bear were hunted in some areas, and mollusks, sea urchins, seaweed and a variety of berries were gathered to supplement the diet.

In addition to *bidarkas*, the Aleut had larger skin-covered open boats called *igilax*. Weapons and tools were made of stone and bone. For heat and light, blubber and oil from seals and whales were burned in stone lamps. Both men and women wore long jackets of bird skin or sealskin,

A lithograph of the 1830s, showing the mode of dress of the inhabitants of the Aleutian Islands.

supplemented by gutskin jackets for kayaking or rainy weather. The men often wore conical wooden hunting helmets and wooden eye shades. For adornment, women tattooed their faces, and both men and women wore stone and ivory labrets.

Ancestors of the Aleut probably entered the Aleutian Islands from western Alaska in about 2000 BC. They engaged in warfare with neighboring Inuit groups on Kodiak Island and Bristol Bay, as well as among themselves. For weapons, they used lances, bows and arrows, wooden shields, and woodslat armor.

In 1741, the Aleuts were visited by a Russian naval expedition led by a Dane, Vitus Bering. They returned to Siberia with seal, sea otter and fox skins, touching off a flood of Russian fur hunters and traders to the Aleutian Islands. The Aleuts were forced by the armed traders to supply furs in massive quantities. A general uprising by the Aleut was cruelly suppressed, and the Aleut population declined precipitously due to disease and conflict with the traders. Some aspects of Aleut culture also declined in this period, and their old religion was replaced by the Russian Orthodox Church by the early 19th century.

As the game supply diminished, the Aleut hunters were forced further afield, bringing them into conflict with neighboring Inuit and Indian

Aleutian-style snowshoes, displayed by Makary Zaochney of Amchitka Island in 1931.

The National Archives

groups. A flotilla of 500 *bidarkas* was reportedly sent to hunt in the Yakutat area of southeastern Alaska in 1794. In 1802, several hundred Aleut were killed by Tlingit warriors in an attack on the Russian fort at Sitka on Baranof Island. By 1831, the dwindling Aleut population of about 2,200 was consolidated on 16 islands, including the previously uninhabited Commander Islands and fur rich Pribilof Islands.

In 1867, the Aleutian Islands, along with Alaska, were purchased by the United States. Fur hunting increased as ships of several nations flocked to the area, driving sea otters to the verge of extinction. The slaughter was brought under control after 1910. During World War II, Attu and Kiska islands were occupied for a short time by the Japanese. In 1958, Alaska, including the Aleutian Islands, became a state of the United States.

In the late 1970s, there were more than 5,000 Aleut, mostly of mixed blood, living on the Alaska coast, the Aleutian Islands, the Pribilof Islands and the Soviet-owned Commander Islands, about 1,000 of whom still spoke the Aleut language. Most of the traditional Aleut culture had long since disappeared, and Aleuts engaged in wage work at fisheries, canneries and military installations. Commercial sealing was still carried on, particularly in the Pribilof Islands.

BIBLIOGRAPHY: Hrdlicka, Ales. *The Aleutian and Commander Islands and their Inhabitants.* Philadelphia: The Wistar Institute of Anatomy and Biology, 1945.

ALGONQUIN: a group of bands located in the Ottawa valley of Ontario and Quebec, numbering about 3,000-4,000 in the early 17th century. In the late 1970s, there were about 3,000 Algonquin living on 11 reserves north and west of Ottawa, and perhaps another 3,000 people of Algonquin descent scattered throughout the Ottawa valley.

The Algonquin spoke a language of the Algonquian language family, which was named for them. Linguistically and culturally, they were most closely related to the Ojibwa and Ottawa.

Little is known of Algonquin social or political organization, although anthropologists have suggested that they were divided into clans with each person belonging to the clan of his father and required to marry outside the clan. Bands, composed of a number of clans, lived together during the summer fishing season, but probably dispersed in winter to hunt as families or small groups.

In the 17th century, the principal Algonquin bands included: the Wescarini, on the Rouge, Lievre and Petite-Nation rivers; the Matouwescarini in the Madawaska valley; the Keinoche in the Muskrat Lake area; the Kichesipirini on Morrison Island in the Ottawa River; and the Onontchataronon along the South Nation River.

Shamans, with special powers derived from guardian spirits, diagnosed illnesses and cured the sick. Hunters also sought guardian spirits through vision quests, to help them locate game. Algonquin mythology included various supernatural beings such as Wiskedjak, a trickster-culture hero; Windigo, a man-eating creature; Paguk, a rattling skeleton; and the Pugwudgininiwug, a race of powerful little men. Painted wooden structures were erected over the graves of prominent persons, with a wooden upright at one end, bearing a figure representing the deceased.

The Algonquin fished in summer and winter, using hemp nets, probably obtained from the Huron, to fish through holes cut in the ice. They hunted deer, beaver, moose and caribou. Less important were corn, beans and squash, planted in burned-over clearings. Maple sugar was made by some bands.

Birchbark canoes were the main means of transportation, with snowshoes and toboggans used in winter. Birchbark was also used in a variety of sewn containers and in the construction of rectangular dwellings at hunting camps. Clothing was made of deer and moose skins.

Before 1570, relations between the Algonquin and the Iroquois living along the St. Lawrence River were apparently peaceful. At that time, a 30-year war broke out between the Iroquois and various Algonquian groups (including the Algonquin and Montagnais), who were acting as middlemen between the Iroquois and the French traders. By 1603 the Al-

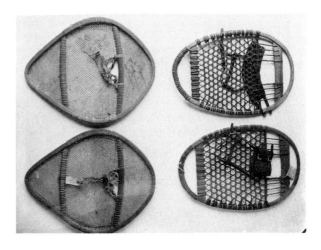

Types of snow-
shoes used by
the Algonquin.

Smithsonian Institution

gonquins had defeated the Iroquois. Allied with the French, they engaged in further battles with the Iroquois in 1609 and 1610.

The Algonquin also attempted to maintain a middleman relationship between the French and Huron, but this strategy failed, as direct relations, bypassing the Algonquin, were established by 1615. In the 1630s, an attempt by the Algonquin to establish trade relations with the Dutch led to war with the Mohawk Iroquois. By the 1640s, the Algonquin were being driven northward and westward by Iroquois raids, finally abandoning the Ottawa valley, temporarily, by 1675. Peace was finally established in 1701.

Missions were established among the Algonquin in 1704 and 1721, but they continued to live primarily by hunting and trapping. In the 19th century, a number of reserves were established in Quebec and Ontario. In the late 1970s, there was one reserve, Golden Lake, in Ontario, and there were ten reserves in Quebec: Barriere Lake, Grand Lake Victoria, Lake Simon, River Desert, Argonaut, Hunters Point, Kipawa, Long Point, Timiskaming and Wolfe Lake. Algonquin were also mixed with Iroquois on Gibson Reserve. About 3,000 Algonquin lived on these reserves, and perhaps another 3,000 of Algonquin descent were scattered around the surrounding countryside. The Algonquian language was still widely spoken.

BIBLIOGRAPHY: Trigger, Bruce G., and Sturtevant, Williams C. (eds.). *Handbook of North American Indians.* vol. 15. Northeast. Washington D.C.; Smithsonian Institution, 1978.

ALSEA: a small Oregon coast tribe located on Alsea Bay and the Alsea and Yaquina rivers. The Alsea belonged to the small Yakonan language family, including the Coos (Hania and Miluk), Kuitsh, Siuslaw and Yaquina, which together numbered about 6,000 in 1780. By the early

20th century, the Alsea and other Yakonan tribes were virtually extinct as identifiable cultures.

The Alsea (or Alsi as they called themselves) were located in at least a dozen small autonomous villages. Each was led by a *kiautc,* or headman, who had little real authority but was respected for his wealth. The *kiautc,* and other men of wealth, occasionally had more than one wife, often marrying sisters.

Also important in the community were shamans, who had supernatural powers acquired from a guardian spirit, through fasting and solitary vigils in lonely places. For a fee, a shaman would cure the sick through a ritual of singing, dancing and sucking out disease-causing objects. For no fee, they also performed such ceremonies as were necessary to make the salmon run. The Alsea believed that after death a person's soul headed north and crossed by canoe into the land of the dead.

The Alsea dwellings consisted of five feet deep pits lined with cedar planks and covered with a low gabled roof. Access was by ladder through the roof. Mats covered the floor, and sleeping platforms lined the outer walls. Three or four families usually occupied the large houses, with mats hung between. Besides permanent villages, the Alsea had more than 20 fishing and hunting camps, where they erected temporary houses of pole and thatch.

Fishing was the major food source and the main occupation of Alsea men. They used an assortment of dip nets, traps, harpoons and weirs to catch chinook, coho and dog salmon as well as steelhead trout, lamprey eel, perch, flounder and herring. The women cut and smoke-dried the salmon for later use. The women also gathered berries, roots, greens and mollusks. Occasionally a whale washed up and was a welcome addition to the diet. The men also hunted small numbers of elk, deer, beaver, quail, grouse and waterfowl, using pits and bows and arrows.

The Alsea made bows of yew or vine maple, arrow tips of bone or flint, and hardwood harpoons tipped with bone or horn. An otter skin was commonly used as a quiver, and a few men had armor of a double layer of elkskin.

Rushes and split roots were twined to make bags, large carrying baskets and other containers, while cooking vessels and dishes were carved of maple and alder. Both men and women wore skirts of shredded bark and fur robes in winter, as well as ear, nose and hair ornaments of dentalia shells, which were a form of wealth.

The Alsea were protected from early contact with outsiders by a treacherous bar across the Alsea River. By the early 1850s, settlers began to drift into the area from the Willamette Valley. The United States government began taking Alsea lands in 1856, establishing part of the area as the Siletz Reservation and opening the rest to settlers. The reservation was greatly reduced in size in 1876, and the remaining land allotted to individual tribal members after 1892.

What recognition the U.S. Government granted to them as a tribe was officially terminated in 1956. By the 1970s, very few Alsea remained, having been largely assimilated into the surrounding population.

BIBLIOGRAPHY: Drucker, Philip. "Contributions to Alsea Ethnography." *University of California Publications in American Archaeology and Ethnology.* vol. 35, 1939.

ANGMAGSSALIK INUIT: *See* EAST GREENLAND INUIT.

APACHE: a group of linguistically and culturally related Athapascan tribes who ranged over southern Colorado and Kansas, eastern Arizona, New Mexico, western Texas and northern Mexico in the late 17th century, with a total population at that time of about 5,000. In the late 1970s, there were more than 17,000 Apache located on reservations in Arizona and New Mexico.

The Apache tribes spoke closely-related dialects of the Apachean language, a member of the southern branch of the Athapascan language family. The name Apache was probably derived from *apachu*, a Zuñi term meaning "enemy," which they applied to the Navajo, who were closely related to the Apache. The Apache and Navajo both referred to themselves as Diné, meaning "the people."

Culturally, the Apache were composed of two main divisions: the Eastern Apache, including Jicarilla, Lipan, Mescalero, Chiricahua and Kiowa Apache, and the Western Apache, including the Cibecue, White Mountain, Coyotero, Northern Tonto and Southern Tonto. The Kiowa Apache, long associated with the Kiowa, are usually considered separately.

The various Apache tribes were loosely organized politically, with no overall tribal leadership. Occasionally they functioned as bands, but the more usual political unit was the small local group composed of several extended families. Leaders of these groups, whose positions were mainly advisory, were chosen for their proven leadership ability and skill at hunting and raiding.

The main social unit was the extended family. Residence was generally matrilocal, *i.e.*, a newly-married couple became a part of the woman's family. Polygamy, practiced by all of the Apache, most commonly entailed a man marrying sisters or his brother's widow. In addition to the extended family, the Western Apache were also organized into matrilineal clans similar to those of the Navajo, with whom they had close ties.

The Apache had a rich mythology and a complex set of deities and spirits, including the Sky, Earth, Sun, Moon, Sun Boy, Child of the Water, White Painted Woman, the Water People and the Mountain Spirits. The latter, also called Gans, were impersonated by masked dancers, who performed at such important ceremonies as the four-day girls' puberty rite. Other ceremonies, performed by shamans, related to curing, hunting, cultivation or rainmaking. The Apache buried their dead or placed them in caves or rock clefts, and buried or burned the possessions of the deceased.

The Western Apache and the Chiricahua usually lived in dome-shaped wickiups thatched with grass, which were covered with skins in cold weather. The other Eastern Apache groups used both the wickiup and, when involved in buffalo hunting, the Plains-style buffalo skin tipi.

The Eastern Apache were primarily hunters and gatherers, although some of the groups engaged in agriculture. The Western Apache cultivated fairly extensive fields of corn, beans and squash, and also engaged in hunting and gathering. All of the Apache hunted deer, elk, antelope, mountain sheep, birds and other small game, and some of the Eastern tribes became expert buffalo hunters as well. Wild foods, important to all the Apache tribes, varied with the environment. The Mescalero depended heavily on mescal from the agave plant. Other gathered foods included mesquite beans, pine nuts, prickly pear, locust blossoms, palmetto, wild persimmon, pecans, yucca fruit, chokecherries, raspberries and juniper berries, as well as a variety of other fruits, seeds, nuts and roots.

The Apache made a wide assortment of fine basketry, both coiled and twined, including cradles, pitch-lined water jars, carrying baskets and other containers. Clothing was made from finely-tanned skins and sometimes decorated with fringes and beadwork.

Smithsonian Institution National Anthropological Archives

An Apache girl filling a water jar —a photograph probably taken by Edward S. Curtis in about 1903.

Library of Congress

Geronimo, the famous Apache leader, pictured with his family at Fort Sill, Oklahoma, in 1895, a decade after the Apache wars ended.

The Apache began migrating from their northwestern Canada homes southward along the eastern slope of the Rocky Mountains probably sometime after 1000 AD. By the late 16th century, they were in Colorado, Kansas and New Mexico. By the mid-17th century, the Eastern Apache acquired horses, becoming skilled raiders, traders and buffalo hunters. In the 18th century, the Eastern Apache were driven from the Plains by Comanche and Caddoan tribes, who had acquired arms from the French.

Moving southward, both Eastern and Western Apache stepped up their alternate raiding of and trading with Spanish settlements in New Mexico and Mexico. As the Spanish were succeeded by the Mexicans and the Americans in the 19th century, attempts at accommodation failed, and years of warfare followed. Placed on reservations in the 1870s, various bands, driven by fear and dissatisfaction, broke loose. The years of raiding and eluding the U.S. Army which followed became known as the Apache Wars. The surrender of Geronimo's Chiricahua band in 1886 effectively marked the end of Apache resistance.

In the late 1970s, there were 17,000 Apache, living on four reservations. The Western Apache occupied Fort Apache and San Carlos reservations in eastern Arizona; the Jicarilla lived on the Jicarilla Reservation in northern New Mexico, and the Mescalero, Lipan and Chiricahua shared the Mescalero Reservation in southern New Mexico. A small group of Chiricahua also resided in Oklahoma.

The Apache retained many of their tribal traditions as well as their

Apache babies
in cradle boards.

The National Archives

language. Some crafts, such as basketry and leatherwork, were being re-vived. Lumbering, stockraising and tourism were important contributors to their economy.

See also: *Chiricahua, Jicarilla, Kiowa Apache, Lipan, Mescalero* and *Western Apache.*

BIBLIOGRAPHY: Mails, Thomas F. *The People Called Apache.* Englewood Cliffs, New Jersey: Prentice Hall, Inc., 1974.

APACHE, WESTERN: five Apache groups located in eastern Arizona in the early 19th century, when they numbered about 4,500. In the late 1970s, there were about 12,000 Western Apache divided between the San Carlos and Fort Apache reservations in Arizona.

The five groups, which included the San Carlos, White Mountain, Northern Tonto and Southern Tonto, all spoke Apache dialects belonging to the southern branch of the Athapascan language family. Culturally, the Western Apache were closely related to the Navajo, who spoke a similar language, as well as to the plains Apache tribes.

The smallest political unit among the Western Apache was the extended family, which camped, hunted and migrated seasonally to harvest wild foods together. Several extended families often joined together to form a local group, which was led by a headman. In later times, larger bands were occasionally led by chiefs and subchiefs.

Socially, the Western Apache were divided into clans, each person inheriting the clan of his mother with marriage forbidden inside the clan. A couple usually lived with the bride's family, and a man and his mother-in-law were forbidden to look at each other or speak to each other. Polygamy existed among those who could afford it, each wife usually having a separate dwelling.

A four-day puberty rite was held to welcome each girl into womanhood. These were major social events, sponsored by the girl's family at great expense. The girl was counseled by an older woman, and a male singer conducted the ceremonies, which included feasting, rituals and dancing by the *gan* dancers. The *gans* represented the Mountain Spirits, characters from Apache mythology who formerly inhabited the earth.

Other supernatural beings included the creator god, Life Giver, White Painted Woman, Child of the Water, Killer of Enemies, and the trickster, Coyote. Men and women shamans had supernatural powers with which they could ward off evil, prophesy the future, and cure the sick. Certain shamans specialized in such ailments as snakebite, owl sickness or the effects of lightning. Songs, prayers and the use of sacred objects were included in the curing ritual, and the shaman also usually left a prescription of taboos to be observed.

Western Apache playing a hoop and pole game at San Carlos, Arizona, in about 1899.
Smithsonian Institution National Anthropological Archives.

The Western Apache usually lived in dome-shaped lodges, or wicki-ups, of mesquite, willow or cottonwood poles thatched with bear grass tied on with yucca cord. In cold or rainy weather, the lodges, which were constructed by the women, were sometimes covered tightly with skins. Brush ramadas were used for summer cooking and as sunshades.

The Western Apache cultivated some corn, beans and squash, and made a mild corn beer called *tulupai*. The women also gathered pine nuts, acorns, mesquite pods, seeds, agave, sumac berries, raspberries, strawberries, grapes and currants. The base of the agave plant was baked in rock-lined pits for several days to make a sweet nutritious food called mescal. Trips to the desert were made in July to harvest the fruit of the saguaro cactus.

The men used deerhead disguises and turkey feather decoys in stalking those animals, and also hunted antelope, elk, javelin, rabbit, porcupine and mountain lion. Bows were sinew-backed and made of mulberry, oak or locust. Arrow tips were often merely fire-hardened wood or cane. Lances, warclubs and rawhide slings were also used.

The Western Apache made both twined and coiled basketry items of fine quality, including bowls, storage jars, burden baskets and pitch-covered water jars. Vegetable dyes were used to make geometric and animal designs in the basketry, and walnut shells were used as brown dye

**A White Mountain
Apache
Mountain Spirit
or devil dancer
(1927)**

Smithsonian Institution National Anthropological Archives.

A White Mountain Apache wickiup—a photograph probably taken by Edward S. Curtis in about 1903.

for deerskin storage bags. Other crafts included hooded cradle boards and black or dark gray pottery with rounded or conical bases. Buckskin clothing included thigh-high moccasins, which were folded down to the knee to make a pocket for carrying items.

The various Apache groups probably came from the north into the southwest in about 1200 AD. By the mid-17th century, they had acquired Spanish horses and were engaging in raids on Mexican settlements for captives and plunder. The United States took over the area after 1846, and established the White Mountain Apache Reservation in 1871. After 1897, this was divided into the Fort Apache and San Carlos reservations.

In the late 1970s, the Western Apache totaled more than 12,000 living on the two southeastern Arizona reservations. Tribally-owned cattle herds were of major importance on both reservations, as was the tribally-owned Fort Apache Timber Company. Asbestos was mined on San Carlos. Both reservations had developed major tourism facilities amid the beautiful lake and mountain scenery, including a ski resort and more than 1,000 campsites and lakeside cabins.

Many Western Apache traditions remained strong in the late 1970s, including the celebration of girls' puberty rites. A museum and culture center had been established at Fort Apache, and there was a revival of interest in language and crafts.

BIBLIOGRAPHY: Baldwin, Gordon C. *The Warrior Apaches.* Tucson: Dale Stuart King, 1965; Goodwin, Grenville. *The Social Organization of the Western Apache.* Tucson: The University of Arizona Press, 1969.

APALACHEE: an extinct tribe of northwestern Florida. The Apalachee were one of the larger, more prosperous tribes of this region, numbering, in the mid-17th century, 6,000 to 8,000 people, located in eight towns between the Aucilla and Apalachicola rivers along Apalachee Bay.

They spoke a language of the Muskogean linguistic family similar to Choctaw. The name Apalachee is probably from a Choctaw word meaning "people on the other side."

The Apalachee were among other tribes who moved into the southeastern U.S. from somewhere west of the Mississippi River sometime around AD 1300. These groups brought with them a tradition of building temple mounds, around which each town was organized. The most important towns were Iniahica, Ivitachuco and Calahuchi.

The Apalachee were primarily an agricultural people, growing corn, beans, peas, pumpkins, and squash. Corn was the main crop and, cultivated twice a year, it provided a stable economy. One Spanish chronicler of the 1539 Hernando DeSoto expedition tells of marching for two leagues through continuous fields of corn in Apalachee territory.

Hunting and gathering also added to the food supply. Wild fruits, berries and mollusks were gathered, and Spanish accounts mention large amounts of dried fish and dried venison. Pottery found in archaelogical sites indicates that extensive trade was carried on with other tribes, particularly the Timucua of northern Florida.

Apalachee territory was crossed in 1528 by the ill-fated Spanish expedition led by Pánfilo de Narváez. The Apalachee were less than hospitable to this group and the later DeSoto expedition. But by the mid-17th century they had been mostly converted to Catholicism by Spanish missionaries. Each of the tribe's eight principal towns had a Catholic mission and continued to prosper.

The beginning of the end for the Apalachee came in 1703-04, when a force of about 50 South Carolina militia and 1000 Creek Indian mercenaries led by Col. James Moore attacked and destroyed four Apalachee towns. Some 200 Apalachee were killed and 1400 others (including 100 slaves) were taken back to Carolina as prisoners.

Of the survivors of the raid, some fled to St. Augustine; others sought the protection of the French at Pensacola, and the rest scattered. Various bands drifted westward to Alabama and Louisiana or joined with other tribes who eventually migrated to Oklahoma. By the early 19th century, the Apalachee as a tribe were extinct.

BIBLIOGRAPHY: Fairbanks, Charles H. *Ethnohistorical Report on the Florida Indians.* New York: Garland Publishing, Inc., 1974

ARAPAHO: an Algonquin tribe located between the Platte and Arkansas rivers in eastern Colorado and southeastern Wyoming in the mid-19th century, when they numbered about 3,000. In the late 1970s, there were about 6,200 Arapaho, located mostly in Oklahoma and Wyoming.

Arapaho was derived from a Pawnee term meaning "he who trades," and referred to their position as middlemen in the trade between northern and southern plains Indians. They called themselves Hinanaeina, meaning "our people." According to tradition the Arapaho were formerly composed of five subtribes, or bands, one of which split off and became the Gros Ventre. The Arapaho were originally located between the headwaters of the Mississippi and the western end of Lake Superior. At that time, they grew corn and lived in permanent villages. Moving gradually westward onto the plains, they gave up agriculture and became nomadic buffalo hunters.

After moving to the plains, the Arapaho were divided into four bands, which wintered separately along wooded streams, keeping track of each other through messengers. In late spring, when the buffalo began gathering in large herds, the bands came together to hunt communally and to celebrate their sacred ceremonies.

There were four chiefs, but no principal chief. Decisions of the four were enforced by a soldier-police group, which also kept order during the communal buffalo hunts. There was a series of age-graded societies for the men, and there was one women's group, the Buffalo Lodge society. Societies cut across band lines, and there was a great deal of intermarriage among the bands. Polygamy was practiced, with men often marrying sisters and their brother's widow. The mother-in-law taboo prohibited men from looking at or speaking to their mother-in-law, and vice versa. The same taboo was somewhat less rigid for a woman and her father-in-law.

The most venerated object, and the symbol of the whole Arapaho tribe, was the sacred pipe. The keepers of the sacred pipe always pitched their tipi in the center of the Arapaho camping circle. When the tribe moved, the sacred pipe always headed the line of march. The most important tribal ceremonies of the Arapaho were the Sun Dance and celebrations related to the sacred pipe. When an Arapaho died, he was dressed in his best and laid in state for all to see. The body was then taken by horse to a nearby hill and buried. The grave was covered with brush, and the best horse of the deceased was killed. The mourners cut their hair, wore old clothes and lightly gashed their arms and legs.

The Arapaho of the plains had no permanent settlements, but moved from place to place in search of the buffalo. Their homes were portable buffalo skin tipis, made by the women. Along the interior walls there were willow frame beds covered with skins. In addition to shelter, the buffalo provided food and some items of clothing, including warm robes for winter. The buffalo meat was cut into strips by the women and dried, and some of it was pulverized and mixed with chokecherries and melted fat to make pemmican. Other game included elk, antelope, deer and various small animals, but buffalo was the preferred meat. Pups were sometimes eaten as a delicacy. Meat was boiled in a hole in the ground lined with a skin and filled with water and hot rocks. The diet was supplemented by gathering roots and berries. They had no agriculture except for cultivation of tobacco.

After the Arapaho obtained horses, the main means of hunting buffalo was by surrounding them on horseback. Each household averaged about ten horses, some used only for hunting or war, and others used as pack horses. They also used dog travois for transporting goods.

When they migrated from the northern woodlands, the Arapaho gave up some of their former crafts, such as pottery and basketry. They continued to produce intricate quillwork, applying it to buffalo robes. They learned to make cups and spoons from buffalo horns and carved bowls from cottonwood knots. Arrows were made by specially skilled old men, working in assembly line fashion.

During some unknown period in their history, the Arapaho from the upper Mississippi Valley migrated west to the upper Missouri River and then drifted southeastward onto the Plains, at some point separating from the Gros Ventre. Much of the movements of the Arapaho were made in company with the Cheyenne with whom they were closely allied. Warfare was frequent, with the Crow, Ute and Wind River Shoshoni their usual enemies.

Around 1835, the Arapaho divided, with the larger part moving south to the Arkansas River in eastern Colorado, becoming the southern Arapaho. The main attraction in that area was the trading post known as Bent's Fort. By 1840, the southern Arapaho had made peace with the other southern plains tribes, and sometimes joined with the Kiowa and Comanche in their raids on Texas and Mexico. In 1861, the southern Arapaho ceded all their lands for a reservation in Indian Territory (Oklahoma). The land initially assigned to them was unsatisfactory, and, together with the southern Cheyenne, their were assigned new lands along the North Canadian and upper Washita rivers.

Around 1890, the Arapaho were important supporters of the Ghost

Powder Face,
a northern
Arapaho
war chief.

The National Archives

Dance movement, which gradually waned after the Wounded Knee massacre. In 1890, the Arapaho and Cheyenne agreed to sell their Oklahoma reservation and to receive individual allotments of 160 acres each, thus opening up 3-1/2 million acres of their land to settlers. In 1937, the southern Arapaho and Southern Cheyenne were formally organized as the Cheyenne-Arapaho Tribes.

In 1868, the northern Arapaho signed a treaty with the United States at Fort Laramie, resulting in attempts to settle them with the southern Arapaho in Indian Territory. The few that went south could not adjust to the climate and other conditions and returned to the north. In 1878, the Arapaho were given the southeastern part of the Wind River Reservation in Wyoming, together with their former enemies, the Shoshoni. In 1907, this reservation was allotted in severalty, 160 acres to each individual. The remaining lands of the reservation were retained in joint ownership by the Arapaho and Shoshoni tribes.

In the late 1970s, the jointly-owned tribal land of the Wind River Reservation exceeded 1.7 million acres. Stock-raising was the main source of tribal income. At that time, there were about 3,700 northern Arapaho and 2,500 southern Arapaho. The tribal language was still spoken, more commonly among the Wyoming group than the Oklahoma group. A northern Arapaho family were caretakers of the sacred pipe, which was still the tribal symbol. Each year in July, the Sun Dance was held in Wyoming, participants including both northern and southern Arapaho.

BIBLIOGRAPHY: Elkin, Henry. *The Northern Arapaho of Wyoming.* New York: D. Appleton-Century Co., 1940; Kroeber, A.L. "The Arapaho." *Bulletin of American Museum of Natural History.* vol. 18, 1902-07; Trenholm, Virginia C. *The Arapahoes, Our People.* Norman: University of Oklahoma Press, 1970.

ARIKARA: an agricultural Caddoan tribe who moved progressively north along the Missouri River from Kansas into the Dakotas, in the late 17th century. They numbered perhaps 3-4,000 in the late 18th century, before smallpox epidemics took their toll. In the late 1970s, some 800 Arikara descendants remained, living with the Mandan and Hidatsa tribes at Fort Berthold Reservation in North Dakota.

The Arikara were the northern extension of the Caddoan lingusitic family, closely related to the Skidi Pawnee, from whom they separated around the 17th century. In the late 1970s a few Arikara still spoke the language. Their tribal name meant "horn," related to their custom of wearing their hair with two pieces of bone standing up on either side like horns. They called themselves Tanish, or the "original people."

The Arikara were a loosely organized confederacy of subtribes, each with a separate village and name. The head chief of the tribe was assisted by the tribal council, which was made up of village chiefs.

Many Arikara religious festivals were associated with corn and its planting, cultivation, harvesting, etc. They believed in a supreme deity who shared his powers with four assistants. Fasting, visions, sacred ceremonies and personal sacred bundles were important aspects of their religious life. The priesthood was hereditary in certain families, while other families enjoyed prestige as the caretakers of one of the tribal medicine bundles. These were a collection of sacred items such as sacred pipes, tobacco, perfect ears of corn and skins of various birds and animals.

The Arikara usually buried their dead in a sitting position, wrapped in skins, with the face painted red. A horse was sometimes killed over the mound grave, and a year of mourning was observed.

The Arikara located their villages on bluffs overlooking the Missouri River. In later times, they were fortified by timber stockades, reinforced with earth and surrounded by ditches. Arikara homes were semi-subterranean earth lodges about 40 feet in diameter, housing two or three families. They took a great deal of labor to construct, but were waterproof and lasted 10-20 years. A heavy wooden framework was covered with willow branches interwoven with grass and covered with a layer of mud or clay. Houses were grouped around a larger earth lodge that served as the medicine lodge, used for ceremonial gatherings. The Arikara also had portable skin tipis which they took along when hunting or traveling.

The Arikara were predominantly agricultural, growing eight or nine varieties of corn, beans, squash, pumpkins and sunflowers. They fertilized their crops and rotated their fields. Their surplus corn they traded to the Cheyenne and other tribes for buffalo robes, skins and meat. Some of this they exchanged with traders for guns, cloth, iron utensils and other goods, with the women usually doing the trading. The Arikara also hunted buffalo, deer and antelope to a certain extent, fished using traps, and gathered berries and other wild foods.

For crossing the Missouri and other rivers, the Arikara used round bull boats made by stretching a buffalo hide over a willow frame about four feet in diameter. They also made snowshoes for winter travel. The Arikara made hoes from the shoulder blade bones of a buffalo and spoons and bowls from the horns. Weapons included buffalo hide shields, flint knives, spears and bows with arrows tipped with flint or horn. They also produced stone mortars, pottery cooking vessels and excellent basketry.

The Arikara probably originated somewhere in the southwest, and, in the 17th century, began moving north with the Skidi Pawnee, from whom they separated in Nebraska. The Arikara moved northward along the Missouri River. In 1770, French traders found them south of the mouth of the Cheyenne River, at war with the Dakota. They suffered a smallpox epidemic in the 1780s and by about 1803, they occupied only three villages, between the Cannonball and Grand rivers in the Dakotas.

By the early 1820s, the Arikara found themselves at war with the U.S. Army. They retreated to join their Pawnee relatives on the Loup River in Nebraska for a few years, returning in about 1835. The Arikara and surrounding tribes were severely reduced by smallpox in 1837. By 1862, they had joined the Mandan and Hidatsa tribes, old trading partners, at Like-a-Fishhook village in a bend of the Missouri River. Around 1870, the area was set aside for the three tribes as Fort Berthold Reservation. In 1887, most of the land was allotted in severalty.

In the 1950s, the Garrison Dam was built, flooding about 25 percent of the reservations, including the best croplands and most of the homes and roads. In the 1970s, tourism facilities were established by the tribes

The Arikara chief
Pashtuwa-chta:
a drawing by
the 19th century
Swiss artist
Karl Bodmer.

The National Archives

on Lake Sakakawea, the reservoir formed by the dam. In the late 1970s, there remained 45,000 acres of tribally owned land and 350,000 acres of allotted land, belonging to individuals of the tribes. Some traditions, such as the Warbonnet Dance, were still observed by the 800 or so Arikara descendants living on the reservation.

BIBLIOGRAPHY: Work Progress Administration. *Arikara Indians.* Vermillion, South Dakota: University Museum, 1941.

ASSINIBOIN: a Siouan tribe living between Lake of the Woods and Lake Winnipeg in the 17th century, numbering about 10,000 at that time. In the late 1970s, there were more than 6,000 Assiniboin living in Montana, Alberta and Saskatchewan. They spoke the Nakota dialect of the Dakota language and, according to tradition, were originally part of the Yanktonai Dakota and lived with them in northern Minnesota. Assiniboin is an Ojibwa term meaning "he who cooks with stones."

The Assiniboin were organized into as many as 30 bands, each with its own chief, chosen for his popularity, ability and family connections. Each band had a council, whose decisions were carried out by the *akitcita,* a sort of police made up of the most responsible warriors. There were other men's societies and dance societies that were socially and ceremonially important.

Religious leadership was provided by various types of physicians, priests and sorcerers, both men and women, who used drums, gourd rattles, charms, songs and incantations. The most important cetemony of the Assiniboin and other Plains Indians was the annual Sun Dance, for which a large medicine lodge was constructed. Their supreme deity was Wakonda, creator of all things; but the sun, thunder and other deities were also worshipped. Dreams, sacrifices, feasting, dancing and the ritual purification of the sweat lodge were all important elements of their religious life.

The Assiniboin placed their dead on tree scaffolds. Dead warriors were dressed in war-dress, their faces painted red, weapons placed beside them, and a horse killed for their use in the afterlife. Women were supplied with the skin-dressing tools and other implements they might need. Mourners wailed, cut their hair, presented a disheveled appearance, and sometimes slashed their arms or legs. Meanwhile, the dead spirit departed for a paradise in the south, where the weather was always warm, the game abundant and there were no quarrels or war.

Assiniboin villages consisted of as many as 200 skin lodges or tipis. A medium-size tipi housing two to four families had a circumference of about 30 feet and was made from 12 dressed buffalo hides sewn together. Hunting and war parties made temporary shelters of brush and boughs.

The Assiniboin economy depended primarily on hunting. Buffalo, the most important game, were hunted in several ways. After the acquisition of horses, the communal hunt on horseback using bow and arrow was the most common method. They sometimes drove the buffalo into giant pens, where they were easily slaughtered. The women went along on hunts to help dress the meat, cutting it in thin strips which were hung up to dry. Elk, deer, bighorn sheep, antelope and wolves were also hunted, but the buffalo was the major supplier of food, shelter, bone tools and horn utensils.

Meat was usually roasted on a spit over the fire, although, while on hunting trips, the men liked to cook by digging a hole and lining it with a skin. This was filled with water, and red-hot rocks were placed in it to boil the water and cook the meat. The diet was supplemented by gathering wild turnips, acorns, grapes, plums and berries.

When the early Assiniboin traveled, they used dogs carrying packs or dragging travois. Early accounts tell of as many as 500 dogs employed in one journey by a large group. The Assiniboin were fond of visiting each other and friendly tribes such as the Cree. Horses later became very important, wealth often being counted by the number of horses owned. Snowshoes were used in winter, and bullboats and rafts were used to cross rivers.

The Assiniboin cooking utensils included clay and wood pots, as well as dippers and spoons of horn. They made flint hatchets and bone

An Assiniboin
placating the
spirit of a slain
eagle. A photo-
graph taken in
about 1900 by
Edward S. Curtis.

Library of Congress

knives, but spears and bow and arrow were the principal weapons. Crafts included intricately designed quillwork on clothing and pictographic writing on tree bark.

The Assiniboin may have separated from the Yanktonai in northern Minnesota by the late 16th century. By the mid-17th century, they had reached the area around Lake Nipigon and Lake of the Woods. In the late 17th century, the Assiniboin moved westward and joined the Cree in the Lake Winnipeg area. In 1775 they were reported along the Saskatchewan and Assiniboine rivers. They hunted a vast area of the northern Plains, frequently at war with the Dakota, Crow and Gros Ventre.

In 1780, a smallpox epidemic reduced their population by about 300 lodges. By this time, the Assiniboin were deeply engaged in the fur trade, particularly with the Hudson's Bay Company posts. In 1836, an even worse epidemic of smallpox killed 4,000 Assiniboin, as well as thousands of other Indians in that region.

The Assiniboin signed treaties with the U.S. in 1851 and 1855, which assigned them lands in western Montana. By the late 19th century, the Assiniboin occupied Fort Belknap Reservation, with the Gros

Building an Assiniboin sweat lodge. The framework of the house is constructed from the slender branches of trees.

Ventre, and Fort Peck Reservation, with the Dakota. In the winter of 1883-84, several hundred Assiniboin died at Fort Peck when rations were not delivered. In the early 20th century, lands were allotted to tribal members, and parts of the reservations were opened to homesteaders. In the 1870s, the Canadian Assiniboin were assigned to reserves in Alberta and Saskatchewan.

In the late 1970s, the largest concentration of the 1,500 or so Canadian Assiniboin was at the Stony Reserve in Alberta, while smaller groups were scattered at other reserves in Alberta and Saskatchewan. The U.S. Assiniboin, at the Fort Belknap and Fort Peck reservations, numbered about 4,500. Many tribal traditions were still strong among the Assiniboin.

BIBLIOGRAPHY: Lowie, Robert H. "The Assiniboine." *Anthropological Papers of the American Museum of Natural History.* no. 4, 1910.

ATAKAPA: an extinct tribe of the Tunican language family, located along the Louisiana-Texas coast from Vermilion Bay to Trinity Bay, numbering about 2,500 in 1600. Those who lived along Trinity Bay were called Akokisa by the Spanish. Atakapa is a Choctaw word meaning "man-eaters," derived from reports of cannibalism and ritual sacrifice of their enemies.

According to an Atakapa creation legend, man originally came from the sea, having been cast up on the shore inside of large oyster shells.

According to another legend, their ancestors were deposited by a flood on the mountaintops of northwest Texas.

The Atakapa lived in coastal fishing villages, locating the houses of their chief and shaman on top of shell mounds. Houses were built of poles interwoven with vines, with a smoke hole left in the top of the conical roof. Beds were made of driftwood covered with moss and skins.

The Atakapa subsisted mainly on fish, shellfish, wild plants and some corn. They hunted with spears and bone-tipped darts, occasionally going to the interior to hunt buffalo. They fished in the lagoons from their hollow log canoes, sometimes using poisons to stupefy the fish, causing them to rise to the surface. Alligators were occasionally caught and cooked whole, and their oil used as mosquito repellant and sunburn lotion.

By the 16th century, the Atakapa were engaged in regular trade with their neighbors. Dried fish was traded to the Avoyel for flint, some of which the Atakapa passed on to the Karankawa for pottery jars. The Atakapa also supplied the interior tribes with dried fish, shark's teeth and feathers (heron, crane, and pelican), in trade for animal skins and pottery.

By 1760, the Atakapa had begun selling some of their lands to French settlers. In 1779, they supplied the Spanish governor with warriors to attack British forts on the Mississippi. Until about 1836, the eastern Atakapa were concentrated on the Mermentau River, Louisiana, and the western Atakapa at Indian Lake (Lake Prien), Louisiana. By the mid-19th century, most of the tribe had succumbed to white man's vices and diseases, or been absorbed into the surrounding population.

BIBLIOGRAPHY: Dyer, V.O. *The Lake Charles Atakapas.* Galveston, 1917.

ATSINA: *See* GROS VENTRE.

AVOYEL: *See* NATCHEZ.

BAFFINLAND INUIT: a central Inuit (Eskimo) group located on Baffin Island in the Canadian Northwest Territories in the early 19th century, numbering more than 1,000. In the late 1970s, there were perhaps several hundred Baffinland Inuit, mostly located near various trading posts such as Pangnirtung on Cumberland Sound. They spoke a dialect of the Inuit (Eskimo) language, which was spoken, with minor variation, from Alaska to Greenland. The name Eskimo was derived from an Abnaki Indian term meaning "raw meat eaters," whereas the term Inuit, meaning "people," was their own name for themselves. The Baffinland Inuit were nomadic hunters with no real political organization. The main economic and social unit was the nuclear family, plus usually one or more other relatives. Religious leadership was provided by *angakok*, or shamans, whose powers derived from certain guardian spirits. According to their mythology, Sedna a woman at the bottom of the sea, controlled all the marine animals. *Angakok* had the power to visit Sedna and propitiate her and the spirits of offended animals. *Angakok* could also cure the sick, recover lost souls and control the weather.

In hard times, the Baffinland Inuit sometimes thought it necessary to abandon the sick or aged. When a person died, his body was immediately wrapped in skins and covered with rocks, and on the fourth day, hunting weapons and food were brought to the grave. The tent of the deceased was sometimes destroyed, and various taboos were observed.

In the winter, Baffinland Inuit built one-and two-family snow houses, using bone snow knives to cut blocks, which were placed in an inward leaning spiral until they formed a dome. Skin tents were used in summer.

They followed a seasonal cycle based on the hunting of marine mammals. Seals and whales were hunted with harpoons in summer from kayaks and *umiaks* (larger, skin-covered open boats). In winter, seals were hunted at their breathing holes. Other game included caribou as well as birds, taken with nets, and fish, caught with hooks. There were many taboos and ceremonies connected with hunting.

Cooking pots and blubber lamps for heat and light were carved from soapstone, and dishes, trays, spoons and ladles were made of wood. Animal and human figures were carved from wood and ivory. Winter transportation included wooden sleds and snowshoes, consisting of round wooden frames criss-crossed with thongs. Clothing made of caribou or seal skin, fit loosely to allow evaporation of perspiration. For maximum insulation, inner garments were worn with the hair side in, and outer garments with the hair side out. Boots of caribou or seal skin were worn over inner stockings.

The first European mariner to visit Baffin Island was Martin Frobisher in 1576, followed by William Baffin in 1616. The Cumberland Sound area, a long inlet on the eastern side of the island, was the most populous area, with eight villages of about 200 each in 1840. In the 19th century, whaling centers were established on the island by the Americans, Scottish and British. Many Inuit were employed at the stations, where they were introduced to manufactured items. With the later decline of the whaling stations, the Inuit returned for a time to their scattered settlements.

In the 20th century, trading posts were established on the island at

Cape Dorset, Lake Harbour, Frobisher Bay, Pangnirtung, Clyde, Pond Inlet and Arctic Bay.

BIBLIOGRAPHY: Boas, Franz. "The Eskimos of Baffinland and Hudson Bay." *Bulletin of the American Museum of Natural History.* vol. 15, 1901.

BANNOCK: a small Shoshonean tribe located in southeastern Idaho and western Wyoming in the early 19th century, when they numbered about 2,000. The Bannock were formerly a band of the Northern Paiute, and spoke a language of the Shoshonean division of the Uto-Aztecan linguistic family. In the late 1970s, the Bannock and Shoshoni tribes were located together on the Ft. Hall Reservation in Idaho, with a total population of about 3,200.

The Bannock were loosely organized into semi-nomadic bands, which ranged along the Snake River. The various band chiefs inherited their office through the male line, subject to community approval.

There were both men and women shamans, whose powers were either inherited or obtained in dreams, who cured the sick, conducted ceremonies and controlled the weather. Principal ceremonies included the Scalp Dance, Grass Dance, Circle Dance and Bear Dance. They buried their dead among the rocks, dressed in their best clothes and wrapped in a blanket, with their heads pointed west. Souls went west along the Milky Way on their journey to the land of the dead. The favorite horse of the deceased was killed, and mourners cut their hair, gashed their legs and observed a year of mourning.

For winter houses, and while traveling, the Bannock used buffalo skin tipis, with pictures depicting personal exploits painted over the door. Dome-shaped grass houses with a willow framework were used in summer, and a similar structure covered with earth served as a sweathouse.

The annual economic cycle of the Bannock called for salmon fishing in the spring on the Snake River, seed and root gathering on Camas Prairie in the summer, and a fall communal hunting trip to Montana for buffalo. Fish were caught with harpoons, weirs, hooks and basket traps below Shoshone Falls. Plant foods gathered included camas, yampa, pine nuts and a variety of seeds.

The Bannock were mainly horsemen, but they also used snowshoes and rafts of tule rushes. Their material culture included simple pottery, horn utensils, willow basketry for containers and cradles, buckskin bags, salmon skin bags, fur blankets, duck feather blankets and clothing of finely-tanned deerskin. The men wore moccasins, leggings and fringed

A young Bannock
warrior—a photo-
graph taken by
Major Lee
Moorhouse
in about 1902.

Smithsonian Institution National Anthropological Archives

shirts, and carried eagle feather fans for ceremonial occasions. Women
wore dresses, moccasins, knee-length leggings and necklaces of elk-teeth.
In cold weather, both wore robes of buffalo, elk or wildcat.

Enemies of the Bannock included the Blackfoot and sometimes the
Crow and Nez Perce. Their weapons included bows of wood and
mountain sheep horn, stone tipped arrows and spears, buffalo hide
shields and a *pogamoggan,* or war club. War horses, which they obtained
in trade from the Nez Perce, were painted with white clay and decorated
with feathers.

In the early 18th century, the Bannock acquired horses and became
skillful equestrians and warriors. Together with the Shoshoni, they
hunted buffalo, conducted raids and fought their common enemy, the
Blackfoot. With the discovery of gold in California, and the opening of
the Oregon Trail, a flood of miners and immigrants came through Bannock land. In the mid-19th century, the Bannock were decimated by
smallpox, and their pastures along the rivers were destroyed by wagon
trains. The Bannock and Shoshoni together fought in vain to protect
their lands. In 1868 they signed the Fort Bridger Treaty and agreed to
move to Fort Hall Reservation. Reservation life was difficult, and the
loss of their lands, the disappearance of the buffalo, insufficient rations,
and other incidents led the Bannock to revolt in 1878. By 1880, the
uprising had been put down, and the Bannock returned to Fort Hall.

By the late 1970s, there were about 3,200 Bannock and Shoshoni, living together on or near the 500,000-acre Fort Hall Reservation in southeastern Idaho.

BIBLIOGRAPHY: Madsen, Brigham D. *The Bannock of Idaho.* Caldwell, Idaho: The Caxton Printers, 1958.

BEAVER: an Athapascan tribe which, in the late 18th century, roamed the prairies of Alberta and British Columbia, in the Peace River area from the mountains in the west to the Peace River Falls about 40 miles downstream from Fort Vermilion, numbering about 1,500 at that time. In the 1970s, there were about 750 Beaver, living on various reserves in the traditional area.

They spoke a Northern Athapascan language related to that of the Sarsi and the Sekani. Culturally, they were similar to the Chipewyan and the Slave, their neighbors to the east and north, respectively. They were also known as the Tsattine, or "dwellers among the beavers," after the plentiful supply of those animals along the Peace River, which was called, by the Indians, the river of beavers.

The Beaver were a nomadic tribe, living in three-pole conical skin tipis of caribou or moose skins, or sometimes in temporary brush shelters, with no permanent dwellings. They were loosely organized into three or four autonomous, geographically defined groups or bands, each with its own general hunting territory and head man. The basic social and economic unit was the family or extended family. Newly married couples lived with the woman's family, and their children belonged to the man's family. Some polygamy was practiced, and women were generally relegated to carrying the heavy loads when the band moved.

Religion centered around guardian spirits acquired in dreams as a result of special preparation and fasting. Shamans acquired supernatural powers from especially powerful guardian spirits, and cured the sick by singing, blowing and sucking disease-causing objects from the body. The most important ceremony was a semiannual festival in which food was sacrificed on a special fire to assure a plentiful supply of similar food in the future. The dead were placed in a roll of birchbark and left on platforms or in trees. Widows cut their hair and often cut off finger joints, and widowers gashed their chests and put arrows through their arms or legs. Relatives of the deceased destroyed or gave away their possessions.

For subsistence, the Beaver relied on hunting, fishing and gathering. Moose were called with cone-shaped trumpets of birchbark and shot with bow and arrow. Buffalo were hunted communally, caribou were shot, rabbits were snared, and beaver were speared after confining them by fences around their lodges. Fish were caught with babiche (rawhide) nets, traps and, in winter, by hook-and-line through the ice.

Transportation in their constant wanderings was by birchbark canoe, snowshoes and toboggans, made of two thin boards curved up in front. They used knives of moose horn and beaver incisors for carving, and made willow bows and birch arrows with flint or moosehorn heads. Other material culture included birchbark dishes, caribou skin bags, and baskets of spruce bark or of spruce roots, woven tightly enough to hold water for cooking. Their clothing was usually of moose skin, consisting of moccasins, leggings, breechclout (for men) and a long coat reaching to knee level. For winter, the hair was worn inside, and for summer, the skins were dressed.

The Beaver apparently split off from the Sekani at some pre-historic time, moving onto the prairies as the Sekani moved into the mountains to the west. Subsequently, the Sarsi, in turn, split off from the Beaver. By the mid-18th century, the Beaver occupied the entire Peace River valley to Lake Athabaska, as well as part of the valley of the Athabaska River, before being driven west again by the Cree in about 1760. By 1876, when they first contacted Canadian traders, they were already obtaining arms and other trade goods indirectly, through other tribes. Subsequent years brought increasing trade, especially furs, and other contact with whites and eventual assignment to reserves.

In the 1970s, there were about 750 Beaver living on various reserves in Alberta and British Columbia in their traditional area, with land totaling about 57,400 acres. They were grouped into 5 bands: Clear Hills, Boyer River and Heart Lake in Alberta, and Fort St. John and Hudson Hope in British Columbia.

BIBLIOGRAPHY: Goddard, Pliny E. "The Beaver Indians." *Anthropological Papers of the American Museum of Natural History.* vol. 10, 1916.

BELLABELLA: a branch of the Kwakiutl living on Milbank Sound, British Columbia, numbering around 330 in 1901. The Bellabella were probably a group of previously independent tribes which banded together sometime in the historic period. In the 1970s, there were about 1,100 Bellabella descendants, living mainly in Bella Bella, B.C.

The Bellabella spoke the Heiltzuk dialect of the Kwakiutl language, a member of the Wakashan language family. Their tribal name was probably derived from an Indian pronunciation of Milbank. They were divided into three septs, or subtribes: Kokaitk, Oelitk and Oealitk, and three matrilineal clans, the Eagle, Raven and Killer Whale.

Culturally, the Bellabella were similar to the rest of the Kwakiutl tribes. Their social life revolved around secret societies, potlatches, and their rich mythological inheritance. Their mythology included a

A Bellabella mask.

folk hero, Raven, and a creator god, Chief Above. According to a creation myth, in the beginning there was only moonlight, and no sun. Chief Above created people and then created the sun, which was too hot, causing the earth to burn up. The people then prayed to Chief Above, who created a new sun, located higher in the sky.

The Bellabella lived in villages of cedar plank houses, often decorated with carved totem poles and clan crests. Their economy centered around salmon fishing, and gathering of wild foods. Dugout canoes were used extensively for travel, fishing, trade and warfare.

Before domination by Europeans, the Bellabella were apparently very warlike, fighting at various times with the Bella Coola, Haida and other Kwakiutl tribes. As Europeans moved into the area, their history followed that of other tribes in the area, with decline in population due to warfare and disease and eventual assignment to reservations.

In the 1970s, there were about 1,100 Bellabella, living on numerous small reserves in British Columbia, principally in the town of Bella Bella. Total area of land included in the reserves was 3,381 acres, of which 1,622 were in Bella Bella itself. Fishing was still important to the economy, but much of the old culture was gone. Many of the old myths were being forgotten, and the Bellabella religion had been essentially replaced by Christianity.

BELLA COOLA: a northwest coast tribe occupying the shores of the Bella Coola River and its tributaries in British Columbia, numbering about 1,400 in 1780. By the 1970s, they numbered about 600, mostly living on a reserve at Bella Coola, British Columbia.

The Bella Coola spoke a language of the Salishan language family, although they were surrounded by Kwakiutl, from whom they acquired some aspects of their culture. Their tribal name was derived from *bixula*, a term of unknown meaning applied to them by the Kwakiutl. They were also known as the Tallion nation, from the name of one of their towns.

The Bella Coola were formerly divided geographically into five groups: Kinsquit, Bella Coola proper, Nohalk, Talionk and Noothlakamish. The main political unit, however, was the autonomous village community, of which there were about 45, each ruled by a chief and having its own traditions. In order to preserve village traditions intact, marriages outside the village were forbidden.

The Bella Coola had a complex social structure, composed of chiefs, shamans, aristocracy, commoners and slaves. Chiefs obtained power by accumulating wealth and giving potlatches—ritualistic displays and distribution of gifts, which were at the center of village ceremonial life. Two ceremonies, the *kusiut* and the *susau'k* were conducted in fall and winter, respectively, often accompanied by potlatches. The *susau'k* were dramatizations of various legends, and the *kusiut* related to initiations into secret societies—the Laughers, the Throwers and the Cannibals being the most important.

The ceremonies were based on their complex religion and mythology. The Bella Coola believed in five worlds: two heavens, upper and lower, earth and two underworlds, upper and lower. Upper heaven was ruled by a supreme female deity, Qama'its, and lower heaven was occupied by a secondary deity, Alk'una'm, the sun Senx, and numerous lesser deities. When a person died, his soul went to the upper underworld. He then had the option of ascending to heaven, but at risk of being sent back to earth. Death the second time meant permanent exile in the lower underworld. According to a creation myth, in the beginning, the mountains were larger and the earth uninhabitable. Qama'its came down, conquered and shrunk the mountains and made the earth habitable.

Bella Coola material culture centered around wood. They carved intricate wooden masks for their ceremonies, painting them with ground up colored rocks mixed with fish oil. Their houses were of cedar planks, with entrances often through intricately carved house posts. They also carved out excellent cedar log canoes with adze and fire. Cedar bark was woven into cloaks, hats, leggings, aprons, baskets and mats, and braided into ropes and fishing lines.

Their economy was based on fishing, hunting and gathering, with

Smithsonian Institution National Anthropological Archives.

A totem pole before a gable-roofed house in Bella Coola village, British Columbia, Canada, in about 1900.

some trade. They caught salmon and eulachon (candle-fish) with nets woven from stinging nettles, and supplemented the diet with various berries and roots. Wild goats, captured, shorn and then set free, provided wool. They traded fish products with eastern Plateau Indians for furs and buckskin, and later to European traders for cloth, muskets, powder and shot, knives, axes and rum.

The Bella Coola probably settled in the present territory in about 1400, driving out some Kwakiutl. Later years were filled with conflict with the neighboring Kwakiutl villages. First contact with Europeans was with the explorer Alexander Mackenzie in about 1793. There was limited contact with white traders, until 1851, when gold was discovered in the area, and a main route to the gold fields led through Bella Coola territory. Smallpox and liquor then took toll, weakening the tribe and resulting in widespread starvation. Decline continued through the 19th century. In 1867, Hudson's Bay Company established a post, and in 1883 a Methodist mission was established. Around 1884, potlatches were made illegal, and in 1894 a large number of Norwegian colonists settled in the area. In 1930, logging industry moved into the area, and in 1950, the first road was completed over the mountains to the outside.

In the 1970s, there were about 600 Bella Coola, mostly living on a reserve in Bella Coola, British Columbia. The ceremonial life had deteriorated considerably. The traditional dances were still performed to some extent, and woodcarving was produced for sale to tourists.

BIBLIOGRAPHY: Boas, Franz. "The Mythology of the Bella Coola Indians." *Memoirs of the American Museum of Natural History.* 1898; Kopos, Cliff. *Bella Coola.* Vancouver: Mitchell Press Limited, 1970.

BEOTHUK: an extinct tribe located in Newfoundland, numbering perhaps 500 in the early 17th century. The Beothuk were driven to extinction by white incursions and warfare with the Micmac in the early 19th century. Whether the Beothuk language belonged to the Algonquian language family or to a separate family was still unresolved in the late 1970s.

The Beothuk occupied small camps of three or more wigwams, each housing several nuclear families. A leader headed each camp or group of camps. Celebrations included 24-hour wedding feasts. When a man died, he was buried with his weapons and tools. Carved wooden figurines, thought to have religious significance, were among the grave goods. The body of the deceased was either placed in a wooden box on a scaffold, laid on the floor of a burial hut, or placed in a cave, rock crevice or rock pile.

The Beothuk made conical wigwams of birch bark on a pole frame. A smokehole was located above the central fireplace, and trenches in the floor were used as beds. They also built dome-shaped skin-covered sweat lodges and racks for drying salmon and storing canoes. For storage, they used bark-lined pits and both conical and ridge-roofed storage houses.

Beothuk economy was based on fishing, hunting and gathering. They fished for salmon, harpooned seals, snared birds and gathered bird's eggs, shellfish and roots. In winter, they hunted migrating caribou with spears, sometimes driving them into the water and giving chase in canoes. The meat was preserved by freezing or smoking.

For transportation, the Beothuk used birchbark (and occasionally caribou skin) canoes, distinctively shaped with high pointed bow and stern and high pointed sides at midship. Snowshoes and hand-drawn sleds were used in winter. Dishes, boxes, buckets and cooking vessels were made from sewn birch or spruce bark. Both men and women wore caribou skin robes, supplemented by leggings, moccasins, mittens and hats. Cold weather clothing was made with the hair side in. For adornment and as an insect repellent, the Beothuk wore red hair and body paint made from powdered red ocher and grease. Early European explorers, on meeting the Beothuk thus adorned, reportedly coined the term "red Indians."

The Beothuk were traditionally friends with the Montagnais of Labrador, but were enemies of the Labrador Inuit (Eskimo).

Beothuk territory was visited by European explorers beginning in the late 15th century. In the 17th century, British, French and Micmac Indian fur trappers began settling on Labrador. Early friendship with the Micmac ended when the French began offering bounties on the Beothuk. By the early 19th century, the Beothuk were finally driven to near extinction by disease, starvation and European and Micmac raiding parties. The survivors probably fled to the Montagnais on Labrador.

BIBLIOGRAPHY: Howley, James P. *The Beothuks or Red Indians.* London: Cambridge University Press, 1915; Winter, Keith. *Shanaditti: The Last of the Beothuks.* North Vancouver, British Columbia: J.J. Douglas, Ltd., 1975.

BILOXI: a small tribe formerly located in Mississippi around Biloxi Bay. Along with the Ofo Indians they were the only speakers of languages of the Siouan linguistic family in this area. Both tribes probably migrated to this area from somewhere in the Ohio valley.

The Biloxi probably never numbered more than 400. The name translated means "first people." French visitors to the Biloxi village on the Pascagoula River in 1700 described it as having 30 or 40 cabins surrounded by an eight foot palisade. Three square watch towers, ten feet on a side, provided additional protection.

On the death of a chief, the tribe would immediately dry the body before a fire. The bodies of the leaders would then be placed inside the village temple along with those of their predecessors. There was an elaborate system of kinship with descent through the female line.

Biloxi material culture included implements of horn and bone, bowls of wood and pottery, and basketry. For adornment feather headdresses, bones and bird beak necklaces, nose rings and earrings were worn, and some tattooing was practiced.

The Biloxi lived together at times with the Pascagoula Indians. After the French lost control of the area to the British in 1763, the Biloxi moved with the Pascagoula across the Mississippi River into Louisiana. Some joined the Tunica Indians around Marksville, while others went to Texas and eventually Oklahoma.

By the late 1970s, a few Indians in the Marksville area could trace their lineage as Biloxi, usually mixed with Tunica, Ofo, Choctaw, or Pascagoula.

BIBLIOGRAPHY: Dorsey, James Owen. *The Biloxi Indians of Louisiana.* Salem: Salem Press, 1893.

BLACKFOOT: a confederacy of three Algonquian tribes located on the northern Plains, numbering about 15,000 in 1780. In the late 1970s, the Blackfoot had a population of about 14,500, living mostly in Montana and Alberta. The Blackfoot confederacy, also known as the Siksika, was composed of the Blackfoot proper, the Blood and the Piegan. Siksika, a Cree term meaning "blackfoot people" may have referred to black-dyed moccasins or to moccasins blackened by the ashes of prairie fires.

The Blackfoot proper, or Northern Blackfoot, occupied territory from the northern branch of the Saskatchewan River south to the Battle River. The Blood, who called themselves Kainah, or "many chiefs," were located between the Battle and Bow rivers. The Piegan, or Pikuni, meaning "small robes" or "poorly dressed robes," were located along the foothills of the Rocky Mountains, south of the Marias River.

Each of the three tribes were organized into autonomous bands, with the Piegan having at least 23, the Blood 7 and the Blackfoot at least 6. In the winter, the bands lived separately, usually in sheltered river valleys. In summer, the bands would gather by tribe to hunt buffalo and celebrate the Sun Dance. Each band was led by a head man, who gained his position by sponsoring social events, helping the poor and showing bravery in warfare. The head men together formed the tribal council and selected the tribal chief. Each of the three tribes was completely autonomous, although very closely linked by culture and language.

Blackfoot social organization was rather complex. The men were divided by age into a series of military societies known collectively as *ikuhnuhkahtsi,* or "all comrades." There were also numerous dance associations and religious societies, to which both men and women belonged, each with its own regalia and ceremonies. Among the Blood and Northern Blackfoot, there was a women's society called the Malaki.

The Blackfoot religion was very rich in both group ceremony and personal expression. Medicine bundles, consisting of collections of sacred objects, were owned by individuals, as well as bands and societies. Group ceremonies, such as the annual Sun Dance, were occasions for personal sacrifice and offerings. The Sun Dance consisting of at least four days of dancing , feasting and sacrifice, was sponsored by a woman, as an expression of gratitude for some favor. The woman, known then as the medicine woman, purchased, with her husband, a medicine bundle and organized the ceremony, including the construction of the medicine lodge.

Two Blackfoot—a Blood (left) and a Piegan (center)—with a Kutana (right): a drawing by Karl Bodmer.

Usually the dead were placed on a tree scaffold and a horse was killed for the journey to the land of the dead. When a Blackfoot died in his tipi, however, it was often used as a burial tipi. Mourners cut their hair, affected a disheveled appearance and sometimes slashed their arms or legs or cut off fingers.

The skin tipi was the usual house style of the Blackfoot and other nomadic Plains Indians. In the early days, these portable dwellings were dragged by dogs pulling travois. With the advent of the horse, longer tipi poles could be carried.

The women constructed and put up the tipi while the men often painted them with star constellations and other designs. Other duties of women included dressing of hides, making clothing, gathering, cooking, storing food, carrying wood and water and all work connected with packing and moving camp. Women owned the tipis, travois, household implements and the horses they rode.

The Blackfoot were primarily buffalo hunters, but supplemented their diet by gathering wild foods, such as turnips, potatoes, onions, cherries, plums and berries. Meat and plant foods were usually dried and stored. Pemmican was made of dried, pounded meat mixed with dried berries or chokecherries and stored in skin bags. The surplus was sold to traders. One pound of pemmican was considered by some to be equivalent to five pounds of meat in food value.

Bureau of Indian Affairs

Building a tipi on the Blackfoot reservation in Montana.

They also hunted or trapped deer, elk and antelope, but buffalo was the preferred game, providing them with food, shelter, clothing, tools and utensils. More than 60 uses for buffalo were known to the Blackfoot. They hunted buffalo in several different ways, including stampeding them over cliffs, driving them into impoundments, surrounding a herd on horseback, and, on occasion, individual stalking. Bulls were usually taken in spring and cows in autumn. After the Blackfoot acquired horses, the surround was the most common method. Bow and arrow were the preferred weapons, even after the introduction of firearms.

Containers of various shapes and sizes were made of skins, often with designs painted on them. Other decorative arts included quillwork and beadwork, usually applied to clothing. Women wore long one-piece skin dresses belted at the waist, and men wore skin shirts, leggings and moccasins. Men wore a lock of hair down the middle of their foreheads to their noses. Caps, with horns, were made from bird or weasel skins.

The Blackfoot may have once lived among Algonquin tribes farther east but by the time of the coming of Europeans, they had lived for many years as hunters on the northern Plains. They probably acquired horses from southern tribes between 1725 and 1750. Eventually the Blackfoot acquired large numbers of horses enabling them to range over a vast area in search of the buffalo, from the northern branch of the Saskatchewan River, south to the headwaters of the Missouri in Montana. The Blackfoot, friendly with the Gros Ventre and Sarsi Indians, warred with most of the other neighboring tribes, including the Flathead, Nez Perce, Assiniboin, Crow and Cree.

By the late 18th century, they were engaged in the fur trade. In 1781-82, they were hit by a smallpox epidemic, and again in 1839, 1869 and 1870. These epidemics, as well as the measles, which struck in 1864, severely reduced the Blackfoot population. Between 1851 and 1878, they ceded their lands in treaties with the United States and Canada. The Blackfoot Reservation was established in western Montana, and three other reserves were established in Alberta, Canada.

In 1883, the last great buffalo herd was destroyed, and the following year some 600 Montana Blackfoot, mostly Piegan, died of starvation. In the 1880s drought foiled both U.S. and Canadian Blackfoot attempts at raising crops. Stock raising, begun in the 1890s, was more successful.

In the late 1970s, there were about 6,500 Blackfoot, mostly Piegan, living in or near the northwestern Montana reservation. Of the 950,000 total acres, 120,000 acres were tribally owned, and 775,000 allotted to individuals. The annual North American Indian Day celebration drew Indians from both the U.S. and Canada.

In Alberta, about 8,000 Blackfoot lived on the Piegan, Blackfoot and Blood reserves, the latter being the largest in Canada. Both U.S. and Canadian Blackfoot still celebrate curing ceremonies, medicine bundle openings and other traditional ceremonies.

BIBLIOGRAPHY: Mcfee, Malcolm. *Modern Blackfeet.* New York: Holt, Rinehart, and Winston, Inc. 1972; Wissler, Clark. "Material

Bureau of Indian Affairs

A Blackfoot
medicine lodge
—probably a
Sun Dance
lodge.

An 1891 photograph of a Brulé camp on the Brulé River, near Pine Ridge, South Dakota.

Culture of the Blackfoot Indians." *Anthropological   Papers of the American Museum of Natural History*, *no. 5*, 1910.

BLOOD: a northern plains Algonquian tribe of the Blackfoot confederacy. *See* BLACKFOOT.

BRULE: the second largest subdivision of the Teton Dakota, located near the headwaters of the White and Niobrara rivers in South Dakota and Nebraska, in the mid-19th century, numbering about 3,000 at that time. Brulé is the French translation of Sichangu, by which they were known, meaning "burnt thighs." The Brulé were divided into Upper Brulé and Lower Brulé, which were subdivided into about 13 bands. In the late 1970s, Brulé descendants numbered about 8,000 mostly located on or near the Rosebud and Lower Brulé reservations in South Dakota. (See also *Teton* and *Dakota*).

BIBLIOGRAPHY: Hyde, George E. *Spotted Tail's Folk*. Norman: University of Oklahoma Press, 1937.

BUNGI: *See* OJIBWA.

Antelope—a
Caddo Indian.

Smithsonian Institution National Anthropological Archives.

CADDO: a loose confederacy of up to 25 small tribes, living along the Red River in Louisiana and Arkansas and in eastern Texas in the 18th century, with a total population of about 8,000. In the late 1970s, there were about 1,200 Caddo descendants residing in Oklahoma. The Caddo were comprised of several groupings or sub-confederacies, including the Hasinai, Kadohadacho and the Natchitoches. The Hasinai, called Texas or Tejas by the Spanish, lived in eastern Texas and numbered about 3,000 in the 18th century. The Kadohadacho, or Caddo proper, lived along the Red River in Louisiana and Arkansas, with a population of about 2,500, and the Natchitoches lived along the Red River in Louisiana, numbering about 1,800. There were also at least two other tribes, Adai and Eyish, with populations of several hundred each. All were members of the southern branch of the Caddoan linguistic family.

Caddo comes from the Caddoan word *caddi* meaning "chief." Each tribe was headed by a *caddi*, who was assisted by *canaha* and other lesser grades of officials. The Hasinai were ruled by a head chief or high priest called *xinesi* or *chenesi*. All offices and titles were hereditary through the male line.

The Caddo worshipped a supreme deity called Ayanat Caddi, as well as numerous lesser spirits, including the sun. Throughout the year, there were numerous ceremonies held in conjunction with planting, the ripening of the green corn, harvesting and hunting. Fasting, prayer, sacrifice, dancing and music were all important elements of these celebrations.

When a person died, he was buried along with any scalps he had taken in life, so his enemies would serve him in the afterlife. Food and water were placed in the grave. A man was buried with his tools and weapons, while a woman was buried with her household utensils. Those killed in warfare were cremated. A fire was kept burning by the grave for six nights, after which time the person's spirit traveled southward to the House of Death, where all were happy.

The Caddo had two types of houses. One type was conical, up to 60 feet in diameter, consisting of a pole framework covered with grass thatch. The other type was the earth lodge, similar to those of their linguistic relatives, the Pawnee and Arikara. These had a heavy wood frame, covered with brush, cane, sage grass and a layer of earth or clay. Houses were grouped about an open area used for dances, games, ceremonies and other gatherings.

The Caddo were both agriculturists and hunters. They grew two corn crops a year and saved the best ears for seed. They grew beans, staking them up with reeds to increase their yield. Nuts, acorns, mulberries, blackberries and pomegranates were gathered, along with persimmons, which were made into bread. Deer, bear, buffalo, raccoon and turkey were the principal game, with deer being stalked by hunters wearing stuffed deer heads.

Bows were made of the osage orange, a favorite wood which the Caddo exported, along with salt, to other tribes. For transportation, they used dugouts, cane rafts, and in later times, horses. The Caddo produced fine basketry, woven mats, feather mantles and cloth of mulberry bark. They were best known, however, for their excellent pottery, reportedly second only to that of the Pueblo Indians. For adornment, they wore nose rings and elaborate tattoos, in animal, bird and flower designs.

The Caddo may have originated in the southwest. By the time they were visited by the DeSoto expedition in 1540-41, they had migrated east, occupying the Red River Valley in Louisiana and Arkansas and lived along the Sabine, Neches, Trinity, Brazos and Colorado rivers in eastern Texas.

In the 18th century, the area became a battleground for the French and Spanish, who turned Caddo villages into armed garrisons. European diseases brought extinction to many Caddo tribes. In 1835 the Louisiana Caddo ceded all their lands in a treaty with the U.S. and joined the Caddo tribes in Texas. At this time, however, Texans were bent on driving out all Indians, and the Caddo were forced to flee to Indian Territory (Oklahoma) in 1859.

A reservation was established north of the Washita River and occupied by Caddo, Wichita and Delaware tribes. Around 1901, tribal lands were allotted to individuals. The three tribes together had about 61,000 acres of allotted land and 2,370 acres of tribal land.

In the 1970s, the Caddo descendants in Oklahoma numbered around 800. Although they had essentially been assimilated into the rest of society, they had retained many of their songs and dances and still conducted traditional ceremonies throughout the year.

BIBLIOGRAPHY: Swanton, John R. "Source Material on the History and Ethnology of the Caddo Indians." *Bureau of American Ethnology Bulletin*. no. 132, 1942.

CAHUILLA: a southern California group located southwest of the San Bernardino Mountains in the late 18th century, numbering between 4,000 and 6,000 at that time. In the late 1970s, there were about 900 Cahuilla descendants, mostly living on or near ten small reservations in southern California.

Cahuilla may have been derived from *kawiya,* meaning "master." The Cahuilla language belongs to the Takic division of the Uto-Aztecan language family.

The Cahuilla had two divisions, or moieties, Wildcat and Coyote, each of which were composed of a number of clans. A person inherited the clan of his father, and was required to marry outside his clan and moiety. The hereditary head of the clan was both a religious and political leader, who supervised economic and ceremonial activities.

Curing of illnesses was performed by male shamans, using super-natural powers, and female doctors, using their knowledge of medicinal plants and other remedies. The Cahuilla believed that each person had a soul spirit which lived on after he died, journeying to the land of the dead.

Villages were located near water courses and were composed of dome-shaped brush shelters or rectangular thatched houses. In addition there were acorn granaries, a sweathouse and a ceremonial house used for curing, dances and other gatherings.

Hunting, gathering and some agriculture provided the Cahuilla with a varied diet. Rabbits and other small game were trapped or hunted with bow and arrow. Six varieties of acorns were gathered, along with pine nuts, cactus bulbs, and various seeds, berries, roots and greens. They also cultivated some corn, beans, and squash. Cahuilla crafts included the making of baskets of various shapes for different uses, such as winnowing, carrying and storage.

Cahuilla baskets.
Smithsonian Institution

In the late 18th century, contact began between the Cahuilla and the Spanish. By the early 19th century, some Cahuilla worked seasonally on Spanish cattle ranches, returning to their villages in the off season. They maintained their autonomy until severely reduced by a smallpox epidemic in 1863. Between 1877 and 1896, they were scattered to numerous reservations.

In the late 1970s, there were about 900 Cahuilla descendants, located on or near about eight reservations. Much of Cahuilla culture had been lost or modified, but there was a growing interest in the traditional way of life. Cahuilla language classes were popular; some religious ceremonies were still performed, and the Malki Museum of Cahuilla culture was established at Morongo Reservation.

BIBLIOGRAPHY: Hooper, Lucille. "The Cahuilla Indians." *University of California Publications in American Archaeology and Ethnology.* vol. 16, 1920; James, Harry C. *The Cahuilla Indians.* Los Angeles: Westernlore Press, 1960; Kroeber, A.L. "Ethnography of the Cahuilla Indians." *University of California Publications in American Archaeology and Ethnology.* vol. 8, 1908.

CALUSA: an extinct Muskogean-speaking tribe of Florida Indians who dominated the lower Gulf Coast from southern Tampa Bay to Cape Sable and all the islands and keys between. They numbered about 3,000 in 1650 but had disappeared as a tribe by the early 19th century.

Calusa culture was most noted for its extensive building of high, flat-topped shell mounds on which were constructed temples and homes of their chiefs. Carefully laid down in layers, shells were also used to make roadways and canals.

Calusa villages, numbering about 50 in the mid-17th century, were built on shell mounds along bayous and streams. Houses were of wattle and daub with palm thatched roof and were sometimes built on pilings near the water. Small mulch gardens were cultivated, but fishing and hunting were the main sources of food. Hooks, spears, nets and traps were all used for fishing.

The Calusa were fine artisans, producing delicate woodcarvings of animals and intricate inlaid work with tortoise shell and sharks' teeth. They made tools such as adzes, scrapers, hoes, hammers, knives, saws, rasps, and awls of various materials such as antlers, shells, sharks' teeth, fish bones, and coral.

Calusa men were tall and wore their hair tied in a top knot with a short rim of hair encircling the crown. Breech clouts which sufficed most of the year were supplemented with deerskin garments in winter. Women wore clothing made from Spanish moss treated until it was soft and fine. Elaborate tattooing and body painting were practiced, especially by chiefs. Beads, pendants, and ear buttons of shell, wood, or bone were also popular.

Materials found at some Calusa archaelogical sites have been carbon dated to 1450-1140 BC. The Calusa probably had some contact with the Southern Death Cult tradition found among the tribes of the Gulf region about AD 1200. They practiced ceremonial human sacrifice, usually of captives taken in warfare.

Intrepid sailors, the Calusa plied the Florida Gulf Coast and carried on a canoe trade with Cuba and perhaps the Yucatan. It was a fleet of 80 Calusa canoes that drove off Ponce de Leon in 1513.

But the Spanish did eventually gain a foothold in Florida. Wars between the Spanish and the British along with their Indian allies led to the final destruction of the Calusa as a tribe. Several hundred reportedly fled to Cuba in the early 19th century. The remaining Calusa joined with the Seminole and shared their fate.

BIBLIOGRAPHY: Voegelin, Byron D. *South Florida's Vanished People*. Fort Myers Beach, Florida: The Island Press, 1943.

CARIBOU INUIT: a group of small central Canadian Arctic tribes located in the southern part of the Barren Grounds west of Hudson Bay in the late 18th century, when they numbered about 500. In the late 1970s, a small number of Caribou Inuit (Eskimo) remained in their traditional territory.

The Caribou Inuit were so-named for their almost total dependence on caribou hunting. Although they fished and hunted for other animals, failure to connect with the migrating caribou herds could spell disaster. They spoke the Inuit (Eskimo) language, which was spoken, with minor variations, by Inuit peoples from Alaska to Greenland. The name Eskimo was derived from an Abnaki Indian term meaning "raw meat eaters," whereas the term Inuit, meaning "people," was their own name for themselves.

Political organization among the Caribou Inuit was minimal, with certain mature men attaining respect through hunting skill and personal appeal. Their advice was sought on such matters as where or when to move camp.

The family was the basic unit, with newly-married couples living with either set of parents. Polygamy was occasionally practiced; a widow often married the brother of her deceased husband. Religious ceremonies emphasized hunting rites, such as leaving a piece of meat as an offering to a slain caribou's soul. Ceremonial and social dances were performed to the accompaniment of tambourine, drums and singing. When a person died, his body was wrapped in a skin and placed within a circle of stones along with various grave goods. The relatives observed a mourning period which included ritual purification and numerous taboos.

The Caribou Inuit built snow houses in winter, and used conical caribou skin tents the rest of the year. Snowhouses were usually built by two men working together. One man cut the snow into blocks with a snow knife, while the other man, working from inside, laid the blocks in an ascending spiral until they formed a dome. A block of clear freshwater ice was set in place over the door to act as a window. To avoid cold drafts, the long entry passage, with storage areas on the side, was dug at a lower level than the house.

Inside was a platform of snow, covered with willow mats and skins, which served as table, chairs and bed. A smaller platform was used for storage. Off to the side a small room with a smokehole in the roof served as a kitchen. For summer dwellings, women put up skin tents over a framework of poles. Brush windbreaks were constructed as work areas.

The most important season was autumn, when the caribou began migrating in vast herds. At this time, the Caribou Inuit gathered to hunt where the herds crossed the rivers, and to take advantage of the autumn fish runs. Winter was spent camping near their food caches and ice fishing on the inland lakes. A very few Caribou Inuit living near the coast also hunted seal and walrus in small numbers. Polar bears, wolves, wolverines and foxes were hunted for their furs.

In spring they hunted ptarmigan and various waterfowl and caught trout using hooks, weirs and spears. Birds' eggs and an assortment of berries were gathered in summer, which was also the trading season.

Hunting weapons and techniques included bow and arrow, caribou lances, harpoons, slings, bolas, nets, snares and pitfalls. Kayaks were

Anoteelik, a
Caribou Inuit,
wearing caribou-
skin clothes and
holding a
caribou spear
(1947).

Smithsonian Institution National Anthropological Archives.

used for transportation as well as for hunting caribou.

Winter transport was the dog sled, the wooden runners of which were covered with a smooth layer of frozen peat, which was kept coated with ice so the sleds would slip easily over the snow. Warm clothing was made from caribou skins, while utensils, ladles and trays were made of bone, wood and soapstone.

Between 1769 and 1772, the Caribou Inuit were visited by a Hudson's Bay Company expedition led by Samuel Hearne. In the late 18th century they began trading regularly with traders at Churchill. In trade with the Chipewyan Indians to the south, the Caribou Inuit exchanged caribou skins and soapstone for moccasins, pyrite and snowshoes. In the late 19th century, they often traveled 300 miles to trade at the post on Reindeer Lake, but by the early 20th century, a series of trading posts were established on nearby Neultin Lake. In 1946-47, a estimated one-third of the Caribou Inuit starved when they failed to make contact with the caribou herd.

BIBLIOGRAPHY: Birket-Smith, Kaj. "The Caribou Eskimos." *Report of the Fifth Thule Expedition 1921-24*. vol. 5, 1929.

CARRIER: an important northern Athapascan tribe living in British Columbia, north of the Chilcotin tribe, around Eutsuk, Francis, Babine and Stuart lakes and the headwaters of the Fraser River, numbering about 8,500 in the late 18th century. In the 1970s, about 4,600 Carrier remained, divided into 16 bands, scattered around British Columbia.

The Carrier spoke a language of the Athapascan family, and called themselves Takulli, or "people who go upon the water." The name Carrier was derived from their custom of each widow carrying the cremated remains of her dead husband with her for three years in a birchbark satchel. During this period, she was forbidden to marry and was in servitude to her husband's family.

The Carrier comprised three subdivisions—Southern (or Lower), Northern (or Upper) and Babines—which were composed of autonomous villages, each led by a chief, or *meotih*. They were also divided into phratries and 19 bands or clans, each with its own territory and hunting grounds. They had a complex society, composed of hereditary nobles, commoners, and a few slaves. Descent of property and titles was sometimes through the male and sometimes through the female line. The *meotih*, whose office was inherited, had as chief responsibilities the settling of disputes over hunting and fishing territory and the giving of potlatches, which were extravagant feasts highlighted by the display and distribution of family wealth.

The Carrier apparently believed in an impersonal supreme being, but more important were a multitude of good and bad spirits, the latter roaming the world causing sickness and other evils. Shamans cured ills and recovered lost souls through powers obtained from guardian spirits acquired by fasting and dreaming in special places. The Carrier believed in reincarnation, as well as life after death, either in a shadowy underworld or somewhere in the west.

The Carrier were semisedentary, living in fixed villages but traveling seasonally for hunting and fishing. They build multi-family, rectangular pole-frame lodges, with gabled roofs, covered with bark or brush. For winter the Southern division used a similar dwelling, which they excavated to a depth of one-and-a-half feet and covered with a layer of earth.

The Carrier economy was based on fishing, hunting and gathering of roots and berries. The men took caribou, deer, bear, beaver, marmot and rabbit, using bow and arrow as well as eight different kinds of snares. Salmon were caught in rivers in the summer, and carp and other fish were caught in lakes through the ice in the winter.

Carrier crafts included many articles of wood. Canoes and cooking vessels were made from birchbark. For overland travel, they used snowshoes as well as birch board toboggans towed by dog teams. In warfare, they carried shields of wood slats or moosehide covered with fine pebbles.

Men wore leggings, moccasins and a robe, often going without clothes in warm weather. Women wore aprons and moccasins. For special ceremonies, nobles wore beautiful *chilkat* blankets, obtained from the Tsimshian in trade. Women wore stone labrets, or lip plugs, for adornment.

First contact with Europeans was with the Scottish explorer Alexander Mackenzie in 1793. In 1806, Fort St. James was built in Carrier territory, becoming a popular trading post. In 1842, a Catholic missionary, Father Demers, arrived, apparently successfully converting many to Catholicism. After that time, the increased influx of white traders, miners and settlers took its toll, bringing a population decline due to epidemics throughout the rest of the 19th century.

In the 1970s, about 4,500 Carrier were divided into 16 small bands, living on a number of small reserves in their old territory in British Columbia. The bands, each with their own reserves, were: Burns Lake, Cheslatta, Ulkatcho, Takla Lake, Stuart-Trembleur Lake, Stony Creek, Stellaque, Quesnel, Omineca, Necoslie, Nazko, Moricetown, Lake Babine, Kluskus, Fraser Lake and Fort George. Total acreage of all reserves was 63,000. Principal sources of income for tribes in the area were lumbering and trapping.

BIBLIOGRAPHY: Morice, A.G. "Carrier Sociology and Mythology." *Transactions of the Royal Society.* Ottawa: 1892. Jenness, Diamond. "Indians of Canada." *Bulletin of the Canadian National Museum.* no. 65, 1960.

CATAWBA: a nation of great hunters and warriors who lived along the Catawba River in the Carolinas. In their wanderings, they ranged northward to the Great Lakes, south into Georgia and westward into Cherokee territory.

The largest of the Carolina tribes after the Cherokee, the Catawba numbered about 6,000 in the early 17th century. Smallpox epidemics and warfare with larger tribes reduced the Catawba population to about 500 in 1780. As disease and warfare took their toll, the Catawba absorbed other small neighboring tribes, including the Cheraw, Sugaree, Waxhaw, Congaree, Santee, Pedee, and Wateree. In the late 1970s, some 400 Catawba of mixed blood lived on or near the Catawba state reservation near Rock Hill, South Carolina.

The Catawba, also called Issa or Esaw, spoke an eastern Siouan language, of which only a few words were known in the late 1970s. The name Ossa or Esaw is translated as "people" or "people of the river."

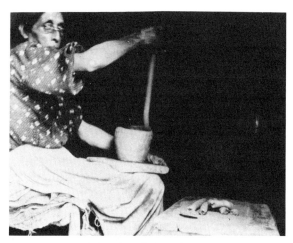

Martha Jane
Harris a Catawba,
on the Catawba
Reservation,
South Carolina,
(1913).

Smithsonian Institution National Anthropological Archives

Early accounts of Catawba towns note the presence of temples similar to those of other southeastern Indians. Houses were usually bark covered cabins, with fields nearby. Women did the work of cultivating corn, beans, squash and gourds while the men ranged far in their search for buffalo, deer, elk and bear. Passenger pigeons and fish caught in traps supplemented the diet. The advent of the British trader greatly changed the life of the Catawba. Desired goods such as guns, cloth, metal tools, axes, pots, knives, beads, tinder boxes and blankets caused the Catawba to range increasingly further in their hunting. The major Indian trails—the 500 mile route between Virginia and Georgia and the trail westward to the Cherokee—crossed through Catawba territory. These were adopted as trade routes by the British traders. In the mid-1700s, at the peak of the trading, packhorse trains with as many as 100 animals could be seen moving along the ancient Indian trails. The result was constant warfare with their old enemies, the Shawnee, Iroquois and Cherokee. This, along with major smallpox epidemics in 1738 and 1759 brought about the decline of the Catawba. In 1756, Chief Haigler, best known of the Catawba leaders, campaigned to stop the selling of alcohol to his tribe by the white traders.

By 1763 the formerly large holdings of the Catawba had been reduced to a 15-mile-square reservation assigned them by the British. By 1840 they had sold all but one square mile of their lands.

In the late 1970s, they lived on a somewhat larger plot of land along the Catawba River, having purchased more land in the mid-20th century. They then had a flourishing pottery industry using traditional methods and clay from the riverbanks.

BIBLIOGRAPHY: Brown, Douglas Summers. *The Catawba Indians:*

The People of the River. Columbia: University of South Carolina Press, 1966.

CAYUGA: one of the five tribes of the Iroquois Confederacy, located along the shores of Cayuga Lake in New York state. The Cayuga had a population of about 1,500 in 1660. In the late 1970s there were about 2,500 descendants of the Cayuga in Canada, and several hundred more in New York, Wisconsin, and Oklahoma. In their Iroquoian language, their name translates as "the place where the locusts are taken out."

The Cayuga, like the other Iroquois, were divided into clans. A person inherited the clan of his mother and was forbidden to marry within his own clan. Clan leaders, who represented their clan at the village and tribal councils, were nominated by the women of the clan.

The Great Council of the Iroquois, which met in the autumn of each year and in time of emergency, was made up of 50 sachems (chiefs). The Cayuga were entitled to ten of these hereditary titles. Iroquois decisions at the village, tribal and Confederacy levels were unanimous, arrived at by discussing a question until a consensus was reached.

The Cayuga had a number of religious festivals throughout the year, many of which were connected with agriculture, such as the Green Corn ceremony, in which they gave thanks for the arrival of the harvest season. Probably most important was the eight-day Mid-Winter Ceremony or New Year's Festival. Held in late January or early February, this ceremony symbolized a new beginning for the tribe, as new fires were laid and old grievances forgotten.

Other important rites included ceremonies to cure the sick, usually conducted by a group such as the False Face Society, with their humorously grotesque, carved wooden masks. Another important ceremony was the family condolence rite. The Cayuga buried their dead in a sitting position, surrounded by food and utensils that would aid them in their journey along the Milky Way. A fire was kept burning for three days, and, on the tenth day, the condolence ceremony was held, symbolizing the departure of the spirit for the land of the dead.

Cayuga villages were usually built on a hill near a lake or stream, and were composed of both single family homes and multiple family long-houses. Elm or basswood bark covered a pole framework, and smoke-holes were left in the roof above each firepit.

Corn, squash, pumpkins, beans and gourds, all grown by the women, were the main crops. Corn, cooked in a variety of ways such as soup, breads, succotash, puddings and stews, was the staple. The corn was dried and stored in bark-lined cellars, and the husks woven into mats and baskets. The women gathered various seeds, nuts, berries, greens, maple sap and mushrooms from the surrounding forests, where the men hunted

A Cayuga mask.

and trapped deer, elk, bear, moose and beaver. Nets, traps, bone hooks and harpoons were all employed in fishing.

The Iroquois League, or Five Nations Confederacy, was formed in about 1450 by the semi-legendary heroes Dekanawida, perhaps a Huron, and Hiawatha, a Mohawk living among the Onondaga. They managed to convince the Cayuga, Seneca, Oneida, Onondaga and Mohawk to abandon intertribal warfare with each other, thus freeing the various tribes to concentrate on trade and rivalry with tribes outside the League.

The 17th century was filled with warfare, as the Iroquois defeated the Huron, Erie, Neutral, Susquehanna and other surrounding tribes to gain control over the region which blocked westward expansion by the Europeans. This strategic location embroiled them in war between the French, English, and Americans in the 18th century. The Cayuga sided with the British in the American Revolution, and had their towns and crops destroyed in Gen. Sullivan's raid of 1779.

During and after the war some Cayuga migrated to Canada, while others scattered among the other New York Iroquois. In 1817 some of these moved to the Sandusky River in Ohio, along with other Iroquois and Delaware. They became known as the Seneca of Sandusky, and eventually moved to Indian Territory (later Oklahoma). Some other Cayuga joined the Oneida in moving to Wisconsin in 1832.

In the late 1970s, the Wisconsin and Oklahoma Cayuga were well-intermingled with the other Indian and white populations. Some of the 200 Cayuga in New York, and those on the Six Nations Reserve in Brant County, Ontario still maintained some of their Iroquois traditions.

BIBLIOGRAPHY: Wait, Mary Van Sickle and Heidt, William, Jr. *The Story of the Cayugas*. Ithaca, New York: De Witt Historical Society of Tompkins County, Inc., 1966.

CAYUSE: a small, but powerful, Plateau tribe occupying the head-waters of the Walla Walla, Umatilla and Grand Ronde rivers in Oregon and Washington in the 18th century, when they numbered about 500. They were very powerful for the size of the tribe, possessing great numbers of horses and dominating lesser neighboring tribes. By the 1970s, they were mixed among the population of about 1,000 on the Umatilla Reservation, near Pendleton, Oregon.

The Cayuse originally spoke a language of the Sahaptian division of the Penutian linguistic family. Their close alliance and frequent trade with the Nez Perce in the 1800s, however, gradually led to their adopting the Nez Perce language (also Sahaptian), which was a sort of lingua franca of the area. They also had a special language which was used only by chiefs for high tribal occasions. Their name was derived from the French term *cailloux,* meaning "people of the stones or rocks." They called themselves, however, Waiilatpus, or "superior people."

The Cayuse were organized into three autonomous bands, each led by a chief and, at times, a war chief. The three band chiefs formed the tribal council. There was little formal organization within the bands. They were semi-nomadic, roaming the Plateau on hunting trips and raids, living in mat lodges and portable hide tipis.

Religious leadership and curing were the duties of shamans, who received their power from *tamanowas,* or spirits, who appeared to them on long solo journeys made during their boyhood. They cured illness by blowing or sucking on the body of the patient, accompanied by chanting. Beaver, Coyote and the Great Creator Spirit, Honeawort, were important in their mythology. A creation myth says the Cayuse sprang from the heart of a large beaver trapped in the Palouse River. The Nez Perce and the Walla Walla sprang from other parts of the beaver. Principal ceremonies were related to food supply and preparation for battle. The latter included fasting, purging themselves, sweat baths, pipe smoking, speeches, dancing, shows of equestrian feats and putting on war paint.

Cayuse economy was based on the horse, which was used for trans-

Chief Upamine, a Cayuse headchief.

The National Archives.

portation in their trade and warfare. Fifteen to twenty horses per person was common, with some wealthier Cayuse having herds of up to 2,000. The term "cayuse" came to mean Indian pony. Their economy was based on trade, hunting and the exacting of tribute from weaker tribes. They obtained salmon from the western tribes, and elk and buffalo meat from the Nez Perce and other eastern neighbors.

After the 1800s, they traded horses as well as beaver and otter furs to whites for guns, kettles, axes, etc. They hunted deer with bow and arrow by surrounding them on horseback. Gathered wild foods, particularly camas roots, supplemented the diet.

Cayuse crafts included ornate saddles, bridles and stirrups. They also made fine basketry of various grasses and brush. Their clothing was of tanned antelope or elk skins—the women wearing long dresses and the men wearing shirts and leggings. Fringes and quillwork were used for decoration.

Before obtaining horses, in about 1750, the Cayuse were a minor, pedestrian tribe. They probably lived with the Molala, before separating sometime in the early 1700s. At that time, they apparently lived on the John Day River, a tributary of the Columbia, in Washington, in constant struggle with surrounding tribes, especially the Northern Paiute and the Northern Shoshoni. Upon acquiring horses, the Cayuse expanded northward and eastward, into the valleys of the Walla Walla, Umatilla and Grand Ronde rivers, subjugating the Walla Walla tribe.

First contact with whites was probably with Lewis and Clark in 1806. In 1838, a mission was founded at the present site of Whitman, Washington. Believing it to be the source of an epidemic among them, the Cayuse destroyed the mission in 1847. After this time, there was almost constant struggle with the whites.

By 1850, few Cayuse were left, as a result of wars, disease and intermarriage with the Nez Perce. In 1855, after war broke out with the whites, they were assigned by treaty, along with the Umatilla and Walla Walla, to the Umatilla Reservation. In 1877, some Cayuse joined the Nez Perce under Chief Joseph in war against the whites.

In the 1970s, the Cayuse were mixed with Umatilla and Walla Walla among the 1,000 Indians on or near the 245,789-acre Umatilla Reservation near Pendleton, Oregon. Their economy was basically agricultural, and most of the old culture was disappearing. They did, however, celebrate an annual roots feast and an Indian Festival of Arts.

BIBLIOGRAPHY: Ruby, Robert H., and Brown, John A. *The Cayuse Indians: Imperial Tribesmen of Old Oregon.* Norman: University of Oklahoma Press, 1972.

CHASTACOSTA: a small Athapascan-speaking group located in southwestern Oregon in the early 19th century. By the late 19th century, they were virtually extinct as a people, although there were probably a few Chastacosta descendants remaining in the late 1970s.

The Chastacosta were one of about ten small Athapascan language groups in the area. The total population of these groups in the mid-19th century was estimated at 5,600. Their name was derived from Shista Kwusta, their name for themselves, the meaning of which is unknown. The Chastacosta occupied between 20 and 30 tiny villages and fishing camps near the confluence of the Rogue and Illinois rivers.

In 1856, when war broke out on the Rogue River between settlers and the Indians, the remaining 153 Chastacosta were placed on Siletz Reservation in western Oregon. By 1937, only 30 Chastacosta remained.

CHEHALIS: a group of small Washington coast tribes located on the

Chehalis River and the south side of Grays Harbor, Washington, in the late 18th century, when together they numbered about 1,000. In the late 1970s, remaining tribal members were included in the 400 Chehalis, Chinook and Northwest Coast tribes on the Chehalis and Shoalwater Reservations.

Chehalis, meaning "sand," was the name of the village at the entrance to Grays Harbor, and was applied to neighboring groups speaking the same language. The language of the Chehalis belonged to the coastal division of the Salishan language family. By the mid-19th century, the Chehalis and Chinook were essentially intermingled.

CHEMEHUEVI: a small nomadic tribe that roamed between southern Nevada and the Tehachapi Mountains of California in the early 19th century, when they numbered perhaps 800. In the late 1970s, there remained about 400 Chemehuevi, living mostly in California and Nevada.

The Chemehuevi called themselves Nuwu, or "people," and spoke a language of the Shoshonean division of the Uto-Aztecan linguistic family. They were originally an offshoot of the Southern Paiute. The Kawaiisu of California were, in turn, an offshoot of the Chemehuevi.

Little is known of the social organization or religion of the Chemehuevi. There were many bands, each with its own chief, whose powers were limited. Their religion was largely influenced by their more powerful neighbor, the Mohave. Favorite mythological characters included Coyote and his elder brother, Puma. The Chemehuevi buried their dead, and burned the possessions of the deceased, along with gifts.

The Chemehuevi subsisted mainly by hunting and gathering, although they grew a few crops along the Colorado River. The men hunted small game such as rabbits, rats, lizards and gophers, with bow and arrow or by pulling them from their burrows with a crooked stick. Pine nuts, yucca dates and various seeds were gathered. Material culture of the Chemehuevi included excellent basketry of willow or cottonwood, as well as rafts made of reed bundles.

Before the late 18th century, the Chemehuevi were mostly located in the eastern Mojave Desert region. Later, some of the Chemehuevi moved to the Colorado River, with the approval of the Mohave, who controlled that area. Their population was reduced by smallpox in the early 19th century and in 1853, the California lands of the Chemehuevi were declared public domain.

In 1865, the Colorado River Reservation was established for the tribes of that area, but the Shoshonean-speaking Chemehuevi were reluctant to join the Yuman-speaking tribes there. In 1907, 36,000 acres were reserved for the Chemehuevi in Chemehuevi Valley, California. Subsequently, 7,700 acres of these lands were flooded by the Parker

Smithsonian Institution National Anthropological Archives

A Chemehuevi man using a sleeping shelter, in about 1906.

Dam, to form Lake Havasu. In a 1951 suit, the Chemehuevi were awarded a $900,000 judgement for 3,600,000 acres of land taken from them.

In the late 1970s, there were about 400 Chemehuevi in the California-Nevada area, a few of which were living on the 28,000 acre reservation in San Bernardino County, California. More housing was being constructed on the reservation, and plans were underway to establish tourism facilities and other business enterprises.

BIBLIOGRAPHY: *Chemehuevi Today* 1975-76 Annual Report of the Chemehuevi Program, 2 vols.

CHEROKEE: one of the Five Civilized Tribes, and the largest southeastern tribe at the time of European contact, numbering about 29,000. The Cherokee controlled about 40,000 square miles of territory in the southern Appalachian region, including western North and South Carolina, southwestern Virginia, eastern Tennessee, northern Georgia and northeastern Alabama. They had more than 60 towns in 1700. In the late 1970s, it was estimated there there were more than 135,000 Cherokee descendants, with the largest concentration in Oklahoma and North Carolina.

The Cherokee called themselves Yunwiya, or the "real people." They spoke an Iroquoian language with at least three different dialects. In the late 1970s, one dialect was spoken in Oklahoma, one was spoken by the Eastern Cherokee, and the third was extinct.

The Cherokee were divided into seven clans. Each person inherited the clan of his mother and was forbidden to marry within his own clan. Each village was ruled by a chief, assisted by a council of wise men and a war chief who took charge in time of war. Women held positions of respect within the tribe, often helping in the selection of chiefs, or serving as priestesses with ceremonial duties.

Other religious ceremonies were conducted by shaman known as *adawehi,* who were also adept at curing, having had years of training in the use of medicinal plants. The chief deity of the Cherokee was the sun. Their most important festival, the Green Corn Dance, celebrated the ripening of the new corn and symbolized a new beginning each year for the tribe. Old offenses were forgiven, new fires were laid, and there were games, dancing and feasting.

The Cherokee usually located their villages near streams, sometimes building palisades around them. Each town had its council house, where meetings and ceremonies were held. Houses were constructed of a pole framework covered with woven mats, sometimes plastered over with clay, inside and out.

The Cherokee economy was based on hunting and agriculture, with corn, squash, beans, sweet potatoes and tobacco as the main crops. The men hunted with bow and arrow, blow gun, stone tomahawk and flint knife. Women tended the fields and made the family clothing, from deer and other skins and furs.

The Cherokee probably migrated to the southeast from somewhere in the upper Ohio valley near their Iroquois relatives. Their capital, Echota, was located on the Little Tennessee River near Madisonville, Tennessee. They were visited by the DeSoto expedition in 1540. In about 1700, the Cherokee received their first firearms, as English traders began to penetrate the area.

The Cherokee were involved in a series of wars, beginning in 1711 with one against the Tuscarora who were driven north. They helped to drive the Shawnee from the Cumberland Valley in Tennessee in 1715. Successive wars followed with the Catawba, Creek, Chickasaw and the British. White settlers began pushing into Kentucky and Tennessee by about 1763. Repeatedly forced to cede lands along their eastern and northern boundaries, a group of Cherokee, under Dragging Canoe, established a new settlement near Chattanooga. Known as the Chicka-mauga, they raided white border settlements, and sided with the British during the American Revolution.

In 1794, part of the Chickamauga Cherokee moved to Arkansas where

A Cherokee boy and girl, North Carolina, 1939. The National Archives.

year by year they were joined by more groups and became known as the Western Cherokee. By 1831, they had ceded their Arkansas territory for lands in Indian Territory (later Oklahoma).

In the early 19th century, the eastern Cherokee began to prosper, with extensive fields and livestock holdings. In 1821, Sequoyah, a mixed blood Cherokee, devised a syllabary to represent the Cherokee language. Within a short time the Cherokee were a literate people, reading their own newspaper, the *Cherokee Phoenix*, in their own language.

By this time, intermarriage with whites had produced a sizeable mixed blood population, whose members, apart from Sequoyah, included John Ross, Major Ridge, and other leaders.

Discovery of gold on Cherokee lands in Georgia and the election of Andrew Jackson as President (term of office 1829-37), spelled doom for the eastern tribe as pressure mounted for the removal of all Indians to the west. The Treaty of New Echota, 1835, signed by a few leaders who represented a small minority, ceded the eastern Cherokee lands and provided for their removal to join the Western Cherokee in Indian Territory. In the winter of 1838-39, some 15,000 Cherokee made the journey known as the Trail of Tears, with one-fourth perishing on the way.

About 1,400 Cherokee hid in the mountains to avoid removal and became known as the Eastern Cherokee. A reservation was later established for them in the Smoky Mountains of North Carolina. In the late 1970s, there were more than 5,000 Eastern Cherokee, including about 700 of full blood. Tribal traditions were still strong, and about one-half could still speak the Cherokee language. Basketry and many of the other traditional arts and crafts were still being practiced.

The Western Cherokee re-established their government and, after some years of dissension, prospered again. The lands of the Cherokee and the other Five Civilized Tribes (Choctaw, Chickasaw, Creek and Seminole) were divided among the tribal members under the Allotment Act in 1902.

In the late 1970s, there were more than 24,000 Cherokee living in Oklahoma, in the vicinity of the tribal headquarters at Tahlequah.

BIBLIOGRAPHY: Mooney, James. *Historical Sketch of the Cherokee.* Washington: Smithsonian Institution Press, 1975; Peithmann, Irvin M. *Red Men of Fire.* Springfield, Illinois: Charles C. Thomas, 1964.

CHEYENNE: an Algonquian tribe originally from the Western Great Lakes region, who moved westward to the Plains by the late 18th century, when they numbered about 3,500. In the late 1970s, the tribe was divided into Northern and Southern Cheyenne, with a total population of about 5,500, living mostly in Montana and Oklahoma. Cheyenne is from a Siouan term meaning "people of alien speech," but they called themselves Tsitsista, meaning "the people."

The Cheyenne were organized into 10 or 11 bands, including the Sutaio, a separate tribe which they absorbed after moving to the Plains. The bands lived separately in winter, when food was scarce, and each group needed a wider hunting ground. In summer, the bands came together for communal buffalo hunting and celebration of their sacred ceremonies. A large circular camp was made, with each band having its assigned position in the circle.

Each band had its own chief, and a few esteemed members of each band were chosen as members of the Council of 44, the governing body of the tribe. New Council members, chosen by the Council for a term of ten years, had to be above reproach in their personal and public lives, and were selected for their wisdom, generosity, even temper and bravery. The Council chose one from among its members to be the Sweet

Four Cheyenne elders, photographed by Thomas B. Marquis in 1922: left to right, Laban Little Wolf, Hairy Hand, Porcupine and Big Beaver.

Medicine Chief, or head chief of the tribe. He and four associates chosen by the Council were known as the five sacred chiefs. War chiefs were separate from the council, being chosen from the seven military societies, to which the men of the tribe belonged. The societies were not graded by age; a man could join whichever society he preferred, and, although free to change societies, usually did not. One of the better known groups was the Dog Soldier society.

The Cheyenne believed in a god above and a god below the earth, both benevolent. Heammawehio, the god above, was the creator of all things. The four compass points were represented by four spirits. The two most important ceremonies in Cheyenne religious life were the Renewal of the Sacred Arrows and the Sun Dance. The latter, celebrated by many of the Plains tribes, was taught to them by the Sutaio. The former, according to tradition, was taught to the Cheyenne by their culture hero, Sweet Medicine, who gave them the four arrows given to him by the Great Spirit. Two of the arrows had power over men and two over the buffalo. The sacred arrows were removed from their bundle and restored to good condition in a four-day ceremony held every few years, or more often, particularly in the event that a Cheyenne was murdered by another Cheyenne. Murder was considered a detestable crime, and the murderer was ostracized for life. Female chastity was highly prized among the Cheyenne, and most of the warrior societies had four maids of honor who were virgin daughters of chiefs.

The Cheyenne had priests and doctors skilled in curing through a combination of ritual and knowledgable use of more than 50 medicinal plants. They were usually assisted by their wife or some other woman. When a Cheyenne died, he was dressed in his best clothes, wrapped in robes and placed either on a scaffold, in a tree or on the ground, covered over with rocks. With him were placed his weapons, tools and other things he might need in the afterlife. A horse was sometimes killed for the use of the deceased in the afterlife, and the possessions of the deceased were given away to non-relatives among the mourners.

Cheyenne material culture underwent remarkable changes as the tribe moved to the Plains from their original woodland setting in Minnesota. Before the migration, they gathered wild rice, fished, hunted, grew corn and lived in bark lodges. In the late 18th century, after moving to the Missouri River, they lived in earth lodges and had an economy based on the cultivation of corn, beans and squash. By the early 19th century, however, they were nomadic horsemen, hunters and warriors of the Plains, totally dependent on the buffalo for food, shelter and clothing.

The Cheyenne of the Plains lived in skin tipis, made by the women in communal sewing bees. The women erected the tipis, with appropriate ceremonies, to which a noted warrior might be invited. The women also dressed skins for clothing and gathered wild turnips, berries and prickly pear, to supplement the buffalo diet.

The communal buffalo hunt was a highly organized affair, requiring strict discipline, to avoid prematurely frightening the herd. The buffalo meat was loaded on horses and taken back to camp for the women to cut into strips and hang up to dry. Some of the dried meat was then pulverized and mixed with chokecherries and melted fat to make pemmican, a nourishing, portable food, capable of being stored for several years in skin bags. Antelope, deer, elk, wild sheep and dog were also part of the food supply, but buffalo was preferred and made up the bulk of the diet.

The bones and horns of the buffalo were also used to make spoons, ladles, cups and tools. A woman's tools for preparing skins were often passed down from generation to generation. Men's clothes made by the women included the Plains costume of moccasins, leggings, breechclout, shirt and buffalo robes. Women wore a one-piece dress and moccasins with leggings and a robe added in winter. Clothing was often decorated with quill work, an art usually taught and controlled by the members of the Quillers Society. Before moving to the Plains, the

Cutting out marketable stock from the herd on the Morningstar Ranch, a tribal enterprise of the Northern Cheyenne Indians, Montana.

Cheyenne made pottery, but a nomadic life made less fragile skin containers more practical.

In 1680, the Cheyenne, who were living at that time in Minnesota, visited the French explorer La Salle at his fort on the Illinois River. In the 18th century, they moved west to the Sheyenne River area of North Dakota where they suffered attacks from the Ojibwa. In the late 18th century, they lived along the Missouri River, near the present North and South Dakota borders, and were associated with the Arikara, Mandan and Hidatsa.

The Cheyenne were encountered in the Black Hills by the 1804 Lewis and Clark expedition. Soon afterward, the Dakota drove them westward to the upper Platte River area of Montana. In 1832, the Bent's Fort trading post was established on the Arkansas River in southern Colorado, and a large part of the tribe moved south, making the trading post their headquarters and becoming known as the Southern Cheyenne. Meanwhile, the rest of the tribe remained in the upper Platte and Yellowstone River areas of Montana and Wyoming, and were known as the Northern Cheyenne. The division was formalized by the 1851 Fort Laramie Treaty with the United States.

From 1832 to 1840, the Southern Cheyenne fought with the Kiowa. In 1864, volunteer troops under Col. J.M. Chivington attacked the peaceful village of Chief Black Kettle on Sand Creek, Colorado, killing about 300 Cheyenne. Black Kettle was killed in 1868, in an attack on his village along the Washita River, by U.S. troops under Col. George Custer. From that time until 1875, the Southern Cheyenne fought together with their allies, the Kiowa, Arapaho and Comanche, to hold the southern Plains against the flood tide of settlers who were protected by the U.S. Army. Although assigned to a reservation along with the Arapaho in 1869, the participated in uprisings until 1875, when some of their warriors were sent to Florida as prisoners of war.

The Northern Cheyenne joined with the Dakota tribes in resisting the encroachment of goldseekers and settlers on their lands. In 1876, together they defeated part of the Seventh Cavalry in the Battle of Little Big Horn. After that, the U.S. Army began rounding up the Northern Cheyenne and taking them south to the Cheyenne-Arapaho reservation in Indian Territory (Oklahoma). Finding conditions intolerable, several hundred Northern Cheyenne, under Little Wolf and Dull Knife, headed back north in 1878, hotly pursued and fighting much of the way. About 64 Cheyenne were killed along the way or attempting to escape after they were captured. In 1884, the government finally relented and granted them a reservation on the Tongue River in southeastern Montana.

In the late 1970s, there were about 5,500 Cheyenne, living mostly in Oklahoma and Montana. The Cheyenne language was still spoken by both groups and many tribal traditions preserved. The Peyote religion, in the rituals of which peyote, a hallucogenic cactus bean, is used, had a strong following. The Southern Cheyenne were keepers of the Sacred Arrows and Northern Cheyenne delegates attended renewal ceremonies.

(See also *Cheyenne, Northern* and *Cheyenne, Southern.*)

BIBLIOGRAPHY: Grinnell, George Bird. *The Cheyenne Indians.* 2 vols. New Haven: Yale University Press, 1923; Hoebel, E. Adamson. *The Cheyennes: Indians of the Great Plains.* New York: Henry Holt and Company, 1960.

CHEYENNE, NORTHERN: the northern division of the Cheyenne tribe. They were formerly the Cheyenne who remained in the Yellowstone and Platte rivers area, when part of the tribe moved south to the Arkansas River in 1832. In 1851, the Treaty of Fort Laramie made formal recognition of the two tribal divisions.

In the late 1970s, about 3,000 Northern Cheyenne lived on or near the 434,000 acre Northern Cheyenne Reservation, on the Tongue River in Big Horn and Rosebud counties in southeastern Montana. Some 263,000 acres were tribally owned and 171,000 acres were allotted to individuals.

Stumphorn, a Southern Cheyenne, and his family, (1890).

Mineral resources, stockraising and farming were the main sources of tribal income.

(See also *Cheyenne.*)

BIBLIOGRAPHY: Marquis, Thomas Bailey. *The Cheyennes of Montana.* Algonac, Michigan: Reference Publications, 1978.

CHEYENNE, SOUTHERN: the southern division of the Cheyenne tribe. They were formed when some of the Cheyenne moved south from the Platte River region to the Arkansas River in 1832, to be near Bent's Fort trading post. The division was formalized by the 1851 Fort Laramie Treaty.

In 1869, the Southern Cheyenne and the Southern Arapaho were assigned a reservation together in Indian Territory (Oklahoma). This land was allotted to individual tribal members in 1891-92. In the late 1970s, about 2,500 Southern Cheyenne, mostly engaged in farming, lived in western Oklahoma, closely associated with the Southern Arapaho.

(See also *Cheyenne.*)

BIBLIOGRAPHY: Wright, Muriel H. *A Guide to the Indian Tribes of Oklahoma.* Norman: University of Oklahoma Press, 1951.

CHICKAHOMINY: a tribe located on the Chickahominy River in Virginia. They were a member of the Powhattan Confederacy of 30 tribes, which was organized in the tidewater Virginia area in the early

Smithsonian Institution National Anthropological Archives.

Chickahominy Indians paying annual tribute to the governor of Virginia: Richmond, Virginia, December 10, 1919.

17th century. Chickahominy has been variously translated as "coarse pounded corn people" or "clearing." They were reportedly ruled by their priests and were not under as tight control as other tribes of the Confederacy. In 1608 the tribe numbered about 900, but by 1722 they had been reduced to 80 by disease and warfare.

In the late 1970s they were the largest group of Indians remaining in Virginia, residing mostly along the Chickahominy River in New Kent and Charles counties. Although they did not have a reservation, the Chickahominy still functioned as an organized tribe with their own chief and tribal council.

BIBLIOGRAPHY: Hodge, Frederick W., ed. "Handbook of American Indians North of Mexico." *Bureau of American Ethnology Bulletin.* no. 30, 1907-10.

CHICKASAW: a tribe of great hunters and warriors whose towns were located near the headwaters of the Tombigbee River in northeastern Mississippi, but who ranged far and wide over the whole Mississippi valley region. The Chickasaw, along with the Cherokee, Choctaw, Creek

Chickasaw stickball and racquet. Smithsonian Institution

and Seminole, were one of the Five Civilized Tribes which were removed to Indian Territory (now Oklahoma) in the 1830s.

Numbering about 5,000 in 1600, the Chickasaw were much less numerous than at least two of their neighbors, the Cherokee and Choctaw, which both had populations in excess of 20,000. The Chickasaw, nevertheless, were able to claim vast hunting grounds in western Kentucky and Tennessee and northern Alabama and Mississippi. According to tribal traditions the Chickasaw and Choctaw were once one tribe; and the close similarity of their Muskogean languages seems to bear this out. The Chickasaw language was still spoken in the 1970s.

The Chickasaw were divided into two moieties, or divisions, which were in turn divided into numerous clans. A person inherited the clan of his mother and was forbidden to marry within that clan. The head chief, or High Minko, was chosen from the Minko clan, and was aided by a counsel of advisors made up of clan leaders and tribal elders. Other leadership was provided by the *hopaye,* the two head priests, one from each division of the tribe. These presided at all religious ceremonies and helped the tribe interpret life in spiritual terms.

The supreme deity of the Chickasaw was Ababinili, a composite of the Four Beloved Things Above: Sun, Clouds, Clear Sky, and He That Lives in the Clear Sky. There were other lesser deities and a whole range of witches and evil spirits. The *aliktce,* or healers, were in charge of dealing with the latter with the aid of potions, teas and poultices derived from various herbs, roots and berries.

The Chickasaw believed in a hereafter in which the good would go to their reward somewhere in the heavens while the evildoers would wander forever in the land of the witches. When a person died, a grave was dug under the house; and the body, with its face painted red, placed in a sitting position surrounded by his worldly possessions. The deceased would face west, since in that direction lay the path to judgement.

Chickasaw towns and villages were laid out compactly in times of war, but were spread out in peacetime. A council house in the central area was used for meetings and ceremonies, along with the council ground which was used for open-air gatherings and ball games. Each family had a summer house, winter house and storage building for corn and other supplies. The summer houses were rectangular, with walls of woven mats and a thatched or bark roof. The winter houses were circular, about 25 feet in diameter, and were excavated three feet below the surface of the ground. The pine log and pole framework was plastered with a mixture of clay and dried grass, which was then whitewashed inside and out. Furnishings included beds and seats, wooden dishes, utensils and clay pots.

The division of labor in Chickasaw society called for men to do the hunting, fishing, house building, boat building, tool making and war making. Women were responsible for all agriculture, food gathering and household chores. The Chickasaw, due to their great success in warfare, often had help with the work in the form of numbers of slaves taken as captives in their battles.

The men were very competent hunters, ranging far and wide and employing great skill in tracking, trapping and using animal calls and decoys. Deer was the most favored game after the buffalo were gone from the southeast; and bear was prized for the skins and fat. The men caught fish by throwing a poison made with buckeye or green walnut hulls into a deep hole in the stream and spearing or grabbing the drugged fish when they came to the surface.

The women collected wild strawberries, persimmons, nuts, acorns, honey and onions. They also dried grapes and plums to make raisins and prunes, and made tea from sassafras root.

Smithsonian Institution National Anthropological Archives.

Sho-ni-on, a mixed blood Chickasaw, a picture published in 1877.

Chickasaw men painted their faces for ceremonies or making war. They shaved the sides of their heads leaving a roach which they soaked in bear grease. A breech clout was the main item of dress, supplemented with deerskin shirts or bearskin robes in colder weather and high deerskin boots for hunting. The women wore dresses of finely tanned deerskin and had their long hair tied up neatly.

In the winter of 1540-41 the Chickasaw had an unwelcome visit by an expedition of Spanish treasure-seekers led by Hernando DeSoto. After finally driving them away the Chickasaw managed to avoid European contact for the next hundred years or so. In the late 17th century English traders began working their way into the Mississippi valley with their cotton cloth, metal tools, knives, guns, iron pots and other goods. As the Chickasaw became more and more dependent on these appurtenances of civilization, they widened their hunting grounds to obtain more and more skins for trade, which resulted in war with the Choctaw and other neighboring tribes.

In the early 18th century the French, moving north from the Gulf of Mexico tried to establish their control over the Mississippi valley. The next 60 years saw constant warfare between the British-backed Chickasaw and the French with their Indian allies, with the Chickasaw usually getting the best of it. This period, however, took its toll on the once powerful tribe. Many warriors were lost in battle; and, although their numbers were replaced by captives taken in war, the Chickasaw spirit was diluted. Some 200 Natchez were adopted after being nearly wiped out by the French in 1729. Other new blood came into the tribe by way of the many English traders who took Chickasaw wives. The children of these marriages, inheriting the clan status of their mothers, often became very powerful in tribal affairs because of their ability to deal with both worlds.

By the late 18th century the scene had changed and the Chickasaw found themselves caught between American and Spanish interests. The Louisiana Purchase and the Spanish cession of Florida made it clear that it was the Americans that the Chickasaw and other eastern tribes would have to deal with eventually.

By the early 19th century the Chickasaw, finding game growing scarce, had settled down to being successful farmers. Some started cotton plantations with field labor performed by black slaves, of which the tribe owned more than a thousand.

White settlers flooding into the area at this time coveted the Indian lands. Between 1801 and 1832 the Chickasaw signed a series of treaties giving up their lands and agreeing to migrate to Indian Territory (now Oklahoma), where some 5,000 Chickasaw and 1,000 slaves were subsequently settled on land bought from the Choctaw Nation. Concentrating on agriculture, the Chickasaw were producing a surplus by 1843. By the 1850s they had set up sawmills, blacksmith shops, newspapers and schools.

During the Civil War, the Chickasaw fought on the side of the Confederacy. After the war more white settlers began pouring into Indian Territory. In 1906 the tribal governments of the Five Civilized Tribes were dissolved, preparatory to the admission of Oklahoma to statehood the following year.

By the late 1970s the Chickasaw were well assimilated into non-Indian society, with about 7,000 (including 300-500 full-bloods) living in Oklahoma. The tribal headquarters was at Ardmore, and about 1,261 acres of tribally owned land remained, with about 95,000 acres of allotted land. There was growing interest in Chickasaw arts and crafts, and Chickasaw language classes were being held.

BIBLIOGRAPHY: Baird, W. David. *The Chickasaw People,* Phoenix: Indian Tribal Series, 1974; Gibson, Arrell M. *The Chickasaws.* Norman: University of Oklahoma Press, 1971.

CHILCOTIN: a seminomadic Athapascan tribe located along the headwaters of the Chilcotin River and in the Anahim Lake area in British Columbia, numbering about 3,500 in the late 18th century. In the 1970s, there were about 1,400 Chilcotin, living mostly somewhat east of there, on a number of reserves in the valley of the Chilcotin River. The Chilcotin, or Tsilkotin, spoke a language of the Northern division of the Athapascan language family, similar to that of their close cultural relatives, the Carrier. Their name translates as "people of Young Man's (Chilcotin) River."

They were composed of apparently autonomous bands, or villages, each led by a chief, or head man, the number of bands varying between three and six during the historical period. Because of their location, they were a transition tribe between the highly structured Northwest Coast culture and the loosely organized culture of the interior tribes. Both hereditary and non-hereditary chiefs were found, and men could rise to chieftaincy by acquiring wealth and giving potlatches (gift distributions). They had a complex social structure, composed of three classes: nobles, commoners and slaves. The nobles, but apparently not the commoners, were divided into two clans, of which the more powerful was the Raven.

Religion was centered around guardian spirits obtained at adolescence. The dead were cremated, buried or placed under piles of stones or brush. When a noble died, his family gave a memorial potlatch, at which they distributed all his possessions, and erected a wooden pillar over the grave carved to represent his clan crest.

The Chilcotin dwellings were small semisubterranean houses, or rectangular pole-frame houses, walled and roofed with bark or brush and an overall layer of earth. They hunted caribou, bear, mountain goat, mountain sheep, marmot and rabbit. Salmon were obtained from the Shuswap, in exchange for dried berries, furs and in later times, snowshoes. From the Bella Coola, they obtained dentalium shells and goat wool blankets.

Chilcotin crafts included bark canoes, both coiled and birchbark baskets, rush mats, wooden boxes and stone pestles for pounding berries. Clothing was typical of the skin clothing of the interior tribes—leggings, breechclout or skirt, belt, robe, cap and moccasins.

The original location of the Chilcotin was apparently around Anahim Lake. Over the years, they gradually moved eastward into the Chilcotin River valley. They had considerable intercourse with the Bella Coola, Kwakiutl and Carrier, and were often at war with the Carrier and the Shuswap.

First European contact was with the Scottish explorer Alexander Mackenzie in 1793. In 1829, Fort Chilcotin was founded in their territory, bringing them into contact with Canadian traders. In 1862, a smallpox plague decimated the Chilcotin, and some moved to the vicinity of Alexandria and the Fraser River and merged with the Shuswap and Carrier. By 1900, most of the Chilcotin were located on three reserves in the Chilcotin River valley, and were essentially acculturated, living lives similar to the non-Indians in the area. A few bands, however, still led a seminomadic, traditional life in the mountains to the west, and were known as Stone Chilcotin or "Stonies."

In the 1970s, there remained about 1,400 Chilcotin, living on various reserves in the Chilcotin River valley in British Columbia, grouped into six bands: Alexandria, Alexis Creek, Anaham, Nemeiah Valley, Stone and Toosey. Total land reserved to the Cholcotin was around 41,800 acres. There were also some Chilcotin descendants mixed in with Shuswap and Carrier on their reserves.

BIBLIOGRAPHY: Jenness, Diamond. "Indians of Canada." *National Museum of Canada Bulletin.* no. 69, 1960.

CHINOOK: a group of northwest coast tribes located on both sides of the lower Columbia River, and in the adjoining coastal area, in the late 18th century, numbering more than 2,000 at that time. They were driven to near-extinction by epidemics in the 19th century. By the later 1970s Chinook descendants were mixed with the Chehalis and other tribes on the Chehalis Reservation in Washington.

The various tribes and divisions (including the Chinook, Clatsop,

A Chinook lodge in Oregon in about 1840. From Charles Wilkes' *Narrative*, (1838-42).

Clackamas, Kathlamet and Wahkiakum) spoke dialects of the Chinookan language, which is divided into Upper and Lower Chinook. Also spoken in the region was the trade language called Chinook Jargon, which was based on the Chinook dialect plus words from Nootka and other Indian languages. After white traders came into the area, a large number of English and French words were added to the jargon, which became the lingua franca from Alaska to California.

The Chinook occupied more than 30 villages, each led by a chief. There were three classes: an upper class, a commoner class, and a slave class. The upper class was composed of chiefs and their families, prominent shamans, warriors and traders. Slaves were obtained by raiding or in trade, from tribes in the Willamette Valley or Puget Sound area.

Important ceremonies included first salmon rites, puberty ceremonies for girls, and potlatches (gift distributions). Adolescents sought guardian spirits in personal quests, involving fasting and praying in remote places.

The Chinook located their burial grounds on islands or near the water. The body of the deceased was wrapped in cattail mats and placed along with his possessions, in a canoe up on posts, with another canoe inverted over the burial canoe. A slave was sometimes killed and buried nearby, to serve as a servant in the afterlife. Mourners cut their hair and never again spoke the name of the dead.

The Chinook built semisubterranean cedar plank houses from 20 to 100 feet long. The gabled roof was covered with bark or planking, and the floor was planked or covered with cattail mats.

Salmon fishing was the principal economic activity. The men caught five varieties of salmon, as well as steelhead trout, herring, sardines and smelt using sieve nets, dams, weirs and two-pronged spears. Three-hundred pound sturgeon were caught with hook and line from canoes.

The women gathered an assortment of roots, as well as acorns, grapes, blueberries, strawberries and cranberries. The men hunted deer, elk and small game, by stalking and use of pitfalls.

The Chinook made, by the twining method, an assortment of baskets and other containers, as well as basketry hats. Dishes and spoons were made of wood, horn or shell. Cradles were carved of wood, some with a hinged board for flattening the infant's head to conform with Chinook standards of beauty.

The Chinook built fine canoes, of a single cedar or fir log up to 50 feet long, accommodating as many as 30 persons. Carved wooden images five feet high adorned the bow and stern. Pointed-blade paddles were carved of ash and wielded with great dexterity by both men and women.

The Chinook were the great traders of the region. They exchanged canoes, dried salmon, berries and blubber with both upriver and coastal tribes for furs, dried meat, camas, slaves, and dentalia shells. The latter, horn-shaped shells called *hiqua*, were the standard medium of exchange throughout the region.

Smallpox and other diseases seriously reduced the Chinook population in 1782-83, 1830-33 and again in 1853. By the mid-19th century, the Chinook were essentially integrated with the Chehalis and other neighboring tribes. They were placed on Grande Ronde, Shoalwater and Chehalis reservations. In the late 1970s Chinook descendants were among the several hundred residents of the Chehalis and Shoalwater reservations.

BIBLIOGRAPHY: Ray, Verne F. *Lower Chinook Ethnographic Notes.* Seattle: University of Washington, 1938; Ruby, Robert H. and Brown, John A. *The Chinook Indians.* Norman: University of Oklahoma Press, 1976.

CHIPEWYAN: the most numerous Athapascan tribe in northern Canada in the 17th and 18th centuries, numbering around 3,500 in 1670. They were a nomadic tribe, ranging over territory in Alberta, Saskatchewan, Manitoba and the Northwest Territories, north of the Churchill River between Great Slave Lake on the west and Hudson Bay on the east. In the 1970s, there were about 5,600 Chipewyan descendants scattered among a number of reserves in the same area.

The Chipewyan spoke a language of the Athapascan language family, which was named for one of their divisions. Their tribal name is a Cree

A Chipewyan
tipi—a photo
by Edward S.
Curtis.
Library of Congress

word meaning "pointed skins," referring to parkas or shirts they wore,
which were pointed and decorated with tails, front and back. A French
name for them was Montagnais, not to be confused with the Algonquian group of the same name in southeastern Canada.

The Chipewyan were composed of four or five geographical divisions:
Athabaska (or Chipewyan proper), Desnedekenade, Etheneldi (or
Caribou Eaters), Thilanottine, and possibly the Tatsanottine (Yellowknives). The latter were culturally very similar, but are considered by
some to be an independent tribe. Each division had a number of autonomous bands, each led by a chief with limited authority. There were no
tribal or division chiefs.

The Chipewyan religion centered around guardian spirits, which were
obtained in dreams and needed for success in life. Shamans cured ills,
which were caused by witchcraft, using powers given them by especially
powerful guardian spirits. The Chipewyan had no deities, but believed
that all people and animals had souls or spirits. Many myths were told
about animal spirits, particularly Raven and Caribou.

They seldom buried their dead, usually simply abandoning the bodies.
The soul of the dead traveled in a stone boat to a beautiful island where
game was plentiful. The good reached the island, but the bad had their
boat sink, and they struggled in the water forever.

The Chipewyan lived in temporary villages, usually near the edge of
the woods, following the caribou herds in their migrations. Their
dwellings were conical caribou skin tents, later replaced by canvas tents

of ridgepole construction. In winter, they piled mounds of snow around the base.

They were primarily hunters, with no agriculture and relatively little gathering of wild foods. Caribou was the principal game, supplying many necessities besides food and clothing. They speared caribou in the lakes and rivers in the summer and snared and shot them with bow and arrow in the woods in the winter. They also hunted buffalo, musk-ox, moose, bear and small game. Second to caribou, however, fish were most important, with trout, whitefish, pike and others caught with weirs, clubs, spears, bone hooks and nets of hide thongs (babiche). The meat was eaten in various ways, including raw, boiled, roasted, smoked, and dried and pounded into pemmican. After a Hudson's Bay Company post was opened at Churchill, fur trapping for trade became very important.

Important material culture included babiche snowshoes and birchbark canoes, necessary for their nomadic existence. They also made toboggans, 8 to 14 feet long, of split and curved planks of wood. Birchbark vessels were used for boiling food, using hot stones, and caribou hide was made into lines, snares, nets and clothing. Eight to ten caribou skins were required for a typical wardrobe—robe, shirt, leggings, breechclout, cap, mittens and moccasins. For ornamentation, they tattooed parallel bars across each cheek, painted their bodies with red ocher, and decorated their clothing with quills.

The Chipewyan are believed to have migrated at some time from the Rocky Mountains. By 1717, when the Hudson's Bay Company founded a post at Churchill, they were living in the area of the Peace River, fighting with the Cree to the south and probably the Inuit to the north. Decades of fighting followed, as they expanded both south and north. They dominated the Yellowknives and Dogrib by denying them access to the Churchill trading post. In the late 1700s, a lasting peace was established. The population declined over the years, however, due to malnutrition and epidemics, including one in 1791 which destroyed a reported 90 percent of the tribe. At about this time, many European traders came into the area, making trapping for trade an important part of their economy. In the mid-19th century Catholic and Protestant missions were established.

By the 1970s, the Chipewyan had been assigned reserves, scattered around the area in Alberta, Saskatchewan, Manitoba and the Northwest Territories. Their total population of 5,600 was spread among 16 bands: Cold Lake, Fort Chipewyan (or Chipewyan), Fort McKay, Fort McMurray, Janvier, Peter Pond Lake, Portage LaRoche, Stony Rapids, Lac la Hache, Fond du Lac, English River, Churchill, Barren Lands, Snowdrift, Resolution and Yellowknife. Some of these bands also included Cree. The total area of the reserves was around 337,000 acres.

The bands were no longer nomadic, and lived in fixed villages of log or wood frame houses. Hunting of caribou in summer, fishing in the fall, and especially trapping for furs in the winter and spring were still important to the economy, but were performed with more modern equipment. The old religion had been mostly replaced by Christianity, although a few of the old beliefs and myths still had significance. The Chipewyan language was still in everyday use, although some children were learning English in school.

BIBLIOGRAPHY: Birket-Smith, Kaj. "Contributions to Chipewyan Ethnology." Fifth Thule Expedition Report, no. 5., 1930; Jenness, D. "Indians of Canada." *Bulletin of the Canadian National Museum.* no. 65, 1960.

CHIPPEWA: See OJIBWA.

CHIRICAHUA: an Apache tribe located in southeastern Arizona, southwestern New Mexico and neighboring Mexico in the early 19th century, when they numbered about 1,000. In the late 1970s, there were about 500 Chiricahua living in Oklahoma, and about 2,500 Chiricahua, Mescalero and Lipan Apache lived together on the Mescalero Reservation in New Mexico.

The tribal name is an Apache term meaning "great mountain." The Chiricahua spoke a language belonging to the southern branch of the Athapascan language family. There were three Chiricahua bands: the Eastern (or Warm Springs), the Central and the Southern. Famous leaders included Cochise, of the Central band, Geronimo and Juh, of the Southern band, and Mangas Colorado, Victorio, Nana and Loco, all of the Eastern band.

The bands were composed of extended families, each with its own leader. The most respected family leader, noted for his wisdom and ability in warfare, was recognized as band leader, although there were sometimes more than one. The bands were too scattered and mobile for any unified tribal organization, but there was always friendship between bands.

On a personal level, there was a certain amount of visiting and intermarriage between bands. The Chiricahua practiced polygamy, including the marrying of sisters to one man or a man marrying his brother's widow. It was taboo for a man to speak to his mother-in-law, and a punishment for a wife's adultery was nose clipping.

The Chiricahua believed in numerous supernatural figures, including

White Painted Woman and her son, Child of the Water. Many tales were told about the trickster, Coyote, and about the Mountain Spirits who dwelled within mountains. These were represented by masked dancers in such important ceremonies as the girl's puberty rites. This four-day ceremony, sponsored by the proud parents, was an important occasion for a social gathering, with feasting, dancing and rituals performed in a tipi-like brush shelter built for the occasion. The girl wore a special deerskin dress, and was attended by an older woman, while a male "singer" conducted the ceremonies. An adolescent boy's coming of age required going on four raids as an apprentice warrior. There were also both male and female shamans who specialized in certain ceremonies and types of cures.

When a Chiricahua died, his face was painted red and his body wrapped in skins and buried the same day. Burial was usually in a cave or under a pile of rocks, in an obscure place which was not visited again. Personal possessions of the deceased were either buried or destroyed; his favorite horse was killed; his house was burned, and sometimes the entire camp moved. Mourners cut their hair, wore old clothes and never pronounced the name of the dead again.

For dwellings, the Chiricahua women built dome-shaped wickiups of poles covered with grass thatch, adding a covering of hides in rainy weather. There was a smokehole in the roof over the central fireplace.

Hunting and gathering were the main economic pursuits. The men hunted deer and antelope with bow and arrow, using deer-head or antelope-head disguises. Elk, mountain sheep and mountain goats were less frequently hunted, and badger, beaver, otter and wildcat were hunted only for their furs. Small boys developed their hunting and tracking skills on cottontail rabbits, opossums, squirrels and birds.

Family groups often made journeys of several days to take advantage of various plant foods as they came in season. While the men hunted, the women gathered agave, mesquite beans, pine nuts, cactus fruit, yucca, acorns, seeds, juniper berries, sumac berries, raspberries and grapes. Nuts and seeds were usually ground to flour, and berries dried and stored in cakes. The base of the agave, or century plant, was placed in a pit lined with rocks and baked for several days. The result was a sweet, nutritious food called mescal, which could be dried and stored for later use. In later times, the Chiricahua grew a little corn, using some of it to make a mild beer called *tiswin*.

Crafts of the Chiricahua included basketry, pottery and tanning of hides. They produced both coiled and twined basketry, using mulberry, sumac and other plant materials, with designs made with various vegetable dyes. Pitch-covered water jars, seed parching trays, storage containers, burden baskets and winnowing trays were among the basketry items made. They also made gourd spoons, dippers and dishes, as well as deerskin moccasins and skirts for women.

Ancestors of the Chiricahua and other Apache groups probably began drifting from the north into the southwest by about 1200 AD. Spanish expeditions began crossing Apache territory after 1540, and decades of raids and counter raids between the two groups followed.

In 1858, the United States Overland Mail Route began coming through Chiricahua territory without incident. In 1861, however, the previously friendly leader, Cochise, was mistakenly arrested for a kidnapping incident. He escaped, but several of his men were killed, touching off ten years of warfare between the Chiricahua and U.S. troops. In 1873, Cochise was persuaded to settle his people on a reservation in southeastern Arizona, where he died in 1874. Shortly thereafter the Chiricahua were moved to the San Carlos Reservation, against their will, along with other Apache groups. They broke out, and another ten years of warfare ensued, with the Chiricahua bands led by Victorio and Juh. In 1883, Gen. George H. Crook finally persuaded the Chiricahua to return to the reservation. Some of the bands soon bolted again, and several more years of raiding and fighting were led by Geronimo and Chihuahua. Surrender came in 1886, and 340 Chiricahua men, women and children began a 27-year term as prisoners of war, successively at Fort Marion, Florida, Mount Vernon Barracks, Alabama, and Fort Sill, Oklahoma. In 1913, they were given the choice of remaining in Oklahoma or going to the Mescalero Reservation in southern New Mexico. About 87 remained in Oklahoma, and were allotted 80 acres of land apiece, while 171 went to New Mexico.

In the late 1970s, the 500 or so Chiricahua Apache in Oklahoma lived around the town of Apache as small farmers and stock-raisers.

On the Mescalero Reservation, the 2,500 Chiricahua, Mescalero and Lipan were partly intermarried. Lumber, cattle-raising, and tourism were major sources of tribal income. A ski resort and campgrounds were located in the beautiful mountains of the reservation. The various Apache dialects were still spoken, especially at home, and there was a continuing interest in Apache traditions and crafts.

BIBLIOGRAPHY: Opler, Morris Edward. *An Apache Life-Way*. New York: Cooper Square Publishers, Inc., 1965.

CHITIMACHA: a tribe known for its beautiful and complex basketry who have inhabited the Louisiana Gulf Coast around Grand Lake since about 600 BC. In the late 1970s, remnants of the Chitimacha tribe lived on or near a 262-acre state reservation in the same area. The tribe, which numbered 3,000 in 1700, was by then reduced to about 300.

Chitimacha baskets.

Smithsonian Institution National Anthropological Archives.

The Chitimacha, whose name may mean "men altogether red," spoke a language not belonging to any other linguistic family. The last Chitimachan speakers died out in the mid-20th century.

Chitimacha villages with populations of 500 or more dotted the shores of Grand Lake, Grand River and Bayou Teche. Houses were simple, made of wooden pole frames and palmetto thatch. A fairly complex political system was developed with a head chief in the main town and a subchief in each village. There were also holy men who were in charge of religious ceremonies and medicine men who were responsible for curing the sick.

These officials and their families made up an elite class. Members almost always married within the nobility, for to marry a commoner was to become a commoner. Women had an unusual amount of power and authority, serving as medicine women and occasionally subchief or even chief.

The Chitimacha version of the creation is that, in the beginning, it was a watery world, until the Great Spirit directed the crawfish to dive down and bring up mud to form the earth. Major religious ceremonies were held in a 12-foot-square dance temple on Grand Lake. A six-day midsummer festival was held annually, during which young males were initiated into manhood.

Men did the hunting and fishing, using blowguns, fish traps and hook and line. Catfish, bass, crab, turtles, shrimp, alligator and deer were plentiful. Women were responsible for raising beans, pumpkins, melons and sweet potatoes and for gathering water lily seeds.

The Chitimacha made highly sophisticated cane basketry dyed black and yellow with dyes made from black walnuts and certain roots. They were famous for a double weaving technique, the art of which is mostly lost. They were also skilled at pottery and metalworking.

The coming of the French to the region marked the decline of the tribe. The French declared war on the Chitimacha in 1706. By the time peace was made in 1718, the tribe was greatly reduced. The survivors were relocated on "reservations" by the French or forced into slavery. An influx of Acadians from Canada into the area in the late 18th century marked a further dilution of the tribe through intermarriage with the newcomers. Catholicism began to replace the Indian religion.

In the late 1970s, most of the 300 members of the tribe made their living off the reservation, the men usually working in the nearby oilfields or the fishing or lumbering industries. There was a new tribal center on the reservation and a renewed interest in Chitimacha crafts and culture.

BIBLIOGRAPHY: Hoover, Herbert T., *The Chitimacha People,* Phoenix: Indian Tribal Series, 1975.

CHOCTAW: the largest single tribe in the southeast, except for the Cherokee. Both tribes, along with the Chickasaw, Seminole, and Creek were later known as the Five Civilized Tribes. Located in central and southern Mississippi and southwestern Alabama, the Choctaw probably numbered 20,000 at the time of first European contact. In the late 1970s about 17,000 Choctaw lived in Oklahoma, and another 4,000 remained in Mississippi.

The Choctaw spoke a Muskogean language very close to that of the Chickasaw. In the late 1970s, both of these languages were still spoken. According to one tribal tradition, the two tribes were once one and migrated together from somewhere in the West led by two brothers, Chahtah and Chikasah. At some point the group split, taking the names of their respective leaders.

Compared to some other tribes in the southeast, the Choctaw seemed to lack a complex political or religious system. They were, however, a highly practical and successful people, growing enough food so that they were able to export to their neighbors, even though their lands were smaller. The Choctaw were also known as a peace-loving people, preferring to settle disputes through discussion and consensus, or perhaps a stickball game, rather than by war. They did, however, defend their towns tenaciously when the need arose.

There were three districts, each headed by a chief, but there apparently was no head chief over the whole tribe. Each town had a chief and a warchief, subservient to the district chiefs. District council meetings were held, and occasionally councils of the nation, usually accompanied by great displays of oratory, feasting, dancing and games. The Choctaw were very fond of social events and game playing and emphasized them in their religious festivals as well.

United States Travel Service

A stickball contest at Philadelphia, Mississippi, during the annual Indian Fair.

They had a number of deities, including the sun and fire, and celebrated the Green Corn Dance as did other tribes of the region. Their ancient culture was of the Mississippi moundbuilders. Their most famous mound, Nanih Waya located in Winston County, is 50 feet high and covers an acre of land. According to one tradition, the Choctaw, and perhaps the neighboring tribes, all issued forth from a cave or hole beneath this sacred mound.

They believed in the immortality of the soul and had elaborate burial customs designed to help the deceased to find the way to the land of the dead. The body was wrapped in skins, and bark and placed on an elevated platform along with food, drink, clothing, utensils, ornaments, and anything the person might need for his journey. A dog was killed to be his companion and, in later times, a pony so that he might ride. A fire was kept burning for heat and light, and mourning and wailing went on for a specified length of time. When the body was taken down, after anywhere from one to six months, it was cleaned, placed in a bark coffin and taken to the bone house. When the bone house was full, the bones were taken out and buried, and mounds built over them.

Town planning was not as formal among the Choctaw as among their neighbors, the Creek. Towns along the borders of their territory were compact and fortified, while towns in the central areas were more spread out and informal. There was usually a public area for meetings, ceremonies and dancing and an area for playing ball.

Stickball and other games were very important to the Choctaw, often being used as a method of settling disputes. Very rough and freewheeling, the game was played on a field two or three hundred yards long, with two upright split logs at either end as goal posts. Points were scored by hitting the uprights with the skin-covered ball using only their *kapucha,* two hickory sticks each with a webbed cup on one end. Several hundred players might play at once and the stakes sometimes included all the personal property of each team.

Women would sometimes have their own ball game after the main event and reportedly were very skilled. Women held an honored position in the tribe, although they did perform a large share of the field work as well as making clothing and preparing and storing food.

The Choctaw cleared their field by cutting and burning, and grew corn, beans, pumpkin, and melon in enough abundance that they sold the surplus to their neighbors. The men hunted deer, bear (for fat), turkey, squirrel, beaver, otter, raccoon, opossum, and rabbit. They fished using spears, nets and poisons to stun the fish. Fruits, nuts, seeds, and roots of various types were also gathered to supplement the diet.

Their material culture and mode of dress resembled that of their southeastern neighbors. One distinguishing feature was that both men and women wore their hair long in early times, and were thus referred to by other tribes as the "long hairs." Tattooing and head flattening were both practiced.

The Spanish DeSoto expedition of 1540 marked the first Choctaw encounter with Europeans. It was, however, the French with whom the Choctaw allied when the carving of empires out of the American wilderness began. In the early 18th century, through trading and gifts, the French managed to enlist their support in wars with the Natchez and Chickasaw. The Choctaw became involved in the rivalry between the French and the British, resulting in a Choctaw civil war in 1750, between supporters of the two sides.

When the Americans succeeded to all former claims on the area by the French, British and Spanish, white settlers poured into the Gulf region and began pressuring for a removal of all Indians to the West. Tecumseh, the Shawnee chief tried to enlist the Choctaw and other southern tribes in a final stand against white expansion, but the Choctaw chief Pushmataha, seeing the futility of the situation, counseled against it. Although the Choctaw had never fought against the United States, they were forced to cede their lands in a series of treaties, starting in 1801 and culminating in the Treaty of Dancing Rabbit Creek in 1830. The main removal of the Choctaw, some 350 miles westward, took place between 1831 and 1833. Cholera and blizzards took a terrible toll on the journey west.

Adapting themselves to the harsh and wild frontier, the Choctaw made remarkable progress in the next 30 years: adapting their agriculture to new conditions and technology, setting up schools with the aid of missionaries, and setting up a constitutional form of government. The Choctaw tribal government, along with those of the other Five Civilized Tribes, was dissolved to make way for the new state of Oklahoma, formed out of Indian Territory in 1907.

By the late 1970s, there were about 17,000 Choctaw living in Oklahoma with about 10,100 acres of tribally owned land and another 134,300 acres of allotted land. In Mississippi there were still some 4,000 descendants of Choctaw who had not been removed to the West. Tribal landholdings amounted to 17,400 acres spread over seven counties, with the headquarters at Pearl River in Neshoba County. The tribal traditions and Choctaw language were reportedly stronger among the Mississippi groups. At the Choctaw Fair held each July or August in Philadelphia, Mississippi, tribe members gathered to dance, display their crafts, celebrate and play stickball once again.

BIBLIOGRAPHY: Debo, Angie, *The Rise and Fall of the Choctaw Republic.* University of Oklahoma Press, Norman, 1934, 1961. Swanton, John R. "Source Material for the Social and Ceremonial Life of the Choctaw Indians." *Bureau of American Ethnology Bulletin.* no. 103, 1931.

CHUMASH: a large southern California group occupying the coastal region around Santa Barbara in the late 18th century, estimated to number between 10,000 and 18,000 at that time. In the late 1970s, there were less than 50 Chumash descendants living on a small reserve in southern California, while an unknown number were assimilated into the general population.

The Chumash consisted of at least six geographically separated groups, speaking related languages of the Hokan linguistic family: Barbareño, Ventureño, Ynezeño, Purisimeño, Obispeño and the Island language. The names were derived from the name of a Spanish mission in each area. Chumash territory extended south from Estero Bay to Malibu Canyon, and included the channel islands of San Miguel, Santa Rosa, Santa Cruz and Anacapa.

Little is known of the traditional social organization of the Chumash, since they were missionized by the Spanish by the late 18th century. Villages were led by chiefs, whose limited authority was based on heredity and wealth. Shamans, who received their powers from a

Sinforosa, a
Chumash of
Piro Canyon,
California,
pictured in about
1870-1880.

Smithsonian Institution National Anthropological Archives.

guardian spirit, cured the sick through use of herbs, chants, charmstones and a tube used for sucking out the cause of the illness. The Chumash buried their dead face down in a flexed position, in a gravesite within the village, marking the graves with rows of stones or planks.

Villages were composed of groupings of hemispherical houses, some up to 50 feet in diameter. They were constructed of poles covered with a thick layer of interwoven grass. Reed mats were used as floor covering, partitions and mattresses. Other structures included storehouses, a sweathouse and an open-air ceremonial enclosure.

Acorns were the major food source for most of the Chumash, the nuts being ground into flour for mush or cakes. Pine nuts, cherries, and a variety of roots, bulbs, seeds and berries were also gathered. The Chumash men hunted mule deer with bow and arrow, rabbits with throwing sticks and other small game using snares and deadfalls. Groups along the coast and on the islands depended more on shellfish, fish, waterfowl and occasional washed up whales. Seines, dip nets and hook and line were used in fishing.

The Chumash made excellent lightweight canoes, from 12 to 25 feet in length, of wood planks lashed together and caulked with asphalt, which they skillfully maneuvered with double-bladed paddles. Woodcarving also included plates, bowls and boxes, usually of oak or alder. They also made finely decorated basketry, including waterbottles, with insides sealed with asphalt. The Chumash were also known for their highly imaginative and abstract rock paintings, which were probably produced in connection with religious ceremonies.

The first Spanish mission in Chumash territory, San Luis Obispo, was established in 1772, to be followed by San Buenaventura, Santa Barbara, La Purisma Concepción and Santa Ynez. By the early 19th century, the Chumash were completely missionized, and their native culture was fast disappearing. Their population declined sharply due to disease and general despondency. After the Mexican government secularized the missions, settlers took over most of the lands, and the remaining Chumash scattered. In the late 1970s, less than 50 Chumash descendants lived on a small reserve near Santa Ynez, in Santa Barbara County, California, while an unknown number of others were assimilated into the general population of southern California.

BIBLIOGRAPHY: Landberg, Leif C.W. *The Chumash Indians of Southern California.* Los Angeles: Southwest Museum, 1965.

COCHITI: a Keresan tribe and pueblo located 30 miles south of Santa Fe, New Mexico, with a population of about 500 in 1700. In the late 1970s the pueblo, located on the same site, had a population of about 1,000. The Cochiti spoke a language of the Keresan family, along with the Santo Domingo, San Felipe, Santa Ana, Zia, Laguna and Acoma.

The leadership of the pueblo included the traditional religious leaders, who wielded the real power, and the secular officials, whose offices dated from Spanish times. The cacique, who was appointed for life by his predecessor, was the religious leader and guardian of the tribal traditions. He appointed for one-year terms the war captains and other officers under him. The secular government, consisting of the governor, lieutenant-governor and *fiscales,* was appointed by the leader of one of the secret societies and was directed by the traditional leadership.

Each person belonged to a clan, inheriting membership in the same clan as his mother, and usually marrying outside the clan. There were two *kivas,* or religious centers: Squash and Turquoise. An individual usually belonged to the *kiva* of his father, although after marriage, a woman joined the *kiva* of her husband.

All men of the pueblo belonged to a *katcina* (kachina) society, and participated in masked dances performed to bring rain. Other dances and ceremonies were performed to insure abundant crops and the well-being of the pueblo. Shamans, called *chaiani,* used their supernatural powers to cure illness, set bones, control the weather and insure good hunting.

When anyone died, a shaman was called in to remove the soul from the

A Sun Dance being held at the Cochiti pueblo, New Mexico, in 1888.
A photograph by C.F. Lummis.

body, which remained in the house for four days before making its way
westward to Wenimatse, the land of the dead. The body was buried on
the day of death, along with a bundle of clothing, food, beads and other
items.

Late 16th century Spanish visitors to Cochiti reported two and three-
storied houses, with the lower story of basalt blocks and the upper stories
of adobe. Two circular *kivas* were also noted. The Spanish also found
the Cochiti men cultivating fields of corn, beans and pumpkins along the
flood plain of the Rio Grande. The women gathered pine nuts, yucca
fruit and juniper berries.

The men also hunted rabbits in communal drives, using throwing
sticks. Mountain lion, deer, antelope and bear were hunted, and
occasionally the Cochiti and Santo Domingo men would travel together
to the Pecos River area to hunt buffalo.

Crafts of the Cochiti included drums, pottery and basketry as well as
shell and turquoise ornaments. From skins, men made moccasins,
leggings and shirts. Other items of clothing were woven of cotton, and
later wool. Sandals were made from yucca.

According to Cochiti tradition, the Pueblo peoples all originally
emerged from the earth at a place in the north called Shipapu and settled
in the Rio de los Frijoles. (Ancient cliff dwellings could still be found in
this area, now Bandelier Natyional Monument, in the late 1970s.)
Gradually they spread southward to separate pueblos along the Rio
Grande.

The Cochiti lived with the San Felipe tribe at Kuapa, 12 miles northwest of the present Cochiti, but later divided to form separate pueblos. The Cochiti occupied various other sites before 1598, when they were visited at the present site by a Spanish expedition led by Juan de Oñate.

In the early 17th century, a mission was established, later called San Buenaventura, and European livestock, fruits and vegetables were introduced. The Cochiti took part in the Pueblo Revolt of 1680, and abandoned their pueblo between 1683 and 1692 to live at the fortified village of Potrero Viejo, along with some of the other Keresan peoples. In the early 19th century, the Cochiti were subjected to various epidemics and Apache raids on their livestock.

In the late 1970s, Cochiti pueblo occupied 28,700 acres and had a population of about 1,000. In spite of Spanish and American contact, the cultural traditions of the Cochiti were still very strong. The traditional style of government still operated, religious ceremonies were performed by the various secret societies, and the Cochiti language was still spoken. Crafts produced included pottery and the famous Cochiti aspen and cottonwood drums.

BIBLIOGRAPHY: Dumarest, Noel. "Notes on Cochiti, New Mexico." *Memoirs of the American Anthropological Association,* no. 6, 1919; Goldfrank, Esther Schiff. "The Social and Ceremonial Organization of Cochiti." *Memoirs of the American Anthropological Association,* no. 33, 1927; Lange, Charles H. *Cochiti: A New Mexico Pueblo, Past and Present.* Austin: University of Texas Press, 1959.

COCOPA: a southwestern tribe located near the mouth of the Colorado River in Mexico in the late 18th century, when they numbered about 3,000. In the late 1970s, there were about 1,500 Cocopa living in southwestern Arizona, Baja California and Sonora, Mexico.

The Cocopa called themselves Xawil Kunyavaei, "those who live on the river," and spoke a language belonging to the Yuman division of the Hokan language family. They lived in small settlements of 10 to 12 families along both the Colorado and Hardy rivers, near their confluence.

The Cocopa were organized into clans, or *shamul,* each with a clan leader called *shapai axany,* or "good man." Other leaders included dance leaders, funeral orators and war leaders, the latter receiving their power through dreams. There were also shamans, both male and female, who used supernatural powers to specialize in treating such things as arrow wounds, broken bones, burns and soul loss.

The Cocopa believed the world was created by twin gods, Sipa and

Komat. Important religious ceremonies included girls and boys puberty rites, at which time girls had their chins tattooed and boys had their noses pierced. Also important was the Karuk, or mourning ceremony, in which the dead were memorialized in a six-day rite. The bereaved burned clothing and food and gave gifts to those attending. The Cocopa cremated the dead, and burned their possessions and house along with food and gifts. A funeral orator instructed the dead person to leave the earth for the happier land of the dead. Mourners cut their hair and never again spoke the name of the deceased.

For cold weather, the Cocopa built conical excavated houses of pole framework covered with thatch and earth. In later times, they made rectangular houses of wattle and daub. Brush shelters were used in summer. Other structures included sunshades for cooking and granaries on stilts, for storing corn.

Cocopa agriculture depended on the flooding of the river, which occurred about May. In July, the Cocopa planted their crops in the alluvial mud. Principal crops were squash, pumpkins and four varieties of corn. In later times, watermelons, introduced by the Spanish, were also planted. Before the harvest, shooing flocks of birds away from the fields was a major activity of men, women and children. They also gathered mesquite, blue palm fruit, screw beans, agave, tule and various seeds. Tule stems and roots were cooked or eaten raw and tule pollen was mixed with corn to make mush or bread.

The men fished for mullet, bass and other fish with nets, and hunted mule deer, rabbits, ducks, geese and quail. In season, the Cocopa would make a raft trip to an island in the Hardy River to harvest wild rice. Large rafts were made with a section of clay floor on which a fire could be built. They also made small rafts of tule stalks lashed together, and transported babies and other valuables across rivers in large pottery ollas (jars with globular bodies).

Cocopa women made pottery with red and black designs, and both men and women wove storage baskets, carrying baskets, cradles and other items. Gourds were used to make rattles, dishes and canteens. Minimal clothing, made from inner willow bark, was supplemented in cold weather with rabbitskin blankets. Both men and women wore their hair long and loose, and wore face paint as adornment and protection from sunburn.

The ancestors of the Cocopa probably came from the north, settled along the Colorado River and, by the 16th century, were forced downriver by the Yuma and Mohave, toward the Gulf of California. They were visited by various Spanish expeditions in the 16th, 17th and 18th centuries. Their traditional enemies were the Quechan, Yuma, Kamia and Mohave, while their allies were the Maricopa and Pima. For

A Cocopa and dwelling: a photograph taken at Hardy River, Lower California, in 1909.

weapons they used bow and arrow, war clubs, short lances and deerskin shields.

In the mid-19th century, some of the Cocopa moved upriver to trade, and with the Gadsden Purchase of 1853-54, came under U.S. jurisdiction. In this period, steamboats were introduced on the Colorado River. Cocopa Indians served as pilots through the treacherous areas and sold wood to fuel the boats. The coming of the railroad to the region ended that era, and the Cocopa lapsed into relative poverty.

In 1917, the Cocopah Reservation was established in southwestern Arizona. In the 1960s, conditions on the reservation began improving. By the late 1970s, there were about 500 Cocopa and other Indians living on or near the reservation which consisted of two separate sections. A housing project was in progress, and a ceremonial building had been completed. There were about 800 other Cocopa living in Baja California and Sonora, Mexico, and a few in the Imperial Valley of California. The Cocopa language was still spoken in many Cocopa homes.

BIBLIOGRAPHY: Gifford, E.W. "The Cocopa." *University of California Publications in American Anthropology and Ethnology.* vol. 31, 1933; Williams, Anita Alvarez de. *The Cocopah People.* Phoenix: Indian Tribal Series, 1974.

COEUR D'ALENE: an interior Salish tribe of the western Plateau region. They inhabited the headwaters of the Spokane River upstream from Spokane Falls, including Coeur d'Alene Lake, in the 18th century, numbering probably around 3,000 at that time. In the 1970s, the tribe numbered about 700, living on and around the Coeur d'Alene Reservation in northern Idaho.

The Coeur d'Alene spoke a language of the interior division of the Salishan language family, similar to that of the Kalispel and the Pend d'Oreilles. They also used a sign language known to the various tribes in the area. They called themselves Skitswish or Schee-chu-umsh. The name Coeur d'Alene, a French term meaning "awl heart," was reportedly once used by a chief in describing a trader's heart.

The Coeur d'Alene were organized into three geographical divisions—the Coeur d'Alene River, Spokane River, and Coeur d'Alene Lake—each of which comprised a number of autonomous bands. Each band was composed of several families, led by an elected chief. There was originally no tribal organization, however later conflicts with other tribes and Europeans caused them to organize and select a tribal chief.

Religion centered around guardian spirits, obtained in vision quests. Shamans had especially powerful guardians, who gave them curing and other supernatural powers. They believed in a host of mythical creatures inhabiting the world around them, including dwarfs, giants, ghosts of the dead, and human creatures who could turn themselves into trees. The trickster Coyote, was said to have given the earth its present form. To ward off misfortune, prayers were offered to forces of nature such as the wind, sun, rain, snow, etc. Festivals varied from simple family gatherings to large feasts similar to the potlatch of the Northwest Coast tribes. The dead were wrapped in blankets in a flexed position and buried in the earth or under rock slides.

The Coeur d'Alene were semisedentary, originally living in conical mat lodges housing from one to three families. Winter dwellings were excavated about two feet. Communal long lodges were used for temporary gatherings, and dome-shaped sweathouses were constructed of bent willow sticks covered with bark or grass and earth. After buffalo hunting became important, portable skin tipis became the prevalent dwelling as the tribe became more nomadic.

The economy was based on hunting and gathering, with no agriculture. Prior to acquiring horses and becoming buffalo hunters, deer was the principal game. Also important were elk, antelope, moose, sheep, bear, and various small game, as well as salmon and other fish caught with gaffs, hooks, traps and nets. Women gathered camas, wild onions, and other bulbs, roots, seeds and berries. Crafts included basketry, made by coiling from cedar roots or twining from hemp, bark

A group of Coeur d'Alene at Plummey, Idaho; a photograph taken on July 4, 1922.

and light twigs. Other craftwork included elk or buffalo hide shields, cedar bark canoes, skin bags and pouches, soapstone pipes, and various tools and implements of stone and antler. Clothing was of deer, elk or antelope skins, decorated with quills and fringes. A typical wardrobe included moccasins, leggings, cap, breechclout and shirt (for men), dress (for women), and robe for cold weather.

The Coeur d'Alene migrated from their homes in British Columbia sometime in the prehistoric period, adopting much of Plateau culture but maintaining some aspects of Northwest Coast culture. They claimed a large territory in Idaho, Washington and Montana, expanding as they acquired horses and became nomadic hunters and warriors. By about 1805, when they met Lewis and Clark, they numbered about 3,000.

The early 1800s saw population decline due to warfare with other tribes and Europeans, and by 1850, there were only around 500. In 1858, they were defeated in a war with the U.S. Army. In the 1880s, a gold rush brought increased pressure from miners and settlers, resulting in the Coeur d'Alene being forced to cede more than 3,500,000 acres in treaties in 1887 and 1889, and to endure confinement to a reservation.

In the 1970s, about 700 Coeur d'Alene lived on or near the 69,328-acre Coeur d'Alene Reservation in northern Idaho. About 19,756 acres of land were tribally owned, and about 49,572 acres were allotted to individuals. The principal sources of income were farming, grazing and lumbering. A 5,000-acre tribal farm enterprise was established in 1972. Most of the tribal culture was gone, and the old religion had been essentially replaced by Christianity.

BIBLIOGRAPHY: Teit, James A. "The Salishan Tribes of the Western

Plains." *Bureau of American Ethnology Annual Report*. no. 45, 1930; *Coeur d'Alene Indian Reservation—Human and Natural Resource Supportive Data*. Billings: U.S. Department of the Interior, Bureau of Indian Affairs, 1976.

COLUMBIA: a Salishan tribe located along the east bank of the Columbia River between Fort Okanogan and Point Eaton, Washington, in the late 18th century, numbering at least 800 at that time. In the late 1970s, about 350 Columbia descendants were intermingled with the many other tribes located on the Colville Reservation, Washington. (See *Colville*.) An unknown number were assimilated into the general population of central Washington.

Culturally, the Columbia closely resembled neighboring Salishan tribes, including the Sanpoil and Okanagon (*q.q.v.*). They, spoke a language of the Salishan family, and were also known at various times as the Sinkiuse, Isle de Pierre and Moses' Band. The latter name was derived from the great chief, Moses, their leader in 1879, when the Columbia Reservation was established. In 1883-84, the reservation was abolished, and they were given the choice of taking individual allotments of 640 acres or moving to the Colville Reservation. Four bands of the Columbia-Sinkiuse chose to follow Chief Moses to the Colville Reservation, while others accepted allotments, becoming intermixed with the surrounding population.

BIBLIOGRAPHY: Teit, James Alexander. "The Middle Columbia Salish." *University of Washington Publications in Anthropology*. No.2, 1928.

COLVILLE: a Salish tribe living in Washington on the Colville River and the Columbia River between Kettle Falls and Hunters, in the late 18th century, numbering about 2,500 at that time. In the 1970s, there were about 1,600 Colville mixed among the approximately 5,500 Indian population on and around the Colville Reservation in northeastern Washington. The tribe gave their name to the reservation, although there were members of at least ten different Salishan tribes and one Sahaptian tribe located there.

The Colville were named after the river and Fort Colville, a Hudson's Bay Company post at Kettle Falls. They were also called Basket People, because of their use of large basket traps at Kettle Falls to catch salmon. They were also called Chaudière by traders, as well as Shuyelpee, a corruption of their own name for themselves. They belonged to the Okanagon group of the Interior division of the Salishan language family. Culturally, they were closely related to the other members of the group, which also included the Okanagon, Lake and Sanpoil.

In about 1806, the Colville were visited by Lewis and Clark, who called them Wheelpoos. In the early 19th century, many traders came to the area, including the Pacific Fur Company, and in 1825, Hudson's Bay Company founded Fort Colville. By the mid-1800s, increasing non-Indians in the area brought conflict and disease. In 1853-54, a smallpox epidemic struck, and in 1858-60, there was considerable friction caused by miners crossing Colville lands on their way to the newly discovered gold fields on the Fraser River.

In 1872, the Colville Reservation was established, setting aside 2,886,000 acres for the Colville and other non-treated tribes in the area. Other tribes assigned to the reservation were the Okanagon, Sanpoil, Lake, Kalispel, Spokane, Coeur d'Alene and other scattered bands. Trouble with settlers, as well as inter-tribal friction over land rights, marked the early years of the reservation. In 1892, about 52,000 acres were allotted in severalty to some Indians, and in 1900, about 1,500,000 acres were opened to settlers. Allottment continued, and by 1914, another 333,000 acres had been allotted to 2,505 Indians. In 1916, nonallotted lands were opened to settlement, which was stopped by legislation in 1935. In 1938, the various tribes were organized into the Confederated Tribes, led by a 14-member business council. In 1956, a bill restored to the tribe some of the land which had been sold to non-Indians.

In the 1970s, there were about 1,600 Colville living on and around the Colville Reservation, mixed with the total Indian population of around 5,500. The reservation encompassed 1,011,495 acres, of which 937,240 were tribally-owned and 74,248 were allotted to individuals. They lived similarly to their non-Indian neighbors, and were essentially acculturated. Stock raising, farming, logging and seasonal wage labor were the most important sources of income.

BIBLIOGRAPHY: Teit, James A. "The Salishan Tribes of the Western Plateaus." *Bureau of American Ethnology Annual Report.* no. 45, 1927-28.

COMANCHE: a Shoshonean tribe which had migrated from the mountains of Wyoming to the southern Plains by the late 18th century, when they numbered between 7,000 and 10,000. In the late 1970s, there were about 4,000 Comanche living in Oklahoma.

Comanche was probably derived either from a Ute term meaning "enemy" or the Spanish *camino ancho* meaning "broad trail." They called themselves Numinu, meaning "the people," while the Siouan tribes referred to them as the Padouca.

Above and right: Comanche hunting buffalo. Drawings by George Catlin, from his *Letters and Notes*, (1844).

The Comanche were loosely organized into about 13 autonomous bands. The bands cooperated with each other, but there was no tribal chief or tribal council. There were only minor cultural differences between bands, and anyone could leave or join a band at will.

Each band had a chief or head man, and the leading men of the band served as his councillors. The major bands included the Penateka (Honey-eaters, or Wasps), Quahadi (Antelopes), Nokoni (Wanderers), Yamparika (Yap-eaters) and the Kotsoteka (Buffalo-eaters). The Penateka, the southernmost band, were the largest.

Polygamy was practiced, especially the marrying of sisters and the marrying of a brother's widow. Punishment of adulterous wives included nose-clipping.

The Comanche had a number of deities, including a creator, the Sun, the Earth and the Moon. A favorite character in Comanche legends was Coyote, a trickster and brother to the Comanche. Because of this relationship they ate neither coyote nor dog. The Comanche did not celebrate the Sun Dance, which was popular with most of the other plains tribes, but they did perform an Eagle dance and a Beaver ceremony. Medicine men were important for their ability to cure the sick and intercede for a person with the spirit world. Young men went to secluded mountain tops to fast, pray and seek a vision of their guardian spirit. Upon their return, medicine men helped them to interpret their vision, explained any taboos that were indicated, and helped gather items for

personal medicine bundles, in which the powers of the vision resided.

The Comanche believed in an afterlife for all except those who died in the dark or were scalped, strangled or drowned. The dead person was dressed in his best clothing, his face painted vermilion and eyes sealed with red clay. The body was placed in a flexed position in a cave, crevice or shallow grave surrounded by rocks and stakes. The mourners cut their hair, gashed themselves, gave away their possessions, burned the tipi of the deceased and never again pronounced his name.

The Comanche lived in portable buffalo-skin tipis, made by the women. Buffalo was the main food source along with elk, black bear, antelope and deer. Meat was roasted over a fire, boiled in a skin-lined pit filled with water and red-hot rocks, or made into pemmican. They neither grew crops nor fished. To supplement the meat diet, the women gathered wild potatoes, persimmons, plums, grapes, currants, mulberries, walnuts and pecans.

Buffalo were hunted by driving them over cliffs, by individual stalking or in communal hunts, in which the herd was surrounded by men on horseback. The Comanche were highly skilled horsemen, credited with such feats as hanging over the side of their horse for protection in battle, while shooting at their enemy from under their horse's neck. They acquired vast herds of horses through buying, trading, breeding, raiding and capturing wild horses. Packhorses were used to pull travois made of tipi poles and loaded with their possessions. They painted the heads and tails of their warhorses red before battle, which, with their painted riders, presented a spectacular sight.

Comanche warriors painted their faces red and wore buffalo horn headdresses and knee-high boots of buffalo hide. Long hair was made even longer with the addition of horsehair. They carried lances and buffalo-hide shields, both decorated with feathers.

Until the late 17th century, the Comanche lived by hunting and gathering in the Rocky Mountain region of Wyoming and northern Colorado, with their Shoshoni relatives. They kept up their friendship with the Shoshoni even after moving south to the North Platte River. By about 1700, they were ranging southward from the Platte to the headwaters of the Arkansas River.

Sometime before 1705, the Comanche acquired horses, and, by 1750, they had sizeable herds. About this time, they were allied with the Caddo and were enemies of the Kiowa. By 1790, however, they had made a lasting peace with the Kiowa, and the two tribes became raiding partners.

Pressure from the Dakota and the lure of raiding targets in Texas and Mexico brought both tribes farther south by the early 19th century. Horses, cattle, booty and captives were the prizes sought by Comanche raids as far south as Durango, Chihuahua and Zacatecas in Mexico. Constant raids and warfare with the Apache took their toll, but the Comanche constantly replenished their population by adopting captive women and children, both Indian and white. Besides the Apache, whom they drove from the southern Plains, they also counted among their enemies the Utes, Pawnee, Osage, Tonkawa, Navajo, and Texans.

Their most bitter wars were probably those with the Texans in the 1840s and 1850s. In 1846, Texas became a state, and decided to remove all Indians from its boundaries. Around 1850, the Penateka band agreed to settle on a reservation in Indian Territory (now Oklahoma), but the northern bands continued to try to protect their territory. In the late 1850s, the Texans renewed their war of extermination against the northern' bands and the Kiowa, with units of Texas Rangers sometimes raiding into Indian Territory.

During the Civil War, both sides courted the Indians with promises in return for their friendship. An 1864 campaign led by Kit Carson against the Comanche was a total failure. In 1865 the Comanche and Kiowa signed a treaty on the Arkansas River with the U.S. government, which reserved a large part of western Oklahoma for them and their allies. The government failed to keep the agreement, and the Plains tribes rose up in protest.

By the 1867 Medicine Lodge Treaty, the Comanche agreed to accept reservations in Indian Territory, but the government again failed to keep squatters off Indian lands. Reservation life was difficult for those used to a free, nomadic life, and hostilities continued until 1875, when Quanah Parker finally surrendered, with his Quahadi band. Reservation lands were allotted in 1892, 160 acres to each tribal member.

In the late 1970s, the Comanche were represented as a tribe on the

Kiowa-Comanche-Apache Intertribal Business Committee. The 4,000 or so Comanche descendants were scattered around Oklahoma, most of them living in the communities of Lawton, Fort Cobb, Anadarko, Apache, Mountain View, Hogart, Cache and Gotebo. There was interest in tribal ceremonies and dances, and work was being done on developing a written form of the Comanche language.

BIBLIOGRAPHY: Wallace, Ernest and Hoebel, E. Adamson. *The Comanches: Lords of the Southern Plains.* Norman: University of Oklahoma Press, 1952.

COMOX: an important group of Coast Salish tribes occupying the east coast of Vancouver Island, British Columbia, including both sides of Discovery Passage, in the 18th century. They were the northernmost group of the Coast Salish, and as such were culturally a transition between the Salish and the neighboring Kwakiutl. In 1780, they were estimated to number around 1,800, but had dwindled to about 85 in 1970, living in the same area on four small reserves.

The Comox spoke a dialect of the Coast Salish division of the Salishan language family, sharing that dialect with their close cultural relatives, the Seechelt. Comox is a version of the name given to them by the Lekwilok, a neighboring Kwakiutl tribe, and its significance is unknown. Their name for both themselves and their dialect, however, was Catlo'ltx.

The Comox were divided into a number of subdivisions, including the Comox proper, Clahuse, Eeksen, Homalke, Kaahe, Kakekt and Sliammon, and possibly the Klamatuk. They lived in fixed villages, each headed by a chief called a *seam.* Society was composed of four classes: princely, nobles, commoners and slaves. There were apparently no clans, and the principal social division was the extended patrilineal family. Family wealth and privileges were inherited patrilineally, passing from father to sons.

Religious leadership was provided by shamans and various secret societies, borrowed from the Kwakiutl. A central concept in their religion was obtaining of a guardian spirit to help one throughout life. These spirits appeared in dreams or visions brought on by quests, such as fasting or feats of physical endurance. Shamans received supernatural curing powers in special kinds of visions.

The Comox lived in fixed villages of multi-family cedar plank houses, often over 100 feet long, sometimes decorated with carved totem poles and family crests. Inside was usually one fire for every two families, with a smoke hole in the roof for each fire.

The economy of the Comox was based mainly on fishing, especially for salmon, through use of weirs, dip-nets and harpoons. Halibut, cod, herring, sturgeon and eulachon (candle-fish) were also taken. They had no agriculture, but relied upon gathering of berries, fruits, edible green leaves and seaweed to supplement the diet. Deer and elk were hunted with snares as well as bow and arrow, but salmon was by far the most important food.

In fishing, as well as for traveling and making war, they used large cedar dugout canoes, carved with stone adzes and chisels. Wars with other tribes were often between fleets of warriors in canoes, armed with spears and bows and arrows.

In early times, there were Comox near the north end of Vancouver Island, and probably further north along the coast. They were frequently at war with the Kwakiutl to the north and other Coast Salish to the south, at times allying themselves with the Lekwilok. By 1895, the Kwakiutl had pushed them south, to the present-day area of the town of Comox. Their first European contact was probably with the explorer Juan de Fuca, in about 1752. Subsequently, there was relatively little contact with other Europeans until about 1843, when Victoria was founded, followed shortly by an influx of miners. The population of the Comox then declined due to disease and warfare. Their lands were taken over by whites and they were eventually assigned to reserves.

In the 1970s, there were few Comox left, their population being approximately 85 in 1970. They lived on four small reserves on Vancouver Island—Comox, Goose Split, Puntledge and Salmon River—with a total acreage of 7,040.

CONESTOGA: *See* SUSQUEHANNA.

COOS: a small Oregon coast tribe located along Coos Bay and Coos River in the early 19th century, numbering about 1,500 at that time. A few Coos descendants probably remained in the late 1970s, although essentially mixed with the general population.

Their name has been variously interpreted as meaning "south," "lake," or "inland bay." The Coos spoke two dialects, Hanis and Miluk, of the Yakonan language family. Other groups belonging to this family included the Alsea, Kuitsh, Siuslaw and Yaquina. Linguists formerly classified Hanis and Miluk as a separate language family, which they called Kusan. The neighbors of the Coos included the Umpqua to the north and the Kalapuya to the east.

In 1805, Lewis and Clark estimated their population at 1,500, located in two villages, Melukitz on the north side of Coos Bay and Anasitch on the south side. In 1857, after war broke out between Indians and settlers on the Rogue River, the Coos were moved to Port Umpqua. Around

1861, they were moved again to Yahatc Reservation. In 1876, Yahatc was opened to settlers, and the majority of the Coos emigrated to the mouth of the Siuslaw River, rather than allowing themselves to be sent to Siletz Reservation. In 1914, about 30 speakers of the Miluk dialect remained.

COPPER INUIT: a central Canadian Arctic tribe located on Victoria Island and along Coronation Gulf, numbering about 800 in the late 18th century. In the late 1970s, there were still about 800 Copper Inuit (Eskimo), located in several communities in their original territory.

The Copper Inuit were so-named by explorers as a result of their use of native copper in various tools and weapons. To neighboring tribes, they were known as the Kitlinermiut. They spoke the Inuit (Eskimo) language, which was spoken, with minor variations, by Inuit peoples from Alaska to Greenland. Their name Eskimo was derived from an Abnaki Indian term meaning "raw meat eaters", whereas the term Inuit, meaning "people", was their own name for themselves.

The Copper Inuit were loosely organized into a number of local groups, each vaguely associated with a general territory. Membership in these groups was fluid, with families or individuals coming and going at will. The basic unit was the nuclear family, composed of a man, woman and their children. Often two families would form an association in which they shared food or labor. These relationships were not based on kinship, but rather a hunting or other partnership between the men. Wife exchange was sometimes practiced within such partnerships.

Shamans cured illness, which was caused by evil spirits or the displeasure of the dead. In early times, the Copper Inuit buried their dead in heavy stone vaults, but in later times they left the bodies exposed to the elements, surrounded by a ring of stones. Implements of the deceased were broken and placed with the body.

The Copper Inuit were nomadic hunters who followed a seasonal migration cycle. From November to May, they gathered in bands of from 50 to 200 to hunt seal out on the ice of Coronation Bay. They lived in temporary villages of snow houses, which were moved every few weeks in search of the seals. Two men could build a snow house in about one hour. One man cut blocks with a snow knife, while the other, working from within, laid the blocks in an ascending spiral until they formed a dome.

In May, they moved to the land, cached their winter equipment, and broke up into small hunting groups of a few families. During summer, they hunted caribou and musk ox, fished, traded and gathered raw materials such as wood, soapstone and copper. During the wet season of spring and early summer, they pitched skin tents on oval rings of turf to keep the water out.

In autumn, the Copper Inuit gathered along the coast to hunt caribou, which migrated in large herds at that time. Autumn was also the time for repairing winter equipment and sewing warm clothing in preparation for the winter migration out onto the ice. Dwellings at this time were skin tents built over triangular tent pits from four to eight feet deep.

The Copper Inuit used wooden dog sleds and skin toboggans for transportation over the snow, and skin kayaks propelled with a double-bladed paddle for water transport. Fish were taken with wooden weirs and traps, as well as hooks, gaffs and three-prong spear hooks, all of copper. Other copper items included ice chisels, snow knives and arrow points. Other tools were made of bone, stone and wood. Snow goggles were made of ivory or bone.

The Copper Inuit were perhaps descendants of a Thule Culture people who migrated into the area in about 1000 AD from Alaska. Although visited by several British expeditions in the late 18th and early 19th century, they remained isolated from European influence for a while longer. In the early 19th century, they began obtaining iron from the Netsilik to the east in trade for soapstone and copper. Other European goods began reaching them indirectly, and probably influenced ways in which they put their native copper to use in tools and implements. European diseases also reached them indirectly, through other tribes.

In the late 1970s, there were about 800 Copper Inuit living in the communities of Coppermine, Holman, Cambridge Bay and Bathurst Inlet, along Coronation Gulf and Victoria Island.

BIBLIOGRAPHY: Jenness, Diamond. "The Life of the Copper Eskimos." *Report of the Canadian Arctic Expedition.* vol. 12, 1922; McGhee, Robert. "Copper Eskimo Prehistory." *National Museums of Canada Publications in Archaeology.* no. 2, 1972; Rasmussen, Knud. "Intellectual Culture of the Copper Eskimos." *Report of the Fifth Thule Expedition 1921-24.* vol. 9, 1932.

COSTANOAN: a central coast California group occupying the region around and south of San Francisco Bay in the late 18th century, when they numbered about 10,000. In the late 1970s, there remained only about 200 Costanoan descendants, living in California.

Costanoan, Spanish for "coast people," refers to a group of eight languages belonging to the Penutian language family. Politically, the Costanoan were divided into numerous tribelets, consisting of one or more villages, each of which were headed by a chief and council of elders. The office of chief was inherited through the male line and could be held by a woman if there were no male heirs. Chiefs were responsible for directing ceremonial and economic activities, such as hunting, fishing and gathering.

A Costanoan basket.

Smithsonian Institution

Socially, the Costanoan were divided into clans which belonged to one of two divisions, the Deer or Bear moieties. The Costanoan prayed to the sun and other deities, and their dreams were interpreted in religious terms by shamans. Other powers of the shaman were controlling the weather and diagnosing and curing disease. The Costanoan either buried or cremated their dead, whose souls journeyed to a land across the sea. Widows cut their hair and covered their heads with ashes or asphalt, and the possessions of the deceased were buried or burned.

The Costanoan built dome-shaped houses of pole framework, thatched with tule, grass or ferns. In some areas they made conical houses of redwood slabs or bark. Sweathouses were dug into the side of a stream bank and used by both men and women.

The Costanoan had a widely varied diet, procured by hunting, fishing and gathering. They gathered acorns, as well as seeds, nuts, berries, grapes, roots, greens, insects and honey. Salmon, steelhead, sturgeon and lamprey were caught in nets and traps or speared at night by bonfire light. Washed up whales and sealions were also eaten. They stalked deer, using deerhead disguises, and also hunted elk, antelope, bear, mountain lion and small game.

The Costanoan made canoes of tule, for fishing and duck hunting, which they propelled with double-ended paddles. Other crafts included twined basketry, used for making fish traps, winnowing trays, sifters and various containers. Clothing was minimal, the men going without and the women wearing tule or buckskin aprons. They wore robes of rabbitskin, deerskin or duck feathers in cold weather.

In the late 18th century, seven Spanish missions were established in Costanoan territory, and most of the Indians were compelled to give up their traditional existence to labor in the mission fields. Between 1770 and 1832, the population of the Costanoan fell from about 10,000 to less than 2,000, due to disease, hardship and declining birthrate. After the Mexican government secularized the missions, in about 1835, some Costanoan worked on ranches, while others tribed to return to a hunting and gathering existence. Most became mixed with the white and Indian population. The Costanoan languages were essentially extinct by the early 20th century. In the late 1970s, there remained perhaps 200 Costanoan descendants, living in California.

BIBLIOGRAPHY: Heizer, Robert F. ed. *The Costanoan Indians.* Cupertino: California History Center, DeAnza College, 1974.

COWICHAN: an important group of 41 Coast Salish tribes located in British Columbia in the 18th century, on the southeast coast of Vancouver Island and on the lower Fraser River, upstream to Spuzzum. In 1780, they probably numbered around 5,500. In the 1970s, they numbered around 1,500, living in British Columbia on the Cowichan Reserve plus eight other small reserves.

The Cowichan spoke a dialect of the Coast Salish division of the Salishan language family. They called themselves Kawutson, which refers to a certain rock on a mountain at the entrance to the Cowichan River.

The Cowichan were composed of two groups: the Cowichan of Vancouver Island and the Fraser River Cowichan, also known as the Stalo. These were composed of a number of autonomous communities, or villages, each headed by a chief, who attained power by inheritance or by accumulating wealth. A class system, with nobles, commoners and slaves was prevalent. The communities were composed of patrilineal families, with both family wealth and privileges passed from father to sons. Marriage was usually with someone outside the village, with brides purchased by exchange of gifts between families.

When a girl reached puberty, she undertook a vigil, fasting alone on a blanket for four days. If a young man joined her in this vigil, and if he was satisfactory to her parents, he was allowed to marry her.

The Cowichans had a complex mythology, and ceremonial life centered around the potlatch, a ritualized display and distribution of wealth characteristic of all the tribes of the area. Potlatches were held at any opportunity—birth, death, naming of a child, etc. They were accompanied by feasting and dancing, with shamans performing dances depicting various ancestors and creatures in their mythology. Potlatches for the dead were presided over by an effigy of the dead person. The Cowichan believed that the dead went toward the rising sun, and that after three days, the soul would return and tell a sleeping relative that all is well with the deceased and mourning should end. The dead were wrapped in skins and placed in cedar boxes or canoes on scaffolds. Mourners cut their hair, and the name of the dead was not spoken for a number of years. A creation myth says that the first Cowichan man, Stufsun, dropped to earth at a point in the vicinity of a falls in the Cowichan River.

The Cowichan lived in villages, sometimes stockaded, of large multi-family houses—often whole villages in one dwelling. They were of cedar plank construction, from 40 to 100 feet long and 20 to 40 feet wide, divided into compartments for different families.

At various times of the year, the Cowichan left their permanent villages to collect food, often living in temporary mat sheds. Travel was almost exclusively by large cedar dugout canoes, which they maneuvered very skillfully. After wintering in their permanent villages, they canoed, in February and March, to Salt Spring Island to take herring with large rakes. In May, they went to various small islands to gather camas, a type of water lily bulb, before returning to Vancouver Island. In June, they went to the Fraser River for sockeye salmon, using nets towed by canoes. In October, they returned to their permanent villages in time for the beginning of the November run of dog salmon, which were caught by weirs and traps. Winter was then devoted to hunting deer and elk, trout fishing and, above all, ceremonies and potlatches.

The Cowichan, like other Coast Salish tribes, were short in stature. The women wore skirts of woven cedar bark, and, at home or in their daily work, the men went without clothes. They added skin robes for formal occasions and for winter wear. Sea otter robes were especially prized, as well as goat hair blankets, which were used as a medium of exchange, along with dentalium shells. Necklaces of dentalium shells were worn for ornamentation by both men and women, along with ear pendants of abalone shell.

In early times the Cowichan were frequently at war with the Klallam, who conducted headhunting expeditions among them. Many wars were on water, with the Cowichan using their heavy canoes to ram and sink the enemy. They were also at war with the Kwakiutl tribes, particularly the Lekwilok, and their occasional allies, the Comox. The Cowichan also conducted slave raids south to the Puget Sound tribes, such as the Skagit and the Snohomish.

First contact with Europeans was probably with the explorer Juan de Fuca in about 1592. In the early 19th century, the Hudson's Bay Company traded in the area, and in 1843 Victoria was founded, followed a few years later by a rush of miners into the area. Subsequently the Cowichan population declined due to disease and white pressure, eventually leading to their assignment to reserves.

In the 1970s, there were about 1,500 Cowichan living in British Columbia on the Cowichan Reserve and eight other small reserves, with land area totalling 6,161 acres.

BIBLIOGRAPHY: Curtis, Edward S. *The North American Indian.* vol. 9. Norwood, Mass: Plimpton Press, 1907-30.

CREE: an important Canadian Algonquian tribe occupying a large territory south of Hudson Bay in the early 17th century, numbering about 15,000 at that time. After becoming involved in the European fur trade and acquiring firearms, they expanded both east and west, occupying a vast area from Labrador westward to Great Slave Lake and southward into northern Montana and North Dakota. In the late 1970s, there were about 75,000 Cree, including numerous bands connected with reserves in Quebec, Ontario, Alberta, Manitoba and Saskatchewan, as well as one group on a reservation in Montana.

The mutually intelligible dialects of the Cree language belong to the central division of the Algonquian language family. Cree was a short form of Kristenaux, a French corruption of one of their own names for themselves. In post-European-contact times, there were two major divisions, the Woodlands Cree and the Plains Cree, who had migrated west to the Plains in the 18th century. The Maskegon or "Swamp People" were a branch of the eastern Cree, who were later sometimes classed as a separate tribe. The Cree were most closely related to the Ojibwa, from whom they may have separated at some early date.

Most of the year, the Woodlands Cree were organized into small hunting groups of one or more families. For a few weeks each summer, they congregated in bands for ceremonies, feasting and councils. In later times, summer gatherings were held in the vicinity of a Hudson's Bay Company trading post.

The Woodlands Cree believed all things in nature, including themselves, had *manitou,* or spirit power. They were careful not to offend the spirits of the animals on which they depended. Numerous ceremonies, sacrifices and taboos were designed to propitiate animal and other spirits. Cree mythology included the culture hero Wisatkatcak and other characters such as Otter (the buffoon) and Thunder. Adolescent boys sought guardian spirits through fasting ordeals. The Cree also had a secret Medicine Society, probably borrowed from the Ojibwa. They buried their dead wrapped in bark, and placed some of the weapons, tools and other property of the deceased on the grave.

Smithsonian Institution National Anthropological Archives

A group of Cree with white men in the interior of Fort Pitt, Canada. The photograph was probably taken in 1884, by J.O. Cote. In 1885, in one of the rare wars to occur between Canadians and Indians, Chief Poundmaker and his Cree followers supported the second Riel rebellion, which was suppressed. Louis Riel and his Métis, (people of mixed Indian and French Canadian ancestry), opposed the building of a coast-to-coast railroad and the settlement which accompanied it.

The Woodlands Cree constructed both conical and dome-shaped dwellings of birchbark or skins on a pole frame. They also made a larger, rectangular two-fire dwelling covered with bark or skins. Sweat lodges, used in case of illness, were made of skin laid over a willow-pole frame.

Although they often were forced to rely on rabbit for food, the Cree also hunted moose, bear, caribou, beaver, lynx, geese and ducks. The coastal Cree also hunted seals, and occasionally whales, using harpoons. Other hunting equipment included bow and arrow, spears, traps and snares. Fish were caught with nets, spears and hooks, and some roots and berries were gathered.

Pemmican was made from dried meat or fish, pulverized and mixed with caribou fat and stored in caches on scaffolds. The Cree made cooking vessels of birchbark, wood and soapstone. Wood was carved into bowls, trays, spoons, cups and cradleboards. Birchbark canoes were the main means of transportation, but snowshoes, toboggans and Inuit (Eskimo) dogsleds were used in winter. Clothing included painted and fringed moose-skin leggings, moccasins, breechclouts, shirts and dresses. They also had robes, mittens and caps of beaver and caribou skin, as well as woven rabbit skin blankets for winter.

The Cree who gradually spread westward to the prairies and Plains in the 18th century soon became dependent on buffalo, which were far easier to hunt than woodland game. When the large buffalo herds split up to forage in winter, the Plains Cree also dispersed into small groups to

Cree women (1903).   The National Archives

follow them. In summer, the groups formed large camps and hunted the buffalo in communal drives. There were 8-12 bands among the Plains Cree, each led by a head man. The position was often hereditary, particularly if the heir was known for his hunting ability, bravery in war, oratory and generosity. Each band also had a warrior society.

The Plains Cree observed the mother-in-law taboo common to the Plains tribes. Marriage was formalized by the girl's family presenting the couple with a fully-equipped tipi. The groom, who had already received a horse from his prospective father-in-law, was presented with a pair of moccasins by his new bride. Wife exchange was sometimes practiced between close male friends, establishing a special bond between the two men.

Adolescent boys were sent to pray and fast in solitude, in hopes of obtaining spirit power through a vision. Shamans cured the sick with aid of their spirit powers. Sun, Thunder, Bear and Buffalo were among the more important spirits. In late June or early July, each band, or several bands together, would gather to celebrate the Sun Dance, an important ceremony among the Plains tribes. Mortuary customs included tree scaffold burial, tipi burial and, among the eastern bands, the construction of gable-roofed board houses over graves.

Buffalo provided the Plains Cree with food, shelter, clothing, bow-strings, containers, tools and fuel. In summer communal hunts, the

Smithsonian Institution National Anthropological Archives

A Cree demonstrating moose calling with a bark horn in about 1927.

buffalo were driven into brush impoundments, and in winter, they were often driven into marshes or deep snow. Other game, less important because of the easy availability of buffalo, included elk, beaver, rabbit, and birds. Fish were sometimes caught using weirs, fishing platforms and spears. Roots and berries were also gathered to supplement the diet. Both pit and platform caches were used to store food, and horses and dog travois were used to transport goods.

In the early 17th century, the Cree were living in the region between Hudson Bay and Lake Superior, spending their winters in the forests and gathering on the shores of either of those two bodies of water for a few weeks in the summer. They were friendly with the Ojibwa, but they fought with the Iroquois and Dakota to the south, the Athapascan tribes to the west, and Inuit (Eskimo) groups in the north. By the mid-17th century, the Cree were acquiring French trade goods through Huron and Algonquian middlemen.

Around 1667, the Hudson's Bay Company established a trading post in Cree territory. As they acquired firearms and trade goods, the Cree began extending south and west. In the late 17th century, they formed a close association with the Assiniboin, cemented by numerous inter-marriages. Smallpox epidemics in 1737 and 1781 wiped out some Cree groups in the Winnipeg area.

By the mid-18th century, the Cree had acquired horses, which enabled them to spread westward to the Rocky Mountains and southward into the Missouri Valley in Montana by 1800. By the mid-19th century, the Cree controlled much of the area north of the Missouri, while the Assiniboin held sway to the south.

Smallpox epidemics and warfare with the Blackfoot in the 1850s, however, brought a quick decline of the Cree. In the 1870s, treaties were made with the Canadian government, establishing some Cree reserves. The Cree were involved in the 1885 Riel Rebellion, with some of the rebels returning to their former Montana lands. In 1916, Rocky Boy's Reservation, named for a Cree-Ojibwa chief, was established for Cree and Ojibwa Indians in Montana.

In the late 1970s, about 75,000 Cree lived on various reserves in Ontario and Quebec. There were also about 1,800 Cree-Ojibwa living on or near the 107,600-acre reservation in Chouteau and Hill counties, Montana.

BIBLIOGRAPHY: Mandelbaum, David, G. "The Plains Cree." *Anthropological Papers of the American Museum of Natural History.* vol. 37, 1940; Skinner, Alanson. "Notes on the Eastern Cree and Northern Saulteaux." *Anthropological Papers of the American Museum of Natural History.* vol. 9. 1911.

CREEK: also known as Muscogee, the major tribe in an alliance of southeastern Indians known as the Creek Confederacy, which was probably formed as a defense against other large Indian groups to the north. The Creek were probably named for their tendency to settle along creeks and streams.

The Creek were known as one of the Five Civilized Tribes, along with the Cherokee, Choctaw, Chickasaw, and Seminole. According to their own traditions they migrated to the southeastern United States from somewhere to the northwest. They spoke the Muskogean language, which was still spoken in the late 1970s.

At the time of European contact the Creek Confederacy, located mostly in the present states of Alabama and Georgia, numbered about 22,000 of whom 18,000 were Muscogee. Other major tribes in the Confederacy at that time were the Apalachicola, Hitchiti, Okmulgee, Alabama, Yuchi, Koasati, and Tuskegee. Later, various other tribes and bands joined the Confederacy. The Creek eventually were relocated in Indian Territory (now Oklahoma). By the late 1970s they numbered about 26,000.

The Confederacy was divided into two groups. The Upper Creek were located along the Coosa and Tallapoosa rivers in Alabama, and the Lower Creek lived on the Chattahoochee and Flint rivers in Georgia. Together they occupied about 50 towns, each led by a chief (*miko*), subchief, and counsellors. These were chosen on the basis of merit rather

Me-na-wa, a
Creek: a
lithograph
from a painting
by Charles Bird
King: first
published in
McKenney and
Hall's *The Indian
Tribes of North
America*,
(1836-44).

Smithsonian Institution National Anthropological Archives.

than heredity. The council had the responsibility of presiding over town meetings, serving as a court of arbitration, seeing to public works, arranging annual festivals, and often deciding whether or not to wage war.

Subordinate to the town council was the *tustunugee* or war chief, who usually led war parties. The towns were known either as white towns, those dedicated to peace ceremonies, or red towns, those dedicated to ceremonies of war. Warriors might come from either red or white towns. A matrilineal clan system prevailed, in which each person belonged to the clan of his mother and was strictly forbidden to marry within his own clan. There were more than 40 clans among the Creek, bearing such names as Deer, Alligator, Corn, Beaver, Wind, etc. A given town might have as few as four or as many as 25 different clans.

The Creek had numerous advisors for religious consultation. There were medicine makers, prophets, and weather shamans, to name a few. Medicine makers attended schools where under a skilled teacher they learn the curative powers of herbs, roots, sweat baths, fasting, chants, etc. Prophets were usually the younger of twins and had powers of clairvoyance. Weather shamans were sometimes held responsible for their lack of control and faulty predictions.

The supreme being of the Creek religion was the "Master of Breath" who ruled over the Land of the Blessed Dead. The dead were buried beneath their houses in a sitting position, surrounded by their possessions. The dead person's spirit followed the Milky Way to the land of the dead. Many perils beset the traveler of this path, and only those who had led a worthy life found their way.

The principal festival in the Creek religious year was the busk or Green Corn Dance, held for four or eight days in midsummer to celebrate the ripening of the new corn. This ceremony symbolized a new beginning. A new fire was lighted in the town square and all household fires were re-kindled from it. There was fasting and a forgiving of all grudges and crimes (except murder and a few others) committed during the previous year. Dancing, feasting, and ritual cleansing in the river were followed by an address by the *miko* concluding the annual festival.

Each village was laid out around a central square which contained a rotunda—a round pole and mud building used for council meetings. Also in the central area was a public square used for dancing and ceremonies and a field for stickball games. Surrounding this central area were the family homes. A fairly well off Creek family would have four buildings of its own: an enclosed winter house, an open summer house, a building used for food storage below and entertaining guests above, and a storehouse for hides and goods.

Agriculture was a mainstay of the economy, with corn, beans, pumpkins, squash and sweet potatoes as the chief crops. Common fields were owned by the town, with plots marked off for each household. Hoes and digging sticks were the main tools until English traders introduced the plow, which was readily taken up by the Creek.

Hunting was important both for food and the skins it provided. Hunting parties would sometimes be gone as long as six months, preserving the meat and treating the skins as they went. Women went along to help with these chores.

Pottery and the weaving of baskets and mats were also the responsibility of the women as well as spinning, weaving and making of clothing. Men made most of the tools, weapons and dugout canoes.

The Creek quickly availed themselves of trade goods brought by the Europeans and soon became very dependent on the traders for cotton cloth, steel knives, guns, iron pots, etc. Many traders intermarried with the Creek and the resulting children came to hold positions of leadership, based on the tribal clan affiliations of their mothers and the schooling often provided them by their fathers.

The Spanish under DeSoto were the first Europeans to encounter the Creek. The Creek, however, later allied themselves with the English, fighting at various times against the Spanish, French, Americans and their assorted Indian allies. Tomochichi, a Yamacraw chief of the Creek Savannah River in 1733, and later accompanied him to London to meet King George II, (reigned 1727-60).

The Creek were becoming prosperous farmers when they became involved in the American Revolution on the side of the British. After the war they were forced to give up large parts of their land to white settlers. The War of 1812 caused civil war among the Creek, the "Red Stick" faction led by William Weatherford supporting the British, while William McIntosh led the "loyalist" supporters of the United States. Both leaders were of mixed Creek and Scottish ancestry.

The "Red Stick" forces were badly beaten at the Battle of Horshoe Bend in 1814 by a composite force of militia, armed settlers, Creek and other Indian tribes led by Andrew Jackson. Both Creek factions lost, having to cede once more large areas of their lands. The remaining Creek lands were wrested away by fraud, forgeries, illegal treaties and burning out by white settlers.

Some Creek fled to Florida to join with the Seminole, while others staged a last ditch uprising in 1836. The majority, however, gave up and were sent west to Indian Territory (later Oklahoma). In 1836-37, some 14,000 Creek successfully made the journey west, while another 3,500 died along the way.

In the West the Creek began to rebuild their towns, re-establish tribal government and grow crops again. They accepted missionaries in order to gain schools for their children. In 1889 they once again felt the white man's greed, as large tracts of their land were opened to settlers.

By 1906 the tribal governments of all the Five Civilized Tribes, which had been functioning for three-quarters of a century on the model of the United States Constitution, were dissolved to make way for the new state of Oklahoma created out of Indian Territory in 1907. Tribal lands were allotted to individuals, a disaster that resulted in 95 percent of the Five Tribes land passing into non-Indian hands by the mid-1970s.

In the late 1970s there were 26,000 Creek living in Oklahoma and another 600 in Alabama. The latter were descendants of those who had refused to be removed to the West. Tribal lands included 4,061 acres, with tribal headquarters at Okmulgee, Oklahoma. Although largely assimilated into white culture they still used the Muscogee language, they celebrated the Green Corn Dance, and the young men still played stickball.

BIBLIOGRAPHY: Green, Donald E. *The Creek People.* Phoenix: Indian Tribal Series, 1973; Spencer, Robert F., Jennings, Jesse D., et al. *Native Americans.* (Ch. X by Theodore Stern). New York: Harper & Row, Publishers, 1965.

CROW: a Siouan tribe living in southwestern Montana and northern Wyoming in the late 18th century, numbering about 4,000 at that time. In the late 1970s, there were about 5,000 Crow, living mostly in south-

A Crow woman
preparing a
buffalo skin:
a photograph by
Edward S. Curtis,
titled "In the
Canyon," (1908).

Library of Congress

eastern Montana. The Crow called themselves Absaroke, the name for a
bird no longer found in the region. The Crow and the Hidatsa formed a
sub-family of the Siouan language group, and the two tribes formerly
lived together.

The Crow were subdivided into about 13 clans, each headed by a man
distinguished for his war record. The governing body of the tribe was a
council of chiefs. Chiefs attained that title by performing four specific
deeds: leading a successful war party, counting coup by touching an
enemy, taking an enemy's weapon from him, and cutting loose a horse
picketed in the enemy's camp. One member of the council was chosen to
be head of the camp, and each spring one of the men's military societies
was appointed as the police force. Their duties included keeping order in
camp, enforcing the discipline of the buffalo hunt and preventing war
parties from setting out at inopportune moments.

Some of the men's societies were the Foxes, Lumpwoods, Crazy Dogs
and Big Dogs. Sometimes in the spring, rival societies would engage in
wife-capturing, usually of wives known to be willing captives. Most girls
were married before puberty, and marriage was almost always outside
the clan. The mother-in-law taboo prohibited a man from looking at or
talking to his mother-in-law. The same held generally for a woman and
her father-in-law.

The Crow believed in a vital force that was found in all nature. The
most important tribal ceremonies were the Medicine Lodge, or Sun
Dance, ceremony and the ceremonies of the Tobacco Society. The latter

were held three times during the year—at initiation, spring planting and harvest. Old Man Coyote, who taught them many things, was the culture hero of the Crow. He was also a trickster and was the subject of many lively tales. According to tradition, in the beginning there was a watery world ruled by First-Maker, who bid a duck dive down and bring up some mud. From this mud, the earth and men were created.

When a Crow died, his body was taken out the side of the tipi rather than the door, or someone else in the tipi would also die. The body was dressed in its best clothes, painted and placed on a scaffold. When decomposed, it was taken down and buried among rocks or in a cave. When a great chief died, a tipi was erected over his scaffold and all left to the elements. Mourners gave away their property, cut their hair and sometimes gashed their legs or cut off fingers.

The Crow lived in skin tipis, which varied in size and required anywhere from seven to twenty buffalo skins to make. When a woman desired a new tipi, she usually commissioned a woman specially skilled in designing and cutting. She would then invite her friends to a sewing bee, perhaps serving them berry pudding or some other favorite dish. Crow tipis were of four-pole construction, as opposed to the three-pole types of some other plains tribes. They were often 25 feet high and the large ones could accomodate 40 people. The rear of the tipi, opposite the door, was the place of honor where the owner or a special guest sat. A draft screen around the lower inside was painted with pictures recounting the owners brave deeds. Adjacent to the tipis there were usually round arbors of boughs and foliage, which provided shade in summer.

While living on the plains, the Crow had no agriculture other than tobacco, although formerly, when they lived on the Missouri River with the Hidatsa, they had raised corn. Buffalo was the main source of food. The three usual ways of hunting the buffalo were driving them over a cliff, driving them into an impoundment, or surrounding them on horseback. The Crow were skilled horsemen, training their children almost from infancy.

Deer were also taken by stalking the animal while wearing a deerskin and head. Meat was roasted over the fire, cooked in the ashes or boiled in a skin-lined pit with hot rocks. Cooking fires were started using a firedrill. Some meat was cut into strips and dried, and sometimes pulverized and mixed with dried chokecherries and melted fat to make pemmican. To supplement the basically meat diet, women dug edible roots with digging sticks, gathered rhubarb, berries, plums and grapes.

Crow material culture was similar to that of other Plains tribes. The Crow made their bows from hickory, ash and, occasionally, elkhorn. Bow and arrow makers were skilled specialists. The Crow made spoons and cups from buffalo horn and carved bowls from wood, as well as fleshers and scrapers and other tools from stone and bone. Skin rafts were used to cross rivers. Women's dresses were highly ornamented with elk's teeth and ermine trim. Favorite games included gambling, hand games and the hoop and pole game.

The Crow and Hidatsa probably originated in the Lake Winnipeg region, moving south to the Plains in about 1550. They probably lived together on the Missouri River, later dividing and then coming back together on the Missouri, where they lived by hunting and growing corn.

Leaving the Hidatsa, the Crow moved westward to southwestern Montana and northern Wyoming, where they lived along the Yellowstone, Bighorn, Powder and Wind Rivers. Two divisions developed, Mountain Crow and River Crow, based on preference of location. The Crow served as middlemen in the horse trade, bringing trade goods to the Shoshoni, in exchange for horses to be traded to tribes farther east.

In 1833, the Crow were hit by smallpox. In 1851, they were given a 38.5 million acre reservation in Montana which was greatly reduced in 1868. In the 1860s and 1870s, many Crow served as scouts for the U.S. Army in its wars against the Dakota, old enemies of the Crow. By 1883, the buffalo were gone and the Crow Agency was moved to the Little Big Horn River, in southeastern Montana.

In the late 1970s there were about 5,000 Crow, mostly living on or near the 1.5 million acre Crow Reservation, which included about 1.2 million acres of land allotted to individuals. Agriculture, ranching, tourism and manufacturing were all important in the tribal economy. Custer Battlefield National Monument, located on the reservation, was a major tourist attraction. A re-enactment of the Little Bighorn Battle was held each year, along with the Crow Fair and Rodeo. Crow was the first language of the reservation, and traditional Crow games and sports were still popular. The Sun Dance and Tobacco Society ceremonies were still performed.

BIBLIOGRAPHY: Lowie, Robert H. *The Crow Indians.* New York: Farrar and Rinehart, Inc., 1935.

CUSABO: an extinct group of about ten subtribes located along the South Carolina coast between Charleston Harbor and the Savannah River.

The ten subtribes (Coosa, Edisto, Wando, Etiwa, Kiawa, Stono, Ashepoo, Combahee, Wimbee, Escamacu) numbered about a total of 2,800 in 1600. All the subtribes were Muskogean language speakers. The tribal name Cusabo has been translated as "Coosa River people."

An early visitor to one of their villages reported seeing a circular building 200 feet in circumference with walls 12 feet high and a roof thatched with palmetto. Inside was a raised seat or platform for their chief.

The Cusabo were visited in 1521 by two Spanish caravels from Santo Domingo under Lucas Vazquez de Ayllón. The Spanish enticed the Indians aboard and then raised anchor, carrying away about 70 to be sold as slaves in Cuba. One Cusabo taken back to Spain by Ayllón told tales of the fabulous wealth of a place called Chicora where gold and precious gems littered the ground. Ayllón returned with six vessels and 500 colonists in futile search of the fabled land, but hardships and starvation drove them off.

As the English moved into the area the Cusabo gradually ceded more and more of their land to the colonists. They fought in the Yamasee War in 1715-16 and the survivors went either to Florida with the Yamasee or moved further inland to merge with the Creek, marking the end of the Cusabo as a tribe.

BIBLIOGRAPHY: Swanton, John R. "The Indians of the Southeastern United States." *Bureau of American Ethnology Bulletin.* no. 137, 1946.

DAKOTA: the largest tribe of the Siouan linguistic family, numbering about 25,000 in the late 17th century, when they were located in Minnesota and Wisconsin. In the following century, they moved westward onto the Plains, some divisions spreading as far west as eastern Wyoming and Montana, exchanging the lifestyle of a woodlands people for that of nomadic buffalo hunters. In the late 1970s, Dakota

Library of Congress

Dakota scraping a hide: a photograph by Heyn, (1899).

A Dakota,
Kicking Bear,
teaches his
son to shoot a
bow and arrow:
a photograph
by Herman Heyn,
(1900).

Library of Congress

descendants numbered about 40,000, located mostly on reservations in South Dakota, North Dakota, Montana, Nebraska and Minnesota.

The Dakota were also known as the Sioux, derived from an Ojibwa term, Nadowe-is-iw, meaning "adder," thus "enemy." They called themselves Oceti Sakowin or "Seven Council Fires," referring to their seven political divisions: Mdewakanton, Sisseton, Wahpeton, Wahpekute, Yankton, Yanktonai and Teton.

The Dakota were also divided into three different dialect groups, Dakota, Nakota and Lakota, all three terms meaning "allies." The Santee or Eastern group, composed of the Mdewakanton, Sisseton, Wahpeton and Wahpekute, spoke the Dakota dialect. The Yankton and Yanktonai make up the Wiciyela or Middle group and spoke the Nakota dialect. The Teton or Western group, which composed more than half the tribe, had seven subdivisions: Oglala, Brulé, Hunkpapa, Miniconjou, Sans Arcs, Sihasapa (or Blackfoot) and Two Kettle (or Oohenonpa.) These all spoke the Lakota dialect.

The Dakota probably migrated from the Ohio valley to the western Great Lakes region, where they were frequently at war with the Ojibwa. Pressure from this tribe, who were early recipients of French firearms, plus the lure of the great buffalo herds, induced the Dakota to move westward. The Teton were the first to leave the Minnesota region, about 1700, and spread the farthest west. They were soon followed by the Yankton and Yanktonai, who occupied a middle position between the western Teton and the eastern Santee groups, who remained in the Minnesota, Wisconsin and eastern South Dakota region.

See also: *Santee, Teton, Yankton, Yanktonai. Mdewakanton,*

Sisseton, Wahpeton, Wahpekute, Oglala, Brulé, Hunkpapa, Miniconjou, Sans Arcs, Sihasapa, and *Two Kettle.*

DELAWARE: the most important Algonquian confederacy at the time of European contact—referred to as "grandfather" by the other Algonquian tribes. Numbering about 11,000 in 1600, they occupied the Delaware River basin, including most of New Jersey and Delaware, as well as eastern Pennsylvania and southeastern New York. Between 1742 and 1867, the Delaware gradually migrated westward in a succession of no less than eight moves. In the late 1970s the Delaware were scattered, with identifiable groups being found in Oklahoma, Kansas, Wisconsin and Ontario.

The Delaware spoke a language of the Algonquian language family, which a few people still spoke in the 1970s. They referred to themselves as Lenni Lenape, meaning "the common people" or "real men." There were three geographical divisions—Munsee, Unami, and Unalachtigo—each with its own dialect and territory. The Munsee occupied the highlands; the Unami were located downstream from the Munsee, and the Unalachtigo were along the ocean. After European contact, the Unalachtigo lost their territory first and merged with the other two. Munsee and Unami became political designations and were often mistaken as separate tribes from the Delaware.

Before European contact the Delaware had some 30 to 40 communities, mostly located along the Delaware River and its various tributaries. Each village was autonomous, having its own chief and councillors. Chiefs were hereditary with succession through the female line. A chief very often nominated his successor from among those eligible.

Chiefs served as religious as well as political leaders of their villages. The Delaware believed in a creator or "Great Spirit" which they called Manitou. They celebrated at least five religious festivals each year, the most important being the Bear Sacrifice. This festival, in which a bear was captured and ceremonially sacrificed, lasted for 10 to 12 days in late January or early February. Other important festivals included the Maple Sugar Dance (March), the Planting Ceremony (May), the Strawberry Dance (June) and the Green Corn Ceremony, celebrating the beginning of the harvest (September).

Ceremonies were usually held in the Big House, a long structure supported by a wooden center post and other posts on which ceremonial masks were carved. Singing and dancing, to the accompaniment of deerskin drums and turtleshell rattles, were important elements of the Big House ceremonies.

The Delaware believed in the immortality of the soul. When a person died, his spirit left his body but lingered in the vicinity for a certain

The interior of a Big House of the Delaware, showing the center post in the foreground, (1932).

number of days, before going on to the afterlife. Mourners blackened their faces and buried the dead person along with some of his possessions. Details of the burial customs varied from village to village and generation to generation.

The Delaware built several types of dwellings or wigwams: circular with a dome roof; rectangular with an arched roof made of saplings tied together at the top, and rectangular with a ridgepole and pitched roof. There were smoke holes in the roof for the fires kept burning inside. Platforms along the wall at several levels served as seats, beds and storage areas. Dried corn, tobacco and herbs were strung from the ceiling.

Corn was the staple food, with beans, squash and pumpkin also important. Seasonal hunting trips were made to the hunting grounds used by each village or band. Game included black bear, white-tailed deer, rabbit, squirrel, ducks and geese. Muskrat, beaver and otter were trapped and fish caught with nets, spears and weirs. The coastal Delaware gathered clams, oysters and other shellfish. Nuts, berries, herbs, roots and maple sap for sugar were all collected to round out the diet. Corn was prepared in numerous ways. It was roasted, boiled, and

**Black Beaver,
a Delaware:
a photograph
by Alexander
Gardner,
(1872).**
The National Archives

pounded into cornmeal for bread, as well as made into soup, mush and dumplings. It was also mixed with beans to make succotash, or laced with nuts, dried fruits, or maple sugar for special flavor.

Cooking and food gathering was the women's domain, along with planting and harvesting, making clothing of skins and furs, gathering wood and weaving baskets. The men cleared the fields, built wigwams, made weapons and tools, hunted, fished, made dugout canoes and protected their families. The old people made wampum, pottery and fishnets, and helped with dressing skins and furs.

Delaware men wore deerskin breech clouts in summer and added a bearskin robe and buckskin leggings in cold weather. Women wore short deerskin skirts and also added bearskins or feather robes, leggings and moccasins in winter. Bear grease was used to dress the long braids of the women and the short roaches or scalp locks of the men. Pendants, strings of wampum and earrings were worn by both sexes. Tattooing and body painting added further adornment.

Delaware history before 1600 was passed down orally from generation to generation. There also existed, however, a written record in the form of pictographs, painted or carved on sticks or bark, known as the Walam Olum. The pictographs told the story of the Delaware from the earliest time, and a later manuscript interpreted the pictographs and told the story in the Delaware language. The actual wood or bark record was lost and doubt cast on the authenticity of the manuscript in the early 19th century. More recent scholars, however, have taken a more open-minded view of the manuscript, regarding it as a modern interpretation of an ancient record, well worth further study.

The Delaware were among the first Indians to come into contact with the Europeans in the area, being visited by Henry Hudson in 1609. A dependence on European trade goods soon changed the material culture of the Delaware as well as that of neighboring tribes. Iron pots, metal tools, knives, guns and cloth were greatly desired and caused rivalry among the various tribes for hunting grounds.

Rivalry also occurred among the various European powers for the Indian fur trade, with the Dutch and Swedes being replaced in 1664 by the English. In 1683 the famous treaty between the Delaware, represented by Chief Tamanend, and the English Quaker leader William Penn probably took place on the tribal council ground at Shackamaxon. The Delaware considered Penn their friend, but a later dispute with his successors over a treaty signed with him in 1686 led to the notorious Walking Purchase of 1737. The boundary of the land cession was to be established as the distance a man could walk in a day and a half. Professional "walkers" were hired who, with the aid of provisions supplied by packhorse, ran a distance of nearly 60 miles in the time allotted.

In the early 18th century, the Delaware were dominated by the Iroquois Confederacy, who sold more of their lands to the English. By 1742, part of the Delaware had moved from their homelands to the Susquehanna River near Wyoming, Pennsylvania. In 1751, the Huron invited the Delaware to settle in eastern Ohio along the Muskingum River, where they began to set up prosperous farms. Soon, however, hostilities broke out between the Delaware and the whites along the Ohio frontier. In 1782 about 100 Christianized Delaware were massacred by Kentucky frontiersmen at the Moravian mission of Gnadenhütten.

In 1789, responding to the increasing bitterness of the Ohio frontier, a band of Delaware crossed the Mississippi and received permission from the Spanish governor to settle in Missouri, while another band moved to Canada. Those who remained in Ohio became the core of resistance to further white encroachment, but were defeated along with their Indian allies in the Battle of Fallen Timbers in 1794. The Treaty of Greenville in 1795 was the first of many treaties in which the Delaware were forced to give up their lands in Ohio and Indiana, always with the "guarantee" of land elsewhere.

A reservation was set aside for them in eastern Kansas at the fork of the Kansas and Missouri rivers in 1829. Here the Delaware once again

A Delaware war club.

settled into frontier life—setting up farms and working as trappers, hunters and guides for the fur trade companies. But pre-Civil War Kansas was a place of turmoil, and the Delaware signed a treaty in 1866 agreeing to remove to the Cherokee lands in Indian Territory (now Oklahoma). They were preceded by other Delaware bands who had drifted into the region as early as 1812, including some who went there after first settling in Texas.

In Indian Territory, the Delaware became citizens of the Cherokee Nation, giving up their own tribal status. Their lands were allotted in severalty along with those of the other Oklahoma tribes.

In the late 1970s, there were very few full-blooded Delaware Indians left, several hundred with at least one-quarter Delaware blood, and thousands of part Delaware. The main body resided in Oklahoma, largely mixed with the white population but represented in tribal affairs by the Delaware Tribal Business Committee. Another Oklahoma group known as the Delaware Tribe of Western Oklahoma resided around Anadarko. There were no Delaware reservations in the state. Little of Delaware culture remained, although a few could still speak the language, and powwows and dances were still held.

In the late 1970s some Delaware also lived near Ottawa, Kansas, as well as on the Stockbridge-Munsee Reservation in Shawano County, Wisconsin. The latter were descendants of the Munsee who had joined the Stockbridge (Mahican) in purchasing a reservation there from the Menominee in 1832.

In the late 1970s, there were also three groups of Delaware in Ontario. About 250 lived on the Six Nations Reserve in Brant County— descendants of Delaware who had migrated with the Cayuga from New York in the late 18th century. Another 300 Delaware, descendants of a group known as the "Moravians of the Thames," occupied a reserve of 3,000 acres in Kent County. Near London there was a third reserve where about 1,000 Delaware formerly known as the "Munsees of the Thames" occupied about 2,700 acres. Among the Canadian Delaware, there remained a few who could speak the language, but most of the tribal culture had been lost.

BIBLIOGRAPHY: Weslager, C.A. *The Delaware Indians.* New Brunswick, New Jersey: Rutgers University Press, 1972; Speck, Frank G. *The Celestial Bear Comes Down to Earth.* Reading, Pennsylvania: Reading Public Museum and Art Gallery, 1945.

DIEGUEÑO: See TIPAI-IPAI.

DOGRIB: a nomadic Athapascan tribe living, since the mid-19th century, between the Great Slave and Great Bear lakes, in the Northwest Territories, Canada. They probably numbered around 1,250 in the late 17th century, and numbered about the same in the 1970s.

They spoke a Northern Athapascan language similar to that of the Slave, called themselves Thlingchadinne, or "dog flank people." The name derives from their tribal creation myth in which a woman delivered offspring which were fathered by a man who turned into a dog by night, passing this trait on to his offspring, who founded the tribe.

The Dogrib were organized into four nomadic autonomous bands, following the caribou herds in their migrations. Leadership and organization was minimal, probably consisting of headmen for each band, with limited authority. Like other tribes of the area, they often abandoned the old and infirm in times of hardship, although they treated their women with kindness. Men changed their name with the birth of each child.

Religion centered around spirits believed to inhabit lakes, rivers, and other aspects of nature. Success in life depended on acquiring, in visions or dreams, a guardian spirit. Shamans cured sickness and foretold the future, through powers obtained from especially powerful guardian spirits. The dead were placed on scaffolds, with streamers attached to the scaffolds to amuse the dead person's spirit and keep it from wandering. One year later, the remains were buried, accompanied by a memorial service.

The Dogrib usually lived in portable skin tipis like the Chipewyan, but sometimes built winter huts of poles and brush similar to those of Mackenzie River tribes. Life was geared to following their principal game animal, the caribou. Although they were basically woodlands people, they made frequent short trips into the barren lands for caribou, which they speared in lakes or snared after driving into pounds. Other game included musk-ox, moose and birds. Muskrat, mink, and fox were trapped for furs, especially after the advent of the European fur trade. They were not partial to fish, but caught some whitefish, trout and others. Clothing was of skins, similar to that of the other tribes in the area—shirt, breechclout, leggings and moccasins.

The Dogrib were probably at one time south and east of their present location, having been first contacted by traders in about 1744, on the Seal River, near Hudson Bay. Until 1823 they were dominated by the Yellowknife, whom they almost annihilated that year. By the mid-19th century, they had been gradually forced northwest of Great Slave Lake by the Cree. Fur trading was important throughout the 1800s, and Dogrib settlements grew up around various trading posts established in the area. Particularly important was Fort Rae, founded in 1852 by the Hudson's Bay Company on Great Slave Lake, around which the tribe has more or less centered since that time. In 1879, the first permanent mission, established near Fort Rae, brought the introduction of agriculture. Fishing also became more important as game became more scarce. In 1910, a shortage of caribou caused some starvation. In 1930, gold was found at Great Bear Lake, bringing some short-lived prosperity.

In the 1970s, the Dogrib were essentially acculturated, living much like their non-Indian neighbors, although the Dogrib language was still spoken. They were governed by a strong chief and council and were apparently reasonably well-off, relying on wage labor as well as the traditional pursuits of hunting, fishing and trapping. A handicraft business at Rae had been formed to provide income for the women.

BIBLIOGRAPHY: Anders, G. *Rae-Lac La Martre*. Ottawa: Department of Indian Affairs and Northern Development, June, 1969.

DWAMISH: a small group of Coast Salish, occupying, in the late 18th and early 19th centuries, an area near the present city of Seattle, Washington. Originally, they occupied one village on the shores of Lake Washington, near its outlet, but later the name was applied to an allied group of small tribes, including the original Dwamish, the Suquamish and others. The city of Seattle was named after one of the great chiefs of this confederation. In the late 18th century, the total population of the confederacy was probably around 1,200. By the 1970s, they were extinct as a group, although a few descendants probably remained, mixed with Snohomish, among the 630 Indians on the Tulalip Reservation in Snohomish County, Washington.

"Lifting over the daylight"—part of a Dwamish ceremony: a photograph taken at Tolt, King County, Washington in July 1920.

The Dwamish spoke a language of the Nisqualli group of the Coast Salish division of the Salishan language family. They were composed of a number of small villages, scattered on the shores of Lake Washington, near the outlet, and on the Dwamish and Black Cedar rivers. The villages were relatively autonomous, each being led by a chief and composed of one or more patrilineal families. Chiefs probably obtained power by wealth or inheritance, as was generally the case in the Coast Salish culture.

The culture of the Dwamish was apparently similar to that of the Snohomish, with whom they were eventually incorporated on the Tulalip Reservation. They were both part of the Northwest Coast culture, which relied on fishing and gathering for food, and on cedar for houses and canoes. The canoes were used for travel, fishing, and making war. Tribes of the area had elaborate social structures, based on family wealth, and consisting of noble, commoner and slave classes. Religious life centered around a rich mythology, and on curing by shamans, who received their powers in dreams or visions. Vision quests to obtain a lifelong guardian spirit were important.

Historically, the Dwamish and other Puget Sound tribes were engaged in continual warfare with the northern tribes such as the Cowichan. First contact with Europeans probably occurred with the explorer Juan de Fuca in about 1592, with little further contact until about 1792, when George Vancouver visited the area, followed later by expeditions of the Hudson's Bay Company.

The early 18th century was a difficult time, with encroachment of settlers on their territory and at least one disastrous war with the Cowichans, when a large fleet of Puget Sound canoes was totally destroyed. In 1853, the territory of Washington and the town of Seattle, which was named after the great chief Seatlh (Seattle), were established.

Seatlh was born in about 1790, and was considered a wise and venerable chief. He was the first signer of the Port Elliott treaty of 1855 between the Puget Sound tribes and the U.S. government, and kept a friendly attitude toward the whites in the general outbreak of 1855 to 1858. He levied a tax on the people of Seattle for the use of his name, based on the Salish belief that mention of a dead man's name disturbs his spirit.

In 1856, the Dwamish were removed to a reserve on the east shore of Bainbridge Island. This land was unsatisfactory, however, having no adequate fishing grounds, and the tribe was assigned, along with other Indians, to a 2,800 acre tract on Holderness Point, on the west side of Elliott Bay. By the end of the 19th century, they had been assigned to the Tulalip Reservation along with the Snohomich and other tribes.

By the 1970s, they were extinct as a group, although a few descendants probably remained, mixed with Snohomish and others on the 5,171 acre Tulalip Reservation, north of Everett, Washington.

EAST GREENLAND INUIT: the eastern-most Inuit (Eskimo) group, located mostly in the Angmagssalik area of eastern Greenland in the late 19th century, when their population had dwindled to about 400. In the late 1970s, there were about 2,000 East Greenland Inuit located in the Angmagssalik and Scoresbysund areas. They spoke a dialect of the Inuit (Eskimo) language, which is spoken with minor variations from Alaska to Greenland. The name Eskimo was derived from an Abnaki Indian term meaning "raw meat eaters." The term Inuit, meaning "people," is their name for themselves.

Informal religious leadership was provided by shamans, whose powers derived from certain "assisting spirits," acquired through trances. The shaman conducted seances, in which he entered into an ecstatic state and called upon his various assisting spirits to help him cure the sick, find lost souls or bring an abundance of game. In early times, the bodies of the dead were thrown into the sea and in times of hardship, old people sometimes threw themselves into the sea.

Aboriginally, the East Greenland Inuit lived in communal houses, with one house, of as many as 50 people, to a settlement. Each house was

**East
Greenland
Inuit
kayaks.**

Smithsonian Institution National Anthropological Archives

headed by a patriarch, although there was no formal organization. Houses were built into the side of a hill, with a long narrow passage leading into the house. Walls were of stone and sod while driftwood was used for posts, beams and rafters. A platform at the back, used for sleeping, sitting and eating, was divided into family compartments by hanging skins. Skins were also used to line the interior and keep out drafts. Floors were of stone, and seal-gut window panes let in light. Seal skin tents were used in summer and on hunting trips.

The East Greenland Inuit depended on the sea for sustenance—hunting seal, walrus, bowhead whale, and catching caplin and other fish. Meat and blubber from seals and whales, eaten raw or cooked, were the main staples. They hunted whales with harpoons in open boats called *umiaks*. Seals were hunted at their breathing holes during winter, and when they came up to bask on the ice in spring. In open water, the East Greenland Inuit hunted seals and walrus from sleek kayaks, reportedly being among the world's finest kayakers. The fish and meat diet was supplemented by mussels, clams, crabs, birds's eggs and berries.

The East Greenland Inuit traveled a great deal, both for hunting and for the enjoyment of traveling. Wooden dog sleds provided winter transportation. Material goods included wooden ladles, trays, snow goggles and finely-crafted buckets as well as cooking pots and blubber lamps made of soapstone.

The clothing of the East Greenland Inuit was basically sealskin, ingeniously made to suit their harsh environment. Jackets with the hair side in were worn next to the body, but loose enough to allow evaporation of perspiration. Completing the costume were outer jackets with the hair outward, short breeches, high boots and long stockings with the hair side in. They sometimes wore inner jackets of fox or bird skins. Gutskin jackets were worn for wet weather and kayaking, and whaling costumes had an air pocket which acted as a lifepreserver. Head-to-toe bearskin costumes were sometimes used for seal hunting, which required long periods of sitting still on the ice.

Greenland was probably first settled more than 4,000 years ago, populated by successive groups from the south and west. Caribou hunters, now known as the Dorset culture, probably entered Greenland by the first century AD. Around 500, a seafaring people arrived, probably originally from northeastern Asia. Known as the Thule culture, they hunted marine life in kayaks and *umiaks.* As the Thule people moved south along the west coast and back north up the east coast, their culture was modified and became known as the Inugsuk culture.

Around 982, a new immigration began from the east. Icelanders, led by Erik the Red, settled in West Greenland, and referred to the earlier inhabitants as Skraelings. These settlements died out in about 1500. Successive waves of people continued to enter Greenland from North America as late as 1865, and European whalers made short visits in the 17th and 18th centuries. Danish colonization began in about 1721.

Eastern Greenland, which had been settled by the 14th century by Inugsuk peoples from Western Greenland, continued to receive successive migrations from that direction. Settlements were made at Angmagssalik, Scoresbysund and Kangerdlugssvaq, but the latter two northern settlements died out for reasons unknown.

Most European settlement was in West Greenland, leaving the easterners essentially isolated until the late 19th century. At that time, the East Greenlanders began migrating to the west, starting a precipitous decline in their population. This trend was halted in 1894 by the establishment of a settlement, including a store, school, church and medical facilities, at Angmagssalik by the Danish government. In 1925, some 85 people from Angmagssalik established a new settlement at Scoresbysund.

In the late 1970s, there were about 2,000 East Greenland Inuit, mostly of pure blood, at Angmagssalik, Scoresbysund and a number of other small settlements along the coast. Seal hunting from kayaks continued to be important, with some modern adaptions, such as the use of guns. The

East Greenland Inuit maintained their language and culture to a large extent.

BIBLIOGRAPHY: Mikkelson, Ejnar. *The East Greenlanders Possibilities of Existence, Their Production and Consumption.* Copenhagen: C.A. Reitzels Forlog, 1944.

EDISTO: a small extinct tribe of the Cusabo group, which occupied the southern South Carolina coastline. The Edisto lived along the lower Edisto River, moving to Edisto Island in about 1587. They may have numbered 1,000 in 1600, and spoke a Muskogean or perhaps a Uchean language.

The villages of the Edisto were marked by a large, circular ceremonial house, wherein the village chief presided. Outside, a tree-lined open space served as the ballfield for chunkey and other games.

The Edisto grew two or three crops of corn each year, as well as pumpkins and melons. They hunted deer, turkey, quail, geese and ducks, and gathered crabs, oysters and other shellfish to supplement the diet.

In 1562, the Edisto aided a group of French Huguenots in an unsuccessful attempt to establish a colony in the area. In 1566, the Spanish established a mission and built Fort San Felipe. By 1576, the Edisto and their neighbors rebelled against the Spanish and burned the fort. The Spanish rebuilt the fort, but finally abandoned the post in 1587.

In 1663 and 1666 the Edisto entertained English exploring parties, and in 1670, an English colony was established. The Edisto, weakened by disease and attacks by neighboring tribes, passed from view about 1715.

BIBLIOGRAPHY: Milling, Chapman J. *Red Carolinians.* Columbia: The University of South Carolina Press, 1969.

ERIE: an extinct sedentary tribe inhabiting the south shores of Lake Erie in the early 17th century. They were once very populous and powerful, numbering possibly as many as 14,500 and occupying land south to the Ohio River, east to present day Ripley, New York, and west to the Maumee River in Ohio. In the 1650s, they were destroyed as a tribe by the Five Nations Iroquois Confederacy.

The Erie spoke a language of the Iroquoian language family, similar to that of the Huron. The Huron translation of their tribal name is "it is long-tailed," in reference to the animal skin robes, complete with tail, which they wore. The Erie were known to the French as the Cat Nation.

Little is known about their political organization, although it was apparently similar to that of the Huron. The Erie religion consisted of worship of various types of spirits. To honor their ancestors, they held a Feast of the Dead over the graves, each year at the end of summer. They buried their dead in rectangular graves or mass burial pits near or within their villages, occasionally marking them with wooden posts or stone slabs. Few items, other than pottery or ornaments, were buried with the bodies. Women kept watch over the graves for three days after burial to ensure that the spirit had gone to the land of the dead.

The Erie villages, from one to several acres in extent, were located along rivers which emptied into Lake Erie. They were fortified by wooden stockades or earthen walls, with houses surrounding an open space with a large fireplace in the center. This central area, with its constantly burning fire, was used for war and peace councils, dances and other public gatherings. Houses were constructed of wooden post framework, covered with bark.

Agriculture, hunting and fishing were all practiced extensively. The women cultivated corn, squash, beans and sunflowers. The men hunted with bow and arrow, living in animal skin shelters when on extended hunting trips. Canoes and snowshoes were used for travel. Game included deer, moose, elk and turkeys. Deer were the most important, supplying many essentials such as clothing, arrowpoints, etc., as well as food. The men also caught fish with bone hooks, spears and weighted nets, while the women gathered nuts, berries, grapes, wild plums and various roots.

A typical meal consisted of meat (usually deer) and some form of corn. Corn was boiled, roasted and ground into meal for use in bread and soup. Soups were also made by boiling turtles and various mollusks.

The Erie were great warriors, using bow and arrow, including poisoned arrows, and knives and hatchets of chipped stone. In their wars with the Iroquois, they may have used firearms.

By the early 1600s, the Erie, who may have originated in the upper Mississippi Valley, were very numerous in the Lake Erie basin. The first and almost only European contact was with Jesuit missionaries.

By the 1640s, there was considerable conflict between the Erie and the Iroquois Confederacy, mainly with the Seneca, over hunting grounds. In the final war between these enemies, begun in 1652, Erie power was broken and the people destroyed, dispersed or led into captivity to be absorbed by the Iroquois tribes. In one major battle, 3,000 to 4,000 Erie were defeated by 1,800 Iroquois warriors at the fall of the Erie town of Riqué. Throughout the war, the Erie fought well, but the guns of the Iroquois, supplied by Dutch and English traders, made the difference that spelled the end of the Erie as a tribe.

BIBLIOGRAPHY: Lupold, Harry F. *The Forgotten People: The Woodland Erie.* Hicksville, New York: Exposition Press, 1975; Vietzen, Raymond C. *The Immortal Eries.* Elyria, Ohio: Wilmot Printing Company, 1945.

ESKIMO: *See* INUIT.

FIVE CIVILIZED TRIBES: *See* CHEROKEE, CHICKASAW, CHOCTAW, CREEK and SEMINOLE.

FLATHEAD: an Interior Salish tribe located in western Montana and Idaho, north of the Gallatin River, between the Rocky Mountains in the west and the Little Belt Range in the east, in the 17th and 18th centuries. Population estimates for that time range from 600 to 3,000. The Flathead, also known as the Salish proper, comprised, together with the Spokan and Kalispel (or Pend d'Oreilles), the Flathead group of Interior Salish. In the 1970s, the Flathead were mixed with Kalispel and Kutenai on the Flathead Reservation in western Montana, with a total population of about 3,500 in the late 1970s.

The Flathead spoke a language of the Interior division of the Salishan language family, calling themselves Se'lic, meaning "people." The name Flathead derives from the fact that, unlike some other related tribes, they did not practice head deformation, leaving the top of the head flat, rather than sloping back from forehead to crown.

The Flathead were a loose organization of bands, composed of several related families who camped together. Each band was led by a chief and assistant chief, selected on the basis of wisdom, influence, bravery and other leadership qualities. There may have been a few hereditary chiefs in earlier times. There was also a tribal chief, and he and the band chiefs made up the tribal council. In later years, authority became more centralized, and bands and their chiefs became less important, eventually disappearing and being replaced by tribal subchiefs and "small" chiefs.

Religious life centered around guardian spirits, necessary for success, obtained in dreams or visions. At puberty, young men fasted, prayed, exercised and kept vigils to this purpose. Shamans had especially strong guardian spirits, enabling them to see the future and to insure good hunting. The Flathead believed in three worlds—an upper, in which the good chief Amo'tken resided, the earth, and a lower world, in which the evil one Amte'p lived. Good souls went to live with Amo'tken and bad ones with Amte'p. An important mythical character was the culture hero Coyote, who was sent by Amo'tken to make life easier for people. A great number of dances and ceremonies were regularly held, including the Sun Dance, Medicine Dance, Praying Dance, Harvest Dance, Hunting Dance, First Fruit Ceremony, Marrying Dance, a woman's dance, and war dances. The dead were covered with skins and robes and placed on a scaffold until ready for burial in graves. The pole on which the corpse was transported to the gravesite was used as a grave marker, and offerings were tied to it.

A 19th-century lithograph showing the mode of crossing rivers used by the Flathead and other Indians.

Two principal types of houses were originally used, both made of mats on a wood frame. A long lodge, sunk a foot in the ground, was used in winter camps for dances, meetings and ceremonies. They lived mostly in one, two or three family conical dwellings of similar construction. Temporary brush shelters were used in the mountains on hunting trips. After acquiring horses, buffalo hunting became important, and skin tipis essentially replaced the mat dwellings.

The Flathead hunted buffalo on the Plains, and elk, deer, antelope and other game in the mountains. A favorite buffalo hunting technique was the communal surround. Trout, salmon, and whitefish were caught with hook and line, nets, weirs and traps. Wild foods, including camas, bitterroot, and various other bulbs, roots and berries were important.

Material culture included pole rafts, birchbark containers, coiled cedar root baskets and bags woven of strips of skin. Their clothing was of the northern Plains type, usually of buffalo skin, including robes, shirt (or dress for women), leggings, breechclout, moccasins and cap or headband.

The Flathead and other Interior Salish probably migrated at some time from British Columbia, and may have extended further eastward into the plains at one time, before being pushed west by the Blackfoot into western Montana by about 1600. In later years, they gradually pushed further westward, eventually being centered around Flathead Lake and extending into Idaho. Around 1700, they acquired horses, and buffalo hunting became more important than before. In the 18th century, wars with the Blackfoot and smallpox epidemics (1760-70 and 1781) severely decreased their population.

After the visit of Lewis and Clark in 1805, fur trapping for trade became important. Missions were established in Flathead territory after 1841. In 1855, the Flathead ceded their lands in Montana and Idaho for a reservation around Flathead Lake, although very few relocated there until 1872. Conditions there were not good, with other tribes being moved into the reservation and the buffalo fast disappearing. One band, led by the great chief Charlot, refused to relocate, holding out in the Bitterroot valley until about 1890. By 1909, some of the land had been allotted to individuals, and some opened up for sale to settlers.

In the 1970s, the Flathead were mixed with Kalispel and Kutenai on the 1,244,000-acre Flathead Reservation in western Montana, among the total population of around 3,500. About half of the land was non-Indian owned, especially the better agricultural land. Log and wood frame cabins had replaced the traditional homes. Important sources of income were forestry, sawmills, and tourist facilities, including a lodge and a hot springs bathhouse. The tribe was governed by a 10-member council.

BIBLIOGRAPHY: Fahey, John. *The Flathead Indians.* Norman: University of Oklahoma Press, 1971; Turney-High, Harry Holbert. "The Flathead Indians of Montana." *Memoirs of the American Anthropological Association.* no. 48, 1937. Teit, James A. "The Salishan Tribes of the Western Plateaus." *Annual Report of the Bureau of American Ethnology.* no. 45, 1927-28.

FOX: an Algonquian tribe, closely related to the Sauk, who lived in the area of Lake Winnebago, Wisconsin, at the time of the arrival of the French, whom they bitterly opposed. They numbered about 2,500 in 1650. By the late 1970s, there were about 600 Fox descendants, living mostly near Tama, Iowa and with the Sauk in Oklahoma.

The Fox called themselves Meskwakihug, or Meskwakie, meaning "people of the red earth. " The Algonquian language of the Fox, closely related to that of the Sauk and the Kickapoo, was still spoken in Fox homes in Iowa in the late 1970s.

The Fox were divided into about 14 clans, each person inheriting the clan of his father and forbidden to marry within his own clan. The Midewiwin, or Grand Medicine Society, played an important role in the religious and social life of the tribe. The Fox believed in numerous spirits or manitou, the most important of which was Wisaka, who created the earth and men, and who lived somewhere in the north.

Important festivals included the green corn feast at the beginning of harvest and the adoption ceremony. When a person died, a person of the same sex and approximate age was adopted by the deceased person's family. The adoptee took over the duties and privileges of the deceased.

Fox mortuary customs included scaffold burial, burial of a warrior seated on a dead enemy, and burial in a sitting position. Sacred tobacco was sprinkled in the grave, and a sacrificed dog was placed by the grave as a companion for the spirit of the deceased.

The Fox, as the Sauk, lived in large bark-covered lodges near their cornfields in the summer. In winter they moved to smaller, reed-mat houses in sheltering woodlands near their hunting grounds. Several varieties of corn, beans, pumpkins and squash were grown by the women. Honey, acorns, berries, fruits, nuts, and wild potatoes were gathered. The Fox hunted bear, deer and turkey in their Wisconsin lands, and as they moved west to the Mississippi, they became great buffalo hunters.

According to Fox traditions, their original homeland was along the southern shore of Lake Superior; although, previous to that, they may have lived with the Sauk around Saginaw Bay in eastern Michigan. By 1640, they had settled in the Green Bay area, where they made themselves unpopular by requiring a toll from French traders paddling their canoes along the Fox River. The French, in turn, angered the Fox by supplying their enemies, the Dakota and Ojibwa, with firearms.

Between 1712 and 1737, Fox and French fought constantly and bitterly, with the Fox close to being wiped out by war and disease on several occasions. As the Fox and Sauk were driven south by the French and Ojibwa, they moved into lands from which they had driven the Illinois tribes. By 1780, the Fox and Sauk were living on the Mississippi near the Rock River, and their hunting parties were ranging far west of the Mississippi in search of buffalo.

In 1804, a band of Sauk ceded Sauk and Fox lands east of the Mississippi to the United States. The Fox moved across the river, where they were joined by the Sauk, after Black Hawk's War (1831-32), in which a few Fox had participated. Lead mines owned by the Fox near Dubuque were illegally seized. The Fox had mined 3-4,000 lbs. annually which they sold to traders. In 1842, the Fox and Sauk sold their remaining lands and moved to a reservation in Kansas. Between 1856 and 1859, after a dispute with the Sauk, most of the Fox returned to Iowa, and settled near Tama, eventually accumulating some 3,000 acres.

In the late 1970s, the Iowa Fox numbered about 600, many of whom still spoke the language and retained many tribal traditions. In 1867, the Fox who stayed with the Sauk moved to Indian Territory (Oklahoma), where they were virtually assimilated into the surrounding culture by the late 1970s.

BIBLIOGRAPHY: Hagan, William T. *The Sac and Fox Indians.* Norman: University of Oklahoma Press, 1950; Jones, William. "Ethnography of the Fox Indians." *Bureau of American Ethnology Bulletin.* no. 125, 1939.

GABRIELINO: an extinct southern California group. They occupied the region around present-day Los Angeles and the islands of Santa Catalina, San Nicolas and San Clemente in the late 18th century, numbering perhaps 5,000 at that time.

The Gabrielino language belongs to the Takic division of the Uto-Aztecan language family. The name was derived from the San Gabriel mission established by the Spanish in the area.

The Gabrielino were composed of numerous autonomous tribelets, occupying a village or village cluster and headed by a chief. The office of chief was inherited through the male line and could be held by a woman if there were no male heirs. A chief's duties included arbitrating disputes, leading war parties, guarding the sacred bundle, and seeing to the general welfare of the community.

Religious leadership was provided by shamans, who had the power to cure the sick, control the weather, interpret dreams, find lost objects and cause a person to sicken and die through use of witchcraft. The Gabrielino had numerous deities, including the sun, the moon and a creator god. They also believed in a number of other sacred beings, such as Crow, Raven, Owl and Eagle, as well as spirits who resided in springs, lakes and other aspects of nature.

The most important Gabrielino ceremony was the eight-day annual mourning ceremony. Elements of the ceremony included singing, dancing, visiting, feasting, naming of children born during the year, and the making of life-size images of the dead, which were burned on the eighth day. The Santa Catalina Gabrielino buried their dead, while most of the other groups cremated their dead, along with their possessions.

The Gabrielino built large circular multi-family houses, covered with tule mats. Each village also had an earth-covered sweathouse and a roofless ceremonial enclosure. Hunting, fishing and gathering provided a diet which varied with the location and environment, and included acorns, pine nuts, shellfish, tuna, swordfish, sharks, sea lions, deer and small game. Gabrielino crafts included both coiled and twined basketry, as well as pottery, carved pipes, ornaments and cooking utensils of steatite (soapstone).

Early contacts between the Gabrielino and the Spanish in the 16th and 17th centuries were peaceful. In 1771, however, San Gabriel mission was established, and by 1800, most Gabrielino groups were compelled to forsake their traditional existence to work in the mission fields. Their population was severely reduced by disease and hardship, which led to Indian revolts, including one led by Toypurina, a chief's daughter, in 1785.

In the 19th century, the Gabrielino were further reduced by epidemics and submerged by waves of Mexican and American settlers. By 1900, Gabrielino culture was essentially eradicated.

BIBLIOGRAPHY: Johnston, Bernice Eastman. *California's Gabrielino Indians.* Los Angeles: Southwest Museum, 1962.

GOSIUTE: a small Utah tribe living southwest of the Great Salt Lake in the early 19th century, numbering about 300 at that time. In the late 1970s, there were about 300 Gosiute in the Utah area. The Gosiute language belongs to the Shoshonean division of the Uto-Aztecan family, and is most closely related to the language of the Western Shoshoni.

The Gosiute lived mostly in small groups around the edge of the Great Salt Lake Desert, with concentrations along Deep Creek and in Skull and Tooele Valley. Social and political organization was relatively simple. Male and female shamans, sometimes with hereditary powers, cured the sick by smoking, singing, sucking out poison or going into a trance to find a lost soul. Certain shamans had power to charm an antelope, as an aid to the hunters.

Important ceremonies included the Pine Nut Dance, the Circle Dance and girls' puberty rites. The dead were either buried with their belongings or cremated in their dwellings. In winter, the Gosiute lived in conical dwellings of pole framework, covered with bark or brush. They also used sagebrush summer shelters, as well as cave or rock shelters.

The territory of the Gosiute provided, for the most part, a meager subsistence based on hunting and gathering. The women used seed beaters to gather more than 30 types of edible or medicinal seeds and fire-hardened digging sticks to dig wild onions, sego lily and yampa. Chokecherries, serviceberries, black currants and raspberries were gathered and dried, along with occasional pine nuts, which were stored in caches lined with juniper bark. Crickets and locusts were roasted by driving them into grass-filled pits, which were then set on fire. Fish were occasionally caught barehanded or with baskets.

In hunting, the Gosiute used an assortment of nets, snares, traps and deadfalls as well as throwing stick and bow and arrow. Bows were made of cedar or mountain mahogany, and the poisoned arrow tips were made of obsidian, quartz or flint. Rabbits, the most important animal food source, were usually hunted communally, by driving them into nets. Other small game included squirrels, prairie dogs, gophers, lizards, snakes and sage hen. Large game, including deer, mountain sheep, bear and elk were occasionally hunted in the mountains, and antelopes were driven into sagebrush corrals in the valleys.

The Gosiute used cottonwood, willow or serviceberry wood to make a variety of basketry, including storage containers, burden baskets, pitch-lined water bottles, winnowing trays, bowls and hats. Spoons and dippers were made of bone or wood. Warm weather clothing was minimal, and rabbitskin robes or capes were added in winter.

In the early 19th century, the Gosiute were targets for Ute slave raiders. By the mid-19th century, Mormon settlers, and later miners and ranchers, began to move into Gosiute territory. In 1914, two reservations were established in northwestern Utah and adjacent Nevada.

In the late 1970s, there were about 300 Gosiute, with 200 living on or near the reservations and another 100 or so mixed with the general population. Goshute Reservation, located on the Utah-Nevada border, included about 108,000 acres, while Skull Valley Reservation in Tooele County comprised 17,000 acres. Many Gosiute lived off the reservation and were employed by ranchers, farmers and other commercial enterprises.

BIBLIOGRAPHY: Malouf, Carling. "The Gosiute Indians." in *Shoshoni Indians*. New York: Garland Publishing, Inc. 1974.

GROS VENTRE: an Algonquian tribe living in the Milk River area of northern Montana, numbering about 3,000 in the late 18th century. In the late 1970s, about 2,000 Gros Ventre and Assiniboin lived together on Fort Belknap Reservation in north central Montana.

The Gros Ventre spoke a language closely related to that of the Arapaho, and were probably part of that tribe sometime before 1700. Gros Ventre, a French term meaning "big belly," probably derived from an incorrect interpretation of sign language. They were also known as Gros Ventre of the Prairie to distinguish them from the Hidatsa, who were sometimes known as the Gros Ventre of the Missouri. The Blackfoot referred to them as Atsina, possibly meaning "gut people," while they called themselves Haaninin, perhaps meaning "lime men" or "chalk men."

The Gros Ventre were composed of 12 fairly autonomous bands, each with its own chief, although, in the distant past, there had been a tribal chief. In winter, to follow the buffalo, the bands camped separately in the timber. In summer, when the buffalo gathered in large herds, the Gros Ventre bands came together for communal buffalo hunting and celebration of the Sun Dance and other tribal ceremonies. They camped in a circle with an opening facing east, each band having its assigned place in the camp circle.

Each person belonged to the band of his father, and usually married outside the bands of both parents. Girls were usually married at age 11 or 12, often to older men. Men usually did not marry until age 20, or so. Polygamy was common, as was divorce. The usual mother-in-law taboo was enforced, forbidding a man and his mother-in-law to look at each other, speak to each other, or be in the same tipi with each other.

As boys grew to be men, they entered a series of age-graded societies, each with its own dances, costumes and paraphernalia. There were two warrior societies, the Star and Wolf. Some men became doctors by fasting in order to receive special powers. Cures were effected through a combined use of medicinal plants and various rituals.

When a Gros Ventre died, his body was wrapped in a burial robe and placed in a tree, in a cave or on a high rock. Female mourners cut their hair and sometimes made gashes on their legs.

The Gros Ventre lived in skin tipis, which were made by the women. A woman wishing to have a new tipi invited her friends to a feast and sewing bee. The tipis were made snug in winter by piling snow around the outside edge and placing a liner along the inside bottom edge. The women also made the clothing, usually of deer or elkskin, dressing the skins with a mixture of brains and liver.

To keep up with the buffalo herd, the Gros Ventre would move camp six or eight times each summer. Dog and horse travois were used to transport the tipis and other belongings. If a river had to be forded, makeshift rafts were made, using the tipi covers and poles. In early times the Gros Ventre hunted buffalo by driving them into chutes, but in later times, they usually surrounded the herd on horseback. The women cut the meat in strips and hung it on drying racks, storing some in strips and making the rest into pemmican, which was stored in skin bags.

Fresh meat was roasted over the fire or boiled, using a hole in the ground lined with a skin and filled with water and red-hot rocks. Buffalo was the favorite meat, although deer and elk were also eaten, and puppies were considered a delicacy. The diet was supplemented with rhubarb, saskatoon berries, birds' eggs and other wild foods. They did not eat fish.

Bows were made of cherry or ash wood, and the Gros Ventre shot holding bow either vertically or horizontally, according to personal preference. Shields were made of toughened buffalo hide.

The Gros Ventre dressed in the usual Plains Indian fashion, with leggings, breechclouts, shirts and moccasins for the men, and dresses for the women. In winter, they added caps of buffalo skin with ear flaps tied under the chin, and hunters wore buffalo skin mittens tied together with a string which passed behind the neck, allowing removal of the mittens while shooting.

The Gros Ventre were probably formerly a band of the Arapaho, although it is unclear when and where they separated. In the 18th century the Gros Ventre were located on the Canadian Plains, slowly moving south by the latter part of the century to occupy the region between the Saskatchewan and Missouri rivers. From 1818 to 1823, they moved south to join the Arapaho, but subsequently moved back north.

In the mid-19th century, the Gros Ventre joined the Blackfoot in fighting the Crow but in 1867, they were allied with the Crow in a

Gros Ventre
chiefs—a
photograph
taken in 1907-08
by Edward S.
Curtis
Library of Congress

disastrous fight with the Blackfoot. Other Gros Ventre enemies included the Shoshoni and Flathead, while their friends usually included the Arapaho, Cheyenne and Cree.

In the 1880s, the Gros Ventre and Assiniboin were placed on the Fort Belknap Reservation in northern Montana. In the late 1970s, there were about 2,000 Assiniboin and Gros Ventre living on or near the 600,000 acre reservation. A Labor Day Indian Celebration was held each year in September and a Mid-Winter Fair in February.

BIBLIOGRAPHY: Flannery, Regina. *The Gros Ventres of Montana.* 2 vols. Washington: The Catholic University of America Press, 1953; Kroeber, A.L. "Ethnology of the Gros Ventre." *Anthropological Papers of the American Museum of Natural History.* vol. 1, 1907.

HAIDA: a large powerful Northwest Coast group living on the Queen Charlotte Islands, British Columbia, and Prince of Wales Island, Alaska, numbering about 9,800 in the late 18th century. In the 1970s, about 1,400 Haida were divided between the Masset and Skidegate bands on Queen Charlotte Islands; about 190 lived in Hydaberg Village, Alaska, and about 400 were mixed with Tlingit at Angoon, Alaska. The Haida, who spoke a number of dialects that constituted the Haida division of the Athapascan language family, called themselves Xa'ida, meaning "people."

The Haida were composed of three divisions: the Kaigani on Prince of Wales Island, and the Gao-haidagai and Gunghet-haidagi on the north and south ends, respectively of the Queen Charlotte Islands.

A Haida village at Howkan, Alaska, in about 1896.   Library of Congress

Each of these were in turn subdivided into autonomous villages led by hereditary chiefs. The Haida were divided into two matrilineal phratries—Raven and Eagle, each of which was subdivided into twenty matrilineal clans. The clan was the basic social and political unit, and each clan had certain prerogatives such as rights to certain lands, names, songs, dances and totemic crests. Each clan had up to 12 households, containing as many as 30 or more persons in one dwelling, forming the basic economic unit. Prestige of families and individuals depended on wealth, and rich households often had numbers of slaves, obtained in raids on the mainland tribes, especially the Tlingit, Tsimshian and Bellabella.

Religion centered around shamans, who, by virtue of their supernatural power, were more powerful than the chiefs. Important to their religion were various myths, especially those featuring Raven, the Haida culture hero. Principal ceremonies were potlatches—ceremonial display and distribution of personal or family wealth—usually given to obtain status or to validate hereditary rank or privilege. They buried their dead in carved cedar mortuary houses elevated on poles, or less often, in caves. Mortuary boxes for noted chiefs and shamans were ornately carved and painted.

Haida villages consisted of rows of gabled cedar plank houses facing the sea, each with a large totem pole next to the entrance. Masterpieces of construction, they were as much as 60 feet wide by 100 feet long and were built communally, using stone adzes, wooden wedges and basalt or jade hammers. On completion, the owner held a potlatch for the workers.

The Haida depended mainly on fishing, although some hunting, gathering and trading contributed to the economy. Salmon was the staple food, and summer months were spent traveling to meet the runs of the various species. Other fish caught were eulachon (candlefish) and halibut. Sea otters, sea lions, and fur seals were hunted for furs and food.

The outstanding Haida craftwork centered around wood. They built sea-going cedar dugout canoes—up to 70 feet long and 8 feet wide, often ornately carved and painted. The Haida made excellent weapons, including bow and arrow, bone-tipped spears, clubs and wooden helmets and body armor. Finely-carved masks were made for their ceremonial life. Baskets were woven of split spruce roots. Clothing was made from otter and other furs, or woven of cedar bark and other vegetable fibers. They also carved excellent tools and utensils of argillite.

According to tradition, the earliest Haida settlements were on the east side of Queen Charlotte Islands. By the early 1700s, they had expanded to Prince of Wales Island, and grown very powerful, raiding for slaves and plunder all along the coast.

Spanish, French, British and American expeditions visited the area in the late 18th century, followed by numerous traders. Haida culture was disrupted by white men's diseases and vices and the decimation of the animal population. In 1869, the Hudson's Bay Company founded a post at Masset. In 1882, reserves were established for the Haida on Queen Charlotte Islands. By about 1900, the Haida had been reduced to about one-tenth of their aboriginal population. In the early 1900s, commercial fishing and canneries were introduced, and a logging boom occurred. Increased supervision by the Canadian government was somewhat tempered by more liberal policies after the 1940s.

In the 1970s, about 1,400 Haida lived on Queen Charlotte Islands, along with 3,500 non-Indians, and about 588 lived at Hydaberg and Angoon villages in Alaska. The many small villages of former times were consolidated into fewer large villages, such as Skidegate and Masset. The old-style houses had largely been replaced with more modern ones, although some villages such as Skedans still looked somewhat as they did in the old days. Salmon fishing, forestry and woodcarving were important sources of income. Many Haida traditions were preserved, while others, such as totem pole carving and the holding of winter potlatches, were being revived.

BIBLIOGRAPHY: Swanton, John R. "Contributions to the Ethnology of the Haida." *Memoir of the American Museum of Natural History.* Volume V, 1905; Brink, J.H. Van Den. *The Haida Indians.* Leiden, The Netherlands: F.F. Brill, 1974; Harrison, Charles. *Ancient Warriors of the North Pacific.* London: H.F. & G. Witherby, 1925.

HAN: an Athapascan tribe located along the upper Yukon River on both sides of the Canada-Alaska border in the early 19th century, numbering about 1,000 at that time. In the late 1970s, several hundred Han descendants were still located along the Yukon on both sides of the border.

The Han spoke a language of the Athapascan family closely related to that of the Kutchin and were sometimes referred to as the Han-kutchin. They were composed of about four bands, each led by a chief, whose position was sometimes hereditary, and a men's advisory council. Chiefs, who were generally wealthy and capable, were in charge of directing hunting activities.

Socially, the Han were divided into two moieties or tribal divisions, composed of matrilineal clans. Each person inherited the clan and moiety of his mother and was restricted from marrying within either. Infant betrothal was sometimes practiced. At puberty, girls were secluded for a year in a hut about a mile from the village and were required to wear a hood. Feasting and ceremonies were held to celebrate the first game killed by a young boy and the arrival of the first salmon. Potlatches, or ceremonial gift distributions were held as memorials to the dead.

Religious leadership was provided by powerful shamans, whose aid was sought for success in hunting and warfare and for curing the sick and ending famine. The Han usually cremated their dead and hung the ashes in a wooden receptacle in a tree. The bodies of chiefs were sometimes placed on a platform, between two halves of a hollowed-out log.

The Han built permanent winter houses of squares of moss on a wood and pole frame. Dome-shaped skin-covered lodges were used on trips. Both house styles usually accommodated two families.

Fishing was the main economic activity, and each village had nearby fishing camps along the river. Weirs, traps, dip nets and spears were used to catch salmon, pike and grayling. Winter was spent hunting for caribou, moose, beaver, lynx and rabbit, using bow and arrow, snares and deadfalls. Corrals were constructed to trap migrating caribou. Blueberries and cranberries were gathered to supplement the diet.

For transportation, the Han built large, stable birchbark canoes and occasionally moosehide boats. In winter, they used snowshoes and sleds pulled by dogs and women. Babies were carried in a birchbark cradle chair. They made birchbark buckets, wood and sheephorn spoons, babiche (rawhide) bags and water tight baskets woven of tamarack root decorated with quillwork. Caribou skin clothing included shirts for men, with points hanging down front and back, and longer shirts for women, pointed in front. Moccasins and mittens were usually of moose skin, and robes were of rabbit, caribou or mountain sheep skin. Quillwork decorated the clothing, and tattooing, face paint and ear and nose ornaments were used for adornment.

In the early 19th century, the Han traded with Russian fur traders, and, after the establishment of Fort Yukon trading post in 1847, with the Hudson's Bay Company. In the latter 19th century, their population was reduced by disease. In 1896-97, the Han were swamped by the Klondike gold rush, which brought some 30,000 miners and others flooding into the area centered at Dawson. This boom was shortlived, however, and the population dropped abruptly in the early 20th century. In the 1970s, the several hundred Han descendants along the Yukon were essentially acculturated.

BIBLIOGRAPHY: Osgood, Cornelius. "The Han Indians." *Yale University Publications in Anthropology*. no. 74, 1971.

HANO: *See* TANO.

HARE: a nomadic Athapascan tribe who ranged over a vast area of Alberta, the Yukon Territory and even Alaska in the 19th century, numbering about 750 before European contact. Since the late 19th century, they have occupied territory east of the Mackenzie River and north and west of Great Bear Lake, numbering about 715 in the 1970s.

They spoke a language of the Northern division of the Athapascan language family similar to that of the Slave. They were also called Kawchodinne, meaning "people of the great hares," derived from their reliance on the Arctic hare for food and clothing.

They were grouped at various times into varying numbers of geographical divisions or bands. In 1876 there were five divisions: Nigottine, Kattagottine, Katchogottine, Satchotugottine and Nellagottine. Each band was nomadic, autonomous, and loosely organized, probably led by a chief of limited authority.

Religion centered around guardian spirits, with shamans providing leadership by virtue of powers obtained from especially powerful spirits. A Hare creation myth tells how the world was created by a muskrat and a beaver. Festivals included lunar feasts at each new moon and memorial services for the dead, one year after death. The dead were wrapped in blankets or moose skins and deposited in cages above ground. Relatives cut their hair and destroyed or gave away their property.

Dwellings, suitable for their nomadic life, were of simple construction of brush and spruce boughs on a rectangular pole frame. In summer simple lean-tos were often used, and in the 19th century, some Hare had caribou skin tipis. Subsistence was mostly by fishing and hunting, with caribou, hare and musk-ox as the most important game.

Hunting and fishing implements included bow and arrow, babiche (rawhide) snares and willow bark nets. Other material culture included stone adzes, ice chisels made of caribou antler and knives with stone or beaver-tooth blades. Household goods included wood or bark dishes and woven baskets of spruce roots and willow twigs, often woven tightly enough to hold water for cooking.

First contact with Europeans was with the Scottish explorer Alexander Mackenzie, who found the Hare living on the Peace River in 1802. Subsequently, they experienced increased contact with traders as they migrated between there and Alaska. They traded principally at Fort Norman and Fort Good Hope in the Great Bear Lake area. Since the late 1800s, they have occupied the territory north of Great Bear Lake, and by 1900, had become essentially acculturated. In the 1970s, there were about 715 Hare in two bands, Fort Franklin and Fort Good Hope.

BIBLIOGRAPHY: Jenness, Diamond. "Indians of Canada." *National Museum of Canada Bulletin.* no. 65, 1960.

HASINAI: *See* CADDO.

HAVASUPAI: a Yuman tribe occupying Cataract Canyon, a side branch of the Grand Canyon in northwestern Arizona. The Havasupai, who also ranged over surrounding areas of the canyon rim and the Colorado Plateau since the 14th century, probably never numbered more than 300 until the 1900s. In the 1970s, there were more than 500 Havasupai, most of whom lived on the Havasupai Reservation in Cataract (or Havasu) Canyon.

Havasupai means "people of the blue-green water." They spoke a Yuman language very close to that spoken by the Walapai, of whom they are an offshoot. Culturally, however, they were influenced by both the Walapai and the Hopi.

The family was the basic socio-economic unit of the Havasupai. Chiefs, whose main functions were to advise and admonish, attained their position through demonstrated ability, sometimes coupled with heredity. Religious leadership was provided by shamans, who received their powers in dreams. There were several types of shamans, with supernatural power to cure or control weather or medical knowledge in such areas as setting bones and treating snakebites.

The Havasupai borrowed many religious traditions from the Hopi, including planting ceremonies, rain dances, prayer sticks and masked dances. In years of good harvests they often invited the Walapai, Hopi and Navajo to their harvest dance. The Havasupai cremated their dead.

A Havasupai home, Truxton Canyon Agency, Arizona. Bureau of Indian Affairs

From April until October, the Havasupai lived down in the bottom of their steep-sided limestone and red sandstone canyon. Using irrigation techniques learned from the Hopi, they grew corn, beans, squash, melons and peaches. They lived in conical pole-frame wickiups with thatched sides and earth and thatch roof. Other structures included, sweat lodges, brush sun shades and stone storage houses built into the base of the cliffs. When Cataract Creek flooded, they took refuge in caves and rock shelters higher up.

In October, after harvesting their crops, gathering various wild foods, and sealing up the surplus food in storage houses or caves, they ascended to the rim for the winter. They ranged widely over the Colorado Plateau. The women gathered mesquite pods, pine nuts, seeds, juniper berries, honey, yucca and agave. The men held rabbit drives, stalked antelope wearing antelope head disguises and hunted deer and mountain sheep. In winter, they tracked the animals in the snow. Winter homes resembled summer homes with an overall layer of earth.

The Havasupai made an assortment of both twined and coiled basketry items, including seed beaters, conical burden baskets, seed parching trays, cradle board hoods and pitch-coated water bottles. Plain pottery bowls were made, and ladles were made from sheep horn. Skins, tanned by the men, were made into clothing, including belted tunics, breechclout, leggings and moccasins for men, and full-length aprons for women. Red ocher was used for making face paint as well as for trade with the Pueblo tribes.

Havasupai trading partners and friends included the Hopi and the Walapai. Their enemies were the Yavapai and Western Apache, who periodically attacked them in their canyon.

The Havasupai had probably settled in their canyon home by the 14th century. Around 1780, a number of Hopi, fleeing drought conditions in their area, took refuge with the Havasupai for a time. The Havasupai Reservation was established in 1880 and reduced in 1882. Much of their former hunting and foraging area was lost to the Navajo, Hopi and settlers.

Some land taken from the Havasupai by the United States government in the early 20th century was partially restored by Congress in 1974. By the late 1970s, the Havasupai had constructed tourist lodges, restaurants and campgrounds, and were giving guided tours of their beautiful canyon with its several spectacular waterfalls.

BIBLIOGRAPHY: Hirst, Stephen. *Life in a Narrow Place*. New York: David McKay Company, 1976; Spier, Leslie. "Havasupai Ethnography." *Anthropological Papers of the American Museum of Natural History*. vol. 29, 1928.

HIDATSA: a Siouan tribe living in North Dakota near the confluence of the Missouri and Knife rivers in the late 18th century, numbering about 2,500 at that time. In the late 1970s, some 1,000 Hidatsa descendants shared a reservation with the Arikara and Mandan a short distance upriver. The Hidatsa were known to the Mandan as Minitaree, meaning "they crossed the water."

The Hidatsa were composed of several loosely associated bands, including the Hidatsa proper, the Awatixa and the Awaxawi. They were also divided into about seven clans, each person inheriting the clan of his mother. Villages were ruled by a village council, chief, and warchief. Men belonged to a series of age-graded military societies between adolescence and old age.

There were also a number of religious societies responsible for various ceremonies. The Naxpike, or Sun Dance, was the most important ceremony, and included prayers, fasting and self-torture. The preserving of medicine bundles, or collections of sacred objects, and the seeking of visions through fasting were important aspects of Hidatsa religion. When a person died his remains were placed on a scaffold, along with food, weapons and a few personal items. Mourners cut their hair, and if the deceased were a great chief, all the fires in the lodges were put out.

Drawing of an Hidatsa village.

The Hidatsa built their villages of earth lodges along the river. The lodges, 40 feet in diameter, housed two or three families. A heavy wooden framework was covered with willow branches interwoven with grass, with an outer layer of mud or clay. Smaller versions deep in the woods were used in the winter, and skin tipis were used while travelling or hunting.

The Hidatsa relied on both hunting and agriculture, with corn and buffalo meat the preferred foods. The women grew corn, squash, beans and pumpkins, while old men tended a small tobacco crop. Corn was stored in bell-shaped caches, dug sometimes as deep as eight feet in the earth. They were lined with logs and grass, with a ladder for access and a covering of earth to make them invisible to raiders.

Besides meat, the buffalo supplied the Hidatsa with hides for blankets and boats, horn for spoons and tools and bones for hoes and other items. The Hidatsa gathered berries and chokecherries, which they dried, and sap from the box elder, which they used to make sugar. To obtain feathers for adornment, they hunted eagles from a pit covered with brush with bait placed on top.

The Hidatsa are very close linguistically to the Crow, and, according to tradition, the two tribes separated in the late 17th century, with the Crow moving further west. In the late 18th century, the Hidatsa lost population through a smallpox epidemic and warfare with the Dakota.

When visited by Lewis and Clark in 1804, they were reduced to several villages on the Knife River, near a grouping of Mandan villages.

After the disastrous smallpox epidemic of 1837, the remnants of the two tribes moved north, settling, in 1845, at a bend of the Missouri River in a village called Like-a-Fishhook, in 1862, they were joined by the Arikara and, in about 1870, the area was set aside for the three tribes as Fort Berthold Reservation. In 1887, most of the land was allotted in severalty.

In the 1950s the Garrison Dam was built, flooding about 25 percent of the reservation, including the best croplands and most of the homes, schools and roads. In the 1970s, tourist facilities were established by the tribes on Lake Sakakawea, the reservoir formed by the dam. By that time, there remained 45,000 acres of tribally owned land and 350,000 acres of allotted land, belonging to individuals of the tribes.

BIBLIOGRAPHY: Bowers, Alfred W. "Hidatsa Social and Ceremonial Organization." *Bureau of American Ethnology Bulletin.* no. 194, 1965.

HITCHITI: a small extinct tribe of the Creek Confederacy, located in western Georgia on the east bank of the Chattahoochee River. They numbered about 60 warriors in 1738.

Hitchiti may have meant "to look upstream" in the Creek language. A Muskogean language, Hitchiti was spoken by several other tribes as well, including the Oconee who became the nucleus of the Seminole nation. The Hitchiti were absorbed by the Creek, though maintaining their own language and culture for some time.

BIBLIOGRAPHY: Swanton, John R. "The Indians of the Southeastern United States." *Bureau of American Ethnology Bulletin.* no. 137, 1946.

HOH: *See* QUILEUTE.

HOPI: a Shoshonean people occupying a number of pueblos in northeastern Arizona, with a population of about 2,800 in 1680. In the late 1970s, the Hopi Reservation, completely surrounded by the Navajo Reservation, included about ten villages with a total population of about 7,200. The Hopi were the western-most of the Pueblos, and were the only Pueblo Indians who spoke a language of the Shoshonean language family. Hopi was derived from their name for themselves, Hopitu, meaning "peaceful ones." They were also known as the Moqui.

As a result of centuries as sedentary agriculturalists—growing corn, beans and squash and occupying stone and adobe towns—the Hopi developed a complex social structure and an extremely rich ceremonial life. Socially they were divided into about 12 phratries, or tribal divisions, each of which was subdivided into numerous clans. A person inherited the clan and phratry of his mother, and was restricted from marrying within the clan or phratry of either his mother or father. Residence was matrilocal, a newly-married couple going to live with or near the woman's family. The clan, an important social and religious unit, could own land and dispense it to its members to use. Each clan also had a house where ceremonial paraphernalia was kept and rituals were held.

Hopi religion included such deities and spirits as the Sun, Earth Mother, Sky Father, the Moon, the Horned Serpent and the numerous *katcina* (katchina) societies, which were associated both with clan ancestors and rain gods.

Among the most important ceremonies were masked dances in which the *katcina* were impersonated for the purposes of bringing rain. Small children believed the masked dancers were actually gods who had come to visit their pueblos. Both boys and girls, at about age eight to ten, were initiated into the *katcina* cult, through a rite of fasting, praying and being whipped with a yucca whip. Each child had a ceremonial mother (girls) or father (boys) who saw them through the ordeal.

The Hopi had numerous other societies, including four men's societies, three women's societies, and societies concerned with curing, clowning, war and weather control. All boys were initiated into one of the four men's societies—Kwan, Ahl, Tao or Wuwutcimi—usually joining the society of their ceremonial father. These rites were usually held in conjunction with the Powama ceremony, a four-day tribal initiation rite for young men, usually held at planting time. Puberty rites for girls included the dressing of their hair into the "squash-blossom" or "butterfly" whorls, worn on each side of the head. Girls wore their hair in this fashion until marriage, when they rearranged it in braids.

The most important ceremony of the year was the Soyal, or Winter Solstice, which celebrated the Hopi world view and recounted their migration legends. At harvest time, the Niman festival was held. Popularly-known were the weather-control ceremonies of the Snake and Antelope societies, in which live snakes were used.

When a Hopi died, his hair was washed with yucca suds and decorated with prayer feathers, and his face was covered with a mask of raw cotton, symbolizing clouds. A man was wrapped in a deerskin blanket and a woman in her wedding blanket, and the body was buried in a sitting position along with food and water. Corn meal and prayersticks were later placed in the grave, and a stick was stuck into the ground as a ladder for the spirit of the deceased. The land of the dead was thought to be located somewhere in the Grand Canyon.

A Hopi woman having her hair dressed: a photograph taken in about 1900 by Henry Peabody.

With the exception of Oraibi, which dates from about the 12th century, the present-day pueblos of the Hopi are of comparatively recent origin. Earlier Hopi villages, which predated Spanish times, were located at the foot of Black Mesa. During the Pueblo Revolt (1680), they were relocated on top of the mesa as a defensive measure. These mesa-top pueblos consisted of one and two-story houses of sandstone plastered with adobe. There were also subterranean rectangular *kivas*, or religious centers, which were entered through a hatchway in the roof. The inside walls of the *kivas* were painted with murals of figures and geometric designs.

The Hopi grew corn, beans, squash and cotton, with corn the staple food. The men planted anywhere there was water—in the flood plains along small intermittent streams, near springs, and even on sand dunes which would hold small amounts of water. The women gathered pine nuts, prickly pear, yucca, berries, currants, nuts and various seeds.

U.S. Department of the Interior. National Park Service.

Ruins at the Wupatki National Monument, Arizona. The prehistoric red sandstone pueblos at Wupatki were built by a group of farming Indians, from whom the modern Hopi are believed to be partly descended. "Wupatki" means "long house" in the Hopi language.

Mescal (the fleshy leaf base and trunk of some species of agave) was obtained in trade from tribes to the north as a supplement to the diet. The Spanish introduced wheat, chilies, peaches, melons and other fruit. The men hunted deer, antelope, elk, rabbits and other small game. The women made fine pottery, and the men spun and wove cotton cloth into ceremonial costumes, clothing and textiles for trade.

The Hopi are descendants of the Anasazi, or "ancient ones," who occupied cliff dwellings scattered across the southwest, before drought conditions brought them to the Black Mesa region. Oraibi, the oldest Hopi pueblo and, with Acoma, one of the oldest continuously occupied villages in the United States, was established in about 1150. The villages of Walpi, Awatovi, Shongopovi and Mishongnovi were all established in the foothills at the base of the mesa or on terraces below the mesa top.

In 1540, a Spanish expedition under Coronado visited the Hopi and in about 1629 a mission was established at Awatovi, followed by missions at the other four villages. The Hopi joined the Pueblo Revolt of 1680. After the revolt, Spanish attempts to restore the mission at Awatovi en-

The main ruin of Wupatki: a photograph taken in 1935. The Wupatki ruins have been occupied longer than other ruins in the vicinity. The extreme dryness of the climate and excellent drainage have preserved wood, textiles, and other materials to an unusual extent. Rooms in this structure are dated between 1087 and 1197 AD. The buildings were abandoned around 1250 AD.

raged the other villages, which forced abandonment of the village in 1700. Thereafter, the Spanish left the Hopi alone.

During the period of the Revolt, Walpi was moved to the top of First Mesa for defensive purposes, and Shongopovi and Mishongnovi were re-established on Second Mesa. Around 1700, the Tano, a Tewa tribe, fleeing the Spanish, were asked to join the Hopi as an ally against raiding Ute. They built a pueblo on First Mesa known as Hano, or Tewa village.

In the mid-18th century, Sichomove was founded on First Mesa, and Shipaulovi on Third Mesa. In the 1870s, Moenkopi, an Oraibi farming area located 40 miles to the west, was established as a separate town. Kiakochomovi, or New Oraibi, was settled in 1890. In 1906, Oraibi, divided into two factions, settled its dispute with a "push-of-war," in which the winners pushed the leader of the losers over a line. The losing conservative faction left Oraibi and founded Hotevilla. The following year, Bakabi was founded by a group from Hotevilla.

Hopi women.

In the late 1970s, about 7,200 Hopi lived in northeast Arizona, on a 2,470,000 acre reservation, completely enclosed by the Navajo Reservation. A Hopi Cultural Center had been established on Second Mesa, along with an Arts and Crafts Guild. The Hopi made excellent pottery, textiles, *katcina* dolls, silverwork and coiled and wicker baskety. The ancient traditions and ceremonies continued to be a vital force in Hopi daily life.

BIBLIOGRAPHY: Eggan, Fred. *Social Organization of the Western Pueblos.* Chicago: The University of Chicago Press, 1950.

HUALAPAI. *See* WALAPAI.

HUNKPAPA: a subdivision of the Teton Dakota, located from the Big Cheyenne River to the Yellowstone River and west to the Black Hills in the mid-19th century, numbering about 2,900 at that time. Their name meant "at the end of the circle," referring to their position in the great camping circle of the Teton. Sitting Bull was a chief of the Hunkpapa. In the late 1970s, Hunkpapa descendants were located on the Standing Rock Reservation in North and South Dakota, along with other Dakota tribes. (See also *Teton* and *Dakota.)*

Sitting Bull, chief of the Hunkpapa.   The National Archives

HUPA: a small northwestern California tribe located along the Trinity River in the early 19th century, numbering about 1,000 at that time. In the late 1970s, there remained more than 1,000 Hupa descendants on or near the Hoopa Valley Reservation, located in their traditional territory.

The Hupa spoke an Athapascan language, as did three small,

culturally similar, neighboring groups, the Chilula, Whilkut and North Fork Hupa. The Hupa lived in about 12 villages on both sides of the river. There was no formal leadership, but persons were ranked according to their wealth, which was measured in such items as albino deerskins, red or black imported obsidian blades, headdresses decorated with redheaded woodpecker scalps, and shell currency. These treasures were inherited and were used for paying a bride price, shaman's fee or indemnity to an injured party or his family.

The Hupa believed in numerous spirits and supernatural beings. They celebrated two important world renewal ceremonies, the White Deerskin dance and the Jumping dance. Other ceremonies celebrated the beginning of the salmon run in spring and the acorn season in autumn. Hupa shamans, who performed cures by sucking out the pain, were almost always women.

When a Hupa died, his body was wrapped in deerskin, removed from the house by a hole in the wall, and buried in a shallow, plank-lined grave with a board placed on top. Clothing and utensils, torn or broken, were placed on top of the grave. Close relatives cut their hair and wore grass necklaces as signs of mourning. After five days, the dead person's soul departed for the damp, dark underworld.

Hupa single-family houses were built of cedar planks around a square pit, with an earthen storage shelf along the interior walls. A stone-lined fire pit was located in the center of the house, and there was a smokehole in the three-pitched roof. The women and children slept in the family house, while the men and older boys slept in a subterranean sweathouse, which was also used as a clubhouse and workshop.

Salmon and acorns were the staple foods. The men used nets, weirs and harpoons to catch the salmon, trout, sturgeon and eel, which were then cut into strips and smoke dried. Women gathered acorns in the autumn and used acorn meal to make mush or bread. Berries, nuts, seeds and roots were gathered and small game were trapped or hunted with bow and arrow. Deer and elk were hunted by driving them into the river and pursuing them by canoe.

Clothing was made of deerskin. Women had three vertical stripes tattooed on their chins and wore basketry caps to cushion their foreheadstattooed on their chins, and wore basketry caps to cushion tattooed on their chins and wore basketry caps to cushion their foreheads against the tumpline used to carry burden baskets. Women also made basketry bowls, storage containers and cradles. Men made wooden stools, headrests, platters, bowls and storage chests and tools of stone and bone.

Because of their remoteness, the Hupa were secluded from most European contact until 1850, when the gold rush reached the Trinity River. Miners flooded into the area, and some stayed to homestead. In 1864, a reservation was established for the Hupa in their traditional homeland.

Smithsonian Institution National Anthropological Archives.

Hupa chiefs at the beginning of the White Deerskin Dance—a photograph taken eight miles from the Yurok town of Weitchpec, Humboldt County, California, in about 1890-97.

In the late 1970s, the 87,000 acre Hoopa Valley Reservation was the largest and most populous in California. About 1,000 Hupa lived on the reservation plus a few Karok, Chilula, Yurok, Whilkut, and others. Timber was the main resource of the reservation, and salmon fishing and acorn gathering were still carried on.

The Hupa continued to take pride in their tribal traditions, celebrating the White Deerskin Dance and Jumping Dance biennially and the Brush Dance annually. The Hupa language was still spoken, particularly by the older tribal members.

BIBLIOGRAPHY: Goddard, Pliny E. "Life and Culture of the Hupa." *University of California Publications in American Archaeology and Ethnology.* vol. 1, 1903; Goldschmidt, Walter R. and Driver, Harold E. "The Hupa White Deerskin Dance." *University of California Publications in American Archaeology and Ethnology.* vol. 35, 1940.

HURON: a confederacy of four highly organized tribes, living in Huronia, a region in Ontario near Lake Simcoe, southeast of Georgian

Bay, in the early 1600s. At this time, their population was estimated between 20,000 and 35,000.

They were great traders, traveling far and wide to trade corn, fish, furs, and tobacco with other tribes and with the French. In 1651, the confederacy was destroyed by the Five Nations Iroquois Confederacy and the Huron dispersed. In the late 1970s, about 2,000 descendants still lived in Oklahoma and on a small reservation near Quebec, Canada. Those in Oklahoma called themselves Wyandot and those near Quebec were known as the Huron of Lorette.

The Huron language of the Iroquoian language family is extinct. They called themselves Wendat, which meant "islanders" or "peninsula dwellers." This name survives as the modern day Wyandot. The origin of the name Huron was a French word meaning "boar-like" or "unkempt".

The four tribes of the Huron confederacy—the Attignaouantan (Bear People), Attigneenongnahac (Cord People), Arendahronon (Rock People) and Tohontaenrat (Deer People),—were independent in local affairs, but, for external affairs, were ruled by a council of chiefs from each tribe. The tribes were divided into matrilineal clans, which were in turn divided into families. Both the tribes and clans were ruled by councils of chiefs, while each family was ruled by the senior child-bearing woman. Titles of chieftaincy were hereditary within a family, but the particular candidate for a position was selected by the child-bearing women of the family.

The Huron believed in a complex world of spirits, many of which they worshipped. They also paid close attention to dreams, considering them to be harbingers of good and evil fortune.

Four types of religious festivals were held each year: singing feasts, farewell feasts, thanksgiving feasts and prayer feasts for deliverance from sickness. Each of these lasted from one to fifteen days. Three types of medicine men figured prominently in the festivals; conjurers who claimed to bring sunshine or rain, seers who discovered lost objects and saw the future, and practitioners to cure the sick. Every eight to ten years, they held a Feast of the Dead, the most important festival of all. At this time, the bodies of those who had died in the interim were moved from their village burial grounds and reburied in a common grave with great ceremony.

In the years between the Feasts of the Dead, the body was wrapped in furs and placed in the grave along with food, weapons and ornaments. The spouse of the dead then entered into ten days of fasting and a year of mourning, in which he or she could not remarry.

Villages were constructed near bodies of water, but far enough back from shore to preclude attack by water. The villages were moved whenever the land was worn out from over-cultivation. Often the villages were

Huron moccasins.

fortified with triple stockades of timbers 35 feet high. Houses were constructed of wood pole frames covered with bark, and were 10-15 feet wide and 40-50 feet long, housing eight to ten families.

The Huron economy relied heavily on agriculture and trade. They were the great traders of the northeast—trading with surrounding tribes and with the French. Corn, fish, tobacco and hemp were obtained from the Neutral and the Tionontate (Petun or Tobacco Nation) and traded to northern Algonquian tribes for furs, principally beaver, which the Huron in turn traded to the French for various goods. The Huron monopolized the trade crops of the Neutral and the Tionontati, and kept them isolated from the French to protect their trading empire. They were expert at construction and navigation of birch bark canoes. The Huron roamed far and wide in their trading missions—the men being gone from June through September on trade expeditions.

A typical trade route took them northwest up the Ottawa River, past Lake Timiskaming, and then east along a chain of lakes to the area of Attikameque. All along the route they traded for furs, which they then took south to the French at Three Rivers and Montreal. Often, a longer route took them further still—north to Lake St. John and down the Saguenay River to the St. Lawrence River downstream of Quebec, before returning home by way of the St. Lawrence.

The Huron did little hunting, although they took some deer by driving them into pens. Agriculture was extensively practiced—mostly by the women—corn, squash, beans, sunflowers and tobacco being the principal crops. Fish, nuts and berries supplemented the diet. Huron women made pottery and wicker baskets, while the men made war clubs and bow and arrows.

The Huron were the northern extension of the Iroquois immigration—probably originating from somewhere in the Mississippi valley. The Bear People and Cord people believed they were in the area by 1570. The Rock people and the Deer people joined them soon after, being driven from the north shore of the St. Lawrence River by the Iroquois Confederacy. Over the years, their ranks were swelled by numerous other adopted peoples, some of whom lived as dependent tribes among the Hurons. Their numbers were estimated as high as 35,000, at the peak of Huron power in the 1600s.

When Jaques Cartier visited the Huron along the St. Lawrence River in 1534, they were already at war with the Iroquois. In 1615, Samuel de Champlain found them in Huronia, driven there by their enemies. From that time until 1650, considerable trade with the French ensued, and a number of Jesuit and Récollect missions were established.

In 1648-1650, the Iroquois destroyed the Huron confederacy, and dispersed the people. The principal cause of the war was the fur trade. In 1648, the Iroquois attacked in full force, and by 1650 the Huron empire was crushed. Factors in the defeat included possession of Dutch firearms by the Iroquois and a plague which swept the Huron in 1636-1640.

In June, 1649, 500 Huron began a final retreat to the area of Quebec, where they became known as the Hurons of Lorette. Others fled to the Neutral, where they were captured and destroyed. Some joined the Erie and were dispersed or destroyed when the Iroquois attacked that tribe. Many others were absorbed into the Iroquois confederacy.

One group of Huron fled to the Tiontati, a closely related tribe to the west, and were again dispersed by the Iroquois. A combined group of Tionontate and Huron then fled west, commencing decades of wandering. Their travels took them, in turn, to Christian Island in Lake Huron, Michilimackinac in Michigan, Green Bay in Wisconsin and back to Michilimackinac by 1671. By 1701, they were down to several hundred warriors. But in the next 30-60 years, now called the Wyandot, they achieved a position of prominence in Ohio and southeastern Michigan, claiming virtually all of Ohio north of the Ohio River.

Conflict with the white settlers, however, led to uprisings in 1745 under Orontony and in 1795 under Tarhee, "the Crane," resulting in the loss of two thirds of Ohio—the Indians retaining only the northwest corner of the state. Treaties in 1805, 1807 and 1808 ceded still more lands to the whites.

After the war of 1812, in which they sided with the British, a large tract was confirmed to the Wyandot in Ohio and Michigan. They sold much of the land, however, and by 1819 were reduced to small holdings near Detroit, Michigan, and Sandusky, Ohio. In 1842 the tribe sold its remaining land and relocated in Wyandotte County, Kansas. The treaty of 1855 conferred U.S. citizenship on them, but resulted in forced land sales, rendering them homeless again. In 1859, the Seneca-Cayuga gave them 33,000 acres of their reservation in northeast Oklahoma, to which they subsequently removed.

By the 1970s Wyandot were among the leading citizens of Ottawa County, Oklahoma, numbering about 1,000, most of whom were of mixed blood.

The Hurons of Lorette were, in the 1970s, for the most part assimilated into the white community, while preserving much of their tribal culture and heritage. Located on a reserve called Huron Village, near Quebec, their population was estimated at around 1,050.

BIBLIOGRAPHY: Heidenreich, Conrad. *Huronia.* Toronto, Canada: McLelland and Stewart, Ltd. 1971; Tooker, Elizabeth. "An Ethnography of the Huron Indians, 1615-1649." *Bureau of American Ethnology Bulletin.* no. 190, 1964.

IGLULIK INUIT: a central Inuit (Eskimo) group located north of Hudson Bay in the Canadian Northwest Territory, numbering more than 500 in the late 1970s. Nomadic Arctic hunters, the Iglulik ranged over a large territory, including part of northern Baffin Island, the Melville Peninsula, Southhampton Island and Roes Welcome Sound, between Repulse Bay and Chesterfield Inlet.

Their most important settlement was Igloolik, an island off the northern coast of the Melville Peninsula. The name of the settlement and the people was derived from their habit of using igloos, or snow houses, as dwellings for part of the year. The Iglulik spoke a dialect of the Inuit (Eskimo) language, which is spoken, with little variation, from Alaska to Greenland. The name Eskimo was derived from an Abnaki Indian term meaning "raw meat eaters," whereas the term Inuit, meaning "people," was their own name for themselves.

The Iglulik were divided into three closely related geographical divisions: Iglulingmiut, Aivilingmiut and Tununermiut, living in scattered settlements composed of a few families. An *ihumataq*, or older man who was respected as a hunter, advised each local group on when to move or when to hunt.

Religious leadership was provided by an *angakok*, or shaman, who received his training from an older shaman. The *angakok* conducted seances, in which they called upon their helping spirits to assist them in curing the sick or finding lost souls. *Angakok* had the power to travel to visit the old woman at the bottom of the sea who controlled all the marine animals, or to visit the god of the weather or wind. He would then prescribe certain taboos to insure good weather or good hunting. There were many established hunting-related taboos, such as the forbidding of hunting of both land and sea animals during the same period. When a man died, no hunting was allowed for six days. The body of the deceased remained in the dwelling for three days, before it was wrapped in a caribou skin, removed through a hole in the rear wall, and taken out and covered over with snow.

In former times, the Iglulik had no permanent settlements, although they frequently visited the same places. From October to May, they lived in snow houses and the rest of the year, in sealskin tents. A snow house could be built by two or three men in an hour. A snow probe was used to test the quality of the snow, and an ivory snow knife was used to cut blocks, which were laid in an inward leaning spiral until they formed a dome. A slab of clear ice or pieces of gut-skin were used as a window. A platform of packed snow covered with several layers of skins served as beds. Two snowhouses together were used as a dance house, where the community gathered for singing and dancing to tambourine drums.

The Iglulik followed a seasonal hunting cycle which they varied according to their inclination and the game supply. Typically, the summer was spent hunting whale, seal and walrus from kayaks and *umiaks* (large skin boats). In the fall, some would follow the caribou, while others fished for salmon and trout, using hooks, traps, weirs and spears. Caribou were stalked with bows and arrows or driven into the water and speared from kayaks. In winter the group hunted seals at their breathing holes. Spring was an important time for building up caches of food by hunting seals and walrus basking on the ice.

For winter transportation, they used wooden dog sleds, increasing speed by coating the runners with a mud shoeing which froze and was coated with ice. In summer, dogs were used to carry pack bags. Other material goods included soapstone cooking pots and blubber lamps for heat and light, dippers of musk-ox horn, wood snow goggles and various implements of carved ivory.

Clothing was made of caribou skin, fit loosely to provide for evaporation of perspiration. For maximum insulation, inner garments were worn with the hair side in, and outer garments with the hair side out. Boots of caribou or seal skin were worn over inner stockings. Women applied intricate beadwork to their jackets in later times.

Little is known about the early history of the Iglulik. In the 19th century, whalers began operating in the area, and after about 1889,

Repulse Bay was commonly used as a winter station by whalers. Trading posts and missions were established in the early 20th century.

In the late 1970s, there were more than 500 Iglulik Inuit, many of whom continued their traditional way of life as nomadic hunters. In some areas, certain modern adaptations were made, such as the use of rifles, steel traps and whale boats with engines.

BIBLIOGRAPHY: Mathiassen, Theikel. "Material Culture of the Iglulik Eskimos." *Report of the Fifth Thule Expedition 1921-24.* vol. 6, 1928; Rasmussen, Knud. "Intellectual Culture of the Iglulik Eskimos." *Report of the Fifth Thule Expedition 1921-24.* vol. 7. 1929.

ILLINOIS: a confederacy of Algonquian tribes which, in the late 17th century, occupied southern Wisconsin, northern Illinois and the west bank of the Mississippi River as far south as the Des Moines River. The main tribes of the confederacy included: Kaskaskia, Peoria, Michigamea, Moingwena, Cahokia and Tamora. Little is known of their political and social organizations except that they were divided into clans. They numbered about 8,000 in 1650. By the late 1970s, a few thousand descendants of the Illinois still lived, mostly in Oklahoma.

The Algonquian language spoken by the confederacy died out by the early 20th century. Illinois is from the word Ilinewek, meaning "man."

The Illinois believed in a supreme being, or Manitou, who was "master of all" and dwelled somewhere in the east. Religious ceremonies were conducted by medicine men. Tobacco smoked in a calumet (sacred pipe) was used extensively in religious and social ceremonies. The Illinois believed in an afterlife and, before burial of the dead, wrapped them in skins and placed them on scaffolds.

The Illinois built both semi-permanent and temporary villages. The temporary villages were huts used by hunting parties, while the more permanent villages consisted of cabins, housing from 6 to 12 families. These were built of woven mats on a pole framework, with floors covered with mats.

Although the women grew corn, beans, squash and melons, the Illinois were basically hunters. The men brought in bear, elk, deer, buffalo, beaver and wildfowl, which the women cut in strips and dried or smoked. Weapons included bows and flint-tipped arrows, lances, war clubs, flint knives and buffalo skin shields. Tools and utensils were made of wood, bone, stone and shell. Buffalo and bear wool were spun into yarn for weaving mats and bags. The men wore breechclouts and the women long dresses. Tattooing, body painting, feathers, and jewelry of colored stones and animal teeth were all used as adornment.

The Illinois of the early 17th century occupied a bountiful land of plentiful game and fertile soil. They were peaceful and hospitable. So,

The Illinois—a detail from a 1705 map by Nicholas de Fer. Library of Congress

when some of the Tionontati fleeing the Iroquois came to them in the 1650s, they gave them refuge, thus incurring the wrath of the Five Nations Confederacy. After that, they were under frequent attack by roving Iroquois war parties, one of which destroyed the village of the Kaskaskia on the Vermilion River in 1680.

The Illinois were driven southward by the Fox, Sauk and Kickapoo, who resented their close connections with the French. The Kaskaskia moved from Wisconsin and northern Illinois to southern Illinois in 1700, settling at the junction of the Mississippi and Kaskaskia rivers. In 1698 the Cahokia and Tamaroa were gathered into a mission by the Jesuits near St. Louis, where they were under frequent attack by Chickasaw and Shawnee. They eventually merged with the Kaskaskia and Peoria, becoming extinct as tribes by 1800.

The Michigamea, who had lived along the Sangamon River in Illinois, were pushed south very early by the Dakota, Fox and Iroquois. Marquette and Jolliet encountered them in southeastern Missouri. But, by 1700, they were pushed back north by the Chickasaw and Quapaw to southern Illinois, where they eventually merged with the Kaskaskia and Peoria.

The Moingwena, who had lived on the west bank of the Mississippi near the mouth of the Des Moines River, merged with the Peoria, in the area of present-day Peoria, Illinois, in about 1674. Eventually the Peoria were forced south by Fox, Sauk, and Kickapoo tribes, settling at St. Genevieve near St. Louis in about 1768.

There was constant warfare throughout the 18th century between the Illinois tribes and the Fox, Sauk, Kickapoo, Shawnee and Chickasaw. Disease and white men's whiskey also took its toll, reducing the once mighty Illinois to a few hundred. By 1765, the confederacy had been destroyed and the tribes dispersed.

The Peoria, Kaskaskia and the remnants of the other Illinois tribes signed treaties in 1803, 1818, and 1832, relinquishing their lands to the United States. In exchange, they were given a reservation on the Marais des Cygnes River in Kansas, where they were joined by the Piankashaw and Wea bands of the Miami tribe. In 1867, they gave up their Kansas lands and moved to Indian Territory, where they bought land from the Seneca-Shawnee-Quapaw tribes, in what is now Ottawa County in northeastern Oklahoma.

In 1873, they were joined by the Miami, acquiring the title of United Peoria and Miami. By 1893, their lands were allotted in severalty under the Allotment Act and their reservation divided among the members. In 1940, they were incorporated as the Peoria Indian Tribe of Oklahoma. By the late 1970s, the descendants of the Illinois tribes living in Oklahoma were mostly assimilated into the general population.

BIBLIOGRAPHY: Scott, James. *The Illinois Nation*. Streator, Illinois: Streator Historical Society, 1972-73.

INGALIK: an Athapascan tribe living in the interior of Alaska on the banks of the Kuskokwim, Anvik, Innoko and lower Yukon rivers, numbering around 600 in the 19th century. In the 1970s, there were probably several hundred Ingalik living in the same area. They spoke a northern language of the Athapascan language family, continuing to do so in the 1970s.

The name Ingalik is an Inuit (Eskimo) term for Indian, and has been sometimes used to include all the Athapascan tribes in the Alaska interior, including the closely related Koyukon (*q.v.*), Tanana (*q.v.*), Nebesna (Upper Tanana) and Han (*q.v.*). The semisedentary Ingalik were loosely organized into four geographical groups, each of which consisted of one or more villages.

They had a complex mythology, based upon the belief that all things of nature, such as people, animals, rivers, lakes, and the elements, had spirits, or *yegs*. Religious life centered around a multitude of ceremonies, many of which were intended to increase the numbers of various game animals. Important ceremonies included the Mask Dance, the Dolls Ceremony, the Bladder Ceremony, and, especially, a 14-night Animals Ceremony. They also had potlatches, where were ceremonial gift distributions akin to those of the Northwest Coast tribes.

The Ingalik universe consisted of four levels: earth; "top of the sky"; an upper underworld where the culture hero Raven dwelled; and a lower underworld called "fish tail." When a person died, his *yeg* generally went to the upper underworld, although certain *yegs* went to the other two worlds, depending on the manner of death. The dead were usually placed in wood coffins in coffin-houses or buried in the ground. More

An Ingalik, holding a wooden scoop, takes a fish from a trap—a photograph taken at Anvik, Alaska, in 1898.

rarely, the bodies were cremated. A four-day ceremony was sometimes held, followed by a 20-day mourning period during which certain taboos were observed. Potlatches were often given as a memorial to the dead.

The Ingalik had summer and winter villages, sometimes located across the river from each other. The winter village contained dome-shaped, earth-covered dwellings housing from one to three families. A larger structure was the communal *kachim,* or men's house, a one-room structure with a fireplace in the center and benches around the periphery for sleeping. The men used it for sleep, work, sweat baths, and as a residence for boys. It was also the village ceremonial center. Other structures in the village included racks for canoes and log caches for food, elevated on posts. Summer villages contained houses of spruce planks, spruce bark or cottonwood logs, as well as gabled-roofed smoke houses and fish drying racks. Temporary brush houses were used on trips.

The Ingalik depended on hunting, fishing and gathering for subsistence. Caribou were the principal game, taken by communal surrounds. They also tracked moose with bow and arrow, occasionally speared or snared a bear, and took other game such as wolverines, wolves, lynx and beavers. Lamprey eel were caught through the ice in winter. Other important fish, caught with traps, nets, weirs and spears, were salmon, trout, grayling and blackfish.

Birchbark canoes were used for transportation and fishing, and sleds and snowshoes were used for winter travel. Other items of material culture included stone axes and wedges and wooden bowls. Clothing was of skins, including squirrel skin shirts and trousers supplemented by belts and parkas. One-piece clothing items, combining trousers and footwear, were worn by the women, whereas the men had separate boots. Personal adornment included dentalia earrings, nose pendants and necklaces.

The Ingalik, along with other Athapascan tribes, were probably driven out of Canada by the Cree, settling in Alaska *c.* 1200. They were occasionally at war with neighboring Athapascans and Inuit. A Russian expedition led by Glazunov visited the Ingalik in 1833, and in 1867, the U.S. purchased Alaska from Russia. A trading post was located at Anvik from 1867 to 1880, and Episcopal and Catholic missions were established in the area by 1880. By 1900, the gold rush in Alaska affected the region by increasing boat traffic on the Yukon River.

Recent years have brought only minor changes to the Ingalik. In the 1970s, the Ingalik continued to rely on hunting and gathering pursuits plus some wage work. There were probably several hundred Ingalik among the 6,000 Athapascans living in Alaska. The Ingalik villages, together with a number of other Athapascan villages, were organized into Doyon, Inc., to be eligible for the 1971 Alaska Native Claims Settlement Act.

BIBLIOGRAPHY: Osgood, Cornelius. "Ingalik Material Culture." *Yale University Publications in Anthropology.* vol. 22, 1940.

INUIT: (also known as Eskimo) a group of linguistically and culturally related peoples occupying the coast and islands of Arctic America from Greenland to the Bering Strait, numbering perhaps 60,000 in the 18th century. In the 1970s, there were about 80,000 Inuit, including 25,000 in Alaska, 40,000 in Greenland and 15,000 in Canada.

They spoke the Inuit language of the Inuit-Aleut (Eskimo-Aleut) language family, which had two branches, the Inuk (or Inupik) and the Yuk (or Yupik). The Inuk branch was spoken from Greenland to the Bering Strait, and the Yuk south of the Bering Strait along the Alaskan coastline. The name Eskimo was derived from an Abnaki term meaning "raw meat eaters," whereas the term Inuit, meaning "people," is their own name for themselves.

The Inuit had no tribes, the largest political unit usually being small cooperative hunting groups composed of several families. They depended almost entirely on hunting and fishing for subsistence. Although there was great similarity of culture across the vast geographical range of the Inuit, specific adaptations to the harsh Arctic environ-

Library of Congress

A photograph, taken in 1899, showing Inuit in front of their earth and skin lodge at Plover Bay, North Alaska. Hanging from the lodge are sealskin floats used in whaling.

ment varied somewhat with the game supply in each area. The type of food, shelter, clothing, transport and other aspects of material culture employed were greatly dependent on the raw materials provided by the game animals available and the lifestyle and technology necessary to procure them. The following articles should be consulted on the various geographically oriented Inuit groups: *Baffinland Inuit, Caribou Inuit, Copper Inuit, East Greenland Inuit, Iglulik Inuit, Labrador Inuit, Mackenzie Inuit, Netsilik Inuit, North Alaska Inuit, Polar Inuit, South Alaska Inuit, Southampton Inuit, West Alaska Inuit and West Greenland Inuit.*

BIBLIOGRAPHY: Birket-Smith, Kaj. *The Eskimos.* 2nd ed. New York: Humanities Press, 1958.

IOWA: a Siouan tribe of the Chiwere division, located in eastern Iowa and southwestern Minnesota in the 17th century, numbering about 1,200 at that time. In the late 1970s, Iowa descendants numbered several hundred, living mostly in Kansas and Oklahoma.

The Iowa were closely related to the other two Chiwere division tribes, the Oto and Missouri, and also to the Winnebago. Iowa has been variously translated as "sleepy ones" and "narrow"; however, they called themselves Pahoja, meaning "gray snow."

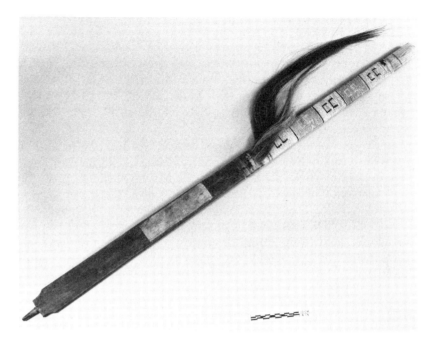

An Iowa pipestem.   Smithsonian Institution

Various house styles were used by the Iowa, including bark-covered pole frame houses, earth lodges and skin tipis for hunting and traveling. The Iowa grew corn, beans and squash, and hunted deer, buffalo, beaver, raccoon, otter and bear. In the 18th and early 19th centuries, they were heavily engaged in the fur trade. They also traded, to other tribes, pipes carved from red pipestone, obtained from the quarries in southwestern Minnesota. Along with the Sauk and Fox, they engaged in lead mining, in the area of present-day Dubuque, Iowa.

The Iowa, according to tradition, originally lived with the Oto, Missouri and Winnebago tribes, somewhere north of the Great Lakes. When migrating south, the Winnebago stopped in the Green Bay region of Wisconsin, while the Iowa, Oto and Missouri continued on south and west. The Iowa separated from the others at the junction of the Iowa and Mississippi rivers, and the Oto and Missouri moved on to the Missouri and Grand rivers.

The Iowa finally settled for a time at the mouth of the Rock River in Illinois. From there they moved to the Des Moines River in northwestern Iowa and to the area around the pipestone quarries in southwestern Minnesota. In the late 18th and early 19th centuries, the Iowa occupied villages near the confluence of the Missouri and Platte rivers. Competition for hunting grounds led to war with the Sauk, Fox and Dakota tribes. These conflicts, plus a smallpox epidemic in 1803, reduced their population to about 800.

The Iowa signed treaties with the United States in 1824, 1825, 1830, 1836 and 1837, ceding all their lands in Iowa, Minnesota and Missouri. In 1836, they were assigned to a reservation along the Great Nemaha River, in southeastern Nebraska and northeastern Kansas. The reservation was reduced in 1854 and 1861. In the late 1870s, part of the Iowa began moving to Indian Territory (Oklahoma), where they were assigned a reservation in 1883.

In the late 1970s, about 700 Iowa descendants lived on or near the Iowa Reservation in Richardson County, Nebraska and Brown County, Kansas, and about 150 lived on allotted lands in Oklahoma. The 1,200 acre reservation included 700 acres of tribally owned land and 500 acres of allotted land. The 150 or so Iowa descendants in Oklahoma lived mostly in Lincoln, Payne and Logan counties, holding about 1,500 acres of allotted land. Both groups of Iowa were virtually assimilated into the surrounding community, but maintained a few of their cultural traditions.

BIBLIOGRAPHY: Gussow, Zachary. *Sac, Fox and Iowa Indians.* New York: Garland Publishing, Inc., 1974.

IROQUOIS: See CAYUGA, MOHAWK, ONEIDA, ONONDAGA, SENECA and TUSCARORA.

ISLETA: a Tiwa tribe and pueblo located three miles south of central Albuquerque, New Mexico, on the west bank of the Rio Grande. With a population of 2,650 in the late 1970s, it occupied the same site as it did when visited by the Spanish explorer, Coronado in 1540. The name Isleta, Spanish for little island, referred to the pueblo's location on a delta or island between the Rio Grande and a small tributary, which later filled in with alluvium. The Isleta, who called their pueblo Shiewhibak, spoke the Tiwa language of the Tanoan language family.

The pueblo was governed by its religious leader, the cacique, who was assisted by the War Chief and Bow Chief. The latter succeeded the cacique who held his office for life. The secular arm of the government, instituted by the Spanish, included the governor, lieutenant governor and other officials appointed by the cacique as liaison between the pueblo and outsiders.

Socially, the pueblo was divided into seven Corn groups, each individual usually being initiated into the same group as his mother. Each individual also belonged to one of two moieties, the Shifun-kavede and the Shure-kavede, sometimes called Black Eye and Red Eye. There were

Isleta playing a game called *patol*, **pictured in 1890.**   Library of Congress

also a number of secret societies, whose powers included controlling the weather, insuring good crops, expelling locusts and curing the sick by means of herbs and massage. Cosmic spirits of the Isleta included the Sun, Moon, Earth, Lightning and Wind. They had a full round of winter and summer ceremonies, performed to bring good weather and bountiful crops. Ceremonies were held either in a ceremonial building called a *kiva* or in the central plaza.

The dead were buried with their head to the south and their feet in the direction of Wimda, the underground world from which they came, and to which they would return. Relatives remained four days in the house of the deceased and then went to the river to bathe and sprinkle meal in the water.

Before the coming of the Spanish, the Isleta men cultivated fields of corn, beans and cotton, irrigating their fields with water from the Rio Grande. The Spanish introduced wheat, alfalfa, onions and various fruits. Isleta men hunted deer and antelope with bows and arrows and rabbits with throwing sticks. Occasionally they ventured to the plains of New Mexico and Texas to hunt buffalo. Crafts included pottery and the spinning and weaving of cotton into belts, leggings and kilts.

The Spanish explorer Coronado visited Isleta in 1540, and the Spanish established a mission there in 1613. The pueblo remained neutral in the 1680 Pueblo Revolt, but was burned by the Spanish in 1681. Some 500 captives were taken, nearly 400 of whom were settled at Isleta del Sur, Mexico, just south of El Paso, Texas. Some of the Isleta who escaped fled to the Hopi, where they remained until 1717. Isleta was rebuilt on the same site by 1718, and had a population of about 300 by 1760. In

1862, Isleta joined with the other pueblos in fighting the Navajo, and in 1886, they participated in their last buffalo hunt on the Plains.

In the late 1970s, Isleta occupied about 211,000 acres, with a population of about 2,650. Located very close to downtown Albuquerque, the Isletans were striving to maintain their cultural traditions. The Isleta language was still spoken; traditional ceremonies and religion were still important in daily life, and Isleta craftsmen produced fine pottery and textiles.

BIBLIOGRAPHY: Parsons, Elsie Clews. "Isleta, New Mexico." *Bureau of American Ethnology Annual Report.* no. 47, 1929-30.

JEMEZ: a tribe and pueblo located on the Jemez River about 45 miles northwest of Albuquerque, New Mexico, numbering about 2,500 in 1680. In the late 1970s their population was around 2,000. The Jemez and the extinct Pecos tribe were the only speakers of the Towa language of the Tanoan language family. The Jemez called themselves Walatowa, or "people of the canyon."

The Jemez were governed by the cacique, a religious leader who was appointed for life by the chiefs of the various ceremonial societies. His duties included coordinating the ceremonial life of the pueblo and taking care of the tribal fetishes. There was also a secular government, including a governor, lieutenant governor, war captains and *fiscales,* who acted as a liaison between the pueblo and the outside world. The secular officers were appointed for one year terms.

The Jemez were divided into matrilineal clans, with marriage forbidden inside the clan. There were also about twenty ceremonial societies, including curing societies, hunter societies, warrior societies and clown societies. In addition, there were two men's societies, Eagle and Arrow, with all men of the pueblo belonging to one or the other. Both men and women were initiated into the *k'ats'ana* cult, and performed masked dances in which they impersonated rain spirits, or *k'ats'ana*, for the purpose of bringing rain for crops. There were two *kivas,* or religious centers, in the pueblo: Squash and Turquoise. An individual usually belonged to the *kiva* of his father, although after marriage, a woman often joined the *kiva* of her husband.

The Jemez buried their dead in graveyards, after sprinkling the body with water, corn meal and corn pollen. Two days after burial, a ceremony using feathered prayer sticks was performed, sending the spirit of the deceased to Wanatota, the land of the dead, where he became a *k'ats'ana.*

The pueblo was composed of one and two-story adobe brick houses, with pine log roofs, adobe floors and plastered walls. The two *kivas,* located in the plaza, were rectangular, with entry through hatchways in the roofs.

The Jemez grew corn, beans and squash, later adding such crops as wheat, melons, chilies and alfalfa, introduced by the Spanish. The men cultivated the irrigated fields and hunted deer, elk and antelope. The women gathered cactus fruits, various greens, and other wild foods to supplement the diet. Eagles were captured for their feathers, and communal rabbit drives were held, as well as occasional trips to the Plains to hunt buffalo. Traditional dress for the women consisted of black cloth dresses, passed over the right shoulder and under the left arm and belted with a bright-colored yarn sash. Moccasins with buckskin leggings completed the costume.

The Jemez tribe occupied perhaps 11 pueblos in the Jemez Valley when the Coronado expedition visited the area in 1541. In the early 17th century, the Spanish established two missions among the Jemez, and by about 1622, induced them to consolidate their 11 pueblos into two. In the mid-17th century, the Jemez joined the Navajo to oppose the Spanish, but the rebellion was put down and 29 Jemez were hanged.

In 1680, the Jemez took a leading role in the Pueblo Revolt, but the following year, they were forced to flee to the mesas. In 1693, they raided the pueblos of Santa Ana and Zia, which had capitulated to the Spanish. The following year, the Spanish were aided by these allies in attacking the mesa-top pueblo of the Jemez, killing about 84 and taking about 360 prisoners. The Spanish burned the pueblo and returned to Santa Fe with the prisoners and large quantities of captured stores. In 1696, the Jemez allied with the Navajo and Acoma to fight the Spanish once again, but they were forced to flee to the Navajo country, where they remained until the early 18th century. When they finally returned, they constructed the present pueblo at or near the original site. Around 1838, the remnants of the Pecos tribe which was on the verge of extinction due to epidemics and Comanche raids, came to live with the Jemez.

In the late 1970s, the Jemez pueblo occupied 88,800 acres with a population of about 2,000. The traditional religion, which was controlled by the cacique, continued to play a vital role in the daily life of the pueblo. Jemez was noted for the excellence of its dancers and its fine craftwork, including weaving, embroidery, water color paintings and yucca basketry.

BIBLIOGRAPHY: Ellis, Florence Hawley. "A Reconstruction of the Basic Jemez Pattern of Social Organization with Comparisons to Other Tanoan Social Structures." *University of New Mexico Publications in Anthropology.* no. 11, 1964; Parsons, Elsie Clews. *The Pueblo of Jemez.* New Haven: Yale University Press, 1925.

JICARILLA: an Apache tribe who made their homes in southeastern Colorado and northern New Mexico, sometimes ranging into Kansas, Oklahoma and Texas. In the late 1970s, there were about 2,000 Jicarilla, located on the Jicarilla Reservation in New Mexico.

The Jicarilla spoke a language of the southern branch of the Athapascan language family. Linguistically, they were closest to the Lipan Apache who were probably an offshoot of the Jicarilla. Culturally, they were more influenced by the Plains and Pueblo tribes than were most other Apache groups. Jicarilla, a Spanish term meaning "little basket," probably referred to their basketry water vessels.

In the 19th century the Jicarilla were divided into two bands—the Llanero, meaning "Plains," and the Ollero, or "Sand People," located east and west of the Rio Grande, respectively. Band membership was important in such things as buffalo hunting or the annual relay race, but the main political unit was the local group, composed of several extended families. The leader, whose position was mainly advisory, was chosen for his hunting and raiding skill.

The main social unit was the extended family. Residence was matrilocal, with a newly-married couple living with the woman's family, although it was taboo for a man to talk to his mother-in-law. Important socio-religious ceremonies included the girls' puberty rites and the Holiness Rite, a five-day curing ceremony performed in a brush enclosure, involving masked dancers, sacred clowns and sand paintings. In some ceremonies, the *hactcin,* similar to the *gan* dancers of other Apache groups, performed masked dances in which they impersonated the Mountain Spirits.

Other ceremonies included pre-hunt rites and the annual autumn relay race between the young men of the two bands. This celebration symbolized the well-being of the tribe and its hope of obtaining an abundant food supply in the coming year. The Jicarilla had a complex mythology, including such characters and deities as Sun Boy, Killer of Enemies, White Painted Woman, Child of the Water, Sky, Earth, Sun and Moon. According to tradition, the Jicarilla people emerged from the underworld at a point near Taos.

The Jicarilla lived in dome-shaped wickiups of pole-frame construction, covered with bark, thatch and, in cold weather, skins. When they were involved in buffalo hunting, they also made Plains style buffalo skin tipis. The Jicarilla lived near the pueblos of Taos and Picuris, and learned from them how to grow corn, beans, squash, pumpkins, peas, wheat and cantaloup. By the early 19th century, they were raising crops along the river bottomlands and building irrigation dams and ditches.

The men also hunted deer, antelope, elk, mountain sheep, turkey, grouse, quail and other small game, using traps as well as bows and

A Jicarilla girl, photographed by Edward S. Curtis, (1904). Library of Congress

arrows. They also went on communal buffalo hunts each year. The women gathered juniper berries, mesquite beans, yucca fruit, chokecherries, prickly pears, acorns, pine nuts and an assortment of other seeds, fruits and roots.

The Jicarilla made pottery of good quality, as well as ceremonial clay pipes. They also made fine basketry, including water vessels sealed with pitch. Their Plains-style skin garments were decorated with beadwork, and bone necklaces and earrings were worn for adornment.

The Jicarilla probably migrated to the southwest from the eastern slope of the Rocky Mountains in northwestern Canada. Traditionally, they were enemies of the Comanche, Cheyenne, Arapaho and Navajo, whereas they were usually on good terms with the Ute and Pueblo tribes. The Lipan probably split off by *c.* 1600.

By 1717, the Jicarilla had been driven out of Colorado and parts of New Mexico by the Comanche. In the 18th century, they retreated southward from the Plains, alternately trading with and raiding the New Mexico settlements. In the early 19th century, they were allied with the Ute against the Comanche, but by 1810, were forced to make peace.

In the 1830s and 1840s, the Jicarilla got into trouble with the United States government by raiding along the Santa Fe trail. They were defeated by U.S. troops in 1854, and for the next 30 years they were pushed from place to place and reservation to reservation. In 1887, they were finally settled on the Jicarilla Reservation in northern New Mexico, in an area known as Terra Amarilla. There they suffered a tuberculosis outbreak in 1890.

In the late 1970s, there were about 2,000 Jicarilla living on the 740,000-acre reservation. There were a number of tribal enterprises, including Jicarilla Arts and Crafts, Jicarilla Buckskin and Leathercraft and various tourism facilities. Crafts included basketry, weaving, painting and beadwork.

BIBLIOGRAPHY: Gunnerson, Dolores A. *The Jicarilla Apaches.* De Kalb, Illinois: Northern Illinois University Press, 1974.

JUANEÑO: *See* LUISEÑO.

KADOHADACHO: *See* CADDO.

KAINAH: *See* BLACKFOOT.

KALAPUYA: a group of small western Oregon tribes occupying the Willamette River Valley in the late 18th century, numbering about 3,000 at that time. Epidemics and warfare with white settlers and other tribes drove the Kalapuya to virtual extinction by the early 20th century.

The Kalapuyan (or Kalapooian) language family comprised three mutually unintelligible dialects. Politically, there were at least nine tribes, or divisions: Calapooya, Santiam, Yoncalla, Luckiamute, Atfalati, Ahantchuyuk, Chelamela, Chepenafa and Yamel (or Yam Hill).

Little is known of their social organization, other than that they lived in numerous tiny villages, led by chiefs, and kept some slaves. Brides were obtained through gifts given to the brides' family, and polygamy was practiced, men usually marrying sisters or their brother's widow.

Religion centered around the personal quest for a guardian spirit, acquired by dreaming, swimming or fasting in lonely places. Shamans cured the sick and performed ceremonies, singing and dancing to the accompaniment of drums, cedar gongs and rattles made of shells or deer hooves. Ceremonies included puberty rites for girls, in which they were required to dance continuously for five nights.

When a Kalapuya died, he was buried with his belongings, sometimes including canoes and horses. Mourners cut their hair, and the widow painted her face red for a month. The house of the deceased was sometimes burned, and his name was never spoken again.

Winter houses of the Kalapuya were of bark, sometimes covered with thatch and earth, up to 60 feet long and housing as many as ten families. Summer or temporary houses were made of grass or boughs.

Fishing, hunting and gathering wild foods provided the Kalapuya with a varied diet. The women collected camas roots, acorns, sunflower seeds, hazel nuts, blueberries, blackberries and strawberries. A small quantity of tobacco was planted in rotten, burnt-out logs. The men hunted deer, elk, bear, beaver and other small game, using decoys, snares and bows and arrows. Fish were taken with spears and traps.

Material culture included dugout canoes between 14 and 30 feet long, of cedar or white fir. They made bows of oak or yew, with flint-tipped arrows, as well as shields and shin protectors of elkhide. Basketry was made of cedar and spruce roots and decorated with animal figure designs. Both men and women wore basketry hats, and women wore aprons of rushes or fringed buckskin. Dentalium shells and face paint were used for adornment.

In 1782-83, an estimated 2,000 Kalapuya were killed by a smallpox epidemic. Between 1830 and 1833, an estimated 75 percent of the Indians of the Columbia and Willamette river valleys were wiped out by a smallpox epidemic, leaving the tribes with little strength to resist the tide of settlers that flooded the area in the 1850s. By treaties in 1854 and 1855, the Kalapuya ceded their Willamette valley lands and were moved to Grande Ronde Reservation, where they dwindled to near extinction by the early 20th century.

BIBLIOGRAPHY: Jacobs, Melville, et al. "Kalapuya Texts." *University of Washington Publications in Anthropology*. vol. 11, 1945; Mackey, Harold. *The Kalapuyas: A Sourcebook on the Indians of the Willamette Valley*. Salem, Oregon: Mission Mill Museum Association, 1974.

KALISPEL: an Interior Salish tribe living on Pend d'Oreille lake and river in eastern Washington and Idaho in the 18th century, numbering probably around 1,600 in 1805. By the 1970s, about 130 Kalispel were living on or near the Kalispel Reservation in Washington, and an indeterminate number were mixed with other tribes on the Colville Reservation in Washington and the Flathead Reservation in Montana.

The Kalispel, also known as the Pend d'Oreilles, together with the Flathead and Spokan, comprised the Flathead group of Interior Salish. They spoke a language of the Interior division of the Salishan language family. The name Kalispel, meaning "camas people," was derived from the name of their principal vegetable food, whereas Pend d'Oreilles, a French term meaning "ear drops," referred to the large shell ear pendants which they wore.

The Kalispel were geographically divided into the Upper Pend d'Oreilles and Lower Pend d'Oreilles, or Kalispelem. The Kalispelem were subdivided into the Lower Kalispel (Kalispel proper), Upper Kalispel and Chewelah, although the latter were considered by some to be an independent tribe.

The Kalispel were loosely organized into bands composed of several related families, who camped together. Each band was led by a chief and an assistant chief selected on the basis of wisdom, influence, bravery and other leadership qualities. There was also a tribal chief who with the band chiefs made up the tribal council. In later years, as tribal authority became more centralized, band chiefs became less important and were eventually replaced by tribal subchiefs and "small" chiefs.

Religious life centered around guardian spirits obtained in dreams or visions and necessary for success in daily life. At puberty, young men fasted, prayed, exercised and kept vigils to this purpose. Shamans had especially strong guardian spirits, enabling them to foresee the future and to insure good hunting. An important mythical character was the culture hero Coyote. The dead were covered with skins and robes and placed on a scaffold until ready for burial. The pole on which the body was transported to the gravesite was used as a grave marker to which offerings were tied.

Two principal types of structures were built, both of mats on a wood frame. A long lodge, sunk a foot in the ground, was used in winter camps for dances, meetings and ceremonies, while they lived mostly in conical dwellings housing one, two or three families. Other types of dwellings included cedar bark lodges, often elevated on platforms, and temporary brush shelters, used in the mountains on hunting trips. After the acquisition of horses, hunting became important, and skin tipis essentially replaced the mat dwellings.

The Kalispel relied mainly on hunting, fishing and gathering for subsistence. They hunted buffalo on the Plains and elk, deer, antelope and other game in the mountains. A favorite hunting technique was the communal surround. Trout, salmon and whitefish were caught by hook

Choitz-Kan, a Kalispel. Drawn by Gustavus Sohon, 1854.

and line, nets, weirs and traps. Wild foods, including camas, bitterroot, and various other roots and berries were important.

The Kalispel made excellent canoes of white pine bark, and were so proficient in their use that the others in the Flathead group called them "paddlers." Material culture included baskets of birchbark and of coiled split cedar roots, as well as bags woven of strips of skin. Their clothing was of the northern Plains type, usually of rabbit or deer skin, including robes, shirt (or dress for women), leggings, breechclout, moccasins, and cap or headband.

The Kalispel, as the other Interior Salish, probably migrated at some time from British Columbia. They lived for a while in eastern Montana, until pressure from the Blackfoot caused them to move west, settling in the Pend d'Oreille Valley, Washington, in the 18th century. There they lived in peace for many years.

The Kalispel were visited by David Thompson, a trader for the Northwest Company, in 1809, who established a trading post among them. A Catholic mission, established in 1843, moved, in 1854, along with some Kalispel, to the area of Lake Flathead, the future site of the Flathead Reservation. The Kalispel remained relatively isolated until 1863, when the discovery of gold in British Columbia brought numbers of miners through their territory. In 1914, pressure from settlers and miners finally resulted in assignment of a 4,629-acre reservation on the east side of the Pend d'Oreille River, which lands were mostly later allotted to individuals, leaving about 150 acres of tribal land. By 1914, the Kalispel had declined to one-tenth of their 1809 population.

In the 1970s, about 130 Kalispel lived on or near the Kalispel Reservation in Washington, and an unknown number were mixed with other tribes on the Colville Reservation in Washington and the Flathead Reservation in Montana. The Kalispel were essentially assimilated into the life of the surrounding communities.

BIBLIOGRAPHY: Carriker, Robert C. *The Kalispel People.* Phoenix: Indian Tibal Series, 1973.

KANSA: a small Siouan tribe living in Kansas, near the Kansas and Missouri rivers, in the 16th century. They had a population of 1,500 in 1700. They spoke a Siouan language similar to the Osage, and, together with the Osage, Quapaw, Omaha and Ponca, formed the Dhegiha branch of the Siouan linguistic family. By the 1970s smallpox and warfare with settlers and neighboring tribes had reduced their numbers to around 800, living in Oklahoma.

The origin of the name Kansa is not clear: Some linguists consider it to stem from a Siouan expression relating to the wind, while others speculate that Kansa derived from the Spanish "escanseques," meaning "the troublesome." They called themselves Hutanga, "by the edge of the shore," relating to a tradition that they once lived on the Atlantic Ocean. They are also known as the Kaw and the Wind People.

The tribe was organized into two moieties, the Nata and the Ictunga. These were subdivided into seven phratries, composed of 16 clans. Each clan included several families, some patrilineal and some matrilineal, with marriage prohibited within a family. Each village was ruled by a chief elected by a common council, with a head chief over all the villages. War chiefs were chosen for military operations. It was not until the 19th century that pressure from the white man, who preferred to deal with one person in their attempts to exploit the Indians, forced them to adopt a hereditary chieftancy system.

The Kansa believed that spirits, or "Waucondah," resided in numerous aspects of nature—sun, earth, etc. Special deities were the Wind Waucondah and Ne-Woh-Kon-Kaga, the spirit of a sacred salt spring in northern Kansas. Visions were very important, induced by fasting and self-torture. A 13 or 14-year-old boy would be taken to a remote site by his father to fast for at least three days. One creation myth relates that the Kansa were created by the Master of Life on a small island, before the rest of the earth was created. They were saved from overcrowding by beavers, muskrats and turtles, who brought up material from the bottom of the great waters to enlarge the island and create the rest of the earth.

The dead were painted, covered with bark, and buried in a sitting position, facing west, together with food and their possessions. A year of

War dance inside a Kansa lodge. An illustration from Edwin James's *Account of an Expedition from Pittsburgh to the Rocky Mountains, Performed in the Years 1819 and '20*, (Philadelphia, 1823).

mourning ensued, including fasting and self-scarification.

The Kansa lived in round or oval wood-framed lodges covered with mats woven of reed, grass or bark. Often they were also covered with earth for added protection. They were 30 to 60 feet in diameter and housed 5 to 6 families. There was a smoke hole in the center and wood platforms covered with skins around the circumference for beds. Skin tipis were used on hunting trips.

The Kansa were basically hunters, with buffalo the principal game, both for the meat and skins for trade. They had a subsistence economy, with a limited amount of agriculture, the women cultivating corn, beans, pumpkins and gathering prairie potatoes. Women also did most of the menial work around the village, with the activities of the men being concerned with warfare and hunting.

According to tradition, the Kansa, along with the other members of the Dhegiha subgroup, originated somewhere in the Southeast, migrating, by way of the Ohio River, to the Kansas and Missouri rivers in Kansas by the early 16th century. During that migration, the group split into five tribes—the Quapaw going south on the Mississippi River, the Omaha, going north up the Mississippi, the Ponca ascending the Missouri River and the Osage going up the Osage River. The Kansa settled near the fork of the Missouri and Kansas rivers, where they were seen by the Spanish explorer Juan de Oñate in 1601.

The 18th and 19th centuries were filled with internal strife, trouble with settlers, and frequent warfare with the Sauk, Fox, Omaha, Osage,

Iowa, Oto, Pawnee and Cheyenne. In 1825, the Kansa ceded all their land in Missouri, and a 2,000,000-acre reservation was granted them in Kansas. In 1846, a treaty ceded all of these lands, and they were removed to a 265,000-acre reservation on the Neosho River further west. Trouble with white settlers led to ceding of these lands in 1873 and removal to a reservation in Indian Territory (now Oklahoma) near the Osage. These lands were allotted in severalty in 1902, and the tribe was dissolved as a legal entity.

In the 1970s, about 800 Kansa lived in Oklahoma, essentially assimilated into the life of the surrounding community. The tribe was governed by a business committee, mostly of full-bloods. A revival was in progress to preserve the tribal heritage. Factionalism was discouraged, and a sense of community was returning.

BIBLIOGRAPHY: Unrau, William E. *The Kansa Indians, a History of the Wind People. 1673-1873.* Norman, Oklahoma: University of Oklahoma Press, 1971; Unrau, William E. *The Kaw People.* Phoenix: Indian Tribal Series, 1975.

KARANKAWA: an extinct tribe that flourished on the Texas Gulf Coast, numbering about 2,800 in 1690. The Karankawa spoke a Coahuiltecan language, and their name may have meant "people walking in the water" in the language of their neighbors, the Lipan Apache.

They were a nomadic people, often packing up their portable huts to move on to a new food supply. Their diet consisted principally of shellfish, wild fowl, turtles, berries, nuts, birds' eggs and roots. Big game was scarce, although they would take an occasional bear, deer, or wandering buffalo. The Karankawa lived for the most part from day to day, storing little.

The men were excellent archers and skillful at maneuvering their dugout canoes. They made knives and tools of stone or shell, and the women made a crude pottery, often rounded on the bottom so it could stand upright in the sand.

Karankawa men were usually described as being exceptionally tall and well-formed, the women as shorter and heavier. The men's hair hung down the back nearly to the waist. They pierced their breasts and lower lips with sharp pieces of cane. In warfare the Karankawa men reportedly painted half their face red and the other half black. Unmarried women painted a single stripe down the forehead, nose and lips, while married women were free to cover themselves with flower, bird, animal and other designs. Both men and women practiced tattooing and head flattening.

The Karankawa lived in small groups, sometimes limited to a single family. They reportedly buried their dead except for doctors who were burned. They engaged in cannibalism, as did some other tribes of this area. There was some Christianization of the tribe by Spanish missionaries.

The Karankawa did not take kindly the incursions of settlers into their homeland, fighting variously with the Spanish, Texans and the pirate band of Jean Lafitte. According to conflicting reports, they were either annihilated or driven into Mexico by the mid-19th century.

BIBLIOGRAPHY: Gatschet, Albert S. *The Karankawa Indians: The Coast People of Texas.* Cambridge, Mass.: Peabody Museum of American Archaeology and Ethnology, 1891.

KAROK: a group located along the middle course of the Klamath River in northwestern California in the mid-19th century, when they numbered about 2,700. In the late 1970s, there were an estimated 3,800 Karok descendants, located mostly in California. Their name is a Karok language term meaning "upstream," as opposed to their neighbors known as Yurok, or "downstream." The Karok had no close linguistic relatives, but have been classified with the Hokan language family.

The Karok were located in three main clusters of villages. There was no other political organization, although certain leaders were recognized because of their wealth. Industry, thrift and acquisition of property were important values among the Karok. Crimes could be atoned for by the payment of shell money to the injured party.

Karok religious ceremonies celebrated the acorn harvest, the salmon run, the deerskin dance and the world renewal. Curing ceremonies were performed by women doctors, who removed a person's sickness by sucking out the evil cause. Other doctors, male and female, cured through the use of medicinal plants.

When a Karok died, his body was buried in a family plot nearby. Shell money and valuables were buried with the deceased, while clothing and tools were hung on a fence built around the grave. After five days, the soul of the deceased went to a place in the sky, and his name was not pronounced again, unless given to a child in the family.

The Karok built family houses and sweathouses of plank construction, dug out to a depth of several feet. Women and children slept in the family houses, while the men slept in the sweathouses, which were taboo for women to enter.

Salmon, deer and acorns were the principal food sources. Salmon were usually caught with a large net from a fishing platform built along the edge of the stream. They also hunted deer, elk, bear and small game. The deer were caught in snares or stalked by hunters wearing deer head masks. Salmon and venison were dried on scaffolds and stored. In the

A Karok warrior
wearing rod armor
and a helmet,
photographed
in the 1890s.
Smithsonian Institution
National Anthropological
Archives

fall, they gathered acorns, which were ground into flour for soup, mush or bread.

Woodworking was an important craft. The Karok cut planking for their houses with stone mauls and horn wedges. Wood was also used for spoons, seats and storage boxes. Other crafts included weaving of vegetable fibers into baskets, containers, cradles and caps. Knives and arrow points were made of obsidian. Bows were made of yew and rod armor vests were used in warfare.

Clothing was made from skins and furs, decorated for ceremonial occasions with fringes, shells and pine nuts. Women wore necklaces and had three vertical lines tattooed on their chins. Both men and women wore basketry caps and sometimes ear and nose ornaments.

The Karok managed to avoid most contact with outsiders until *c.* 1850, when gold miners swarmed into their territory. The seizing of Karok lands and burning of their villages led to clashes that were forcibly put down by military operations, killing at least 100 Karok. No reservations were established for the Karok, although some moved to reservations in Scott Valley. Most remained in their old territory and were gradually assimilated into the general population, their own population drastically reduced by hardship, disease and warfare.

In the late 1970s, only a handful of fullbloods remained, although there were an estimated 3,800 people with some identifiable Karok ancestry. There were signs, including the holding of the world renewal ceremony, of a reviving interest in Karok tradition and culture.

BIBLIOGRAPHY: Bright, William. *"Karok." Handbook of North American Indians.* vol. 8. Washington: Smithsonian Institution, 1978.

KASKA: *See* NAHANE.

KASKASKIA: the principal tribe of the Illinois confederacy, which was located in southern Wisconsin, northern Illinois, and eastern Iowa in the 17th century. The Kaskaskia spoke the same Algonquian language as the other members of the confederacy, which included the Peoria, Machigamea, Moingwena, Cahokia and Tamaroa, For a description of their culture, see the article on the Illinois. Several thousand descendants of the Illinois tribes lived in Oklahoma in the late 1970s. Kaskaskia means "he scrapes it off with a tool," referring to a method of dressing hides or skins.

The main village of Kaskasia, located at the junction of the Vermilion and Illinois rivers, was visited by Marquette and Jolliet in 1673, when it numbered about 74 cabins. Each cabin, constructed of poles covered with reed mats, contained five or six cooking fires, with one or two families to a fire. The interior walls and floors were covered with mats, and corn was stored in pits beneath each cabin.

By 1680, the town had expanded to a population of 6,000-7,000, composed partly of other Illinois tribes who had gathered there for protection from Iroquois war parties, who were roving the western Great Lakes region at that time. The Iroquois burned the village about 1680.

By 1691, the Kaskaskia moved to Lake Peoria, where they lived for a time with the Peoria and Moingwena. In 1700, they moved to southern Illinois, near the Cahokia and Tamaroa tribes, settling at the junction of the Mississippi and Kaskaskia rivers. Here they were able to settle into the sedentary agricultural life which they preferred, raising corn as their staple food. There was also an abundance of game, as well as pecans, mulberries, pawpaws and persimmons for gathering.

French missionaries and traders were active in the villages of the Kaskaskia, bringing European goods, Christianity and a great deal of intermarriage. The close association of the Kaskaskia with the French drew the wrath of other tribes. During the 18th century there was intermittent warfare between them and the Kickapoo, Sauk, Fox, Chickasaw, and Shawnee. By 1765, the Illinois confederacy had been dispersed and their lands divided between the Sauk, Fox and Kickapoo.

Disease and liquor also took their toll, and the Kaskaskia were reduced

A Kaskaskia
Indian—an
illustration
from Collot's
Voyage,
(1826).
Library of Congress

to less than 200 by the close of the 18th century. In 1832, they signed the
Castor Hill Treaty, along with the Peoria and remnants of the other
Illinois tribes, and moved to a reservation in Kansas, where they were
known as the Confederated Peoria Indians. In 1867, under the Omnibus
Treaty, they were forced to leave Kansas and move to Indian Territory
(now Oklahoma). Here the Confederated Peoria, including the Wea and
Piankashaw bands of the Miami, bought lands from the Seneca-
Shawnee-Quapaw, in what is now Ottawa County in northeastern
Oklahoma.

In 1873, they were joined by the Miami, acquiring the title of United
Peoria and Miami. By 1893 their lands were allotted in severalty under
the Allotment Act and their reservation divided among the members. In
1940, they were incorporated as the Peoria Indian Tribe of Oklahoma.
By the late 1970s, there were several thousand descendants of the Illinois
tribes, mostly living in Oklahoma and assimilated into the general population.

BIBLIOGRAPHY: Good, Mary Elizabeth. *Guebert Site.* Wood River,
Illinois: Central States Archaeological Societies, Inc., 1972.

KAWAIISU: *See* CHEMEHUEVI.

KERESAN: *See* ACOMA, COCHITI, LAGUNA, SAN FELIPE, SANTA ANA, SANTO DOMINGO and ZIA.

KICHAI: *See* WICHITA.

KICKAPOO: a midwestern tribe noted for their resistance to white acculturation, fierceness in war, and frequent wanderings. In the 1650s, they numbered around 3,000, occupying land around the Fox and Wisconsin rivers in Wisconsin. In the 1970s, Kickapoo lived in Kansas, Oklahoma and Mexico.

The Kickapoo spoke a language of the Algonquian language family, similar to that of the Sauk and Shawnee. They called themselves Kiwega-paw, meaning ''he who moves about, standing now here, now there.''

The Kickapoo culture was similar to that of the Sauk and Foxes. They were organized into patrilineal clans, with marriage always outside of the clan.

The Kickapoo believed in a supreme being Kicihiata, who dwelled in the sky and created the earth and all things on the earth. Other spirits or *manitou* existed in all things, such as trees, rocks, clouds, sky, sun and earth. Religious life was under the leadership of priests, and centered around a week-long renewal ceremony, and feast in early spring, concerned with the opening and refurbishment of the sacred bundles. Other lesser festivals included the Green Corn Dance and a Buffalo Dance.

The dead were buried in graveyards in or near the villages. They were dressed in travel clothes and positioned with their feet toward the west, in the direction of the land of the dead. They were buried in either stone slab or hollow log vaults, with food and water for the journey.

The Kickapoo had both summer and winter houses. Both houses were oval and had a framework of green saplings, with the summer house being bark-covered and the winter houses being covered with mats woven of cattails. The door always faced east, and there was a smoke hole in the roof.

The economy of the tribes was primarily agricultural, although hunting, fishing and gathering of roots and berries supplemented the diet. Corn, beans and squash were the principal crops, and deer and bear the principal game. Buffalo were also hunted on summer trips west across the Mississippi River, where they became acquainted with the horse.

Their principal crafts were pottery and woodworking. The Kickapoo made fine wood cradleboards, ladles, and bowls, often ornamenting such craftwork with carvings or porcupine quills.

The Kickapoo apparently originated, along with the Sauk and Fox, in eastern Michigan. By the mid 17th century pressure from the Iroquois

Babeshikit,
a Kickapoo
warrior, (1894).

The National Archives

had driven them west to Wisconsin, in the area of the Fox and Wisconsin rivers. They immediately became one of the leaders of the opposition to the French.

From this time until 1763, when France relinquished its claims to the region, the Kickapoo were almost constantly at war with various tribes and with the French. Until c. 1701, allied with the Fox and Mascoutin, they fought the Iroquois. They then fought the French until 1730, when they became French allies and subsequently dispersed the Fox. The Kickapoo, together with the Sauk and Fox, began invading their southern neighbors, the Illinois confederacy c. 1716, and by 1765, had totally dispersed those tribes, dividing their conquered lands among them. About this time, the Kickapoo split into three bands, two migrating to Illinois and one to Texas.

The following years brought struggle against the British, and later against the United States. In 1812, the Kickapoo joined the Shawnee chief Tecumseh in his confederacy, and supported Black Hawk, the Sauk leader, in his uprising some twenty years later. By treaties in 1809 and 1819, they ceded their Illinois land to the U.S. government, and by 1824 were removed to Missouri. In 1832, due to difficulties with squatters, they moved to a new reservation granted them in Kansas.

In 1838, a small band migrated to Mexico. In 1854 and 1862, treaties opened some of the Kansas Kickapoo lands to settlers. By the 1862 treaty the Kickapoo were allotted some of their reservation lands in severalty, with the rest being sold to a railroad company. As a result, a dissatisfied band migrated to join the band in Mexico. In 1873, many of the Mexican group were persuaded to return to Indian Territory (now Oklahoma) and Kansas. Those who remained became known as the Mexican Kickapoo. In 1883 those who returned were granted a reservation of 100,000 acres in Oklahoma. In 1893, the lands were allotted in severalty, under protest by the Kickapoo. By the 1970s only 6,000 acres of allotted land remained.

In the late 1970s, a few hundred Kickapoo remained on reservations in Mexico, about 800 occupied a reservation in Kansas and some 600 lived in Pottawatomi County, Oklahoma. The Kickapoo in all three locations retained a large part of their tribal culture, religion, arts and crafts.

BIBLIOGRAPHY: Gibson, A.M. *The Kickapoos: Lords of the Middle Border.* Norman, Oklahoma: The University of Oklahoma Press, 1963; Ritzenthaler, Robert E. and Peterson, Frederick A. "The Mexican Kickapoo Indians." *Publications in Anthropology of the Public Museum of the City of Milwaukee.* no. 2, 1956.

KIOWA: a southern plains people who originated in the mountains of western Montana, near the headwaters of the Missouri and Yellowstone rivers. They migrated southeast, arriving at the Arkansas and Red rivers by the early 19th century, numbering about 2,000 at that time. In the late 1970s, there were about 3,500 Kiowa, mostly located in southwestern Oklahoma.

Kiowa, meaning "principal people," was derived from Gaigwu or Kaigwu, the name by which they called themselves. The Kiowa language, still spoken in the 1970s, has long been a problem for linguists attempting to classify it, but is probably related to the Tanoan family. The Kiowa had seven divisions or bands, including the Kiowa Apache, who migrated with them from the north. The Kiowa Apache spoke an Athapascan language, but had essentially the same culture and history as the Kiowa.

Each of the bands was fairly autonomous, with its own peace and war chiefs. At various times, however, they had a tribal chief over all the bands. The bands usually lived apart in winter, but camped together in summer to celebrate the Sun Dance. The Kiowa had social classes based on rank attained through military exploits, wealth and religious power. Warriors attained status by "counting coup," which included such heroic acts as touching the enemy, charging the enemy or rescuing a comrade. Lesser credit was attained by killing the enemy or stealing horses.

There were numerous societies, including warrior societies, shield

Three Kiowa, with a drum and a rattle.   The National Archives

societies, dancing societies, sacred societies and two women's societies. Boys under age 12 belonged to the Rabbits Society, and those over 12 joined the Herders, in preparation for their role as warriors. The shield societies, such as the Buffalo Shield or Sun Dance Shield, had special talents and responsibilities, such as setting broken bones, prophesying, curing the sick or performance of certain ceremonies, dances and songs. Among the Plains tribes, the Kiowa were noted as musicians. Religious status was gained by prominence in these activities or by being guardian of items sacred to the tribe.

Kiowa religion centered around the Sun Dance ceremony and the ceremonies associated with the Ten Grandmother Bundles. These were ten collections of sacred items given to the Kiowa, according to tradition, by their culture hero Sun Boy, about whom many tales and legends are told. Young men fasted for four days in hopes of having a vision of a guardian spirit, which would guide and protect them throughout their lives. From the spirit, which might be a certain animal or other natural phenomenon, the person gained special personal power.

When a Kiowa died, he was either buried or his body left in a tipi erected on a hill. The family of the deceased gave away all of his possessions and many of their own. Mourners cut their hair and sometimes gashed themselves or cut off fingers. During the mourning period, the deceased person's family lived by themselves on the fringe of the camp or village.

Kiowa villages were located along streams and composed of portable skin tipis, which were constructed and owned by the women. The Kiowa economy depended on the buffalo for food, shelter and clothing. The men hunted the buffalo in a highly disciplined fashion. No one was allowed to do anything which might alarm the buffalo or jeopardize the success of the hunt. After the hunt, the women butchered the meat, cutting it into strips to dry. These were later pulverized and mixed with dried chokecherries and melted fat to make pemmican. Stored in skin bags, the mixture would keep several years.

Deer, antelope and small game were also hunted, but not bear, which was taboo to kill or eat. Kiowa, like many other Plains tribes, also preferred not to eat fish. Wild potatoes, honey, pecans, and hickory nuts were gathered to supplement the diet. At an annual trading sesion, the Kiowa traded meat, buffalo hides and salt to the Pueblo Indians for cornmeal and dried fruit.

The women dressed the buffalo hides and made warm buffalo robes and moccasins for all. Soft buffalo calfskin was made into leggings, shirts and breechclouts for the men and knee-length leggings, skirts and blouses for the women. The Kiowa, along with the Dakota, also painted pictographs on buffalo skins as a calendric record of the tribe's history.

Before they became great buffalo hunters and warriors of the southern Plains, the Kiowa lived in western Montana, near the headwaters of the Missouri and Yellowstone rivers. The Kiowa Apache probably joined them while they still lived in this area. In the late 17th century, they started drifting southeast, settling near the Crow, with whom they formed an alliance. By the early 18th century, the Kiowa had acquired horses and moved into the Black Hills region. In the early 19th century, they were pushed southward by the Cheyenne and Dakota to eventually occupy an area which included western Oklahoma and adjoining areas of Texas and New Mexico.

By this time, the Kiowa had become highly successful buffalo hunters, horsemen and warriors. Around 1790, they made peace with the Comanche, with whom they subsequently conducted raids as far south as Durango, Mexico. Horses were the main prize. On the Plains, a person's wealth was counted in horses, and, among the Kiowa, nobody walked. They were excellent horse trainers and breeders.

Years of warfare with the Osage, Cheyenne and Arapaho were ended by peace agreements in 1834 and 1840. Until after the Civil War, the Kiowa and their allies put up a strong resistance to the emigration of settlers along the southern overland trails. In 1865, the Kiowa and Comanche agreed to scttlc on a reservation south of the Arkansas River. By 1868 they had been forced onto a reservation around Fort Sill, Oklahoma. They continued, however, to conduct raids into Texas until 1875, when a group of 70 warriors, including 26 Kiowa, were sent to

Florida as prisoners of war.

In 1877, a measles epidemic killed many Kiowa and Kiowa Apache, and in 1879 the buffalo disappeared from the Plains. The last Sun Dance of the Kiowa was held in 1887, and in 1890-91, they were briefly caught up in the Ghost Dance movement. Measles struck again in 1895 and 1902. In 1901, the reservation of the Kiowa, Kiowa Apache and Comanche was allotted in severalty, 160 acres to each individual, and the remaining lands opened to the highest bidders.

By the 1970s, most of the 3,500 Kiowa still lived in Oklahoma, in and around Anadarko, Fort Cobb, Mountain View and Carnegie. The Kiowa language was still spoken although not the old ceremonial dialect. The Gourd Dancers and Blackfeet societies had been revived, and traditional dances and ceremonies were being performed. The Kiowa counted among their number several well-known artists and a Pulitzer Prize winner, N. Scott Momaday.

BIBLIOGRAPHY: Marriott, Alice. *Kiowa Years*. New York: The Macmillan Co., 1968; Mayhall, Mildred P., *The Kiowas*. Norman: University of Oklahoma Press, 1962.

KIOWA APACHE: a southern Plains people of the Athapascan linguistic family who originated in the mountains of western Montana, near the headwaters of the Missouri and Yellowstone rivers. Along with the Kiowa, they migrated southeast, arriving at the Arkansas and Red rivers by the early 19th century, numbering several hundred at that time. In the late 1970s, there were about 600 Kiowa Apache, mostly located in southwestern Oklahoma.

The Kiowa Apache, while belonging to the same language family as the Apache tribes, were never connected with them politically. From early times, they were an integral part of the Kiowa, and shared with them a common culture and history, although they spoke a different language. The Kiowa Apache were called Gattacka by the Pawnee and the French, but they referred to themselves as Nadi'ish-dena, meaning "our people." Their language was still spoken in the 1970s. The Kiowa Apache were one of the seven divisions, or bands, of the Kiowa, and had their own chief and war chief. Each of the bands was fairly autonomous, but usually camped together in summer to hunt buffalo and celebrate the Sun Dance. There was a limited amount of intermarriage between the Kiowa Apache and the other Kiowa bands, with the couple usually living with or near the woman's family. There was some polygamy, with men sometimes marrying sisters or their brother's widow. As with the Kiowa, there were a number of secret, religious, social and dancing societies for both men and women. Boys and girls were all members of the Rabbits dance group.

Pacer's son, a Kiowa Apache: photograph by Soule, (1868-74).

The Kiowa Apache, like the Kiowa, obtained horses by the early 18th century and became great buffalo hunters, horsemen and warriors of the Plains. Their whole economy revolved around the buffalo, which provided food, shelter and clothing. Men killed the buffalo in highly organized hunts. The women butchered, dried and stored the meat and dressed the hides, from which they made tipis and clothing. Wild foods were gathered to supplement the diet, and corn was obtained from the Wichita and Pueblo peoples.

The Kiowa Apache probably joined the Kiowa while they were both still living in Montana. In the late 17th century, they began migrating southeast, settling near the Crow, with whom they formed an alliance. By the early 18th century, they had acquired horses and moved into the Black Hills region. In the early 19th century, the Kiowa and Kiowa Apache were pushed southward by the Cheyenne and Dakota to eventually occupy an area which included western Kansas, eastern Colorado, western Oklahoma and adjoining areas of Texas and New Mexico. Their subsequent history pretty much parallels that of the Kiowa. (See *Kiowa.*)

In the late 1970s, there were about 600 Kiowa Apache living in southwestern Oklahoma, mostly near the towns of Apache and Fort Cobb.

BIBLIOGRAPHY: Mayhall, Mildred P. *The Kiowas.* Norman: University of Oklahoma Press, 1962; Wright, Muriel H. *A Guide to the Indian Tribes of Oklahoma.* Norman; University of Oklahoma Press, 1951.

KLALLAM: a Northwest Coast tribe located along the southern side of the Strait of Juan de Fuca, between the mouth of the Hoko River and Port Discovery Bay, in the late 18th century, numbering about 2,000 at that time. In the late 1970s, about 850 Klallam descendants lived on two reservations in Washington, and others were scattered around the Puget Sound area. A small group was also located on southern Vancouver Island, British Columbia.

They spoke a language of the Coast division of the Salishan language family, closely related to that of the Songish. The Klallam called themselves Nuxsklaiyem, meaning "strong people." They had numerous villages, each led by a chief, who attained his position by virtue of wealth and often inheritance. Chiefs were expected to give feasts and potlatches and arbitrate disputes.

Socially, the Klallam were organized into upper and lower classes. The upper class, consisting of chiefs and their relatives, usually married outside the village and often outside the tribe in order to marry within their class. The Klallam also had slaves, obtained through warfare and trade.

Religion centered around spirits, sought by fasting and praying in secluded places. There were a number of different types of guardian spirits, each with a special type of power. Shamans had powerful guardian spirits which enabled them to cure the sick, find lost objects, exorcise ghosts and recover lost souls.

The most important celebrations were potlatches, by which chiefs or wealthy persons enhanced their prestige by giving away large quantities of material goods. Potlatches were usually given to celebrate marriages, name-giving and girls' puberty rites, and to honor the dead. Klallam burial customs included scaffold, canoe, tree and ground burial. The house of the deceased was usually deserted for a few months, and mourners cut their hair. Widows often married their husband's brother.

The Klallam built cedar plank houses, with both gabled and single-pitched roofs, including a large community potlatch house. Sleeping benches lined the interior walls, with storage areas underneath. Both small single-family and large multi-family houses were used, the latter having extra fireplaces. Temporary rush mat shelters were used while traveling or hunting.

Salmon was the staple food. It was dried, along with clams, for winter use. Humpback and silver salmon, herring, smelt, cod, flounder, eulachon (candlefish), halibut and steelhead trout were caught with weirs, traps, gill nets, rakes and spears. The Klallam, whose favorite fishing ground was the Hood Canal, migrated seasonally with the various runs of fish in different areas. Some whale and seal hunting was done, and fish eggs and shellfish were gathered. Women dug camas and fern roots and collected huckleberries, blackberries, hazelnuts and acorns.

The Klallam built small narrow cedar log canoes for use on rivers and bought large ocean-going canoes from the Makah. Dishes, including 20-foot long serving dishes used at feasts, were carved of maple or alder. They made water buckets of cedar, clamshell spoons and watertight baskets of cedar twigs or roots. Clothing included shredded cedar bark capes and skirts, skin shirts for hunters, and robes of beaver or sea otter skin. Blankets were woven of dog hair or mountain goat mixed with duck down.

The Klallam had a reputation as fierce warriors, their usual enemies being the Snohomish and Dwamish. They stockaded some of their villages and used double-thickness elkskin shirts for armor. In addition to warfare, there was also a good deal of trade, intermarriage and pot-latching with neighboring tribes.

In 1850, some Klallam settled on the Lummi Reservation, and after 1855, others went to the Puyallup Reservation. A small number also moved to the southern end of Vancouver Island around Beecher Bay. Other Klallam, assigned to the Skokomish Reservation in 1855, declined to go and settled instead near Port Angeles and on the Port Gamble Peninsula. These lands were purchased in 1934 and established as reservations in 1968. In the late 1970s, there were more than 500 Klallam on or near the 372-acre Lower Elwha Reservation and about 350 on or near the 1,300-acre Port Gamble Reservation. An unknown number of Klallam descendants were mixed with other tribes on the Lummi and Puyallup reservations.

BIBLIOGRAPHY: Gunther, Erna. "Klallam Ethnography." *University of Washington Publications in Anthropology*. vol. 1, no. 5, 1927.

KLAMATH: a small tribe located in south central Oregon and northern California, along Upper Klamath Lake, Klamath Marsh, and the Williamson and Sprague rivers, in the early 19th century, when they numbered about 1,200. In the late 1970s, there were about 2,000 Klamath descendants, mostly living in Oregon.

The Klamath, with the closely-related Modoc, spoke a dialect of the Lutuami language of the Penutian linguistic family. The origin of their tribal name is unsure, but they called themselves Maklak, or "men."

The Klamath were divided into about seven autonomous tribelets, with a common dialect and culture. There were local chiefs, but, in aboriginal times, shamans were usually more important. Chiefs usually attained their positions through wealth or through skill at leading war parties.

Shamans acquired great spriritual power through fasting, prayer and visions. Either men or women could be shamans, although the majority, particularly the more powerful ones, were men. The Klamath believed in a wide range of spirits, associated with birds, animals and those dwelling in particular places. At puberty and other important times in their lives, individuals would seek special powers from the spirits by going to lonely mountain tops to fast and pray or by diving in lonely mountain pools.

Klamath marriage was formalized by a series of gift exchanges between the two families. A Klamath man occasionally married sisters or his brother's widow. When a Klamath died, his body was wrapped in tule mats and, five days later, taken by canoe to be burned along with his personal property. The house of the deceased was also burned, and his relatives retired to a sweat lodge for several days to be purified.

Klamath multifamily winter dwellings were earth-covered lodges with a heavy wooden framework, while mat-covered dwellings served for summer use or while on food gathering trips. Each village had several winter and summer sweatlodges, of similar construction.

In the spring, most of the Klamath left their permanent winter villages for favorite fishing spots. They fished from dugout canoes and stream bank, using a wide variety of nets and occasionally traps and spears. Fish was their primary food. In summer they moved to meadow areas to gather chokecherries, plums, huckleberries, currants, serviceberries, and a variety of roots. While the women gathered plant food, the men hunted mule deer, antelope and small game. They made bows of juniper or yew and arrowheads of obsidian. From mid-August to late September, they camped near Klamath Marsh to harvest *wokas* or waterlily seeds that were abundant but tedious to process. Several bushels of pods yielded only a few pounds of seeds to be ground into flour. Various foods were dried and stored in communal pits for the long snowy winters.

The Klamath made, usually by twining, a variety of baskets and basketry caps, frequently worn by the women. Both men and women

Wokas, or water-lily seeds, harvested by the Klamath in dugout canoes propelled by long poles: photographed in about 1902.

originally wore fringed aprons of fiber or buckskin. In the mid-19th century, clothing styles of the Plains Indians were adopted. The Klamath practiced frontal head flattening and ear and nose piercing.

The Klamath, along with the Modoc, had a long history of warfare with the neighboring Achomawi, Shasta and Kalapuya. By the 1840s, they were heavily involved in raiding for slaves and plunder, which they exchanged, for horses with the Columbia River tribes to the north. In the 1850s, wagon trains on the Oregon trail brought disease to the Klamath and Modoc territory and frightened away the game.

In 1864, the Klamath and Modoc signed a treaty with the United States, relinquishing their lands in exchange for a reservation on Upper Klamath Lake, on former Klamath land. In 1870, some of the Modoc, feeling unwelcome, left for their former homes, and subsequently became involved in the Modoc war of 1872-73, in which the Klamath took no part.

In 1956, the Klamath Reservation was terminated. In 1961 and 1974, the lands were sold, and the proceeds were divided among the Klamath and Modoc tribal members. In the late 1970s, there were about 2,000 Klamath, mostly living in Oregon.

BIBLIOGRAPHY: Spier, Leslie. "Klamath Ethnography." *University of California Publications in American Archaeology and Ethnology.* vol. 30, 1930; Stern, Theodore. *The Klamath Tribe.* Seattle: University of Washington Press, 1965.

Smithsonian Institution National Anthropological Archives

Mrs. Shachelford, a Klikitat Indian, pictured sitting on a rock, together with baskets.

KLIKITAT: a Plateau tribe occupying the headwaters of the Cowlitz, Lewis, White Salmon and Klickitat rivers in central Washington in the late 19th century, numbering about 700 at that time. In the 1970s, they were mixed with Yakima and other Indians among the 9,000 population on the Yakima Reservation in Washington.

The Klikitat spoke a language of the Sahaptian division of the Penutian language family, similar to that of the Yakima. They called themselves Qwulh-hwai-pum, or "prairie people." Klikitat is derived from a Chinook term meaning "beyond," referring to their location beyond the Cascade Mountains.

The Klikitat were grouped into nomadic bands, each led by a chief. Their culture and economy was similar to that of the Yakima (*q.v.*), relying on hunting, gathering and especially fishing. Salmon and camas bulbs were the principal foods, supplemented by other game, fish, roots and berries. They were also active traders, acting as intermediaries between the coast tribes and those east of the Cascades.

The Klikitat probably originated south of the Columbia River, migrating northward during the pre-historical period. They were met by Lewis and Clark in 1805 on the Yakima and Klickitat rivers. From 1820 to 1830, they expanded south of the Columbia, but were later forced back across the river by the Umpqua. By 1855, pressure from settlers forced the Klikitat to cede their lands under the treaty which established the Yakima Reservation. Subsequent to this time, they intermingled with the Yakima to the extent that by the 1970s, they were no longer distinct as a tribe.

KOROA: *See* TUNICA.

KOYUKON: an Alaskan Athapascan people occupying the valley of the Yukon River between the Anvik and Tanana Rivers, and the Koyukuk and Innoko rivers, numbering about 1,500 in the mid-18th century. They were also called the Koyukhotana, meaning "people of the Koyukuk River." They spoke a language of the northern division of the Athapascan language family, and were culturally related to their Athapascan neighbors, the Ingalik, Tanana and Nebesna, or Upper Tanana. Some authors group all these peoples under the one common term, Tena. (For information on Koyukon culture, see *Ingalik*).

Alaskan Athapascans originated in what is now Canada and were probably driven into Alaska by the Cree. They made contact with European traders and miners in the 19th century, and when mining was at its peak in the area from 1890 to 1910, much traditional culture was lost. In the 1970s, probably several hundred Koyukon lived in a number of villages in their traditional area. They, together with other Athapascans, were organized in Doyon, Inc., to qualify for benefits of the Alaskan Native Claims Settlement Act (1971).

KUTCHIN: a group of Athapascan tribes living on the Yukon River and its tributaries in Alaska, and the Mackenzie and Peel rivers in Canada, with a total population of about 1,300 in the mid-19th century. In the 1970s, there were perhaps 1,000 Kutchin living in Alaska and

Kutchin winter lodges—an illustration from Sir John Richardson's *Arctic Searching Expedition: A Journal of a Boat Voyage Through Rupert's Land and the Arctic Sea,* **(1851): from an original drawing made by A.H. Murray in about 1848.**

about 1,100 on numerous reserves in the Yukon Territory, Canada.

The various tribes spoke dialects of the Kutchin division of the northern Athapascan language family. In their own language, Kutchin meant "those who dwell." Each of the various tribes was known by a place name plus the suffix "kutchin." The tribes generally accepted as Kutchin groups include the Kutcha-kutchin (Yukon Flats), Nakotcho-kutchin (Mackenzie Flats), Natsit-kutchin (Chandalor River), Tatlit-kutchin (Peel River), Tennuth-kutchin (Birch Creek), Tukkuth-kutchin (Upper Porcupine River), Tranjik-kutchin (Black River) and Vunta-kutchin (Crow River). Other tribes considered by some authors to be Kutchin tribes include the Tanana (Tenan-kutchin), Han (Han-kutchin), Tutchone (Tutchone-kutchin) and the Dihai-kutchin. Although probably not actually Kutchin tribes, these groups were culturally very similar to the Kutchin.

The Kutchin were nomadic hunting, fishing and gathering tribes, divided into three clans, Tchit-che-at, Tange-rat-sey and Natsah-i. Each tribe had a chief, who usually had limited authority. Chiefs were either hereditary or chosen for wealth or wisdom, depending on the tribe. Marriage was usually outside the clan and often outside the tribe, with the children belonging to the tribe of the mother. When a son was born, the father received a new name formed by adding the suffix "tee" to his son's name. They had some slaves.

The Kutchin believed that all things had life and that various spirits inhabited the lakes, woods, etc. Shamans, who were often more powerful than chiefs, had supernatural powers enabling them to foretell the future, control the weather and cure the sick. Ceremonial feasts were held to celebrate such occasions as the birth of a child and girls' attainment of puberty. In honor of their deceased, the Crow River tribe gave potlatches similar to those of the Northwest Coast tribes. The dead were either cremated or placed in coffins on platforms, together with various implements belonging to the deceased.

For most of the year, the Kutchin lived mainly in portable elliptical caribou skin tents laid over a pole frame, about twelve feet long and six feet high. From fall through mid-winter, they lived in more permanent semi-subterranean houses of blocks of moss on a wood frame, with gabled roof. Various other types of dwellings were in use, including birchbark tents used in the Yukon Flats in place of caribou skin.

The Kutchin subsisted mostly by hunting and fishing, with caribou the staple along the Mackenzie and Peel rivers and moose and salmon the staples along the Yukon River. Moose and caribou were taken with snares and by stalking with bow and arrow. Salmon, pike and whitefish were caught with hook-and-line, traps and babiche nets. Various berries, rhubarb, and a parsnip-like root were gathered to supplement the basically meat diet.

The Kutchin traveled by birchbark or moose skin canoes, wood sleds, and snowshoes of babiche nets. Their bows were laminated birch and willow strips, tied together with willow shoots. They had containers, many waterproof, of bent wood, birchbark and woven tamarack roots decorated with porcupine quills. Clothing was usually of caribou skin, including shirts, trousers, robes, mittens and caps, decorated with leather tassels and quillwork.

The Kutchin were isolated from the outside world until the Scottish explorer Alexander Mackenzie visited them in 1789. Various other explorers and traders followed, and in 1810 a trading post was established at Fort Good Hope on the Lower Mackenzie. Later, posts were established at Fort McPherson (1839) on the Peel River and at Fort Yukon (1847). In these years of expanded trade, trapping for furs became more important. In the late 19th century, Catholic and Protestant missions were established in the area. The 20th century brought increased contact with the outside world, but with much less impact than on other more accessible tribes.

In the 1970s, about 1,100 Kutchin lived in Canada in six bands: Aishihik, Carmacks, Champagnc, Dawson, Kluane, Mayo and Selkirk. Probably about the same number lived in Alaska in various villages. Some tribes were less nomadic than formerly and had small wood-frame houses typical of the area. The Kutchin, however, were still basically reliant upon the traditional pursuits of hunting, fishing and trapping.

BIBLIOGRAPHY: Osgood, Cornelius. "Contributions to the Ethnology of the Kutchin." *Yale University Publications in Anthropology.* no. 14, 1936.

KUTENAI: a Plateau tribe living in Washington, Idaho and British Columbia, on the Kootenay and Columbia rivers and Arrow Lake, numbering about 1,200 in the late 18th century. They were known for their melodic Kutenaian language, which comprised its own language family, apparently unrelated to that of surrounding tribes. They called themselves San'ka. In the 1970s, about 50 Kutenai lived on the Kootenai Reservation in Idaho; probably several hundred lived, mixed with various Salish tribes, on the Flathead Reservation in Montana, and about 500 lived on various reserves in British Columbia.

The nomadic Kutenai were geographically divided into Upper and Lower divisions and further subdivided into eight autonomous bands. Bands were led by non-hereditary chiefs and assistant chiefs, selected for wisdom and leadership qualities. The Upper division had a war chief as the most powerful chief, followed by a general chief, guide or economic chief, and a hunting chief; whereas the Lower division had a band chief as the most important, followed by a war chief, fish chief, deer chief and duck chief.

Shamans, both male and female, provided important religious and political leadership; in fact a council of shamans chose the chief of the Upper division. With powers obtained from spirits in dreams, they foretold the future and cured illness, through songs, rattles and chants. The Kutenai believed that all things of nature had spirits, presided over by a Master Spirit, or Old Man.

Guardian spirits, secured in youth on vision quests were central to the Kutenai religion and important for success in life. A number of festivals centered on asking help from the various spirits, such as the Midwinter Festival, the Sun Dance and the War Dance. Important participants in the festivals were the three religious societies, the Crazy Dogs, Crazy Owls and Shaman's Society.

The dead were dressed in robes, sewed in blankets and buried, after temporary placement on a platform. The family of the deceased moved his tipi and often gave away his possessions, and his name was never spoken again.

The principal Upper Kutenai dwellings were tipis, either of skins, grass mats, or tule mats. They also built semisubterranean longhouses, probably for winter dwellings or gatherings, of mats on a pole frame, housing 40-50 people. The Lower Kutenai, were less nomadic, made

Mrs. Koostatah,
wife of a Kutenai
chief, in a quilled
costume, holding
a quilled and
beaded legging
she made.

Bureau of Indian Affairs

summer tipis and winter longhouses of Indian hemp on pole frames.

The Kutenai had no agriculture, except for a small amount of tobacco. The Upper Kutenai were primarily buffalo hunters, making several trips to the Plains each year for that purpose, using bow and arrow or driving them over cliffs. The Lower Kutenai were primarily fishermen, catching trout, salmon and sturgeon with weirs, traps and spears. Both Upper and Lower Kutenai also hunted other game such as moose, caribou, elk, birds and rabbits, and supplemented their diet with gathered roots and berries, particularly bitterroot. Fish, game and gathered foods were all dried for winter use. Means of transportation included canoes of pine and other bark, snowshoes and, in the case of the Upper division, horses.

For hunting and warfare, they had cherry and cedar bows, stone knives, clubs with antler points embedded in them, spears and slingshots. Crafts included carved wooden bowls, clay pots, stone pipes, waterproof twined baskets of cedar and cherry roots and birchbark baskets. They were also proficient in leatherwork, making excellent moccasins, sandals, coats and gloves. Clothing was of the Plains type—skin breechclout, moccasins, shirt and leggings for men and skin dress and moccasins for women. Clothing was highly decorated with feathers, quills, paint, squirrel tails, rabbit fur and later, beadwork.

The Kutenai apparently once lived east of the Rocky Mountains, occupying land as far east as MacLeod, Alberta, before being pushed west by the Blackfoot to settle in northern Idaho, Washington and British Columbia. Around 1808, they were visited by David Thompson of the Northwest Company, and a trading post was established in their territory. Later, Hudson's Bay Company came to the area, bringing Christianized Iroquois and, later, missionaries to live among the Kutenai. Good relations with the whites continued, as the Kutenai avoided taking part in Chief Joseph's (Nez Perce) War in 1877. Disease and alcohol, however, greatly reduced their population during this time. In 1895, the Kootenai Reservation was established in northern Idaho and about 100 Kutenai moved to the Flathead Reservation in Montana.

In the 1970s, about 50 Kutenai lived on or near the 2,700-acre reservation in Idaho, and probably several hundred lived among the 3,500 population of the Flathead Reservation in Montana. Another 500 lived on various reserves in British Columbia, divided among four bands: Columbia Lake, Lower Kootenai, Saint Mary's and Tobacco Plains. Essentially acculturated and no longer nomadic, they lived in wood frame houses similar to their non-Indian neighbors. They relied mostly on wage labor for subsistence, although hunting, fishing and gathering were still important in some areas.

BIBLIOGRAPHY: Turney-High, Harry H. "Ethnography of the Kutenai." *Memoirs of the American Anthropological Association.* no. 56, 1941.

KWAKIUTL: a group of Northwest Coast tribes in British Columbia known for their complex social structure. They occupied northern Vancouver Island and the mainland coast from Douglas Channel to Bute Inlet, numbering about 5,000-6,000 in 1750. In the 1970s, about 3,800 Kwakiutl lived on numerous reserves in British Columbia.

The Kwakiutl, together with the Nootka tribes, comprised the Wakashan language family. Their name, Kwakiutl, probably meant "beach on the other side of the water." They were geographically divided into three linguistic divisions, Haisla, Heiltzuk and Southern Kwakiutl (Kwakiutl proper).

They were subdivided into a number of autonomous villages, each led by an hereditary chief. The Kwakiutl had a complex social organization, with four classes: chiefs, nobles, commoners and slaves. The basic unit was the extended family, or *numaym,* with descent usually in the male line (patrilineal), but occasionally matrilineal. Some of the northern tribes, i.e. the Haisla division, however, developed systems of matrilineal phratries similar to those of their northern neighbors, the Tsimshian.

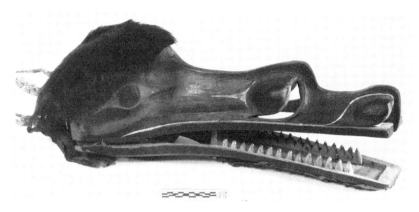

A Kwakiutl mask. Smithsonian Institution

Each *numaym* had certain ranks and privileges, which were usually passed from father to son, such as property, crests, dances, masks and guardian spirits.

Their religion centered around guardian spirits, obtained through prayer or fasting. Associated with various spirits were a number of secret societies, such as the Cannibal, Grizzly Bear, Crazy Man and Warrior societies, each of which performed special dances and ceremonies. The principal ceremonies were traditional Northwest Coast potlatches, which reached their most elaborate development among the Kwakiutl. These consisted of ceremonial display and distribution of family or personal wealth to obtain status or validate certain inherited rights or privileges of the giver of the potlatch. Potlatches were given for numerous occasions: designation of heirs, name-giving, attainment of puberty, marriage, birth, death and initiation of members into secret societies. Potlatches were often given on credit, i.e. by borrowing blankets (the medium of exchange) from a friend or relative, often at 100 percent interest.

Mortuary customs among the southern Kwakiutl included burial in trees, caves or, in the case of noted chiefs, canoes; whereas the northern Kwakiutl cremated their dead.

Kwakiutl villages consisted of rows of cedar beam and plank houses facing the sea. The houses were large, and each held several families, all of one *numaym*. Each village also had one or more ceremonial houses of similar construction. The Kwakiutl traveled between villages and fishing grounds in large carved and painted cedar dugout canoes, often using skin sails.

The Kwakiutl economy relied primarily on salmon, which were caught with weirs, traps, harpoons, and nets dragged between two canoes. Codfish and halibut were caught with hook-and-line, and herring and eulachon (candlefish) were taken with long rakes. Seals and sea lion were speared with harpoons, which were either tied to sealskin floats or to the stern of a canoe. Some elk and deer were hunted with bow and arrow in winter. Gathered foods included sea grass, berries and roots as well as shellfish, sea urchins and cuttlefish.

As with other Northwest Coast tribes, the primary Kwakiutl craft was woodworking. Fine totem poles and ceremonial masks, as well as everyday items such as canoes, dishes and paddles were ornately carved. They also made bent cedar boxes, horn spoons, stone mortars and pestles, baskets of wicker and cedar bark, and cedar bark and rush mats for bedding, seats and boxcovers. Clothing for the Kwakiutl included robes made of tanned skins or woven from mountain goat wool or dog hair. Women also wore a cedar bark skirt and men a shirt, probably of skins. In rainy weather, the women wore large waterproof basketry caps and a waterproof cedar bark cape or poncho. Ear and nose ornaments of bone or abalone shell were worn by all.

According to tradition, the Kwakiutl have been in the same area for a long time, warring with the other coast tribes to the north and south. Around 1775, they were visited by the explorers Bodega and Maurelle. Thereafter, many English and American traders came to trade steel adzes, knives and guns for furs, especially that of the sea otter. In the 19th century, missions were established, but many Kwakiutl retained their traditional religion. Acculturation was accelerated by the outlawing of the potlatch by the Canadian government in the early 20th century. White pressure and diseases took their toll, and by 1904, the Kwakiutl population was reduced to about 2,200.

By the 1970s, there were about 3,800 Kwakiutl, divided into 16 bands in British Columbia: Bellabella, Cape Mudge, Campbell River, Gilford Island, Kitamaat, Kwawkewlth, Kwawwaineuk, Kwiakah, Mamalillikulla, Nimpkish, Nuwitti, Oweekano, Quatsino, Tanakteuk, Tsawataineuk and Turnour Island. The total land area of their reserves was about 25,000 acres. They were somewhat acculturated, but retained many Kwakiutl traditions. They lived mainly in villages similar to those of non-Indians of the area, although still migrating freely between the villages as in former times. Fishing and hunting, both individual and commercial, were still mainstays of the economy. Potlatches, especially those commemorating the dead, were still given, and the Kwakiutl language was spoken.

BIBLIOGRAPHY: Boas, Franz. *Kwakiutl Ethnography.* Chicago: University of Chicago Press, 1960; Boas, Franz. "The Kwakiutl of Vancouver Island." *Memoir of the American Museum of Natural History.* vol. 5. 1909; Rohner, Ronald P. and Rohner, Evelynn C. "The Kwakiutl Indians of British Columbia." *Native North American Cultures: Four Cases.* Holt, Reinhart and Winston, 1966.

LABRADOR INUIT: the southernmost Inuit (Eskimo) group, located along the Labrador-Ungava coast, numbering about 3,000 in the mid-18th century. In the late 1970s, there were more than 800 Labrador Inuit, located in the same area. They spoke a dialect of the Inuit (Eskimo) language which was spoken, with minor variation, from Alaska to Greenland. The name "Eskimo" was derived from an Abnaki Indian term meaning "raw meat eaters," whereas the term Inuit, meaning "people," was their own name for themselves.

The Labrador Inuit were geographically divided into local groups, who were called by the name of the particular area in which they lived plus the suffix *miut.* Local groups were not formally organized, and individuals or families left or joined at will. The groups were usually broken into scattered settlements, with the members coming together in summer just before the annual caribou hunt, or for community feasting whenever a whale was stranded or washed up on their shore.

There was little organization or leadership, other than in such economic activities as whaling, which required at least 12 men to work together, usually under the leadership of the harpooner or the boat owner. The lack of leadership led to frequent conflicts, which were usually resolved by a council of all the men in the settlement. Marriage was both within and outside the local group. Polygamy usually involved a man marrying two related women and there were occasional incidents of polyandry as well.

Religious leadership was provided by *angakok,* or shamans, of both sexes, who called upon their *tuurngaq,* or guardian spirits, to help them

Smithsonian Institution National Anthropological Archives

Deserted snow houses of the Labrador Inuit: photographed in 1882-84.

Smithsonian Institution National Anthropological Archives

Three Labrador Inuit girls, pictured in 1882-84.

cure the sick, assure successful hunting or control the weather. Labrador Inuit mythology included the typical Inuit myth in which Sedna, a woman at the bottom of the sea, controlled all marine life. According to another tradition, a male deity presided over sea animals, and a female deity presided over land animals. To assure successful hunting, it was necessary to propitiate these deities by ceremonies and the observance of taboos. They buried their dead in caribou clothing in a box-like grave of stones. Personal effects of the deceased were broken and placed on the grave.

The Labrador Inuit built semisubterranean winter dwellings, housing up to 20 people, of turf and stone with whale bone and wood supports. Skin partitions separated the various families. Temporary snow houses were also occasionally used, consisting of two or three domed houses, entered by one long, low entry way. From late April to mid-October, sealskin tents were used, with usually two families to a tent.

In autumn, the Labrador Inuit moved inland to hunt the migrating caribou, either with bow and arrow or from kayaks using lances. By November, they usually returned to the coast to hunt migrating whales in open boats called *umiaks*, using large harpoons. Seals were hunted on the sea at their breathing holes in winter, and from kayaks in spring and summer. Salmon, cod and arctic char were taken with hook and spear. Walrus, beluga, polar bear and black bear were also hunted at times.

Wooden dog sleds were used for winter transportation. Other material culture included coiled basketry, whalebone cups, wooden spoons, seal-skin containers, stone kettles and lamps, as well as carved ivory animal figures. Warm lightweight caribou skins were used for winter clothing, sealskin was used for waterproof boots and mittens, and waterproof rain wear was made from gut-skin.

The Labrador Inuit probably entered the Labrador region in the last half of the 16th century. In the late 17th century, they were encountered by traders, with whom they had generally hostile relations. In the 18th century, they began traveling south by boat in the summer to trade with the French, and later the British. After 1764, Moravian missions were established in the area, becoming centers around which the Inuit settled. In this period, diseases and the killing off of whales and other game by white hunters, led to population decline. The Inuit had acquired firearms by 1787, and were engaged in fox trapping for the fur trade by the early 19th century. By 1916, the caribou had been driven to near-extinction, but they started becoming more plentiful again after the 1940s.

In the late 1970s, there were more than 800 Labrador Inuit, living mainly in about six communities in their original area. Common activities were codfishing, wage labor and traditional subsistence hunting.

BIBLIOGRAPHY: Hawkes, E.W. "The Labrador Eskimo." *Canada Department of Mines Memoir*. no. 91, 1916; Taylor, J. Garth. "Labrador Eskimo Settlements of the Early Contact Period." *National Museums of Canada Publications in Ethnology*. no. 9, 1974.

LAGUNA: a Keresan tribe and pueblo located about 45 miles west of Albuquerque, New Mexico, on the south bank of the San Jose River. In 1707, the main pueblo of Laguna had a population of about 330, and four outlying villages had a total population of about 150. In the late 1970s, the old pueblo of Laguna was used largely as a ceremonial center, and a population of several thousand was scattered among seven or eight small farming villages.

The Laguna people, together with their close cultural relatives, the Acoma, spoke a language of the western division of the Keresan family. The eastern Keresan division included Santo Domingo, Santa Ana, San Felipe, Cochiti and Zia. The name Laguna, Spanish for "lake," was inspired by a large pond located west of the pueblo. The people referred to their pueblo as Kawaiku.

Laguna was divided into about 19 clans, with each person inheriting the clan of his mother and marriage forbidden inside the clan. All young men of the pueblo were initiated into the *katcina* (kachina) cult, and took part in masked dances in which they impersonated the rain gods who

Women of Laguna, New Mexico, with decorated pottery, (1902).

brought rain. There were also numerous secret societies, including Clown, Warrior, Hunter and Medicine societies. The Medicine societies performed ceremonies and dances to cure the sick, bring good crops, control the weather and insure the health and well-being of the pueblo.

The heads of the various societies, the *cheani*, were in charge of selecting the cacique, or religious leader of the pueblo. The cacique, appointed for life, performed no other labor, but prayed, fasted and controlled the religious and ceremonial life of the pueblo. He was assisted by two war chiefs. The secular officials of the pueblo, whose offices dated from Spanish times, were elected by the people and included the governor, two assistants and other officers. The secular officials dealt with traders and others outside the pueblo.

When a Laguna Indian died, his face was painted many colors, and he was buried, along with bowls of food and water, with his head to the east. On the third day, a shaman performed a ceremony using feathered prayer sticks, sending the spirit of the deceased to the land of the dead.

According to Laguna tradition, the tribe migrated from somewhere to the north, possibly Mesa Verde, having been forced south by drought conditions. They settled on the shore of the lake, and in the late 17th century were joined by emigrants from Acoma, Zuñi, and the eastern Keresan pueblos.

In the 18th century, Laguna came into conflict with Mexican slavers and Navajo, Apache and Ute raiders. Laguna was later brought into increasing contact with the outside world by its location on the railroad line. In the 19th century, a number of whites married into the pueblo, introducing Protestantism. A split eventually developed in the community, and the conservative faction took their religious paraphernalia and left, some to found the colony of Oraibi at Isleta pueblo and others to join Mesita, an eastern village of Laguna.

In the late 1970s, the Laguna occupied some 450,000 acres of land. The population of several thousand lived in the villages of Casa Blanca, Encinal, Paraje, Mesita, Paguate, Seama and the old pueblo of Laguna. They were one of the largest and most acculturated of the pueblo groups. Money from uranium leases was being invested in civil projects. The traditional culture and language remained important, however, with ceremonies celebrated in the old pueblo and craftsmen producing fine embroidery, pottery and yucca basketry.

BIBLIOGRAPHY: Eggan, Fred. *Social Organization of the Western Pueblos.* Chicago: The University of Chicago Press, 1950; Ellis, Florence H. *Pueblo Indians.* vol. II, New York: Garland Publishing, Inc., 1974.

LAKE: a Salish tribe living, in the late 18th century, in Washington on the Columbia River, from Kettle Falls to the Canadian border, and in British Columbia, in the valley of the Kettle and Kutenai rivers and on the shores of the Arrow Lakes, numbering between 500 and 2,000 at that time. In the 1970s, there were about 260 Lake Indians living on or near the Colville Reservation in northeastern Washington.

The Lake, who were also called the Senijextee, derived their common name from the fact that they lived on the Arrow Lakes. They belonged to the Okanagon group of the Interior division of the Salishan language family. Culturally and historically, they were closely related to the other members of the Okanagon group, which also included the Okanagon, Colville and Sanpoil (*q.q.v.*)

The Lake Indians were apparently a long time in their traditional area. Traditional enemies were the Kutenai, with whom they had at least one great war at some time in prehistory. Initial contact with Europeans was with David Thompson in 1811, with minimal subsequent exposure to traders. In 1872, the Colville Reservation was established, to which a number of Lake were assigned.

In the 1970s, the Lake were extinct as a tribe in Canada, probably absorbed by the Okanagon and neighboring Thompson. There were about 260 Lake living on and around the 1,011,495-acre Colville Reservation in northeast Washington, mixed with the total reservation population of about 3,000 Indians of various tribes.

BIBLIOGRAPHY: Teit, James A. "The Salishan Tribes of the Western Plateau." *Bureau of American Ethnology, 45th Annual Report.* Washington: Smithsonian Institution, 1927-28.

LILLOOET: an interior Salishan tribe located in southwestern British Columbia in the late 18th century, numbering perhaps 4,000 at that time. In the late 1970s, there were about 2,500 Lillooet divided into about ten bands located on or near reserves in British Columbia.

The Lillooet spoke a Salishan language related to that of the neighboring Shuswap and Thompson. They had two main divisions, Upper and Lower, which were each subdivided into bands composed of one or more villages. In early times, each village was composed of a single clan and led by an hereditary clan chief. Other respected persons included war chiefs, hunting chiefs, orators, the wealthy and the generous.

Adolescent boys and girls spent long training periods of fasting, seclusion and physical endurance to prepare them for adulthood. Youths sought visions or dreams of guardian spirits who would give them special powers or talents. Special guardian spirits helped shamans cure the sick and recover lost souls.

Lillooet mythology included the trickster, Old Coyote, as well as such figures as Raven, Eagle, Beaver, Sun, Moon and Thunder. Among the important ceremonies were clan dances, at which carved wooden masks representing the clan ancestor (Wolf, Owl, Frog, Coyote, etc.) were displayed. Special events were commemorated by potlatches, at which the host distributed gifts to his guests as a measure of his prestige.

The Lillooet placed their dead in painted grave boxes or in graves lined with bark or mats. Carved wooden poles and images of the deceased were used to mark the graves.

The Lillooet had several types of house construction, including log and plank communal dwellings housing from four to eight families, semisubterranean circular earth lodges for winter, and bark or mat houses for summer. The earth lodges were constructed of cedar bark and a layer of earth on a wood frame. The clan totem was sometimes painted on the center post, or, in the case of the Lower Lillooet, carved on totem poles placed in front of the houses.

Salmon and other fish, caught with nets, spears, weirs and traps, were the most important food sources. Bear, mountain goat, bighorn sheep, caribou, black bear, beaver, marmot, raccoon, rabbit and squirrel were all hunted, using bows and arrows, traps, deadfalls, snares and hunting dogs. The women gathered roots and berries and dried the meat and fish for later use.

The Lillooet made carved wooden dishes and spoons, birchbark trays and baskets, bags of bark twine and mats of tule and rushes. They made clothing from cedar bark or skins, and wove robes from rabbit skin, goat wool or dog hair. Clothing was decorated with quillwork, and dentalium shells, facepaint and ear and nose ornaments were used for adornment. Both bark and cedar dugout canoes, as well as snowshoes were used for transportation.

The Lillooet engaged in extensive trade with their neighbors and the lower Fraser River tribes. They occasionally fought with the Thompson and other groups, using elkskin or rod armor in warfare. In the mid-19th century, they were hard hit by smallpox, followed by famine. In the late 1970s, the remaining bands included: Anderson Lake, Bridge River, Cayoose Creek, Douglas, Fountain, Lillooet, Mount Currie Pemberton, Samahquam, Seton Lake and Skookum Chuck.

BIBLIOGRAPHY: Teit, James Alexander. "The Lillooet Indians." *Memoir of the Museum of Natural History.* vol. 4, 1906.

LIPAN: an Apache tribe located in Texas in the early 19th century, numbering about 750 at that time. In the late 1970s, Lipan descendants were mixed with the Mescalero and Chiricahua on the Mescalero Reservation in southern New Mexico.

The Lipan spoke a language of the southern branch of the Athapascan language family. Linguistically, they were close to the Jicarilla, of whom they were probably an offshoot. Culturally, the Lipan differed from the Jicarilla by being less agricultural and more nomadic.

The Lipan were organized into two bands for such activities as buffalo hunting, but the main political and economic unit was the local group, composed of several extended families. These groups were led by chiefs, who acted mainly as advisors. Their position was based on demonstrated leadership ability and skill in hunting and warfare.

The main social unit was the extended family. Residence was matrilocal, with a newly-married couple living with the woman's family, although it was taboo for a man to talk to his mother-in-law. Important socio-religious ceremonies included puberty rites for girls. Shamans performed cures, through the use of supernatural powers, and conducted other ceremonies. Lipan mythology was extensive, including many tales about the trickster Coyote.

The Lipan lived mostly in buffalo skin tipis, although sometimes they used pole-frame wickiups covered with thatch or brush. A few families cultivated corn and pumpkins, but the Lipan relied mainly on hunting and gathering. The women collected palmetto, wild persimmon, pecans, yucca, agave, and other roots, seeds and nuts. Frequent moves were made, either by the local group or the extended family, to harvest various wild foods. Although the men hunted deer and small game, the communal autumn buffalo hunt was most important. The buffalo supplied food and shelter, as well as material for clothing, tools, utensils, containers, etc.

By the mid-17th century, the Lipan had acquired horses and had become expert buffalo hunters and raiders, controlling the high plains of eastern New Mexico, northern Texas and southern Kansas. They raided the Tewa pueblos and other peoples as far south as Mexico. By the early 1700s, the Caddoan tribes had acquired firearms from the French and by 1740, they had driven the Lipan south from the Red River.

At this time, the Lipan were also under constant attack by the Comanche, and therefore requested protection from their former enemy, the Spanish. The mission of San Saba was established in 1757, and was promptly destroyed by the Comanche. The Spanish and Lipan became allied in a continuing struggle against the Comanche, as the Lipan moved further south into the Davis Mountains and the Big Bend area of Texas.

In the 1830s and early 1840s, the Lipan were on good terms with the Texans, serving as guides, army scouts and trading partners. They were also valued as allies against the Comanche. But by the late 1840s, however, Texans had determined to rid their borders of all Indians, and adopted an extermination policy. Most of the Lipan were driven into Coahuila state, Mexico.

Between 1903 and 1905, about 35 Lipan were returned to the United States and placed on the Mescalero Reservation. In the late 1970s, the 2,400 population of the reservation included a mixture of Mescalero, Chiricahua, Lipan and other groups.

BIBLIOGRAPHY: Ray, Vern F. and Opler, Morris E. *Lipan and Mescalero Apache in Texas.* Garland Publishing, Inc., 1974.

LUISEÑO: a southern California group located along the coast, south of present-day Los Angeles, in the late 18th century, when they numbered perhaps 10,000. In the late 1970s, there remained about 1,800 Luiseño, living in California. The Luiseño language belongs to the Takic division of the Uto-Aztecan family, and was spoken by Indians associated with San Juan Capistrano mission and San Luis Rey mission, which was the origin of the name Luiseño. The name Juaneño had at times been applied by the members of the group associated with San Juan Capistrano mission.

The Luiseño were organized into tribelets, each occupying a village led by a hereditary chief. The chief was assisted in carrying out his social,

Luiseño basket and mortar.   Smithsonian Institution

economic and religious responsibilities by a council of advisors and shamans.

The Luiseño had a large number of ceremonies, including those connected with hunting, fertility, birth, name-giving, puberty, marriage, death, rain-making, peace, etc. Death ceremonies included burning an image of the deceased, purification of the relatives, feasting and gift-giving. In some ceremonies, they drank a vision-inducing concoction made from jimsonweed.

The Luiseño lived in autonomous villages along the coast or inland along streams. They built conical houses thatched with reeds, brush or bark. Each village also had a semisubterranean earth-covered sweat-house and an open-air enclosure used for ceremonies. Although the Luiseño lived mostly in sedentary villages, they made food gathering trips to other areas. Inland groups came to the coast to fish and collect shellfish, and, in autumn, all the groups settled for several weeks in mountain oak groves to gather acorns.

The staple food was acorns, which were ground into meal for mush and bread. A wide variety of seeds, nuts and berries were also gathered, including sunflower seeds, elderberries, thimbleberries and pine nuts. Controlled burning of certain areas served to increase the yield of seed-bearing plants and provided a method of hunting small game. Deer, rabbit, quail and ducks were hunted with bow and arrow, throwing sticks, traps and snares. Canoes were used in ocean fishing, and traps, nets and poisons were used to catch fish in mountain streams.

Luiseño craftwork included simple pottery and excellent coiled and twined basketry. They also made sand paintings for initiation rites of young boys into the Chingichngish cult. They wore pendants of mica, abalone shell and bear claws, and men wore nose and ear ornaments of cane or bone. Women wore cedar bark aprons, and both men and women were robes of deer, rabbit or otter skin in cold weather.

In the late 18th century, the missions of San Luis Rey and San Juan Capistrano were established by the Spanish. Many Luiseño were brought to the missions, where their culture was replaced or altered by Spanish culture. During this period, and during succeeding periods under the Mexicans and Americans, many died of disease, hardship and ill-treatment.

In the late 1970s, most Luiseño, who numbered about 1,000, lived on or near the reservations of Rincon, Pala, Pauma, Sobaba, Pechanga and La Jolla. The Luiseño language was still spoken, and language classes were popular with the young. Traditional ceremonies were still performed, such as those connected with curing, installing religious leaders, and mourning. Traditional foods, games, song and dances were also still popular.

BIBLIOGRAPHY: Sparkman, Philip Stedman. "The Culture of the Luiseño Indians." *University of California Publications in American Archaeology and Anthropology.* vol. 8, 1908.

LUMMI: a Pacific Northwest Coast tribe located on San Juan and other islands of Puget Sound and the adjacent mainland, numbering pehaps 1,000 in the late 18th century. In the late 1970s, there were about 2,500 Lummi mixed with other groups on the Lummi Reservation in northwestern Washington. The Lummi spoke a language of the Coast division of the Salishan language family.

They lived in semi-permanent winter villages composed of from 5 to 20 longhouses, each housing one or more extended families. Leadership of the houses and villages was based on wealth, family lineage and specialized knowledge and skills. There were three social classes: the nobles, commoners, and slaves, who were either captured in war or purchased. Things of value which could be inherited included ceremonial costumes, masks, rights to perform certain dances, fishing locations, manufactured goods and raw materials. Items of special value included dentalium shells, deer hooves and horn.

Central to Lummi religion was belief in guardian spirits who helped each person acquire special skills or good fortune. Shamans had special powers obtained from their spirits, enabling them to cause or cure sickness. Guardian spirits were obtained during adolescence, through quests involving fasting, hardship and diving in mountain streams where spirits dwelled. Girls underwent four or five day puberty rites, after which they were secluded until marriage. To obtain a bride, a boy's family gave gifts to the bride's family, which were then distributed among the friends of both families. Wealthy men sometimes practiced polygamy. Important ceremonies included First Salmon rites, masked spirit dances and potlatches, at which a host distributed accumulated property to his guests and displayed his wealth and inherited privileges. The giver could anticipate being invited to reciprocatory affairs.

When a person died, his body was dressed in festive clothing, taken from the house feet first and buried. Wealthy people were buried with grave goods in a canoe. The property of the deceased was given away, and relatives observed a four or five day fasting and mourning period.

Lummi winter houses were built of overlapping cedar planks and had a slanted or gabled roof. They were divided into family sections, with a cooking fire in each and benches along the outer walls for sleeping and storage. The house posts were painted and carved with animal and human figure designs. Huts used as steam baths were built near the water. In summer, the Lummi traveled in small groups among the islands, following the seasonal food cycle and living in temporary dwellings of woven cattail mats.

Bureau of Indian Affairs.

Lummi Indians of Washington state in their whaling canoe, during the 1910 annual canoe race.

United States Travel Service

A Lummi canoe race in progress in Puget Sound, near Bellingham, Washington.

Sockeye salmon, caught in nets from canoes, was the most important food source. Other fish included herring, codfish, dog salmon, silver salmon and humpback salmon, taken with traps, weirs, hooks, rakes, dip nets and spears. The fish were dried and stored for later use or trade. In May, camas bulbs were dug on certain islands and cooked in rock-lined pits. Ducks were caught in underwater nets, and deer were taken with nets, pits or bow and arrow. Beaver, otter, muskrat and bear were also occasionally trapped or hunted. Gathered foods included clams, crabs, bulbs and, reportedly, 25 kinds of berries and 16 varieties of roots.

The Lummi men manufactured 30-foot cedar dugout canoes, as well as wooden chests, buckets and carved ceremonial masks. Women wove cedar root baskets and goat wool blankets, and made fish nets and dresses of cedar bark. Men wore goathair blankets or buckskin shirts, with bearskin robes added in winter.

The Lummi traded and intermarried with neighboring tribes as far north as the Fraser River and as far south as the White River. They also engaged in warfare with their neighbors, taking heads and captives when they were victorious. Frequent attacks by Vancouver Island tribes led them to stockade some of their villages. They also dug pitfalls in front of the main entrances to their longhouses.

By 1827, a Hudson's Bay Company trading post had been established in the region, and by mid-century, settlers were entering the area. By 1849, smallpox and warfare had reduced the Lummi population, and they were assigned to a small reservation in their traditional territory. In 1886, the reservation was allotted to individuals, and by the 1950s, 40 percent of the allotted lands were no longer owned by tribal members.

In the late 1970s, there were perhaps 2,000 Lummi, of whom three-fourths lived on the 7,000-acre Lummi Reservation in Bellingham County, Washington. Less than ten still spoke the tribal language, but some traditional ceremonies and festivals were still celebrated, including the annual Stommish water festival. A highly successful aquaculture project, producing salmon, oysters and trout, was begun in the late 1960s.

BIBLIOGRAPHY: Stern, Bernhard J. *The Lummi Indians of Northwest Washington*. New York: Columbia University Press, 1934.

MACKENZIE INUIT: an Inuit (Eskimo) group located in the delta of the Mackenzie River in the northwestern part of the Canadian Northwest Territories, numbering at least 2,500 in the mid-19th century. By 1910, devastating epidemics had reduced them to about 150, essentially mixed with Alaskan Inuit, who had begun migrating into the area in the late 19th century. By the late 1970s, there were about 2,000 Inuit in the Mackenzie delta area.

The Mackenzie Inuit spoke a dialect of the Inuit (Eskimo) language, which was spoken, with minor variation, from Alaska to Greenland. The name Eskimo was derived from an Abnaki Indian term meaning "raw meat eaters," whereas Inuit, meaning "people," was their own name for themselves.

The Mackenzie Inuit were divided into five local groups: Kittegary-umiut, Kupugmiut, Kigirktarugmiut, Nuvouigmiut and Avvagmiut. Some of the groups were led by patrilineally hereditary chiefs. Marriage between the groups was fairly common. Child betrothal and wife exchange were practiced, as well as polygamy, particularly the marriage of a man to sisters.

The Mackenzie Inuit built communal winter dwellings of sod on a log framework, housing about six families each. The houses were either rectangular or cross-shaped, with sleeping platforms in three arms of the cross. In the fourth arm, a trap door led to a subterranean entrance tunnel. When hunting seal or ice fishing, temporary snowhouses were used on the river and sea ice. Conical caribou skin tents were used in summer, with usually two families to a tent. Each village also had one or more men's houses, or *kajigi*, up to 60 feet long, where the men took their meals and worked on their equipment.

Kittigaruit, located at the mouth of East Channel, was the largest summer village, having a population of 800-1,000 during the beluga hunting season. Beluga, a type of dolphin, were a staple food of the Mackenzie Inuit. They were hunted in communal drives by as many as 200 kayakers using harpoons. After drying and storing the beluga meat and oil, the Inuit dispersed to the interior to trade with the Kutchin Indians, hunt caribou from kayaks, or to fish for herring or whitefish using gill nets.

By winter, they had returned to their winter houses, where they lived off their stored food and celebrated their religious ceremonies during the dark days of December. The return of the sun in late January signalled the beginning of the season for hunting caribou, moose, rabbits and seals. Late spring was spent fishing and hunting waterfowl in the delta.

Traders in the late 18th and early 19th century were not welcomed by the Mackenzie Inuit, who, by that time, were already receiving some European trade goods from the North Alaskan Inuit. By the 1860s, both traders and whalers were active in the area. They found the Inuit located in settlements along the East Channel, Tuktoyaktuk Peninsula, Anderson River and Cape Bathhurst. Between 1865 and 1902, the Mackenzie Inuit were devastated by epidemics of scarlet fever, influenza and smallpox.

In the 20th century, they were essentially absorbed by Alaskan Inuit who had migrated to the area. In the late 1970s, there were about 2,000 Inuit living in the Mackenzie River delta, some of whom continued to live by traditional means, such as hunting beluga, caribou and seals, trapping muskrat and mink, fishing and gathering berries. Their way of life was somewhat changed, however, by such modern conveniences as rifles, sewing machines and outboard motors.

BIBLIOGRAPHY: Mc Ghee, Robert. *Beluga Hunters.* St. John's: Institute of Social and Economic Research, Memorial University of Newfoundland, 1974.

MAHICAN: a confederacy of subtribes originally located on both sides of the Hudson River in upstate New York. Of the five main divisions of the tribe, only the Westenhuck, who occupied the Housatonic valley and eventually became known as the Stockbridge Indians, survived as a tribe in the late 1970s.

The confederacy was centered at Schodac on an island near present-day Albany, but 40 villages were scattered north to Lake Champlain, and south to Catskill Creek on the west bank of the Hudson and the Poughkeepsie area on the east bank. The Mahican numbered about 3,000 in 1600. In the late 1970s, the majority of the remnants of the Stockbridge division lived in Wisconsin on the Stockbridge-Munsee Reservation while a few lived in Oklahoma.

The Mahican spoke an Algonquian language, which was practically extinct by the 1970s, and their name meant "wolf." They were organized into three matrilineal clans: bear, wolf and turtle. Each village, or castle, had its own chief and councillors. The head sachem, or great chief, who inherited his office through the female line, was keeper of the *mnoti,* or bag of peace, which contained the tribe's wampum, necessary for conducting business and making peace agreements with other tribes. The head sachem was assisted by three other officials: the "owl," who served as orator and town crier, a "runner," or messenger, and a "hero," who served as war chief.

The Mahican principal deity was Manito, or "Great Spirit." They celebrated the Green Corn Dance each year at the beginning of the harvest season. They believed in the immortality of the soul, and buried their dead with food, dishes, weapons and other provisions they might need. The body was placed in a sitting position surrounded with wood and then covered with earth and stones to make a house-like tomb.

Mahican villages were usually located on a hill near a river, and were often surrounded by a stockade. Their houses or wigwams were either circular or rectangular, with a framework of hickory saplings set in the ground at intervals and tied together at the top. The covering was of overlapping sheets of elm or basswood bark cut from the trees in the springtime and pressed flat. Fire circles dug in the floor were lined with stones. Animal skins hung on the interior walls, and benches lined the sides.

The Mahican were skilled agriculturalists. The men burned and cleaned the fields, while the women planted and cultivated corn, beans and squash. Fields were rotated periodically, and ashes and fish were used as fertilizer.

Corn was the staple crop—several varieties being cultivated, including popcorn. The best corn was saved for seed and the rest stored in bark containers or pits lined with bark. Corn was ground in a mortar made from a burned out oak stump. The meal was sifted, the finer part used to make bread and the course part used in corn soup. Bread was either baked in loaves or made as dumplings. A lightweight, high-energy trail food for hunters and warriors was made from a mixture of fine corn meal and maple sugar, to which water was added before eating.

The men hunted bear, deer, elk, moose, rabbit, squirrel, raccoon, turkey and geese. The meat was hung in strips to dry. Fish were caught with bone hooks, nets and weirs and the surplus smoked or dried. Women and girls gathered waterlily roots, greens, mushrooms, berries and nuts, and made tea from sassafras and wintergreen.

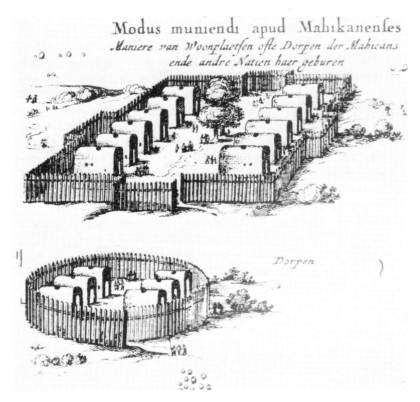

Villages of the Mahican and Delaware, from an old print.

Hunters made bows of hickory or red cedar and arrowheads of flint. Dishes and containers were made of bark, bowls, spoons and ladles of maple, oak or ash. They made simple pottery, including pipes in the shape of heads, as well as baskets of black ash splints, sometimes dyed.

Their clothing, of finely tanned skins, included skirts, breech clouts, shirts, blankets, moccasins and hip-length leggings, often decorated with beadwork or quillwork. Both men and women wore braids dressed with bear grease, although warriors sometimes burned or plucked the sides of their hair leaving a strip down the middle.

Mahican contact with Europeans began with Henry Hudson in 1609. In the 1660s, war with the Mohawk forced the Mahican of the Housatonic valley to move to the Stockbridge, Massachusetts, area where they came to be called Stockbridge Indians. About 1730, pressure from white settlers induced a large number of Stockbridge to move to the Susquehanna River near Wyoming, Pennsylvania. Another group of Stockbridge joined the Oneida in New York after the American Revolution, and migrated with them to Wisconsin.

In the late 1970s, there were descendants of Stockbridge mixed with Cherokee and Quapaw in Oklahoma. In Wisconsin, the Stockbridge-Munsee Reservation in Shawano County included 2,250 tribally-owned acres with a mixed population of about 600. The Mahican language and culture were mostly extinct.

BIBLIOGRAPHY: Dyer, Louisa A. *The House of Peace*. New York: Longmans, Green and Co., 1956.

MAIDU: a northeastern California group located in the region south of Lassen Peak in the early 19th century, when they probably numbered about 9,000. In the late 1970s, there were perhaps 1,500 Maidu descendants, living in northern California.

The Maidu language, belonging to the Penutian family, had three divisions: Northeastern, Northwestern and Southern. The Northeastern were called Konkow, and the Southern were the Nisenan.

The terrain of Maidu territory varied considerably, from river valleys to high mountain meadows. The usual settlement pattern was a cluster of small villages, with the head man and a large dance house or ceremonial chamber located in the central village. Religious leadership was provided by shamans, who interceded with the spirits, interpreted dreams, conducted ceremonies and healed the sick.

The Maidu believed that the world was fashioned by Earth Creator from mud brought up out of the sea by Turtle. Coyote, a trickster figure, brought death and conflict to the once-happy inhabitants. Mortuary customs varied among the Maidu groups. The Nisenan cremated their dead, while the Maidu and Konkow both buried their dead, along with food and gifts. All three groups burned the house and possessions of the deceased immediately after death. For several years after the person's death, annual anniversary mourning ceremonies were held, in which more gifts and offerings were burned.

The Maidu had several house styles, varying with season and location. In the valleys, semisubterranean earth-covered lodges were used in winter, while brush shelters served in summer. Hill peoples made conical winter houses covered with bark or skins, and brush shelters in summer.

Hunting, fishing and gathering supplied the Maidu with a widely varied diet. Acorns, pine nuts and manzanita berries as well as various roots and insects were collected in the proper seasons. Eel, salmon and trout were caught with nets, weirs and spears. Communal deer drives were held, in which the deer were driven over cliffs or past concealed hunters. They also hunted elk, antelope, bear and small game with bow and arrow, spears and knives.

The Maidu produced fine basketry by both the coil and twining methods. They made their scant clothing out of tanned deerskin, adding

Smithsonian Institution National Anthropological Archives

A Maidu altar near Placerville, California, in about 1912.

mountain lion fur robes in cold weather. Other crafts included making of necklaces, earrings and other ornaments of shell, bone and feathers, as well as construction of both dugout and tule canoes.

The Maidu had little contact with the Spanish or trappers of the early 19th century, but in 1833 they were decimated by a white-introduced epidemic.

The arrival of miners and settlers in Maidu territory in the mid-19th century was a further disaster, as lands were lost and food supplies destroyed. Several hundred were forced onto reservations. There was a short revival of Maidu culture and religion in the 1870s.

In the late 1970s, the Maidu were intermingled with other Indians and the white population, so that population estimates were difficult. A few Maidu still spoke the language, made baskets and held private ceremonies, and the Maidu Bear Dance was held annually in Jonesville.

BIBLIOGRAPHY: Beals, Ralph L. "Ethnology of the Nisenan." *University of California Publications in American Archaeology and Ethnology.* vol. 31, 1933.

MAKAH: a Northwest Coast whaling people located at Cape Flattery on the Strait of Juan de Fuca in northwestern Washington, numbering about 2,000 in the late 18th century. By the late 1970s, there were about 1,000 Makah, mostly living in Washington. They spoke a language of the Nootka division of the Wakashan language family, and were closely related to the Nootka of Vancouver Island. They called themselves Kwe-net-che-chat, meaning "people of the point."

They occupied four or five winter villages on both sides of the cape, including Neah, Waatch, Tzues, Ozette and Baada. Socially the Makah were divided into three classes: hereditary nobles, commoners and slaves. Patrilineal lineages controlled various types of inheritable property, such as ceremonial privileges, fishing grounds and berry patches.

The Makah spent the summer concentrating on food gathering activities, and devoted the winter to craftwork and their rich and complex ceremonial life. One important four-day ceremony was the Wolf Ritual, performed with carved wooden masks, in which members were initiated into the secret Klukwalle society.

The acquisition of guardian spirits was central to Makah religion. Leadership was provided by both male and female shamans, who had acquired several guardian spirits which aided them in performing cures. Adolescent boys acquired their guardians by fasting in remote places. Girls were secluded for a time at puberty and observed certain rites. Marriage was contracted with gifts from the boy's family to the girl's family, which were then distributed to friends of both families. Important festivals included potlatches, in which gifts were given and family wealth displayed.

The bodies of deceased Makah were removed through the roofs of the houses and buried in wooden boxes, along with personal items such as fishing or whaling gear or baskets. When a chief died, his slaves were sometimes killed.

Makah winter houses were multifamily longhouses of cedar planks which were sometimes procured in trade from Vancouver Island tribes. The houses were up to 60 by 30 feet and 10 feet high, housing about 40 people. The interiors had benches along the walls for sleeping and storage.

The Makah hunted whale in ocean-going cedar-log canoes with eight-man crews. They were superb canoe men, although their larger canoes were usually obtained from Vancouver Island with its larger cedar trees. Whale hunting took great skill and daring, and boys were taught to handle tiny canoes from childhood. Whaling equipment included harpoons attached to sealskin floats with long whale sinew rope.

Halibut were an even more important food source, often sliced and dried for later use. Salmon, cod and squid were also taken, as well as seals and sea lions. Various waterfowl were hunted, as well as elk, deer and bear, which were prized mainly for their skins. The women gathered greens, roots and an assortment of berries.

The Makah were excellent craftsmen. From wood they carved small and medium-sized canoes, ladles, bowls, and dishes. Boxes were made by steaming and bending wood. The women made fine bark baskets and dog hair blankets. Other clothing was of cedar bark and woven bird down feathers, and rain gear included conical hats and bear skin robes. Nose ornaments, dentalium shell ear ornaments and face paint were worn for adornment.

The Makah served as middlemen in the trade carried on among tribes in their area. The principal items that passed through their hands included dried halibut, sea otter skins, vermilion, whale and seal oil, dentalium shells, dried cedar bark for mats and clothing, canoes, dried salmon and slaves. They were occasionally at war with the Quileute, Klallam and others.

In 1792, the Spanish failed in an attempt to establish a colony on Neah Bay. Well into the 19th century, the Makah were protected from encroachment by settlers by the thick surrounding forests. Around 1860, they gave up whaling for the profits to be made in seal hunting, but were forced to abandon this practice in about 1890, when seal hunting was prohibited. In 1862, the Treaty of Neah Bay established a reservation in their traditional homeland.

In the late 1970s, there were about 1,000 Makah living on or near the 27,000-acre Makah Reservation in Clallam County, Washington.

BIBLIOGRAPHY: Colson, Elizabeth. *The Makah Indians.* Minneapolis: University of Minnesota Press, 1953; Swan, James G. "Indians of Cape Flattery." *Smithsonian Contributions to Knowledge.* vol. 16, 1869.

MALECITE: a small tribe located in the Saint John River valley in southern New Brunswick in the early 17th century, when, together with the Passamaquoddy, they numbered about 1,000. In the late 1970s, there were about 2,000 Malecite descendants connected with seven reserves in New Brunswick.

The Malecite and Passamaquoddy, who spoke dialects of the same eastern Algonquian language, were together known as the Etchemin by early explorers. They were culturally very similar, except that the Malecite concentrated on inland hunting, whereas the Passamaquoddy were sea mammal hunters.

The Malecite gathered in large villages in summer, and dispersed in winter to live in small hunting camps. Local leadership was informal, usually exercised by mature men who were skillful hunters. In the 17th century, they had one supreme hereditary chief who resided at the principal village. With increased European contact, leadership gradually became more formalized, with a hierarchy of peace chiefs and war chiefs. Also important were shamans, who cured the sick and exercised other powers given them by a spirit helper.

The extended family was the most important social unit. Before marriage, a young man was required to spend a year's probationary period serving his future father-in-law and proving himself as a hunter and provider. The Malecite had a rich mythology, centered around Kuloscap, the culture hero. Other supernatural beings included cannibal giants, dwarfs, ghosts and such characters as Turtle and Snowshoe Hare.

The Malecite sometimes palisaded their summer villages, which were composed of both single and multi-family dwellings. Single family dwellings were usually conical pole-frame wigwams, whereas multi-family dwellings and council houses were rectangular lodges with log sides and a birchbark roof.

In the spring, the Malecite returned to their villages to plant corn. Using the village as a base, they made numerous trips to fishing sites to spear salmon, bass and sturgeon. Wild grapes and various roots supplemented the summer fish diet. In late summer, the corn was harvested and either stored in bark-lined pits or taken along when the group dispersed for winter hunting. The Malecite ranged over a large area of Maine, New Brunswick and the Gaspé Peninsula in their search for moose, bear, otter, beaver and muskrat.

Lightweight, maneuverable canoes were made of birchbark and occasionally spruce bark or moose hide. Snowshoes were used for winter transportation. The Malecite made an assortment of containers, baskets, boxes, trays and dishes from birchbark, and sometimes decorated them with quill work.

The Malecite were visited by the French explorer Samuel de Champlain and others in the early 17th century. In the following decades, they became involved with the French fur trade, grew dependent on European trade goods and accepted French missionaries. Extensive intermarriage increased their sympathy toward the French. In the mid-18th century, the Malecite joined with the Passamaquoddy, Abnaki, Penobscot, Micmac and other tribes sympathetic to the French, to form the Wabanaki (Abnaki) Confederacy. By the late 18th century, English colonists crowded into their territory, pushing the Malecite out of their old villages, fishing spots and hunting grounds. Throughout the 18th century, their population declined drastically due to disease and alcohol, before beginning to recover in the 19th century. In the 19th century, efforts were made to establish reserves on remaining Malecite campsites.

In the late 1970s, the 2,000 Malecite descendants were becoming

256 INDIAN TRIBES OF NORTH AMERICA

increasingly interested in maintaining their culture and language and having close relations with the Passamaquoddy and other Indian groups.

BIBLIOGRAPHY: Wallis, Wilson D. and Wallis, Ruth S. *The Malecite Indians of New Brunswick*. National Museum of Canada Bulletin. no. 148, 1957.

MANDAN: a Plains tribe of the Siouan linguistic family who lived on the Missouri River in what is now North Dakota in the early 18th century. They numbered about 3,500, occupying nine villages near the mouth of the Heart River. Their tribal name was given them by the Dakota, but they called themselves Numakiki, or "people." In the late 1970s, several hundred Mandan descendants, some of whom still spoke their traditional language, lived with the Arikara and Hidatsa tribes at Fort Berthold Reservation in North Dakota.

The Mandan consisted of about five bands, each speaking a slightly different dialect. The tribe was divided into two moieties, or divisions, and about 13 clans. A person inherited the moiety and clan of his mother and was required to marry outside these groupings. Inheritance of their earth lodge dwellings and household possessions was also through the female line. Villages were ruled by a council, chief and warchief.

Mandan religious life was particularly rich in ceremonies, the most important of which was the Okipa, which was held in summer. The Okipa, a type of Sun Dance held inside a special lodge, was celebrated to ensure the prosperity of the people and to bring buffalo. The four-day ceremony included fasting, dancing, recounting the tribal history, prayers and self-torture. Young men were suspended on rawhide ropes attached to skewers through their chest muscles. There were many other festivals connected with agriculture and hunting.

The Mandan practiced scaffold burial, although, in early times, earth burials may have been more common. A four-day mourning period was held, and when the bones had dried, the skulls were placed in circles near the village.

The Mandan located their villages on high bluffs above the river, with stockades and barrier ditches on the unprotected side. As many as 150 earth lodges were arranged around an open area used for dances, ceremonies and other gatherings. The lodges, housing two or three families, were about 40 feet in diameter. A heavy wooden framework was covered with willow branches interwoven with grass, with an outer layer of mud and clay. They also had portable skin tipis used for traveling and hunting trips.

Both hunting and agriculture were important to the Mandan economy. The women grew corn, beans and squash, using digging sticks, antler rakes and hoes made from the shoulder blade bone of a buffalo. They

Mandan crossing the ice with their dog-sleds: an illustration published in the 1840s.

traded surplus corn to the Assiniboin for buffalo hides and meat. The Mandan also fished, hunted buffalo and gathered wild foods to supplement the diet. Pottery cooking vessels and fine basketry were made by the women. Dogs were used to pull travois toboggans.

The Mandan probably came to the Missouri River region from somewhere to the southeast, in about 1250. They gradually moved upriver until they reached the mouth of the Heart River, where they were visited by French explorers in 1738. In the late 18th century, their population was severely reduced by smallpox epidemics and warfare with the Dakota. By the time of the 1804 visit of Lewis and Clark, their nine villages had been reduced to two, near the mouth of the Knife River.

Even more severe was the 1837 smallpox epidemic, which nearly destroyed the Mandan, killing all but about 150 out of 1,800. In 1845, the surviving Mandan joined the Hidatsa and moved north to form a village at a bend in the Missouri, which they called Like-a-Fishhook. In 1862, they were joined by the Arikara, and, around 1870s, the area was set aside for the three tribes as Fort Berthold Reservation. In 1887, most of the land was allotted in severalty.

In the 1950s, the Garrison Dam was built, flooding about 25 percent of the reservation, including the best croplands as well as most of the homes, schools and roads. In the 1970s, tourist facilities were established by the tribes on Lake Sakakawea, the reservoir formed by the dam. In the late 1970s, there remained 45,000 acres of tribally owned land, and 350,000 acres of allotted land, belonging to individuals of the tribes.

BIBLIOGRAPHY: Bowers, Alfred W. *Mandan Social and Ceremonial Organization.* Chicago: University of Chicago Press, 1950.

MARICOPA: a Yuman tribe located along the middle Gila River in south central Arizona in the late 18th century, numbering about 3,000 at that time. In the late 1970s, there were more than 12,000 Maricopa and Pima living together on two reservations in south-central Arizona. The Maricopa spoke a Yuman language of the Hokan language family.

They were led by a chief, whose function was mainly to advise, and who usually lived in the strongest village. Although the position of chief was sometimes hereditary in the male line, usually he was recognized for his personal appeal, leadership qualities and certain dreams he had experienced. Dreaming was the source of power among the Maricopa, and all skills and good fortune derived from it. Chiefs, song leaders, dance leaders, war leaders, and shamans all attained their position and power through involuntary dreams. Shamans had special powers in such areas as curing, weather control, aiding fishermen, detecting thieves and locating the enemy.

Socially, the Maricopa were divided into clans, with each person inheriting the clan of his father and marriage forbidden within the clan. A newly-married couple moved in with the groom's family. As part of the marriage customs, the bride spent a day of grinding corn and carrying water for her new mother-in-law. Polygamy was sometimes practiced, including the customs of a man marrying his brother's widow and a woman marrying her sister's widower.

The Maricopa cremated their dead and burned the houses of the deceased. A horse was killed so the deceased would be able to ride westward into the land of the dead. For exceptional chiefs, warriors, orators or singers, mourning ceremonies were sometimes held a few days after death. A dead warrior's most famous battles were re-enacted, and the songs of a dead singer were sung.

The Maricopa men built circular dome-shaped dwellings of thatch and earth over a pole frame. The dwellings were 15-25 feet in diameter and always faced east. There was also a meeting house of similar construction, 30-35 feet in diameter. Other structures included sweat lodges and cylindrical granaries, similar in construction to a coiled basket, about four feet high and four feet in diameter.

The Maricopa grew corn, beans, pumpkins, cotton and later, melons. Men planted and cultivated, and the women did the harvesting. The women also gathered mesquite beans, cholla beans, ironwood nuts, caterpillars, honey, seeds, berries and saguaro cactus fruit, from which a sweet, fermented drink was made. Stone metates were used for grinding the two staple foods, mesquite beans and corn.

The scarcity of big game made hunting less important. Rabbits, however, were hunted by stalking and in communal drives using nets. Fish, second in importance to rabbits as a source of animal protein, were caught with nets or bare hands. Small game were trapped, and an occasional deer or mountain sheep was taken.

The Maricopa women made a large assortment of pottery, including cooking pots, bowls, water jars, parching pans and ladles. Basketry making was confined to coiled burden baskets. Cotton blankets were woven by old men, and breechclouts for men and fringed skirts for women were woven from willow bark. Rabbit skin capes were used in cold weather and sandals were worn on journeys. Personal adornment included face painting and tattooing.

The Maricopa and Yuma lived together along the lower Colorado River until about the 16th century, when the Maricopa broke off and moved gradually up-river to the Gila River. They were visited by various Spanish expeditions in the 17th and 18th century, but with relatively little impact. By about 1800, the Maricopa had moved near the Pima on the middle Gila River, where they were joined by several other groups driven from the Colorado River by the Yuma and Mohave. By about 1838, the Maricopa had absorbed the Halchidoma, Kohuana and Halyikwamai.

Conflicts between the Maricopa and Yuma occurred every few years. Maricopa weapons included bows of mesquite or ironwood, short clubs and small circular hide shields. In 1857, the Maricopa and Pima severely defeated a Yuma and Mohave war party in the last major battle of the Colorado tribes. A reservation was set aside for the Maricopa in 1859, but it was later revoked, and new lands were assigned in 1879 and 1882-83.

In the late 1970s, about 3,000 Maricopa and Pima lived on the Salt River Reservation in south-central Arizona near Phoenix, and about 9,000 Maricopa and Pima occupied the nearby Gila River Reservation.

BIBLIOGRAPHY: Spier, Leslie. *Yuman Tribes of the Gila River.* Chicago: The University of Chicago Press, 1933.

MASSACHUSET: an extinct tribe located along Massachusetts Bay, from Plymouth north to Salem and along the Neponset and Charles river valleys. Numbering about 3,000 in 1600, they included in their territory the area of present day Boston. They spoke an Algonquian language closely related to that of the Narraganset. Massachuset means "at the great hills."

Divided into bands ruled by a sachem, the Massachuset had about 20 villages along the coast in 1614, as reported by Capt. John Smith. Their economy was based on fishing, hunting and agriculture, with corn as the main crop.

In 1617 the Massachuset were decimated by an epidemic that swept through the New England tribes. Reportedly, the Massachuset suffered the most. About this same time, they were attacked by some of their northern neighbors, so that by 1631 their population had dwindled to about 500.

In 1633, they were nearly wiped out by smallpox, and the remainder were gathered into villages with other tribes by Christian missionaries, including John Eliot. Known under the general term "praying Indians," they lost their separate tribal identity.

BIBLIOGRAPHY: Speck, Frank G., *Territorial Subdivisions and Boundaries of the Wampanoag, Massachusett, and Nauset Indians*. New York: Museum of the American Indian, 1920.

MDEWAKANTON. One of the seven divisions of the Dakota, located in northern Minnesota in the late 17th century, numbering about 1,200 at that time. In the late 1970s, there were perhaps 800 Mdewakanton descendants, often mixed with Wahpekute, living in Nebraska, South Dakota and Minnesota.

The language of the Mdewakanton belongs to the Santee or Eastern division of the Dakota language, which is a member of the Siouan linguistic family. The Santee Dakota include also the Wahpekute, Sisseton and Wahpeton. Mdewakanton means "people of the mystic lake."

The Mdewakanton were divided into seven bands, each usually led by an hereditary chief. An élite warrior group, the *akitcita*, acted as a sort of police, keeping order during hunts, games and councils, and acting as messengers and escorts. Religious leadership was provided by both male and female shamans. Shamans usually led hunting and war parties, in addition to performing their other duties of curing the sick, prophesying, forecasting the weather, and interpreting visions and dreams.

The Mdewakanton placed their dead on scaffolds wrapped in skins or blankets. After a few months or years, the remains were taken to tribal burial grounds, and placed in burial mounds along with tools, utensils and weapons. The mounds were usually several feet high and about 15 feet in diameter, although some were as much as 10 feet high and 60 feet in diameter.

Their summer houses were of pole and elm bark construction, with gabled roofs. For winter, they built small, conical houses covered with skins.

After the Mdewakanton were driven from their northern Minnesota villages to the Nebraska plains, they became nomadic hunters, returning

A Mdewakanton Indian—Tshe-ton Wa-ka-wa Ma-ni, or the Hawk That Hunts Walking, also known as Little Crow (the Younger)—was the chief leader of the 1862 Minnesota uprising: a photograph taken in 1858 in Washington, D.C.

to their villages only to plant a few crops, principally corn. Fishing was important, particularly for sturgeon. Wild rice was harvested from canoes. The stalks were tied together to hasten the drying, and a few days later the rice was harvested by letting the grains fall into the canoe. They also gathered maple sugar, berries, wild turnips and potatoes to supplement the diet.

The Mdewakanton, along with the other Santee Dakota tribes, were encountered by French explorers in the Mille Lacs, Minnesota, region in the late 17th century. According to some traditions, previous to that they had lived further north around Lake of the Woods. The Dakota were driven from Mille Lacs by the Ojibwa in about 1750. The Mdewakanton were probably the last to migrate and remained the farthest east, establishing villages along the Mississippi and lower Minnesota rivers. They soon became dependent on the communal buffalo hunt—competing with the Sauk, Fox and other tribes for hunting grounds.

In the treaties of 1837 and 1851, the Santee were forced to cede all of their Minnesota and Iowa lands, except for a reservation along the Minnesota River. The Mdewakanton and Wahpekute occupied the Lower Agency of the reservation and the Sisseton and Wahpeton the Upper Agency. Confined to the reservation, the Santee found themselves at the mercy of dishonest traders, incompetent government agents, and squatters. Numerous incidents finally led to an uprising in 1862 on the Lower Agency. The Upper Agency tribes declared themselves neutral, while the dissidents were led by a Mdewakanton chief, Little Crow. Neither the Mdewakanton nor Wahpekute gave unanimous support to the uprising, however, so it was ended within a few months.

About 38 Santee were executed by hanging, and the government expropriated all Santee lands and property. Many fled to the western Dakota tribes, and to Canada. The rest of the Mdewakanton and Wahpekute were rounded up and herded about, before finally being settled at Crow Creek, South Dakota. During this time, hundreds died of starvation, illness and hardship.

In 1866, they were moved to the Santee Reservation in Nebraska. Drought, locust plagues and smallpox epidemics were some of the conditions faced in the early years of the reservation. In the 1870s, several hundred left the Santee Reservation to settle on the Big Sioux River, near Flandreau, South Dakota. Some of the Flandreau group eventually drifted back to Minnesota, to join other groups of Santee.

In the late 1970s, Mdewakanton descendants made up the majority of the population of the Santee and Flandreau Reservations, each of which had populations of about 300. They were also represented in the Minnesota Santee communities of Prairie Island, Prior Lake and Birch Coulee.

BIBLIOGRAPHY: Landes, Ruth. *The Mystic Lake Sioux*. Madison: The University of Wisconsin Press, 1968; Meyer, Roy W. *History of the Santee Sioux*. Lincoln: University of Nebraska Press, 1967.

MENOMINEE: a tribe of the Algonquian language family, located along the Menominee River between Wisconsin and Michigan in the early 17th century, numbering about 3,000 at that time. In the late 1970s

Setting up a Menominee bark canoe; a picture taken in about 1892-93. The bark covering has been folded around the canoe frame, and stakes have been driven into the ground to hold the bark in place while it is stitched to the frame.

they remained in essentially the same area, occupying a reservation on the Wolf River and numbering about 2,800.

The Menominee were linguistically related to the Ojibwa, and their tribal name meant "wild rice people," in the language of the latter. The Menominee language was still spoken in the late 1970s.

The Menominee were divided into two moieties, or tribal divisions, Bear and Thunderbird, which were further subdivided into perhaps seven clans. Their social organization was disrupted by the arrival of Europeans, and little is known of early patterns except that they were sedentary—living in fishing villages and harvesting wild rice. With the advent of the fur trade, they were scattered into mobile bands of hunters.

Religion was of great importance in Menominee life, and they had a complex set of deities, divided into various strata. At the top was Mecawetok, the supreme force, and just below him were the Thunderers, who were friendly to man. An evil underworld contained such denizens as the Hairy Horned Serpent, the Underground Panther, the White Deer

A Menominee, with snowshoes and a gun, standing with his bride in front of a bark house: a 1908 photograph.

and the Great White Bear. Fasting and dreams were very important to the individual Menominee, as were medicine bundles, containing medicine, charms and other sacred items. The Mitawit, or Grand Medicine Society, borrowed from the Ojibwa, was an important secret society of shamans who specialized in curing.

Burial varied with time and place. In early times, scaffold burials were common, while, in later times, bodies were painted red and enclosed in long pieces of birch bark. They were buried with weapons, tools and ornaments, and three logs were placed over the grave. Mourners blackened their faces with charcoal, and there were feasting and games. In more modern times, coffins were used, and a small house-like structure was built over the grave, with an opening through which food and other grave-offerings could be placed.

When the Menominee began to rely more on hunting, they moved deep into the woods in winter—living in dome-shaped wigwams covered with woven mats. In summer, they often lived along the shores of Green Bay, in rectangular bark-covered cabins of pole construction. A Menominee village usually contained an open field for playing lacrosse. A favorite winter game was snow snake, in which a carved wooden stick was hurled along the top of the frozen snow, to see who could send it the furthest.

In early times, the Menominee lived mainly by fishing and harvesting wild rice. They used hooks, weirs, gill nets and spears, fishing both the streams and the waters of Green Bay. In winter, they fished through holes cut in the ice. Wild rice was gathered from a canoe. One person navigated the canoe while the other used one stick to draw the rice stalks over the canoe and another to beat the heads so the grains would fall into the canoe. The Menominee also grew gardens of corn, beans, squash and tobacco and gathered raspberries, blueberries and sap for maple sugar.

The Menominee made both birch-bark and dugout canoes, and snow-shoes for winter transportation. Other crafts included weaving mats of cattails, rushes or cedar bark, dyed to make various designs. Intricate beadwork was applied to bags, clothing and ceremonial items, and a simple pottery was made.

In about 1634, the Menominee were visited by the French explorer Jean Nicolet. In the 1660s, they and the neighboring Winnebago were nearly overwhelmed by Michigan and eastern tribes, driven into the Green Bay area by the Iroquois Confederacy.

From the 1670s to about 1815, the Menominee were preoccupied by the fur trade—hunting beaver, deer, black bear, wildcat, rabbit, lynx, and buffalo, which roamed into Wisconsin in those days. They traded the furs and skins to Europeans for trade goods.

By the early 19th century, the game was depleted, and most of the tribes were beginning to cede their lands to the U.S. and move west. By 1854, the Menominee had given up all their lands and settled on a reservation on the Wolf River in Wisconsin. Some of their lands were given to various New York tribes as reservations.

In 1961, the Menominee Reservation was terminated, but by 1973 it had been restored. Lumbering, which had begun in the late 19th century, was the major source of revenue. Some 2,800 Menominee descendants lived on or near the reservation and took pride in preserving their tribal integrity, language and traditions.

BIBLIOGRAPHY: Keesing, Felix M. "The Menomini Indians of Wisconsin." *Memoirs of the American Philosophical Society.* vol. 10, 1939.

MESCALERO: an Apache tribe located in southern New Mexico, western Texas and northern Chihuahua, Mexico in the early 19th century, numbering perhaps 800 at that time. In the late 1970s, there were about 2,500 Mescalero, Chiricahua and Lipan Apache living together on the Mescalero Reservation in southern New Mexico.

The Mescalero spoke a language of the southern branch of the Athapascan language family. The name, given them by the Spanish, referred to their custom of making a nutritious food called mescal from the base of the agave plant.

The smallest political unit of the Mescalero was the *gata*, or extended family, which hunted, gathered food and lived together. These were

Economic Development Administration

"The Inn of the Mountain Gods," a ski resort on the Mescalero Reservation in southern New Mexico.

usually led by the oldest capable man, and often banded together to form larger groups, which were led by a *nanta*, or leader who acted as an advisor.

When a Mescalero couple married, they usually lived with the family of the bride and became part of that *gata*, although it was taboo for a man to talk to his mother-in-law. Polygamy was fairly common, with men often marrying sisters. When twins were born, one was usually killed, otherwise, according to tradition, they would both die.

Important religious ceremonies included the four-day puberty rite for girls, sponsored by the girl's family. The celebration included feasting, dancing and performance of rituals in a tipi constructed for the occasion. An adolescent boy's coming of age required going on four raids as an apprentice warrior.shamans performed curing ceremonies and practised witchcraft, as well as using their power to counteract the witchcraft of others. The Mecalero buried their dead in caves or rock clefts far from camp, with their heads towards the west. Some possessions of the deceased were buried with him; the rest were destroyed, and his favorite horse was killed.

The Mescalero lived in buffalo hide tipis similar to those of the Plains Indians. They also sometimes built wickiups of poles and thatch or brush. As the Mescalero acquired horses, and the resulting greater mobility, buffalo hunting became more important. Communal hunts were held in late fall and on into winter. Horse travois replaced dog travois, making it possible to use longer tipi poles. Other game included deer and antelope, which were stalked using deer or antelope-head disguises, as well as elk and mountain sheep.

The Mescalero grew corn, beans and squash, using some of the corn to make *tiswin,* a mild beer. Even when they could grow crops, food gathering, particularly agave, was of major importance. The base of the agave, also known as the century plant, was dug up, placed in a rock-lined pit and baked for several days. The resulting sweet-tasting mescal could be dried and stored for later use. They also gathered mesquite beans, prickly pear, pine nuts, locust blossoms, seeds, nuts, grapes, sumac berries and raspberries.

The Mescalero and other Apache groups first came from the north into the southwest in about 1200 AD. At that time, they were friendly with the Pueblo peoples, and traded them buffalo robes and meat for their agricultural surpluses.

By the early 17th century, the Mescalero had acquired horses and began raiding Spanish settlements in New Mexico, becoming masters of the southern Plains. By the early 18th century, however, the Comanche and Ute, equipped with firearms, began threatening Apache supremacy. Around 1720, Plains tribes wiped out a combined Apache-Spanish force, and in 1727, the Mescalero were forced to abandon their buffalo hunting grounds north of the Arkansas River.

In the late 18th century, the Mescalero made peace with the Spanish and began serving as scouts for their military, living in camps near the Spanish settlements and receiving rations. Epidemics frequently swept their camps in those years. In about 1825, after the Mexicans had taken over from the Spanish, the Mescalero moved north and began raiding New Mexico settlements again.

Around 1852, the Mescalero made a peace treaty with the United States, and in 1873, the Mescalero Reservation in southern New Mexico was established. In the late 1870s, some Mescalero joined with the Chiricahua Apache in their wars with the U.S. Army, and a few shared their fate as prisoners of war. In 1913, the prisoners were released, and about 170, including a few Mescalero, were settled on the Mescalero Reservation.

In the late 1970s, there were about 2,500 Mescalero, Chiricahua and Lipan Apache living on the 460,000-acre reservation. There was some intermarriage among the groups. Lumber, cattle-raising and tourism were the major sources of tribal income. A ski resort and camp grounds were located among the beautiful mountains of the reservation. The various Apache dialects were still spoken, especially at home, and there was a continuing interest in Apache traditions and crafts.

BIBLIOGRAPHY: Opler, Morris Edward. ''An Analysis of Mescalero and Chiricahua Apache Social Organization in the Light of their Systems of Relationship." Ph.D. dissertation, University of Chicago, 1933; Sonnichsen, C.L. *The Mescalero Apaches.* Norman: University of Oklahoma Press, 1973.

MIAMI: an Algonquian tribe, numbering about 4,500, who lived in the Green Bay, Wisconsin area in the mid-17th century, and shortly after that, migrated to the region around the southern end of Lake Michigan. In the late 1970s, 4,200 descendants of the Miami lived in Oklahoma and Indiana. The name Miami was probably derived from an Ojibwa word, *oumamik,* meaning "people of the peninsula." They were also known as Twightwee by the English.

The Miami were divided into six bands: Atchatchakangouen, Kilatika, Mengakonkia, Pepicokia, Wea and Piankashaw. The first three combined and became known as the Miami proper, or Crane Band. The Pepicokia were absorbed by the Wea and Piankashaw, who later acted as separate tribes, having their own tribal councils by 1818.

The Miami had a well-organized political structure, based on the clan system. Each person inherited the clan of his father and was forbidden to marry within his own clan. Each village had a council made up of the chiefs of the various clans. The council elected one of their number as village chief. Delegates were sent from each village council to the band council, which in turn sent delegates to the tribal council. Clan, village, band and tribal chiefs were all chosen on the basis of merit and enjoyed a great deal of respect and authority.

Along with other Algonquian tribes in the region, the Miami had a Midewiwin or Grand Medicine Society, made up of priests who had special magical powers for curing. Lesser shamans also cured with the aid of medicinal roots and herbs. The sun was the supreme deity and "master of life" for the Miami, although lesser spirits or *manito* were also important.

Two of the most important festivals celebrated the fall harvest and the return from the winter hunt. Both were celebrated with feasting, games, dancing and the music of drums, rattles, flutes and whistles. Miami mortuary customs varied, including burial in hollowed out logs, in small sealed log cabins and on scaffolds.

Miami villages usually had a council house for meetings and ceremonies. Houses were constructed of poles covered by rush mats. The Miami were noted for growing a corn superior to that of their neighbors, having a finer skin and whiter meal. They also grew melons, squash, pumpkins and beans. Village life was stable, based more on agriculture than hunting, although communal buffalo hunts were held each year.

In about 1650, the Miami fled beyon the Mississippi to avoid attack by Iroquois war parties that were ranging around the Great Lakes at that

Michikinikwa, or Little Turtle, (1752-1812), a chief of the Miami tribe: from a painting attributed to Gilbert Stuart, (1797).

time. Contact with the Dakota soon brought them back to Wisconsin. By 1669, some of the Miami were established at the mouth of the St. Joseph River in southwestern Michigan. By 1683, they were in a loose trade alliance with the French, who helped negotiate peace between the Miami and Iroquois in 1701.

The Wea band established themselves at the present site of Chicago in 1690. Another group of Miami settled near Detroit in 1691. By about 1712, the Miami in Michigan felt the pressure of the Potawatomi and moved to the headwaters of the Maumee in Ohio. By the mid-18th century, the Wea occupied lands along the middle Wabash, and the Piankashaw had settled along the lower Wabash in Indiana.

In the mid-18th century, the Miami fought to stop the flood of white settlers into the Ohio Valley, but, by 1763, they gave up most of their Ohio lands and concentrated in Indiana. In 1790-91, the Miami and other tribes led by the Miami chief Little Turtle inflicted several defeats on the Americans. But their defeat at the Battle of Fallen Timbers (1794) marked the end of this stage of resistance. By 1827, most of their lands had been taken from them, and some of the Miami began moving to Kansas. The Piankashaw and Wea settled with the Peoria and Kaskaskia. After the Civil War, the various bands in Kansas moved to the Quapaw Reservation in Indian Territory (now Oklahoma).

In the late 1970s, more than 1,200 Miami descendants were registered in Oklahoma, mostly in Ottawa County. The Oklahoma Miami were represented by an active tribal organization. More than 3,000 Miami lived in Indiana, with the largest number in Wabash County.

BIBLIOGRAPHY: Anson, Bert. *The Miami Indians.* Norman: University of Oklahoma Press, 1960.

MICMAC: an Algonquian tribe occupying Nova Scotia, Cape Breton, Prince Edward Island, northern New Brunswick and the Gaspé Peninsula of Quebec in the 16th century, numbering about 4,000 at that time. In the late 1970s, there were more than 10,000 Micmac living on or connected with about 28 reserves in Nova Scotia, New Brunswick, Quebec and Prince Edward Island.

The Micmac spoke an Algonquian language closely related to that of the Malecite, Passamaquoddy and Penobscot. They were divided into bands, each of which camped together in summer but were otherwise scattered into local groups. Local groups were led by a *saxamaw,* who was usually the eldest son of a powerful family. Group membership was flexible, with families or individuals moving in or out fairly freely. Before marriage, a young man was required to spend a two-year probationary period in the wigwam of his prospective father-in-law, proving himself as a hunter and worker.

The Micmac believed in maintaining harmony with the world of nature, particularly the animals on which they depended. They believed in a Great Spirit, identified with the sun, who created the world, as well as in numerous other spirits and beings. Many tales were told of Gluscap, the culture hero-trickster, as well as other creatures such as a cannibal giant, dwarfs, ghosts and witches.

When a person died, a three day mourning period was followed by a feast and burial. In New Brunswick and on the Gaspé Peninsula, the bodies of the deceased were wrapped in bark and buried on an uninhabited island, along with weapons, tools and other personal property. Scaffold burial was practiced on Cape Breton. Relatives cut their hair and mourned for a year.

Dwellings were conical wigwams of bark, skins or woven mats on a

Three Micmac women weaving baskets outside a bark tipi on Prince Edward Island, Canada.

pole frame. Boughs covered with furs were used for sleeping on, and a central fireplace was used for heating and cooking.

The Micmac economy depended on hunting and fishing, and they migrated seasonally with the food supply. Moose were stalked using moose head disguises and birchbark moose calls. Snares, deadfalls, spears and bow and arrow were used in hunting bear, beaver, caribou, rabbit and otter, and seals were taken with harpoons. In spring, they gathered at coastal fishing camps to catch smelt, herring, salmon and cod with hooks, nets, weirs and spears. To supplement the diet, they gathered shellfish, roots, nuts and berries. Meat was roasted or boiled in hollowed-out wooden troughs, using red-hot stones to heat the water. Coiled baskets were made of spruce root, and other containers were made of skin or birchbark decorated with quillwork. They made birchbark canoes, with decked bow and stern and high sides at midship.

By the 17th century, the Micmac, involved with the French fur trade, had begun to acquire considerable quantities of European trade goods, changing their culture significantly. Disease, alcoholism and warfare with the neighboring Malecite and Montagnais also characterized this period. In the 18th century, the Micmac were drawn into the conflict between the French and English. They made peace with the English in 1760, but some hostilities continued for another 20 years, after which reserves were established for the various bands.

During the 19th century, the Micmac continued to trap and hunt, but were also drawn into lumbering, industry, construction, shipping and migrant agricultural work. In the 20th century, their 60 reserves were consolidated to less than 30. In the late 1970s, only about 70 percent of the enrolled members of each reserve were in residence at a given time, as the Micmac, particularly the men, followed a cycle of working off the reservation and then returning for a time. Many engaged in high steel construction work in such cities as Boston. Through strong band governments, the Micmac had gained the initiative in controlling their own affairs. Most Micmac were bilingual, speaking English as well as their own language.

BIBLIOGRAPHY: Wallis, Wilson D. and Wallis, Ruth S. *The Micmac Indians of Eastern Canada*. Minneapolis: University of Minnesota Press, 1955.

MIKASUKI: *See* SEMINOLE.

MINICONJOU: a subdivision of the Teton Dakota, located from the Black Hills south to the Platte River in the mid-19th century, numbering about 2,000 at that time. Their name meant "those who plant beside the stream." In the late 1970s, Miniconjou descendants were located on the

The National Archives

Big Foot's band of Miniconjou at a grass dance on the Cheyenne River, South Dakota: a photograph taken on August 9, 1890.

MINICONJOU MINICONJOU   273

Cheyenne River Reservation in South Dakota, along with other Dakota tribes. (See also *Teton* and *Dakota*.)

MISSISAUGA: *See* OJIBWA

MISSOURI: a Siouan tribe of the Chiwere division, which also includes the Oto and Iowa. In 1780, they numbered about 1,000, living near the junction of the Missouri and Grand rivers. In the late 1970s, descendants of the Missouri lived with the Oto in Oklahoma and had lost their separate tribal identity.

The Missouri called themselves Niutachi, or "people of the river mouth." Missouri was an Algonquian term variously translated as "people having dugout canoes," or "Great Muddy," in reference to the river.

The Missouri culture and lifestyle was similar to that of the Oto. Both lived in villages of earth lodges along the banks of rivers. The women cultivated corn, beans and squash, while the men hunted buffalo, deer and other game.

According to tradition, the Missouri lived in early times with the Oto, Iowa and Winnebago tribes, somewhere in the Great Lakes region. At some point they began migrating south and west, leaving the Winnebago in the Green Bay area of Wisconsin and the Iowa at the junction of the Mississippi and Iowa rivers. The Missouri and the Oto continued on until they reached the junction of the Missouri and Grand rivers, where they had a falling out. According to tradition, the Oto chief's son ran off with the Missouri chief's daughter, causing the tribes to split.

The Oto moved west along the Missouri River to the Platte River, while the Missouri remained at the mouth of the Grand River. In 1693, they began trade relations with the French, which continued for the next century. The Missouri suffered greatly from disease and from raids by tribes to the east, particularly the Fox and Sauk. In 1730, after about 300 of their population were killed in a raid by the Sauk, the Missouri moved across the river, settling near the Osage.

In about 1798, the Missouri were nearly wiped out when the Fox ambushed their canoes on the Missouri River. Many fled to the Oto at this time. By 1829, the remnants of the Missouri were living with the Oto. Numbering about 80 in 1833, they were, however, still ruled by their own chief. The following decades were very difficult, as the two tribes battled cholera epidemics and fought with the Omaha, Pawnee and Dakota for the scarce food supply. By treaties signed in 1830, 1833, 1836 and 1854, the Oto-Missouri ceded all their lands and moved to a reservation on the Big Blue River, between Kansas and Nebraska.

Intra-tribal fighting in about 1880 split them into factions, with the Coyote, or traditional faction, moving to Indian Territory (Oklahoma).

Three Indians—an Oto, a Ponca, and a Missouri: a drawing by Karl Bodmer.

The following year the other group, known as the Quakers, ceded their lands for a reservation near Red Rock in north central Oklahoma. By 1890, the Coyote had gradually joined them there. In 1907, the reservation was allotted to individual tribal members.

In 1955, the U.S. Supreme Court upheld an award of $1 million to the Oto-Missouri in repayment for illegal land settlements. This was divided among the 2,000 Oto-Missouri on the tribal rolls, the two tribes now being so intermarried as to be indistinguishable.

In the late 1970s, there were 28,000 acres of allotted land remaining, as well as 1,700 acres of tribally-owned land. The Oto-Missouri celebrated their traditional dances and ceremonies each year in July. An elementary grammar of the Chiwere language was published in 1975, and Oto-Missouri children were learning their tribal language in school.

BIBLIOGRAPHY: Chapman, Berlin Basil. *The Otoes and Missourias.* Times Journal Publishing Co. 1965; Edmunds, R. David. *The Otoe-Missouria People.* Phoenix: Indian Tribal Series, 1976.

MIWOK: a central California people located in the coastal region between San Francisco and Monterey in the early 19th century, numbering about 22,000 at that time. In the late 1970s, there were about 100 Miwok descendants located on California reservations, and probably several hundred more mixed with the general population.

The aboriginal Miwok were composed of three divisions: Eastern Miwok, Coast Miwok and Lake Miwok, with estimated populations of

19,500, 2,000 and 500, respectively. All spoke languages of the Miwokan subgroup of the Penutian language family. The Eastern Miwok subdivided into five cultural and linguistic groups: the Bay Miwok, Plains Miwok, Northern Miwok, Southern Miwok and Central Sierra Miwok. The latter three contained the bulk of the population.

Politically, the Miwok were organized into tribelets composed of several settlements or hamlets, each led by its own chief. With the exception of the Coast Miwok, each chief inherited his office through the male line. The duties of the chief, who was usually wealthy, included hosting guests, sponsoring ceremonies, settling disputes and overseeing the acorn harvest. There were two other officials, an announcer and a messenger. Among the Coast Miwok, there were in addition, two powerful female officials, who were in charge of various festivals and dances and oversaw the construction of the dance house.

Various types of shamans specialized in certain powers, which they obtained either by inheritance or dreaming. Aside from curing the sick, they also could control the weather, locate missing objects and locate deer for hunters. The Miwok had numerous ceremonies and dances, both sacred and social, which were held in a dance house or assembly house. They had a rich mythology, including many tales about the Trickster culture hero, Coyote. The dead were either cremated or buried, and mourners gathered to weep and wail. Widows cut or singed their hair and rubbed pitch on their face and hair.

House styles of the Miwok varied with the season and location, and included conical pole-frame structures covered with bark slabs, brush, grass thatch or tule mats. Semisubterranean earth lodges were sometimes used as winter homes or assembly houses. Each village also had a sweathouse.

The Miwok traveled seasonally to harvest wild plants, including acorns, greens, pine nuts, buckeyes, berries, seeds and roots. Fish were important in all areas, and included salmon, trout and various shellfish. They hunted deer, elk and bear, as well as smaller game such as rabbit, beaver, squirrel, quail and waterfowl. A variety of traps and snares were used, as well as bow and arrow. Deer were stalked using deerhead disguises, and rabbits were caught in communal drives by herding them into a long net.

The Miwok made excellent basketry in a variety of forms, including seed beaters, winnowing trays, cradles, burden baskets, storage containers and sifters. Rabbitskin blankets were woven, and deerskin was used for men's breechclouts and shirts as well as aprons or skirts for the women. For adornment, they wore ear and nose ornaments, as well as face and body paint. Tattooing and head deformation were also considered marks of beauty.

By the early 19th century, Spanish missions had been established in Miwok territory, and thousands of Indians were forcibly removed to the missions, where many died of disease and hardship. The Spanish encountered some difficulty, however, in their missionizing attempts among the Eastern Miwok, who began conducting organized raids on the missions in the 1820s and 1830s.

By mid-century, the Miwok were inundated by a flood of miners, fur-trappers, ranchers and settlers. The population of the Miwok plummeted from about 22,000 in 1800 to about 5,000 by mid-century. Miwok began laboring in the mines and on farms and ranches, becoming dependent on wages and giving up most of their hunting and gathering activities.

In the early 20th century a few small rancherias were purchased for the Miwok by the U.S. government. In the late 1970s, about 100 Miwok descendants were located on these rancherias, while probably several hundred more lived in or near small towns in the Sierra Nevada foothills.

BIBLIOGRAPHY: Barrett, S.A. and Gifford, E.W. "Miwok Material Culture." *Bulletin of the Public Museum of the City of Milwaukee.* vol. 2, 1933; Corrotto, Eugene L. *Miwok Means People.* Fresno, California: Valley Publishers, 1973.

MOBILE: a large extinct tribe located between the Alabama and Tombigbee rivers in southern Mississippi. They spoke a Muskogean language different from the corrupted form of Choctaw known as the Mobilian trade language. The latter was used as a lingua franca among trading Indians from Florida to Louisiana and north to the Ohio River. Mobile is thought to be derived from a Choctaw word meaning "to paddle." They may have numbered 6-7,000 when encountered by DeSoto in 1540, although they were reduced to 2,000 by 1650.

Their meeting with the Spanish was a disaster. In a day-long battle at their fortified town of Mabila (Mavilla) some 2,500 were killed. Although they fought fiercely and bravely (according to the Spanish accounts), the Mobile were no match for the armored intruders with their firearms and horses.

By the early 18th century the Mobile had moved southward to Mobile Bay, where they came under French influence and were Christianized. By the late 18th century the Mobile had either died out or merged with the Choctaw, with whom they were closely related.

BIBLIOGRAPHY: Swanton, John R. "The Indians of the Southeastern United States." *Bureau of American Ethnology Bulletin.* no. 137, 1946.

MODOC: a small tribe located in northern California and southern Oregon on Lost River, as well as Tule, Klamath and Clear lakes, in the early 19th century, when they numbered about 800. In the late 1970s, there were perhaps 500 Modoc descendants remaining, with about 50 located in Oklahoma and the rest mainly in Oregon.

The Modoc, along with the closely-related Klamath, spoke a dialect of the Lutuami language of the Penutian linguistic family. Their tribal name was derived from Moatokni, or "southerners," as they were referred to by the Klamath. They called themselves Maklaks, or "people."

The Modoc were composed of about 25 villages, each led by a civil chief (*la gi*) and a war chief. A *la gi* was chosen for his wealth, personal following and ability as an orator. Religious leadership was provided by shamans, who received their calling through five nights of appropriate dreams, followed by a five-day quest. Powers of shamans included dream interpretation, curing of illness, weather control and the ability to cause illness or death.

The Modoc believed that their culture hero Kumookumts created the world by weaving it outward from a point on the east side of Tule Lake. They believed also in an afterlife somewhere in the west. When a Modoc died, his body was wrapped in deerskin and burned, along with most of his possessions. His house was often burned, and his name no longer spoken. Widows cut their hair and smeared pitch and ashes on their hair and face.

The Modoc built semisubterranean multifamily winter homes, from 16 to 40 feet in diameter. The dwellings were constructed of a log framework, covered with poles and planks and overlain with tule mats and a thick layer of earth. Entrance was through the smoke hole in the roof. Summer and temporary houses were made of mats over a pole framework.

The Modoc spent the winter in their permanent villages, but they spent spring, summer and autumn nomadically, conducting their fishing, hunting and food gathering activities. The men caught trout, perch and suckers with a variety of nets. They also hunted mule deer, antelope, elk, bear, mountain sheep, duck, geese, quail, rabbits and other small game. Bow and arrow and spears were the usual weapons. The women, meanwhile, followed a seasonal cycle, gathering various roots, greens, fruits, berries and seeds as they ripened. Waterlily seeds (*wokas*) were an important food source, gathered in marshy areas in September and made into flour.

Modoc men and women both wore aprons of buckskin or tule in warm weather, adding leggings, fur robes and hats in cold weather. Some head deformation and piercing of ears and nose was practiced. Charcoal black

The Modoc Indians during the battle of the lava beds. Library of Congress

was used to prevent sunburn and snow blindness. Means of transportation included snowshoes, cedar log dugouts, tule rafts and horses.

In the early 19th century, the Modoc acquired their first horses and a desire for more. As a result, in the 1830s, the Modoc, along with the Klamath, stepped up their raids on the neighboring Achomawi and Shasta, with whom they had long been at war. Slaves and plunder thus acquired were taken to The Dalles of the Columbia River, a great intertribal trading center, to be exchanged for horses with tribes to the north.

The Modoc had their troubles too. In the winter of 1830, they were nearly starved out by snows so deep that finding their food caches was impossible. In 1833, they were affected by a serious epidemic which struck most of the Indian groups in the region, and, in 1847, they were seriously reduced by smallpox.

In the late 1840s, wagon trains on the Oregon trail began coming through Modoc summer hunting grounds, scaring the game away. The Modoc retaliated by attacking wagon trains. In 1851, gold was discovered nearby, and the area was soon flooded with miners, who helped themselves to Modoc land. The Modoc continued their attacks on wagon trains into the 1860s, but in 1864, along with the Klamath, signed a treaty with the United States, relinquishing their lands for a reservation.

The reservation was unfortunately located on former Klamath lands, and the more numerous Klamath made the Modoc feel unwelcome. In 1870, about 150 Modoc left the reservation with their leader Kintpuash (Captain Jack), and returned to their former homes on the Lost River, hoping to be assigned a reservation in that area.

In 1872, war broke out, and the Modoc fled to the lava beds, a labyrinth of rocks and caves south of Tule Lake. There, 80 warriors with their families were able to hold off more than 1,000 U.S. troops and Oregon volunteers. In 1873, during a peace conference, the Modoc killed two members of the U.S. delegation including Gen. Edward Canby. Shortly after, they surrendered, and Kintpuash and the other leaders were executed, while the rest of the band was sent to Indian Territory (Oklahoma).

The Oklahoma band was assigned lands on the northeast corner of the Shawnee reservation. These lands were allotted to individuals in 1890. In 1909, those who wished to were allowed to join the rest of the tribe still located on the Klamath Reservation in Oregon.

In 1956, the Klamath Reservation was terminated. In 1961 and 1974, the lands were sold, and the proceeds divided among the Klamath and Modoc tribal members. In the late 1970s, there were about 500 Modoc descendants remaining, with about 50 living in Oklahoma and most of the others located in Oregon.

BIBLIOGRAPHY: Faulk, Odie B. *The Modoc People*. Phoenix: Indian Tribal Series, 1976; Ray, Verne F. *Primitive Pragmatists: The Modoc Indians of Northern California*. Seattle: University of Washington Press, 1963.

MOHAVE: a Yuman tribe occupying both sides of the lower Colorado River in the late 18th century, numbering about 3,000 at that time. In the late 1970s, about 2,000 Mohave occupied two reservations in their traditional homeland, between Needles, California and Black Canyon.

Their tribal name was derived from Hamakhava, meaning "three mountains," referring to three jagged peaks in their territory known as the Needles. The Mohave spoke a Yuman language of the Hokan language family. They were a warrior tribe, closely allied with the Yuma.

The Mohave, although loosely organized, had a strong sense of tribal identity. They were led by a *kohota,* or chief, whose position was hereditary in the male line. His ruling powers were mainly advisory, but he had the duties of being dance director, scalp custodian and guardian of captives.

The Mohave believed that all knowledge, skills and fortune were derived from dreaming. Hunters, warriors, gamblers and shamans all received their special powers from dreams, which they may have had as an infant, or even before birth. Shamans cured the sick by restoring the patient's lost soul through dreams and songs. The Mohave had about 30 song cycles, each cycle numbering 100-200 songs, based on tales from their complex mythology. The songs were sung for curing, at funerals or merely for entertainment. The Mohave cremated their dead and burned the house and possessions of the deceased. Mourning and wailing was sometimes begun before death occurred, and relatives of the deceased observed certain food taboos for four days after death. For illustrious warriors, special mourning ceremonies were held at a later date.

The Mohave had no large towns or villages, but settled near any arable land. They built flat-roofed houses supported by four posts and covered with arrow weed thatch and sand. They also made cylindrical granaries with flat roofs.

For subsistence, they relied mainly on agriculture, planting their crops along the Colorado River after the annual floods receded. Corn, beans, squash, pumpkins and, after Spanish times, wheat and melons were cultivated. These crops were supplemented by such wild foods as mesquite beans, pine nuts and various seeds and fruits. Fish, caught with a giant scoop, were the primary source of animal protein. Bow and arrow, traps and deadfalls were used to take minor numbers of deer, mountain sheep, rabbits, beaver, raccoon and quail.

The Mohave made an assortment of pottery, including cooking pots, water jars and seed parching pans. Gourds were also used for carrying water, storing seeds and for making rattles. Most basketry was obtained in trade. The Mohave were inveterate traders, sometimes traveling several hundred miles to the Pacific Coast to obtain seashells. They acted as middle men, dealing in pottery, Hopi blankets, gourds, dried pumpkins, seashells and mesquite beans.

The women wore willowbark aprons, whereas the men wore breechclouts. Rabbit skin robes were worn in cold weather, and badger hide sandals were used for traveling. Both men and women adorned themselves with artistic face and body painting and men sometimes wore feathers in their hair.

Warfare was important in Mohave life, with the capture of females the main object. Their usual enemies included the Maricopa and Pima, whereas their frequent allies were the Yuma. Mohave weapons included clubs, circular deer hide shields, mesquite or willow bows, and arrows carried in coyote or wildcat skin quivers.

The Mohave were visited by Spanish expeditions in the 17th and 18th centuries, with relatively little impact. By the early 19th century, however, beaver and otter trappers were hunting in Mohave territory, and in the mid-19th century, they were visited by American exploration

A Mohave woman and child: a photograph by Edward S. Curtis, (1903).

and surveying expeditions. In 1865, the Colorado River Reservation was established for the Mohave and Chemehuevi tribes.

In the late 1970s, more than 1,800 Mohave and Chemehuevi lived on the 164,000 acre Colorado River Reservation, and more than 380 Mohave lived on the 38,000 acre Fort Mohave Reservation located near Needles, California. The Mohave language was still spoken.

BIBLIOGRAPHY: Kroeber, A.L. "Handbook of the Indians of California." *Smithsonian Institution Bureau of American Ethnology Bulletin.* no. 78, 1925; Spier, Leslie. "Mohave Culture Items." *Museum of Northern Arizona Bulletin.* no. 28, 1955.

MOHAWK: the eastern-most tribe of the Five Nations Iroquois Confederacy, located along the Hudson and Mohawk river valleys, north to the St. Lawrence River. From a population of perhaps 5,000 in 1650,

Library of Congress
Hendrick, the Mohawk chief, who was killed at the Battle of Lake George, New York, in 1755.

there were about 9,000 descendants in the late 1970s, residing mostly in Canada, New York, and Oklahoma.

Mohawk, a name applied to them by their enemies, means "man-eater." They called themselves Kaniengehaga, or "people of the place of the flint." In the late 1970s, the Iroquoian Mohawk language was still spoken and was still used as the official language in gatherings of the Iroquois.

The Mohawk were divided into three clans: bear, wolf and turtle. A person inherited the clan of his mother, and was forbidden to marry

A Mohawk man and woman pounding corn, near Brantford, Ontario.

within his own clan. Clan leaders, who represented their clan on the village and tribal councils, were nominated by the women of the clan.

The Great Council of the Iroquois, which met in the autumn of each year and in time of emergency, was made up of 50 sachems (chiefs) from the five tribes (Mohawk, Seneca, Onondaga, Oneida and Cayuga). The Mohawk held nine of these hereditary titles and were referred to as "keepers of the eastern door." Decisions in the Great Council were unanimous, resolved by discussing a problem until a consensus was reached.

Agriculture was the heart of many of the Mohawk religious festivals, such as the Green Corn ceremony, which gave thanks for the arrival of the harvest. At some festivals, curing groups such as the False Face Society wore carved wooden masks with distorted features to drive away illness.

The Mohawk usually located their villages on a hill along a river or stream. One description of a Mohawk town noted 36 longhouses, some 80 to 100 feet long, aligned in street-like rows. They were constructed of bark over a pole framework, each containing four or five firepits. Large quantities of corn and dried salmon were stored within.

Corn was the staple of the Mohawk, supplemented by beans, squash, fish, game and such wild foods as nuts, berries, roots, mushrooms and seeds. Men burned and cleared the fields while women took charge of planting, cultivating and harvesting. The men fished the streams with nets, weir and bone hooks and hunted with traps and bow and arrow.

The Iroquois League, or Five Nations Confederacy, was formed in about 1450 by the semi-legendary heroes Dekanawida, probably a Huron, and Hiawatha, a Mohawk living among the Onondaga. They managed to convince the five Iroquois tribes to abandon intertribal warfare with each other, thus freeing the various tribes to concentrate on trade and rivalry with their non-League neighbors.

In the early 1600s, when the Mohawk obtained Dutch firearms in trade for beaver pelts, they set about dominating their neighbors. Their trading and war parties ranged as far east as the Atlantic, north to Hudson Bay and south into the Carolinas. The 17th century was one of warfare as the Iroquois defeated the Huron, Erie, Neutral, Susquehanna and other surrounding tribes to gain control over the region which blocked the westward expansion of Europeans. This strategic location embroiled them in wars between the French, English and Americans. The Mohawk sided with the English in the American Revolution, and, after the war, most of them followed their chief Joseph Brant (Thayendanegea) to Canada, where they settled on the Grand River.

In the late 17th century, a group of Mohawk and Oneida who favored the French went to live near Montreal. They later moved to Sault St. Louis and became known as the Caughnawaga or "praying Mohawk." Some of these later moved to Ohio with other Iroquois, becoming known as the Seneca of Sandusky and eventually settling in Indian Territory (Oklahoma). Other Mohawk went west as guides and fur trappers and joined tribes in the northwest.

In the late 1970s the St. Regis (U.S.) Reservation had a population of about 2,500 Mohawk. Another 7,000 Mohawk lived in Canada, mostly on either the Caughnawaga Reserve or the Six Nations Reserve, set aside for Brant's followers. There were a few other groups in Ontario, Quebec and Alberta.

The Mohawk, especially the Caughnawaga are world-renowned as "high-steel men," constructing skyscrapers and bridges across the country. Colonies have grown up in the major cities. The Mohawk traditions, however, are still strong, and most return to the reservation frequently.

BIBLIOGRAPHY: Wilson, Edmund, *Apologies to the Iroquois*. New York: Farrar, Straus, Cudahy, 1960.

MOHEGAN: *See* PEQUOT.

MONACHE: a central California group located along the Sierra Nevada in the early 19th century, numbering about 2,000 at that time. In the late 1970s, there were several hundred Monache living in California, in several communities and on the Tule River Reservation. The Monache, also known as the western Mono, spoke a language of the Shoshonean division of the Uto-Aztecan language family. Culturally they were most closely related to the neighboring Yokuts, although they spoke the same language as the Northern Paiute of Owens Valley.

The Monache had six divisions, including the Northfork Mono, Wabonuch, Entimbich, Michahay, Waksachi and Patwisha. These divisions were composed of villages or hamlets each led by its own chief, who usually inherited his office through the male line. The chiefs' duties included arranging ceremonies, with the aid of a messenger, who made announcements, directed dancing and settled quarrels.

Also important in the villages were shamans, who possessed supernatural powers which they used for curing illness. Other individuals could obtain supernatural power from supernatural dream helpers, whom they acquired by swimming on cold winter mornings, visiting secluded spots, or taking *datura,* a concoction made from jimsonweed. When a Monache died, his soul was believed to travel west for two days to the land of the dead. His body was bound in a flexed position and cremated, and the remaining bones were buried. Women mourners singed their hair, and other relatives avoided washing or eating meat or

Library of Congress

A Monache house, with baskets: a photograph by Edward S. Curtis, taken in about 1910.

grease for six days. An annual six-day Mourning Ceremony was held, which included burning effigies of those who had died during the year.

The dwellings of the Monache village were often arranged in a semi-circle and were constructed of either thatch or cedar bark on a pole framework. Thatch was made from strips of brush, which were pounded until they were soft and then twined together. Most villages also had a sweathouse, acorn storehouses on posts and an open area used for dances and assemblies.

The Monache were hunters and gatherers, with acorns, the primary staple, being ground to flour on bedrock mortars. Other plant foods gathered were yucca roots, various seeds, and manzanita berries, used for making cider. The men hunted and trapped bear, rabbits and squirrels, and took deer using deerhead disguises as decoys. They caught fish with traps, weirs, nets and spears, and dried them for later use.

Material culture of the Monache included cooking vessels of both pottery and steatite (soapstone). Both twined and coiled basketry was produced, in the form of an assortment of containers, hats, cradles and other items. Basketry boats about four feet in diameter were used for floating babies and other valuables across rivers. They made bows of juniper and arrows of obsidian. Both men and women wore red and white face and body paint for ceremonies. Deerskin or fiber aprons were the usual apparel for women, with woven rabbit skin blankets in general use for cold weather.

The Monache occupied relatively undesirable territory, and thus remained comparatively isolated from the advance of civilization. As a result, they had a higher survival rate than their neighbors. In the mid-20th century, about 200 Northfork Mono still lived in several communities in California. There were also Monache on the Big Sandy and Cold Springs rancherias in Fresno County, and others were mixed with 350 Indians on the Tule River Reservation, Tulare County, California.

BIBLIOGRAPHY: Gayton, A.H. "Yokuts and Western Mono Ethnography." *University of California Anthropological Records.* vol. 10, 1948.

MONO: *See* MONACHE.

MONTAGNAIS: a group of Algonquian peoples located in Quebec and Labrador and closely associated with the Naskapi, with whom they together numbered about 5,500 in the early 17th century. In the late 1970s, there were about 6,000 Montagnais and 400 Naskapi located in Quebec and Labrador.

Montagnais, a French term meaning "mountaineers," referred to

Smithsonian Institution National Anthropological Archives

A Montagnais camp on Grand Lake, in Labrador, in about 1891.

themselves as Inu, meaning "the people." The Montagnais and Naskapi spoke dialects of the same Algonquian family language. Both groups were nomadic hunters and fishermen, with vast territories extending from the St. Lawrence River and Gulf northward to James Bay and Ungava Bay.

The Montagnais were divided into hunting bands. These were subdivided into groups of from two to six families who hunted together in winter under the leadership of a mature, capable head man. In summer, bands came together to fish or communally hunt caribou. In later times bands controlled hunting, fishing and trapping rights to certain territories. Rights to specific areas were inherited by individuals through the male line.

Marriage was usually outside the band, and men sometimes practised polygamy. Shamans provided religious leadership and cured illness through special powers. The Montagnais buried their dead wrapped in bark, sometimes building a little bark hut over the grave. Memorial feasts were sometimes given for the dead. The Naskapi placed their dead in trees or on scaffolds.

The Montagnais built conical wigwams of birchbark, whereas the Naskapi used caribou skin tipis. In both dwellings, a smokehole was located over the central fireplace. Pole-frame sweat lodges covered with skins were also used by the Naskapi.

The Montagnais hunted moose, caribou, geese, ducks, ptarmigan and grouse. After becoming involved in the fur trade, they concentrated on trapping fox, beaver, marten, mink, bear, lynx, wolf, wolverine and muskrat. In summer, they moved downriver to the coast to spear eels and salmon, harpoon seals and gather berries.

The Naskapi hunted caribou, their principal game, by pursuing them through deep snow on snowshoes or by driving them into water and pursuing them in canoes. They also trapped fox, otter, marten and other small game, and borrowed both ice fishing and seal hunting techniques from the neighboring Inuit (Eskimo). Birchbark canoes, toboggans and large oval snowshoes were the main means of transportation. Babies were carried in soft fur bags lined with dried moss.

The Montagnais wore skin breechclouts, leggings, moccasins and robes. The Naskapi adopted the more tailored, warmer clothing worn by the Inuit, including hooded caribou parkas. In later times, Montagnais women were noted for wearing pointed caps of red and blue cloth.

By the mid-16th century, European traders were frequent visitors. The 17th century brought an increased demand for beaver pelts and other furs, which were exchanged for European trade goods. By 1670, observers noted that cloth, copper kettles, knives, and iron arrowheads had nearly replaced the corresponding aboriginal items.

As the animal population in the area was diminished by both white and Indian trappers, the trade center moved inland from Tadoussac to Quebec and Montreal, leaving the Montagnais in the backwaters. During this time, the Montagnais were also driven northward by the expanding Iroquois, and the Naskapi had frequent conflict with the Inuit. Both groups also suffered greatly from epidemics of smallpox, measles, influenza and periods of starvation.

In the late 1970s, many Montagnais and Naskapi continued to hunt and trap for a living. They usually lived near certain trading posts which supplied them with clothing, sewing machines, rifles, ammunition, canvas tents, canvas canoes, traps and food. White flour had essentially replaced meat as the staple, and the trappers concentrated on obtaining furs rather than hunting for food. Families sometimes accompanied the men inland on their winter hunting trips, remaining at some central point on the trap line of perhaps 30 miles in length. Other times they remained on the coast.

BIBLIOGRAPHY: Harper, Francis. *The Friendly Montagnais and Their Neighbors in the Ungava Peninsula.* Lawrence: University of Kansas, 1964; Leacock, Eleanor. "The Montagnais Hunting Territory and the Fur Trade." *American Anthropological Association Memoir.* no. 78, 1954.

MONTAUK: a small but powerful tribe who occupied the eastern end of Long Island, New York, controlling most of the other tribes on the island except for those on the western end. The name Montauk, which may mean "fortified place," has at times been used to designate this larger grouping of tribes. In this broader sense, the Montauk numbered about 6,000 in 1600. By the late 1970s there were only a few Montauk of mixed blood living on the island.

The Montauk spoke an Algonquian language similar to that of the Natick and other Massachusetts tribes. About 13 of the Long Island tribes formed a protective league against the mainland tribes headed by the grand sachem, or great chief, of the Montauk tribe who lived at Montauk Point.

Houses, or wigwams, were either small and circular or multi-family longhouses. Both were constructed by setting saplings in the ground at intervals, drawing them together at the top and covering the whole with thatch.

The material culture of the Long Island tribes was replaced very early by European trade goods. Wampum, which was used for ceremonial purposes as well as the medium of exchange, was made from shells ranging in color from white to dark purple. The process of cutting, drilling, and polishing the shell was difficult and laborious.

A combination of white men's diseases and raids by mainland tribes led to the early decline of the Montauk. They were made tributaries of the Pequot in the early 17th century and were driven by Narraganset raids to seek protection of the white settlers at Easthampton about 1659. The grand sachem about this time was Wyandanch, whose brothers ruled the Shinnecock and Manhasset tribes.

About 1788, most of the Montauk went to New York to join the Brotherton and migrated to Wisconsin with them in about 1833. Only a few mixed blood Montauk remained on Long Island by the late 1970s.

BIBLIOGRAPHY: Saville, Foster Harmon. *A Montauk Cemetery at Easthampton, Long Island.* New York: Museum of the American Indian, 1920.

MUNSEE: See DELAWARE.

NABESNA: See TANANA.

NAHANE: a group of Athapascan peoples located in northern British Columbia and the southern part of the Yukon Territory in the late 18th century, numbering about 2,000 at that time. In the late 1970s, there were about 1,800 Nahane living in British Columbia and the Yukon

Territory. The Nahane, their name meaning "people of the west," spoke a language belonging to the Athapascan family.

The two major divisions of the Nahane were the Tahltan and Kaska. They were further divided into autonomous bands with fluid membership. Socially, they were divided into two matrilineal exogamous phratries, Raven and Wolf, similar to those of the neighboring Tlingit. Leadership was exercised by mature men who were capable hunters. Young married couples lived with the bride's family, after the groom had spent a year serving his prospective parents-in-law and proving himself as a hunter.

There were many rituals and taboos connected with hunting, and young men sought special hunting powers in dreams and visions. Shamans acquired guardian spirits who aided them in curing the sick. Disposal of the dead was by cremation or covering with brush, after wrapping the bodies in skins. Some groups held potlatches to commemorate the dead, in which the phratries exchanged food and gifts, and wooden masks were displayed. After a period of mourning, a widow sometimes married her deceased husband's brother.

The Nahane used bark or brush dwellings of several styles, including rectangular huts, conical tipis and temporary summer lean-tos. They were primarily hunters, especially of caribou. Mountain sheep and goats, beaver, moose, rabbit, fox, marten, wolverine and lynx were also hunted with bow and arrow, spears, traps and snares. Salmon and other fish were taken with weirs and nets in summer. The women collected roots and berries.

They carved wooden dishes and spoons and used spruce root baskets as cooking vessels. Clothing was of skins, including shirts and leggings with attached moccasins for men, and long dresses, leggings and moccasins for women. Robes were woven of rabbit skin or goat hair, and babies were carried in bags of beaver or other types of fur, lined with dry moss. Clothing was adorned with quillwork, and tattooing and ear and nose ornaments were used for adornment. Spruce bark canoes, snowshoes and caribou skin toboggans were used for transportation.

In the early years of the fur trade, the Tlingit acted as middlemen between the Nahane and the Europeans. By the 19th century, Hudson's Bay Company had established posts in the Nahane area, some of which were destroyed by coast tribes who objected to losing their middleman position.

The Klondike gold rush in the 1870s and the building of the Alaskan Highway in the 1940s both served to break down the Nahane way of life. In the late 1970s, trapping, fishing, guiding and wage labor were the most important economic pursuits. There were about 1,200 Nahane, including Kaska, connected with the Ross River, Laird River and Whitehorse bands, and about 700 connected with the Tahltan band.

BIBLIOGRAPHY: Honigmann, John J. "The Kaska Indians: An Ethnographic Reconstruction." *Yale University Publications in Anthropology.* no. 51, 1954.

NAMBE: a Tewa pueblo located on the Nambe River, 16 miles north of Santa Fe, New Mexico, with a population of about 325 in the late 1970s. The Nambe, along with San Ildefonso, San Juan, Santa Clara, Tesuque and Pojoague, spoke the Tewa language of the Tanoan language family. The name Nambe meant "mound of earth."

Nambe was divided into two moieties or tribal divisions Winter, or Turquoise, and Summer, or Squash—which were further divided into numerous clans. Each person belonged to the clan and moiety of his father. The pueblo was led by two caciques, a summer cacique, who governed from late February until mid-October, and a winter cacique, who was in charge the remainder of the year. The caciques were both the religious and political leaders of the pueblo, controlling the secular officers whom they appointed. The secular government, which dated from Spanish times, included a governor, who served as a liaison between the pueblo and the outside world. Two war chiefs guarded the

Traditional "ramadas" at the Nambe pueblo in New Mexico.

kivas, buildings where ceremonies were held, and carried out instructions of the cacique. There were also a number of secret societies, concerned with war, hunting, crop fertility and curing the sick. Each society had its own dances, rituals and paraphernalia which it used to carry out its special responsibilities.

In the early 17th century, the Spanish established a mission at Nambe. In 1680, Nambe joined most of the other pueblos in rebelling against the Spanish. The Pueblo Revolt, as it was called, was put down by 1692, and the Spanish returned to the area.

By the late 1970s, Nambe pueblo occupied 19,000 acres, with a population of about 325. Due partly to intermarriage, Nambe was very similar to the surrounding Spanish-American communities.

NANTICOKE: an Algonquian tribe which occupied the peninsula between the Delaware and Chesapeake bays. They were related to the Delaware and Piscataway (Conoy) tribes, having probably separated from them at some early date.

A great chief, or sachem, called emperor by the English, ruled over all the Nanticoke. Each village or town was in turn, ruled by a lesser chief, who probably inherited his title through the female line.

They stored the bones of their dead in a log *chiacason,* or burial temple, with shelves for bones and accompanying pipes, beads and ornaments. When the bones were later buried, a spirit dance was held to celebrate the passing of the souls to the afterlife. The Nanticoke were reportedly practitioners of poisoning and witchcraft.

Their villages were built along the banks of streams and were sometimes palisaded. In spring and summer, the Nanticoke concentrated on fishing and agriculture, but after the fall harvest, the entire village moved into the woods to hunt. Crafts included the making of splint basketry and log dugouts. They were known as good traders, and made and used wampum in their dealings with other tribes.

In 1608, the Nanticoke were visited by Capt. John Smith, who noted that they had at least five towns. In 1642, they were declared hostile by the Marylanders, in a feud that continued on and off through most of the rest of that century. The Indians objected to the peddling of liquor in their towns, and to the smallpox and other diseases brought on by their contact with the colonists.

In 1684 the Nanticoke were granted a 5,000 acre reservation between Chicacoan Creek and the Nanticoke River. White encroachment continued, however, so in 1707 another reservation of 3,000 acres was granted on Broad Creek in Delaware. In 1742, as a result of their taking part in the planning of an aborted uprising, the Nanticoke were forced to sign a treaty giving up their right to elect an emperor.

A young Nanticoke
boy with a
hominy mortar,
on Indian River,
Delaware:
a picture
taken before
1912.

Smithsonian Institution
National Anthropological
Archives

In 1747, with the permission of the Iroquois Confederacy, they settled near Wyoming, Pennsylvania; but by 1753, they had moved further up the Susquehanna, to settle at the former Onondaga town of Otsiningo. About that same time, they became a federated tribe of the Iroquois Confederacy and also merged with the Piscatway.

In 1778 about 200 Nanticoke moved to Fort Niagara at the time of the raid of the American general, John Sullivan, against the Iroquois. Most of these moved to Canada with the Iroquois after the American Revolution. In the late 1970s, there were descendants of Nanticoke in Canada, a few mixed with Delaware Indians in Oklahoma and a few mixed with the white population in Delaware.

BIBLIOGRAPHY: Weslager, C.A., *The Nanticoke Indians.* Harrisburg: The Pennsylvania Historical and Museum Commission, 1948.

NARRAGANSET: a powerful New England tribe who controlled most of Rhode Island and subordinated, at various times, the neighboring Niantic, Cowesit and some villages of the Nipmuc. For a short time they even dominated the powerful Wampanoag, who lived across Narraganset Bay, when that tribe was weakened by war and plague in the early 17th century.

Numbering about 3,000 in 1600, the Narraganset were nearly destroyed by warfare and disease, but in the late 1970s, several hundred

Lester Skeesucks,
a Narraganset
Indian, a
picture taken
before 1910.

Smithsonian Institution
National Anthropological
Archives

of their descendants remained. The Narraganset, whose name means "people of the small point," spoke an Algonquian language which died out in the 19th century.

They were ruled at times by a dual chieftainship consisting of a junior and a senior sachem. The most famous of these were Canonicus and his nephew Miantonomo, who ruled about the time the English colonies were being established in Massachusetts and Rhode Island. The office of sachem was inherited through the male line and alliances with sub-tribes and tributary tribes were constantly strengthened by marriage between the various ruling families. The head sachems had absolute power, but governed with the advice of their subschiefs and were responsible for the welfare of all their people.

In religious matters, *powwows* (priests or medicine men) were in charge, using their powers to cure the sick, bring rain or ensure victory in battle. The Narraganset believed in Cautantowwit, the god of all creation, who lived somewhere in the southwest. They also had numerous other spirits, or manitou, who controlled such things as the sun, moon, fire and water. When a Narraganset died, he was buried in mats or skins along with his tools, weapons and food, and was believed to have journeyed to join Cautantowwit in the southwest.

The Narraganset lived in circular wigwams, 10 to 20 feet in diameter, constructed of poles covered with bark. In spring, they moved near their cleared fields, where they planted corn, beans, squash, tobacco and sunflowers. These they dried and stored in pits in the ground. The men trapped and hunted deer, bear, beaver, and other small game. Bone needles were used in making skirts, breechclouts, moccasins and leggings of deerskin and for winter wear, robes, caps and mittens of bear and rabbit skin. Clothing was often adorned with quillwork and tiny wampum beads.

At the time of the founding of the first New England colonies, the Narraganset star was in the ascent. They had been spared the great plague of 1616 which had decimated many of their neighbors, and afterwards they had taken in many of the survivors as well as their territories. The great sachem of the Wampanoag, Massasoit, had even been forced to pay allegiance to Canonicus. The arrival of the English, the plague of 1633, and wars with the Pequot and the Mohegan, however, depleted some of their power.

In 1675-76 the Narraganset joined with their old enemies, the Wampanoag, to drive out the English. The struggle, known as King Philip's war, resulted in the death of hundreds of colonists and the near extermination of the Wampanoag, Narraganset and other smaller tribes. The Narraganset lost 1,000 killed or captured in the Great Swamp Fight in December of 1675. The English managed to take their island fortress, usually impregnable, because an unusually cold winter had frozen the water surrounding it. This broke the resistance, although fighting continued in 1676.

The Narraganset fled to the Mahican and Abnaki tribes. Some who were captured or surrendered were made slaves or indentured servants. Others were settled with the Niantic, who had remained neutral during the war, the two tribes thereafter being called the Narraganset. A reservation was set aside but was gradually diminished until the last lands were sold to the state in 1880.

By 1788, some of the tribe had joined the Brotherton Indians of New York and later moved to Wisconsin. In 1934, the Narraganset remaining in Rhode Island were incorporated under the Indian Reorganization Act. In the late 1970s, several hundred of their descendants remained. The Narraganset held a gathering each year in August, and there was growing interest in Indian welfare and culture as a whole.

BIBLIOGRAPHY: Boissevain, Ethel. *The Narraganset People.* Phoenix: Indian Tribal Series, 1975; Chapin, Howard M., *Sachems of the Narragansetts.* Providence: Rhode Island Historical Society, 1931.

NASKAPI: *See* MONTAGNAIS.

NATCHEZ: an extinct southeastern tribe, which was the largest, most powerful tribe on the lower Mississippi River at the time of European

Natchez Indians holding a harvest festival dance: from Le Page du Pratz, *Histoire de la Louisiane,* **(1758).**

Library of Congress.

contact. The Muskogean-speaking Natchez were a sedentary agricultural people with a complex social system based on worship of the sun. The total population of the tribe was about 4,500 in 1650.

Nine villages were located on St. Catherine's Creek near the present-day city of Natchez, Mississippi. They were ruled by a hereditary chief called the "Great Sun." His subjects were divided into two classes, nobles and commoners, with the nobility being further subdivided into suns, nobles and honored men. All members of the nobility were required to marry commoners, while commoners were free to marry within their own class.

Heredity was traced through the female line. A "Great Sun" would usually be the eldest son of "White Woman," a rank held by the eldest sister of the previous "Great Sun." Each morning the "Great Sun" greeted the rising sun and pointed out the direction it was to travel through the sky. On the death of a "Great Sun," up to 30 of his wives, guards and retainers would submit to death by strangulation, after being partly drugged with tobacco pills.

The body of the dead chief was placed in the Sun temple along with his predecessors. The bodies of nobles were dried on platforms, while commoners were buried near their villages. The Natchez believed in an afterlife based on a person's conduct of his earthly life. Those to be rewarded went to a place where the weather was always good, food plentiful, and there was no war, as all peoples were one, while those to be punished went to a watery world swarming with mosquitoes.

In the main village (called Natchez), there was a ceremonial center consisting of a sun temple and the cabin of the "Great Sun," each built on a mound facing each other. The buildings were of dried mud covered with woven mats on the outside. Three painted wooden birds adorned the temple roof, while a perpetual fire of three hickory logs was kept burning inside. Each of the lesser villages also had a ceremonial center, presided over by a subordinate chief of the sun class.

Agriculture was the mainstay of the Natchez economy, with corn the main crop. They cultivated beans, pumpkins, mushrooms, and later watermelon and peaches and gathered wild rice, berries, wild grapes, persimmons and nuts. Corn was usually pounded into meal in wooden mortars, and made into gruel or bread. They also were famous for persimmon bread. Salt was obtained in trade from Caddoan tribes to the northwest. Men and women both participated in sowing and harvesting of the corn crop. These labors were accompanied by elaborate religious festivals and offerings at the Sun temple.

The men hunted deer, wild turkey and buffalo, with bows and feathered arrows, the tips of which were either fire hardened or made of bone. Small fish were netted, while larger fish were shot with an arrow attached to a line and a wooden float. Fish and meat were preserved by smoke-drying.

Women were highly skilled in crafts, making incised pottery, weaving baskets and nets, and making a fine white textile out of the inner bark of the mulberry tree. This and various animal skins were made into clothing. Dugout canoes, up to 40 feet long, were made by burning out cypress or poplar logs. Adornment of both sexes included face and body tattooing and painting, ear plugs and earrings. Head flattening was also performed by binding infants' heads to their cradleboards.

Canoe parties of Natchez harassed the DeSoto expedition as it passed through the area in 1542. LaSalle visited the Natchez in 1682, and the village of the "Great Sun" was visited in 1700 by French explorers who wrote detailed accounts of what they saw.

The Natchez fought three wars with the French, in 1716, 1723, and 1729, during which time the Indians were greatly reduced and dispersed. After an attack by the French in 1731, 480 Natchez were sold into slavery in Santo Domingo, including the last "Great Sun." Most of the survivors fled north to the Chickasaw. Others moved to South Carolina and eventually joined the Creek and Cherokee. As a tribe the Natchez are now extinct, although their blood is well mixed with other southeastern tribes.

BIBLIOGRAPHY: Cushman, Horatio Bardwell, *History of the*

Choctaw, Chickasaw and Natchez Indians. New York: Russell and Russell, 1972.

NATCHITOCHES: *See* CADDO.

NAVAJO: the largest tribe in the United States in the late 1970s, numbering about 155,000 at that time, mostly located on or near the Navajo Reservation in Arizona, New Mexico and Utah. In the late 17th century, they were located in the same general area, with a population of about 6,000.

The Navajo spoke a language of the Athapascan family, similar to that of the Apache, both tribes having migrated into the southwest from northwestern Canada by about 1200 AD. Navajo was derived from a Tewa word, perhaps meaning "large cultivated fields." The Navajo refer to themselves as Diné, or "the people."

Until modern times, the Navajo had no tribal-wide organization. In the mid-18th century, they were composed of a number of bands, each led by a *natari*, or headman, The *natari*, appointed for life, was assisted by one or more war leaders.

The Navajo were divided into more than 60 clans, with each person belonging to the clan of his mother. Marriage within either mother's or father's clan was forbidden. Each newly-married couple built a hogan

A Navajo ceremonial sand painting, photographed by Edward S. Curtis in 1905.

A Navajo
woman with
a young girl:
Canyon de Chelly
National
Monument,
Arizona.

U.S. Department of the
Interior: National Park Service

near that of the bride's mother, although a man was forbidden to converse with or be in the same room with his mother-in-law. Property was usually inherited through the female line by female descendants. Men sometimes married sisters or other closely related females, each wife having her own home. An important economic and social unit was the extended family, which usually cooperated in such communal tasks as house building, cultivation and stock raising. In later times, a larger unit, known as an "outfit," composed of two or more extended families, worked together on various economic enterprises.

, Navajo deities belonged to a category of beings known as the Holy People, as distinguished from humans, or mere Earth Surface People. Included among the Holy People were Changing Woman (or Turquoise Woman, a sort of Creator-Mother Nature), her husband the Sun, and their children, Monster Slayer and Child of the Waters. Other Holy People, who could be either kindly or malevolent, included the Thunder People, Wind People, Crooked Snake People, Coyote, and others.

Many religious customs of the Navajo were borrowed from the Pueblo Indians, particularly the Hopi. Masked dances, feathered prayer sticks, altars, dry painting (sand painting) and the use of corn meal and pollen were all borrowed and adopted by the Navajo. One important ceremony was the *kinalda*, or girls' four-day puberty rite, during which girls were required to gast, grind large quantities of corn, race eastward at dawn each morning, and dance in an all-night ceremony on the fourth night.

Important parts of Navajo religion were the singing of solemn chants and the performance of sacred dramas by masked impersonators of the Holy People. There were more than 50 curing chants alone, each containing several hundred songs or prayers, carefully memorized by apprentice singers. The function of the great chants was to preserve the harmony of the universe at large and restore the mental and physical health of individuals.

The Navajo had a great fear of the dead and ghosts. When a person died, his body was removed through a hole cut in the north side of the dwelling and buried immediately in a rock crevice. Most of the belongings of the deceased were destroyed or buried with the body, and his hogan was abandoned. In the past, slaves were sometimes killed. The relatives purified themselves by washing and smoking, and observed a four-day mourning period. Meanwhile, the soul of the deceased set out on a four-day journey to an underground afterlife somewhere to the north.

The Navajo built two types of hogans, or dwellings. The earlier one was supported by three forked poles resulting in a conical structure. The later dwelling had a framework of four vertical posts placed in a square. Walls were built up like a log cabin, gradually tapering toward the center to form a dome-shaped roof with an opening left as a smokehole. The

U.S. Department of the Interior: National Park Service

A hogan at Standing Cow Ruins, Canyon de Chelly, Arizona.

Navajo and sheep at Canyon de Chelly, Arizona.

roof, and sometimes the walls, were covered with a layer or packed earth. Other structures in a settlement included sweat lodges, brush corrals, and flat-roofed brush ramadas, or sunshades, for work areas.

The Navajo, who came into the Southwest as a hunting and gathering people, soon learned agriculture from the Pueblo peoples. Corn, beans and squash were later supplemented by fruit trees, oats and wheat, introduced by the Spanish. The women also gathered pine nuts, cactus fruit, wild potatoes, greens and a variety of seeds. Many of the wild plant foods were destroyed when the Navajo began raising livestock, acquired from the Spanish in the 16th century.

The men hunted antelope by driving them into stone and brush corrals. Both deer and antelope were caught by trapping in pitfalls and by stalking with animal head disguises. Eagles were caught by hunters hiding in a pit under a cover of sticks and earth, with a tethered rabbit for bait. Eagle feathers were used for ceremonial purposes. Hunting of deer, bear, antelope and eagle required special ritual observances. A variety of traps and snares were used in hunting, as were throwing sticks and bows of oak and juniper.

Navajo women made fine pottery, including ladles, jars with pointed bottoms, and decorated bowls of various shapes. They also made coiled basketry winnowing trays, food containers, ceremonial baskets, parching trays and pitch-covered water bottles. Early clothing for the Navajo consisted of aprons and breechclouts of woven yucca, later replaced by buckskin. Juniper bark and yucca sandals were also worn. By the mid-18th century, the women were wearing dresses made of two woolen blankets, usually black with stripes of red, yellow or blue, sewn

A Navajo
silversmith,
(1939).
Library of Congress

together and belted. By this time, the men began wearing buckskin shirts, leggings and moccasins. By the late 19th century, voluminous calico skirts and velveteen blouses were popular with the women, and cotton pants and velveteen shirts were worn by the men.

Silver and turquoise jewelry was the favorite adornment. Silverworking, learned from Mexican silversmiths in the 19th century, reached the state of high artistry among the Navajo men. The Navajo women, meanwhile, had learned weaving techniques from the Pueblo Indians, and had begun producing beautiful rugs and blankets using their own imaginative designs, made with natural vegetable, animal and mineral dyes.

By the 13th century, the ancestors of the Navajo and Apache had probably begun drifting into the southwest, by an unknown route, from northwestern Canada. In the late 16th century, Spanish explorers found them settled in northern New Mexico in an area the Navajo called Dinetka, "Home of the People."

By the late 17th century, the Navajo were herding sheep, goats and horses acquired from the Spanish, and were raiding Spanish settlements for food, horses and women. After the Pueblo Revolt in 1680, numbers

**A Navajo
weaver:
Canyon
de Chelly,
Arizona.**

U.S. Department of the
Interior: National Park Service

of Hopi, Jemez and other Pueblo Indians took refuge with the Navajo, bringing their skills in weaving, pottery making and agriculture, as well as religious and ceremonial traditions. Most of the Pueblo returned eventually to their homes, but many stayed to marry and form new clans within the Navajo tribe. In the 18th century, drought brought another influx of Hopi immigrants.

In the early 19th century, the Navajo continued to raid Spanish and New Mexican settlements and to endure reprisal raids. Mexico became independent of Spain in the 1820s, and the Navajo had a new ruler for a short time. By 1848, Mexico had been forced to give up New Mexico to the United States, which was determined to stop all Indian raiding. The Navajo and other tribes were to be concentrated on reservations. In 1863, when the Navajo refused to be moved, U.S. troops under Kit Carson began destroying all Navajo crops, orchards, herds and homes and rounding up the starving survivors. In 1864, some 8,000 Navajo were herded on a forced march of 350 miles from Fort Defiance to Fort Sumner, also known as Bosque Redondo, where they were interned for four years. Some 2,000 died on the march or later during internment, but many escaped back to their homeland.

Navajo working on an irrigation system at Window Rock, Arizona.

In 1868, the Navajo Reservation was established, and the Navajo returned to rebuild their homes and herds and re-establish fields and orchards. In the 1880s, some of the best grazing land and watering places of the reservation were taken for railroad rights of way. Disease, discrimination and alcoholism plagued the Navajo in the late 19th century.

The 20th century was marked by considerable growth in population, reaching around 155,000 by the late 1970s. The discovery of oil on the reservation stimulated development in the early 1920s. Stockraising was so successful that by the 1930s, a stock reduction program was necessary to save the reservation from overgrazing.

In the late 1970s, the resources of the Navajo Reservation were insufficient to support the growing population. Several off-reservation communities had developed to ease the pressure, including Ramah, just south of Gallup, and Canyoncito and Puertocito, southwest of Albuquerque. There was a need to develop new means of livelihood on the reservation to supplement stockraising, subsistence farming and wagework for the government and the railroad, the two major employers.

Tourism was growing, with the addition of several new tribal parks, and silverwork and weaving continued to be important. In the late 1970s, Navajo culture, arts and crafts, language and religion were vital forces in the daily life of "the people."

BIBLIOGRAPHY: Kluckhohn, Clyde and Leighton, Dorothea. *The Navajo.* Cambridge: Harvard University Press, 1946; Kluckhohn, Clyde,

Hill, W.W. and Kluckhohn, Lucy Wales. *Navajo Material Culture.* Cambridge: Harvard University Press, 1971.

NESPELEM: *see* SANPOIL.

NETSILIK INUIT: an Inuit (Eskimo) group located in the Canadian Arctic north of Hudson Bay, numbering about 500 in the 19th century. In the late 1970s, there were several hundred Netsilik Inuit, living in the same area. The Netsilik, whose name meant "people of the seal," spoke a dialect of the Inuit (Eskimo) language, which was spoken, with minor variations, from Alaska to Greenland. The name Eskimo was derived from an Abnaki term meaning "raw meat eaters," while the term Inuit, meaning "people," was their own name for themselves.

The Netsilik were subdivided into a number of small hunting bands, each identified with a particular area. The Netsilingmiut lived around Boothia Isthmus; the Arviligjuarmiut lived around Pelly Bay and Simpson Peninsula; the Arvertormiut occupied the northern end of Boothia Peninsula; the Qegertarmiut were on the southern and eastern ends of King William Island, and the Ilivilermiut were located on Adelaide Peninsula.

The bands were not formally organized, and individuals and families joined or left at will. The extended family, led by the oldest capable male, was the most important unit. Marriage tended to be monogamous. Often, two families would enter into a partnership for seal hunting and food sharing.

Religious leadership was provided by *angakot*, or shamans, who called upon their protecting spirits, or *tunraq*, to help them cure the sick, control the weather, locate game or find lost objects. Apprentice *angakot* received their training and their first *tunraq* from an older *angakot*. The Netsilik believed in numerous deities, spirits, ghosts and monsters, and carried amulets for protection and luck in hunting. Many hunting taboos and ceremonies were observed to propitiate the "woman at the bottom of the sea," who controlled all marine animals.

There were also taboos observed when someone died, including a prohibition of working or hunting during the four or five day mourning period. The body and belongings of the deceased were abandoned, and the survivors moved their camp.

In winter, the Netsilik came together in four or five main villages of snowhouses to hunt seal. Usually, two closely related nuclear families occupied a snowhouse, which could be built by two or three men in an hour. Blocks cut with a snow knife were placed in an inward-leaning spiral until they formed a dome. A thin slab of freshwater ice served as a window, and a platform of packed snow covered with skins and furs served as beds. Conical sealskin tents, anchored with stones, were used as summer dwellings.

The seasonal cycle of the Netsilik called for winter harpooning of seals at their breathing holes on the sea ice, and summer migrations to the interior for fishing and caribou hunting. The migrating caribou were hunted communally, with light spears from kayaks, as they crossed rivers and lakes. Steelhead, lake trout and cod were taken with spears, weirs and leisters (three-pronged spears). They also occasionally hunted polar bear and musk-ox.

For winter transportation, the Netsilik used short sleds pulled by two or three dogs. The wooden runners were shod with a layer of frozen peat coated with ice. They made lamps and cooking pots of soapstone, and oil and water containers from sealskin. Containers for tools were made from salmon skin, and clothing was sewn using needles and caribou-sinew thread.

Winter clothing was made mainly from caribou skins, which were warm, lightweight and soft. For maximum insulation, inner clothing was sewn with the hair side in, and outer clothing with the hair side out. Sealskin was used for waterproof boots, mittens and coats for kayaking.

The Netsilik area was visited by numerous 19th-century expeditions in search of the Northwest Passage to the Pacific. Significant contact with the outside world was not made, however, until the visits of the Roald Amundsen expedition (1903-05) and of Knud Rasmussen, of the Fifth Thule expedition, (1923). By that time, the Netsilik had acquired firearms from the neighboring Iglulik.

In the 1920s, they were engaged in trapping of white foxes for the fur trade. By the 1930s, several missions were established in the area, becoming permanent settlements: Gjoa Haven on King William Island, Spence Bay and Kugardjuk on Pelly Bay. Beginning in the 1950s, the Canadian government established schools and nursing stations in the areas, and English was taught in the schools.

In the late 1970s, the Netsilik youth, through the schools, were rapidly becoming acculturated in some respects. The caribou, hunted both summer and winter, were considerably depleted by the use of guns, and the musk-ox were near extinction. Sealing was carried on in summer using rifles and canoes. With the more individualized hunting methods, the nuclear family was more important than ever as an economic unit.

BIBLIOGRAPHY: Balikci, Asen. *The Netsilik Eskimo.* Garden City, New York: The Natural History Press, 1970.

NEUTRAL: an extinct sedentary tribe inhabiting the northern shore of Lake Erie in the early 1600s. They were quite populous, numbering between 12,000 and 20,000 at that time, and occupying land from both shores of the Niagara River on the east, to the Grand River on the west. They were destroyed as a tribe by the Five Nations Iroquois Confederacy in the 1650s.

The Neutral spoke a language of the Iroquoian language family, similar to that of the Huron, and were called Attiwandaron by the Huron, meaning "those who speak a language slightly different from ours." The name Neutral was coined by the French explorers and missionaries because the tribe was neutral in the wars between the Iroquois and the Huron.

The Neutral were organized into several matrilineal clans, each probably named for an animal. The clans were sub-divided into families, each headed by a woman. The tribe was ruled by a number of chiefs, probably with one great chief ruling over all. The titles of chieftaincy were hereditary within a family, but candidates for the office were chosen by the matron of the family and approved by a council of chiefs.

The Neutral believed in various spirits and demons and when a person died the mourners blackened their faces as well as that of the dead. The body of the deceased was adorned with feathers and trinkets and then placed on an elevated platform. The bones were later stored in the home until mass burial at the feast of the dead. At this feast, dead heroes were often "resurrected" into the body of a live person amidst solemn ceremony. The live person was then endowed with the name, title and respect due the dead hero.

Neutral villages located near enemy frontiers were often surrounded by single or double palisades of vertical poles, with the spaces between them lined with bark. The houses were 40-50 feet long and 10-15 feet wide, made of wood frames covered with bark, and housed 10-20 families.

The tribal economy was based on hunting, agriculture and trade. Men hunted deer, wildcat, black bear and beaver. Women planted corn, beans, squash, and the principal crop, tobacco, and gathered wild apples and chestnuts. They traded tobacco and furs to the Huron and flint for arrowheads to various tribes. They had a monopoly on flint from their quarries located near Point Abino on Lake Erie. The Neutral manufactured flint arrowheads, as well as excellent carved stone pipes. They wore clothing of finely-tanned skins and adorned themselves with tattooing and body painting.

The Neutral probably migrated from somewhere south, along with the Iroquois. By the 1600s, they were well established in the Lake Erie area, and allied with the Andironon and Wenrohronon tribes in a loose confederacy. The first European contact was probably with de Champlain's interpreter, Etienne Brulé, in 1615. Subsequent contact was essentially limited to various Jesuit and Récollect missionaries, as the Huron, who dominated the tribe economically, prevented direct trade of the Neutrals with the French.

In 1650, after having dispersed the Hurons, some of whom had sought shelter with the Neutral, the Iroquois Confederacy turned on the Neutral, and drove them from their lands by 1651. Some joined bands of Huron near Lakes Superior and Michigan; some fled south to the Susquehanna River, while others were captured and absorbed by the Iroquois.

BIBLIOGRAPHY: Wright, Gordon K. *The Neutral Indians: A Source Book*. Rochester, New York: New York State Archeological Association, 1963; Tait, Lyal. *The Petuns: Tobacco Indians of Canada*. Port Burwell, Ontario: Erie Publishers, 1971.

NEZ PERCE: the most numerous and powerful Sahaptian tribe, located along the lower Snake River and its tributaries in western Idaho, northeastern Oregon and southwestern Washington in the early 19th century, numbering about 6,000 at that time. In the late 1970s, about 1,700 Nez Perce were located on the Nez Perce Reservation in Idaho, and descendants of Chief Joseph's band were located on the Colville Reservation in Washington.

The Nez Perce spoke a language of the Sahaptian division of the Penutian language family. Their tribal name, a French term meaning "pierced nose," was a misnomer, since the Nez Perce were not among those tribes who customarily wore nose ornaments for adornment.

The Nez Perce were composed of numerous small, local bands, each consisting of one or more villages plus fishing camps. In later times, the local bands became grouped into larger bands, each with its own chiefs and warchiefs.

Religious leadership was provided by shamans, who cured the sick, controlled the weather, exorcised ghosts and presided at funerals and other ceremonies. Adolescents were encouraged to seek guardian spirits through fasting and vigils on mountain tops. Shamans had such heaven-oriented guardian spirits as Sun, Cloud, Eagle or Fish Hawk. Important ceremonies included guardian spirit dances, in which the participants dressed and acted as representations of their guardian spirits. Nez Perce mythology centered around the culture hero-trickster Coyote. When a person died, his body was dressed in fine clothes and, after two or three days, wrapped in deerskin and buried along with personal possessions. The family of the deceased usually moved their house and cut their hair.

The Nez Perce had a variety of house styles, including both square and conical mat lodges and communal longhouses up to 150 feet in length.

A Nez Perce
baby:
photograph
by Edward S.
Curtis,
in about 1910.

Library of Congress

The latter were of mats on a pole A-frame, with a line of fireplaces down the middle. Other structures included earth-covered sweat lodges, where young unmarried men slept and dance houses for ceremonies and dances. After the Nez Perce acquired horses and began making buffalo-hunting trips to the Plains, some groups adopted skin tipis.

Fish was the staple food, with salmon, trout, eel and sturgeon caught with nets, hooks, spears and traps. The salmon was dried or smoked, and stored for later use. Women gathered camas, wild carrots, wild onions, bitterroot, serviceberries, huckleberries, chokecherries and currants. Deer, elk and mountain sheep were hunted with bow and arrow. Snowshoes were used for hunting in winter.

The Nez Perce made an assortment of basketry items, including watertight vessels, packbaskets, winnowing trays, cups, bowls, mats and hats. Other craft items included horn ladles, wood bowls, skin bags, soapstone pipes, cradleboards and dugout canoes. Clothing was of skins, including moccasins, leggings, breechclouts, shirts, long dresses and women's caps embellished with fringes, quillwork and elks teeth. Elk and buffalo robes were worn for extra warmth, and face paint was used for adornment.

The Nez Perce acquired horses around 1730, and by selective breeding

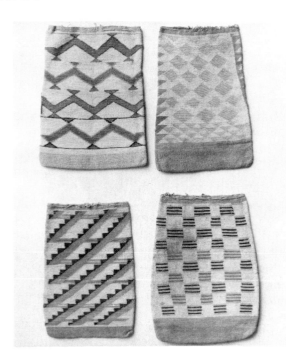

Nez Perce bags.
Smithsonian Institution

developed excellent stock, including the appaloosa. Their vast herds were favorite targets for raids by Plains Indians who had not yet built up their herds. The Nez Perce allied with the Flathead, Coeur d'Alene and Spokan against the Blackfoot, Gros Ventre, Crow and other Plains tribes. Other allies were the Sahaptian tribes, the Cayuse, Umatilla and Wallawalla, with whom they fought the Shoshoni, Bannock and other Great Basin tribes to the south. Weapons of the Nez Perce included: bows of mountain sheep horn, cedar or ash; arrows tipped with obsidian or jasper; elkskin shields, helmets and armor.

After the Lewis and Clark expedition of 1805-06, trappers and traders flooded into the region. The Nez Perce were involved in the fur trade in the 1820s and 1830s, and supplied settlers with needed items in the 1840s. During this time epidemics seriously reduced the Nez Perce population, which fell to about 1,800 by 1850.

In 1855, the Nez Perce and neighboring tribes were induced to sign treaties ceding their lands to the United States in return for reservations. Gold was discovered on the Nez Perce treaty lands, and, in 1863, their reservation was reduced by 75 percent with the loss of the Walowa and Grande Ronde valleys in Oregon. The bands in those areas refused to recognize the treaties or move to the reservation at Lapwai, Idaho.

In 1877, the Nez Perce, led by the chiefs Joseph and Looking Glass, resisted attempts by the U.S. Army to force them onto the reservation. Five months of fighting led to a remarkable 1,200-mile retreat by Joseph's band of about 450 Nez Perce, pursued by several thousand troops. They were finally captured near the Montana-Canada border. Joseph's band was sent to Indian Territory (Oklahoma), where many died before the band was sent to the Colville Reservation in Washington.

In the late 1970s, the Nez Perce Reservation had a population of 1,700 and contained 34,000 acres of tribal land and 53,000 acres allotted to individuals. Many traditions were still observed, including ceremonial dances, root feasts, Indian games, and ceremonies of the Seven Drums Society.

BIBLIOGRAPHY: Haines, Francis. *The Nez Perces.* Norman: University of Oklahoma Press, 1955; Spinden, Herbert Joseph. "The Nez Perce Indians." *Memoirs of the American Anthropological Association.* vol. 2, 1908.

NIANTIC: *See* NARRAGANSET.

NIPMUC: a small Algonquian tribe located in the central plateau region of Massachusetts, between the Merrimack and Connecticut rivers. Nipmuc translates as "freshwater fishing place." Numbering about 500 in 1600, they were extinct as a tribe by the late 18th century.

Their villages had no strong political connection with each other, resulting in their being dominated by their stronger neighbors, the Massachuset, Pequot, Narraganset, and Wampanoag tribes. Tribute was paid to these, as well as to the Mohawk, further west.

The Nipmuc were Christianized by New England missionaries, including John Eliot, who translated the Bible into Indian languages. By 1674 the missionaries claimed ten villages of Christian converts, the largest of which was Hassanamiset (now Grafton).

The Nipmuc located their villages along streams and ponds. Houses were of pole framework covered with mats woven of bark. A smokehole was left in the roof for the cooking fire within, as well as a door at either end.

The women engaged in agriculture and sometimes constructed the wigwams. The men hunted deer, beaver, raccoon and other animals, but the staple food was corn. They grew apples, introduced by the English, in large orchards and made cider. They made clothing of animal skins and furs and wove fine mantles of turkey feathers.

In 1675, the Nipmuc joined with surrounding Indians in King Philip's War, a vain effort to drive out the English. After the war, the Nipmuc were dispersed, some fleeing to Canada or to the tribes along the

Hudson. Those who remained in the vicinity eventually died out or were absorbed by the white population.

BIBLIOGRAPHY: Freeland, Mary DeWitt. *The Records of Oxford.* Albany: Joel Munsell's Sons, 1894.

NISQUALLI: a Northwest Coast group located along the Nisqualli River in northwestern Washington, which, together with the Puyallup and other related groups, numbered about 3,600 in 1780. In the late 1970s, there were more than 850 Nisqualli and other Indian groups living on or near the Nisqualli Reservation in Washington.

The Nisqualli language, belonging to the Coast division of the Salishan language family, was spoken by the Nisqualli, Puyallup, Skagit, Snohomish and Snuqualmie. The Nisqualli had a number of villages along the river, composed of large cedar plank dwellings, each housing from four to eight families. Leadership of each house and village was based on wealth and prestige. They were divided into three classes: nobles, commoners and a few slaves, who were either taken in warfare or purchased from other tribes. Their economic organization included a number of specialists, including hunters, harpooners, canoe makers, warriors and gamblers.

Shamans were specialists who had acquired supernatural powers enabling them to cure the sick and recover lost souls. Adolescent boys made five to ten-day quests in which they fasted and underwent physical hardship in order to gain powers needed for success in life. At puberty, girls fasted, bathed and observed certain taboos. Marriage was formalized through an exchange of gifts between the two families.

The most important Nisqualli ceremony was the *sugwigwi*, or potlatch, during which a wealthy person reaffirmed his status by distributing gifts and displaying his inherited wealth and privileges. Potlatches were held in connection with such events as reburial of the dead. Two methods of interment were used: burial in a canoe hung in trees, and burial in the ground, covering the grave with a small cedar plank shed.

Along the coast of Puget Sound, Nisqualli houses tended to have single-pitch roofs, while those in the river valley were usually gabled. The massive house posts supporting the roof were often painted. Sleeping platforms lined the interior walls and each family had its own fireplace.

The Nisqualli had an abundant food supply, which varied with the location. Salmon, the staple food, as well as herring, smelt, cod, trout and flounder, were caught and smoke-dried for later use. Fishing technology included hooks, traps, weirs, spears, nets and herring rakes. Coastal groups also harpooned seal. Deer, elk, black bear and beaver were also hunted with bow and arrow, snares and pitfalls. Deer, duck and fish were all hunted at night from canoes with a small fire in the stern used to

NISQUALLI 313

attract the game. The women gathered sea foods such as clams, mussels, cockles and fish eggs, as well as greens, seeds, camas, tiger lily bulbs, and an assortment of berries.

The Nisqualli were the only Coast Salish group to acquire a large number of horses, for which they had excellent pasture land. In warfare, they used warclubs, flint-pointed spears and yew bows and arrows. The women made both twined and water-tight coiled basketry, as well as mats of cattails and tule. Cedar bark was used to make clothing and rain capes, sometimes supplemented with skin items such as moccasins and leggings. Face painting and dentalium necklaces were used for adornment and women wore basketry caps.

In 1854, the Medicine Creek Treaty, on which the name of the Nisqualli leader Leschi was probably forged, ceded most of their lands. A 4,700-acre reservation was established in 1857. In 1918, all reservation lands on the east side of the Nisqualli River were made part of Fort Lewis military post.

In 1973, there were 85 Nisqualli on the tribal tolls, and an unknown number not enrolled. In the late 1970s, there were about 850 Nisqualli and Indians of other tribes living on or near the 800-acre Nisqually Reservation, located 10 miles east of Olympia, Washington.

BIBLIOGRAPHY: Smith, Marion W. *The Puyallup-Nisqualli.* New York: Columbia University Press, 1940.

NOOTKA: a group of Northwest Coast whaling tribes located on the western coast of Vancouver Island, British Columbia, numbering about 6,000 in the late 18th century. In the late 1970s, there were about 3,500 Nootka, divided into about 16 bands, living on reserves in their traditional territory.

The various Nootka tribes spoke dialects of the Nootkan language of the Wakashan language family. The three main dialects included Nootka proper, Nitinat and Makah, the latter spoken by a Nootkan tribe on Cape Flattery.

The Nootka were composed of a number of tribes and confederacies occupying permanent winter villages. Socially they were divided into several classes: slaves; commoners; a middle class composed of orators, war chiefs and minor chiefs; and the nobility, including the ranking chief and his family. Rank was based on wealth and inherited privileges. Prestige derived from giving potlatches, in which the host distributed gifts, displayed inherited wealth and recounted the privileges of his lineage. Each gift given was later returned with interest in subsequent potlatches. Privileges and property included both economic and cere-

A Nootka thunderbird and whale memorial, erected to commemorate the death of a chief, at Friendly Cove, Nootka Sound, Vancouver Island, British Columbia, (1903).

monial possessions such as areas on both land and sea and the right to certain rituals, dances, songs, names and ceremonies.

Winter provided leisure time, during which the Nootka developed a rich mythology and a complex ceremonial life. There were numerous categories of spirits and mythological beings, including the Salmon People, Supernatural Canoes, Thunderbird, Wolf, dwarfs, canoe-swallowing sharks and the Sky Codfish who caused eclipses by swallowing the sun. Hunting rites were important, especially those connected with whaling. Special rituals also surrounded the first salmon catch of the season. Potlatches were given to celebrate such events as birth, puberty, marriage and death, and were the means by which a chief transferred his privileges to his children.

Central to Nootka religion was the acquisition of a guardian spirit to guide a person throughout his life, giving him power in the form of special skills, luck or other achievements. Shamans acquired several guardian spirits which helped them to cure the sick, recover lost souls and perform magic. Shaman dances, highlighted by a major potlatch and the use of carved wooden masks, were the major social ceremony.

When a Nootka died, his body was wrapped in a cedar bark blanket and placed in a wooden box, which was removed through an opening in the house wall and placed in a cave or tree or beside a carved wooden memorial to the dead. A feast was held, at which the possessions of the deceased were given away. Slaves were sometimes killed to accompany the wealthy in the afterlife.

Nootka winter homes were large cedar plank multifamily dwellings, with gabled roofs supported by a ridge pole and massive log posts, on which sea lion heads and human figures were carved. Low sleeping platforms lined the walls, and wooden storage chests served as room dividers. Each family had its own fireplace. In summer, when the family migrated to fishing or hunting camps, the wall planks were taken along and used in the smaller temporary houses.

Although the Nootka were intrepid whalers, dog salmon, which ran in the autumn, provided the staple winter food. Coho salmon, sockeye salmon, halibut, herring and cod, caught with hooks, traps and spears, were also important. Whaling from ocean-going cedar log canoes was a highly specialized occupation, only participated in by those with the requisite skills and ritual knowledge. Equipment used included heavy harpoons connected by a long line to sealskin floats. Whale meat, blubber and oil were highly prized.

Seals and sea lions were also harpooned, and ducks and other water fowl were taken with underwater nets and traps. The men also hunted elk, deer, mink, marten and otter using spears, bow and arrow, snares and deadfalls. The women gathered shellfish, sea urchins, roots, huckleberries, thimbleberries, blackberries, salmonberries and cranberries.

Food was dried, smoked, broiled, steamed in pits or boiled in wooden boxes with red hot stones. Dishes, platters, cups, buckets and storage boxes were made of wood. Small canoes were sometimes used for serving food at a large feast. The Nootka made six types of cedar canoes, which were used by tribes throughout the region. Cedar bark mat sails were sometimes added. Cedar inner bark was woven into skirts, robes, rain capes, mats and bags, and spruce root was used for making rain hats and baskets. Ear and nose ornaments were worn, and face paint was used for ceremonies and sunburn protection.

The Nootka engaged in both warfare and trade with their neighbors. They were well-possessed of several valuable trade items, including sea otter pelts, dentalia shell and cedar canoes. After 1774, the Nootka were flooded with European trade goods. European traders' interest in sea otter pelts resulted in the near extinction of that animal by the 1820s. Shark oil for the sawmill industry brought trade to the Nootka again after 1850. In the 1880s, some Nootka men joined fur sealing expeditions bound for the Bering Sea and visited China, Japan and San Francisco as well.

When reserves were established in the late 19th century, the Nootka winter and summer villages and favorite fishing spots were included. By the early 20th century, schools and canneries were established in the area. In about 1913, a law was enacted prohibiting potlatches, which seriously weakened Nootka cultural traditions. In the late 1970s, the 16 Nootka bands had a total population of about 3,500.

BIBLIOGRAPHY: Drucker, Philip. "The Northern and Central Nootkan Tribes." *Bureau of American Ethnology Bulletin*. no. 144, 1951.

NORRIDGEWOCK: a small eastern Abnaki group located in the Kennebec valley of southern Maine. In the early 18th century, they were dispersed or driven into Canada, where they were absorbed by other Abnaki groups. The Norridgewock spoke the Abnaki language of the Algonquian language family.

The Norridgewock were known as the Kennebec in the 17th century, when they occupied numerous towns in the Kennebec valley. They were allied with the French against the English colonists, who destroyed their principal village of Norridgewock in 1729 and again in 1749. At the outbreak of the French and Indian War in 1754, the surviving Norridgewock fled to St. Francis in Quebec.

BIBLIOGRAPHY: Hanson, J.W. *History of the Old Towns, Norridgewock and Canaan*. Boston: 1849.

NORTH ALASKA INUIT: an Inuit (Eskimo) people located along the north Alaska coast and the adjacent tundra and foothills north of the Brooks Range, between Point Hope and Point Barrow, in the mid-19th century, when they numbered 4,000 to 5,000. In the late 1970s, there were about 2,800 North Alaska Inuit, located mostly along the coast and in a few interior settlements along the Kobuk River, near Anaktuvuk Pass in the Brooks Range.

The North Alaska Inuit spoke the Inuit (Eskimo) language, which was spoken, with minor variations, from northern Alaska to Greenland. They were divided into the Tareumiut, who lived along the coast and concentrated on whale hunting, and the inland dwelling Nuunamiut, who depended on the vast caribou herds. The two groups were mutually dependent, trading whale blubber and oil for caribou skins.

The North Alaska Inuit lacked political organization and leadership other than that required by communal economic activities. Among the interior Nuunamiut, caribou hunt leaders were important, whereas among the coastal Tareumiut, the *umealiq*, or boat-owner, provided whale hunting leadership. For a short time each year, membership in a

A North Alaska Inuit hunter, with snowshoes. The National Archives

hunting group or boating party was important, while most of the year, individuals moved about freely.

The family was the basic social unit, consisting of the nuclear family plus a few relatives. Kinship relationships were important, and were extended by marrying outside the kinship group. Successful hunters sometimes had two, or occasionally three, wives. Outside of kinship, the most important relationships were partnerships between two men based on hunting, trading or social activities. Men with such relationships would sometimes exchange wives for short periods, as a sign of the strength of the relationship.

The North Alaska Inuit believed the world was created by Raven, a trickster figure in their mythology. Their religion centered around ceremonies, rites and taboos intended to propitiate the spirits of the animals they hunted. Shamans conducted ceremonies and seances to cure the sick. When a person died, his body was removed through the skylight and abandoned out on the tundra. When food was scarce, old people and newly-born female babies were sometimes abandoned.

Both the Tareumiut and Nuunamiut built semisubterranean houses of sod, with long underground entrance-ways serving as storage areas. The coastal houses were usually a little more elaborate, with interior walls of wood and whale bone. A platform in the main room served as chairs, table and beds, while cooking was performed in a little side room with a smokehole. Well insulated, and heated by small seal oil lamps, the houses were very warm. Seal or walrus gut stretched over a frame served as a translucent skylight.

A larger house of similar construction, called a *karigi,* was used as a men's house, ceremonial house and recreation center. The Nuunamiut also commonly used a dome-shaped house of two layers of caribou skins on a willow pole framework. Both groups also had portable tents, used for hunting trips, and occasionally built temporary snowhouse shelters.

The main activity of the coastal Tareumiut was whale hunting in open skin boats called *umiaks.* This dangerous activity took place for about two months in spring, after which they moved inland to fish, hunt caribou and trade with the Nuunamiut. The interior dwellers hunted the migrating caribou from spring to fall, by driving them into corrals lined with stakes, or into the river, where they chased them in kayaks. Both groups also hunted or trapped wolves, wolverines, foxes, ptarmigans, rabbits and water fowl. In winter, the coastal groups also hunted seal and walrus through the ice.

Women's work included fishing, butchering and storing meat, preparing food, dressing skins and making clothing of caribou skins. For transport in winter, the North Alaska Inuit used wooden dogsleds with iced runners to improve their speed.

The mid-19th century marked the beginning of frequent contact between the North Alaska Inuit and whalers, which lasted until whaling died out in the latter part of the century. Missionaries and traders were active in the region by the early 20th century. Fox hunting, for the fur trade, reached its peak in the 1920s. In the late 1970s, the hunting of whale, seal, caribou and walrus were still of prime importance, with certain modern adaptations such as the use of guns and snowmobiles. The family was still the most important unit in North Alaska Inuit life.

BIBLIOGRAPHY: Spencer, Robert F. "The North Alaskan Eskimo: A Study in Ecology and Society." *Smithsonian Institution Bureau of American Ethnology Bulletin.* no. 171, 1959.

NTLAKYAPAMUK: *See* THOMPSON.

Library of Congress

Red Cloud and his wife: a photograph by Herman Heyn, (1900).

OGLALA. The largest subdivision of the Teton Dakota, located in the mid-19th century in the region north of the North Platte River of South Dakota, including the Black Hills, numbering about 3,600 at that time. Their name meant "to scatter one's own." Red Cloud and Crazy Horse were two of the most famous Oglala chiefs. In the late 1970s, Oglala descendants numbered about 12,000, located mostly at Pine Ridge Reservation, South Dakota. (See also *Teton* and *Dakota*.)

BIBLIOGRAPHY: Hyde, George E. *Red Cloud's Folk*. Norman: University of Oklahoma Press, 1937.

OJIBWA: an Algonquian tribe located north of Lake Huron and northeast of Lake Superior in the early 17th century, numbering perhaps 35,000 at that time. In the late 1970s, they were the most numerous tribe north of Mexico, with about 160,000 Ojibwa descendants living in Michigan, Wisconsin, Minnesota, North Dakota, Montana, Oklahoma, Ontario, Manitoba and Saskatchewan.

The Ojibwa, whose name means "puckered up," referring to their style of moccasin, spoke an Algonquian language. The Ojibwa language had numerous dialects, some of which were spoken by the Ottawa and Algonquin tribes, as well as by the various Ojibwa bands. They referred to themselves as Anishinabe, meaning "people" or "first people."

The Ojibwa were known at various times in various places by a number of other names. The most commonly used of these was Chippewa, used in the United States and southern Ontario in the late 1970s. In northeastern Ontario, the term Mississauga, the name of a band located on the northern end of Lake Huron, was applied at times to most of the southeastern Ojibwa. The Ojibwa living around Sault Sainte Marie were called Saulteur or Saulteaux by the French, names which spread north and west with Ojibwa bands in the 18th and 19th centuries. At the same time, Ojibwa bands moving westward from the Minnesota-Wisconsin-Ontario woodlands to the Plains became known as the Plains Ojibwa, or Bungi. This latter group underwent extreme cultural change in the space of a few generations, as they abandoned most of their woodland culture for the life of the equestrian buffalo hunter of the Plains.

In early historic times the Ojibwa were composed of small autonomous bands, each led by a chief whose influence was based on ability, personal appeal and kinship. Each band was composed of a number of families, usually interrelated. Socially the Ojibwa were divided into from 15 to 23 clans, each named after a totemic animal, bird or fish. Each person inherited the clan of his father and was restricted from marrying inside his clan.

The Ojibwa believed in the Great Spirit, or Gitchi Manito, as well as numerous other *manito,* or spirits, present in all aspects of nature. Ojibwa children were encouraged to seek a guardian or spirit helper, who would aid them throughout their lives. Guardian spirits were acquired through visions obtained by fasting in remote places. The Ojibwa had a rich mythology, which included the culture hero Nanabozho (or Wisakedjak), his brother Wolf, the evil Underwater Panthers, Ice Giants, Sun, Moon, Earth, Thunderbirds and numerous other characters.

The most important ceremony of the Woodlands Ojibwa was the secret Medicine Dance of the Midewiwin, or Medicine Lodge Society. Candidates for society membership, including both men and women,

Bureau of Indian Affairs

An Ojibwa cemetery near Coos Lake, Minnesota. The triangular openings in the ends of the burial huts were made to permit the spirits of the dead to escape and make their way to the afterworld.

were initiated, after payment of certain fees and a period of instruction, in a ceremony lasting several days. Shamans, who cured the sick, had usually attained at least the fourth of the eight degrees of the Midewiwin. Other curing was performed by persons knowledgeable in the use of medicinal plants.

When an Ojibwa died, his body was dressed in good clothing, wrapped in birchbark, removed through an opening in the west side of the wigwam and buried. In later times, a small gable-roofed bark house was built over the grave. The soul embarked on a four-day journey to an afterlife somewhere in the west.

The most common house style of the Ojibwa was the conical or dome-shaped wigwam of birchbark or cattail mats on a pole frame. Small conical sweat lodges were used for treating illness or for ceremonial purification.

In summer, the Ojibwa bands gathered into villages, where they fished, collected wild foods and planted small gardens of corn, beans, squash and pumpkin. They caught fish with nets, bone or wood hooks, and spears, sometimes used at night by birchbark torchlight. In winter, the bands usually broke up into smaller groups and moved to their hunting grounds. Bow and arrow, snares and deadfalls were used to hunt

Bureau of Indian Affairs

Ojibwa at Mille Lacs, Minnesota, in 1936. The wigwam is of the "maple sugar" type: the ridge pole and eight supporting poles being very heavy to support the maple sugar pots. In the fall, leaves are piled around the base of the wigwam to conserve heat.

deer, moose, bear, beaver, lynx, mink, marten, otter, rabbit and, in the northern areas, caribou. Meat was dried, pulverized and mixed with fat and chokecherries or blueberries to make pemmican.

To supplement the diet, they gathered wild foods such as strawberries, juneberries, raspberries, blackberries, cranberries and nuts. For several weeks in spring, gathering maple sap to make mapie sugar was an important activity. In some areas, wild rice in lakes was harvested in the fall by poling a canoe through the rice and gently knocking the grains of rice into the canoe with two sticks.

For the Woodlands Ojibwa, birchbark canoes were the most important means of transportation. Snowshoes were used in winter. Two popular games were lacrosse and snow-snake throwing, in which a polished stick was slid along the top of the crusted snow. Birchbark was used for making dishes, trays and an assortment of containers. Clothing was of buckskin, including breechclouts, leggings, moccasins, dresses and robes, with fringes and quillwork for decoration.

By the early 17th century, French explorers had entered Ojibwa territory around Georgian Bay, soon to be followed by fur traders and missionaries. By the late 17th century, the Ojibwa were becoming heavily

Joe Jackson
of the Saginaw
Chippewa
(Ojibwa)
tribe of Michigan,
making
snowshoes
for sale,
(1965).

Bureau of Indian Affairs

involved with the fur trade, exchanging skins and pelts for guns, cloth, knives, iron kettles, beads, tools and other European items. At this time, pressure from the Iroquois and from French fur traders were factors causing expansion and dispersion of Ojibwa bands.

Some bands moved into the lower peninsula of Michigan, where they were closely allied with the Ottawa and Potawatomi, while others moved westward into northern Wisconsin and Minnesota. The Saulteaux began ranging far north of the Great Lakes, the northern groups becoming culturally influenced by the Cree.

As the well-armed Ojibwa moved into Wisconsin and Minnesota, they displaced the Dakota (Sioux) and other groups. The Ojibwa added wild rice gathering to their woodlands subsistence activities and continued their involvement in the fur trade. Many Ojibwa went west as paddlers for the French voyageurs, and remained there. Ojibwa bands to the north moved westward to Lake Winnebago, Lake of the Woods and Rainy Lake. Ojibwa groups moving into the Red River area displaced the Hidatsa, Arikara and Cheyenne.

With the acquisition of horses, Ojibwa bands moved out onto the Plains to hunt buffalo. By 1830, the Plains Ojibwa, or Bungi, had moved west to northern Dakota, northeastern Montana, southern Manitoba and southeastern Saskatchewan. The buffalo became the main

Catching ripe rice
grain heads with
one stick, a
Chippewa rice
harvester prepares
to thresh them
with another,
so that the rice
will fall into
his boat.

Bureau of Indian Affairs

source of food, shelter, clothing, tools and weapons. They adopted many Plains Indian cultural aspects, including the Sun Dance, soldier societies, men's dance societies, scaffold burials, buffalo skin tipis, communal buffalo hunting and hard-sole Plains-style moccasins. They adopted Plains-style tailored skin clothing, but decorated it with colorful geometric and floral patterned beadwork. Many aspects of Woodlands culture were retained, including the Midewiwin society and sugar making, wherever maple or box elder trees could be found. Deer, moose, elk and caribou were still hunted where available.

In the early 19th century, Ojibwa groups in Michigan and Ontario were forced to cede their lands for reservations, and in the mid-19th century, the Wisconsin and Minnesota bands were forced to do the same. In the 1860s, other Ojibwa groups, mixed with Ottawa, Munsee and Potawatomi, settled in Indian Territory (Oklahoma). In 1869-70, Plains Ojibwa, along with Plains Cree, took part in the Métis rebellion in Manitoba, led by Louis Riel. Soon afterwards the Canadian Plains Ojibwa and northern Saulteaux were assigned reserves. The U.S. Plains Ojibwa were settled on Turtle Mountain Reservation, North Dakota, in about 1892, and, with some Plains Cree, on Rocky Boy's Reservation, Montana, in 1916.

In the late 1970s, about three-fourths of the estimated 160,000 Ojibwa descendants lived in Canada, with about half of these in Ontario. Only about half of the Canadian Ojibwa were listed on tribal rolls or connected with any reserve or band. In both the United States and Canada, many Ojibwa were living in urban areas, but many of these returned frequently to visit families and friends on reserves. There was a growing interest and pride in Ojibwa traditions, culture and language, a surprising amount of which remained after more than three centuries of acculturation.

BIBLIOGRAPHY: Howard, James H. "The Plains Ojibwa or Bungi." *Anthropological Papers of the South Dakota Museum.* (University of South Dakota). no. 1, 1965; Skinner, Alanson. "Notes on the Eastern Cree and Northern Saulteaux." *Anthropological Papers of the American Museum of Natural History.* vol. 9, 1911.

OKANAGON: the principal tribe of a group of culturally related Washington and British Columbia tribes, known as the Okanagon Group and including the Lake (Senijextee), Colville, and Sanpoil (*q.q.v.*), as well as the Okanagon themselves. The Okanagon occupied the Okanagon and Similkameen river valleys and the shores of Lake Okanagon, on both sides of the U.S.-Canada border, numbering about 2,200 in 1780.

In the 1970s, there were about 660 Okanagon on and around the Colville Reservation in Washington and about 1,500 on various reserves in British Columbia. They spoke a language of the Interior division of the Salishan language family, calling themselves Isonkva'ili, meaning "our people."

They were composed of two geographical divisions, the Similkameen and the Okanagon proper, which were subdivided into from five to ten bands. Recent authors have divided them into the Northern Okanagon, in Canada, and the Sinkaietk, in the United States. Each of the bands was autonomous and led by a chief, usually hereditary, with limited power. The real authority rested in an informal council of older men. There were also temporary war chiefs, to lead them in time of warfare.

Religion centered around spirits believed to reside in animals, rocks, plants and all things of nature. Guardian spirits were acquired by youths through visions during periods of seclusion, sweat bathing and physical training, and were essential to success in life. Shamans cured sickness through powers acquired from especially powerful guardian spirits. The principal deity was a creator deity variously called Chief of the Dead, Chief Above or Great Mystery. Important ceremonies included puberty rites for girls, the First Fruit Festival, and various dances—War, Scalp, Guardian Spirit, Marriage and Sun Dances. Coyote was a culture hero important in their mythology.

The dead were wrapped in matting or robes and buried in the ground or in rock slides. Sometimes canoes were placed on the grave or effigies were erected over the grave site. Widows and widowers cut their hair, prayed and wore old clothes. The souls of the dead went to a more pleasant land, somewhere in the south or west.

Winter dwellings were circular, semisubterranean lodges of pole frame construction, 45 feet in diameter, with entry by an opening in the roof. Summer dwellings were above ground, conical in shape, of tule mats on a pole frame. Dome-shaped sweathouses were used by both men and women to purify themselves and by youths as homes during their period of training to acquire guardian spirits. In later times, skin tents replaced the mat summer dwellings for trips to the Plains for buffalo.

The Okanagon were a hunting, fishing and gathering people. Salmon was the staple food, caught with dip nets, seine nets, weirs, traps, spears and hook-and-line. Deer, elk, bear, beaver, and marmot were important game, as well as buffalo, taken on trips across the Rocky Mountains to the Plains. Hunting techniques included drives, stalking, surrounds and the use of dogs. Meat was roasted, boiled or dried for later use. To supplement the diet, they gathered various roots, especially camas and bitterroot, and berries, especially serviceberries, soapberries and huckle-berries, as well as cherries and nuts.

Water transportation was by canoes of birch or other bark. Small round snowshoes were used for winter travel. Weapons included double curved bows of juniper, and arrows with flint heads. Baskets were of cedar bark, or woven spruce roots. Decorated with geometric designs, the latter were often tight enough to hold water for cooking. Other crafts included blankets of goat wool or woven of strips of rabbit fur, as well as woven sacks of rushes, bark and Indian hemp. Clothing was of dressed skins—leggings, moccasins, breechclout (for men) and tunic (for women), with a fur robe added for cold weather.

Traditionally, the Okanagon were once localized near the confluence of the Okanagon and Similkameen rivers in Washington, before expanding to their present location. After acquisition of the horse in the early 1700s, they steadily expanded northward, displacing the Stuwik and the Shuswap. At various times, they allied with the Colville in wars against the Nez Perce and Yakima. First contact with Europeans was probably with traders in the early 19th century.

In 1848, the tribe was divided by the international boundary. In 1858, gold was discovered on the Fraser River, leading to several years of conflict with miners and settlers. In 1872, the Colville Reservation was established, absorbing the U.S. Okanagon, together with other tribes. The Canadian Okanagon were later assigned to a number of small reserves.

In the 1970s, there were about 660 Okanagon (or Sinkaietk) on and around the 1,011,495-acre Colville Reservation in northeastern Washington, mixed in among the total population of about 3,000 of various tribes. There were also about 1,500 Okanagon living on various reserves in British Columbia, grouped into six bands: Lower Similkameen, Okanagon, Osoyoos, Penticton, Upper Similkameen and Westbank. The total land area of the various reserves was about 139,000 acres.

BIBLIOGRAPHY: Teit, James A. "The Salishan Tribes of the Western Plateaus." *Bureau of American Ethnology Annual Report. no. 45,* 1927-28.

OMAHA: a tribe of the Dhegiha division of the Siouan language family, located in northeastern Nebraska in the late 18th century, numbering about 2,800 at that time. In the late 1970s, there were about 1,500 Omaha descendants, mostly located in Nebraska.

The other four members of the Dhegiha language group were the Ponca, Quapaw, Osage and Kansa. The Omaha were the most closely related to the Ponca in language, culture and history. The tribal name, meaning "those going against the current," referred to the tradition which recounted the migration of the Dhegiha peoples down the Ohio River to the Mississippi River. Those who went up the Mississippi (which included all but the Quapaw) at that time were all referred to as Omaha, later splitting into the Osage, Kansa, Ponca and Omaha.

The Omaha had two divisions, each composed of five patrilineal gentes. The two divisions, Sky People and Earth People, were each represented by a principal chief and a sacred pipe, while Omaha tribal unity was symbolized by a sacred pole. A tribal council was composed of seven chiefs, whose responsibilities included maintaining tribal peace and order, dealing with other tribes, and selecting the *wathon,* or leader of the annual buffalo hunt. The council also chose *wanonshe,* or "soldiers," to carry out their orders.

The Omaha had numerous societies, divided into two types, social and secret. Social societies included men's warrior societies, as well as those of a purely social nature. Secret societies, which usually required members to have had a dream or vision, often practiced healing by means of medicinal plants and rituals. Omaha religion emphasized an invisible life force, called Wakonda, through which all things were related to each other.

The Omaha thought the Milky Way was a path made by spirits, on their journey to the realm of the dead. Burial customs included placing their dead on scaffolds or in a tree or burying them in a sitting position facing east. Mounds of earth were placed over the hillside graves.

The National Archives
Omaha boys in uniform at the Carlisle Indian School in Pennsylvania.

The Omaha located their villages along streams, with a nearby hill for a lookout. Their two house styles were earth lodges, which they adopted from the Arikara, and portable skin tipis, used for hunting or set up in sheltered valleys in wintertime. Earth lodges, 20 to 60 feet in diameter, were constructed of a heavy wood framework interwoven with willow branches. A thick layer of grass thatch was placed over this framework and covered with pieces of sod overlapped like shingles. The interior floor was made very smooth and hard by successive treatments of water and fire.

Women, who did all the work of constructing tipis, were aided by the men in the more heavy work of building earth lodges. When household duties became too burdensome, an Omaha man would sometimes marry the sister or niece of his first wife. Women's other duties included dressing skins for shelter and clothing, and growing corn, beans, and squash, which were dried and stored in underground caches.

The summer buffalo hunt was important for more than just the food, shelter and clothing it provided. Hoes and other tools were made of buffalo bones. Containers, round bull boats and shields were made from the tough hides. Other crafts included pottery, woodcarving, quillwork, painting and beadwork.

According to tradition, the Dhegiha group migrated together from the southeast, by way of the Ohio and Wabash river valleys. Reaching the confluence of the Ohio and Mississippi, in about 1540, the Quapaw went downstream, while the other tribes went upstream. The Osage left the group when they reached the Osage River, and the Kansa left to go up the Missouri River. The Omaha and Ponca continued to the upper Mississippi Valley and settled for a time around the Minnesota pipestone quarries. They were soon driven westward by the Dakota to the area of Lake Andes in present-day South Dakota, where the Ponca and Omaha separated. The Ponca continued as far west as the Black Hills before turning back toward the east. They rejoined the Omaha, and the two tribes went down the Missouri to Nebraska, where the Omaha left the Ponca and settled on Bow Creek, Nebraska in the late 17th century.

The Omaha continued to dwell in that area of Nebraska, west of the Missouri River between the Platte and Niobrara rivers, until the mid-19th century. During the early 18th century, the Omaha visited French trading posts far up the Missouri River and on Lake Winnipeg. By the late 18th and early 19th centuries, they were regularly visited by English and American traders, trade goods soon changing many aspects of their material culture.

The Omaha were ravaged by smallpox in 1802, which reduced their population to about 300. In 1854, they were forced to cede all their lands to the United States, and one year later, they moved to a reservation in Dakota County, Nebraska. In 1865, the northern part of the reservation was sold to the Winnebago. Lands were allotted to Omaha tribal members in 1882. In the late 1970s, there were about 1,500 Omaha, mostly living on or near the 40,000 acre Omaha Reservation.

BIBLIOGRAPHY: Fletcher, Alice C. and LaFlesche, Francis. "The Omaha Tribe." *Bureau of American Ethnology Annual Report*, no. 27, 1906.

ONEIDA: one of the tribes of the Iroquois Five Nations Confederacy located in an area in New York state bounded on the north by Oneida Lake and on the south by the upper waters of the Susquehanna River. They numbered about 1,000 in 1677, having lost population through war and epidemics. As with the other Iroquois tribes, the Oneida constantly replaced their dwindling population by adopting captives taken in battles with other tribes. In the late 1970s, their descendants numbered about 5,000, in Wisconsin, New York and Ontario.

Oneida has been translated as "people of the stone set up." They were organized into three clans: Turtle, Wolf, and Bear. Clan membership was inherited from a person's mother, and it was forbidden to marry within one's own clan. Women held a position of respect within the tribe, nominating the chiefs of their clan. These chiefs represented the clan in village council meetings and at the Great Council of the Confederacy, which met in the autumn of each year or in times of emergency. The Oneida were entitled to nine of the 50 sachemships on the council.

The principal Oneida village, Oneniote, was located on a hill and surrounded by a double palisade. The village contained over 60 lodges or longhouses. The multi-family longhouses were of pole and bark construction, and had animal effigies painted on them to mark the various clans. Inside they were divided into family apartments, each with its own cooking fire and benches for sleeping and storage.

Agriculture was the mainstay of the Oneida economy, with corn, beans, pumpkins, tobacco and ginseng as the main crops. Some 1,000 bushels of the latter were raised in peak years for trade with other tribes and Europeans.

While the women handled the agricultural chores, the men hunted for bear, deer and small game, sometimes ranging for long distances over several months' time. The women were often called upon to help bring the meat home and cut it in strips to dry. Fishing was also important, with the surplus of dried salmon being sold to the Mohawk.

The Iroquois League, or Confederacy, was formed in about 1450 by the semi-legendary heroes Dekanawida, probably a Huron, and Hiawatha, a Mohawk living among the Onondaga. They managed to convince the Oneida, Onondaga, Mohawk, Seneca and Cayuga to give up warfare with each other.

The Oneida were in contact with Dutch traders by 1635. By mid-century, they were embroiled, along with the other Iroquois Confederacy tribes, in wars with the French and the Huron. In the late 1600s, recurring battles with the French, as well as recurring smallpox epi-

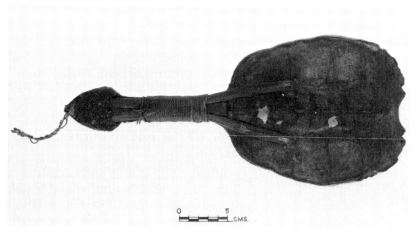

An Oneida turtleshell rattle. Smithsonian Institution

demics, severely reduced their numbers. It was estimated that, at times, over one-half of the tribe was made up of Huron and Algonquian captives.

By 1750, some of the Oneida had begun to drift into the Ohio valley. The rest became embroiled in the French and Indian War and the American Revolution. In the Revolution, they first attempted to remain neutral, along with the Tuscarora, who had come north to join the Iroquois Confederacy in 1722. Later they served as scouts and guides for the Americans, bringing on themselves retaliation from the other Iroquois tribes, who had sided with the British.

After the Revolution, the Oneida were confirmed in their lands by the Americans. In 1792, about 630 Oneida were left in New York. About this time, they began selling their lands and looking for a home further west, free from white encroachment. Most of the other Iroquois, who were loyal to the British, had departed for Canada.

In the 1820s, the Oneida purchased land in Wisconsin from the Menominee Indians, and most of the tribe moved West. Much of the Wisconsin land was subsequently lost through legal fights, treaties and swindles. By the late 1970s, about 2,000 tribally owned acres remained, together with nearly 500 acres of allotted land. About 3,000 Oneida lived on or near the Wisconsin reservation, while another 2,000 lived either in New York, or else in Canada, along the Thames River in Ontario.

BIBLIOGRAPHY: Richards, Cara E., *The Oneida People*. Phoenix: Indian Tribal Series, 1974.

ONONDAGA: one of the Five Nations Iroquois Confederacy, located along the shores of Onondaga Lake, north of Ontario and south to the upper Susquehanna River. They numbered about 1,750 in the 1660s. In the late 1970s, about 800 Onondaga lived in New York state and another 600 in Canada. In the Iroquoian Onondaga language, which was still in use in the late 1970s, Onondaga means "people of the mountain."

The Onondaga were organized into eight matrilineal clans: Wolf, Bear, Beaver, Tortoise, Deer, Heron and Eagle. Clan leaders, who represented their clan on the village and tribal councils, were nominated by the clan matrons. The Great Council of the Iroquois, which met in the autumn of each year and in time of emergency, was composed of 50 sachems (chiefs) from the five tribes (Onondaga, Mohawk, Seneca, Oneida, Cayuga). The Onondaga held 14 of these hereditary titles— more than any other tribe.

In addition, the capital of the Confederacy was located at Onondaga village, and the Onondaga were keepers of the Council Fire. The chief

The Smithsonian Institution National Anthropological Archives

The Onondaga played a leading role in the Iroquois Confederacy. Here chiefs of the Six Nations meet in council: their wampum belts are being explained, (1871). Wampum consisted of beads fashioned from shells and strung together. Wampum belts were originally used to record treaties, or to be used as a form of tribute, as well, on occasion, for purposes of historical record. It was not originally a medium of exchange, but became one after European settlers began to use it as a form of currency.

of the Council, called the Tadodaho, was always an Onondaga. Two other Onondaga sachems acted as his councillors and a third was "keeper of the Council wampum." These responsibilities all date back to the formation of the Iroquois League or Confederacy in about 1450, by the semi-legendary founders, Hiawatha and Dekanawida. The establishment of the League at Onondaga made it not only one of the most important and renowned towns of the Iroquois, but also in North America. At the height of Iroquois power, it was the capital of a government extending from the Hudson River in the east to Lake Michigan in the west, and from Lake Simcoe in the north to the Potomac in the south.

The Onondaga worshipped Ha-wah-ne-u, known as the Creator of the World, Holder of the Heavens, and Master of Breath. Their most important festivals included the maple sugar festival, the corn planting festival, the green corn feast, the harvest festival and the Mid-Winter ceremony. The last, celebrated in late January or early February, was the most important, celebrating the new year with sacrifices and dancing. In early times, the Onondaga placed the bodies of their dead on scaffolds, later burying the bones. In later customs, the dead were buried in bark coffins with moccasins, weapons, and a kettle of provisions.

Onondaga, the main village, was composed of rectangular multi-family dwellings of pole and bark construction, called longhouses. The Iroquois people were often referred to as the "people of the longhouse," symbolic of the Confederacy itself, with the five "families" of the house, stretching east-west across New York state.

A religion that developed among the Iroquois in the early 19th century was called the Longhouse Religion. Founded by a Seneca chief named Handsome Lake, it encouraged a return to the old Indian religion, with some Christian modifications. In the late 1970s the Longhouse Religion was still very vital, particularly on the Onondaga Reservation.

The Onondaga economy, as that of the other Iroquois, was based on hunting, fishing and agriculture. Corn, prepared in numerous ways, was the staple food. After the advent of the European trader, the stone,

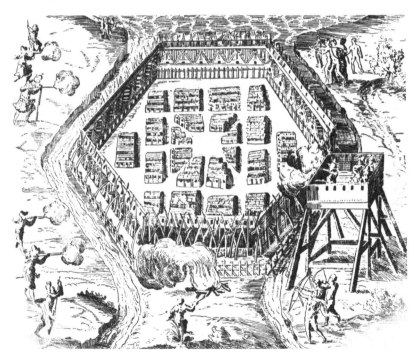

Smithsonian Institution National Anthropological Archives

A palisaded Onondaga town being attacked by the French, under the leadership of Samuel de Champlain, in 1615. This town stood in the town of Fenner, in present Madison County, New York.

bone, and shell tools of the Iroquois were soon replaced by iron implements. Guns, powder, kettles and cloth were among the prized trade goods that spurred the Iroquois to range wide in their hunting parties and eventually eliminate their competition.

The 17th century was filled with warfare, as the Iroquois finally defeated the Huron, Erie, Neutral and Susquehanna. Many captives were absorbed into the Iroquois tribes, until, in 1657, it was said that foreigners outnumbered Onondaga in that tribe. The strategic location of the Iroquois, as they also took possession of the lands vacated by their former enemies, embroiled them in wars between the French, English and Americans in the 18th century. The Onondaga sided with the English in the American Revolution, and many migrated to Canada during or after the war.

In the late 1970s there were 600 Onondaga living on the Six Nations Reserve in Brant County, Ontario. Another 800 lived on or near the 7,300 acre Onondaga Reservation in New York.

BIBLIOGRAPHY: Clark, Joshua V. H. *Onondaga,* Syracuse: Stoddard and Babcock, 1849.

OSAGE: the most important tribe of the Dhegiha division of the Siouan linguistic family, located on the Osage River in western Missouri in the late 17th century, numbering about 6,200 at that time. In the late 1970s, there were about 10,000 Osage descendants, living mostly in northern Oklahoma. Because of the opportunities afforded them by the oil wealth of their lands, however, Osage could be found all over the world.

Their tribal name was derived from a corruption of Wazhazhe, their name for themselves. The other tribes of the Dhegiha family include Omaha, Ponca, Kansa and Quapaw. In the 1970s, the Osage still spoke their language, and classes in it were popular.

The Osage were divided into two divisions, or moieties: the Tzisho, or Sky People, and the Hunkah, or Land People. The moieties were subdivided into 21 clans, each person inheriting the clan of his father. Division chiefs were hereditary in certain clans; the peace chief came from the Tzisho, while the war chief was named from the Hunkah. From the early 19th century, there were also three political divisions: the Great Osage, Little Osage and Arkansas Osage.

The Osage believed in a supernatural life force, Wakonda, which resided in all things on earth and in the heavens. Shamans provided religious leadership, along with the secret religious society, to which both men and women belonged. Important ceremonies included planting, peace and war ceremonies and the Rite of Chiefs, in which the oral history of the tribe was recounted.

Young Osage dancers at an Oklahoma pow-wow. United States Travel Service

A person was required to marry someone of the opposite moiety, and men who married oldest daughters had marriage rights to their younger sisters as well. When an Osage chief or other distinguished person died, he was buried above ground in a sitting position, surrounded by rocks and logs and then covered with earth. Others were buried in the ground along with tools, weapons, food and water. A mourning ceremony, which required the promise of an enemy scalp, followed. This caused a great deal of trouble between the Osage and neighboring tribes.

Osage villages were composed of houses of wood framework covered with woven rush mats or bark. They ranged from 36 to 100 feet in length. In nearby fields, Osage women grew corn, squash, pumpkins and beans. To supplement the diet, they gathered persimmons, pawpaws, grapes, hackberries, hickory nuts, walnuts, pecans and acorns. Men hunted deer, turkey, beaver, prairie chicken and wild cat. They went on carefully organized buffalo hunts, in the early days stampeding the buffalo over a cliff.

Bows were made of the Osage orange tree, which was prized for this purpose. Other crafts included carved wooden cradleboards, cattail and rush mats, buffalo hair bags, and fine deerskin clothing. The Osage men were exceptionally tall and striking in appearance, ornamented with body paint, tattooing, earringsm bracelets and scalplocks.

According to tradition, the Osage and the other Dhegiha tribes migrated westward from the southeast, via the Ohio Valley. By 1673, they were living in two villages along the south fork of the Osage River, one belonging to the Little Osage, the other to the Great Osage. They also had villages on the Missouri and Marmitou rivers. By the early 18th century, they had formed a strong alliance with the French, providing them with deer and beaver pelts as well as slaves, which the Osage captured on raids of Pawnee and Ponca villages. The French accorded the Osage special treatment, because of their strategic location and because they helped the French fight the Fox and other tribes.

The Spanish, who owned the region in the latter 18th century, were a little less deferential, but still recognized the need to be on good terms with the Osage. In 1802, to be near a trading post opened by the Chouteau family, favorite French traders of the Osage, about one-half of the Great Osage band moved to the Arkansas River, near the mouth of the Verdegris, in Oklahoma.

In 1808, the Osage ceded the northern half of Arkansas and most of Missouri to the United States, the Great and Little Osage bands moving to the Neosho River in Kansas. As their old lands began filling up with eastern tribes placed there by the U.S. government, fighting broke out between the Osage and the Cherokee, Choctaw, Chickasaw and others. A village of the Arkansas Osage was burned in 1817. By treaties in 1818 and 1825, the Osage ceded all their lands except for a reservation in Kansas, where all the bands had settled by 1836.

During the Civil War, the Osage fought on both sides, causing division within the tribe. By 1870, the Osage had sold their Kansas lands and bought lands in Indian Territory (Oklahoma). By 1906, the Osage had voted in favor of an allotment plan, which they drew up themselves, providing for their reservation to be divided, allotting 658 acres to each of the 2,229 tribal members, with the tribe retaining all the mineral rights. When great reserves of oil were discovered on the reservation, this proved to be an extremely wise plan. By the 1920s the Osage were famous for their wealth. After an initial spending spree, most of the tribe settled down to a wise management of their finances.

In the 1970s, there were about 300 fullbloods remaining among the approximately 10,000 Osage. Interest was reviving in Osage culture, arts, crafts and language.

BIBLIOGRAPHY: Chapman, Carl H. *The Origin of the Osage Indian Tribe*. New York: Garland Publishing, Inc., 1974.

OTO: a Siouan tribe of the Chiwere division, which also includes the Missouri and Iowa. In 1780, they numbered about 900, living along the Platte River in eastern Nebraska. In the late 1970s, some 2,000 descendants of the combined Oto and Missouri tribes lived mostly in Oklahoma, and many still spoke the Chiwere language.

Oto villages were organized into about 10 clans, each made up of a

An Oto delegation. The National Archives

number of families. A person inherited the clan of his father, but all household property was owned by the women. Each clan had certain responsibilities: a member of the Buffalo clan lead the spring hunt, while the fall hunt was led by a member of the Bear clan. The offices of the clan chief, war chief and priests were hereditary. In early times, the tribal chief was named from the Bear clan.

The Oto believed in an all-prevading spirit called Wakonta. Fasting and visions brought them in closer touch with the spirit world. A number of secret curing societies and dance societies, such as the Medicine Lodge and the Buffalo Doctors Lodge, specialized in various religious ceremonies or types of cures. The bodies of the dead were either placed in a tree or buried in the ground. A four-day mourning period was observed, and a horse was sometimes killed so the deceased could ride to the land of the dead.

Oto villages were composed of from 40-70 earth lodges, each about 40 feet in diameter and dug into the ground two or three feet. The lodges were of a heavy wooden framework interwoven with brush and grass, with an outer layer of clay or earth. Skin tipis were used for hunting trips.

The Oto depended on both hunting and agriculture for food. The women gardened the bottomlands along the rivers, growing corn, beans, squash and melons. The men gave some help in the fields and in gathering wood and water, but hunting was their main activity. They went on buffalo hunts twice a year, in spring and fall, and hunted deer, turkey, racoon and rabbits the rest of the year. While on their hunts, they stored their food in bell-shaped caches in the ground.

According to tradition, the Oto lived in early times with the Missouri, Iowa and Winnebago tribes, somewhere in the Great Lakes region. At some point they began migrating south and west, leaving the Winnebago in the Green Bay area of Wisconsin and the Iowa at the junction of the Mississippi and Iowa rivers. The Oto and Missouri continued on until they reached the junction of the Missouri and Grand rivers, where they had a falling out.

According to tradition, the Oto chief's son ran off with the Missouri chief's daughter, causing the tribes to split. The Oto moved west along the Missouri River, leaving the Missouri behind. Out of this event came the Oto tribal name, derived from *wahtohtata,* translated variously as "lovers" or "lechers."

Between 1680 and 1717, the Oto lived in Iowa, first on the Upper Iowa River and later on the Blue Earth River. From about 1717 to 1854, the Oto lived at various locations along the Platte River and the Missouri River near the mouth of the Platte. They traded with the French and later the Americans. The Oto lost population through warfare with the Pawnee, Fox, Sauk and other tribes and through serious epidemics of smallpox.

By 1829 the Oto had absorbed the Missouri, who had been reduced to less than 100 by warfare and disease. The following decades were very difficult as the two tribes battled cholera epidemics and fought with the Omaha, Pawnee and Dakota for the scarce food supply. By treaties signed in 1830, 1833, 1836 and 1854, the Oto-Missouri ceded all their lands and moved to a reservation on the Big Blue River, between Kansas and Nebraska.

Intra-tribal fighting in about 1880 split the group into two factions, with the Coyote, or traditional faction, moving to Indian Territory (Oklahoma). The next year, the other group, called the Quakers, ceded their lands for a reservation near Red Rock in north central Oklahoma. By 1890, the Coyote had gradually joined them there. In 1907, the reservation was allotted to individual tribal members.

In 1955, the U.S. Supreme Court upheld an award of $1 million to the Oto-Missouri in repayment for illegal land settlements. This was divided among the 2,000 Oto-Missouri on the tribal rolls, the two tribes now being so intermarried as to be indistinguishable.

In the late 1970s, there were 28,000 acres of allotted land remaining and 1,700 acres of tribally-owned land. The Oto-Missouri celebrated their traditional dances and ceremonies each year in July. An elementary grammar of the Chiwere language was published in 1975, and Oto-Missouri children were learning their tribal language in school.

BIBLIOGRAPHY: Whitman, William. *The Oto*. New York: Columbia University Press, 1937.

OTTAWA: an Algonquian tribe located on Manitoulin Island and the Bruce Peninsula on northern Lake Huron in the early 17th century, numbering perhaps 5,000 at that time. In the late 1970s, there were more than 8,000 Ottawa descendants widely scattered around the U.S. and Canada, with concentrations in Ontario, Michigan, Wisconsin and Oklahoma.

The Ottawa spoke a dialect of the Ojibwa language of the Algonquian linguistic family. Their tribal name was derived from the Algonquian word *adawe,* meaning "to trade." They were indeed a great trading people, making commercial expeditions of hundreds of miles and serving as middlemen between the Huron and the western tribes.

By the 17th century, the Ottawa were divided into a number of autonomous subdivisions, each with its own chief or chiefs. These were further divided into local bands or villages, each with its own leadership.

The Ottawa believed the world was created by the Great Hare and controlled by a supreme being called the Master of Life. There were also countless good and evil spirits known as *manito.* During puberty, boys and girls sought, by fasting in secluded places, to acquire guardian spirits through dreams or visions. Shamans had power to intercede with the various *manito* and enlist their assistance in curing the sick. The dead were either buried, placed on scaffolds or cremated, and feasts honoring the dead were held every few years.

The Ottawa built permanent villages of barrel-roofed longhouses of overlapping sheets of bark on a pole frame. Villages were sometimes palisaded for protection. Mat-covered conical lodges were used on hunting trips.

The Ottawa had a diversified economy, based on fishing, hunting, trading, agriculture and gathering of wild foods. They hunted and trapped deer, bear, beaver, birds and other small game and fished the rivers and Great Lakes with nets. They usually split up into small hunting groups in winter, regrouping in spring to plant corn, beans and squash

Smithsonian Institution National Anthropological Archives

An Ottawa chief, Shoppenagon (Little Needle), and his family.

and collect maple sap for syrup. The women were in charge of cultivation as well as the gathering of blueberries, raspberries, strawberries and other plant food. Log mortars and wooden pestles were used for grinding corn meal for soup or bread.

Crafts included making birchbark and leather containers, rush mats, and birchbark canoes, the main means of transport. Weapons included bows and arrows, wooden clubs and circular hide shields. Men's clothing was limited to breechclouts, if anything, in summer, with a fur robe added in winter. Elaborate tattooing and face and body painting, as well as nose and ear ornaments were used for adornment.

In 1615, the Ottawa were visited on Georgian Bay by Samuel de Champlain, and in 1635, on Manitoulin Island, by Jean Nicolet. After the Iroquois defeated the Huron in 1649, they drove the Ottawa west to the Straits of Mackinac and Green Bay. Various bands settled for short periods on Keweenaw Bay and Chequamegon Bay, both on Lake Superior. A group which settled at Lake Pepin near the Mississippi River was driven out by the Dakota (Sioux).

In the 18th century, the Ottawa established settlements at numerous points along the Lake Michigan and Lake Huron coasts, including Saginaw Bay, Beaver Island, Grand Traverse Bay, Little Traverse Bay, the Grand and St. Joseph rivers in Michigan, and the sites of present-day Milwaukee and Chicago. The Ottawa also joined the Huron and numerous other tribes near Detroit. From this base, the great Ottawa chief Pontiac led his unsuccessful attempt to stop the flood of settlers into the Ohio valley.

In the early 19th century, most of the Ottawa were forced out of Ohio and lower Michigan by treaties. Some went to Kansas, some went to Manitoulin and Drummond islands, and others settled in Michigan on reservations or allotted lands in Oceana and Mason counties. On Walpole Island in the St. Clair River, where Ottawa groups had settled in 1796, they were intermingled with Ojibwa and Potawatomi. In 1867, the Kansas Ottawa moved to the Quapaw Agency in Indian Territory (Oklahoma).

In the late 1970s, there were more than 8,000 Ottawa descendants with about 4,500 located in northern Michigan, 3,000 in Ontario and 500 in Oklahoma. The Ottawa language was still spoken by most Manitoulin Island Ottawa and by some Michigan Ottawa.

BIBLIOGRAPHY: Cash, Joseph H. and Wolff, Gerald W. *The Ottawa People*. Phoenix: Indian Tribal Series, 1976; Peckham, Howard H. *Pontiac and the Indian Uprising*. Princeton: Princeton University Press, 1947.

PAIUTE, NORTHERN: a Basin people, who occupied eastern Oregon, northwestern Nevada and adjacent California, south to Owens Valley in the early 19th century, when, together with the Southern Paiute, they numbered about 7,500. In the late 1970s, the two groups together numbered about 4,000, with the Northern Paiute mostly located in Nevada, Oregon and California.

The Northern Paiute, along with the Bannock and Monache, spoke languages of the Mono-Paviotso branch of the Shoshonean division of the Uto-Aztecan language family. For the most part, they lived as extended families, each led by the oldest capable male. In areas of more concentrated population, they formed into bands, led by a headman. Other leaders were chosen to take charge of communal hunts, pine nut gathering and small-scale irrigation projects.

Shamans served as religious leaders and cured the sick by singing, sucking out disease-causing objects and utilizing the power in such

Smithsonian Institution National Anthropological Archives.

Wovoka, ("The Cutter"), also known as Jack Wilson, the famous Northern Paiute "Messiah." Born in 1856 in Mason Valley, Nevada, Wovoka had a vision in 1888, as a result of which he introduced the Ghost Dance, which, it was thought, would result in the disappearance of the white man, and a return to the old Indian ways. This photograph was taken in 1891 by James Mooney, of the Bureau of American Ethnology.

objects as eagle feathers. In their mythology, Wolf was a beneficent creator and culture hero, while his brother Coyote was considered a trouble-maker and source of evil.

Marriages were formalized with an exchange of presents between the two families. Polygamy was practiced, with a man sometimes marrying sisters or his brother's widow. Important ceremonies were the girls' puberty rites and the annual mourning ceremony. The dead were wrapped in skin blankets and buried, along with their most cherished possessions. Houses and other property of the deceased were burned, and mourners cut their hair and effected a disheveled appearance.

House construction varied with the season and locale. Winter homes in the valleys were cone-shaped, with tule mats and sometimes a layer of earth over a pole framework. In the mountains, dwellings were constructed of pine boughs laid along a ridge pole. In summer, brush shelters and sunshades of willow boughs served.

Although the Northern Paiute did not practice agriculture, they did irrigate small plots of wild seed-bearing plants, by constructing dams of boulders and brush and digging channels to divert the water. The seeds were harvested with seed-beaters and conical carrying baskets. In Nevada and Oregon, roots and bulbs, dug with digging sticks, were staple foods, while south of the Humbolt River, pine nuts were a primary food source. In some areas, wild cherries, berries, acorns and insect larvae were collected.

Fish were caught using spears, hooks, nets, baskets and by using a stupefying poison. Deer and mountain sheep were hunted in communal drives. They also hunted and trapped small game, including squirrel, porcupine, waterfowl and rabbits.

Pottery was made, as well as twined and coiled basketry, including containers, cradles and caps to protect women's heads from the tumpline that supported their carrying baskets. Snowshoes were made for winter travel. Men wove rabbit skin blankets on a frame. Face and body paint were worn, along with shell necklaces, for ceremonial occasions.

Early 19th-century trappers enjoyed friendly relations with the Northern Paiute. By mid-century, however, miners were flocking to the area on their way to the California gold fields and the Comstock silver lode near Virginia City, Nevada. Piñon trees, the source of the edible pine nut, were cut down for fuel and housing, and the seed-bearing plants needed for food were destroyed by livestock. Despite Paiute opposition the United States assumed control of Northern Paiute lands in the late 1860s and early 1870s, and established some reservations for them.

In 1888 a Paiute medicine man named Wovoka had a vision in which he was instructed to teach a certain dance which would cause the disappearance of the white man and bring the return of the old Indian ways. He founded the Ghost Dance movement, which spread throughout the Basin and Plains, and farther. It eventually died out after 1890, when Dakota adherents were attacked by the U.S. Army at Wounded Knee.

In the late 1970s, Northern and Southern Paiute together numbered more than 4,000. Their reservations included Duck Valley, Fallon, Fort McDermitt, Las Vegas, Lovelock, Moapa River, Pyramid Lake, Walker River, Winnemucca and Yerington in Nevada; Burns Paiute and Warm

Springs in Oregon; Bishop, Fort Bidwell, Fort Independence and Lone Pine in California; Southern Paiute in Utah; and Kaibab in Arizona. Many other Paiute were scattered among the general population of the area.

BIBLIOGRAPHY: Steward, Julian H. "Ethnography of the Owens Valley Paiute," *University of California Publications in American Archaeology and Ethnology.* vol. 33, 1933; Steward, Julian H. and Wheeler-Voegelin, Erminie. *Paiute Indians.* vol. 3, New York: Garland Publishing, Inc., 1974.

PAIUTE, SOUTHERN: A Basin people located in northern Arizona, southern Utah, southern Nevada and the adjacent area of California in the early 19th century, when, together with the Northern Paiute, they numbered about 7,500. The two groups together numbered about 4,000 in the late 1970s, with the Southern Paiute mostly located in Nevada, Utah, Arizona and California.

The Southern Paiute referred to themselves as Nuwu, meaning "person." They spoke a language belonging to the Plateau Shoshonean division of the Uto-Aztecan language family, as did the Ute and the Chemehuevi. The latter were a relatively recent offshoot of the Southern Paiute. The Southern Paiute had a number of geographic divisions including the Kaibab, Kaiparowits, San Juan, Panguitch, Shivwits, Moapa, Las Vegas, Paranigets, St. George and Panaca.

Politically, however, the largest unit was the extended family, which gathered food, hunted, migrated and camped together. In later times, these camp groups sometimes banded together to conduct raids. Leadership was provided by the oldest capable males, by those with special hunting or food gathering skills, and by shamans who cured the sick and conducted ceremonies.

Important ceremonies included the Circle Dance and girls' puberty rites. Southern Paiute mythology included Wolf, who created the heavens and earth, and his mischievious brother Coyote. In early times, the Southern Paiute cremated their dead, but more recently, they buried them in rock shelters. The possessions of the deceased were burned or buried, and his dwelling was torn down and moved to another location. Female mourners wailed and cut their hair, and the name of the deceased was not spoken again.

Southern Paiute dwellings varied with the season and locale, and included caves, brush shelters and conical houses of pole framework covered with strips of cedar bark. They migrated seasonally, according to the food supply, and were expert at utilizing the resources of their region.

A Southern Paiute woman gathering seeds, photographed by John Hillers, (1873).

The National Archives

Hunting, gathering and a little agriculture were the basis of the Southern Paiute economy. From ancient times, using irrigation, they grew a small amount of corn and squash, but wild plants were of greater importance. Twined seed-beaters were used to knock loose the seeds of goldenrod and various grasses into conical carrying baskets. They dug various roots with digging sticks and gathered pine nuts, yucca dates, cactus fruit, agave, nuts, juniper berries and grasshoppers. Men hunted small game such as squirrels, prairie dogs, lizards, marmots, porcupines and sage hen. Probably most important were rabbits, which were tracked in the snow or driven into 100 yard-long nets placed in a semicircle. Deer, antelope and mountain sheep were hunted with bow and arrow.

Their bows were made of cedar, locust or mountain sheep horn. Other craft work included both coiled and twined basketry, used to make such items as water jars, parching trays, hats, cradles, carrying baskets and a variety of storage containers. Woven rabbit-fur robes were made for winter wear.

The forebears of the Paiute people started moving in the northern Southwest in about 1000, gradually replacing the Hopi Pueblo in that region. They probably learned from the Hopi how to cultivate corn, and continued to trade with them until 1600. In 1776, a Spanish expedition chronicled by Father Silvestre de Escalante passed through Southern Paiute territory. Subsequent Spanish contact had little effect, and the Southern Paiute, unlike the neighboring Ute, did not acquire horses.

In the 19th century, they were plagued with Ute and Navajo horsemen, who came sometimes to trade and sometimes to raid for slaves. The Chemehuevi split off from the tribe and gradually moved into the Colorado River valley. In the 1850s, Mormon settlers began taking over some Southern Paiute lands.

In the late 19th and early 20th centuries, a number of reservations were established for the Northern and Southern Paiute. By the late 1970s, there were more than 4,000 located on a number of reservations. These reservations included: Duck Valley, Fallon, Fort McDermitt, Las Vegas, Lovelock, Moapa River, Pyramid Lake, Walker River, Winnemucca and Yerington in Nevada; Burns Paiute and Warm Springs in Oregon; Bishop, Fort Bidwell, Fort Independence and Lone Pine in California; and Kaibab in Arizona. Many other Paiute were scattered among the general population of the area.

BIBLIOGRAPHY: Euler, Robert C. "Southern Paiute Ethnohistory." *University of Utah Anthropological Papers.* no. 78, 1966; Kelly, Isabel T. "Southern Paiute Ethnography." *University of Utah Anthropological Papers.* no. 69, 1964.

PALOUSE: a Plateau tribe located along the Palouse River in Washington and Idaho in the early 19th century, numbering about 1,600 in about 1805, according to Lewis and Clark. They were closely related

**Wolf Necklace,
a Palouse chief,
(1890).**
The National Archives

culturally and linguistically to the Nez Perce, and were thought by Lewis and Clark to be a band of that group, named Pelloatpallah. Both tribes spoke languages of the Sahaptian division of the Penutian language family.

The Palouse were assigned to the Yakima Reservation by the Yakima Treaty of 1855, but refused to recognize the treaty or move to the reservation, remaining in several small villages along the Snake River. In 1854, they numbered about 500. Some Palouse settled on the Colville Reservation after its establishment in 1872, and their descendants lived there in the late 1970s.

PAMLICO: a small extinct Algonquian tribe located along the Pamlico River in Beaufort County, North Carolina. They were nearly destroyed by smallpox in 1696. The Pamlico fought on the side of the Tuscarora in the Tuscarora War of 1711. After the war, they were reportedly either killed or made slaves by the Tuscarora faction that had fought on the side of the British.

BIBLIOGRAPHY: Swanton, John R. "The Indians of the Southeastern United States." *Bureau of American Ethnology Bulletin*, no. 137, 1946.

PAMUNKEY: the leading tribe of the Powhatan confederacy of eastern Virginia, located at the junction of the Pamunkey and Mattapony rivers. They probably numbered about 1,000 in 1608. The Algonquian language of the Pamunkey died out by the late 18th century,

A Pamunkey bowl.

Smithsonian Institution

but, in the late 1970s, there were still descendants of Pamunkey living on and near a reservation in Virginia.

Pamunkey culture was similar to that of the other Powhatan tribes. They built houses of poles covered with woven mats of bark, and grew corn, beans, pumpkins and fruit trees. Clay pottery and pipes were made and ceremonial robes were woven of turkey feathers.

In 1625, the principal town of the Pamunkey was destroyed by the English, during the war between the colonists and the Powhatan Confederacy.

In 1654 the Pamunkey lost 100 warriors, including their chief, Totoptomoi, while helping the English fight mountain tribes. In 1675, Queen Anne, the widow of Totoptomoi, assisted the English in Bacon's Rebellion. She later became a noted spokesman for her people.

By 1705, the Pamunkey had been reduced by disease and warfare to about 150. In about 1781, a reservation was set aside for them in King William County, Virginia. In the late 1970s, the Pamunkey still retained the 800 acre reservation, with a population of about 35 living on or near the reservation. Basketry, pottery and beadwork were produced for the arts and crafts shop on the reservation.

BIBLIOGRAPHY: Pollard, J.G. "Pamunkey Indians of Virginia." *Bureau of American Ethnology Bulletin*, no. 137, 1894.

PANAMINT: *See* SHOSHONI, WESTERN.

PAPAGO: a nomadic hunting and gathering tribe located in the desert region south of the Gila River of Arizona and extending into Sonora, Mexico. In the late 17th century, they numbered about 6,000. In the late 1970s, they continued to live in the same area, known as the Papagueria, numbering more than 15,000.

The Papago, meaning "bean people," spoke a language of the Piman division of the Uto-Aztecan language family. The Papago and Pima to the north were essentially one people, speaking basically the same language and having a similar culture. The greatest difference between the two groups was due to environmental influence. The Pima had sufficient water from streams to rely on agriculture, while the Papago, with no permanent streams, depended mainly on hunting and gathering for their food supply. The Pima, consequently, were known as the "River People," while the Papago were known as the "Desert People."

Socially, the Papago were divided into two moieties, or tribal divisions, known as Coyote and Buzzard. These were subdivided into about five clans, with each person belonging to the clan of his father. It was forbidden to marry relatives on either parent's side. After marriage, a couple resided with the groom's parents until they had one or more children. Polygamy was practiced, with men often marrying sisters or

A Papago basketmaker.   The National Archives

their brother's widow. Generally all the wives lived in the same household.

Autonomous villages, usually composed of kin, were the main political unit. During the rainy summer months, the villages were located near cultivated fields along intermittent streams. In September, when the streams had dried up, they returned to the foothills to camp near wells and springs, living by hunting and gathering.

The men's council, composed of all adult males, served as the governing body of the village, with older men having the most say. The head man of the village had a number of titles, including Wise Speaker and Keeper of the Fire. His duties included advising, admonishing, calling of council meetings, keeping up the ceremonial house, caring for the sacred fetishes and acting as priest in ceremonies. He trained his own successor, whom he chose subject to the approval of the men's council. Other officials included the village crier, war leader, hunt leader, game leader and song leader. Curing was performed by shamans, both men and older women, who derived their power from dreams.

The principal deities of the Papago were the creator, Earth Maker, and the culture hero, I'itoi. Important ceremonies were the girls' puberty rites and rain ceremonies, at which a sweet intoxicating drink made from saguaro fruit was consumed. Ceremonial orations, handed down through generations, were given. The Papago cremated warriors killed in battle. All others were buried in caves, rock crevices or in little stone houses constructed against the side of a cliff. Weapons, pots, baskets—whatever was appropriate—were buried with the deceased, whose soul went eastward to the land of the dead.

Papago houses were circular, semisubterranean dwellings of pole and thatch, often covered with earth. A ceremonial house called the Big House or the Rain House, was of the same construction, but larger. In summer, the Papago men grew a little corn, beans, and squash in their flood plain fields, while the women gathered wild foods. They harvested their crops and dried them, returning by October to their wells and springs in the foothills. There the men hunted deer, mountain sheep and rabbits, while the women continued to gather mesquite beans, saguaro, cholla beans, agave, yucca and prickly pear. Fall and winter were also time for trading trips. The Papago obtained agricultural products in exchange for dried meat, pigments made from red and yellow ocher, and salt from natural salt pans.

Most craft work was carried on by older people, since younger people were needed for the hard labor of acquiring food. They made a simple red pottery, as well as an assortment of basketry from yucca leaves and other materials. Carrying nets, frame back packs and cradle boards were made, and buckskin was tanned for clothing and trade. Skirts and breechclouts of cotton or buckskin were the usual costume.

In the 16th and 17th centuries, the Papago were visited by various Spanish expeditions. A mission was established in the late 17th century by Father Eusebio Kino, who introduced wheat and livestock. In 1751, a short-lived revolt against the Spanish was led by a Papago, Luis Oacpicagigua. Apache raids, begun in the 18th century, continued intermittently until the mid-19th century. By 1800, the Sobaipuri, a Piman tribe driven out of the San Pedro valley by the Apache, had merged with the Papago.

The 1853-54 Gadsden Purchase, transferring control of the area to the United States, brought settlers into Papago territory. In 1874, the San Xavier Reservation was established, excluding some of the most fertile lands of that area, which had been pre-empted by settlers. In 1882, the Gila Bend Reservation was established, but most Papago continued to live off the reservations. In 1916-17, the Papago, or Sells, Reservation was established, again leaving out the best grazing lands, which had already been taken over by ranchers.

In the late 1970s, there were more than 15,000 Papago. About 9,000 lived on the three reservations in southern Arizona, with a total area of 2,855,000 acres. The 6,000 off-reservation Papago were spread over southern Arizona and northern Sonora, Mexico. The Papago retained more of their tribal traditions and culture than the neighboring Pima.

BIBLIOGRAPHY: Underhill, Ruth Murray. "Social Organization of the Papago Indians." *Columbia University Contributions in Anthropology.* vol. 30, 1939.

PASSAMAQUODDY: a small tribe located along the Maine and New Brunswick coast in the early 17th century, when together with the Malecite, they numbered about 1,000. In the late 1970s, there were more than 1,000 Passamaquoddy descendants connected with two reservations in Maine.

The Passamaquoddy and Malecite, who spoke dialects of the same eastern Algonquian language, were together known as the Etchemin by early explorers. They were culturally very similar, except that the Passamaquoddy were sea mammal hunters, whereas the Malecite concentrated on inland hunting.

The Passamaquoddy gathered in large villages in summer, dispersing

A Passamaquoddy etched birchbark basket.

Smithsonian Institution

in winters to live in small hunting camps. In the aboriginal period, leadership was informal, usually exercised by mature men who were skillful hunters. After European contact, the office of chief became more formalized and was inherited through the male line. The extended family was the most important social unit. Before marriage, a young man was required to spend a year's probationary period serving his future father-in-law and proving himself as a hunter and provider.

The Passamaquoddy had a rich mythology, centered around Kuloscap, the culture hero. Other supernatural beings included giants, dwarfs, ghosts and such characters as Turtle and the Snowshoe Hare. Shamans cured the sick through powers given them by a spirit helper.

In their summer villages, the Passamaquoddy built both single family conical pole-frame wigwams and rectangular multi-family lodges constructed of four or five tiers of logs with a pole and birchbark roof. Of similar construction were council chambers accommodating up to 100 persons. By the 17th century, villages were sometimes palisaded.

In spring the Passamaquoddy gathered at their fishing sites to spear bass, sturgeon and salmon, sometimes at night by torchlight. In summer,

**Passamaquoddy
Indians with
Father Versilljou—
a picture taken
in Maine
circa 1860-75.**

Smithsonian Institution
National
Anthropological Archives

two-man canoe teams hunted seal and porpoise in the Bay of Fundy. Clams, lobsters and sea birds' eggs added variety to the diet, as did the whales which occasionally became stranded in the coastal shallows. In winter, the Passamaquoddy dispersed into small groups to hunt bear, beaver, otter, muskrat and moose, using birchbark moose calls.

Lightweight, maneuverable canoes were made of birchbark and occasionally spruce bark or moosehide. Snowshoes were used for travelling in winter. An assortment of containers, baskets, boxes, trays and dishes were made from birchbark, sometimes decorated with quillwork.

The Passamaquoddy were visited by the French explorer de Champlain and others in the early 17th century. In the following decades, they engaged in the French fur trade, and grew dependent upon European trade goods. In the mid-18th century, the Passamaquoddy joined with the Malecite, Abnaki, Penobscot, Micmac and other tribes sympathetic to the French to form the Abnaki Confederacy. By the late 18th century, English colonists crowded into Passamaquoddy territory, pushing them out of their old villages and fishing and hunting grounds. In 1794, lands were reserved for the Passamaquoddy in Washington County, Massachusetts (later part of Maine).

In the late 1970s, more than 800 Passamaquoddy descendants were connected with the 100-acre Pleasant Point Reservation. Another 200 Passamaquoddy descendants were connected with the Peter Dana Point (Indian Township) Reservation which contained 23,000 acres, 7,000 of which were owned by non-Indians. Both are state of Maine reservations. The Passamaquoddy were becoming increasingly interested in maintaining their language and culture and in having close relations with the Malecite and other Indian groups.

BIBLIOGRAPHY: Erickson, Vincent O. "Maliseet-Passamaquoddy." *Handbook of North American Indians.* vol. 15. Washington: Smithsonian Institution, 1978.

PATWIN: a northwest California group numbering perhaps 3,000 in the early 19th century. By the 1970s, there were only a handful of Patwin descendants, living in California.

The Patwin language, along with Wintu and Nomlaki, compose the Wintuan (or Wintun) division of the Penutian language family. There were numerous Patwin tribelets, consisting usually of a village with several satellite villages. Each village had a chief, who directed economic and ceremonial activities.

The main religious ceremonies of the Patwin were those of the Kuksu cult, in which boys were initiated into a secret society. Shamans cured the sick, usually by sucking out the disease-causing object. If the patient died, his body was wrapped in skins and buried, together with some personal goods.

Patwin dwellings, sweathouses and dance houses were all semi-subterranean, earth-covered structures. Men wore no clothing, while women wore aprons or skirts of shredded bark or tule. The Patwin hunted, fished and gathered to provide a varied diet, including acorns, salmon, trout, deer, elk, antelope, small game and various roots, nuts and berries. They made basketry by both the twining and coil methods.

By the early 19th century, Spanish missions were established among the Patwin. Epidemics in the 1830s severely reduced the Patwin population. Under Mexican rule in the 1830s and 1840s, settlers took over much of Patwin lands. After 1850, under American rule, some were placed on reservations, while others worked as laborers on ranches. Their population continued to dwindle until the 1970s, when there were only a handful of Patwin descendants remaining in California.

BIBLIOGRAPHY: McKern, W.C. "Functional Families of the Patwin." *University of California Publications in American Anthropology and Ethnology.* vol. 13, 1922.

PAWNEE: an important Caddoan confederacy located in the Platte River valley by the late 18th century, numbering about 10,000 at that time. In the late 1970s, they numbered about 1,200 mostly living in Oklahoma. The Pawnee were closely related to the Wichita and Arikara, also of the Caddoan family. There have been various translations of their tribal name, including "horn," "hunter" and "braid."

The four tribes of the Pawnee were the Chaui, Kitkehahki, Pitahauerat, and the Skidi, who were also known as the Loup, or Wolf, Pawnee. The tribes were organized into matrilineal clans. Chiefs, called *lesharo,* inherited their title through the female line. There were governing councils at the village, tribe and confederacy levels, the tribal council being composed of the village chiefs, and the confederacy council made up from the councils of the tribes.

Village chiefs were custodians of the sacred bundles, but the priests were in charge of their use. The Pawnee religion was rich in ceremony and required a large and powerful class of priests and shamans. They believed in a creator or "spirit father" called Tirawa. They also took an interest in various heavenly bodies, particularly the morning and evening stars.

The Skidi periodically made a human sacrifice, preferably a young captive girl, to the morning star, in order to ensure the success of their crops. Other rites included the calumet ceremony, various ceremonies connected with planting, cultivating and harvesting of corn, and the buffalo dance, performed before a hunt. There were also many secret

A Pawnee village: from George Catlin's *Letters and Notes on the North American Indians*, (1844).

societies, each with its own elaborate rituals. The Pawnee buried their dead in a sitting position, covering the graves with mounds of dirt and sod. Burial grounds were usually located on high ground away from the village.

The Pawnee constructed permanent villages of earth lodges, and used several types of temporary housing while hunting or traveling. The round earth lodges were excavated several feet and were about 60 feet in diameter. A heavy wooden framework was interwoven with a wickerwork of brush and grass, and then covered over with a thick layer of earth. A smokehole was left in the roof for the fire, which was kept burning in the center. Some of the lodges had sleeping quarters partitioned off by means of mats or wickerwork. Temporary housing consisted of grass lodges, skin-covered huts, and skin tipis.

The Pawnee grew corn, beans and pumpkins and hunted buffalo in well-organized, communal hunts. They wove baskets and mats and produced a fine, incised pottery.

The Pawnee, according to some traditions, migrated from the southwest. By the mid-16th century, they had probably reached north central Kansas and, in the following century, probably settled on the Loup fork of the Platte River in Nebraska. According to Arikara tradition, the Arikara and the Skidi Pawnee had migrated together until reaching this point, where they separated, after which the Arikara moved up the Missouri River. The Skidi were later joined on the Loup by the other three Pawnee tribes.

From the mid-17th to the 18th century, the Pawnee were continually at war with the Apaches, who carried off many Pawnee women and children to sell as slaves to the Spanish. In the 18th century, the Illinois and other eastern tribes conducted the same sort of raids, selling the Pawnee slaves to the French. It was practiced to such an extent that *pani* became the term for slave, of whatever tribe.

However, the Pawnee, being somewhat off the beaten path of explorers and traders, did manage to avoid direct contact with Europeans longer than most tribes. With the acquisition of horses, they became great horse raiders. By the 1750s, they were trading with the French, and soon a regular east-west trade route ran through Pawnee territory. This marked the beginning of their decline. The Skidi, who had eight villages in 1725, were reduced to one by the 1800s.

By 1849, the Pawnee were reduced to about 4,500 by cholera and warfare with the Dakota. They ceded all their lands to the United States in treaties of 1833, 1848 and 1857, except for a reservation along the Loup fork. Many Pawnee served as scouts for the U.S. Army during this period. By 1876, they had ceded their Nebraska reservation and moved to a reservation in Indian Territory (Oklahoma).

Part of the Pawnee reservation was allotted to tribal members in 1892, with the rest opened to homesteaders the following year. The Pawnee were reduced to about 650 by 1906.

By the late 1970s, there were some 1,200 Pawnee descendants living in Pawnee and Payne counties, Oklahoma. Some 22,500 acres of allotted land and about 700 acres of tribally-owned land remained. The Pawnee still performed their tribal dances at a powwow held each year.

BIBLIOGRAPHY: Hyde, George E. *The Pawnee Indians.* Norman: University of Oklahoma Press, 1951.

PEND D'OREILLES: *See* KALISPEL.

PENNACOOK: a small confederacy of Algonquian tribes, mostly extinct by the late 17th century. In the early 17th century, they occupied the Merrimack River valley of central New Hampshire and the neighboring areas of northeastern Massachusetts and southern Maine. The Pennacook tribe, the most influential of the confederacy, numbered about 500 at that time. Other tribes in the confederacy included the Wamesit, Agawam, Nashua, Souhegan, Amoskeog and Winnepesaukee. Pennacook has been variously translated as "the crooked place" or "at the bottom of the hill."

The Pennacook tribes lived mostly in small fishing villages of from 50 to 300 people, each with its own chief. The confederacy was led by a great sachem, the best known of whom was Passaconaway who had risen from *powwow,* or medicine man, to chief. The Pennacook believed in an afterlife somewhere in the southwest, and buried their dead with weapons and tools necessary for the journey.

The women raised corn while the men hunted and fished for sturgeon, salmon and shad. Tools and weapons were made from turtle shell, clam shell, wood, bark and stone. Pendants and other ornaments were made from horn and fishbone.

The Pennacook were visited by Capt. John Smith in 1614. About that same time, they suffered loss of population from a serious epidemic and war with the Abnaki Indians of Maine. Passaconaway, who became sachem in about 1629, submitted to the jurisdiction of the colony of Massachusetts in 1644.

The Pennacook were among the tribes influenced by the missionary John Eliot. In 1653, a reservation was set aside for them. The Pennacook attempt to remain neutral during King Philip's War (1675-76) resulted in their being attacked by both sides. Wannalancet, the son and successor of Passaconaway, led 200 of his followers deep into the woods to avoid involvement. While they were gone, their lands were stolen and, upon their return, some of them were sold into slavery in the West Indies.

In 1680, the Pennacook were badly defeated in a war with the Mohawk. By about 1686, the Pennacook had sold their remaining lands and begun to disperse—some to live with the Mahican in New York, some to live with tribes in Maine, while others remained in the area. But the largest number went with Wannalancet to join other tribes at Saint Francis, Quebec.

BIBLIOGRAPHY: Bouton, Nathaniel. *History of Concord.* Concord: Benning W. Sanborn, 1856.

PENOBSCOT: an eastern Abnaki tribe located along Penobscot River and Bay in the early 18th century, numbering about 1,000 at that time. In the late 1970s, there were about 1,000 Penobscot descendants living on or near the Penobscot Reservation in Maine.

They spoke the Penobscot dialect of the eastern Abnaki language of the Algonquian language family. The name Penobscot, meaning "it flows on rocks," referred to the river on which they lived. They were culturally similar to the other eastern Abnaki (*q.v.*) tribes.

The Penobscot were divided into patrilineal family groups, which usually gathered together in summer camps or villages to fish and hunt. In winter, they divided again into small hunting groups, each with its own territory.

**Susan Dana,
a Penobscot,
(1970).**

Smithsonian Institution
National Anthropological
Archives

Shamans provided religious leadership and cured persistent illnesses which didn't respond to medicinal plant remedies. Penobscot mythology centered around the culture hero Gluskabi and the trickster figure Raccoon.

Penobscot dwellings were usually conical lodges of overlapping birch-bark sheets on a pole frame. Fishing, hunting and gathering of wild foods were important to the Penobscot economy. Fishing technology included spears, weirs, basketry traps and nets. Moose, deer, bear, beaver, otter and mink were stalked with bow and arrow or trapped with deadfalls and snares. Both fish and meat were dried and stored for later use. They also gathered shellfish, berries, grapes, cherries and maple sap for syrup.

A variety of baskets, cooking vessels and other containers were made from birchbark, and spoons and ladles were carved from wood. The birchbark (and occasionally moose-hide) canoe was the main means of transportation. In winter, snowshoes were used for travel. Clothing was of tanned skins, and included moccasins, leggings, breechclouts and coats for men. Women, in addition, also wore long skirts.

In the 16th century, the Penobscot were visited by various European explorers, becoming involved in the fur trade by the 17th century. Between 1607 and 1615, the Penobscot were at war with the Micmac to the north. In the 17th and 18th centuries, they fought several wars against the English colonists and were drawn into the conflict between the French and English.

By the mid-18th century, the Penobscot had joined with the other Abnaki tribes, as well as the Malecite, Passamaquoddy and Micmac, to form the Abnaki (Wabanaki) confederacy, an alliance against the English and their Iroquois allies. The Penobscot were the only Abnaki group not driven northward into Canada in the ensuing war, although they did lose most of their territory to English settlers.

In the late 1970s, the 4,440-acre Penobscot Reservation consisted of 146 islands in the Penobscot River. Only Indian Island was inhabited year-round, and the village of Old Town was the main population center. The reservation was under the state rather than the federal government, and the tribe was represented in the Maine legislature by an elected non-voting delegate. There were a few remaining speakers of the Penobscot dialect, and some craftwork was still produced.

BIBLIOGRAPHY: Speck, Frank G. *Penobscot Man: The Life History of a Forest Tribe in Maine.* Philadelphia: University of Pennsylvania Press, 1940.

PEORIA: an important tribe of the Illinois Confederacy, located in southern Wisconsin, northern Illinois and eastern Iowa in the late 17th century. The confederacy included the Peoria, Kaskaskia, Moingwena, Michigamea, Cahokia, and Tamaroa, all of which spoke the same Algonquian language and shared a similar culture. (For a description of their culture, see the article on the Illinois.) In the late 1970s, several thousand descendants of the Illinois tribes were living in Oklahoma. Peoria has been translated as "he comes carrying a pack on his back."

The Peoria lived around Prairie du Chien, Wisconsin, until probably mid-17th century, when they joined the Moingwena, in the area of present-day Peoria, Illinois. Here they were encountered by Marquette and Jolliet in 1673. In the 1700s, the Illinois Confederacy was dispersed and the Peoria were forced south by the Kickapoo, Fox and Sauk, who resented their friendship with the French. In about 1768, they settled at St. Genevieve, near St. Louis.

The Peoria, Kaskaskia, and the remnants of the other Illinois tribes signed treaties in 1803, 1818 and 1832, relinquishing their lands to the United States. They settled on the Marais des Cygnes River in Kansas, where they were joined by the Piankashaw and Wea bands of the Miami tribe. In 1867, they gave up their Kansas lands and moved to Indian Territory, where they bought land from the Seneca-Shawnee-Quapaw Indians, in what is now Ottawa County in northeastern Oklahoma.

In 1873, they were joined by the Miami, acquiring the title of United Peoria and Miami. By 1893, their lands were allotted in severalty under

James Charlie, a Peoria.

Smithsonian Institution
National Anthropological
Archives

the Allotment Act and their reservation divided among the members. In 1940, they were allowed to incorporate as the Peoria Indian Tribe of Oklahoma. By the late 1970s, the descendants of the Peoria, and other Illinois tribes living in Oklahoma, were mostly assimilated into the general population.

BIBLIOGRAPHY: Scott, James. *The Illinois Nation.* Streator, Illinois. Streator Historical Society, 1972-73.

PEQUOT: a powerful Algonquian tribe of Connecticut, also known as the Mohegan after about 1637. The Pequot and Mohegan were one tribe, numbering about 4,000 in 1600, before splitting into two tribes in the early 17th century.

The Pequot occupied most of Connecticut east of the Connecticut River, including the upper valley of the Thames River and its tributaries. The Mohegan laid claim to this territory after the destruction and dispersal of the Pequot, in the Pequot War of 1637. Pequot had been translated as "destroyers" while Mohegan means "wolf." The last speaker of the Pequot-Mohegan language died in the early 20th century. Descendants of the Pequot held two small reservations in eastern Connecticut in the late 1970s. A few Mohegan descendants also remained in Connecticut and Wisconsin.

The Pequot were ruled by a grand sachem, or hereditary chief. Lesser chiefs, called sagamores, each had a band of followers loyal to them. There were 26 sagamores under the last grand sachems of the Pequot.

Religious leadership was provided by *powwows*, or medicine men, who cured the sick and banished evil spirits through the use of herbs, roots, prayers and song. Sweathouses were also used in healing.

The Pequot had a supreme deity. There were also lesser deities with specific responsibilities and areas of control.

They buried their dead wrapped in skins and woven mats, and provided them with tools, weapons and food to take on their journey to the land of the dead.

Pequot villages were usually located on a hill, and were often palisaded as a defensive measure. Houses were from 20 to 40 feet in length, of pole construction covered with bark. An open space was left in the center of the village for games and gatherings. Temporary villages were sometimes built near the sea in summer, for fishing and shellfish gathering, and in the woods during the hunting season.

Women and children did the work of cultivating corn and beans, while men usually grew the tobacco. Hunting was important both for food and for obtaining skins and furs for clothing. Besides deer, bear, beaver and otter, a large variety of wild fowl was hunted, including quail, turkey, pigeon,

A Pequot wooden doll.

Smithsonian Institution
National Anthropological
Archives

ducks and geese. Bows were made of hickory and arrows tipped with flint. Fish were caught with spears, bone hooks, and nets of Indian hemp. Strawberries, blackberries and huckleberries were among wild foods gathered. A typical meal might be succotash (corn and beans) with some meat cooked in it, and cornmeal cakes wrapped in leaves and baked in hot ashes.

The Pequot used both the light and maneuverable birchbark canoe and the heavier log dugout to negotiate their waterways. Crafts included the making of basketry from wood splints and rushes, the carving of wooden bowls and spoons, and the making of wampum. The latter, tiny beads of polished and drilled shell, were used in both trade and political dealings with other tribes.

The Pequot probably came into Connecticut from the northwest shortly before 1600, defeating the tribes living in that area. They may have been related to the Mahican of the Hudson Valley.

In the early 17th century, a powerful subchief, Uncas, the brother-in-law of the grand sachem Sassacus, broke off from the Pequot, together with his followers, who then became the Mohegan. In 1637, when the Pequot War with the English broke out, the Mohegan and the Narraganset joined the English in attacking a Pequot town on the Mystic River. Some 600 Pequot were killed. The main body of the tribe fled to the southwest, but most were captured and sent into slavery in the West Indies, or made captives of the Mohegan and the Narraganset. Some fled to the tribes of Long Island, which were tributary to the Pequot. Sassacus and others fled to the Mohawk, and were killed. The Pequot who surrendered were forced to pay an annual tribute of wampum, and were forbidden ever to organize again as a tribe.

The Mohegan, their numbers swelled by the defeated Pequot, laid claim to the Pequot territory. In 1657, they were at war with the Narraganset. In King Philip's War of 1675-76, the Mohegan aided the English once again. Following the war, they were the only remaining New England tribe of importance. But the Mohegan, too, soon declined. In the late 18th century, the Mohegan, along with the Mahican, Wappinger, Narraganset and Montauk tribes, moved to Oneida country in New York, establishing the town of Brotherton. In the early 19th century, the Brotherton group, along with the Stockbridge and Oneida Indians, migrated to Wisconsin. In 1832, a reservation was established for them on Lake Winnebago. The land was later divided and sold, and the Indians were absorbed by the surrounding white community.

Two small Pequot reservations were established in Connecticut. By the late 1970s, about 200 Pequot-Mohegan descendants remained in Connecticut. The Eastern or Stonington Pequot held 220 acres in North

Stonington, and the Nameaug or Western Pequot held 175 acres in Ledyard.

BIBLIOGRAPHY: Peale, Arthur L. *Uncas and the Mohegan-Pequot.* Boston: Meador Publishing Company, 1939.

PIANKASHAW: *See* MIAMI.

PICURIS: A Tiwa tribe and pueblo located about 40 miles north of Santa Fe, New Mexico, numbering about 3,000 in the mid-17th century. By the late 1970s, the population of the pueblo had diminished to about 200.

The Picuris spoke a language of the Tiwa division of the Tanoan language family. Other Tiwa tribes included Taos, Isleta and Sandia. The Picuris referred to their pueblo as Walana or Pingultha. They were located in a remote, mountainous area, and served as a link between the other pueblos and the Plains Indian tribes, often trading with the Apache.

In 1591, Picuris was visited by the Spanish explorer Castaño de Sosa, who reported buildings seven to nine stories high. Also reported were underground *kivas,* or ceremonial houses, about 20 feet in diameter, entered through a hatchway in the roof. The Picuris men planted fields

Smithsonian Institution National Anthropological Archives

The castillo at the pueblo (village) of Picuris, New Mexico, (1899).

of corn, beans, gourds, squash, cotton and tobacco, in spite of a short growing season which sometimes froze the corn crop. The Spanish introduced wheat, alfalfa, chilies, peaches, apples and plums. The men hunted elk and deer with juniper bows, and occasionally made extended forays to the Plains to hunt buffalo.

In 1621, the Spanish established the mission of San Lorenzo at Picuris. In 1680, Picuris joined the Pueblo Revolt, supplying one of the leaders, Luis Tupatu. The pueblo was abandoned until the Spanish reconquered the area in 1692. The northern pueblos rebelled again in 1696, but the rebellion was quickly put down.

In the early 18th century, the Apache, under pressure from the Comanche, began raiding the northern pueblos. By the mid-18th century, the population of Picuris had dropped to about 400, plus about 50 resident Europeans. In the late 18th century, the pueblo population was further reduced by Comanche raids and smallpox epidemics. A succession of churches was built in Picuris, with the present-day church dating from about 1776. By the mid-19th century, the population of the Picuris area had risen to about 800, of which only about 140 were Indians. In 1858, the United States Congress confirmed the 1689 Spanish land grant on which the Picuris Indians had lived for over 600 years.

In the late 1970s, the people of Picuris were striving to maintain their traditions. A tribal museum and craft center had been established. Among the crafts produced in the pueblo was a gold-flecked cookware made from micaceous clay found in the area.

BIBLIOGRAPHY: Schroeder, Albert H. "A Brief History of the Picuris Pueblo." *Adams State College Series in Anthropology.* no. 2, 1974.

PIEGAN: *See* BLACKFOOT.

PIMA: a sedentary tribe living in the Gila and Salt River valleys of southern Arizona in the late 18th century, numbering about 2,500 at that time. In the late 1970s, there were more than 12,000 Pima and Maricopa living together on two reservations in southern Arizona.

The Pima called themselves Aatam, meaning "the people," and spoke a language of the Piman division of the Uto-Aztecan language family. The Pima and their southern neighbors, the Papago, were essentially one people, speaking basically the same language and having a similar culture. The main difference between the two was a result of environmental influence. The Pima had sufficient water from streams to rely primarily on agriculture, whereas the Papago, having no permanent streams, were forced to rely mainly on hunting and gathering. The Pima were often referred to as the "River People," whereas the Papago were called the "Desert People."

Economic Development Administration

The Arts and Crafts Center at the Gila River Indian Community, Sacaton, Arizona.

Socially, the Pima were divided into two moieties, or divisions, called Red Ants and White Ants. These were subdivided into about five clans, with each person belonging to the clan of his father. Marriage was usually outside both parents' families. After marriage, a couple lived with the groom's parents until they had one or more children of their own. Polygamy was practiced, with men often marrying sisters or their brother's widow. Generally all wives lived in the same household.

The village was the main political unit, led by a head man and a council composed of all the adult males of the village. The head man, who lived either in or next to the council house, advised and exhorted the people, arbitrated disputes, and took care of the sacred items of the village. He usually trained a male relative as his successor, subject to approval of the council. Other officials included a messenger, announcer, war leader and hunt leader.

Among the deities of the Pima were Earth Maker, I'itoi and Coyote. Important ceremonies inclided a harvest festival, at which an intoxicating beverage made from the fruit of saguaro cactus was consumed, and a victory dance, held after a successful battle. Warriors who had killed an enemy were required to undergo a 16-day purification rite, in which they fasted, painted their faces black and remained apart from the tribe. The Pima buried their dead in rock crevices, or seated in a stone hut, along with weapons, tools and food. The house of the deceased was burned, and his soul set out on a four-day journey eastward to the land of the dead.

The Pima built dome-shaped houses of thatch and earth on a pole

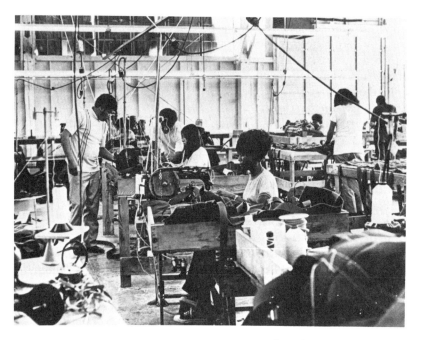

Pima Indians at work for the Gila River Industrial Commission on the Gila River Indian Reservation in Arizona.

frame. In summer, a simple open-sided brush arbor was used. A low, rectangular council house was large enough to accommodate a meeting of all the village adult males. Other important structures were cylindrical bins used to store mesquite beans.

The Pima grew corn, beans, squash and cotton along the streams, constructing miles of irrigation ditches. Wheat, introduced by the Spanish, later became important. The men dug the irrigation ditches and cultivated the fields, and the women harvested the crops. The women also gathered a variety of wild foods, including mesquite beans, saguaro fruit, prickly pear fruit, yucca, ironwood nuts and a variety of seeds. Squash was cut in strips and dried. Seeds and corn were parched and ground to meal on a cottonwood mortar or a stone metate, for use in gruel or cakes. The basically vegetable diet was supplemented by fish, caught with nets, and various game such as deer, mountain sheep, antelope, rabbit, peccary, badger, quail and beaver.

Hunting bows were of osage orange or willow, whereas bows for warfare were of mulberry. Other weapons included clubs and circular hide shields. The women wove basketry items using the coil method, and made pottery jars, bowls and other items, and the men wove cotton belts and blankets. Women wore skirts of cotton, deer skin or willow bark, and men wore breechclouts of cotton or deer skin. Sandals for traveling were made of sheep or deer skin. The Pima were unusually tall, and adorned themselves with tattooing, turquoise ear ornaments and red, yellow and white body paint.

In the 17th and 18th centuries, the Pima were visited by various Spanish explorers, who introduced wheat, melons, cattle and horses. Around 1800, the Maricopa, fleeing from the Yuma and Mohave, settled near the Pima. Allied with the Maricopa, the Pima fought the Yuma, Mohave and Yavapai and endured continual raiding by the Apache.

The 1849 gold rush brought miners streaming through the Pima territory, many being assisted and guided by the Pima. In 1870, a reservation was established for the Pima and Maricopa on the Gila River, and in 1879, the Salt River Reservation was established.

In the late 1970s, there were about 9,000 Pima and Maricopa living on the 372,000-acre Gila River Reservation, and another 3,000 on the 49,000-acre Salt River Reservation, both near Phoenix. The Pima were essentially acculturated, through a century of close contact with non-Indian Americans.

BIBLIOGRAPHY: Russell, Frank. "The Pima Indians". *Annual Report of the Bureau of American Ethnology*. no. 26, 1908.

PIRO: a large extinct pueblo tribe of New Mexico, estimated to have numbered about 9,000 in the early 17th century, but reduced to about 60 by the early 20th century. They spoke a Tiwa language of the Tanoan language family.

The Piro were composed of two geographical divisions. The larger consisted of about 6,000 people occupying 14 villages along the Rio Grande north of San Marcial in Socorro County. The smaller division occupied 11 villages in the vicinity of the salt lagoons east of the Rio Grande.

According to contemporary accounts, the Piro pueblos consisted of two to four story houses. In addition, each town had two kivas, or religious centers, built mostly underground, with entry through openings in the roofs. The Piro men raised turkeys and cultivated large irrigated fields of corn, beans, gourds and tobacco. Women ground corn on large flat rocks, using the meal or flour to make a variety of breads. Clothing was made from dressed skins and woven cotton.

Little is known of life in their towns before the coming of the Spanish in the late 16th century. Shortly thereafter, the villages of the Piro were consolidated, partly for protection from Apache raids, and partly to make missionization easier for the Spanish.

By the late 17th century, the Piro had been reduced to about four villages. They did not take part in the Pueblo Revolt in 1680, and the inhabitants of the remaining Piro pueblos retreated with the Spanish to El Paso, Texas. They eventually established the villages of Socorro, Texas, and Senecu del Sur, in Chihuahua, Mexico, where about 60 of their descendants lived in the early 20th century.

BIBLIOGRAPHY: Hodge, Frederick Webb. "Handbook of American Indians." *Bureau of American Ethnology, Bulletin.* no. 30, 1907-10.

POJOAQUE: a small Tewan tribe and pueblo on the Rio Grande, 18 miles northwest of Santa Fe, New Mexico, numbering about 79 in the early 1700s. In the 1970s, their population was around 100.

The Pojoaque spoke the Tewa language of the Tanoan language family. Their traditional culture was probably similar to that of other Tewan tribes, including the San Ildefonso, San Juan, Santa Clara, Nambe and Tesuque (*q.q.v.*).

The Pojoaque had a relatively peaceful existence until initial contact with Spanish explorers. In the 17th century, the mission of San Francisco was founded at Pojoaque. The town was abandoned after the Pueblo Revolt of 1680 and the revolt of 1696, but was resettled in 1706 by order of the governor of New Mexico. At this time the mission of Nuestra Senora de Guadalupe was established. It was reduced to visiting status in 1760, but restored as a mission in 1782.

In 1885, land grants previously made by Spain to the Pojoaque were confirmed by the United States. In the 1970s, about 100 Pojoaque lived on a reservation of 11,599 acres, governed by a governor, lieutenant governor and council. The Pojoaque were essentially assimilated into the surrounding Spanish-American culture.

POLAR INUIT: the northern-most Inuit (Eskimo) group, located on the northwest coast of Greenland between Cape York and Cape Alexander and numbering about 250 in the late 19th century. In the late 1970s, there were more than 500 Polar Inuit, living in the same area. They spoke a dialect of the Inuit (Eskimo) language, which was spoken, with minor variations, from Alaska to Greenland. The name Eskimo was derived from an Abnaki Indian term meaning "raw meat eaters," whereas the term Inuit, meaning "people," was their name for themselves.

The Polar Inuit had no real political organization. Socially, they were divided into households composed of a nuclear family plus one or more relatives. Informal religious leadership was provided by one or more *angakok,* or shamans, whose powers derived from certain "assisting spirits," acquired through trances. The *angakok* conducted seances, in which he entered an ecstatic state and called upon his various assisting spirits to help him cure the sick, find lost souls or bring an abundance of wild game.

The Polar Inuit had a rich mythology, which included such spirits and deities as the Old Woman of the Sea, who controlled all the marine animals; the Sun woman and her brother the Moon, whose whittling on walrus tusks caused snow; plus giant kayaks, an animal with an iron tail, a giant worm and a giant bear. Many taboos and ceremonies were connected with hunting, the activity on which their lives depended. Breaking of any taboos would cause illness and possibly death.

When a person died, his body was removed through the window and buried under rocks, along with broken implements, weapons, toys or whatever was appropriate to the person. The name of the deceased was not spoken again until it was given to a new baby. In times of hardship, the old were sometimes abandoned, often at their own request, as were newborn girl infants.

The Polar Inuit had several house styles, including sealskin tents for spring and summer, temporary snowhouses for winter hunting, and the more usual winter house of stone and sod. The latter was very snug, with the interior lined with sealskins and the exterior waterproofed by a layer of turf kneaded with oil and blubber. A long narrow passage way, lower than the interior of the house, provided storage and acted as an air lock to keep out cold drafts. One or two seal gut-skin windows let in light. The main room was largely occupied by a platform of sandstone or slate slabs, covered with grass and furs and used as a table, chairs and beds. Snowhouses used in winter hunting camps were constructed of blocks of snow cut with a snow knife. Two or three men could make a snow house in an hour, laying the blocks in an inward-leaning spiral to form a dome.

Meat and blubber from seal and walrus were the staple foods. Most of the year, the Polar Inuit could hunt these animals out on the sea ice, harpooning them at their breathing holes in winter or as they basked on the ice in spring. In the short period of open water in summer, they hunted them from kayaks, introduced in 1860 by immigrants from Baffin Island. Polar bear were hunted on the ice, using dogs to corner them. Caribou were hunted by driving them into stone corrals or by driving them into the water and hunting them from kayaks. Sea birds were taken with snares, long nets on poles or bird darts. Foxes, hares, and eider ducks were all trapped or snared for their fur or skin. There was no hunting in the dark months of December and January.

Wooden dog sleds with iced runners were the most important means of transport. Wood was also used to make snow goggles and snow-beaters for brushing snow off clothing before entering dwellings. Trays

Smithsonian Institution National Anthropological Archives

Inuit building a snow house in Arctic Canada, (circa 1913-18).

and utensils were made of walrus bone or musk-ox horn. They used carved soapstone cooking pots and blubber lamps, which provided both heat and light.

Women made the clothing, chewing the skins so they would remain soft under the frigid Arctic conditions. Outer jackets were made of sealskin or fox skin, and inner jackets were of bird skin or sealskin. Sealskin boots, white for women, were worn over sealskin stockings. Hunters sometimes wore bearskin over-boots, to enable them to move silently over the ice.

Greenland was probably first settled more than 4,000 years ago, populated by successive groups from the south and west. Caribou hunters, belonging to the Dorset culture, probably entered Greenland by the first century AD. Around 500, a seafaring people arrived, probably originally from northeastern Asia. Known as the Thule culture, they hunted marine life in kayaks and *umiaks* (large skin-covered open boats). Polar Inuit culture was an amalgam of the cuture of these early groups with that of successive waves of immigrants who arrived as late as 1865.

The British explorer John Ross, who visited the Thule area in 1818, was probably the first European encountered by the Polar Inuit. In 1892, American explorer Admiral Robert Peary explored northern Greenland, followed by a number of Danish and other explorers. In the 1950s, a United States air base, located at Thule since World War II, was expanded. The noise of the aircraft frightened walrus, seals and polar bear in the area, prompting the Polar Inuit to move 90 miles north to Kanak (Thule Village.)

In the late 1970s, there were more than 500 Polar Inuit of relatively pure stock, continuing to live the life of nomadic Arctic hunters. Seal hunting was still the main means of livelihood, with some modern adaptations, such as the use of motor boats and rifles. Trading of fox furs and walrus tusks was also important. Traditional culture and language continued to be vital forces in Polar Inuit daily life.

BIBLIOGRAPHY: Ekblaw, W. Elmer. "The Material Response of the Polar Eskimo to the Far Arctic Environment." *Annals of the Association of American Geographers.* vol. 17, Dec., 1927; Holtved, Erik. *Contributions to Polar Eskimo Ethnography.* Copenhagen: C.A. Reitzels Forlag, 1967; Rasmussen, Knud. *The People of the Polar North.* London: Kegan Paul, Trench, Trubner and Co., Ltd., 1908.

POMO: a group of northern California peoples occupying the Russian River valley, northward to Clear Lake and westward to the coast, in the early 19th century, probably numbering between 13,000 and 20,000 at that time. In the late 1970s, there remained about 1,000 Pomo descendants, living in California.

The various Pomo peoples spoke seven mutually unintelligible languages of the Pomoan linguistic family: Southern Pomo, Central Pomo, Northern Pomo, Eastern Pomo, Northeastern Pomo, Southeastern Pomo and Southwestern Pomo (also known as Kashaya). The seven groups were culturally similar, but not identical.

The Pomo groups were generally divided into tribelets, composed of one or more bilaterally related kinship groups with from 100 to 2,000 members. Tribelets, led by headmen or minor chiefs, were generally autonomous, although occasionally several would form a confederacy.

The Pomo had a complexity of religious beliefs and ceremonies. They practiced the Kuksu cult, in which gods and ghosts were impersonated in dances performed by members of a secret society. The various dances of the annual ceremony were related to curing, group well-being, fertility and initiation of young boys into the society. Other public ceremonies included a woman's dance and celebration of the ripening of various crops such as strawberries and acorns.

Pomo dead usually lay in state for four days, during which time friends and relatives brought gifts to be burned. The body was cremated along with the gifts, at a special place on the edge of the village. The house and personal possessions of the deceased were also sometimes burned. Mourners cut their hair, wailed and sang songs of mourning.

Pomo house structure varied with the environment. Those along lakes

A Pomo woman
beating seeds
from bushes:
a photograph
probably taken
by Edward S.
Curtis, in
about 1924.

Smithsonian Institution
National Anthropological
Archives

built circular houses of tule (rushes), while those in timber areas built conical houses covered with redwood bark slabs. Both single and multi-family houses were used. Most villages had semisubterranean sweathouses, where the men took daily sweat baths, and also a large community house for dances and ceremonies.

The Pomo had a varied diet, the emphasis varying with the environment of each group. Those near lakes took large numbers of fish by various nets, traps and weirs, while other groups emphasized acorn-gathering. The Pomo gathered some seven kinds of acorns, along with buckeyes, pepperwood nuts, and various greens, roots, bulbs and berries. They also hunted deer, elk, antelope, water fowl and other small game. Most foods were dried and stored for later use.

Clothing was minimal and made from skins, tule, and shredded redwood or willow bark. Tule was a versatile material used for making moccasins, leggings, mats, boots and houses. The Pomo made a wide variety of fine basketry, using both coil and twining methods. Weapons and tools were made of stone, bone and wood.

In the early 19th century, the Pomo first encountered Europeans. In 1811, a Russian settlement was established at Fort Ross, which employed about 100 Pomo as agricultural laborers. Spanish missions were established in the region after 1817. In the 1830s and 1840s thousands of Pomo died of cholera and smallpox, and thousands more were killed by Mexican military expeditions or sold into slavery.

After 1850, under the Americans, settlers, miners and ranchers flooded into the area, taking over Pomo lands. In the 1860s, many Pomo were forced onto reservations at Round Valley and Mendocino.

In the late 1970s, there were more than 1,000 Pomo living in California, mostly on about 23 small rancherias. Many were employed as seasonal farm laborers. The extended family was still the main social unit, although some of the rancherias were becoming politically organized. The Pomo languages were still spoken, and many traditional ceremonies performed, accompanied by feasting, singing, dancing and the wearing of ceremonial regalia.

BIBLIOGRAPHY: Barrett, S.A. *"Material Aspects of Pomo Culture." Bulletin of the Public Museum of the City of Milwaukee.* vol. 20, 1952.

PONCA: a Siouan tribe living in the area of Knox County in northeastern Nebraska, by the late 17th century, numbering around 3,000 at that time. Together with the Kansa, Omaha, Osage and Quapaw, they formed the Dhegiha subgroup of the Siouan linguistic family. In the 1970s, about 2,350 Ponca lived in Nebraska and Oklahoma. They spoke a language similar to the Omaha, with whom they sometimes lived and to whom were culturally related. Ponca, meant "sacred head" in their language which, by the 1970s was only spoken by the older people.

The Ponca were organized into two moieties, Chighu and Wazhazha, each of which were subdivided into four clans. They were ruled by hereditary chiefs whose duties included political, religious and military leadership. During the communal buffalo hunt, the chiefs were aided in keeping order by the very powerful buffalo police.

The Ponca worshipped the great spirit Wakanda, and believed that all things had supernatural power, *xube*, to some degree. One especially important object was the sacred pipe, which, according to tradition, was carved of the red stone, catlinite, when the Ponca lived in Minnesota. The original pipe was lost, but replacements were used, especially in the Pipe Dance. Other important celebrations included the Medicine Lodge Ceremony, the Sun Dance, and the War Dance. A ball game, shinny, using a sacred ball of deerskin stuffed with horsehair, had religious significance. Vision questing, through self-torture and fasting, was also important.

The early Ponca buried their dead in graves, wrapped in a buffalo robe, with food, moccasins and other articles. Later, on the Plains, scaffold burial became more important. Up to a year of mourning ensued. Dead persons who had led exemplary lives went to We-Noch-a-te, the town of brave and generous spirits; while unworthy deceased went to the town of poor and useless spirits.

The Ponca lived in fixed villages of earth lodges or hide-covered lodges, including a central ceremonial earth lodge. The lodges always

A Ponca delegation, before 1877.   The National Archives

faced east, to catch the morning sun. The towns were located on bluffs overlooking rivers, with gardens in the fertile bottomlands. Often the towns were fortified by stockades of cottonwood logs and earth. Skin-covered tipis were used during the semiannual communal buffalo hunts.

The tribal economy was mostly agricultural, with corn, beans, squash, pumpkins and tobacco being the principal crops. Fishing, hunting of buffalo, gathering of wild foods, and, after the late 18th century, fur-trapping was also important. Twice each year the Ponca held communal buffalo hunts, using bow and arrow or stampeding them over cliffs. Bow and arrow were also used in warfare, as well as wooden war clubs and shields made from the tough hide of the neck of the buffalo. Other Ponca crafts included woodcarving, making a blue clay pottery of good quality, and weaving mats and baskets from willow and bullrush stems. They also produced quillwork and beadwork in floral and geometric designs. Their clothes were of buffalo skins—moccasins, leggings and breechclout for men and a one-piece dress for women. A buckskin shirt, robe or blanket, fur cap and mittens were added for cold weather.

The Ponca, together with the others of the Dhegiha group, probably migrated from the southeast by way of the Ohio River valley. Around 1540, they arrived at the Mississippi, with the Quapaw going south and the rest going upstream. The Osage and Kansa left the group at the mouth of the Osage River, while the Ponca and Omaha continued on to Minnesota, where they settled on the Big Sioux River. Driven from this area by the Dakota, they traveled to the Lake Andes area of present-day South Dakota, where the Ponca and Omaha separated. The Ponca continued west as far as the Black Hills, and eventually turned east again. They rejoined the Omaha and went down the Missouri to Nebraska, finally, by 1673, settling near the Niobrara River. There the Omaha left them, finally settling on Bow Creek.

The Ponca were encountered by Lewis and Clark in 1804, at which time their numbers had been reduced to about 200 by smallpox. In 1817 and 1825, they signed treaties of friendship with the U.S. government, and in 1858, a 126,000 acre reservation was granted them.

In 1877, the Ponca were removed to Indian Territory (now Oklahoma) and assigned a 101,000 acre reservation. Dissatisfaction with this arrangement resulted in an appeal to Congress in 1881, led by Standing Bear, which restored to the Ponca 26,000 acres of their old lands in Nebraska. In 1908, the Oklahoma lands were allotted in severalty. Subsequently, most of the lands were eventually sold or leased to whites. In the 1950s, the Nebraska Ponca were "terminated," i.e. no longer recognized by the U.S. government as a tribe.

In the 1970s, about 2,000 Ponca lived in Oklahoma, on 17,400 acres of individually owned and 875 acres of tribally owned land. About 350 Ponca lived in Nebraska. They were largely acculturated into white society, with little of the old culture remaining. The northern (Nebraska) Ponca were almost completely intermixed with Santee Dakota, Yankton and white, and their ancient Nebraska lands were being flooded and eroded by a dam system on the Missouri River. The southern Ponca tribe was governed by a seven-member committee, established in 1950, and by a tribal chairman selected by the committee.

BIBLIOGRAPHY: Howard, James H. "The Ponca Tribe." *Bureau of American Ethnology Bulletin.* no. 195, 1965; Jablow, Joseph. *Ethnohistory of the Ponca.* New York: Garland Publishing, Inc., 1974.

POTAWATOMI: a tribe of the Algonquian language family, located along the eastern shores of Lake Michigan in the early 17th century, numbering between 3,000 and 4,000 at that time. In the late 1970s, there were about 13,000 Potawatomi descendants, living in Oklahoma, Kansas, Wisconsin, Michigan and Ontario.

They were closely related culturally and linguistically with the Ottawa and Ojibwa, and their tribal name reportedly meant "people of the place of the fire," in the Ojibwan language. The Potawatomi referred to themselves as Weshnabek, or "the people."

The Potawatomi were organized into 30 or more different clans,

**Potawatomi:
a photograph
by Brady
and Handy.**
Library of Congress.

with each person inheriting the clan of his father. Villages were ruled by a chief, who was responsible to a council of elders.

Religious leaders included three classes of shaman: doctors, diviners (*chaskyd*) and advisor-magicians (*wabino*). Religion was an intensely personal matter, with vision-seeking, through fasting, of prime importance in each person's life.

The Potawatomi also had many festivals and ceremonies such as the Medicine Dance, War Dance and Sacred Bundle Ceremony. The Medicine Dance was performed by members of the Midewiwin, or Grand Medicine Society, a secret curing society.

The Potawatomi believed in an afterlife somewhere in the west. Burial customs varied with time and place. In early times, the Hare clan practiced cremation, while other clans employed scaffold burials. In later times, persons were buried amid personal items they might need for their journey, and a shelter was built over the grave. The family of the deceased might ceremonially adopt a person to take his place.

Villages were usually built along streams and were composed of large bark-covered lodges or smaller mat-covered, dome-shaped wigwams, both constructed over a pole framework. An open field for playing lacrosse was usually found nearby.

The Potawatomi had a diversified economy. They raised corn, beans, peas, squash, melons and tobacco in their gardens, at times selling a surplus to traders. After the harvest each year, they would break into smaller groups for their winter hunt, which lasted several months. Deer, elk, bear and beaver abounded as did fish, which were caught with nets,

A group of Potawatomi and Ojibwa from Walpole Island, on the Canadian shore of the St. Clair River, dividing Michigan from Ontario. This drawing was made when the group visited England in 1856. Pe-ot-e-kie-sic, the "chief of the Walpole tribe," (the third man from the right), offered to help the British fight the Russians in the Crimean War (1854-56) by raising a band of warriors, but his offer was declined. The *Illustrated London News*, which published this picture, regretted this, saying that the "red men, with their unerring rifles and wonderful means of approaching the enemy unseen and unheard, would have been admirable scouts."

weirs or traps. Maple sap was gathered in spring to be boiled into syrup and sugar. Beechnuts gathered in autumn were pounded into flour. The women made pottery and men made fine birchbark canoes. Clothing was made of skins and furs decorated with paint and quillwork. Men practiced tattooing, and both men and women used body paint.

According to tradition, the Potawatomi originally migrated from somewhere northeast of Michigan, settling along the eastern Lake Michigan shore. By 1641, they were driven west by the Neutral, Huron and the Five Nations Iroquois Confederacy.

In 1642, the Potawatomi fled for a short time to Upper Michigan, and then to the Green Bay area of Wisconsin. There they served as middlemen in the French fur trade. In the late 1600s, the Potawatomi began moving south into lands vacated by the Illinois tribes, and eastward to occupy lands formerly held by the Miami. By about 1714, they had spread across northern Illinois and southern Michigan.

In the late 1700s, the Potawatomi joined the struggle for the Ohio valley. They helped the Ottawa chief Pontiac fight the English (1763-64), and joined the Miami in their victories against the Americans in 1790-91, as well as in their defeat at the battle of Fallen Timbers in 1794.

In the succession of treaties following the 1794 defeat, Potawatomi lands were gradually whittled away. In 1800 they had about 100 villages, spread over Wisconsin, Illinois, Michigan and Indiana. By the 1830s, the Potawatomi lands had been mostly ceded and removal had begun. Various bands were moved to Missouri, Iowa, Kansas and finally Indian Territory (Oklahoma). Hundreds of Potawatomi resisted removal and remained in Wisconsin and Michigan. Hundreds more fled to Canada and established communities and reserves all along the eastern shore of Lake Huron.

In the late 1970s, there were some 13,000 descendants of Potawatomi. The Citizen Band of Potawatomi in Oklahoma alone listed 11,000 on its rolls, with about 1,500 of them living within the Shawnee Agency. Most of these were virtually assimilated into the surrounding culture. In Kansas, the more conservative Prairie Band of Potawatomi retained many aspects of tribal traditions and counted 2,100 on their rolls, including some 700 on or near the reservation.

In the late 1970s, there were also scattered communities of Potawatomi in Wisconsin, Upper and Lower Michigan and Ontario. Some 200 Potawatomi lived with Ottawa and Ojibwa, on the Walpole Island Reserve in the St. Clair River, retaining much of their language and culture.

BIBLIOGRAPHY: Clifton, James A. *The Prairie People.* Lawrence, Kansas: The Regents Press of Kansas, 1977; Clifton, James A. *A Place of Refuge for All Time.* Ottawa: National Museums of Canada, 1975.

A 1624 engraving of Powhatan, who "held this state and fashion when Captain John Smith was delivered to him a prisoner," in 1607.

Library of Congress

POWHATAN: an Algonquian confederacy of 30 tribes located along the eastern shore of the Chesapeake Bay in Virginia. The confederacy numbered about 9,000 at the time of the founding of Jamestown in 1607, and played an important role in the history of that colony. The confederacy had some 200 villages in 1607, but this number was reduced to 12 by 1705 through disease and warfare with the colonists. By the late 1970s, there remained a few hundred Chickahominy, Pamunkey and others of mixed blood living in Virginia.

The name Powhatan means "falls on a current of water" and the town known by that name was located on a falls of the James River near present-day Richmond. The colonists applied the name to the whole confederacy, as well as to Wahunsonacock, the founder of the confederacy, who made his home in the town of Powhatan.

Villages were often enclosed by palisades ten to twelve feet high. The long, narrow houses were made of bent saplings, covered with bark and woven mats. Several families lived in each of the houses, which sometimes reached 36 yards in length.

Three varieties of corn were grown, as well as beans, pumpkins and fruit trees. The Powhatan were skilled in basketry, beadwork, pottery and weaving of ceremonial clothing from turkey feathers. They also carved images of their chief deity, Okee. The Powhatan believed in the immortality of the soul, and when a chief died, his bones were wrapped in skins and placed on a scaffold and burned. Others were buried in the ground.

The first encounter of the Powhatan with Europeans was with a short-lived Spanish Jesuit mission established among them in 1570. By the early 17th century the confederacy had grown from 8 to 30 tribes under the leadership of Wahunsonacock. The marriage of his daughter, Pocahontas, to John Rolfe, one of the colonists, helped foster a period of peace between the Indians and the English.

Relations with the colonists deteriorated after the death of Wahunsonacock in 1618. In 1622 his brother, Opechancanough, led an attack which destroyed all English settlements except Jamestown, which had received warning. Fourteen years of bitter warfare followed, in which the Powhatan were greatly reduced. Peace was made in 1636, but incursions by the colonists brought war again in 1641. Opechacanough was killed in 1644, ending the confederacy.

In the late 1970s there was a Pamunkey state reservation of 800 acres in King William county, Virginia, with a population of about 40. Chickahominy, the largest Indian group remaining in Virginia, lived along the Chickahominy River in New Kent and Charles counties.

BIBLIOGRAPHY: Speck, Frank G. *Chapters on the Ethnology of the Powhatan Tribes of Virginia.* New York: Museum of the American Indian, 1928.

PUEBLO: a general term for all the Indians who occupied permanent stone or adobe villages (pueblos) in New Mexico and Arizona, and were descended from the cliff-dwelling Anasazi peoples. The 80-odd pueblos founded by the early Spanish explorers were reduced to about 25 by the late 1970s.

While similar, the Pueblo peoples were neither linguistically nor culturally uniform. In the modern pueblos, four language families were represented. The Hopi spoke a language of the Shoshonean division of the Uto-Aztecan family, and the Zuñi alone comprised the Zuñian family. The Keresan language family had two divisions: the western division, including Acoma and Laguna, and the eastern, or Rio Grande division, composed of Cochiti, Santo Domingo, San Felipe, Santa Ana and Zia. The Tanoan language family was represented by the Tewa, Tiwa, Towa, and Piro divisions. The Tewa included San Juan, Santa Clara, San Ildefonso, Tano (Hano) and Pojoaque. The Tiwa pueblos in-

A typical Pueblo dome-shaped "beehive" baking oven, introduced in Spanish times: a photograph taken in 1908.

cluded Taos, Picuris, Sandia and Isleta. In the 1970s, Jemez was the only remaining Towa pueblo, and the Piro pueblos were extinct except for tribal remnants in Texas and Mexico.

Culturally, the pueblos were usually divided into two groups: western and eastern, or Rio Grande. The western group included the Zuñi, Hopi (including Hano), Acoma and Laguna and the eastern group included the remaining Tewa, Tiwa, Towa and Keresan pueblos. Cultural differences between the two groups, however, were not distinct, with Jemez and the Keresan pueblos considered as transitional.

In pre-Spanish times, the pueblos were largely theocratic societies, governed by the heads of the various religious societies. The Spanish required the pueblos to institute a set of secular officials, including a governor, lieutenant governor, war captains, *fiscales*, etc. Appointed by the religious leaders of the pueblo, the secular officials served mainly as liaison between the pueblo and the outside world.

Among the Rio Grande pueblos, the people were divided into two moieties, or divisions, variously termed Summer and Winter or Squash and Turquoise. Each moiety had its *kiva*, or ceremonial building, around which religious and social activities centered. Among the western pueblos, clans were more important, with each clan responsible for certain ceremonies and religious paraphernalia. Secret societies were important in all pueblos, with each society having responsibility for certain ceremonies related to curing, hunting, agriculture, clowning or weather control.

Most pueblos had a tribal-wide *katcina* (kachina) society into which all men and sometimes women were initiated. This society's most important function was the performance of masked dances in which rain gods, or *katcina*, were impersonated. The *katcina*, who were also related to tribal ancestors, had more importance in the drier western pueblos than in those along the Rio Grande.

Marriage among the Pueblos was monogamous, although divorce, in pre-Spanish times, was easily obtained. In the western pueblos, newly-married couples lived with the wife's family, and the houses were owned by the women and inherited through the female line.

According to most traditions, the Pueblo peoples emerged from the earth through a hole in the ground located somewhere to the north. Upon death, a person's spirit returned to this place of origin, sometimes called Shipapu. The Pueblo usually buried their dead, sometimes burying or burning possessions of the deceased.

The dwellings of the Pueblo were compact stone or adobe apartment houses, often built around a central plaza. In pre-Spanish times, they were sometimes as many as seven stories high, built in terrace-fashion, with each succeeding story one room smaller than the one below.

The Cliff Palace at Mesa Verde, Colorado. The Pueblo Indians are descended from the original Anasazi inhabitants who built these dwellings.

U.S. Department of the Interior:
National Park Service

Another view of the cliff dwellings at Mesa Verde.

Common sights on the terraces were corn drying in the sun and dome-shaped beehive baking ovens, introduced during Spanish times.

The upper stories were reached by ladders, which could be pulled up as a defensive measure. There was no entrance at ground level to the lowest story, which was entered through a hole in the roof. Roofs were constructed of tree limbs covered with grass and mud. Floors were of flagstones or packed adobe. Men constructed the dwellings, and women plastered the walls with adobe inside and out and whitewashed the interior walls. Ceremonial rooms, or *kivas*, were either circular or rectangular, and could be either above ground or semisubterranean, with entry through a hatchway in the roof.

Agriculture, the main means of subsistence, often required extensive irrigation. In the drier western pueblos, cultivation was intensive, and every available drop of water was utilized. Corn was the staple crop, but beans, squash, pumpkins, cotton and tobacco were also grown, and the Spanish introduced wheat, chilies, alfalfa and a variety of fruit trees. Women tended small gardens of vegetables and gathered seeds, roots, pine nuts, cactus fruit and other wild plant foods.

The men hunted deer, elk and antelope with bow and arrow, and in

U.S. Department of the Interior: National Park Service

Ruins of buildings at Chaco Canyon, once inhabited by the Anasazi, ancestors of the present-day Pueblo.

some pueblos, they made occasional hunting trips to the Plains for buffalo. Communal drives were held to hunt rabbits, using throwing sticks, for both food and ceremonial purposes.

The Pueblo women produced probably the finest pottery north of Mexico, as well as excellent basketry. Men wove beautiful cotton textiles for ceremonial costumes, everyday clothing and trade. After the Spanish introduced sheep and other livestock, women's dresses were made of dark wool, belted with brightly-colored yarn belts. Moccasins and knee-length deerskin leggings were also worn.

The ancestors of the pueblo people were the Anasazi, whose ancient cliff-dwellings may be seen in the ruins of Mesa Verde, Chaco Canyon, Kayenta and numerous other sites. Drought conditions in the 13th century, and perhaps warfare with Plains tribes, were the probable reasons for the abandonment of these dwellings and the southward migration of their peoples.

New towns were built along the Rio Grande and its tributaries and further west at Zuñi and Hopi. About 200 pueblos had been consolidated to about 80 by the time of the first Spanish expeditions into the area in about 1540. By the early 17th century, many Spanish missions had been established, and Spanish colonists were beginning to occupy Pueblo

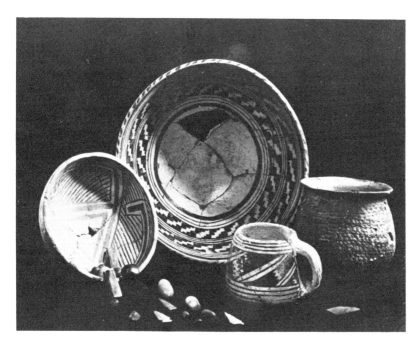

Bowls from Mesa Verde.   U.S. Department of the Interior: National Park Service

lands. Enforced tributes of corn, craft items and labor, coupled with attempts to stamp out the traditional Pueblo religion, led to revolt.

In 1680, after several minor rebellions, the pueblos cooperated in a general revolt, led by Popé, a San Juan Indian, and others. Of the 2,350 Spanish colonists and 33 missionaries in the area, about 375 colonists and 21 priests were killed in the revolt. The others were allowed to flee safely to El Paso, although the missions were destroyed. The Spanish returned in 1692 and re-established control, except for a short rebellion in 1696.

In the 18th and 19th centuries, the pueblos endured raids by Plains tribes, the ravages of epidemics and the change of overlordship from Spanish to Mexican to American. Through it all, they maintained their religion and culture, principally by maintaining absolute secrecy in such matters.

In the late 1970s, the traditional culture of the Pueblos persisted, with overlays and trappings of Catholicism and of Spanish and American culture. Most important rites were still held in secret, with a full calendar of traditional ceremonies being held every year. Some colorful dances were open to the public. Most people were bilingual, speaking English as well as their native language. The older people often spoke Spanish as well as other Pueblo languages. Six pueblos elected their civil officials,

U.S. Department of the Interior. National Park Service

Pottery found at the Aztec Ruins National Monument, New Mexico.

but religious leaders continued to be most influential in the more traditional pueblos. Most of the pueblos belonged to the All Indian Pueblo Council, which met regularly to deal with the common problems of the pueblos.

Adobe homes were still predominant, often modernized by glass windows, first-story doors, plumbing and electricity. A revival of Pueblo crafts, begun in the early 20th century, continued. Fine silver and turquoise jewelry, as well as excellent pottery, weaving and basketry were being produced.

See also: *Cochiti, Hopi, Isleta, Jemez, Laguna, Nambe, Picuris, Piro, Pojoaque, Sandia, San Felipe, San Ildefonso, San Juan, Santa Ana, Santa Clara, Santo Domingo, Tano, Taos, Tesuque. Zia,* and *Zuñi.*

BIBLIOGRAPHY: Dozier, Edward P. *The Pueblo Indians of North America.* New York: Holt, Rinehart and Winston, Inc.; Sando, Joe S. *The Pueblo Indians.* San Francisco: The Indian Historian Press, 1976.

PUYALLUP: a Northwest Coast group located along the Puyallup River and Commencement Bay in northwestern Washington in the late 18th century. Together with the Nisqualli (*q.v.*) and other related tribes, they numbered about 3,600 in 1780. In the late 1970s, there were about 4,400 Indians residing in Pierce County, Washington, of which about 200 lived on or near the Puyallup Reservation.

The Puyallup spoke the Nisqualli language of the Coast division of the Salishan language family. Their culture closely resembled that of the Nisqualli.

In 1855, the Puyallup and other Puget Sound tribes were assigned reservations under the provisions of the 1854 Medicine Creek Treaty. Some of the lands were subsequently allotted to individuals. In 1904, restrictions on allotted land were ended, resulting in the eventual sale of much of the land to non-Indians. In the late 1970s, the reservation included only 33 acres.

BIBLIOGRAPHY: Smith, Marian W. *The Puyallup-Nisqually.* New York: Columbia University Press, 1940.

QUAPAW: a tribe of the Dhegiha division of the Siouan language family, residing near the mouth of the Arkansas River in the late 17th century, numbering about 2,500 at that time. In the late 1970s, there were 1,600 Quapaw, mostly living in Oklahoma. Their tribal name means "downstream people" and refers to the tradition that the Dhegiha tribes migrated west through the Ohio Valley, and, upon reaching the Mississippi, the Quapaw turned downstream, while the others turned upstream. They were also known as Arkansea.

The Quapaw had two divisions, or moieties, subdivided into 22 patrilineal clans. Each village was governed by an hereditary chief and council of elders. In later times, there was a chief of the whole tribe. The Quapaw worshipped a great overall spirit, called Wakonda, as well as numerous lesser spirits. One of their most important ceremonies was the Pipe Dance, the beauty of which greatly impressed the French explorer, Marquette. The Green Corn Dance, celebrating the beginning of the harvest, was also important.

The Quapaw buried their dead both in the ground and above ground, covered with a mound of rocks and earth. The deceased was furnished with tools, weapons and an eagle feather was placed in his hand.

Quapaw villages, located near the junction of the Mississippi and Arkansas rivers, were built on mounds of earth and sometimes palisaded. Their long, dome-roofed houses were covered with cypress bark and housed several families. They grew three crops of corn a year, as well as beans, squash, gourds and tobacco. Persimmons, walnuts, mulberries and plums were gathered.

The men hunted deer, buffalo and fowl, and fished with weirs and nets. Crafts included making walnut and cypress dugout canoes and carved stone pipes. The Quapaw also made excellent painted and incised pottery, which they traded to neighboring tribes.

The Quapaw villages on the Mississippi were the turn-around point for the 1673 Marquette-Jolliet expedition which was searching for a route to the Pacific Ocean. The Quapaw informed the explorers that the Mississippi flowed into the Gulf of Mexico and, furthermore, that the tribes downriver were unfriendly. By the end of the century, other French explorers found the Quapaw decimated by smallpox and warfare.

In the 18th century, as allies of the French, the Quapaw became involved in their warfare with the Chickasaw. By 1800, the Quapaw were reduced to three small villages of about 1,000 total population on the Arkansas River. Warfare, disease, alcoholism and intermarriage had all weakened the tribal strength. In 1818, they ceded their claims to southern Arkansas, southern Oklahoma and northern Louisiana to the United States, reserving about one million acres in Arkansas. By 1824, they were forced to give this up, too, and went to live with the Caddo on the Red River in Louisiana. After having their crops flooded twice, resulting in starvation, they began to drift back to Arkansas.

In 1833, they were finally given lands in Indian Territory (Oklahoma) and Kansas, but later had to cede those in Kansas. The remainder of the 19th century was difficult for the Quapaw, with many hardships due to forced moves, disease and the Civil War. In 1893 the Quapaw divided their own reservation lands, the only tribe to do so, allotting 200 acres to each of the 240 tribal members.

In 1905, rich lead and zinc deposits were discovered on some of the Quapaw lands. A flock of miners and unscrupulous adventurers rushed to the area. A few Quapaw became quite wealthy from mining leases, and a flurry of wild spending followed in the 1920s.

In the 1970s, about 300 of the 1,200 tribal members were of one-quarter or more Quapaw blood. Most engaged in farming or business; a few were wealthy, and a few were poor, with most somewhere in the middle. Quapaw tribal dances were still performed each year.

BIBLIOGRAPHY: Nieberding, Velma Seamster. *The Quapaws*. Miami, Oklahoma: Dixons, Inc. 1976.

QUILEUTE: a Northwest Coast whaling tribe located along the Quillayute River, Jackson Creek and Hoh River in northwestern Washington, numbering about 500 in the late 18th century. In the late 1970s, there were about 400 Quileute, including members of the Hoh subtribe, living on or near two reservations in their traditional territory.

The Quileute, with the extinct Chimakum tribe, spoke the only known languages to belong to the Chimakuan language family. In the late 1970s there were less than 15 Quileute who still spoke the language, but work was in progress on a Quileute dictionary and language instruction materials.

The basic unit of the Quileute was the extended family or household, led by a chief whose prestige was derived from inherited wealth and privileges. There were three social classes: nobles, commoners and slaves, the slaves being obtained in warfare or trade. The wealthy sometimes had several wives. Marriage was contracted through an exchange of gifts between the two families.

Religion centered around guardian spirits, sought by adolescents through purification, fasting and visiting remote places, to give them power in the form of skills, luck or achievements. Shamans acquired several guardian spirits enabling them to cure the sick and recover lost souls. Quileute mythology included the culture hero Qwaeti, Thunderbird, Earth Shaker, Blue Jay and the trickster character Raven. There were a number of secret societies, including those for warriors, fishermen, hunters, shamans and whalers. Each society had certain knowledge and rituals necessary to the performance of these occupations. Members were initiated in six-day ceremonies which included dances in which carved wooden masks were worn.

Other important ceremonies included First Salmon rites and potlatches, which were given to celebrate births and weddings and as memorials to the dead. Potlatches were hosted by a wealthy man, and included a ceremonial gift-giving and recitation of the lineage and inherited privileges of the host.

The Quileute buried many of their dead on James Island. The bodies of the deceased were wrapped in mats or dog hair blankets and buried in a canoe or a hollow log. On the second anniversary of death, the remains were reburied in a wooden box, and a memorial potlatch was given.

Quileute villages, located at the river mouths and several points upstream, were composed of multi-family cedar plank houses, about 60 feet long by 40 feet wide, with a single-pitch roof. Sleeping platforms lined the interior walls, and each family had its own fireplace.

The Quileute were reportedly second to none as seal hunters. They also hunted sea lions, sea otters and porpoises. Whaling crews, having observed the proper rituals, braved the ocean in cedar log canoes, using heavy harpoons attached to sealskin floats.

In spite of the emphasis on sea mammals, fish provided the staple food. Salmon, herring, steelhead trout, halibut and cod were caught with traps, weirs, spears, drag nets, dip nets and gill nets. Far less important were various inland game animals, taken with bow and arrow, snares and deadfalls. Women gathered crabs, mussels, clams, seaweed, salmon eggs, fern roots, camas bulbs, greens, wild cherries, crabapples, grapes and a wide assortment of berries.

The Quileute made canoes and boxes from cedar, dishes and platters from yew and alder, hemlock bark buckets, water-tight spruce-root baskets and cattail mats and baskets. Clothing included shredded cedar bark skirts and capes, as well as spruce root rain hats. Tattooing and ear and nose ornaments were used for adornment, and head-flattening was practiced by the nobility. Face painting was used for ceremonies, mourning, adornment and sunburn protection.

The Quileute were frequently at war with the Makah, but around 1850, they were at peace with them long enough to learn their whaling techniques. The Quileute did not welcome early explorers, preferring their privacy. They signed a treaty with the United States in 1855, but the Quileute and Hoh Reservations were not established until 1889 and 1893, respectively. In 1889, a fire destroyed the village at LaPush, including all the sacred masks and other ceremonial equipment, baskets and hunting implements. About 1904, the last whale was taken, and in the 1930s, sealing was abandoned.

In the 1970s, there were about 320 Quileute living on or near the 600-acre Quileute Reservation located at LaPush, Clallam County, Washington. Another 80 Quileute (or Hoh) were located on or near the 450-acre Hoh Reservation in Jefferson County. Salmon, halibut, steelhead and smelt fishing were still important, and a few cedar canoes were still in use. Potlatches were held to celebrate name-giving, marriages and memorials to the dead, and traditional Quileute songs and tales were still heard.

BIBLIOGRAPHY: Pettitt, George A. "The Quileute of LaPush 1775-1945." *University of California Anthropological Records.* vol. 14, 1950; Powell, Jay and Jenson, Vickie. *Quileute.* Seattle: University of Washington Press, 1976.

QUINAULT: a Northwest Coast tribe located along the Quinault River and adjacent coastline of Washington in the late 18th century, numbering about 800 at that time. In the late 1970s, Quinault descendants were mixed with other Northwest Coast tribes on the Quinault Reservation at Taholah, Washington.

The Quinault spoke a language of the Coast division of the Salishan language family. Their tribal name was derived from the name for their largest settlement, Kwinail, located on the site of the modern-day village of Taholah.

The Quinault had about 20 villages, each led by a chief, whose functions included advising, admonishing and sponsoring feasts and potlatches. His power was based on wealth, family, maturity and personal appeal. The villages were composed of households of from two to six families, each household occupying a large house owned by the head of

Quinault working in a fish processing plant at Tahola, Washington.

one of the families. There were two main classes: nobility, composed of chiefs and their families, and commoners, although the distinction between them was somewhat blurred. The Quinault also had a few slaves, obtained in warfare or trade.

Religion centered around guardian spirits, sought by children from age eight, through daily bathing, physical training and fasting in lonely places. Girls were secluded for five months at puberty. Shamans had powerful guardian spirits, which assisted them in curing the sick, finding lost souls and exorcising ghosts. Quinault mythology included Misp, who created the world and made it fit for habitation, and Xwoni Xwoni, the trickster buffoon. Many taboos and ceremonies were connected with salmon, the staple food. Important celebrations, included potlatches, by which chiefs or wealthy persons enhanced their prestige by giving away large amounts of material goods.

Quinault burial customs included wrapping the body in mats and placing it in a canoe, with a second canoe sometimes inverted over it, or placing it in a wooden box on posts. Personal items and utensils were usually placed with the body. Surviving spouses usually remarried into the family of their deceased wife or husband.

The Quinault built gable-roofed cedar plank houses with a platform in front where men gathered to talk and work. Sleeping platforms and storage shelves ringed the interior walls. While on hunting trips, temporary bark or brush shelters were used.

The Quinault were located on an excellent salmon fishing river, and caught sockeye, king, silver, dog and humpback salmon, as well as steelhead trout, smelt, candlefish, halibut, cod, sole and herring. Fishing technology included dip nets, harpoons, hooks and drift nets used from canoes, and each village had at least one weir which it carefully maintained. A few men, who had the proper guardian spirit, engaged in whaling. Eight-man crews with special gear and training hunted whales in ocean-going canoes usually obtained from the Makah or Nootka. Seal, sea otter and sea lion were also hunted, as well as land animals such as elk (using elk calls), bear, deer, beaver, wildcat, wolf, marmot, rabbit, mink and ducks. Camas, roots, berries, razor clams, rock oysters, mussels and crabs were also gathered from land and sea.

The Quinault made wooden boxes, platters, dishes, bowls and spoons, as well as baskets of cedar root and cedar bark. Blankets were woven of both rabbit skin and dog hair. The men often went without clothing, donning moccasins and leggings for hunting, and women wore skirts of grass or shredded bark. Cedar bark was woven into hats, and rain capes were made of rushes. Face painting and tattooing were used for adornment.

The Quinault traded and intermarried a good deal with neighboring tribes. They made their own cedar log river canoes, but often obtained

A Salish horseman at Flathead Reservation, Montana.

Bureau of Indian Affairs

whaling canoes from the Makah, along with whale oil and dentalium shells. In exchange, they provided dried salmon, sea otter skins and dried elk meat.

In the early 19th century, the Quinault were severely hit by a smallpox epidemic. In 1855 they ceded all of their lands to the United States, except for a small reservation, which was enlarged in 1873.

In the 1970s, the Quinault were mixed with Chinook, Chehalis and Cowlitz, among the 2,000 population of the 189,000-acre Quinault Reservation. Salmon fishing continued to be the main economic pursuit, including a highly successful tribally-owned fish marketing enterprise.

BIBLIOGRAPHY: Olson, Ronald L. "The Quinault Indians." *University of Washington Publications in Anthropology*. vol. 6, 1936.

SALISH: *See* FLATHEAD.

SANDIA: a Tiwa tribe and pueblo located 12 miles north of Albuquerque, New Mexico, on the east bank of the Rio Grande. With a population of 300 in the late 1970s, it occupied the same location as it did when visited by the Spanish explorer Coronado in 1540.

The name Sandia was Spanish for "watermelon," but the Indians referred to their pueblo as Napeya or Nafiat, meaning "a dusty or sandy

Smithsonian Institution National Anthropological Archives

A view of the pueblo of Sandia, New Mexico, in 1879.

place.'' The Sandia, along with Isleta, Taos and Picuris, spoke the Tiwa language of the Tanoan language family.

Sandia was also visited by Juan de Oñate in 1598, and shortly thereafter became the seat of the mission of San Francisco. In the early 17th century, Sandia was one of about eight Tiwa pueblos, with a total population of about 6,000 along that stretch of the Rio Grande. By the latter part of the century, these had been consolidated into four pueblos, including Sandia, which had an estimated population of 3,000, and Isleta, with a population of 2,000.

In 1680, Sandia joined Taos, Picuris and most of the other pueblos in rebelling against the Spanish. The Sandia abandoned their pueblo and fled to the Hopi for safety. There on the Second Mesa, north of Mishongnovi, they built the village of Payupki, where they remained until 1792. At that time, they returned and rebuilt Sandia, which had been burned by the Spanish in 1681.

In the late 1970s, Sandia pueblo occupied about 22,800 acres with a population of about 300. The traditional culture and language were still important to the people. Annual ceremonies included the Corn Dance in June and the New Year's Dance.

SANETCH: See SONGISH.

SAN FELIPE: a Keresan tribe and pueblo located about 30 miles southwest of Santa Fe, New Mexico, with a population of about 2,300 in the late 1970s. They called their pueblo Katishtya, and spoke a language of the Keresan family. Other Keresan tribes included the Cochiti, Santo Domingo, Santa Ana, Zia, Laguna and Acoma.

The leadership of the pueblo included the traditional religious leaders, who wielded the real power, and the secular officials, whose offices dated from Spanish times. The cacique, who was appointed for life and was the head of the Flint and Koshari societies, was the religious leader of the pueblo. He was the guardian of tribal traditions and keeper of the various fetishes.

The cacique annually appointed two war captains and eight helpers to implement his authority. The secular arm of the government included the governor, lieutenant-governor and other officers, who were appointed for one year. They dealt with those outside the pueblo, and were often mistakenly thought by outsiders to be the real rulers of the pueblo.

There were three curing societies, Flint, Giant, and Cikame, who performed cures either individually or as a group. A curing ceremony often involved restoring a heart stolen by witches. All men in the pueblo belonged to one of three *katcina* (kachina) groups, who performed masked dances to bring rain, usually in spring and summer. Harvest dances were performed in the fall.

Bureau of Indian Affairs

An English language class at San Felipe pueblo, in New Mexico.

Each person belonged to a clan, inheriting membership in the same clan as his mother and usually marrying outside the clan. There were two *kivas*, or religious centers: Squash and Turquoise. An individual usually belonged to the *kiva* of his father, although after marriage, a woman joined the *kiva* of her husband. When a person died, his body was usually buried within 24 hours, and his possessions were buried or destroyed. Ceremonies were held on the fourth day, by which time the soul had departed for the land of the dead.

According to tradition, the Cochiti and San Felipe peoples lived together in prehistoric times at several locations, including Kuapa, about 12 miles northwest of the present Cochiti. They were forced south and separated by pressure from the Tewa peoples.

By 1540, when visited by the Spanish explorer Coronado, the San Felipe had established a pueblo, which they called Katishtya, on the present-day site at the foot of Tamita mesa. A Spanish mission was located there in the early 17th century. In 1680, the San Felipe took an active part in the Pueblo Revolt, but fled to the fortified town of Potrero Viejo, along with some of the other Keresan peoples. When they returned in 1693, they re-established Katishtya on the summit of the Black mesa, for defensive purposes. But by the early 18th century, they had relocated it at the base of the mesa, the site of the present-day San Felipe.

In the late 1970s, the population of the 49,000-acre pueblo was about 2,300. Although influenced by Spanish and American contact, the culture and traditions of San Felipe were still strong. Religious ceremonies and dances were held throughout the year; the language was still vital and the government of the cacique continued to rule in traditional affairs.

BIBLIOGRAPHY: White, Leslie A. "The Pueblo of San Felipe." *Memoirs of the American Anthropological Association.* no. 38, 1932.

SAN ILDEFONSO: a Tewa tribe and pueblo located 20 miles north of Santa Fe, New Mexico, on the east bank of the Rio Grande, with a population of about 350 in the late 1970s. They have been at approximately the same location since before the coming of the Spanish in the late 16th century.

The San Ildefonso called their pueblo Powhoge, meaning "where the water cuts through." The San Ildefonso, along with the San Juan, Santa Clara, Nambe, Tesuque and Pojoaque, spoke the Tewa language of the Tanoan language family.

The tribe was divided into two moieties, or divisions, Summer and Winter, which were further subdivided into clans. Each person usually belonged to his father's moiety, but women often joined the moiety of their husband when they married. In the past there were as many as 58 clans, with clan membership also inherited from one's father.

The most important leaders of the pueblo were the Winter cacique and Summer cacique. These religious leaders were chosen by their predecessors, and were in charge of the religious and ceremonial life of the pueblo, as well as controlling the secular government of the pueblo through officials appointed by themselves. Secular officials included the governor, two lieutenant governors, and a war captain, whose duties included dealing with outsiders. There were also a number of societies—the Kossa, or clowns, the War Society and the Medicine societies. Each society had its own dances and ceremonies which they performed for various purposes such as bringing rain, curing the sick or insuring a bountiful corn crop or successful hunt.

When a person died, he was buried with his feet in the direction of Sipofene, the place in the north where the Pueblo peoples emerged from the earth, and to which their spirits returned. His possessions were buried or broken, and placed on the grave, along with food. For four days, the relatives remained in the house of the deceased with his spirit, which was sent on the fifth day to Sipofene.

The pueblo consisted of one and two-story adobe houses and three

San Ildefonso women husking corn.   The National Archives

kivas, or religious centers, one round and two rectangular. An earlier pueblo was composed of two and three-story dwellings around a central plaza.

The men of San Ildefonso cultivated fields of corn, beans and squash and hunted deer and rabbits. The women gathered pine nuts, prickly pear cactus fruit, yucca seed pods and various roots, as well as cedar, sumac and juniper berries.

Weapons included obsidian knives, war clubs, rabbit sticks, leather slings and bows of cherry, cedar or elk antler. The men dressed skins, sewed moccasins, wove baskets, and decorated pottery made by the women.

According to tradition, ancestors of the San Ildefonso lived at Otowi, an extensive prehistoric pueblo on a nearby mesa, consisting of terraced structures containing two to four-story houses with a total of 750 rooms. Drought conditions finally forced the people to move to the valley.

In 1598, the San Ildefonso were visited by the explorer Juna de Oñate, and the Spanish established a mission there in 1617. In 1680, the San Ildefonso took a prominent part in the Pueblo Revolt. The Spanish returned in 1692, and the San Ildefonso retreated in 1694 to the top of Huerfano mesa, from which they held off four successive attacks. Finally, after a four-day siege, they were forced to surrender.

In the succeeding centuries, the San Ildefonso defended themselves against attacks by Navajo, Comanche and Kiowa raiders. In the early

20th century, a new plaza was built, dividing the pueblo into two sections.

A pottery-making revival was begun in the early 20th century, when men from San Ildefonso assisted in the excavation of prehistoric ruins on the Pajarito Plateau. Pottery fragments found in the excavations were carefully studied by the women potters of San Ildefonso, who began experimenting to reproduce some of the old designs and styles. Many excellent potters developed their talents, the best known being Maria Montoya Martinez. Her famous black-on-black ware and other styles were decorated by her husband, Julian Martinez, and later, by her son, Popovi Da.

In the late 1970s, San Ildefonso occupied 26,000 acres, with a population of about 350. Most of the women, including Maria Martinez and her family, were involved in pottery-making, and many of the men decorated pottery or did paintings. Traditional ceremonies, religion, and the Tewa language, were still strongly maintained.

BIBLIOGRAPHY: Whitman, William. *The Pueblo Indians of San Ildefonso.* New York: Columbia University Press, 1947.

SAN JUAN: a Tewa tribe and pueblo located, since the early 16th century, 25 miles northwest of Santa Fe, New Mexico, on the east bank of the Rio Grande. In the late 1970s, San Juan Pueblo, occupying 12,000 acres, had a population of about 1,700.

The San Juan spoke a Tewa language of the Tanoan language family. Other Tewa pueblos included San Ildefonso, Santa Clara, Nambe, Tesuque, Tano (Hano) and Pojoaque. The San Juan referred to their pueblo as Oke'onwi.

San Juan was organized into about 33 clans and two moieties, or tribal divisions. Each person usually belonged to the clan and moiety of his father. The two moieties, Summer (or Squash) and Winter (or Turquoise) each had a *kiva*, or ceremonial building. There were also a number of societies, including Curing societies, Hunter societies, War societies, Clown societies and societies concerned with weather control. All boys and girls were initiated into the Ohuwa (equivalent to the *katcina* cult of other pueblos), in which masked dancers impersonated cloud gods for the purpose of bringing rain.

In traditional and religious affairs, San Juan was ruled by two caciques, one for summer and one for winter. A war chief and two assistants aided the caciques in organizing the ceremonial life of the pueblo. Secular officials, whose offices dated from Spanish times, were appointed to one-year terms by the caciques. The main secular official was the governor who, with the advice of the caciques, dealt with the world outside the pueblo. He was assisted by two lieutenant governors, an *alguacil* (peace officer) and *fiscales,* who looked after the church.

The San Juan Turtle Dance.   Bureau of Indian Affairs

According to tradition, the San Juan occupied the nearby ancient ruins of Pioge, Sajiuwingge and Pajiuuingge, before establishing themselves at their present site in the early 16th century. In 1598, San Juan was visited by a Spanish expedition led by Juan de Oñate, who established the first capital of New Mexico there. A mission was established soon after, but the capital was moved to Santa Fe in 1610.

Friendly relations existed between the Indians and the Spanish until the Spanish required the Indians to provide food and labor and attempted to quash the Indian religion. In 1675, the Spanish whipped 47 San Juan Indians convicted of witchcraft, among them a medicine man named Popé. In 1680, the Pueblo Revolt broke out, led by Popé and others, and the Spanish were forced to flee to El Paso. In 1692, they returned and restored themselves to power, except for minor outbreaks in 1696. Around 1782, San Juan and Santa Clara pueblos were severely reduced by epidemics. In 1858, the United States Congress confirmed the 1689 Spanish land grant.

In the late 1970s, the San Juan pueblo was governed in civil matters by a governor and the tribal council. The Indians of San Juan had intermarried with the Spanish to a greater extent than any of the other pueblos. The cacique still had charge of religious and cultural matters. The Tewa language was still spoken, and ceremonies such as the Corn

Economic Development Administration

Making adobe bricks at San Juan, New Mexico.

Dance were performed annually. The women of San Juan were well known for their excellent pottery.

BIBLIOGRAPHY: Ortiz, Alfonso. *The Tewa World.* Chicago: The University of Chicago Press, 1969.

SANPOIL: a Salishan group located near the confluence of the Columbia and Sanpoil rivers in Washington in the late 18th century, numbering about 1,600 at that time. In the late 1970s, Sanpoil descendants were mixed with Nespelem, Colville and other Plateau groups on the Colville Reservation in northeastern Washington.

The Sanpoil and the neighboring Nespelem spoke the same language, belonging to the Interior division of the Salishan language family, and shared a similar culture as well. They were divided into autonomous villages, each led by a chief and sub-chief, whose offices tended to be hereditary. Chiefs arbitrated disputes, gave advice and presided over the village assembly. Other officials included a messenger, a spokesman and the salmon chief. The latter, often a shaman, who had the salmon as his guardian spirit, directed the building of salmon weirs and traps.

Religion centered around guardian spirits, sought through fasting, praying and feats of endurance such as running and swimming. Shamans had guardian spirits to aid them in curing the sick. The most important ceremonies were the five-day First Salmon rites and the Mid-Winter ceremonies. Girls were secluded for ten days at puberty, during which they fasted and went out only at night to run. Marriages were formalized by an exchange of gifts between the two families. The Sanpoil believed the land of the dead was located at the end of the Milky Way. They wrapped the body of the deceased in deerskin and buried it along with personal items. The family of the deceased observed certain taboos, purification rites and a period of mourning.

In winter, the Sanpoil lived in circular semisubterranean lodges from 10 to 16 feet in diameter, with flat or conical roofs. A wood frame was covered with planks or mats and a layer of grass and brush. Over this was spread a layer of earth, preferably water-resistant clay. In spring, the village broke into groups of several families to dig roots and to fish for salmon, living in conical mat shelters. In later times, large gabled mat houses were also used in winter. Sweatlodges of grass and earth on a willow frame were located near the river.

Fish was the staple food. Silver, dog, king, and humpback salmon, as well as trout and sturgeon, were caught with traps, weirs, nets and spears. The women gathered shellfish, salmon eggs, camas, roots, nuts, seeds, and berries. In fall, hunting parties went to the mountains for deer, elk, bear, rabbit, antelope and fowl. Women went along to help dress and carry the game. Meat and fish were dried and made into pemmican. The Sanpoil carved dishes and spoons of wood and wove cedar roots into coiled basketry water containers, berry baskets and cooking utensils. In early times, they made crude sun-dried pottery vessels covered with fish skin. Mats were made from tule and various grasses. Clothing—breechclouts or aprons, ponchos and Indian hemp leggings for men—was of woven bark fibers, later replaced by tailored buckskin clothing introduced from the Plains. Fur robes were worn for warmth, and earrings, necklaces and face paint were used for adornment.

The Sanpoil and Nespelem were unusually peaceful people, rarely even engaging in counter raids when occasionally attacked by the Shuswap, Coeur d'Alene or Nez Perce. In the late 18th century, they were decimated by smallpox, measles and influenza epidemics. Again in 1846 and 1852-53, they were hard hit by smallpox. The Sanpoil remained in their own territory living their traditional lives until 1872, when they were placed on the Colville Reservation, along with other Plateau tribes. In 1910, there were about 234 Sanpoil. In the late 1970s they were intermingled among the population of more than 4,500 of the Confederated Tribes located on or near the million-acre Colville Reservation in Ferry and Okanagon counties, Washington.

BIBLIOGRAPHY: Ray, Verne F. "The Sanpoil and Nespelem." *University of Washington Publications in Anthropology.* vol. 5, 1933.

SANS ARCS. A subdivision of the Teton Dakota, located west of the Missouri River between the Grand and Heart rivers in the mid-19th century, numbering about 1,400 at that time. Sans Arcs is the French translation of "Itazipcho," the name by which they were known, meaning "without bows." In the late 1970s, Sans Arcs descendants were located on the Cheyenne River Reservation in South Dakota, along with other Dakota groups. (See also *Teton* and *Dakota*.)

SANTA ANA: a Keresan tribe and pueblo located about 25 miles north of Albuquerque, New Mexico. The old pueblo, called Tamaya, was located on the north bank of the Jemez River about eight miles above its confluence with the Rio Grande, with a population of about 340 in 1700. In the late 1970s, the old pueblo was used mainly for ceremonial occasions and celebrations, and the population of around 500 was located at Ranchos de Santa Ana, about 10 miles southeast. The Santa Ana people spoke a language of the Keresan family, as did the people of Santo Domingo, San Felipe, Cochiti, Zia, Laguna and Acoma.

The traditional head of Santa Ana was the cacique, who served as the religious leader and as the intermediary between the pueblo and the spirit world. He was guardian of the tribal fetishes and other sacred items.

**Black Eye,
a Sans Arc,
(1872).**
The National Archives

Santa Ana pueblo, New Mexico, in 1879.

Other religious leaders included the assistant to the cacique and two war priests, *masewi* and *oyoyewi,* appointed for one-year terms. The secular officials, also appointed by the cacique for one-year terms, included the governor (or *dapop*), lieutenant governor, *capitani* (headman), and *fiscales* (prosecutor). These officials, whose offices were instituted by the Spanish, served as liaison between the pueblo and the outside world, but the actual government of the pueblo rested with the religious leaders.

The religious centers of Santa Ana were the two *kivas,* designated Squash and Turquoise. Each individual belonged to one or the other, according to his clan affiliation. Both men and women belonged to the *katcina* (kachina) dance groups, which performed masked dances impersonating rain gods who lived in the west at Wenima. There were also a number of secret societies, including the Warrior, Hunter and Medicine societies.

When a person died, his body was usually buried that day in the churchyard, with a bunch of turkey feathers in each hand and under his head. Bread and other items were also buried with him. The person's spirit lingered for four days until sent by a shaman to the land of the dead, where it became a *katcina* (deified ancestral spirit).

Houses were built of adobe brick plastered over inside and out and whitewashed inside. The flat roofs were of brush or planks covered with earth, and floors were of hard-packed clay. The two stone *kivas* were circular, with about 10 feet of the building above ground and four feet below, and were entered through a hatchway on the roof.

Before the coming of the Spanish, the Santa Ana raised corn, beans, squash and cotton, weaving the cotton into clothing and ceremonial costumes. The men cultivated the fields and hunted deer, antelope and elk. Rabbits were hunted in communal drives, with some of the meat given to the cacique to use for sacrificial offerings to the tribal fetishes. Young eagles were captured and raised for their feathers, and bear and mountain lion were hunted for their skins. Occasional trips were made to the Plains area to hunt buffalo. The women did the indoor work, plastered the houses, ground the corn to meal, and made fine pottery.

According to tradition, the various Pueblo peoples originally emerged from the earth at a place in the north called Shipapu, gradually moving southward. The Santa Ana eventually settled on a mesa in the Jemez River area, not far from San Felipe, calling their pueblo Tamaya.

The Spanish visited the pueblo in 1598, and soon after established the mission of Santa Ana. In 1680, the Santa Ana joined in the Pueblo Revolt, and the Spanish burned their town in 1687. By 1692 the Santa Ana submitted to the Spanish, and re-established their pueblo of Tamaya at its present site. Fighting with the Spanish continued, however, until 1696.

In the 18th century, Santa Ana purchased five tracts of land to the southeast, on both sides of the Rio Grande, and began cultivating crops there. The tribe began spending spring and summer near their fields, or ranchitos, and returning to the pueblo in fall and winter. Gradually permanent homes were built on the new lands, and the ranchitos eventually became the year-round residence of the people.

By the late 1970s, the old pueblo was deserted, and the population of about 500 resided at Ranchos de Santa Ana, where the houses were of a similar construction, but more modern. On holidays and for ceremonial occasions, everyone returned to the old pueblo to celebrate their traditional dances and ceremonies.

BIBLIOGRAPHY: White, Leslie A. "The Pueblo of Santa Ana, New Mexico." *American Anthropologist.* vol. 44, 1942.

SANTA CLARA: a Tewa tribe and pueblo located 25 miles north of Santa Fe, New Mexico, on the west bank of the Rio Grande, with a population of about 1,250 in the late 1970s. The Santa Clara, along with the San Ildefonso, San Juan, Nambe, Tesuque and Pojoaque spoke the Tewa language of the Tanoan language family. They referred to their pueblo as Kapo'onwi.

The ancestors of the Santa Clara and other Tewa groups lived in the

Santa Clara Indian women, with a baby, (1916). The National Archives

Puye cliff dwellings, which were carved out of a mesa near the present pueblo. The dwellings, which extended for many hundreds of yards, were occupied into the historical period. Drought conditions were among the factors that forced the Tewa to move down to the Rio Grande.

In the early 17th century, the Spanish established a mission at Santa Clara, later granting the tribe their land. The original Spanish land grant was confirmed by the United States Congress in 1858, and subsequent grants brought the total acreage of the pueblo to 45,700 acres in the late 1970s.

By the late 1970s, the Santa Clara had opened their ancient dwellings at Puye to visitors. The pueblo was also famous for excellent pottery. More than 75 Santa Clara women were involved in pottery-making, and were assisted in painting the pottery by a number of the men. Other craftwork included textiles and embroidery. The Tewa language and tribal religion, under the guidance of the cacique, the traditional religious leader, were still vital in the daily life of the pueblo.

SANTEE: the eastern division of the Dakota, living in northern Minnesota in the late 17th century. The four Santee groups—the Mdewakanton, Wahpekute, Sisseton and Wahpeton—together numbered about 5,000 at that time. In the late 1970s, Santee descendants could be found in North and South Dakota, Minnesota, Montana, Alberta and Saskatchewan numbering perhaps 5,000.

The Santee spoke the Dakota dialect of the Dakota language, which belongs to the Siouan language family. Santee was derived from Isanati, meaning "knife." (See *Mdewakanton, Wahpekute, Sisseton* and *Wahpeton.*)

BIBLIOGRAPHY: Meyer, Roy W. *History of the Santee Sioux.* Lincoln: University of Nebraska Press, 1967.

SANTO DOMINGO: a Keresan tribe and pueblo located 25 miles southwest of Santa Fe, New Mexico since about 1700, when they numbered about 200. In the late 1970s, Santo Domingo was one of the largest and most traditional of the New Mexico pueblos, with a population of more than 2,800.

The Santo Domingans, who called their pueblo Kiuw, spoke a language of the Keresan family. Other Keresan tribes included the San Felipe, Cochiti, Santa Ana, Zia, Laguna and Acoma. The Santo Domingo language was still spoken in the late 1970s.

The religious and political head of the pueblo was the cacique, who was chosen for life to be the guardian of the sacred traditions of the tribe. He appointed two war chiefs, *Masewi* and *Oyoyewi*, and ten helpers, or *gowatcanyi*, for one-year terms to carry out his directives. There was also a secular arm of the pueblo government established during Spanish rule to deal with outsiders. This consisted of a governor (*dapop*), lieutenant governor, *capitani* (head man), and *fiscales* (prosecutor), appointed to one-year terms by the head of the Cikame society.

There were a number of different secret societies in Santo Domingo, including four curing societies, a Hunters' society who performed the buffalo and deer dances, and the Koshairi and Quirana societies. All men of the pueblo belonged to one of the *katcina* (kachina) societies, whose members performed masked dances to bring rain. Each person belonged to a clan, inheriting membership in the same clan as his mother. Marriage was usually outside the clan, but within the pueblo.

According to Santo Domingo tradition, the Pueblo peoples originally emerged from the earth at a place in the north known as Shipapu. When a person died, he was buried the same day, and his spirit returned to Shipapu. Four days after burial, a shaman performed ceremonies in which food and other offerings were wrapped in a blanket and buried.

Religious ceremonies were usually held in one of two *kivas,* round buildings with entry through a hatchway in the roof. An individual usually belonged to the *kiva* of his father, although after marriage, a woman joined the *kiva* of her husband.

Houses and *kivas* were constructed of stone blocks, quarried by the men and plastered over with adobe by the women. The interconnected one and two-story houses were entered by ladders leading to hatchways on the roof. Corn, beans, squash and cotton were grown by the men in irrigated fields. The women made fine pottery.

According to tradition, the Pueblo tribes formerly lived together in cliff dwellings at Rito de Frijoles (Bandelier National Monument), and spread southward along the Rio Grande, establishing the separate pueblos. The Santo Domingo people were visited by several Spanish expeditions in the late 16th century. Known originally as Gipuy, the pueblo was renamed Santo Domingo in 1591 by Gasper Castaño de Sosa. Juan de Oñate brought the pueblo under Spanish control in 1598. By the early 17th century, a church was built, and European livestock, fruits and vegetables were introduced. In 1680, Santo Domingo took an active part in the Pueblo Revolt, but its people were forced to retreat north with some of the other Keresan tribes to a fortified town, Potrero Viejo. By 1683, they had returned to Santo Domingo, although rebellion continued until 1696.

During the 17th century, several early sites of the pueblo were destroyed by floods. The present site which has also had a number of flood disasters, was established in the early 18th century. In the late 18th century some people from Tano pueblo, whose village had been decimated by Comanche attacks and smallpox, joined Santo Domingo. In 1858, the United States Congress confirmed the original land grant of about 70,000 acres, made by the Spanish in 1689.

In the late 1970s, the culture and traditions of Santo Domingo remained strong. Government was carried on in the traditional manner; religious ceremonies were still vital to daily life, and the Santo Domingo language was widely spoken. Important craftwork included exquisite turquoise and shell jewelry and fine pottery.

BIBLIOGRAPHY: White, Leslie A. "The Pueblo of Santo Domingo." *Memoirs of the American Anthropological Association.* no. 43, 1935.

SARSI: an Athapascan tribe located near the upper Saskatchewan and Athabaska rivers in Alberta in the late 18th century, numbering about 600 at that time. In the late 1970s, the Sarsi band, located near Calgary, numbered about 500.

The Sarsi (or Sarcee) spoke a northern Athapascan language similar to that of the Beaver tribe to the north, with whom they once formed a single tribe. The Sarsi were composed of bands, each comprising a number of closely-related families which hunted and camped together. Band membership was fluid, and bands continually formed and disbanded or were absorbed by other bands. Each band was led by a man

**Jim Big Plume,
head chief of
Sarsi.**
Smithsonian Institution
National Anthropological
Archives

whose prestige was recognized by consensus of the group, although this position was mainly advisory. There were no tribal chiefs in aboriginal times.

Girls belonged to their mother's band, whereas boys over age ten belonged to their father's band. Marriage was formalized by an exchange of gifts between the two families. Polygamy was practiced, usually a man marrying sisters or his brother's widow. A man and his mother-in-law were prohibited by taboo from speaking to each other.

There were five male societies, each of which held a four-day dance in August. All young men usually joined the Mosquitoes first, later joining one or more of the others. The society dances and the Sun Dance were the most important tribal ceremonies. Sun Dances were nine-day ceremonies sponsored by some honorable woman to fulfill a vow. They included the building of the Sun Dance Lodge (on the fifth day), dancing, singing, fasting, feasting, prayers and voluntary self-torture by young warriors.

Important aspects of Sarsi religion were the obtaining of power through dreams and visions and the care and ritual connected with medicine bundles (collections of sacred objects). When a person died, his body was wrapped in skins and placed on a scaffold, along with clothes, utensils and other possessions, and his horse was killed. Chiefs or noted warriors were sometimes left in their tipi, which was then abandoned.

The Sarsi lived in buffalo skin tipis, made and set up by the women. In summer, the tribe camped together to hunt buffalo and hold ceremonies. Buffalo were hunted in communal drives in which they were either driven over a cliff or into brush corrals or pounds. The rest of the year, the tribe broke into bands or small hunting parties, occasionally gathering for a tribal winter buffalo hunt. The buffalo provided the Sarsi with food, shelter, clothing, tools, bowstrings, containers and other necessary items. A simple pottery was made in early times.

By the early 18th century, the Sarsi had separated from the Beaver and moved southward to the region of the upper Saskatchewan and Athabaska rivers. In the late 18th century, Hudson's Bay Company trading posts were established near the Sarsi, and firearms became readily available. By the early 19th century, the Sarsi allied themselves with the Blackfoot to the south for protection from the Cree and Assiniboin. Warfare with the Cree lasted until 1875.

In the 19th century, the Sarsi were struck by numerous epidemics, including smallpox in 1836 and 1870 and scarlet fever in 1856. In 1877, they and the Blackfoot signed a treaty with the Canadian government reliquishing their lands. In 1880, about 450 Sarsi in five bands were settled on a reserve near Calgary, Alberta. In the late 1970s, the Sarsi band numbered about 500.

BIBLIOGRAPHY: Jenness, Diamond. "The Sarcee Indians of Alberta." *National Museum of Canada Bulletin*. no. 90, 1938.

SAUK: an Algonquian tribe whose final resistance to removal from their lands in Illinois was known as Black Hawk's War. In early times, the Sauk made their homes around Saginaw Bay in eastern Michigan, from which they were expelled by the Ojibwa, eventually settling around Green Bay, Wisconsin. French explorers and missionaries first visited them here in about 1667. The Sauk probably numbered about 3,500 at that time. By the late 1970s, their 1,500 or so descendants lived mostly in Oklahoma, mixed with Fox Indians.

Sauk, or Sac, is the short form of Osakiwug, by which the tribe called itself, meaning "yellow earth." Linguistically, as well as culturally, the Sauk were closely related to the Fox and the Kickapoo. In the late 1970s, the Sauk Algonquian language was still spoken among older members of the tribe.

The Sauk tribe was divided into two moieties or divisions, Oskukh and Kishko, black and white. The moieties were further subdivided into about 12 clans, each person inheriting the clan of his father and forbidden to marry within his own clan. The tribe was governed by a council made up of hereditary civil chiefs, one of whom was given first rank.

The Sauk forces being shelled by the steamer *Warrior* at the battle of
Bad Axe, on the Mississippi, south of La Crosse, Wisconsin, during
the Black Hawk War in 1832.

The Sauk believed in a number of deities, the most important of which
was Wisaka, the founder of the Medicine Dance. Other spirits included
the South Wind, Fire, and Earth Spirit, who was grandmother to the
Sauk. Among the festivals held each year were planting feasts, the
festival celebrating ripening of the green corn and the fall feast, which
preceded the annual hunt.

In the Sauk afterlife, a dead person's soul followed the Milky Way
(White River) and, if it was quick enough to get past the guardian spirit
and his watch dog, it crossed the river on a log and reached the land of
the dead. Mourners blackened their faces with charcoal, and a dead
chief's face was painted green.

The Sauk had both summer and winter villages. One summer village
was described in 1817 as having over 100 lodges, housing 1,000 warriors
and their families. The lodges were of pole construction covered with
bark, about 40-60 feet long. Women tended corn fields, along with
gardens of pumpkins, beans, squash and melons. They gathered fruit,
berries, wild potatoes and nuts, just as they had gathered maple sugar
and wild rice in their earlier homes near the Great Lakes.

After the harvest, the surplus food was sold to traders and the rest
dried, wrapped in bark containers and placed in pits, carefully concealed
with sod. The Sauk then migrated to their winter homes, situated in a
sheltered location near good hunting grounds. Winter homes were
smaller and more snug than the summer ones, covered with tightly woven
reed mats and lined with mats and skins.

The men hunted bear, deer, buffalo, beaver, otter, raccoon, wild cat, muskrat and mink—trading most of the pelts to French traders. Traditional weapons included bow and arrow, spear or lance, and war-clubs.

In about 1733, the Sauk and the Fox were both pushed southward by the Menominee, the Ojibwa and the French, settling on the banks of the Mississippi River on lands formerly held by the Illinois. There, the Fox altered their material culture, exchanging bark canoes and snowshoes for bullboats and horses. They became skilled buffalo hunters and cultivated extensive fields of corn. In 1804, one band of Sauk signed a treaty ceding the Illinois lands of the Sauk to the United States. Angered, the rest of the Sauk refused to move. In 1831-32, pressure from the white settlers finally resulted in a war between the Sauk, led by Black Hawk, and the Illinois militia. In the final battle, Black Hawk's forces were shelled by the steamer *Warrior* while trying to cross the Mississippi at the mouth of the Bad Axe River, south of La Crosse, Wisconsin. Those who made it across were attacked by the Dakota on the other side.

Later, the Sauk and the Fox drove the Dakota out of Iowa and took over their lands. In 1842, they ceded these lands to the U.S. and accepted a reservation in Kansas. The Sauk ceded their Kansas lands by an 1867 treaty and moved to Indian Territory (Oklahoma). In 1890, part of their reservation was allotted in severalty to tribal members, and some 380,000 acres were opened to white settlement.

In the late 1970s, the Sauk and Fox Tribe of Oklahoma retained about 800 acres of tribally owned land and were governed by a business committee. Some 18,000 acres of allotted land were owned by the 1,800 or so Sauk descendants living in the area.

BIBLIOGRAPHY: Hagan, William T. *The Sac and Fox Indians.* Norman: University of Oklahoma Press, 1958; Skinner, Alanson, *Observations on the Ethnology of the Sauk Indians.* Milwaukee: Public Museum of the City of Milwaukee, 1923.

SAULTEAUX: *See* OJIBWA.

SECOTAN: an extinct Algonquian tribe reported to be located, in 1584, between Albemarle Sound and the Pamlico River in North Carolina. They were probably absorbed by the Machapunga, who occupied that area at a later date.

The Secotan grew beans, peas, melons, pumpkins and three carieties of corn. They also were expert fishermen, using spears and traps.

The Secotan lived in palisaded villages of from 10 to 30 houses, constructed of a pole framework covered with bark or rush mats. A temple housed a wooden idol called Kiwasa, and also served as a storage

A Secotan village;
a watercolor by
John White,
(1585-87).

Library of Congress

place for the bones of their dead rulers. A drawing of their main village was made by a member of the Sir Walter Raleigh expedition, who visited the Secotan in 1584.

BIBLIOGRAPHY: Hodge, Frederick W., ed. "Handbook of American Indians North of Mexico." *Bureau of American Ethnology Bulletin.* no. 30, 1907-10.

SEECHELT: a Northwest Coast tribe located in British Columbia on Jervis and Seechelt inlets, Nelson Island and the southern part of Texada Island in the Strait of Georgia, in the late 18th century, numbering about 1,000 at that time. In the 1970s, there were about 475 Seechelt attached to the Seechelt reserve adjacent to the summer resort town of Sechelt.

They spoke a language of the Coast division of the Salishan language family. The Seechelt were composed of four divisions: Tuwanek, Skaiakos, Kunechin and Tsonai, the latter two reportedly of Kwakiutl lineage. Their culture closely resembled that of the Comox (*q.v.*) and other neighboring Northwest Coast tribes.

BIBLIOGRAPHY: Barnett, Homer G. *The Coast Salish of British Columbia.* Eugene, Oregon: The University Press, 1955.

SEKANI: an Athapascan tribe located in British Columbia along the upper Peace, Parsnip and Finlay rivers in the early 19th century, numbering about 1,000 at that time. In the late 1970s, there were about 450 Sekani belonging to two bands in British Columbia.

The Sekani, or "people of the rocks," spoke a language of the Athapascan language family. They were composed of a number of autonomous bands, each led by a man respected for his maturity and hunting ability, but with no real authority. For a short time, in the 19th century, the Sekani adopted the phratries and matrilineal social organization of the coastal tribes. Young married men were required to hunt for their parents-in-law for the first year of marriage or until their first child was born.

Religion centered around guardian spirits, as with other Athapascan tribes of the area. At puberty, girls were secluded, and boys sought animal or bird guardian spirits, through fasting and dreaming in remote places. Shamans usually had wind and thunder among their guardian spirits, assisting them in curing and causing illness. The Sekani usually cremated their dead or covered them with the brush hut in which they had lived. Prominent men were placed in coffins or hollow logs, which were placed on raised platforms or in trees. Later, a memorial feast was given by the nearest male relative.

The Sekani had no permanent villages, but constructed temporary conical spruce bark lodges and lean-tos of brush, skin or bark. Primarily hunters, they used bow and arrow, spears, snares and moose jawbone clubs to take moose, caribou, mountain sheep, bear, beaver, marmot, grouse, geese and ducks. Although fish were considered second-rate, their fishing technology included nets, weirs, bone fishhooks, three-pronged spears, ice fishing and night fishing from canoes with pine torches. Trout and whitefish predominated. Blueberries and saskatoon berries rounded out the diet.

They used dishes and cooking vessels of spruce bark, with wood or horn spoons. Food was stored in skin bags, which were sometimes left in tree caches. Clothing was of skins, including aprons, long shirts and kneelength leggings for women and shirts and leggings for men. Robes, caps, fur-lined moccasins and mittens were worn in cold weather, and babies were carried in rabbit or groundhog fur bags. Adornment included quillwork, fringes, tassels, bearclaw necklaces and face paint.

The Sekani may have been united with the Beaver, or Tsattine, in aboriginal times. By the late 18th century, conflict with the Beaver and Cree on the east had induced the Sekani to spread westward to the area of Takla and Bear lakes, When they attempted to move southward, they were driven back by the Carrier and Shuswap. In 1805 and 1826, trading posts were established in the area, after which white trappers and miners came, game diminished, and the Sekani became subject to alcoholism and disease.

In the late 1970s, the two remaining Sekani bands, McLeod Lake and Finlay River, numbered about 450 and were centered around two Hudson's Bay Company posts, Fort McLeod on McLeod Lake and Fort Grahame on the Finlay River.

BIBLIOGRAPHY: Jenness, Diamond. "The Sekani Indians of British Columbia." *National Museum of Canada Bulletin.* no. 84, 1937.

SEMINOLE: a tribe of Florida Indians composed of a combination of Oconee, Yamasee, Creek and other Indians who fled to that area from Georgia and South Carolina. They were referred to as Seminole by 1775. They numbered about 5,000 in 1821 when Florida was ceded by Spain to the United States. In the late 1970s they numbered more than 6,000, with about two-thirds living in Oklahoma and the remainder in southern Florida.

The name Seminole is variously translated as "runaway" or "pioneer" or said to be a corruption of the Spanish word *cimarrón,* meaning "wild" or "untamed."

Two Muskogean languages are spoken by the Seminole: Hitchiti, spoken by the Mikasuki division of the Seminole, and Muskogee. Most of the Seminole living in Florida can still speak their own language while many of those living in Oklahoma cannot.

Hitchiti-speaking Oconee Indians from southern Georgia who moved into northern Florida in the early 18th century formed the nucleus for the Seminole. They were joined in 1715-16 by Yamasee Indians fleeing the Carolinas after the Yamasee War. Northern Florida had been previously largely depopulated of its major Indian tribes, the Apalachee and Timucua, by disease and raids by English-supported northern tribes. The disastrous Creek War of 1814 brought a new influx of Indians, some of whom joined the Seminole while others formed new towns of their own.

Although the Seminole retained their Creek culture and Muskogean languages, they were usually scattered in settlements too small to re-establish the complex town and clan structure they were accustomed to. In Florida they grew the traditional crops of corn, beans, squash, and

A Seminole family in a canoe, in about 1900.   Library of Congress

tobacco, but also depended more on fishing, hunting and gathering. They also acquired a few new crops from the Spanish—sweet potatoes, melons, and oranges—and they domesticated stray Spanish cattle.

The Seminole villages, being across what was then an international border, became refuges for runaway black slaves from the United States. The black refugees were aided and protected by the Indians—sometimes settling among them, and other times forming their own new towns.

Raids into Florida for slaves by the state militias brought on the First Seminole War (1817-18), which resulted in the cession of Florida to the United States in 1821. Under the Treaty of Moultrie Creek (1823), the Seminole were forced to give up their lands in northern Florida for a reservation of about 4 million acres in the central part of the state.

As American settlers poured into the new territory, there was pressure to have all the Indians removed to the West, as was being done with the other eastern tribes. A highly controversial treaty was signed at Payne's Landing in 1832, under which the Seminole were to be removed to lands in Indian Territory (now Oklahoma). Seminole leaders Osceola, Wild Cat, Alligator, and Arikepa denounced the treaty as illegal, after which the Second Seminole War (1835-42) began. The Indians fled south to the swamps of the Everglades, from which they conducted a guerrilla war. Osceola was captured while parleying under a flag of truce and died in prison a few months later. They war dragged on until 1842, with some 4,500 Seminole finally being removed to the West.

The Third Seminole War (1855-58) was the final attempt to move the Indians from Florida, convincing another 123 to relocate in the West.

But about 300 Seminole just moved deeper into the Everglades, determined to stay.

A nomadic existence had been developed by these people during the long years of war. They continued to live in small camps of not much more than an extended family—a woman, her husband, her daughters and their husbands, children and grandchildren. The Seminole had preserved and emphasized their matrilineal Creek heritage.

Open-sided houses on stilts (*chickees*) were built of cypress poles thatched with palmetto. A central cookhouse with a dirt floor served the whole camp. A favorite dish was *sofkee,* hominy boiled with wood ash (for flavoring) to make a soup or thin gruel. This too was part of their Creek heritage, as were the Green Corn Dance, ball games and other customs and religious ceremonies.

Isolated from the rest of the tribe, and indeed from most of the rest of the world, in their Everglades enclave, the Florida Seminole adapted to their environment and learned new skills and crafts. They developed a flat, very shallow-draft canoe, ideally suited for negotiating the swamps of the Everglades.

The women created a distinctive and colorful style of clothing called patchwork. Begun around the turn of the century when the first hand-turned sewing machines became available, the patchwork consisted of small strips of different colored material sewn into long strips which were sewn onto garments in intricate patterns. Both men's and women's clothing were thus adorned, with patchwork styles constantly undergoing change. Women also wore pounds and pounds of beads around their necks, and men very elaborate turbans.

By the late 1970s, 2,000 Florida Seminole lived on four reservations: Big Cypress (42,700 acres), Brighton (35,805 acres), Hollywood (480 acres), and the Miccosukee Reservation (333 acres), a 500-foot wide, five-mile long strip of land known as the Tamiami Trail. The Seminole also had hunting and fishing rights on the 104,000-acre Florida State Reservation. The chief sources of income for the tribe were cattle raising, tourism, crafts, farming and forestry. Increasingly *chickees* were being replaced with concrete block houses, but the people still wore their colorful patchwork, at least for formal occasions.

In the late 1970s, the Seminole Indians in Oklahoma numbered about 4,000, holding about 35,443 acres of allotted land. The tribal headquarters was at Wewoka, and tribally held land included 320 acres. The western Seminole still performed some of their traditional ceremonies and dances, but no longer practised many of the old crafts and skills.

BIBLIOGRAPHY: Fairbanks, Charles H. *The Florida Seminole People.* Phoenix: Indian Tribal Series, 1973; McReynolds, Edwin C. *The Seminoles.* Norman: University of Oklahoma Press, 1957.

SENECA: the largest, most powerful and westernmost of the tribes that made up the Iroquois Confederacy. At the height of their power, the Seneca numbered about 5,000, occupying the territory from Lake Ontario in the north to the upper reaches of the Allegheny and Susquehannah rivers in the south and from Lake Erie on the west to Seneca Lake on the east. In the late 1970s, there were about 300 living on the Six Nations Reserve in Canada and about 4,000 located on or near three reservations in western New York state. Seneca is an Algonquian word meaning "people of the stone." The Seneca, whose Iroquoian language was still spoken in the 1970s, referred to themselves as "the people of the hill."

The Seneca were organized into eight matrilineal clans: Wolf, Turtle, Beaver, Bear, Deer, Heron, Snipe and Hawk. Clan chiefs, who represented their clans at councils, were nominated by the women, subject to the approval of the men of the clan. Women also owned property and, when captured, were ransomed for twice the amount for men.

Each Seneca village had a council made up of clan chiefs while the Seneca tribal council was composed of the village council chiefs. The Great Council of the Confederacy met at the Onondaga capital, in the autumn of each year and in times of emergency. The Council was composed of 50 sachems, 8 of whom were Seneca.

The chief deity of the Seneca was "Earth Holder," while lesser spirits included Sun, Moon, Morningstar, Whirlwind and Thunderer. The most important religious festival was the Midwinter Ceremony, held each year in late January or early February. The eight-day ceremony included the sacrifice of a white dog on the fifth day and participation by the False Face Society. This was a society for curing the sick which wore carved wooden masks with comically distorted features. Other important Seneca festivals celebrated planting season and the ripening of strawberries, raspberries, beans, and the green corn.

According to some creation myths of the Seneca, their tribe originated from a hole in the top of a hill at the head of Canandaigua Lake. They believed in the immortality of the soul and buried their dead usually in a sitting position.

The Seneca built multifamily dwellings from 18 to 200 feet in length and 12 to 18 feet high. The longhouses were constructed of a pole framework covered with elm, basswood or hemlock bark. They were usually occupied by related families or members of the same clan, with the clan matron in charge.

The Seneca were primarily agricultural people, growing a dozen varieties of corn which they prepared in as many different ways, including corn soup, hominy, breads and pudding. Corn and beans were stored in bark chests or bark-lined pits in the ground, and squash and corn were

Red Jacket:
a famous
Seneca orator,
(circa 1756-1830).

Smithsonian Institution
National Anthropological
Archives

hung in the longhouses to dry. The men burned and cleared the communal fields, while the women did the planting, cultivating and harvesting.

Seneca men ranged far and wide on hunting parties, often being gone several months at a time. Snowshoes and elm bark canoes were used for travelling, and wooden backpack frames served to carry heavy loads. Before the coming of the Europeans the usual weapons were bows and arrows, stone axes and knives, and blowguns. By the late 17th century, however, European trade goods had virtually replaced traditional weapons and tools.

The Iroquois League, or Five Nations Confederacy, was formed in about 1450 by the semi-legendary heroes Dekanawida, probably a Huron, and Hiawatha, a Mohawk living among the Onondaga. They managed to convince the Seneca, Onondaga, Mohawk, Oneida and Cayuga to give up warfare with each other.

The early 17th century was rife with warfare between the Iroquois Confederacy and the Huron-French alliance. Between 1648 and 1656, the Iroquois defeated the Huron, the Neutral Indians, and the Erie. Much of the fighting was done by the Seneca, who were the largest and westernmost of the Five Nations.

In the late 1600s Seneca war parties ranged beyond the Ohio Valley in

Cornplanter,
a famous Seneca
chief who fought
the Americans
during the War of
Independence, and
who later ceded
land to the U.S.
by treaty.
He died in 1836.

Smithsonian Institution
National
Anthropological
Archives

wars with the Illinois and Miami, adopting members of tribes they defeated.

In 1722, the Iroquois Confederacy became the Six Nations, with the addition of the Tuscarora.

Most of the Iroquois League sided with the British in the American Revolution, except the Oneida and the Tuscarora. During and after the war, a large part of the Seneca moved to Canada. Those who remained were forced, in 1797, to cede all but 200,000 acres of their land to the U.S. In 1799 a Seneca religious leader arose named Handsome Lake, who preached a return to the Indian religion.

In 1838 the Seneca lost most of their remaining land in an illegal treaty. In the late 1970s, the remaining Seneca lands in the United States consisted of the Allegany (30,000 acres), the Cattaraugus (21,680 acres), and the Oil Springs (640 acres) reservations in western New York, and the Tonawanda Reservation (7,500 acres), near Buffalo. About 4,000 Seneca lived on or near these reservations and some 300 more lived in Canada on the Six Nations Reserve in Brant County, Ontario.

In the late 1970s, there was a growing interest in Iroquois culture and a strong revival of the Longhouse Religion, especially at Tonawanda Reservation.

BIBLIOGRAPHY: Abrams, George H.J. *The Seneca People.* Phoenix: Indian Tribal Series, 1976; Wallace, Anthony F.C. and Stein, Sheila C.

The Death and Rebirth of the Seneca, New York: Alfred A. Knopf, 1969.

SERRANO: a southern California group located in the San Bernardino Mountains and adjacent part of the Mojave Desert in the late 18th century, when they numbered between 1,500 and 2,500. In the late 1970s, there remained about 100 Serrano descendants, mostly living on two reservations in southern California.

The name Serrano was derived from a Spanish term meaning "mountaineer" or "highlander." The Serrano language, which was still spoken by a few in the late 1970s, belongs to the Takic division of the Uto-Aztecan language family.

The Serrano had two divisions, or moieties, Wildcat and Coyote, each of which was composed of a number of clans. A person inherited the clan of his father, and was required to marry outside his clan and moiety. The clan, which was the main political unit, was headed by the *kika,* who provided religious, political and economic leadership. Shamans also conducted ceremonies, interpreted dreams and cured by sucking out offending objects and administering medicinal plants.

The Serrano believed in twin creator-gods and a whole hierarchy of supernatural beings and spirits. They cremated their dead and burned most of the possessions of the deceased. A second burning of the remaining possessions was held within a month by the mourners, accompanied by singing and dancing.

Their villages were composed of houses constructed of tule mats on willow frames. Other structures included granaries, semisubterranean sweathouses and a large ceremonial house where the *kika* lived.

Hunting and gathering supplied most of the Serrano diet, which included acorns, pine nuts, yucca roots, mesquite and cactus fruit. The men hunted deer, mountain sheep, antelope and small game using bow and arrow, traps and curved throwing sticks. They produced beautifully decorated coiled basketry.

In the early 19th century, most of the Serrano were removed to Spanish missions, where they became intermingled with other Indian groups. In the late 1970s, Serrano descendants numbering about 100, were mostly located in California, on Morongo Reservation in Riverside County, and San Manuel Reservation in San Bernadino County, where they participated in pan-Indian ceremonies and activities.

BIBLIOGRAPHY: Bean, Lowell John and Smith, Charles R. "Serrano," *Handbook of North American Indians.* vol. 8. Washington: Smithsonian Institution, 1978.

SHASTA: a group located on the California-Oregon border and numbering about 2,000 at the time of European contact. The Shasta, together with the Konomihu, Okwanuchu and New River Shasta, made up the Shastan division of the Hokan language family. By the late 1970s, there were only about 50 Shasta remaining in California and Oregon, and the other three Shastan tribes and their languages were nearly extinct.

The Shasta were divided into villages, each with a headman whose duties included keeping peace and mediating disputes. His wife held a similar position among the women. Shamans, who cured through use of supernatural powers, were usually women. There were also women who cured using their knowledge of medicinal plants.

Each family had rights to certain hunting or fishing places, inherited through the male line. Marriage, usually contracted outside the village, required payment of a bride price.

Shasta winter homes were rectangular, about 16 by 20 feet in size, and were excavated to a depth of about three feet. The dwellings had side walls of packed earth and end walls of wood, and housed one, two or more families. Of similar construction, but larger, was the community house, used for various gatherings and as a guest house. Each village also had a sweathouse built near a stream. Families lived in brush shelters in spring and summer and bark houses during acorn gathering season.

The Shasta buried their dead in family burial plots, and burned or buried the possessions of the deceased. A widow cut her hair and covered her face and head with pitch mixed with charcoal. It was believed a dead person's soul traveled eastward along the Milky Way to the home of Mockingbird, a figure in Shasta mythology. Another important mythical figure was Coyote, the trickster and culture hero.

Hunting, fishing and gathering provided the Shasta with a widely-varied diet, in which venison and acorns were staple foods. Acorns and pine nuts were gathered by both men and women, while women gathered roots, seeds, bulbs, insects and numerous kinds of berries. Men hunted deer, bear and small game by stalking and by the use of pits and traps. They fished, mostly for salmon, trout and eels, using spears, nets and traps.

The clothing of the Shasta was made of deerskin and shredded willow bark. Adornment included shell necklaces, ear and nose ornaments, face and body paint and tattooing. The Shasta made tools and utensils of wood, bone, stone and obsidian, as well as containers of rawhide and basketry and bowls of wood and soapstone. For transportation, they made snowshoes, pine dugout canoes and tule rafts. Weapons included bow and arrows, knives and rod armor vests.

The Shastan groups had trade and social relations with each other, broken by occasional feuds. They sometimes fought the Achomawi and Wintu, and banded together in retaliatory raids against the Modoc. By the 1820s, fur trappers had entered Shasta territory, soon followed by settlers. Clashes followed, bringing on the Rogue River wars of the early 1850s. The surviving Shasta were forced onto Grande Ronde and, later, Siletz Reservation. Seeking solace, the Shasta became involved in several late 19th century religious movements, including the 1870 Ghost Dance, the Earth Lodge cult and the Big Head cult.

In the late 1970s, of the 50 or so remaining Shasta, a few lived on California or Oregon reservations, while the rest were mixed with the general population.

BIBLIOGRAPHY: Holt, Catherine. "Shasta Ethnography". *University of California Anthropological Records*. vol. 3, 1946.

SHAWNEE: an Algonquian tribe known for being in the forefront of resistance to white expansion in the Ohio Valley in the early 19th century. The Shawnee moved frequently, and the various divisions of the tribe were divided and reunited on and off throughout history. In 1650, they numbered about 3,000 and occupied the Cumberland River valley in Tennessee, although they had probably originated further north. They were most closely related to the Fox, Sauk and Kickapoo. In the late 1970s, there were about 2,000 Shawnee living mostly in Oklahoma, a few of whom still spoke the Shawnee language.

Shawnee means "southerner," probably relating to the division of the tribe which migrated to the Savannah River area in about 1674. The Shawnee were also known as Shawano and Satana.

The tribe was divided into five divisions: Chillikothe, Kispokotha, Piqua, Hathawekela and Spitotha. Within the divisions were as many as 12 clans, named for various animals. Each person inherited the clan of his father. Clan and division chiefs were hereditary, to a large extent, while war chiefs were selected. Women occupied positions of respect, sometimes conducting ceremonies and often using their knowledge of medicinal plants and herbs in curing.

The Shawnee had a supreme deity sometimes referred to as Moneto. In some cosmologies he had two assistants, a grandmother and her grandson, the former being the deity most concerned with the welfare of the Shawnee. The Piqua (or Peckwwe) division of the tribe was in charge of religious ceremonies. The Bread Dance, held at planting time, was an important occasion for dancing, feasting and praying for bountiful crops. Dancing was performed to the accompaniment of flute, drums and deer-hoof rattles.

Shawnee burial customs varied from place to place and time to time throughout their history. In the early 19th century, the dead were

Tecumseh, the Shawnee leader, (1768-1813), killed at the battle of the Thames River in Ontario: from a pencil sketch by a French trader, Pierre Le Drue, in about 1808.
Smithsonian Institution
National Anthropological
Archives

commonly buried in the ground on a slab of wood or stone, and sacred tobacco was sprinkled into the grave. A Condolence Ceremony was held for the deceased person's family. If the deceased was a man, a Replacement Ceremony was held, about a year later, in which his widow chose a new husband.

As the Shawnee changed locations, their house styles varied, according to the available materials. In the Ohio Valley, in the 18th and 19th centuries, they built *wegiwa* (wigwams) of a pole framework covered with elm or birch bark.

Women sometimes built the *wegiwa,* and were responsible for planting and cultivating crops, dressing game, gathering wood, cooking and storing food. Several varieties of corn were grown and cooked in numerous ways. Strawberries, dewberries, plums, cherries, grapes, pawpaw, persimmon, and maple syrup were among the wild foods gathered. Hunting, fishing and protection of the tribe were the chief duties of the men.

Between 1678 and 1694, the Piqua division of the Shawnee left the Cumberland Valley and settled in Pennsylvania. In the early 18th century, they were joined by the Hathawekela, who had tired of dealing with white settlers and fighting the Catawba.

About 1714, the Shawnee who had remained in the Cumberland Valley were finally forced out by the Chickasaw and Cherokee and finally settled, in about 1730, on the north bank of the Ohio River, occupying lands from the Allegheny River in Pennsylvania, southwest to the Scioto River in Ohio. In the mid-18th century, they were joined by the main body of the Shawnee, who had been living in Pennsylvania.

Between 1763 and 1793, the Shawnee were the core of resistance to westward expansion of white settlers into the Ohio Valley, fighting against both the English and the Americans. In 1793, having been pushed north to the Miami River, a large group of Shawnee and Delaware moved to Cape Girardeau, Missouri, where they were given land by the Spanish government.

In 1794, the Shawnee and their allies, the Delaware, Ottawa, Miami, Potawatomi and others, were defeated at the Battle of Fallen Timbers. The following year, by the terms of the Treaty of Greenville, they were forced to cede most of their lands in Ohio and southern Indiana. The Shawnee were dispersed again—to Missouri, Indiana and the Auglaize River in Ohio.

Tecumseh and his brother, Tenskwatawa, were important leaders of the Shawnee at this time. Tenskwatawa, known as the Shawnee Prophet, preached a return to Indian ways and abandonment of white men's goods and ideas. Tecumseh, meanwhile, attempted to forge an Indian alliance of all the tribes in the region, to fight the westward march of settlers. In 1811, while Tecumseh was in the South gathering support among the Creek and other tribes, the Indian forces at Tippecanoe, Indiana, were decisively defeated. Tecumseh himself was killed fighting American forces at the Battle of the Thomas River, in Ontario, in 1813.

In 1825 the Missouri Shawnee moved to a Kansas reservation, where they were joined by the Ohio Shawnee in about 1831. About 1845 Shawnee from Kansas, Louisiana, Arkansas and Texas gathered on the Canadian River in Oklahoma where they became known as the Absentee Shawnee. Another group, who had lived with the Seneca in Ohio in 1867, settled in Ottawa County, Oklahoma, where they became known as the Eastern Shawnee. The main body of the Shawnee were incorporated with the Cherokee in 1869.

In the late 1970s, the Shawnee of Oklahoma, numbering more than 2,000, were mostly assimilated with their Indian and white neighbors. Some of the cultural traditions were still observed, and the Shawnee language was still spoken by the older people.

BIBLIOGRAPHY: Galloway, William Albert. *Old Chillicothe.* Xenia, Ohio: The Buckeye Press, 1934; Trowbridge, C.C. *Shawnese Traditions.* Ann Arbor: University of Michigan Press, 1939.

SHINNECOCK: one of the main tribes of Long Island, New York, located between Shinnecock Bay and Montauk Point. In the late 1970s, the Shinnecock still occupied a 400-acre reservation deeded to them in 1703, three miles southwest of Southampton on their ancient homeland.

The Shinnecock were part of the Montauk confederacy, and their most famous chief, Nowedonah, was a brother of Wyandanch, the grand sachem of the Montauk in the mid-17th century. Nowedonah in 1640 granted eight square miles of land at Southampton to English colonists from Massachusetts for 16 coats and 60 bushels of corn, to be paid after the first harvest.

Women held a respected position with the tribe. The sister of Nowedonah, Quashawan, succeeded to the chieftaincy of the Shinnecock about 1667. Women had the responsibility of cultivating fields, dressing skins and gathering shellfish, wild strawberries, various roots and herbs. They knew the medicinal value of many plants and practiced fertilization of their cornfields by burying two fish in each hill of corn.

Whale meat was also important in the diet. The Shinnecock were whalers before the advent of the Europeans. As many as 100 men would set out in dugouts, attacking the offshore whales with harpoons and bow and arrow, finally dragging them ashore. The whale were valued for their meat, oil used for lighting, and fins used in religious ceremonies. By the early 18th century, the larger boats and whaling methods of the white men had replaced those of the Indians. The Shinnecock joined whaling crews out of Sag Harbor and sailed the world.

When whaling died out with the discovery of petroleum in Pennsylvania, the Shinnecock lost an important source of income. Some joined the Brotherton Indians in New York and later moved with them to the Oneida reservation in Wisconsin in the mid-19th century. In 1876, ten of the remaining Shinnecock men on Long Island were drowned in a tragic attempt to salvage the sailing ship *Circassian* as it foundered off Bridgehampton.

In the late 1970s, about 200 mixed-blood Shinnecock lived on or near the Long Island Reservation. The last speakers of their Algonquian language had died out by the early 20th century. There was little left of the Shinnecock culture, although a Labor Day Powwow was held annually.

BIBLIOGRAPHY: Hunter, Lois Marie. *The Shinnecock Indians.* Islip, New York: Buy Brothers, 1950.

SHOSHONI, NORTHERN: a division of the Shoshoni peoples located in eastern Idaho, northern Utah, western Montana and eastern Oregon in the early 19th century, when they numbered about 3,000. In the late 1970s, there were about 3,000 Shoshoni and Bannock

U.S. Department of the Interior. National Park Service
A Northern Shoshoni wickiup on Wigwam Creek, Yellowstone National Park.

located on or near the Fort Hall Reservation in southeastern Idaho. Other divisions of the Shoshoni were the Western, and the Wind River, or Eastern, and their offshoot, the Comanche. The Shoshoni all spoke a language of the Shoshonean division of the Uto-Aztecan language family. The name "Snake" was applied to various bands of Shoshoni, although they referred to themselves as *Nomo*, or "people."

The Northern Shoshoni were divided into bands which came together at certain times of the year for councils, celebrations and communal buffalo hunting. At such times they were led by a principal chief and a number of minor chiefs.

Various medicine men specializing in curing certain ailments, using medicinal roots herbs, charms and sweat lodge treatment. Their supernatural power was acquired through dreams, visions and visits to secluded mountain spots known to be inhabited by spirits. Northern Shoshoni wrapped their dead in blankets and placed the bodies in crevices in the rocks. The soul of the deceased departed for the land of Coyote and Wolf, two important figures in Shoshoni mythology. Mourners cut their hair, gashed their legs, killed a horse of the deceased, and abandoned his tipi.

Their economy depended on fishing, food gathering and annual trips to the Plains to hunt buffalo. They spent summers along the tributaries of the Columbia River, fishing for salmon, as well as sturgeon and trout. Fishing techniques included nets, weirs, basket traps and spears, and attracting the fish at night with torches.

The Sun Dance of the Northern Shoshoni: the morning of the third day, (1910).

Women gathered chokecherries, service berries, and sunflower seeds, which they dried and made into cakes. With digging sticks, they collected prairie turnips, yampa and camas, placing the latter in pits with hot rocks for several days until they were dark brown and sweet. Grasshoppers, crickets and ants were roasted in trays with burning coals.

Large game such as mountain sheep and antelope were also hunted, the latter by being chased in relays by hunters using fresh horses. Most important, however, was the annual September buffalo hunt, when the various Shoshoni bands joined with the Bannock or Flathead in migrating to the Plains through the territory of their enemies, the Blackfoot and Crow. Adding to their economy was trade with the Flathead, Nez Perce and Cayuse, with whom they traded buffalo skins ans salmon, for horses and mules.

The Northern Shoshoni used bows of cedar, elkhorn or sheephorn, with poison-tipped arrows carried in an otterskin quiver. Obsidian was used for knives and arrowheads. They sometimes wore antelope skin armor and carried shields of heat-toughened bull buffalo neck skin, along with Pogamoggans, or warclubs.

Material culture included bowls and pipes of soapstone (steatite), and both coiled and twined basketry, made of sagebrush bark and roots. They also produced buckskin bags with painted geometrical designs, as well as clothing decorated with quillwork and beadwork. In winter, buffalo skin moccasins, with the hair inside, were worn, along with robes made from skins of antelope, deer, buffalo or bighorn sheep.

In the 18th century, the Northern Shoshoni had acquired horses and moved for a time from Basin onto the northern Plains. Towards the end of the century, however, they were driven back by the Blackfoot, who had acquired firearms. After that, buffalo hunting was limited to annual trips.

With the discovery of gold in California, and the opening of the Oregon Trail, a flood of miners and immigrants came through Shoshoni lands. Wagon trains destroyed the pasture land along the rivers and scared away the game. The Shoshoni and Bannock fought unsuccessfully to protect their lands, but they were eventually placed on Fort Hall Reservation, along with the Bannock. In the late 1970s, there were about 3,000 Shoshoni and Bannock, living together on or near the 500,000 acre Fort Hall Reservation in southwestern Idaho.

BIBLIOGRAPHY: Lowie, Robert H. "The Northern Shoshoni" *Anthropological Papers of the American Museum of Natural History.* vol. 2, 1909; Murphy, Robert F. and Murphy, Yolanda. "Shoshone-Bannock Subsistance and Society." *Anthropological Records of the University of California.* vol. 16, no. 7, 1960.

SHOSHONI, WESTERN: a division of the Shoshoni peoples, located in Idaho, Utah, Nevada and California in the early 19th century, when they numbered about 2,000. Other divisions of the Shoshoni included the Northern, and Wind River (or Eastern), and their offshoot, the Comanche. In the late 1970s, Western Shoshoni descendants were mixed with Paiutes on two Nevada reservations, with a total combined population of about 1,000. The Shoshoni spoke a language of the Shoshonean division of the Uto-Aztecan linguistic family.

The Western Shoshoni included the Gosiute (*q.v.*), Cumumbah, Tosawis, Tukuarika (or Sheepeaters) of Yellowstone, and Koso (or Panamint) of Death Valley, California. The territory of the Western Shoshoni included central and western Idaho, northwestern Utah, central and northeastern Nevada, and Death Valley and Panamint Valley of California, largely barren and unproductive areas. They were sometimes referred to as "Diggers," from their habit of digging plant roots with a stick as an important means of subsistence. Another name applied was Shoshoko, meaning "walkers," to distinguish them from the horse-owning Shoshoni.

Social and political organization of the Western Shoshoni was not complex. The basic unit was the small kinship group, which gathered food, led by the oldest able male. *Bugahant*, or medicine men, served as religious leaders. The principal deity was Apo, the sun, while man was believed to have been created by Coyote. When a person died, his spirit returned to the land of Coyote. The mourners buried the deceased and destroyed his property, either at that time or in a later mourning ceremony.

Winter dwellings of the Western Shoshoni were earth mounds, in which the smoke-hole also served as the entrance. Summer dwellings were simple brush shelters. The Western Shoshoni subsisted mainly by gathering plant food, hunting small game and fishing. It was a nomadic existence, moving from area to area as the various plant foods ripened. Gathered seeds were ground to meal with metates and made into cakes, which were dried in the sun and stored in the ground. The Western Shoshoni also gathered berries, nuts and roots, which they dug up with fire-hardened digging sticks. Snares, pitfalls and nets, as well as bow and arrow, were used to hunt rabbits and other rodents, while grasshoppers were collected in communal drives.

Material culture of the Western Shoshoni included excellent basketry. Summer clothing was simple, with men wearing a breechclout and women a sagebrush fiber apron. Rabbit skin blankets were used in winter.

The Western Shoshoni, unlike the Northern and Wind River Shoshoni, never acquired horses to any extent, and thus never developed the buffalo-hunting culture of their kinsmen. They remained fairly isolated until 1858, when the discovery of the Comstock silver lode brought miners treking through their territory. Ranchers followed, their cattle destroying the seed-bearing plants so critical to Shoshoni subsistence.

In the early 1860s there were clashes between settlers and the Indians, after which the Indians were forcibly put down by the U.S. Army in 1862. In 1877, Duck Valley Reservation was established for the Western Shoshoni, who were joined by some Paiute in 1886.

In the late 1970s, there were about 900 Western Shoshoni and Paiute located on or near the 293,000-acre Duck Valley Reservation on the Nevada-Idaho border. Another 100 Western Shoshoni were located in central Nevada, on or near the 3,800 acre Duckwater Reservation, which had been established in 1940. The language of the Western Shoshoni was still in use, but their traditional culture was mostly forgotten.

BIBLIOGRAPHY: Trenholm, Virginia Cole and Carley, Maurice. *The Shoshonis*. Norman: University of Oklahoma Press, 1964.

SHOSHONI, WIND RIVER: a division of the Shoshoni peoples located in western Wyoming in the early 19th century, numbering about 2,000 at that time. The famed Comanche were an offshoot of the Wind River Shoshoni. Other divisions of the Shoshoni included the Western and Northern. In the late 1970s, there were about 3,000 Wind River Shoshoni, living on or near the Wind River Reservation in west-central Wyoming.

Wind River Shoshoni, with Chief Washakie, (seated, center).

The Wind River Shoshoni, also known as the Eastern Shoshoni, spoke a language of the Shoshonean division of the Uto-Aztecan language family. They were also referred to in later times as Washakie's Band, after their most famous principal chief. Their territory included the valleys of the Wind, Green and Big Horn rivers.

In winter, the Shoshoni would separate into bands, camping mostly in the Wind River valley, under the leadership of the various band chiefs. In spring, they came together for the spring buffalo hunt, and in early summer, they celebrated the Sun Dance. At this time they were led by the head chief, whose power was mostly based on his personal prestige.

In summer, the Shoshoni again broke into bands for plant food gathering and small scale hunting. Aside from buffalo the principal game were elk, beaver and mule deer, but they also hunted antelope, mountain sheep, moose, bear, jackrabbit, ducks, geese and sage hen. In the spring, they caught fish, mainly trout, using traps, weirs, dams and spears. Plant foods were an important part of the diet, including camas, wild onions, currants, gooseberries and sunflower seeds. In fall, when buffalo grew fat, bands came together for highly-disciplined communal hunts.

Besides food, the buffalo provided material for robes, tipis, bags, saddles, cradles, glue, bowstrings, tools and fuel. Buffalo skin tipis, the usual dwelling of the Wind River Shoshoni, were made by the women and decorated by their husbands with pictures of their brave war deeds. Buffalo hides were also used to make a sort of sled for winter travel.

In about 1700, the Wind River Shoshoni acquired horses, and soon expanded from the Basin area into the Plains area. About this time, the Comanche broke off and began moving southward toward Texas. About 1750, the Blackfoot and other Plains tribes began acquiring firearms and used them to drive the Shoshoni southwestward back into the Basin.

Between 1810 and 1840, the fur trade era was at its peak and the Shoshoni sold as many as 2,000 buffalo skins a year, for a variety of trade goods. When settlers flocked through Shoshoni territory in the 1850s and 1860s, the Wind River band, under Washakie, exhibited great patience and restraint. By the Fort Bridger Treaty of 1863, they were given 44 million acres in central Wyoming, which was subsequently reduced to about 1.9 million acres. In 1878, the northern Arapaho were also placed on the Wind River Reservation.

In the late 1970s, the two tribes on the reservation numbered about 6,700, including about 3,000 Shoshoni.

BIBLIOGRAPHY: Shimkin, D.B. "Wind River Shoshone Ethnography." University of California *Anthropological Records,* vol. 5, 1947.

Smithsonian Institution National Anthropological Archives

Chief Washakie's autobiographical account, drawn on an elk skin.

SHUSWAP: an Interior Salish tribe of British Columbia, located in the valleys of the Fraser, North Thompson and South Thompson rivers, numbering perhaps 7,000 in the early 19th century. In the late 1970s, there were about 4,000 Shuswap attached to 18 bands in British Columbia. They spoke a language of the interior division of the Salishan language family, closely related to that of the Lillooet, Thompson and Okanagon tribes to the south.

The Shuswap were composed of about seven autonomous bands. The southern and eastern bands each had their own hereditary chief, whose main functions included advising, admonishing and regulating food procuring activities when necessary. These bands also had war chiefs, hunt chiefs, dance chiefs and a few other leading men respected for their oratory, wisdom, wealth or generosity.

The northern and western bands, which had a similar organization in earlier times, adopted a Northwest Coast system by the 19th century, similar to that of the neighboring Carrier and Chilcotin tribes. They were divided into three classes: nobles, commoners and slaves. The nobility, which included the families of chiefs, all belonged to hereditary crest groups, including Raven, Wolf, Eagle, Beaver and Grizzly Bear. Commoners belonged to non-hereditary dance groups and associations. Slaves, obtained in warfare or trade, were owned by all Shuswap bands.

Adolescent boys underwent a training period of fasting, praying and dancing in secluded places, seeking guardian spirits to give them special hunting or shamanistic powers. Shamans had powerful guardian spirits, who aided them in restoring lost souls and curing the sick. Curing techniques included massage, blowing on the diseased part of the body, incantations, sprinkling water and prescribing certain taboos. Girls were secluded at puberty, during which time they practiced basketmaking and other crafts. They fasted, prayed and went out only at night to run, exercise and bathe.

Shuswap celebrations usually included feasting, dancing, singing, drumming and ceremonial smoking of tobacco. Among the characters of Shuswap mythology were dwarfs, giants, wind people, Old One and the trickster character, Coyote. When a person died, he was buried with his personal possessions, and offerings were hung on poles next to the grave. A small tent-like structure was sometimes built over the grave.

For winter use, the Shuswap built semisubterranean houses, some of which had several chambers. In summer they used conical mat lodges in the valleys, and rectangular bark-covered dwellings in more wooded areas. Some of the bands were quite nomadic, while others were nearly sedentary, depending on the food supply, which was primarily salmon in some areas and game in other areas.

Salmon, trout and sturgeon were caught with nets, weirs, spears, hooks and basket traps. Bow and arrow, snares, traps and spears were used in hunting deer, elk, caribou, marmot, mountain sheep, hare, beaver, grouse, bear, moose, ducks and geese. Fish and meat were dried or smoked for later use. Salmon eggs, roots, serviceberries, soapberries and blueberries were important additions to the diet.

The Shuswap made dishes, cups, trays and baskets from birchbark, coiled basketry of cedar or spruce roots and bags from skin or woven grass. Skins and furs were used for making clothing, including shirts, robes, leggings, breechclouts, moccasins, caps and mittens. Clothing was decorated with fringes and shells. For travel, the Shuswap used bark canoes, some dugouts, snowshoes and horses, introduced in 1780.

Warfare was common in the 18th century, often engaged in autonomously by various bands, without tribal involvement. Enemies included various bands of the Lillooet, Okanagon, Thompson, Cree, Chilcotin, Sekani and Carrier. Defensive weapons included rod armor, elkskin vests and shields. There was also considerable inter-tribal in slaves, dentalium shells, moose skins, deerskins, roots and salmon. With the establishment of Hudson's Bay Company trading posts in the early 19th century, furs, skins, moccasins, dried roots, berries, meat and salmon were exhcanged for European blankets, cloth, glass beads, steel traps, axes, knives, copper and iron kettles, and firearms.

Fighting between the tribes ended in about 1862. About the same time, a smallpox epidemic struck the Shuswap and their neighbors, wiping out whole villages. Measles, scarlet fever, whooping cough and influenza further diminished the population.

In the late 1970s, the 18 Shuswap bands were assigned about 146,000 acres of reserve land in British Columbia. Hunting, trapping and fishing were still carried on, although traditional housing had been replaced by log cabins and canvas tents, and traditional staple foods had been replaced by potatoes, flour, rice and beans.

BIBLIOGRAPHY: Teit, James Alexander. "The Shuswap." *Memoirs of the American Museum of Natural History.* vol. 4, 1909.

SIHASAPA: a small subdivision of the Teton Dakota, located west of the Missouri River, between the Heart and Grand rivers, South Dakota, in the mid-19th century, numbering about 1,300 at that time. Their name meant "blackfoot," referring to black moccasins which they wore. They are not to be confused with the Algonquian Blackfoot confederacy. In the late 1970s, Sihasapa descendants were located on the Cheyenne River Reservation in South Dakota and the Standing Rock Reservation in North and South Dakota. (See also *Teton* and *Dakota*).

SIKSIKA: *See* BLACKFOOT.

SINKIUSE: See COLUMBIA.

SIOUX: See DAKOTA.

SISSETON: one of the seven divisions of the Dakota, located in northern Minnesota in the late 17th century, numbering about 2,500 at that time. By the late 1970s, there were perhaps 2,000 descendants of Sisseton, living mostly in North and South Dakota and Minnesota.

The language of the Sisseton belongs to the Santee, or Eastern, division of the Dakota language, which is a member of the Siouan linguistic family. The Santee Dakota also include the Wahpeton, Mdewakanton and the Wahpekute. Sisseton has been variously translated as "swamp village," "lake village" and "fishscale village."

The Sisseton were divided into seven bands, each ruled by an hereditary chief and council. An elite warrior group, the *akitcita*, acted as a sort of police—keeping order during, hunts, games and councils, and acting as messengers and escorts. Religious leadership was provided by both medicine men and women, whose powers included prophesying, curing the sick and forecasting the weather.

The Sisseton believed in Wakan Tanka, the Great Spirit and creator of the universe, as well as a number of other gods and spirits. Vision quests and ritual purification through use of a sweat lodge were important religious elements. The Sisseton, who were the most westerly of the Santee, had adopted some Plains ceremonies such as the Sun Dance. They placed their dead on scaffolds or in trees. The bodies were wrapped in skins or blankets, placed with their head toward the south and accompanied by their personal effects, weapons, cooking utensils, etc. For a dead warrior, a horse might be killed for his use in the afterlife. Murdered persons were buried in the ground face down. Mourners cut their hair and slashed themselves with knives.

When in the woodlands, the Sisseton lived in bark-covered summer lodges and skin or mat-covered winter homes. When they moved westward to the prairies, however, they sometimes used skin tipis.

Agriculture, hunting and fishing were all important to the economy. They grew corn, beans, squash and pumpkins in small amounts and gathered wild rice, maple sugar, fruits and berries. They speared fish at night by the light of pitch torches, and, in the winter, fished through the ice. They trapped muskrat, otter, beaver and mink and hunted bear, deer and elk, but as the Sisseton moved further west, they turned more to buffalo. Well-organized buffalo hunts were led by four hunt leaders, who kept strict discipline, to insure the success of the hunt. Bow and arrow were the main hunting weapons.

The Sisseton made dugout canoes, and carved ceremonial pipes from catlinite. Other crafts included weaving of rushes into mats, and decorating clothing and other items with beadwork and quillwork in geometric and animal designs.

Early French explorers found the Sisseton and other Santee occupying the Mille Lacs, Minnesota area in 1680. In subsequent years, the Santee were regularly at war with the Ojibwa, who drove them out of the Mille Lacs region by about 1750.

By 1800 the Sisseton had moved west into lands vacated by the Teton Dakota. Their main villages were at Lake Traverse and along the Minnesota River, but they ranged far in all directions on their hunting trips.

By the mid-19th century, the press of settlers was so great that the Santee were forced to cede all their Minnesota and Iowa lands in treaties of 1837 and 1851. They retained a reservation along the Minnesota River, with the Wahpeton and Sisseton occupying the Upper Agency and the Mdewakanton and Wahpekute the Lower Agency. When an uprising broke out on the Lower Agency in 1862, the Wahpeton and Sisseton tried to remain neutral. After the uprising, however, all the Santee lands and property were confiscated and many neutrals taken prisoner. Many Wahpeton and other Santee fled to the Plains or to Canada.

Around 1867, two reservations were established for the Wahpeton and Sisseton: the Sisseston Reservation, near Lake Traverse in South Dakota, and the Fort Totten Reservation, on Devil's Lake between North and South Dakota. Locusts and drought made farming difficult. By 1892, the Sisseton Reservation was divided, with 300,000 acres allotted to tribal members and nearly 600,000 acres opened to homesteaders. Much of the allotted lands were later sold or leased to non-Indians.

In the late 1970s, the Wahpeton and Sisseton were closely connected and intermarried. Wahpeton descendants could also be found on the Santee Reservation in Nebraska, on reserves in Canada, and among the Santee who gradually drifted back to their homelands in Minnesota.

BIBLIOGRAPHY: Blackthunder, Elijah, et al. *Ehanna Woyakapi: History of the Sisseton Wahpeton Sioux Tribe.* Sisseton, South Dakota: Sisseton-Wahpeton Sioux Tribe, Inc., 1972.

SKAGIT: a Northwest Coast group located along the Skagit River and Whidbey Island in northwestern Washington, numbering, together with the neighboring Swinomish, about 1,200 in the late 18th century. In the late 1970s, there were about 750 Skagit and Swinomish in Washington state. The Skagit spoke a language of the Coast division of the Salishan language family, and called themselves Hum-a-luh, meaning "the people."

They were divided into the Upper and Lower Skagit, the latter occupying the lower Skagit River valley and sharing Whidbey Island with the Swinomish and the former located further up the Skagit River. They lived in small autonomous winter villages, with little political organization, but socially divided into three classes: upper, lower and slaves. Certain informal leaders were influential due to their status as wealthy men of respected lineage.

Central to the Skagit religion was the acquisition of guardian spirits to guide each person throughout life and aid him in developing his skills and talents. Shamans usually had several spirits who aided them in curing and in recovering lost souls. Their mythology included a culture hero and such trickster characters as Raven, Mink and Coyote, the latter borrowed from Plateau Indians. Skagit ceremonial life, carried on mostly in the winter, was rich and complex and was accompanied by music, singing and dancing. Potlatches, or ceremonial gift distributions, were held to mark such events as puberty, marriage, name-giving, funerals, reburial and memorial services for the dead.

When a person died, he was wrapped in cedar bark mats and buried on the fifth day in a shallow grave. The wealthy were buried in canoes, along with some of their possessions. The family of the deceased gave away his possessions and abandoned their house for a time. Widows and widowers cut their hair and, after a time, usually married someone from the family of their dead spouse.

In winter, the Skagit lived in permanent villages strung along the river, comprised of multifamily longhouses of overlapping red cedar planks. Inner house posts were carved and painted to represent the owner's guardian spirit. Sleeping platforms were around the inside walls, with storage shelves above. Each family, or two, had a fireplace for cooking and drying meat, and fish hanging from the rafters to smoke-dry. Villages usually had at least one sweathouse of brush and skins over a pole frame.

In summer, the Skagit lived in temporary shelters of cattail mats, which they took with them as they migrated to various fishing, hunting or food gathering locations. Salmon was the staple food, taken with spears, nets, hooks and weirs during their runs between May and November. King, chinook, humpback, dog and sockeye salmon were baked, boiled or grilled, as well as dried or smoked for later consumption. Other sea food included herring, smelt, flounder, cod, clams, oysters, mussels and crabs. The men also hunted deer, elk, mountain goat, geese and ducks as well as bear, beaver, snowshoe rabbit, raccoon and otter. The women dug camas bulbs, tiger lily bulbs and picked a variety of berries, which they dried and stored.

The men made canoes of red cedar logs, which they poled when going upstream. They also carved wooden bowls, dippers and buckets and made wooden boxes by bending steamed wood. The women made fine baskets, sometimes water-tight for cooking. Both Lower and Upper Skagit wore clothing of cedar bark and cattails, the Upper Skagit also using skin garments similar to those of Plateau Indians. Blankets were made of mountain goat hair. Nose ornaments, tattooing and face painting were all used for adornment, and the wealthy classes practiced head flattening.

The Skagit were essentially a peaceful people, trading and intermarrying with their neighbors, although sometimes being drawn into conflict. By 1792, Skagit territory had been visited by both Spanish and English exploring expeditions. The Hudson's Bay Company established trading posts in the region by 1825. The Lower Skagit lands were soon taken over by European settlers, who took up permanent residence on Whidbey Island by 1850. In 1855, the Swinomish Reservation was established for the Skagit, Swinomish and others by the Point Elliott Treaty.

The Upper Skagit were more isolated, and remained in their own area until 1897, when the Washington National Forest was created partly on their land, and they were restrained from fishing, hunting and cutting wood. In about 1907, some Skagit were allotted lands on the Suiattle River and removed to that remote area.

The Upper Skagit continued using canoes as primary transportation into the 1920s. By the 1940s, wage work, logging, and agriculture were more important than traditional subsistence activities. In the late 1970s, there were about 575 Skagit, Swinomish and others located on the 3,000-acre Swinomish Reservation in Skagit County, Washington, and perhaps another 175 Upper Skagit living in the Suiattle River area. Some fishing, hunting and berry gathering were still carried on, and a few women made baskets. The language was still spoken, and a few shamans reportedly still practiced. Guardian spirit dances were held and traditional music, dancing and folktales continued to be important.

BIBLIOGRAPHY: Bennett, Lee Ann. "Effect of White Contact on the Lower Skagit Indians." *Washington Archaeological Society Occasional Paper.* no 3, 1972; Collins, June McCormick. *Valley of the Spirits.* Seattle: University of Washington Press, 1974.

SKOKOMISH: *See* TWANA.

SLAVE: an Athapascan group occupying the western side of Great Slave Lake and the Slave River south to Lake Athabaska in the early 18th century, numbering about 1,250 at that time. In the late 1970s, there were about 3,500 Slaves located in the Mackenzie River valley between Great Slave Lake and Fort Norman, in Canada's Northwest Territories.

Two Slave
Indian boys
on the Hay
River,
Mackenzie,
Canada,
(1903).
The National Archives

The Slave, as other Athapascan language speakers, referred to themselves as Diné, meaning "the people." The Cree, who drove them northward in the 18th century, called them Awakanak, meaning "slaves," and they were also known as Etchareottine, meaning "people dwelling in the shelter."

The Slave were composed of a number of autonomous bands, with little formal leadership other than temporary war leaders and an informal council of hunters. Shamans provided religious leadership, curing the sick through the aid of their guardian spirits. All persons sought to acquire a guardian spirit through dreams, but shamans had especially strong spirits, who gave them special "medicine," or power.

Newly-married men were required to hunt for their parents-in-law for the first year or so of their marriage. Observers noted that the Slave took unusually good care of their aged and infirm, and women were treated with kindness and respect. They either placed the bodies of their dead on scaffolds or covered them with leaves or snow and built a small hut over them. The souls of the dead were aided by an otter and a loon in crossing to the other side of a great lake, where they began life anew.

Their winter dwellings were low, tent-shaped log cabins chinked with moss. In summer, two conical lodges of brush or spruce bark were sometimes placed together so two families shared a fireplace.

Fish and game were about equally important in the Slave diet. Woodland caribou and moose were stalked with bow and arrow and spears. They used snares, traps and caribou antler clubs to take beaver and other small game, and caught fish with hooks and willowbark nets. An assortment of berries supplemented the diet.

Cooking vessels were made of spruce bark or woven spruce roots. Clothing was of skins, including moccasins, leggings and shirts adorned with fringes. Leather headbands were decorated with quillwork and white ermine fur. Women wore basketry caps of woven spruce roots and carried their babies in bags made from woven rabbit fur. Men wore nose ornaments and caribou antler necklaces for adornment.

For transportation, the Slave used birch or spruce bark canoes and, occasionally, moose hide canoes. Snowshoes were used in winter along with toboggans of beaver hide or bent birch wood.

In the early 18th century, the Slave were driven by the Cree from their homes along the shores of Lake Athabaska. They fled northward to Great Slave Lake, and from there spread along the Mackenzie valley to Fort Norman. In 1789, they were visited by the Scottish explorer Alexander Mackenzie, who was soon followed by traders and missionaries.

In the late 1970s there were about 3,500 Slave located in the Yukon Territory, Alberta and British Columbia. Reserves belonging to the Slave in Alberta and British Columbia totaled about 100,000 acres.

BIBLIOGRAPHY: Honigmann, John J. "Ethnography and Acculturation of the Fort Nelson Slave." *Yale University Publications in Anthropology.* no. 33, 1946; Mason, J. Alden. "Notes on the Indians of the Great Slave Lake Area." *Yale University Publications in Anthropology.* no. 34, 1946.

SNAKE: *See* SHOSHONI, NORTHERN.

Snohomish dugout canoes in Washington state. A larger type of this canoe was used for whaling.

SNOHOMISH: a small Northwest Coast group located on the southern end of Whidbey Island and around the mouth of the Snohomish River in northwestern Washington, numbering about 350 in 1850. In the late 1970s, about 700 Snohomish, Snuqualmie and members of other groups lived together on the 5,000-acre Tulalip Reservation in Snohomish County, Washington.

The Snohomish spoke a dialect of the Nisqualli language of the Coast division of the Salishan language family. Culturally, they were similar to other Coast Salish groups, which included the Dwamish, Lummi, Nisqualli, Puyallup and Skagit (*q.q.v.*).

SNUQUALMIE: a small Northwest Coast group located along the Snoqualmie River in northwestern Washington, numbering about 225 in the mid-19th century. In the late 1970s, about 700 Snuqualmie, Snohomish and members of other groups lived together on the 5,000-acre Tulalip Reservation in Snohomish County, Washington.

The Snuqualmie spoke a dialect of the Nisqualli language of the Coast division of the Salishan language family. Culturally, they were similar to other Coast Salish groups, which included the Dwamish, Lummi, Nisqualli, Puyallup and Skagit (*q.q.v.*).

SONGISH: a group of linguistically related Northwest Coast tribes located on Vancouver Island, British Columbia, and San Juan Islands, Washington, in the late 18th century, numbering about 2,700 at that time. In the 1970s, there were about 1,000 Songish connected with seven Vancouver Island reserves.

The Songish language belonged to the Coast division of the Salishan language family. The Songish group included the Songish proper, the Sanetch and the Sooke. Culturally they closely resembled neighboring Coast Salish tribes, including the Klallam and Cowichan (*q.q.v.*).

BIBLIOGRAPHY: Barnett, Homer G. *The Coast Salish of British Columbia.* Eugene, Oregon: The University Press, 1955

SOUTH ALASKA INUIT: a number of Inuit (Eskimo) groups located along the southern Alaska coast from Kodiak Island to Controller Bay, numbering about 10,200 in the late 19th century. In the late 1970s, there were about 2,000 Inuit located in the same general area. They spoke the Suk dialect of the Yuk (or Yupik) branch of the Inuit (Eskimo) language. The name Eskimo was derived from an Abnaki Indian term meaning "raw meat eaters," whereas the term Inuit, meaning "people" is their own name for themselves.

The South Alaska Inuit included three major groups. The Koniagmiut, located on Kodiak Island and the adjacent mainland, were the largest, numbering about 8,000 at the time of first European contact. The Unixkugmiut, numbering about 600, occupied the tip and eastern side of the Kenai Peninsula. Adjoining them were the Chugach, who lived eastward along the coast to Controller Bay, with a population of about 1,600.

The family, which cooperated in subsistence activities, was the most important economic unit. Chugach communities or groups of communities were often led by a chief and assistant chief, both inheriting their offices through the male line. Chiefs, who were wealthy and were supported by the work of others, led war parties and hunting parties and guided the subsistence activities of the community. The Chugach and the Koniagmiut had slaves, which they captured in raids on the Eyak and Tlingit Indians, as well as each other.

An important leader among the Koniagmiut was the dance leader, who taught children dances and was responsible for directing ceremonies. Shamans were important among the South Alaskan Inuit, as among all Inuit, for their powers of curing the sick, controlling the weather and assuring successful hunting. Raven was an important figure in their mythology, as the creator of light.

Among the Chugach, a two week Memorial Feast for the Dead was held about every two years and included feasting and gift exchange. The Chugach and Koniagmiut both sometimes mummified their dead, and the Koniagmiut sometimes killed a slave to serve the deceased in the afterlife.

Most of the Koniagmiut lived on Kodiak Island, with its sheltered bays and abundant marine life, making it one of the most densely populated areas north of Mexico in aboriginal times. They had large stable villages composed of multifamily subterranean dwellings with log corner posts and plank walls. The main room, used for cooking and storage, had a central fireplace and smokehole. Sleeping compartments were also used for sweat baths.

The Chugach built small rectangular plank-sided houses for winter, and a variety of dwellings for summer, including bark shelters and skin boats turned over. They also built a multifamily summer house similar to that of the Koniagmiut. Very little is known about the culture of the Unixkugmiut.

The Koniagmiut were primarily whale hunters and salmon fishermen, although they also depended on seals, sea lions and halibut. The Chugach were also whalers and fishermen, using log weirs, traps and darts to catch several varieties of salmon.

In fall, they hunted mountain goat with bow and arrow and snared fox, otter and mink. Bears were taken with snares and deadfalls, or stalked by hunters wearing bearskin disguises.

Whaling was highly specialized, and required esoteric knowledge of techniques and accompanying ritual. Whalers used two-hole kayaks, or *bidarkas*, with the hunter in front and the paddler behind. The whale was wounded with a slate-bladed lance, tipped with aconite poison, after which the hunters went home and waited for the dead whale to drift ashore. Seals and sea otters were also harpooned from kayaks. Cod and halibut were caught with barbed hooks, herring and candlefish with dip nets, and birds with nets and bows and arrows. To supplement the diet, they gathered foods such as clams, cockles, mussels, sea urchins, berries, roots and kelp.

Transportation included the one, two and three hole kayak, although the latter was probably not aboriginal. They also used *umiaks* (skin-covered open boats), plank toboggans pulled by dogs, and pack bags carried by dogs. Other crafts included spruce-root baskets with geometric designs, wooden spoons and dippers and oblong wooden eating bowls with painted designs.

For clothing, the Chugach wore long parkas of animal or bird skin, shirts of caribou skin obtained in trade, and rain gear of eagle skin or gut. Long boots were made from sea lion skin, salmon skin or the entire leg skin of a brown bear, including paw and claws. They wore conical basketry hats made from spruce roots, decorated with dentalia shells and sea lion whiskers. The Koniagmiut preferred parkas of marmot and ground squirrel and wore wooden sun visors. The women were tattooed, and both men and women wore nose and ear ornaments and labrets.

The South Alaskan Inuit engaged in both trade and warfare with their neighbors. The Koniagmiut had fortified positions, complete with food caches, to which they could retreat when attacked. The Chugach had wooden slat armor and reportedly used portable log screens which 30 men could use as a shield.

In 1784, the Russians established a fur trading post at Three Saints Bay on Kodiak Island. By the early 19th century, the Koniagmiut population had been reduced by half by the severe treatment and servitude forced on them by the fur traders. A smallpox epidemic in 1837-38 killed about 700, reducing the population of the island to about 2,000 by mid-century. In the late 19th century, hunters and traders from many nations flocked to the area, causing the near-extinction of the highly-prized sea otter. By the early 20th century, fishing had replaced furs as the main source of income of the area.

In the late 1970s, there were about 2,000 South Alaska Inuit, with about 1,500 living on Kodiak Island. They were largely assimilated into the surrounding population, and generally preferred to refer to themselves as Aleut. For the purpose of the Alaska Native Claims Settlement Act, they were organized into the Chugach Natives, Incorporated, including the villages of English Bay, Port Graham, Seldovia and

Tatilek, and Koniag, Incorporated, including Akhiok, Karluk Kodiak, Larsen Bay, Old Harbor, Ouzinkie and Port Lions.

BIBLIOGRAPHY: Clark, Donald Woodforde. *Koniag Prehistory.* Stuttgart: Verlag W. Kohlhammer, 1974; Hrdlicka, Ales. *The Anthropology of Kodiak Island.* Philadelphia: The Wistar Institute of Anatomy and Biology, 1944.

SOUTHAMPTON INUIT: an extinct Inuit (Eskimo) group located on Southampton Island, at the entrance to Hudson Bay, in the Canadian Northwest Territories. Known also as the Saglirmiut, they numbered about 57 in the late 19th century, and were wiped out by an unknown epidemic in 1902-03.

The Southampton Inuit were partly isolated from outside contact by dangerous reefs surrounding the island. Although many whalers and explorers were in the area, they were rarely visited, and consequently, comparatively little is known about their culture.

They lived in winter huts constructed of the skull caps of whales. The interior of the dwelling had a central platform of limestone, on which limestone blubber lamps were placed. Beds were located around the outside wall. Skin tents were used in summer, and storehouses of limestone slabs were used for storing split salmon. They sewed the bodies of their dead in skins and buried them in a rock grave.

Food sources included whales, seals, walrus, salmon and birds. They made knives of bone and flint, and arrows with flint tips. For transportation, they made a curious sort of boat or raft from three inflated seal skins connected with inflated intestines. They also had sleds with runners made from whale jawbones. Other material culture included cups made of wood and whalebone, limestone cooking pots, wooden snow goggles, and ivory combs and hair ornaments. The men wore their very long hair tied in a large ball above the forehead.

Most existing information on the Southampton Inuit is from a description given by George Comer, an American whaler who visited the island in 1898 and collected a number of items. Since the demise of the Saglirmiut, the island has been taken over by the Aivilingmiut of the Iglulik Inuit group.

BIBLIOGRAPHY: Boas, Franz. "The Eskimos of Baffin Land and Hudson Bay." *Bulletin of the American Museum of Natural History.* vol. 15, 1901.

SPOKAN: an Interior Salish tribe occupying the Spokane River valley in Washington in the 18th century, numbering about 600 in 1805. In the 1970s, there were about 580 Spokan descendants on the Spokan Reservation in eastern Washington, and an indeterminate number mixed with other tribes on the Colville Reservation in Washington and the Coeur d'Alene Reservation in Idaho.

The Spokan, together with the Flathead and Kalispel, comprised the Flathead group of Interior Salish. They spoke a language of the Interior division of the Salishan language family. The Spokan were also known as the "Sun People," a mistranslation of their tribal name.

They were composed of three geographical divisions, Upper, Lower and Southern (or Middle) Spokan. These were further subdivided into bands, composed of several related families who camped together. Each band was led by a chief and an assistant chief, selected on the basis of wisdom, influence, bravery and other leadership qualities. Often a number of bands would winter camp together, forming a village and selecting a village chief. There may have been a few hereditary chiefs in earlier times. There was also a tribal chief who with the band chiefs made up the tribal council. In later years, as tribal authority became more centralized, band chiefs became less important, eventually being replaced by tribal sub-chiefs and "small" chiefs.

Religious life centered around guardian spirits obtained in dreams or visions and necessary for success in daily life. At puberty, young men fasted, prayed, exercised and kept vigils to this purpose. Shamans had especially strong guardian spirits, enabling them to foresee the future and to insure good hunting. An important mythical character was the culture hero Coyote. A great number of dances and ceremonies were regularly held. The dead were covered with skins and robes and placed on a scaffold until ready for burial. The pole on which the corpse was transported to the grave site was used as a grave marker to which offerings were tied.

Two principal types of structures were built, both of mats on a wood frame. A long lodge, sunk a foot in the ground, was used in winter camps for dances, meetings and ceremonies, whereas the people lived mostly in conical dwellings housing one, two or three families. Temporary brush shelters were used in the mountains on hunting trips. After acquiring horses, buffalo hunting became important, and skin tipis essentially replaced the mat dwellings.

The Spokan engaged in hunting, fishing and gathering for subsistence. In the mountains they hunted elk, deer, antelope and other game, and they crossed the mountains to hunt buffalo on the Plains. A favorite hunting technique was the communal surround. The most important food, however, was salmon, which, along with trout and whitefish, were caught with hook and line, nets, weirs and traps. These were smoked and dried in elevated sheds and stored for use during the off-season. Wild foods, including camas, bitterroot, and various other roots, and berries were important.

The Spokan used few canoes, unlike the others in the Flathead group, usually traveling the rivers instead on pole rafts. Types of containers included baskets of birchbark and of coiled split cedar roots, as well as

**Chief Gary,
a Spokan,
on horseback.**

The National Archives

bags woven of strips of skin. Their clothing was of the northern Plains type, usually of buffalo skin, including robes, shirt (or dress for women), leggings, breechclout, moccasins, and cap or headband.

The Spokan, together with the other Interior Salish, probably migrated at some point from British Columbia. In the mid-18th century, they were located in Washington, often making buffalo hunting trips to the Plains with horses they acquired, about that time, from the Kalispel. Around 1800, they were decimated by smallpox, so when encountered by Lewis and Clark in 1805, they were considerably reduced in numbers. After that time, many traders came to the area, and fur trapping became important. In the mid-1800s, missionaries started coming to the Spokan. Trouble with settlers led to war in 1858. The Spokan, allied with the Coeur d'Alene, Yakima and Palouse, achieved some early victories, but were later put down by U.S. troops. In 1872, the Colville Reservation was established, which became home for some Spokan, and, in 1881, the Spokane Reservation was established.

In the 1900s, times were hard for the Spokan. Pollution of the rivers gradually stopped salmon fishing as a source of livelihood. In 1940, Corlee Dam was built, preventing salmon from ascending the Spokane River.

In the 1970s, about 580 Spokan lived on the 137,000-acre Spokane Reservation in Washington, and an unknown number lived mixed with other Indians on the Colville Reservation in Washington and the Coeur d'Alene Reservation in Idaho. On the Spokane Reservation, they were essentially acculturated and assimilated into the surrounding population.

BIBLIOGRAPHY: Teit, James A. *"The Salishan Tribes of the Western Plateaus." Annual Report of the Bureau of American Ethnology.* no. 45, 1927-28; Roy, Prodipto. *Assimilation of the Spokane Indians.* Washington Agricultural Experiment Stations, Institute of Agricultural Science, Washington State University, 1961.

SQUAMISH: a Northwest Coast group located on Howe Sound and Burrard Inlet, north of the mouth of the Fraser River in southwestern British Columbia, numbering about 1,800 in the late 18th century. By the late 1970s, there were about 1,200 Squamish living on various reserves in British Columbia.

The Squamish spoke a language of the Coast division of the Salishan language family, and were culturally similar to other Coast Salish groups. They lived in numerous villages of cedar plank houses about 60 feet long and 20 feet wide. Sleeping platforms were along the four sides, and the interior posts and beams were carved with the figures of men and animals. As a precaution against raids, a secret passage under the sleeping platforms led to a subterranean room.

The Squamish lived in an area of abundant food supply, enabling them to subsist on summer food gathering and concentrate on craftwork and ceremonial life in winter. Central to religious life was the acquisition of guardian spirits, necessary for success in life. Adolescent boys usually sought such spirits by fasting in remote places or diving in mountain pools or streams. Girls observed an eight-day puberty rite, during which they secluded themselves, observed various taboos and fasted. The Squamish commemorated important occasions by giving potlatches, at which gifts were distributed, and inherited privileges, such as the singing of inherited songs, displayed.

Salmon and other fish were taken using seines and reef nets, and the surplus was smoke-dried and stored. Principal game included seal, elk, deer and bear. Women gathered clams, roots, bulbs, greens and berries, drying the latter in cakes for storage.

Canoes, the main means of transportation, were made from cedar logs. Other crafts included carving of wooden dishes and weaving of wool blankets and cedar bark bags with checkered patterns. Shredded cedar bark was used for summer clothing, and buckskin clothing was used for mountain hunting and winter wear.

In 1792, the Squamish were visited by the British explorer George Vancouver. A succession of smallpox epidemics reduced their population to a few hundred by the late 19th century. In the late 1970s, there were about 1,200 Squamish living on various reserves in southwestern British

Columbia, but only a few older people still spoke the Squamish language.

STALO: *See* COWICHAN.

STOCKBRIDGE: *See* MAHICAN.

SUSQUEHANNA: an important Iroquoian tribe located along the Susquehanna River in New York, Pennsylvania and Maryland. Now extinct, they numbered about 5,000 in 1600. They were known at various times by several different names, including Sasquehannock, Conestoga, Andaste and Minquas.

The Susquehanna were composed of at least six clans: Wolf, Heron, Turtle, Owl, Bear and Fox. They were ruled by a sachem or chief, with spiritual leadership by medicine men who effected cures and otherwise dealt with the spirit world. They buried their dead with a stone or block of wood under their heads, or in a sitting position, surrounded by food, weapons, tools and wampum.

The Susquehanna built their towns along the river, surrounded by a palisade of poles 25-30 feet high, interwoven with branches and reeds. Their houses were 20-180 feet long, constructed of hickory poles covered with overlapping pieces of birch, ash or chestnut bark. Smoke holes were left in the roof for the cooking fires inside, and the floors were lined with mats and furs. They had sweathouses dug in the earth near the river and lined with clay. A sick person sat in the house surrounded by heated rocks and, after sweating for awhile, plunged in the cold river.

Hunting, fishing and agriculture were all important in the Susquehanna economy. They had extensive fields of corn, and stored the dried corn in clay-lined pits dug on a hill. They also grew beans and peas and gathered acorns, walnuts, strawberries, mulberries and billberries. Women were in charge of planting and gathering, while the men hunted deer, beaver, otter, fox, raccoon and turkey.

The women made incised pottery, wove baskets and mats, and made nets and rope from Indian hemp. The women adorned themselves with earrings and tattooing, and the men wore war paint of red, green, black and white stripes. The women wore their hair long, while the men wore theirs long on one side and short and bristly on the other.

The Susquehanna were described as "giants" by Capt. John Smith, who saw them in 1608. They soon after became heavily engaged in trade with the Dutch and Swedish (who called them Minquas), exchanging beaver and otter pelts for guns, powder, iron knives, axes, hoes, kettles and liquor.

They were often involved in warfare with the Delaware (1623-34), with the Patuxent and Piscataway (1630-44) and with the Maryland settlers

A Susquehanna town: an engraving, circa 1600, probably by Théodore de Bry.

(after 1642). Their most dangerous foe, however, was the powerful Iroquois Confederacy, to the north, who called them the Andaste. After years of warfare, the Iroquois conquered the Susquehanna in 1675-76 and forced them to settle near the Oneida in New York.

Years later they were allowed to return to the Susquehanna Valley, but by then it was filling up with displaced eastern tribes under the protection and domination of the Iroquois. Through warfare and disease, the Susquehanna had dwindled to about 20 in 1763, and were known to white settlers in Pennsylvania as Conestoga Indians. In December of that year, the remaining Susquehanna were murdered by a gang of frontier rangers, known as the Paxton Boys, in retaliation for Indian raids that had taken place in western Pennsylvania.

BIBLIOGRAPHY: Witthoft, John and Kinsey, W. Fred, III., eds. *Susquehannock Miscellany*. Harrisburg: The Pennsylvania Historical and Museum Commission, 1959.

SWINOMISH: *See* SKAGIT.

TAENSA: *See* NATCHEZ.

TAHLTAN: *See* NAHANE.

TAKELMA: a southwestern Oregon tribe which, together with the Latgawa, composed the tiny Takilman linguistic family, numbering about 500 in the late 18th century. Both tribes were virtually extinct by the early 20th century.

The Takelma and Latgawa were located along the middle course and northern tributaries of the Rogue River. Takelma, meant "those dwelling along the river," in their language, while Latgawa meant "those living in the uplands."

The Takelma occupied more than 15 tiny villages, each headed by a chief, who usually acquired his position through hereditary wealth. Religious leadership was provided by both male and female shamans, who obtained their spiritual powers from guardian spirits acquired through fasting and dreaming. Takelma mythology included a culture hero, Daldal, and the familiar trickster character, Coyote.

The winter dwellings of the Takelma were semisubterranean, of pine plank construction, with a smokehole in the roof above the central fireplace. Sweathouses used by the men were of similar construction, but smaller. Simple brush shelter dwellings were used in summer, while visiting favorite fishing or hunting spots.

The four major foods of the Takelma were salmon, venison, acorns and camas roots, which were supplemented by pine nuts, manzanita berries and other wild plants and game.

The Takelma made an assortment of twined basketry containers, as well as caps worn by the women. Both men and women wore red, white and black face paint. Women tattooed three stripes on their chin, while men tattooed marks on their arms, for measuring strings of dentalia shells, a form of wealth used as a medium of exchange throughout the area. When a Takelma man wished to marry, usually outside the village, dentalia shells were an important part of the gifts given the bride's family.

BIBLIOGRAPHY: Hodge, Frederick W., ed. "Handbook of American Indians North of Mexico." vol. 2. *Bureau of American Ethnology Bulletin,* no. 30, 1907-10.

TAKULLI: *See* CARRIER.

TANAINA: a group of Alaskan Athapascan tribes or divisions occupying 14 settlements on the shores of Cook Inlet and its tributaries, numbering about 3,000 in 1805. The various divisions were culturally related, although not identical, forming a transition between the interior Athapascan tribes and the Northwest Coast cultures. They spoke an Athapascan language closely related to that of the Ingalik, and were also known as Knaiakhotana or Tekanin-Kutchin. In the 1970s, there were probably several hundred Tanaina, living in a number of villages in their traditional area.

They were geographically and culturally divided into four areas: Kachemak, Kenai-Tyonek, Upper Inlet and Iliamna-Susitna, each having slightly different cultures. They were socially organized into two exogomous moieties or phratries, which were subdivided into matrilineal clans—five in one moiety and ten in the other. The village was the political unit, each headed by a chief. The chiefs were usually the wealthiest men, and in most areas, the office was hereditary. In the Iliamna-Susitna area, however, they could be supplanted by men who gave greater potlatches (ceremonial gift distributions).

The traditional religion of the Tanaina centered around spirits believed to exist in all of nature. Shamans mediated between man and the spirits, and used powers given them by spirits to cure sickness and foretell the future. The shaman was very powerful in the village, serving as doctor, prophet, high priest and, often, chief. A creation myth says that the culture hero Raven created two women who founded the two Tanaina moieties. Principal celebrations were the First Salmon ceremony and potlatches for the dead. The dead were cremated and the remains either buried, hung in a sack in a tree, or put in boxes elevated on posts. The possessions of the deceased were given away, and 10 to 20 days of strict mourning followed. The "shadow-spirit" of the dead remained on earth for 40 days before retiring to the underworld.

The Tanaina lived in winter villages of *barabaras*—rectangular, gabled semisubterranean dwellings from 10 to 100 feet in length. The walls were of log-cabin type construction, thatched with grass and covered with dirt, and the roof was of spruce bark or planks, sometimes covered with thatch. The main room had a fireplace with smoke hole and a sleeping platform for single men and boys, under which slept the married couples. Adjoining rooms included a sweat lodge and a sleeping room for the elderly. Summer houses were similar, but of simpler design and lighter construction. Temporary houses of various types, such as spruce boughs over a bent alder frame, were often used on trips.

The Tanaina, like other northern Athapascans, were fishermen, hunters and gatherers, with no agriculture. Fish, particularly salmon, was the staple food. They caught five kinds of salmon using weirs, traps, spears and drag nets of alder poles and spruce root line. They also caught halibut and catfish on bone hooks, and eulachon (candlefish) with dip nets. Important game were sea mammals—seal, sea otter, and beluga. Land animals included caribou, which were taken by the use of dogs or by communals surrounds, as well as bear, moose, mountain goat, beaver, rabbit, and other game. Clams, mussles, seaweed, spruce and birch fiber, and many kinds of berries and roots were gathered to supplement the diet.

Hunting technology included two types of spruce bows, spears, knives, clubs, traps, deadfalls and slingshots. They travelled using kayaks and umiaks, which they acquired from the Inuit, and which supplanted the older traditional birchbark canoes and moose skin river boats. The Tanaina women produced spruce root baskets (sometimes waterproof), clay lamps, finely-tanned skins, and plaited rabbitskin blankets. Clothing for both sexes was a one-piece knee-length garment of tanned caribou or sheep skin with the hair removed, plus a shirt and knee-boots of the same material. For cold weather, the garment had footwear attached, and a parka and mittens were added. Ornamentation included tattooing and face painting.

The Tanaina were probably long time residents on Cook Inlet, occasionally at war with the Koniagmiut Inuit at the lower end of the inlet. First European contact was probably with Capt. James Cook in 1778, followed by a number of English traders throughout the rest of the 18th century. In 1786, the Russian settlement of Kasilof was established, and in 1791, a Russian redoubt was established at Kenai. Years of Russian dominance followed, marked by continual strife between Russians and Indians and by the establishment of the Russian Orthodox Church. Disease, particularly a smallpox epidemic in 1838, as well as foreign pressure severely reduced their population throughout the 19th century. In 1867, the U.S. purchased Alaska, and the Tanaina were left alone until about 1900, when the discovery of gold brought numbers of miners and settlers into the area. Foreign influences, such as canneries and trading posts, multiplied, bringing increased acculturation and decline of the game supply.

By the 1970s, they were essentially acculturated, dressing and living very much like their non-Indian neighbors. At this time, there were probably several hundred Tanaina, living in a number of villages in the Cook Inlet area of Alaska.

BIBLIOGRAPHY: Osgood, Cornelius. "The Ethnography of the Tanaina." *Yale University Publications in Anthropology.* no. 16, 1937.

TANANA: an Alaskan people occupying the valley of the Tanana River and its tributaries, numbering about 500 in the late 18th century. They were also called Tenan-kutchin by some authors, who considered them to be Kutchin tribes. They were composed of two geographic divisions, the Lower Tanana, or Tanana proper, and the Upper Tanana, or Nebesna. They spoke a language of the Northern division of the Athapascan language family, and were culturally closely related to their

Athapascan neighbors, the Koyukon and Ingalik (*q.q.v.*). Some authors group all these peoples under the term, Tena.

Alaskan Athapascans originated in Canada and were probably driven into Alaska by the Cree. In the 19th century, contact began with European traders and miners, and when mining in the area reached its peak between 1890 and 1910, much of the traditional culture was lost. In the 1970s, probably several hundred Tanana lived in a number of villages in the traditional area. They, along with other Athapascans, were organized into Doyon, Inc., to qualify for the Alaskan Native Claims Act.

BIBLIOGRAPHY: McKennan, Robert A. "The Upper Tanana Indians." *Yale University Publications in Anthropology.* no. 55, 1959.

TANO: a southern Tewa tribe located in the Galisteo basin south of Santa Fe, New Mexico, between the 14th and late 17th centuries. After the Pueblo Revolt (1680-92), some of the Tano migrated to Hopi territory, where they established Hano pueblo on First Mesa and became known as the Hopi-Tewa. In the 1950s, the 400 or so Hopi-Tewa still maintained their language and culture.

The Tano probably moved to the Gallisteo basin from Mesa Verde in about 1350 due to drought conditions. They established about 10 villages with total population estimates ranging between 1,400 and 4,000. The Tano came into contact with Keresan tribes, and the Apache, who alternately raided them and traded with them. Between 1540 and 1590, they were visited by five separate Spanish expeditions. Spanish colonization began shortly thereafter, and the Tano, being near Santa Fe, bore a heavy burden of supplying food and labor to the newcomers. These requirements, along with Spanish attempts to stamp out their religion, made the Tano prominent supporters of the Pueblo Revolt in 1680. Reportedly, the Tano alone laid siege to Santa Fe for five days, before being aided by the Tewa and northern Tiwa. Some 300 Tano were killed, and 47 were captured and later executed.

With the withdrawal of the Spanish, the Apache began raiding the Gallisteo area, and the Tano were forced to move to Santa Fe and the Tewa towns north of there. When the Spanish returned in 1693, many of the Santa Fe Tano were made slaves of the soldiers and colonists. The others fled to the Tewa pueblos. In 1696, the people of two former Tano towns, San Cristobal and San Lorenzo, took part in a second rebellion, after which they fled to join the Hopi. By 1706, other Tano groups had gathered in the Galisteo basin, where they lived until Comanche raids and smallpox forced the survivors to take refuge at Santo Domingo pueblo.

According to tradition, the Hopi invited the Tano to live with

A Tano altar of prayer plumes, (1913).   Smithsonian Institution

them and protect them from Ute raiders, which they did. In the early 18th century, the Spanish attempted unsuccessfully to force the Tano to return to their homes.

The Tano settled down to life among the Hopi, managing to maintain their own language and culture, while borrowing some Hopi social organization. The Tano were organized into seven clans. Each person inherited the clan of his mother and was forbidden to marry within his own clan. Upon marrying, a couple lived with the woman's family. Women owned all the houses and fields, and inheritance was through the female line.

There were two *kivas,* or religious centers, with clan membership determining *kiva* membership. All boys and girls were initiated into the *katcina* cult by whipping. Masked dances were performed in which *katcina,* or rain gods, were impersonated for the purpose of bringing rain. The most important rite was the Winter Solstice ceremony, and all boys of the pueblo were initiated into the Winter Solstice Society. There were a number of other societies, of which curing societies were among the most important.

The history of the Tano since the early 18th century has been closely linked with that of the Hopi. Together they endured Navajo raids, drought and disease. After the early years of mutual suspicion, they gradually developed a complementary relationship in which the rich Hopi ceremonial life came to be appreciated by the Hopi-Tewa (Tano), and the greater ability of the Hopi-Tewa to deal with the outside world was recognized by the Hopi. Marriage between the two groups gradually became more common, although the Hopi-Tewa continued to maintain their separate language and culture.

BIBLIOGRAPHY: Dozier, Edward P. "The Hopi-Tewa of Arizona." *University of California Publications in American Archaeology and Ethnology.* vol. 44, 1954; Eggan, Fred. *Social Organization of the Western Pueblos,* Chicago: University of Chicago Press, 1950.

TAOS: a Tiwa tribe and pueblo located 55 miles northeast of Santa Fe, New Mexico in the late 17th century, numbering about 2,000 at that time. In the late 1970s, more than 1,500 occupied the pueblo, which was still located on the original site, on both sides of Taos Creek. The Taos spoke a Tiwa language of the Tanoan family, which also included Picuris, Isleta and Sandia. The Taos referred to their pueblo as Ilaphai, or "red willow place."

Socially, Taos was organized into six *kiva* groups, each infant being given to the *kiva* of his parents choice. At adolescence, boys were initiated into their *kiva* group, after an 18-month instruction period during which they lived at the *kiva.* Initiation culminated in a pilgrimage to the sacred Blue Lake for ceremonies, which included making offerings of feathers, corn meal and corn pollen. Girls' puberty rites included ceremonies in which they ground corn, observed food taboos and changed their hairstyle.

The religious leader of Taos was the cacique, who, along with the tribal council, had power in traditional matters. The council was composed of the heads of all the *kivas* plus the secular officials, which were appointed by the religious leaders. Secular officials included the governor, lieutenant-governor, war captains and *fiscales* (prosecutors), who served one-year terms. The governor and his officers arbitrated disputes, kept order in the pueblo, and organized work. Announcements for planting crops, work on irrigation diteches, and preparations for festivals and ceremonies were called out from the governor's rooftop.

Most ceremonies were connected with the various *kivas*, and included the Deer dance, Bear People ceremony, Turtle dance and the annual August pilgrimage of all the adults to Blue Lake. The Taos sacred world included the Sun, Moon, Earth Mother and numerous other deities and spirits, including the souls or spirits of ancestors. There were both male and female shamans, who often specialized in certain types of cures, such as relieving ailments, bone setting and exorcism of witches.

When a person died, he was dressed in his best clothes and buried along with food. Members of his household remained in the house for four days. After that time prayer feathers and corn meal were set out for the spirit of the deceased, which then departed for the Ipiwinitonau, the underground land of the dead.

Taos girls filling water jars at a river: a photograph probably taken by Edward S. Curtis.

The pueblo of Taos consisted of two house groupings, North Town and South Town, facing each other across Taos Creek. The terraced adobe brick dwellings were up to five and six stories high, with each succeeding story smaller by one room width than the one below. The roofs were of poles and branches covered over with grass and earth. Women plastered the finished houses which were constructed and usually owned by the men. The lower stories were entered through a hatchway on the roof, reached by a ladder which could be pulled up as a defensive measure. In addition to dwellings, there were seven detached semisubterranean ceremonial rooms, or *kivas*, one of which later fell into disuse.

The men cultivated fields of corn, beans and squash, and the women tended small gardens or gathered wild foods. Wheat, oats and melons were introduced by the Spanish. The men held rabbit drives which were organized by the war captains. Deer were hunted with bow and arrow, and in winter, parties of 20-30 men sometimes went to the Plains to hunt buffalo. Turkeys were hunted for food and feathers, and captured baby eagles were raised for their feathers. The women had numerous uses for corn, including corn meal baked in husks and thin wafer bread baked on a hot, greased rock.

In pre-Spanish times, they made clothing of dressed skins. Later the women adopted the common Pueblo dark wool dress, which crossed over the right shoulder and under the left, and was tied with a red and green yarn belt. Moccasin-boots completed the costume.

According to tradition, the Taos emerged from a hole in the earth

**Taos Indians
in ceremonial
dress.**

U.S. Travel Service

somewhere to the north. The ancestors of the Taos were probably among the residents of the Chaco Canyon cliff dwellings. When drought struck that area in the 13th century, they moved into Taos Valley, living in pit-houses which were similar to the *kivas* of later times.

Members of the Coronado expedition visited Taos in 1540, and by the early 17th century, the Spanish established the mission of San Geronimo. Land-grabbing by Spanish colonists, required tributes of corn, enforced servitude and attempts to stamp out their religion led the Taos to stage several small rebellions prior to 1680. In that year, Taos played a prominent role in the general Pueblo Revolt, led by Popé, a San Juan medicine man, headquartered at Taos. The Taos, Picuris and other nearby tribes besieged Santa Fe, finally forcing the Spanish to flee to El Paso.

When the Spanish returned in 1692, some of the Taos fled to the mountains, and others to the Kiowa. The Spanish sacked the abandoned pueblo in 1693, after which the Taos returned and began rebuilding. A short-lived revolt broke out again in 1696.

Taos, being the northernmost pueblo, had always served as a gateway to the Plains and center for trade between the Pueblo and Plains tribes. There was some intermarriage between the Taos and Plains tribes, and Taos men braided their hair and wore leggings similar to Plains fashions.

Taos also suffered from raids by Comanche and Ute in the late 18th century.

By that time, Taos was an important trading point on the Santa Fe Trail. In the 1836 New Mexico revolt against Mexico, a Taos Indian served as governor of the rebel government for two months. In 1847, the Taos Indians, encouraged by the Mexicans, staged a rebellion against the new American government, killing about 15, including the New Mexico governor, Charles Bent. U.S. troops put down the rebellion, killing 150 Taos and executing 15.

In 1906, the U.S. government took 50,000 acres of Taos Indian land, including their sacred Blue Lake, and added it to Carson National Forest. In 1970, after decades of battles, the U.S. Congress finally restored the land and lake to the Taos people.

In the late 1970s, Taos pueblo still maintained its five and six story dwellings, although the upper levels were used mainly for storage. Doors and glass windows had been added, but the basic adobe architecture remained unchanged. The traditional ceremonies and religion continued to flourish, with added elements of Catholicism and Peyote religion.

Many of the Taos had summer homes near their fields or in the nearby towns of Fernando de Taos or Ranchos de Taos. The beauty of the area attracted artists, skiers and tourists, who came to see public performances of the Deer, Turtle and Sun-Down dances. Taos craftsmen were especially known for their drums and moccasins, and also produced woodcarving, weaving, pottery and rabbit-skin blankets.

BIBLIOGRAPHY: Parsons, Elsie Clews. *Taos Pueblo*. Menasha, Wisconsin: George Banta Publishing Company, 1936; Smith, M. Estellie. "Governing at Taos." *Eastern New Mexico University Contributions in Anthropology*. vol. 2, 1969.

TAWAKONI: *See* WICHITA.

TESUQUE: the southernmost Tewa tribe and pueblo, located eight miles north of Santa Fe, New Mexico, with a population of about 250 in the late 1970s. The Tesuque, along with the Santa Clara, San Ildefonso, San Juan, Nambe and Pojoaque, spoke the Tewa language of the Tanoan language family. Tesuque, or Tatunge, has been variously translated as "cottonwood tree place" and "dry, spotted place."

The Tesuque were composed of two tribal divisions, or moieties: Winter and Summer. Each moiety was headed by a cacique, who also served as religious leader of the whole pueblo for half of the year. Secular officers of the pueblo were appointed by the cacique. The Tesuque were further divided into clans. Each individual inherited the clan of his father, and was forbidden to marry within his clan.

In the early 17th century, the Spanish established a mission at Tesuque. During the Pueblo Revolt (1680-92), the Tesuque abandoned their pueblo, returning later to build a new one nearby. The new pueblo was composed of one and two-story communal adobe buildings, which remain to the present day.

In the late 1970s, Tesuque pueblo included 16,800 acres, with a population of about 250. The Tewa language was still widely spoken, and traditional ceremonies, including the Deer and Eagle dances, were performed throughout the year.

TETON: the largest of the seven divisions of the Dakota, constituting over half the Dakota population of about 25,000 in 1780. Formerly a woodlands people located in the northern Minnesota region in the 17th century, the Teton had migrated, by the mid-19th century, to the Plains of western Dakota, northwestern Nebraska, northeastern Wyoming and southeastern Montana.

The Teton were subdivided into seven sub-tribes: Oglala, Brulé, Hunkpapa, Miniconjou, Sans Arcs, Sihasapa (or Blackfoot) and Two Kettle (or Oohenonpa). These sub-tribes became more autonomous after the migration to the Plains and were themselves subdivided into bands and sub-bands. The Teton, or Western Dakota, represented the westernmost extension of Dakota language speakers, while the Middle division was termed Yankton and the Eastern division, Santee. The Teton, sometimes referred to as the Teton Sioux, spoke the Lakota dialect of the Dakota language, which belongs to the Siouan linguistic family.

The material culture of the Teton underwent drastic change in their

Tesuque Indians.   Bureau of Indian Affairs

westward migration. In Minnesota, they were a woodlands people, living in pole-frame lodges covered with bark or woven mats, gathering wild rice and maple sugar, fishing, and hunting woodland game. Their main means of transportation were birchbark canoes. In winter they travelled on snowshoes. In the Plains, Teton life was centered around the buffalo, which provided food, shelter, clothing, tools, containers and numerous other items. Acquisition of horses in the early 18th century made the Teton nomads, ranging far and wide in search of the great herds.

On the Plains, each of the Teton sub-tribes had its own leadership and government, and acted independently, They fought most of the neighboring tribes but did not war on each other. In winter the sub-tribes split into bands or even smaller units called *tiyospaye*, because of the scarce supply of food and feed for their horses at that time of year. From 5 to 20 related families would winter in a sheltered valley, hunting the available game and using their supply of food that had been dried and preserved the previous summer. Winter was the time for making and repairing tools and weapons, doing craftwork and making clothing.

In summer, the various bands would gather to hunt buffalo and to celebrate the Sun Dance. Not much is known about the political organization of some of the Teton sub-tribes during the summer camp. Among the Oglala , however, there was a chief's society composed of the leading men over 40 years old. This group elected seven chiefs, who held office for life. The seven delegated their authority to four "shirt-wearers," who were the councillors and chief executives and served for life. The seven also chose four *wakikun,* with one-year terms, who were in charge of organizing and controlling the camp. The *wakikun* were assisted by the *akitcita*, a sort of police who kept order in the camp, enforced decisions and oversaw the buffalo hunt.

In a Teton summer camp, more than a dozen different societies functioned for both men and women, including dance groups, craft groups and warrior societies. Each had its own songs, dances, ceremonies and regalia. The Sun Dance, held in mid-summer, required four days of preparation for the four-day ceremony. Fasting, prayer, dancing, feasting and self-torture were all important elements of the ceremony, which was celebrated by most of the Plains tribes.

The Teton believed in a supreme force which they called Wakan Tanka. They also had a complex hierarchy of deities, including the Sun, Earth, Thunder, the four compass points, etc. Vision quests were an important means by which each person received a guardian animal spirit, who protected him all his life. There were various types of priests and shamans who interpreted visions, conducted ceremonies and effected cures through the use of medicinal plants and various rituals. The Teton buried their dead on high hills or placed them on scaffolds or in trees. A

**Chief Runs-the-
Enemy,
a Teton Dakota.**
The National Archives

dead warrior's favorite horse was usually killed and his weapons and personal effects placed with him. Mourners gave away some of their possessions, cut their hair and often slashed themselves.

When the Teton moved onto the Plains, they adopted the skin tipi for both summer and winter use. About 12 buffalo skins made an average size tipi. The women dressed and sewed the skins for the tipis, set them up and took them down when it was time to move, which was frequently. The women also owned the tipis. Polygamy was fairly common, a man usually marrying sisters. They might all live together, or each woman might have a separate tipi.

The Teton depended entirely on hunting and gathering for their food supply, engaging neither in agriculture nor fishing. The wild foods they gathered included prairie turnip, potatoes, onions, chokecherries, plums and strawberries. The dried chokecherries were mixed with dried and pounded meat to make pemmican, which would keep several years.

Mrs. Red Thunder, a Teton, with her children, in front of a tipi, (1897).
Smithsonian Institution
National Anthropological
Archives

Buffalo meat was cooked on a spit or boiled in a buffalo skin filled with water and red-hot rocks.

Buffalo were hunted in several different ways including stalking, driving over cliffs, or setting grass on fire and surrounding them. After the Teton acquired horses, sometime before 1742, the communal buffalo hunt, surrounding the herd on horseback, was the most common method. When the hunt was over, the women would butcher the meat and carry it back to camp. Uses for buffalo were not limited to meat for food and hides for clothing and tipis. The sinews were used for bowstrings and thread, bones for tools, hair for weaving bags and belts, horns for spoons and ladles, hooves for rattles, and the chips for fuel.

The women were skilled in the dressing of hides for various purposes. For clothing, they used deer or elkskins, which were lighter weight, using buffalo hides for winter robes, moccasins, shields and assorted containers. Fine quillwork in geometric patterns decorated clothing and bags. In later times, this was largely replaced by beadwork. Painting was done on tipis, skin bags and buffalo robes. The Teton painted pictographs on hides as a calendric record of events.

Normal dress for Teton men included breechclout and moccasins in warm weather, supplemented with a shirt, leggings and buffalo robe in colder weather. Their long hair was braided and face and body painted for ornamentation. Feathers and feather headdresses were worn, not merely as ornamentation, but to signify certain deeds of bravery performed by the wearer. Women wore long one-piece dresses tied with belts, short leggings and moccasins. Their hair was parted in the middle, with the parting often painted vermilion, and was also often braided. Face paint and ear ornaments were popular.

The Dakota probably originated as a tribe in the Ohio valley and migrated from there to the western Great Lakes. Sometime before 1650 they had settled near the western end of Lake Superior and in the upper Mississippi Valley. They were frequently at war with the Ojibwa, who drove them southward to the Mille Lacs region of Minnesota. Continued pressure from the Ojibwa, who were early recipients of French firearms, plus the lure of the buffalo herds, induced the Dakota to move westward.

The Teton, led by the Oglala and Brulé, probably began migrating in the late 17th century. By 1700, they were reported living in southwestern Minnesota and hunting buffalo. Successively they moved to the Big Stone Lake area between Minnesota and South Dakota and then to the Sioux and James rivers area of eastern South Dakota, driving out the Omaha.

By the mid-18th century, the Teton had moved to the Missouri River valley, driving the Arikara further up that river. About 1765, they entered the Black Hills region, displacing the Cheyenne and Kiowa. About 1822, they joined with the Cheyenne in driving the Crow out of the eastern Wyoming region above the North Platte. From 1820-40 the fur trade was at its height in this region, and the Teton were the main suppliers. Contact with whites was still limited mostly to traders at this point, and the Teton were able to supply themselves with the conveniences of trade goods while remaining in relative seclusion.

After 1841, however, wagon trains began moving through Teton territory west to Utah, Oregon and California. Although only passing through, the trains frightened away the buffalo and destroyed the grasslands and wood supply along the river valleys. The Teton began attacking the wagon trains, until a treaty was signed near Fort Laramie in 1851, in which the U.S. government defined and recognized the claims of the various tribes to the region, while the Indians agreed to permit the wagon trains to have free access.

In 1854, a combined force of Oglala, Brulé and Miniconjou destroyed a posse of 30 white men who fired on their village. The following year, troops led by Col. William S. Harvey retaliated by destroying a peaceful Brulé village at Ash Hollow, Nebraska.

By 1865, the Dakota, Cheyenne, Arapaho and other northern Plains tribes had allied themselves in an attempt to prevent the building of more roads and railroads through their territories. In 1866 a combined force of Teton, Cheyenne and Arapaho destroyed 80 soldiers led by Capt. William J. Fetterman. The following year, the Teton lost hundreds of warriors in a battle known as the Wagon Box Fight. In 1868, Red Cloud, an Oglala chief, signed a second treaty at Fort Laramie, in which the

U.S. government agreed to stop building roads through Teton territory and set aside the western part of South Dakota as a reservation.

The following few years of peace were ended by the discovery of gold in the Black Hills and the rush of prospectors to this area. The Teton refused to cede the area, which included lands sacred to them. In 1876, after defeating part of the Seventh Cavalry, led by Col. George A. Custer, at the Battle of Little Bighorn, the Teton were forced to give up the Black Hills and settle on the reservation. In 1889, the reservation was broken up into five smaller reservations. That year, the Dakota and other tribes joined in the Ghost Dance movement, which was suppressed by the arrest and murder of Hunkpapa chief Sitting Bull and by the Wounded Knee massacre in 1890.

In the late 1970s, the five Teton reservations were: Pine Ridge (Oglala), Rosebud (Brulé and Two Kettle), Lower Brulé (Lower Brulé), Standing Rock (Hunkpapa and Sihasapa), and Cheyenne River (Miniconjou, Sans Arcs, Two Kettle, and Sihasapa).

(See also *Oglala, Brulé, Two Kettle, Hunkpapa, Sihasapa, Miniconjou* and *Sans Arcs.*)

BIBLIOGRAPHY: Ewers, John C. *Teton Dakota Ethnology and History.* U.S. Dept. of the Interior, National Park Service, 1938.

TEWA: See NAMBE, POJOAQUE, SAN ILDEFONSO, SANTA CLARA, TANO, and TESUQUE.

THOMPSON: a large Salishan tribe occupying the valleys of the Fraser, Thompson, and Nicola rivers in southwestern British Columbia, numbering about 5,000 in 1780. In the 1970s, there were about 2,800 Thompson, scattered among 15 bands in their traditional area. They spoke a language of the Interior division of the Salishan language family similar to that of the Shuswap, and were also known as Ntlakyapamuk, from their own name for themselves.

The Thompson Indians occupied a number of villages, grouped geographically into the Lower Thompson band, located downstream of Cisco on the Fraser River, and the Upper Thompson division, consisting of four bands, upstream. Bands were autonomous groups of related families, led by an hereditary chief, of limited authority. The real authority rested in a council of the older men. There were also temporary war chiefs to lead them in warfare.

Religion centered around guardian spirits acquired in youth through vision quests which included periods of seclusion and fasting. Shamans cured ills with the aid of especially powerful guardian spirits. An important deity was the Chief of the Dead. Important ceremonies included a First Salmon festival, a ghost or circle dance, and puberty rites for girls. At puberty, girls purified themselves by daily prayers, bathing and rubbing their bodies with fir branches. The dead were buried in the ground or in rock slides.

Winter dwellings were circular semisubterranean pole-frame lodges 45 feet in diameter, entered through an opening in the roof. Summer dwellings were either oblong or circular lodges of rush mats on a pole frame, built above ground. They also had dome-shaped sweathouses, used by both men and women for purification, and also used by youths as a home during their period of fasting to acquire guardian spirits.

The staple food of the Thompson was salmon, caught with dipnets, seine nets, weirs, traps, spears and hook-and-line. They also took various game, including deer, elk, bear, beaver, marmot and caribou. Hunting techniques included drives, stalking, surrounds and the use of dogs. Meat was either roasted, boiled or dried for later use. Various roots, especially camas and bitterroot, and berries, especially serviceberries, soapberries and huckleberries, as well as nuts and cherries, were gathered to supplement the diet.

Birchbark canoes provided water transportation, and small round snowshoes were used in winter. Bows were of the double-curved type, made usually of juniper. Basketry was of birchbark or of cedar roots, often woven tightly enough to hold water for cooking, and decorated with geometric designs. Other crafts included weaving of blankets of goat wool or strips of rabbit fur. Clothing was of dressed skins—leggings, moccasins, breechclout (for men) and tunics (for women). A fur robe was added in cold weather.

Trading partners of the Thompson included the neighboring Okanagon, Lake, Colville and Sanpoil. Former enemies were a small Athapascan tribe on the Nicola river called the Stuwik, whom they absorbed by about 1800. First contact with Europeans was probably first with Simon Fraser in 1809, and then with traders of the Northwest and Hudson's Bay Companies. More injurious to the tribe, however, were the miners who came after the 1858 discovery of gold. Throughout the late 19th century, disease, especially a smallpox epidemic in 1863, and pressure from non-Indians caused a severe drop in the population to about 1,800 in 1906.

In more recent years, conditions improved and the population increased again. In the 1970s, there were around 2,800 Thompson Indians living in their traditional territory on various reserves totalling about 105,000 acres. They were grouped into 15 bands: Boothroyd, Boston Bar, Coldwater, Cook's Ferry, Kanaka Bar, Lower Nicola, Lytton, Nicomen, Nooaitch, Oregon Jack Creek, Shackan, Siska, Skuppah, Spuzzum and Upper Nicola.

Farming was important to the economy, but the traditional pursuits of hunting, fishing and trapping were still followed. Other sources of income were wage labor and the sale of crafts such as basketry.

BIBLIOGRAPHY: Teit, James A. "The Thompson Indians of British Columbia." *Memoirs of the American Museum of Natural History.* vol. 2, 1900.

TIGUA: *See* TIWA.

TILLAMOOK: the principal Salishan tribe located along the Oregon coast in the early 19th century, numbering about 2,200 at that time. By the early 20th century, the Tillamook were virtually extinct as a tribe, although in the late 1970s there were still a few Tillamook descendants in the Oregon area.

The Tillamook language belonged to the Coastal division of the Salishan language family. They were more often called Killamook, a Chinook term meaning "people of Nekelim (or Nehalem)." The Tillamook were divided into four dialect groups: Tillamook proper, Salmon River, Nestucca and Naalem.

Occupying the Oregon coast from Nehalem to the Salmon River, the Tillamook lived in numerous tiny villages, each headed by a chief, whose position was based on wealth. Shamans provided religious leadership, interpreted dreams, performed ceremonies and cured the sick.

The Tillamook believed that the land of the dead was located somewhere to the west, and that reaching it required a canoe. When a person died, his body was placed in a plank box and put into his canoe, which was painted red and set on forked poles. Another canoe was inverted over the first, and cordage was wrapped around the two. The tools and equipment of the deceased were hung on poles nearby.

At puberty, boys were sent to the woods for 10 days to seek a guardian spirit. Their future occupation—hunter, warrior, fisherman, canoe builder, shaman—was based on whatever type of spirit appeared to them on this quest. Girls also sometimes sought a guardian spirit through fasting, isolation and dancing. Ceremonies included the first-salmon rites and those connected with birth and death.

Tillamook babies were placed in a canoe-shaped cradle, and a head presser was applied for the first year, to achieve the flattening considered a mark of beauty.

The Tillamook built long, rectangular, cedar-plank winter houses with slanted roofs, usually housing several families. Summer houses and storehouses were made of woven mats, and sweathouses were constructed of pole framework covered with hemlock bark and a layer of earth.

The hunting-fishing-gathering economy of the Tillamook produced a varied diet. Salmon, trout and herring were roasted, smoked or dried for

Tillamook Indians, in about 1898.

Smithsonian Institution National Anthropological Archives

later use. Elk, blacktail deer, waterfowl and other small game were hunted with bow and arrow, spears and traps. Along the coast, they obtained clams, mussels, crabs and an occasional washed-up whale, especially prized for its oil. Women gathered an assortment of roots, greens and berries.

Tillamook canoes ranged from 50-foot, 30-man seagoing craft, with images carved on bow and stern, to smaller types used on the rivers. Men and women were both adept at navigating the smaller canoes.

Epidemics in the first half of the 19th century reduced the Tillamook population from more than 2,000 to less than 200. By the early 20th century, Tillamook culture was virtually extinct, and only a few speakers of the language remained.

BIBLIOGRAPHY: Boas, Franz. "Notes on the Tillamook." *University of California Publications in American Archaeology and Ethnology.* vol. 20, 1923; Sauter, John and Johnson, Bruce. *Tillamook Indians of the Oregon Coast.* Portland, Oregon: Binfords & Mort, Publishers, 1974.

Timucua Indians depositing their crops in the public granary: from an engraving by Théodore de Bry, after a drawing by Jacques le Moyne, who visited Florida in 1564-65.

TIMUCUA: an extinct group of closely related tribes, also known as Utina, which occupied most of northern Florida. The Timucuan group (including the Timucua, Saturiba, Yustaga, Potano, Tocobaga, Mayaca, and Marracou) numbered about 13,000 in 1650, living in more than 40 towns and villages. The Timucua spoke a language usually classed with the Muskogean linguistic family.

They were organized by clans, and some of their chiefs were hereditary. Among their deities they worshiped the sun and moon, at times offering human sacrifice. Their priests were powerful and served also to cure the sick and improve the weather. When a priest died, his body and all his possessions were placed in his house, and the house was burned. A chief who died, however, was buried and his house and possessions burned. Under Spanish rule in the 1600s, the Timucua became Christian.

Villages of the Timucua were compactly built and fortified with a surrounding stockade complete with guardhouse. A large four-sided building used for town gatherings and ceremonies stood in the center. The houses were round, built of poles thatched with palmetto.

Two corn crops a year were planted, in March and June. First, the fields were burned-over, and then holes for the seed poked in the ground with a stick. The harvest was stored in common granaries and dispensed as needed. Hunting and gathering were also important, the men using

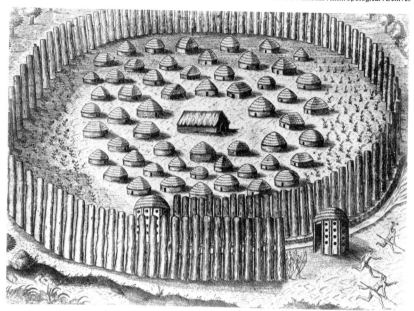

A fortified Timucua town: from an engraving by Théodore de Bry, after a drawing by Jacques le Moyne, who visited Florida in 1564-65.

Timucua Indian hunting deer with decoys made of the head and skin of the deer: from an engraving by Théodore de Bry, after a drawing by Jacques le Moyne.

bow and arrow, darts and clubs to hunt alligators, deer, buffalo, rabbit and various small game. Shellfish and wild fruits were gathered, and a bread was made out of cooti root (arrow root). The women wove a variety of baskets and mats.

The Timucua were described as tall and well-formed and distinguished by elaborate red, black and blue tattooing all over their bodies. They also covered their bodies with bear grease, perhaps partly as a protection from the sun. The men wore their long hair tied up in a knot, which they used as a handy place to keep their arrows while hunting.

The Timucua, expert boat builders and sailors, carried on a canoe trade with Cuba. Various Spanish expeditions visited Timucua territory in the early 16th century. By the latter part of the century, the Spanish had come to stay and, in the early 1600s, reported the Timucua firmly under their control. However, the most complete information on the Timucua in the pre-colonial period comes from the reports of a 1564-65 French expedition led by René de Laudonnière and the drawings of the artist accompanying the expedition, Jacques Le Moyne.

European diseases reduced the Timucua greatly as did a rebellion in 1656. Their final destruction, however, was caused primarily by raiders from the north—Creek, Yuchi, and Catawba Indians aided by the English—who, in the early 18th century, burned and destroyed most Timucua and Apalachee towns and carried off hundreds as slaves. A once numerous people, the Timucua were extinct as a tribe by the mid-18th century.

BIBLIOGRAPHY: Fairbanks, Charles H. *Ethnohistorical Report on the Florida Indians.* New York: Garland Publishing, Inc., 1974.

TIONONTATI: an Ontario tribe located south of Nottawasaga Bay of eastern Lake Huron in the early 17th century, numbering perhaps 8,000 at that time. In the late 1970s, Tionontati descendants, mixed with the Huron and other groups and known as the Wyandot, lived in Oklahoma and numbered about 1,000.

The Tionontati, whose name meant "place of the hills," spoke an Iroquoian language similar to that of the Huron. They were also known as the Petun, or Tobacco Nation, for their large fields of tobacco.

The Tionontati were divided into two groups, designated Wolf and Deer, each of which occupied several villages. Of the total of eight or ten villages, the principal Deer and Wolf villages were Ekarenniondi and Ehure respectively.

Culturally and linguistically, the Tionintati were most closely related to the Huron band of Attignaouantan. They lived in sedentary villages and grew large quantities of corn and tobacco, exporting the latter to the

Huron. The Tionontati also had friendly relations with the Ottawa, an Algonquian tribe to the west, as well as with the Iroquoian Neutral nation.

In the early 17th century, the Tionontati were closely allied with the Huron, who acted as middlemen in trade between them and the French. In the 1640s, the Tionontati were drawn into the rivalry between the Huron and the Iroquois Five Nations Confederacy. Their village of Ehwae was partly destroyed, probably by Iroquois, in 1640. In 1648-49, the Huron towns were destroyed by the Iroquois, and some of the survivors fled to the Tionontati. In 1649, the Tionontati were also destroyed, and the combined Huron and Tionontati survivors began a 200-year saga of wandering that brought them finally to Oklahoma, where their descendants lived in the late 1970s under the name Wyandot. (See *Huron*).

TIPAI-IPAI: a southern California people occupying the region on both sides of the boundary between California and Baja California in the late 18th century, when they numbered more than 3,000. In the late 1970s, there were perhaps 1,500 Tipai-Ipai descendants, living in California.

The terms Tipai and Ipai, both meaning "people," have been applied, since the 1950s, to two linguistically-related groups formerly known as Kamia and Diegueño. The latter name was derived from the Spanish mission located in the area, San Diego de Alcala. The language, still known as Diegueño, spoken by the Tipai-Ipai belongs to the Yuman division of the Hokan language family.

A Tipai-Ipai woman pounding meal: a photograph taken in the 1890s.

The Tipai-Ipai were composed of autonomous bands or tribelets, usually made up of a single patrilineal clan, headed by a clan chief and his assistant. Shamans provided religious leadership by performing ceremonies, interpreting dreams, controlling the weather and curing the sick.

The most important religious ceremony of the Tipai-Ipai was the *kaurk,* a clan mourning ceremony. The four to eight day ceremony included gift-giving, dancing and feasting, and culminated in the burning of lifelike images of the dead, painted and dressed in traditional clothing. The Tipai-Ipai cremated their dead and believed in an afterlife somewhere to the south.

House styles of the Tipai-Ipai varied with the season and environment. Winter houses included dome-shaped dwellings of pole framework covered with thatch, bark or pine slabs, while brush shelters often served as summer houses. Caves were sometimes used as winter homes in the mountains, while dwellings of pole and palm-leaf thatch were used in the desert.

Flour made from six varieties of acorns was the staple for most Tipai-Ipai, although they also made flour from mesquite beans and the seeds of sage, pigweed, peppergrass, flax and buckwheat. Other wild foods utilized included cactus, agave, clover, cherries, plums, elderberries, manzanita berries and prickly pear. In spring, summer and fall, the various bands moved with the food cycle, ending with acorn gathering in the mountain groves from September through November. The women did most of the seed gathering, while the men hunted small game and an occasional deer with bow and arrow and throwing sticks.

The Tipai-Ipai made a wide assortment of basketry and pottery used in the various stages of food collecting, processing, storing and cooking. They also used granite mullers, or pestles, for grinding seeds and acorns, and clay pipes for smoking cultivated tobacco.

In 1769, the Spanish established the presidio and mission of San Diego de Alcala among the Tipai-Ipai. There were numerous revolts against the sedentary way of life imposed by mission agriculture, which contrasted with their former semi-nomadic life as hunters and gatherers.

Under the Mexicans and Americans, the Tipai-Ipai lost their best lands to settlers. After 1875, they were settled on about 12 small, poor reservations. In the late 1970s, there were about 1,500 Tipai-Ipai descendants living in southern California and northwestern Baja California, with about one-third actually living on reservations. All dialects of the Diegueño language were still spoken, and Tipai-Ipai traditions were overlain with Spanish, Mexican and American customs.

BIBLIOGRAPHY: Spicer, Leslie. "Southern Diegueño Customs." *University of California Publications in American Archaeology and Eth-*

Tlingit in dancing costumes, Chilkat, Alaska.   Library of Congress

nology. vol. 20, 1923; Gifford, E.W. "The Kamia of Imperial Valley." *Bureau of American Ethnology Bulletin,* no. 97, 1931.

TIWA: *See* ISLETA, PICURIS, SANDIA and TAOS.

TLINGIT: a Northwest Coast group occupying the southeastern Alaska coastline from Yakutat Bay to Cape Fox, numbering about 10,000 in the mid-18th century. In the late 1970s, there were more than 9,000 Tlingit located in their traditional area. The Tlingit language probably belongs to the Athapascan language family.

The Tlingit occupied numerous villages on both the mainland, including parts of the interior river valleys, and the islands, including the northern end of Prince of Wales Island. The abundant food supply gave them leisure time in winter to develop a complex social system and a religious life rich in ceremony and mythology.

The Tlingit were divided into two moieties, Wolf and Raven, which were further subdivided into clans. Both moieties and clans were matrilineal and exogamous, which meant that each person belonged to the clan and moiety of his mother and was restricted from marrying within either. Clans were composed of a number of lineages or family groups, descended through the female line.

The Tlingit lived in large cedar plank dwellings occupied by a number of related families. A boy, at about age ten, went to live in the house of his mother's brother, thus joining the other males of his lineage. When a couple married, they usually lived in the house of the groom's father. The oldest male in a house, the *yitsati,* was designated as "keeper of the house." He served as the ceremonial leader, represented the house in clan councils and conducted trade relations. Within a village, the two ranking *yitsati* from opposite moieties were designated *ankaua,* or village leaders.

Inherited privileges, such as the rights to certain songs, dances, ceremonies or territories, including fishing grounds, sealing grounds, berry patches, beaches, etc., were the basis for the prestige accorded a lineage. Lineages worked constantly to enhance their prestige, through acquisition and distribution of material wealth. Each individual was ranked socially according to the prestige of his lineage. The Tlingit also had a number of slaves, mostly Coast Salish people obtained in trade from the Haida or Tsimshian, who in turn, got them from the Kwakiutl. They also had some other slaves, taken as captives in warfare with neighboring tribes or other Tlingit groups.

Religious leadership was provided by shamans, who used power given them by guardian spirits to cure the sick, recover lost souls and aid war parties. Adolescent boys also sought guardian spirits, which usually appeared to them in dreams, visions, or trances, after a regimen of bathing and fasting in remote places. Tlingit mythology included the culture hero-trickster character Raven, who stole the sun, water and fish and gave them to the Tlingit. Girls at puberty were secluded behind a screen for four months to a year, after which a potlatch was given to recognize their new status as marriageable young women.

Potlatches were important ceremonies held to enhance the prestige of a lineage through ceremonial gift-giving and display of lineage wealth and privileges. They usually lasted several days at least, and included feasting, dancing, singing, theatricals and the giving away of various gifts, including slaves and ceremonial copper shields. In early times, slaves, especially purchased for the potlatch, were more often killed or set free than given away. In post-European-contact times, blankets and money became the principal gifts.

Tlingit arts and crafts were tied to ceremonial and religious life. Dancers wore carved wooden masks with moveavle features, including blinking eyes, opening mouths and protruding tongues. Ceremonial dress included wooden crest hats carved with the crest animal of the clan and worn by the clan leader. Chilkat robes of mountain goat wool and cedar bark string, which originated with the Tsimshian but were highly developed by the Chilkat division of the Tlingit, depicted totemic designs in yellow, blue-green, black and white.

When a Tlingit died, he was cremated, and the ashes were placed in a wooden box in the clan graveyard, where totem pole memorials were erected in honor of the dead. Alternatively, the ashes were placed in the totem pole standing in front of the house of the deceased.

Tlingit houses were built of yellow cedar or spruce planks, with carved center posts and a gabled roof. The bottom figure of the totem pole in front of the house often had an open mouth, which served as the doorway. Sleeping platforms ran along the walls, and ceremonial equipment was kept behind a large screen at the back painted with totemic crests. One corner of the house was often made into a sweat bath.

Food was abundant, and varied with the location of the various Tlinglit groups. Fish was usually most important, including salmon, cod, halibut, herring and candlefish (eulachon), caught with hooks, weirs, traps, spears and nets. Men harpooned seal, sea otter and sea lion, and women gathered seafoods such as clams, mussels, oysters, sea urchins, seaweeds and sea birds' eggs. Bow and arrow, snares, pitfalls and deadfalls were used to hunt deer, mountain goat, black bear, porcupine, snowshoe rabbit, ducks and geese. Fox, wolf and wolverine were trapped for their furs. Interior groups also hunted moose, caribou, bighorn sheep and brown bear. Land foods gathered included wild rice, wild celery, rhubarb, roots, currants and a variety of berries.

U.S. Department of the Interior.   National Park Service

A Tlingit totem pole at Sitka national Monument, Alaska.

For sea transportation, the Tlingit used large red cedar dugout canoes, which were either obtained from the Haida or made by themselves on Prince of Wales Island. On rivers, they used smaller cottonwood dugouts. The Tlingit were excellent wood workers, making helmets, dishes, boxes and other containers, as well as their houses, canoes, totem poles, masks and hats. The women wove spruce root and cedar bark basketry, as well as Chilkat robes. The central and southern Tlingit wore mostly shredded bark clothing, whereas the northerners wore warmer buckskin garments, including leggings and moccasins in cold weather. All groups used cedar bark rain ponchos, caps, and skin or fur robes in cold weather.

The Tlingit were inveterate traders, with other tribes and with each other. Products of the interior groups included moose and caribou hides, moccasins and copper, while coastal mainland groups offered dressed skins and furs, eulachon oil, horn spoons, baskets and Chilkat blankets. The island groups produced seal oil, dried salmon, halibut, venison and shellfish. Warfare was also common, among themselves as well as with other tribes. Weapons included bow and arrow, daggers, spears, clubs, sharpened canoe paddles (for naval warfare), stick armor and wooden helmets.

After 1741, the Tlingit were visited by a procession of Russian, English, American and French naval expeditions. In 1799, the Russians built a fort at Sitka, which was subsequently destroyed by the Tlingit and rebuilt in 1804. Another Russian outpost was established in 1802 at Wrangell. A serious smallpox epidemic killed hundreds of Tlingit from 1836 through 1840. Around 1854, the Chilkat Tlingit destroyed a Hudson's Bay Company post in the Yukon valley, considering the post an infringement on their territory.

In 1867, the United States bought Alaska from the Russians. Gold strikes in the 1870s and 1896-97 brought miners flooding into the area, bringing disease and alcohol. The Tlingit found wage work in mines and salmon canneries.

In 1912, the Alaska Native Brotherhood was founded by the Tlingit, becoming a strong force for acculturation, as well as for Indian rights. In its early years, this organization opposed such traditional customs as potlatches, an attitude which was reversed by the 1970s. In the late 1970s, there were more than 9,000 Tlingit living in their traditional area, with concentrations in such towns as Klawak, Kake, Yakutat, Hoonah, Wrangell, Klukwan and Sitka. Fishing and hunting were still important economic activities.

BIBLIOGRAPHY: Krause, Aurel. *The Tlingit Indians.* Seattle: University of Washington Press, 1956. (1885); Laguna, Frederica de. "Under Mount Saint Elias: The History and Culture of the Yakutat

Tlingit." *Smithsonian Contributions to Anthropology.* vol. 7, 1972; Oberg, Kalervo. *The Social Economy of the Tlingit Indians.* Seattle: University of Washington Press, 1973.

TOLOWA: a northwestern California group occupying the Pacific coast region from the Oregon boundary south to Wilson Creek in the early 19th century, numbering about 2,400 at that time. In the late 1970s, the Tolowa descendants, numbering perhaps 200, were intermixed with both Indian and white population. The Tolowa spoke an Athapascan language, as did the nearby Hupa, although the languages were mutually unintelligible.

Prestige among the Tolowa was attained by the acquisition of wealth, the wealthiest man in a village usually being acknowledged as headman. Wealthy men might have several wives. Men often married sisters and sometimes the widow of their brother.

Women could attain status as shamans, who cured the sick by dancing, trances, incantations and sucking out the evil pain. Important religious ceremonies were connected with the catching of the first salmon, smelt or sea lion. When a Tolowa died, his body was removed through a loose plank in the side of the house, wrapped in tule mats and buried along with shell beads and other objects. The Tolowa occupied about eight permanent coastal villages most of the year. Their family houses were of redwood planks, with a central excavated area used for cooking and sleeping quarters for women and children. A ground level ledge around the interior wall was used for storage. The men and adolescent boys slept in the sweathouses, which were also used for gambling, weapon-making and other male activities.

The Tolowa were more dependent on the sea for food than their neighbors, the Karok, Yurok and Hupa. Smelt and sea lions were important, as were edible seaweed, shellfish and eggs of various shore birds. In earlier times, the Tolowa made 40-foot redwood canoes for offshore fishing and sea lion hunting expeditions. In autumn, the Tolowa moved inland to fish for salmon and to gather acorns. Women took charge of drying and storing the food and transporting it back to the permanent villages on the coast.

Tolowa crafts included making wild iris fishnets, tule mats and basketry of various vegetable fibers. Various tools were made of stone, bone and wood. Material wealth was reckoned in such treasures as large obsidian knives, head-dresses of redheaded woodpecker scalps, and necklaces of dentalium shell beads.

In the late 18th century, according to Tolowa tradition, one of their villages was wiped out by an epidemic contracted from European explorers. Further contact with whites was limited until about 1850, when the California gold rush reached the area. The 1870 Ghost Dance

movement reached the Tolowa in 1872, and was popular for about 10 years. In subsequent years, the Tolowa population was greatly reduced by measles and cholera. They were relocated on small reservations and rancherias, where they intermarried with other Indian groups. By the late 1970s, few traditionally oriented Tolowa remained.

BIBLIOGRAPHY: Drucker, Philip. "The Tolowa and their Southwestern Oregon Kin." *University of California Publications in American Anthropology and Ethnology,* vol. 36, 1937.

Delia, a Tolowa woman, Lake Earl, California, 1901.
Smithsonian Institution
National
Anthropological
Archives

A Tonkawa drum.   Smithsonian Institution

TONKAWA: a nomadic tribe of hunters who roamed over east central Texas until moving to Indian Territory (Oklahoma) in the late 19th century. They numbered about 1,600 in the late 17th century but, by the late 1970s, only about 40 Tonkawa remained on a reservation in Oklahoma.

They spoke a language now classed as a separate, Tonkawan, linguistic family. The tribal name may mean "they all stay together." Historically the tribe consisted of a score of autonomous bands living principally on game such as deer, bear and buffalo. This diet was supplemented with seeds, nuts, roots, acorns, herbs and prickly pear, as well as fish, shellfish and rattlesnake meat.

The Tonkawa worshipped numerous deities, religious customs keeping them from eating wolf or coyote. There is strong evidence that the Tonkawa engaged in cannibalism, as did some other tribes of this area.

The Tonkawa lacked a social or political cohesiveness. Their scattered villages of skin tipis were highly portable and were moved frequently in the continual search for game and food. The Tonkawa were noted as swift runners, expert bowmen and horsemen. In a region of shifting alliances, they were frequently at war with the Apache or Comanche.

In warfare the men wore protective hide vests and feathered helmets, carried hide shields and painted themselves with red, green, yellow and black paints. Both men and women tattooed and painted their bodies. The women cut their hair short and the men wore it long, braided down the back. Earrings and pendants were worn as ornaments.

The buffalo were of great importance to the Tonkawa, being a source of food and many other necessities. The horns were used for spoons and cups, tendons for thread and bowstrings, the hooves for glue, the tail hair for rope, and the hide for saddles, bridles, shields, shirts, tents, footwear and blankets. As the Comanche gradually cut the Tonkawa off from the buffalo, they relied increasingly on deer.

The Tonkawa fought sporadically with the Spanish. They later allied themselves with the U.S. in fighting against the Comanche.

When Texas voted to deport all its Indians, the Tonkawa moved to a reservation in Indian Territory (now Oklahoma). There about half the remaining 300 were killed in a raid by other Indian tribes in 1862.

In the late 1970s, the Tonkawa numbered about 40, living on or near a reservation of 481 acres in Kay County, Oklahoma.

BIBLIOGRAPHY: Jones, William Kirkland. *Notes on the History and Material Culture of the Tonkawa Indians.* Washington: Smithsonian Press, 1969.

TSIMSHIAN: a Northwest Coast group located along the Nass and Skeena rivers and intervening coast and islands in western British Columbia, numbering about 8,500 in 1835. In the late 1970s, there were more than 9,000 Tsimshian located in British Columbia and Alaska. The Tsimshian language was a member of the Penutian language family.

They were divided into three groups, each speaking a different dialect: the Tsimshian proper, located along the coast and islands and lower Skeena River; the Niska, located along the Nass River; and the Gitskan, located along the upper Skeena River. These were subdivided into numerous autonomous local groups, centered about a village or villages and sometimes referred to as tribes.

Socially, the Tsimshian were divided into four phratries: Eagle, Wolf, Raven (Frog-Raven among the Gitksan) and Killer Whale (Fireweed among the Gitksan). Each person belonged to the phratry of his mother and was restricted from marrying inside his phratry. The phratries were composed of lineages, or groups of families related to each other through the female line. Each lineage controlled a defined territory and owned

A Tsimshian animal bowl.   Smithsonian Institution

such inherited property as houses, totem poles, fishing banks, berry patches, beaches, ceremonies, songs, dances and names. Lineage heads, usually the oldest male, were in charge of ceremonies and food gathering activities.

Marriages were contracted with an exchange of gifts between the families, and the couple went to live with the husband's family. At puberty, wealthy girls were secluded for several months to a year, others for a lesser period. Adolescent boys sought guardian spirits, which usually appeared to them in a dream, vision or trance after following a regimen of bathing and fasting in remote places. Shamans had several guardian spirits which aided them in diagnosing and curing illness. Tsimshian mythology included numerous spirits and supernatural beings, such as the tricksters Raven, Mink and Blue Jay.

The abundant food supply gave the Tsimshian leisure time in winter to devote to arts, crafts and the development of a complex ceremonial life. They had secret societies, borrowed from the Kwakiutl, into which members were initiated in winter ceremonies. The most important ceremonies were potlatches held as memorials to the dead and in connection with such important events as marriage and name-giving. The purpose was to enhance the prestige of a particular lineage by the ceremonial distribution of gifts and display of the wealth and privileges of that lineage. The potlatch lasted several days at least, and included feasting, dancing, singing and theatrics as a prelude to the gift giving.

Slaves, obtained as captives in war or bought from other tribes, were an important gift, in later times replaced by blankets and money.

The Tsimshian built large multi-family cedar plank houses with gabled roofs. Along the interior walls were platforms used as beds, seats and storage. Carved or painted wooden chests were also used as storage, and dried food was hung from the rafters. Each family had its own cooking fire. Forts were occasionally built on hills or promontories. At summer fishing and hunting sites, they sometimes lived in temporary lean-tos.

Salmon was the most important food, and smokehouses were built at their fishing sites to preserve the salmon for winter use. Silver salmon, sockeye salmon, humpback salmon, herring, cod, halibut and candlefish (eulachon) were all caught, the latter prized for its oil. Seals and sea lions were also harpooned for their oil. Among the land game were bear, deer and mountain goat. The women gathered berries, shellfish, seaweed, greens, roots and crabapples.

For sea transportation, the Tsimshian used long cedar canoes, usually obtained from the Haida. Along the rivers, smaller dugouts, bark canoes and rafts were used. Snowshoes were used in winter.

The Tsimshian were expert woodworkers, carving intricate totem poles with fantastic animal and human faces as memorials to the dead. Other wood items included masks, food dishes, boxes and other containers. They also cold-hammered native copper into tools and ceremonial items. Tsimshian women were the originators of Chilkat robes, which were made from mountain goat wool and yellow cedar bark, woven into black, yellow, blue-green and white designs representing lineage crests. Clothing for both men and women included skin aprons, cedar bark robes and conical spruce basketry hats, supplemented by fur or skin robes in winter. Adornment included ear ornaments and labrets (lip plugs) for women.

In the late 18th century, the upriver Tsimshian groups began moving closer to the coast to trade with Russian, American and English fur traders. In 1834, Hudson's Bay Company built Fort Simpson trading post on the Tsimshian peninsula. Many Tsimshian dismantled their winter homes and rebuilt them on either side of the post, forming a settlement which numbered 2,300 by 1857.

In 1862, the missionary William Duncan led a group of 50 Tsimshian to Metlakatla, where they established a new town complete with cooperative store, sawmill, boatbuilding plant and a schooner so the Tsimshian could trade directly with Victoria. In 1881, Duncan was dismissed in a disagreement with church authorities. He obtained permission to settle his colony in Alaska, and in 1887, he and 825 Tsimshian moved to Annette Island, where they established New Metlakatla. In 1891, the U.S. Congress set aside the Annette Island Reserve.

The Tsimshian remaining in British Columbia were brought into closer contact with the outside world by discovery of gold in 1867, and by the completion of the railroad between Prince Rupert and Hazelton. By the late 19th century, their sea-going canoes had been replaced by European-style sailboats. These were in turn replaced by motorboats in the mid-20th century, although dugout canoes were still used in the interior.

In the late 1970s, there were more than 1,000 Tsimshian located on the 86,000-acre Annette Island Reserve, where the salmon industry and logging were important to the economy. The Tsimshian in British Columbia numbered more than 8,000, grouped in about 16 bands. Fishing and hunting were still very important.

BIBLIOGRAPHY: Garfield, Viola E. "Tsimshian Clan and Society." *University of Washington Publications in Anthropology.* vol. 7, 1939; Smith, Marian W., ed. "The Tsimshian: Their Arts and Music." *Publications of the American Ethnological Society.* no. 18, 1951.

TUBATULABAL: a central California group located in the southern Sierra Nevada foothills in the early 19th century, when they probably numbered between 500 and 1,000. In the late 1970s, there remained about 50 Tubatulabal living in California.

In their language, Tubatulabal means "pine nut eaters." Their language of which few speakers remained in the late 1970s, is a subgroup of the Uto-Aztecan linguistic family.

The Tubatulabal were divided into three autonomous bands: Pahkanapil, Palagewan and Bankalachi. Each band was headed by a *timiwal,* or chief, who was chosen by the oldest males. The *timiwal* arbitrated disputes, represented the band in dealings with other bands or groups, and organized war parties.

The Tubatulabal believed in numerous supernatural spirits, often in animal form. In Tubatulabal mythology, Coyote was a culture hero and trickster. The jimsonweed was believed to have special powers and was used by shamans in effecting cures. Other curing methods included singing, dancing, smoking tobacco and sucking out disease-causing objects. Shamans, who inherited their powers, could be either male or female, but only the former could cure. The power of female shamans was confined to witchery.

When a Tubatulabal died, his body was wrapped in tule mats and buried in a shallow grave. Within two years, a mourning ceremony was held, in which a tule image of the deceased was destroyed, along with most of his possessions.

In winter, domed houses of brush and mud were used, with tule mats and skins serving as bedding. In warmer months, open-sided brush shelters were used. Most villages also had a brush and mud sweathouse.

Acorns, pine nuts, and fish were the staple foods, but a wide variety of other foods supplemented the diet. The women gathered seeds, berries, roots and bulbs, while the men hunted deer, bear, antelope, mountain sheep, mountain lion and small game, with bow and arrow, traps and snares. They caught fish by driving them into corrals built of stones placed in the river. Two men inside the corral caught the fish and threw them on the bank.

Tubatulabal craftwork included fine basketry, made by both the coiled and twined methods, and pottery, produced from a local red clay. Deer-skin was tanned to make moccasins, vests, aprons and sleeveless coats for colder weather.

Beginning in the late 18th century, the Tubatulabal came into contact with whites while on trading trips to the coast. By the mid-19th century, miners, ranchers and settlers had begun taking over their lands. In 1893, survivors of the Pahkanapil and Palagewan bands were allotted lands in the Kern and South Fork Kern valleys. Epidemics of measles and influenza struck in 1902 and 1918, respectively, further reducing their population.

In the late 1970s, the remaining Tubatulabal, mostly located in the Kern valley of California, lived lives similar to those of their non-Indian neighbors.

BIBLIOGRAPHY: Voegelin, Erminie. "Tubatulabal Ethnography." *University of California Anthropological Records.* vol. 2, 1938.

TUNICA: a tribe formerly located on the lower Yazoo River in Mississippi. They numbered about 2,000 by the late 17th century, but, by the late 1970s there were only a few surviving members, living in the area of Marksville, Louisiana.

The Tunica spoke a language unrelated to any other linguistic family. Tunican speakers included also the Yazoo, Koroa and a few other tribes. The last Tunican speakers died out in the 20th century. The name has been translated as meaning "those who are the people."

The Tunica were mainly an agricultural people, although they also hunted deer and buffalo. When persimmons were in season these became almost a staple food, being baked into a persimmon bread. A division of labor was observed in which the men did all the planting, harvesting and dressing of skins. Women performed all the indoor work, including making a fine, glazed pottery and an excellent fabric out of mulberry bark.

The Tunica built their temples on top of mounds and placed earthen figures inside. They celebrated the Green Corn feast and worshipped the sun, among their deities. Their dead were buried in the ground with their heads toward the east. Four days of fasting and mourning were followed

Smithsonian Institution National Anthropological Archives

Tunica Indians: Buffalo Tamer, with three Natchez scalps. With him are the widow and the son, Jacob, of the previous chief, killed by the Natchez in 1731. A drawing by A. de Batz, New Orleans, 1732.

by a ritual cleansing in the river. They practiced tattooing and head deformation, and the women blackened their teeth.

The Tunica supported the French in the 18th century, but fought with the Chickasaw, Alabama and Houma tribes. By the 19th century, they were dispersed, some to Oklahoma and Texas and the rest to the Marksville area where a few Tunica of mixed blood still lived in the late 1970s.

BIBLIOGRAPHY: Haas, Mary Rosamond. *Tunica Texts.* Berkeley: University of California, 1950.

TUSCARORA: a tribe who joined the Iroquois Confederacy in the early 18th century, after having been driven from their homes in North Carolina. Numbering about 5,000 in 1600, the Tuscarora occupied extensive lands along the Roanoke, Tar, Pamlico, and Neuse rivers. In the late 1970s about 600 Tuscarora lived on or near the Tuscarora Reservation in Niagara County, New York and another 700 lived on the Six Nations Reserve in Ontario, Canada.

They spoke an Iroquoian language, referring to themselves as Skaroo'ren meaning "hemp gatherers." By the 1970s, the Tuscarora language was reportedly quite different from that spoken by the tribe when it lived in North Carolina. It was also mutually unintelligible with Mohawk, the language spoken at gatherings of the Iroquois Confederacy.

Both the language and culture of the Tuscarora underwent changes in the course of their migration from North Carolina to New York. The earlier culture was modified to suit their new life in the north as members of the Iroquois League.

In North Carolina, the Tuscarora believed that the soul was immortal and, after death, found its way to a paradise somewhere in the west. In early times, they buried their dead on scaffolds and placed the dried bones in a village bonehouse. Later, coffins were made of woven rushes, cane, or bark and placed in the ground. Spring planting and harvest festivals were held, as well as war and peace celebrations.

In the north, the Tuscarora forgot their old religion and were gradually Christianized. In the 20th century there was a growing interest in the Longhouse Religion of the Iroquois begun by the Seneca chief, Handsome Lake, in the early 19th century.

In the south, the Tuscarora built round lodges of poles covered with cypress or cedar bark. In the north, they adopted the Iroquois custom of building multi-family longhouses divided into compartments, each with its own cooking fire, beds, and storage area.

Both before and after migrating north, corn was the staple food of the Tuscarora, supplemented by beans, squash, and such nuts, fruits and berries that could be gathered. The men fished the streams and hunted deer, bear, rabbit, raccoon, partridge, pheasant, geese and ducks.

In North Carolina, the Tuscarora men made cypress log canoes, bows of black locust, hoes from animal bones, and dishes and spoons from the wood of the tulip or gum trees. The women made clay pots for cooking

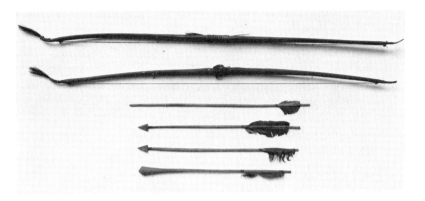

Tuscarora bows and arrows.   Smithsonian Institution

and food storage, clothing of animal skins, and wove mats and baskets from bark and Indian hemp. By the time they had settled in New York, many of these items had been replaced by European trade goods and the skills necessary to make them had been forgotten.

Before living in North Carolina, the Tuscarora originated somewhere to the north. Just when they migrated south is not known, but a standard guess is about 1400. In North Carolina, they fought at various times with the Catawba, Creek and Cherokee, the larger tribes of that area. As white colonists poured into the Carolinas, all of the tribes suffered greatly, having their lands taken from them, being cheated by traders, and being sold into slavery. They were also reduced in number by smallpox and other diseases to which they had no immunity. Between 1711 and 1713, the Tuscarora and their Indian allies—the Coree, Pamlico and Machapunga and other tribes—waged a war of desperation on the settlers. Neoheroka, a palisaded town of the Tuscarora, was finally destroyed with a loss of about 950 Indians. Totally demoralized, the Tuscarora sought the protection of the Five Nations Iroquois Confederacy, who invited them to come northward.

In 1722 the Tuscarora, sponsored by the Oneida, officially joined the Iroquois Confederacy, thereafter known as the Six Nations, and adopted much of the Iroquois culture and organization. They were organized into eight matrilineal clans similar to those of the other Iroquois tribes. Women had the power of nominating chiefs of the clan, subject to the approval of the clan and the council of chiefs or lords. Some of the Tuscarora stayed in Pennsylvania awhile before finally moving to New York, while others attempted to remain in North Carolina. Not until 1802 was the migration complete.

A Tutchone carved wooden fish, (the Dog Salmon), with the carved figure of an Indian inside it, from Sitka. A watercolor representation of the original carving, "made by an Indian from the interior," (1878).

The Tuscarora and Oneida, who wished to remain neutral during the American Revolution, were attacked by the other tribes of the Confederacy. Tuscarora who sided with the British were given lands on the Six Nations Reserve in Brant County, Ontario. Those who remained neutral were granted the lands they already occupied in New York state, which had been given them by the Seneca.

In the late 1970s the Tuscarora Reservation included 5,700 acres, nine miles northeast of Niagara Falls. Life on the reservation was similar to that of the surrounding white community.

BIBLIOGRAPHY: Johnson, F. Roy. *The Tuscaroras.* 2 vols. Murfreesboro, North Carolina: Johnson Publishing Company, 1967-68.

TUTCHONE: an Athapascan tribe living along the Yukon River, from Fort Selkirk to the Deer River, in Yukon Territory, Canada, numbering around 1,100 in the late 19th century. In the 1970s, there were probably several hundred Tutchone, living in their traditional area.

The Tutchone spoke a language of the Athapascan language family, and called themselves "crow people." Their language, culture, and probably their history, was similar to that of the Kutchin (*q.v.*). Some authors have identified them as a Kutchin tribe, referring to them as the Tutchone-Kutchin.

TUTELO: a small tribe of the eastern Siouan linguistic family, who lived in Virginia, along the upper James and Rappahanock rivers. By the late 1970s, they were extinct as a tribe, although a few Tutelo descendants could be found living among the Cayuga in Canada. The Tutelo were closely related to several other small Siouan tribes of Virginia, including the Saponi, Keyauwee, and Occaneechi, which together numbered about 750 in 1701. Tutelo, and its variant forms, was a term applied to the southeastern Siouan tribes by the Iroquois.

The Tutelo were noted for a particular mortuary custom known as the spirit adoption ceremony, in which a living person was adopted by the deceased person's family. The adoptee, the same age and sex as the deceased, was given the clothes of the deceased and took on his privileges and responsibilities. Through the adoptee, the spirit of the deceased was brought back to life for one night during the ceremony, so that he could be honored and feasted by his family, before starting his journey for the land of the dead.

When the Tutelo lived in Virginia, their subsistence was based mainly on gathering of wild foods and hunting buffalo, elk, bear and other game.

In the 17th century, the Tutelo were engaged in warfare with the Powhatan tribes of Virginia. In the latter part of that century, they came under repeated attack from the tribes of the Five Nations Iroquois Confederacy, particularly the Seneca. The Tutelo moved south into North Carolina and later back into Virginia, still under attack by the Iroquois.

In 1722, at a council in Albany, peace was made between the Iroquois and the southeastern Sioux tribes. Soon afterward, the Tutelo and Saponi moved to Shamokin on the Susquehanna River in Pennsylvania, under the protection of the Iroquois. In 1753, the Tutelo were accepted into the Confederacy along with the Nanticoke and Delaware, being allowed to attend meetings of the Great Council of the Confederacy as observers.

In 1771, the Tutelo moved to lands given them by the Cayuga three miles below Cayuga Lake. When the Iroquois sided with the English in the American Revolution, the towns of the Cayuga and Tutelo were destroyed in a raid by Gen. Sullivan. Most of the Tutelo moved to Canada with the Cayuga and settled on the Six Nations Reserve on the Grand River. They were almost totally wiped out by cholera epidemics in 1832 and 1848. The survivors were absorbed by the Cayuga, and the Tutelo language died out in the late 19th century.

BIBLIOGRAPHY: Speck, Frank G. *The Tutelo Spirit Adoption Ceremony.* Harrisburg: Pennsylvania Historical Commission, 1942.

TWANA: a Northwest Coast group located along the Hood Canal in northwestern Washington, numbering about 1,000 in the late 18th century. In the late 1970s, there were about 450 Twana living on the Skokomish Reservation in Mason County, Washington. The Twana spoke a language of the Coastal division of the Salishan language family, and referred to themselves as Tuadhu.

They had about nine autonomous winter villages, the largest being Skokomish, at the mouth of the Skokomish River. Socially the Twana were divided into three classes: nobles, commoners and slaves. There were no formal political officials, but the ranking noble-class male had considerable prestige and influence. Rank was based on wealth and lineage.

A wealthy man often had multiple wives, who were frequently sisters. Marriage was contracted by the payment of a bride price to the bride's family, which was later repaid in reciprocal gifts to the groom's family. Each person usually married outside his village, and the couple lived with the groom's family.

In winter, the Twana had leisure time to devote to their ceremonial and religious life. All-important was the acquisition of a guardian spirit, which would give an individual power in the form of luck, skills and achievement. Adolescent boys were encouraged to seek their guardian spirits through a quest which included ritual purification, physical toughening, fasting and visiting remote places. Shamans had several guardian spirits who enabled them to cure the sick and perform magic. Spirit dances, accompanied by drums and rattles, were among the most important Twana ceremonies. Other ceremonies included First Salmon rites and potlatches, in which a wealthy host distributed gifts and displayed his inherited wealth and privileges.

The Twana buried their dead the day after death, removing the body through the side wall. The rich were buried in canoes set on posts five or six feet above the ground. Widows cut their hair, and a memorial feast was held, at which the possessions of the deceased were given away.

Twana villages were composed of large, multi-family cedar plank houses with gabled roofs, as well as smaller houses with single-pitched roofs. Sleeping platforms along the wall were covered with rush mats, and there was a fire pit for each family. Each village usually had a large gabled building used for potlatches and other gatherings. In summer, they left their permanent villages to hunt, fish and gather food, living in temporary rectangular dwellings of cattail mats over a pole frame.

The Twana lived amidst an abundant food supply, with salmon the staple food. King, silver, humpback, and dog salmon, as well as steelhead trout, halibut and cod, were caught with spears, weirs and dip nets. Next in importance were seals, taken with harpoons and nets. They gathered various mollusks and hunted waterfowl at night, using a small fire on the stern of the canoe. They also took elk, deer, black bear, beaver and muskrat with bow and arrow, snares and pitfalls. The women gathered shellfish, roots, berries, nuts, greens and camas bulbs. Surplus food was dried or smoked and stored for the winter.

The Twana made five types of cedar canoes, sometimes adding a sail of rush mats. Two canoes were sometimes connected by a platform to carry heavy loads. Snowshoes were used by hunters and packbaskets were used for carrying. Cedar bark clothing was supplemented in cold weather with animal fur blankets, buckskin clothing, moccasins, mittens and goat hair blankets obtained in trade. Adornment included ear ornaments and face paint for ceremonies.

The Twana engaged in considerable trade with their neighbors, exchanging baskets, furs and food for slaves, whale meat, dentalium shells, sea otter pelts and goat skin blankets. They were frequently raided by the Kwakiutl and other groups. The Twana developed close relations with the Klallam, intermarrying and adopting some Klallam ceremonies.

Between 1790 and 1850, contact with Europeans was essentially limited to trade. In 1850, settlers began entering Twana territory in numbers, and after the 1855 Treaty of Point-no-Point, the Twana were placed on the Skokomish Reservation. The Indian Shaker religion became popular after 1882. In the late 1970s, about 450 Twana lived on or near the 5,000-acre reservation.

BIBLIOGRAPHY: Elmendorf, William W. *Structure of Twana Culture.* New York: Garland Publishing Inc., 1974.

TWO KETTLE: a small subdivision of the Teton Dakota, located along the Cheyenne, Moreau and Grand Rivers of South Dakota, in the mid-19th century, numbering about 800 at that time. Their tribal name Oohenonpa meant "two boilings," hence the popular name Two Kettle. In the late 1970s, Two Kettle descendants were mixed with other Dakota on the Cheyenne River and Rosebud reservations of South Dakota. (See also *Teton* and *Dakota.*)

UMATILLA: a Sahaptian tribe located along the Umatilla and Columbia rivers in Oregon in the late 18th century, numbering, together with the neighboring Wallawalla, about 1,600 at that time. In the late 1970s, Umatilla descendants were among the more than 1,000 Indians of several tribes located on or near the Umatilla Reservation in northeastern Oregon.

The Umatilla spoke a language of the Sahaptian division of the Penutian language family, and were culturally similar to the other Sahaptian tribes, including the Nez Perce, Cayuse, Wallawalla and Yakima (*q.q.v.*).

By the mid-19th century, the Umatilla and other neighboring tribes were hard hit by smallpox and other diseases brought to their area by trappers, traders, miners and settlers. In 1855, the Sahaptian tribes were forced to cede their lands to the United States in exchange for reservations.

In the late 1970s, the 245,800-acre Umatilla Reservation near Pendleton was the home of more than 1,000 Umatilla, Wallawalla and Cayuse.

The Confederated Tribes of the Umatilla Reservation took an active role each year in the Pendleton Roundup, a world-famous rodeo, Indian encampment and pageant.

BIBLIOGRAPHY: Planning Support Group, United States Bureau of Indian Affairs. *The Confederated Tribes of the Umatilla Indian Reservation.* Billings, Montana, 1976.

UMPQUA: a small Oregon coast tribe located along the North Umpqua River in the mid-19th century. At that time, their population, greatly reduced by epidemics, was estimated at about 400. By the 1970s, they were virtually extinct as a tribe, although a very few Umpqua descendants remained. The Umpqua were one of more than ten small tribes in the area, speaking languages of the Athapascan language family. Their name has been variously translated as "thunder" or "high and low water."

Little is known of their social organization. Their winter villages consisted of semisubterranean circular dwellings, constructed of poles covered with either cedar planks or slabs of cedar bark. Summer houses were covered with woven mats or skins. They buried their dead in a

Little Chief, an Umatilla.
The National Archives

"Princess
Umpqua,"
of the Umpqua
tribe,
circa 1900.

Smithsonian Institution
National
Anthropological
Archives

sitting position, encased in cedar bark, and burial houses of cedar planks
were constructed over the graves.

Umpqua economy was based on fishing, hunting and gathering. The
men caught salmon by netting them from fishing platforms as well as by
using spears, seines and weirs. The women cut and dried the salmon,
some of which they pulverized and mixed with dried berries and fat, to
make a fish pemmican.

The women also gathered an assortment of berries and acorns, as well
as camas bulbs, which they dug with digging sticks. The men hunted elk,
deer and small game, using pitfalls, snares and bow and arrow. Bows
were made of yew, and arrows were tipped with obsidian.

Between 1836 and 1852, the Hudson's Bay Company maintained a
trading post at Fort Umpqua, which the tribe frequented, although they
were never heavily engaged in the fur trade. Settlers began moving into
the valley during this period. The Umpqua and other tribes in the area
were so reduced by smallpox and other epidemics that they provided little
resistance. In 1855-56, the Umpqua were moved to Grande Ronde Reservation, where they dwindled to less than 100 by the late 19th century.

BIBLIOGRAPHY: Bakken, Lavola J. *Land of the North Umpquas.*
Grants Pass, Oregon: Te-Cum-Tom Publications, 1973.

UTE: a powerful Basin tribe occupying western Colorado and eastern Utah in the early 19th century, numbering about 4,500 at that time. In the late 1970s, about 4,000 Ute were located on three reservations—two in southwestern Colorado and one in northeastern Utah. The languages of the Ute, Southern Paiute and Chemehuevi belong to the Plateau Shoshonean division of the Uto-Aztecan language family. The Ute referred to themselves as Nunt'z, meaning "the people."

Before the Ute acquired horses in the 18th century, they were organized into small hunting and gathering groups consisting usually of a single extended family. With the advent of horses, larger bands formed for purposes of communal buffalo hunting and raiding. Eventually seven autonomous bands emerged as the Ute confederacy: Uncompahgre (or Tabeguache), Mouache, Capote, Weminuche, Uintah, Yampa or Parianuch. Family groups continued to have their own leadership, but each band has a chief and council.

Shamans, who derived their power from dreams, could control the weather and cure the sick, using drum, rattles and a medicine kit of herbs and paraphernalia. Ute ceremonies included the Bear Dance and later the Sun Dance. They had musical instruments such as flute, rasp and drums, and were noted for the excellence of their singers and drummers.

Polygamy was practiced, usually consisting of a man marrying sisters or the widow of his brother. When a person died, his body was wrapped in buckskin and placed in a rock crevice, with the head toward the west. His possessions were burned or buried, and his horses were killed or the mane and tail cut. Mourners cut their hair and dressed in ragged clothing.

In early times, the Ute used two types of primitive brush shelters and conical pole-frame shelters, covered with juniper bark or tule. When they became buffalo hunters, they began using buffalo skin tipis, which were made and set up by the women and decorated with painted designs by the men. The families, and later bands, gathered in sheltered areas in the winter, and split up to hunt small game and gather wild foods in spring and summer.

Buffalo were hunted communally in the fall, although not all Ute ever acquired horses or became buffalo hunters. After 1830, the buffalo had virtually disappeared from Ute territory, so hunt leaders led the hunters north to Wyoming. Besides food, the buffalo provided tipis, robes and other clothing, glue, containers, bone for tools, sinew bowstrings and numerous other items.

Plant food gathering remained an important part of the economy, especially seeds collected with seedbeaters and carrying baskets. They also collected pine nuts, yampa, strawberries, blackberries, raspberries and grasshoppers. Elk were tracked in deep snow with snowshoes, antelope were driven over low cliffs and rabbits were hunted with throwing sticks, or driven into long nets. Deer, bear, beaver, ducks and sage hen were also hunted. Coyote, wolf and wildcat were sometimes taken for their furs, but not eaten. Baby eaglets were taken from their nests and raised for their feathers.

They made bows of cedar, chokecherry or sheephorn, as well as flint knives and buffalo skin shields. Other crafts included making of numerous basketry items and pottery cooking vessels and water jars. Cups and ladles were made of horn and sleeping mats were woven of tule. The Ute had finely-tanned buckskins, which they traded or used for clothing. Other clothing was made of twined sagebrush bark, and blankets were made of rabbit and other skins. Men wore beaver or weasel caps in winter and rawhide eye shields for bright sun. Face painting, tattooing and ear ornaments were all used for adornment.

In 1776, a Spanish expedition chronicled by Father Silvestre de Escalante passed through Ute territory. The following years brought slave traders, trappers, mountain men, fur traders and miners to the area. Ranchers and settlers soon followed, bringing about confrontations between whites and Indians. Livestock found grazing on former Ute lands were considered fair game by Ute raiders. The Ute also fought the Comanche along their common border.

In 1863, the United States government called a council of the Ute bands, to convince them to move west of the continental divide. Ouray, an Uncompahgre chief who spoke English and Spanish as well as several Indian dialects, was made spokesman for the Ute. In 1868, they agreed to move, providing that Colorado, west of the divide, was reserved for the Ute. This agreement was cut short with the discovery of gold in the San Juan Mountains, which brought miners flooding into the area. The western Colorado lands were ceded by treaty in 1873.

In 1877, the Southern Ute Reservation was established along the Colorado-New Mexico border, for the Mouache, the Capote and the Weminuche bands. The first two merged to form the Southern Ute Tribe, taking allotments on the eastern part of the reservation. The Weminuche, calling themselves the Ute Mountain Tribe, took the western part of the reservation and became stockraisers.

The Uintah, Uncompahgre, Yampa and Parianuch were assigned to the Uintah and Ouray Reservation in northwestern Utah, becoming known as the Northern Ute. In 1950, the Confederated Ute Tribes won a 31 million dollar judgement against the U.S. government for lands taken, the money being divided between the Northern, Southern and Mountain Ute.

In the late 1970s, oil and gas leases and stockraising were the major sources of tribal income, which was used greatly to improve living conditions on the three reservations. Extensive tourist facilities were being built, including campgrounds, motels, restaurants, museums and craft shops. The Ute language was still widely spoken, and the Bear Dance and Sun Dance were performed annually.

BIBLIOGRAPHY: Opler, Marvin Kaufmann. *The Southern Ute of Colorado*. New York: D. Appleton-Century Co., 1940; Smith, Anne M. *Ethnography of the Northern Utes*. Santa Fe: Museum of New Mexico, 1974.

WACO: *See* WICHITA.

WAHPEKUTE: one of the seven divisions of the Dakota, located in northern Minnesota in the late 17th century, numbering about 800 at that time. In the 1970s, there were Wahpekute and Mdewakanton descendants living together on reservations in Nebraska, South Dakota and Minnesota.

The language of the Wahpekute belongs to the Santee or Eastern division of the Dakota language, which is a member of the Siouan linguistic family. The Santee Dakota also include the Mdewakanton, Wahpeton and Sisseton tribes. Wahpekute means "shooters among the leaves." Wahpekute culture was similar to that of the Mdewakanton, with whom they were closely associated.

In the late 17th century, the Wahpekute along with the other Santee Dakota groups, were encountered by French explorers in the Mille Lacs, Minnesota region. After the Santee were driven out of that area by the Ojibwa in about 1750, the Wahpekute became nomadic, living at times on both sides of the Minnesota River and on the Des Moines, Cannon and Blue Earth rivers. On their buffalo hunts, they ranged from the Mississippi to the Missouri River.

In the 1840s, a rivalry between chiefs resulted in a band led by Wandesapa leaving the main group. In 1857, the renegade band, led by Inkpaduta, killed a number of white settlers in Minnesota and Iowa, resulting in greatly increased friction between the Santee and the settlers.

By the 1837 and 1851 treaties, the Santee had to cede all of their Minnesota and Iowa lands, except for a reservation along the Minnesota River. The Mdewakanton and Wahpekute occupied the Lower Agency of the reservation and the Sisseton and Wahpeton the Upper Agency. Confined to the reservation, the Santee found themselves at the mercy of dishonest traders, incompetent government agents, and squatters. Numerous incidents finally led to an uprising in 1862 on the Lower Agency. The Upper Agency tribes declared themselves neutral, while the dissidents were led by a Mdewakanton chief, Little Crow. Neither the Mdewakanton nor Wahpekute gave unanimous support for the uprising, however, so it was ended within a few months.

About 38 Santee were executed by hanging, and the government expropriated all Santee lands and property. Many fled to the western

Dakota tribes and to Canada. The rest of the Mdewakanton and Wahpekute were rounded up and herded about, before finally being settled at Crow Creek, South Dakota. Hundreds died of starvation, illness and hardship during this time.

In 1866, they were moved to the Santee Reservation in Nebraska. Drought, locust plagues and smallpox epidemics were some of the conditions faced in the early years of the reservation. In the 1870s, several hundred left the Santee Reservation to settle on the Big Sioux River near Flandreau, South Dakota. Some of the Flandreau group eventually drifted back to Minnesota to join other groups of Santee.

In the late 1970s, Mdewakanton descendants made up the majority and Wahpekute the minority, on the Santee and Flandreau Reservations, each of which had populations of about 300. They were also represented in the Minnesota Santee communities of Prairie Island, Prior Lake and Birch Coulee.

BIBLIOGRAPHY: Meyer, Roy W. *History of the Santee Sioux.* Lincoln: University of Nebraska Press, 1967.

WAHPETON: one of the seven divisions of the Dakota, located in northern Minnesota in the late 17th century, numbering about 1,200 at that time. In the late 1970s, there were perhaps 2,000 descendants of Wahpeton, living mostly in South Dakota, North Dakota and Minnesota.

The language of the Wahpeton belongs to the Santee, or Eastern, division of the Dakota language, which is a member of the Siouan linguistic family. The Santee Dakota include also the Mdewakanton, Wahpekute and Sisseton. Wahpeton means "dwellers among the leaves."

The Wahpeton were divided into seven bands, each ruled by an hereditary chief and a council. An elite warrior group, the *akitcita,* acted as a sort of police, keeping order during hunts, games, and councils, and acting as messengers and escorts. Religious leadership was provided by both male and female shamans, whose powers included prophesy, curing the sick and forecasting the weather.

The Wahpeton believed in Wakan Tanka, the Great Spirit and creator of the universe, as well as a number of other gods and spirits. They had a secret Medicine Lodge Society, which performed the Medicine Dance several times each year. Drums, deer hoof rattles, whistles and sacred tobacco pipes carved of red stone were important elements of their ceremonies. In early times, the Wahpeton buried their dead, but later they changed to the practice of placing their dead on scaffolds, a custom they may have adopted from the Sisseton.

**Other Day,
a Wahpeton,
(1858).**

Smithsonian Institution
National
Anthropological
Archives

Wahpeton had summer houses of bark on a pole framework, with gabled roofs. Winter houses were smaller hemispherical lodges, covered with mats or skins. Both men and women helped construct houses, while women grew corn, beans, squash and pumpkins.

As the Wahpeton and other Santee tribes moved farther south and west, they relied more on buffalo hunts on the prairies. Hunting of deer, elk and bear was also important, as was the trapping of beaver, muskrat, mink and otter. Wild rice, maple sugar, fruits and berries supplemented the diet.

The Wahpeton made birchbark canoes and wove bags of cedar or basswood fiber. They wove rushes and produced elaborate floral and animal designs in quillwork and later beadwork.

Early French explorers found the Wahpeton and other Santee in the Mille Lacs, Minnesota, area in about 1680. They were almost continually at war with the Ojibwa, who succeeded in pushing them out of the Mille Lacs region by about 1750. Around 1800, the Wahpeton moved to above the mouth of the Minnesota River, and by 1849, they had moved further upriver and were composed of an upper and lower division, totaling about 1,500 in population.

By this time, the press of settlers was so great that the Santee were forced to cede all their Minnesota and Iowa lands in 1837 and 1851. They retained a reservation along the Minnesota River, with the Wahpeton and Sisseton occupying the Upper Agency and the Mdewakanton and Wahpekute the Lower Agency. When an uprising broke out on the Lower Agency in 1862, the Wahpeton and Sisseton tried to remain neutral. After the uprising, however, all the Santee lands and property were confiscated, and many neutrals taken prisoner. Many Wahpeton and other Santee fled to the Plains or Canada.

Around 1867, two reservations were established for the Wahpeton and Sisseton: the Sisseton Reservation, near Lake Traverse in South Dakota, and the Fort Totten Reservation on Devil's Lake between North and South Dakota. Locusts and drought made farming difficult. By 1892, the Sisseton Reservation was divided, with 300,000 acres allotted to tribal members and nearly 600,000 acres opened to homesteaders. Much of the allotted lands have since been sold or leased to non-Indians.

In the late 1970s, Wahpeton and Sisseton were closely connected and intermarried. Wahpeton descendants could also be found on the Santee Reservation in Nebraska, on reserves in Canada, and among the Santee who gradually drifted back to their homelands in Minnesota.

BIBLIOGRAPHY: Black Thunder, Elijah, et al. *Ehanna Woyakapi: History of the Sisseton Wahpeton Sioux Tribe.* Sisseton, South Dakota: Sisseton-Wahpeton Tribe, Inc., 1972.

WAILAKI: an Athapascan group located in northwestern California along the Eel River in the mid-19th century, when they numbered about 2,700. In the late 1970s, they were extinct as a tribe, although a few Wailaki descendants lived on the Round Valley Reservation in Mendocino County, California.

The Wailaki, along with their close neighbors the Mattole, Lassik, Sinkyone and Nongatl, spoke a southern Athapascan language. Wailaki was a Wintu term meaning "north language." The Wailaki had three main subdivisions: the Tsennahkenne (Eel River Wailaki), Bahneko (North Fork Wailaki) and Pitch Wailaki (located further up the North Fork of the Eel River). Within these three subdivisions were at least 19 tribelets, living in more than 95 tiny villages.

A tribelet chief inherited his office from his father and probably held it for life. Chiefs settled disputes, provided food for ceremonial occasions, and were entitled to extra wives.

Wailaki religious beliefs included a creator god known as Ketanagai ("night traveler"). Wailaki shamans reportedly could see and communicate with Ketanagai. There were various types of shamans, both men and women, whose powers included curing the sick, prophesying the future and finding lost souls and other objects. Their techniques included dancing, singing, smoking tobacco, and sucking poisons out of the sick person's body. Wailaki ceremonies included those connected with salmon fishing, acorn gathering and puberty rites for girls. When a Wailaki died, he was buried with his head to the east in a deep grave, which was later piled with stones.

Winter houses·of the Wailaki were circular, with a conical roof, and constructed of slabs of redwood, fir or bark. A cooking fire was located in the center of the excavated floor. The Wailaki also built brush shelters for summer living and sweathouses heated by direct fire.

Acorns and game, including deer and elk, were the major food sources. They made basketry, by both the coil and twining methods, creating such items as containers, bowls, caps and quail traps.

Before the mid-19th century, the Wailaki had little contact with whites, but when they did it was catastrophic. Punitive raids in 1861 and 1862 nearly exterminated them. By the late 1970s, a few Wailaki descendants remained, mixed with other California tribes on the Round Valley Reservation.

BIBLIOGRAPHY: Kroeber, A.L. "Handbook of the Indians of California." *Bureau of American Ethnology Bulletin,* no. 78, 1925.

WALAPAI: a Yuman tribe located near the great bend of the Colorado River in northwestern Arizona in the late 17th century, when they numbered about 700. In the late 1970s, there were about 1,000 Walapai living on the Hualapai Reservation at Peach Springs, Arizona.

The Walapai, meaning "pine tree people," spoke a Yuman language of the Hokan language family. Linguistically and culturally, they were closest to their offshoot, the Havasupai. They were primarily a hunting and gathering people, similar to the Basin tribes in the simplicity of their social, religious and political organization.

There was no tribal chief but, rather, a number of head men who attained respect and prominence in a particular geographical area or within a certain band. The position of head man was sometimes hereditary in the male line, but was more often based on personal appeal and ability as a warrior and orator. They had little authority, their main functions being to advise and exhort their people.

Both male and female shamans, who acquired their power from dreams, performed curing ceremonies, for which service they were paid in buckskins. They sang to the accompaniment of gourd rattles, blew on the patient and sucked out the disease-causing object. Unsuccessful shamans were occasionally killed by the family of the deceased patient. The Walapai cremated their dead, burned the house of the deceased and

**A Walapai
woman with a
tattooed chin,
(in about
the 1880s).**

Smithsonian Institution
National
Anthropological
Archives

killed his horse. In the 19th century, the Walapai adopted the Mohave mourning ceremony, in which a pantomime of warfare was performed in honor of the dead.

The Walapi lived on oval dome-shaped huts of thatch or juniper bark over a pole frame. They also built sweathouses and sunshades. The Walapai engaged in some agriculture, cultivating corn, beans, squash and pumpkins near springs and streams, occasionally using irrigation ditches. The poor soil and arid conditions made them far more dependent on hunting and gathering, however, and they left their permanent villages in spring and summer, to follow the seasonal ripening of the various plant foods.

The women gathered cactus fruit, agave, yucca, pine nuts, honey, quail eggs and a wide variety of seeds, berries and roots. The men held rabbit drives using nets; stalked antelope wearing antelope head disguises; and hunted deer, mountain sheep and small game. Meat was dried and stored in skin bags. Agave was roasted in pits to make sweet, nutritious mescal, which was dried in sheets and stored. Corn was made into mush, soup or bread, and pumpkins were dried in long strips.

The Walapai made an assortment of coiled and twined basketry, including burden baskets, seed beaters, seed parching trays, pitch-covered water bottles and cradle hoods. Simple pottery items included cooking pots, dishes, water jars and clay pipes. They made aprons, shirts and breechclouts from skins, sandals from yucca, and blankets and other clothing from bark fiber and rabbitskin. For adornment, they used red ocher face paint, and the women tattooed their chins. Weapons used by the Walapai in their constant warfare with the Yavapai included mulberry bows, clubs and hide shields.

The ancestors of the Walapai probably entered the southwest by the 13th century, settling along the middle Colorado River and ranging through the Hualapai, Yavapai and Sacramento valleys of present-day Arizona. They were inveterate traders, dealing in Pacific Ocean shells, Havasupai corn and Mohave horses, as well as red ocher, mescal and dressed skins of their own production.

In 1883, the Hualapai Reservation was established in Arizona. In 1970, there were about 1,000 Walapai, mostly full bloods, living on the nearby 1000-acre reservation. The language was still spoken by the older people, and the younger people were learning it in classes at school. The tribal council was composed of an hereditary chief and eight elected

Smithsonian Institution National Anthropological Archives

A Wallawalla Indian, Rosa Paul, standing beside a tipi with her husband and child.

representatives. Timber, livestock, wage work, tourism and the sale of baskets were the main sources of income.

BIBLIOGRAPHY: Kroeber, A.L., ed. "Walapai Ethnography." *Memoirs of the American Anthropological Association.* no. 42, 1935.

WALLAWALLA: a Sahaptian tribe located in Oregon and Washington, along the Wallawalla River and the Columbia River near its confluence with the Snake River, in the late 18th century, numbering together with the Umatilla about 1,600 at that time. In the late 1970s, Wallawalla descendants were among the more than 1,000 Indians of several tribes located on or near the Umatilla Reservation.

The Wallawalla, whose name means "little river," spoke a language of the Sahaptian division of the Penutian language family. They were culturally similar to the other Sahaptian tribes, including the Nez Perce, Cayuse, Umatilla and Yakima (*q.q.v.*).

By the mid-19th century, the Wallawalla and neighboring tribes were hard hit by smallpox and other diseases brought to their area by trappers, traders, miners and settlers. In 1855, the Wallawalla and other Sahaptian tribes were forced to cede their lands to the United States in exchange for reservations.

In the late 1970s, the 245,800-acre Umatilla Reservation near Pendleton was the home of more than 1,000 Umatilla, Wallawalla and Cayuse. The Confederated Tribes of the Umatilla Reservation took an active role each year in the Pendleton Roundup, a world-famous rodeo, Indian encampment and pageant.

BIBLIOGRAPHY: Planning Support Group, United States Bureau of Indian Affairs. *The Confederated Tribes of the Umatilla Indian Reservation.* Billings, Montana, 1976.

WAMPANOAG: a powerful New England tribe which controlled southeastern Massachusetts from Cape Cod to Narraganset Bay, including the islands of Nantucket and Martha's Vineyard. It was their assistance which insured the survival of the Plymouth Bay colony.

The Wampanoag, including the tributary tribes on the islands, numbered about 5,000 in 1600. In the late 1970s, several hundred Wampanoag descendants could be found mostly in the area of Martha's Vineyard. Also known as Pokanokets, the Wampanoag were Algonquian language speakers. Their name meant "eastern people" or "coastal people."

They were ruled by a chief sachem whose office was hereditary. The sachem had absolute power, but usually made decisions on the advice of his sagamores, village chiefs or clan chiefs. Religious leadership was provided by powwows, priests or medicine men, who were in charge of

"King Philip,
grand sachem
of the
Wampanoag.

Smithsonian Institution
National
Anthropological
Archives

curing, improving the weather, interpreting dreams and general inter-
cession with the world of spirits.

The Wampanoag believed in numerous deities, including gods of the
sun, moon, fire and sea. But over all was their supreme deity who lived
somewhere in the west, where the souls of the dead went. The
Wampanoag buried their dead wrapped in woven mats and surrounded
with the possessions he might need or enjoy in the hereafter. Mourners
blackened their faces with soot and hung the dead person's skin coat or
robe over the grave. As it deteriorated, it marked the passing of the
departed's soul to the land of the dead.

The Wampanoag had about 30 villages when the Pilgrims arrived.
These were usually located along bays, rivers or springs of running
water. The principal towns were Sowams, Montaup and Kickemiut.
Villages consisted of wigwams clustered around an open space, used for
ceremonies and other gatherings. Often there was a sweathouse built
into the side of a hill near a pond or stream.

Wigwams were either circular or rectangular, up to 100 feet long. They were constructed of poles covered with birchbark, hickory bark or woven mats. For warmth, they were often dug several feet below ground and lined with pine needles, cattails or the like. The smoke from the cooking fire escaped through a hole in the roof. Large baskets provided storage, and bunks lined with skins were against the walls.

Hunting, fishing, gathering and agriculture combined to put food on the Wampanoag table. Corn, beans, pumpkin and squash were grown by the women. Men grew tobacco and hunted bear, deer, beaver, raccoon, quail, partridge and wild turkey. The fruits of the sea were not ignored, as lobsters, clams, oysters, crabs and mussels were all gathered and steamed over hot rocks. Grapes, cherries, huckleberries and acorns were also gleaned from the countryside. A lightweight trail food was made from parched corn and maple sugar, to which water was added before eating.

Dugout canoes, which could hold 10 to 15 men, were made of hollowed out trees. Weapons and tools were crafted of stone, bone and shell, while cooking dishes were made of stone and clay. Baskets and mats were woven of rushes and various grasses. White wampum was made from the periwinkle shell, and black or purple from the quahog. The wampum beads were used for adornment, as well as for trade and negotiations with other tribes.

The Pilgrims found the Wampanoag in somewhat of a decline in 1621. They had been warred on by the Penobscots in 1615, suffered a great plague in 1616, and in that weakened state been forced to submit to Narraganset overlordship. These were the circumstances under which Massasoit, the Wampanoag grand sachem, made a treaty of peace and friendship with the English. In those early years, the Wampanoag provided large amounts of material assistance and technical advice to the Pilgrims, giving them seed to plant and showing them how to fertilize their hills of corn with dead fish.

The peace lasted more than 50 years and was renewed by Massasoit's son, Pometacom or Metacomet, who became grand sachem about 1662, and was known to the English as Philip. During this period, white colonists poured into Wampanoag territory, cutting forests which sheltered their game. Indian lands were stolen and white men's diseases and vices further weakened all the New England tribes.

Philip, in an attempt to save his people, plotted with the Narraganset and other tribes to drive the English out. Before they could adequately prepare, war was precipitated by some of the younger warriors. King Philip's War (1675-76) resulted in the killing of hundreds of settlers and the near extermination of the Wampanoag and Narraganset tribes.

The remaining Wampanoag were either captured and enslaved or fled either to the interior or to the tribes on Nantucket and Martha's

Vineyard, which had remained neutral during the war. In the late 1970s, there were several hundred Wampanoag descendants, mostly living in the area of Martha's Vineyard.

BIBLIOGRAPHY. Travers. Milton A. *The Wampanoag Indian Federation.* New Bedford, Massachusetts: Reynolds-DeWalt, 1957.

WAPPINGER: an extinct confederacy of Algonquian tribes located along the east bank of the Hudson River from Manhattan to Poughkeepsie, and eastward to the lower Connecticut River valley. The western Wappinger tribes in the New York area numbered about 3,000 in 1600, while the eastern tribes in Connecticut numbered about 1,750. They were related to the Delaware to the south and the Mahican to the north.

The Wappinger, translated as "eastern people," were composed of nine tribes: Wappinger, Manhattan, Wecquaesgeek, Sitsink, Kitchawank, Tankiteke, Nochpeem, Siwanoy and Mattabesec. Their economy consisted of hunting, fishing and agriculture, with corn as the staple crop. They were noted for their manufacture of wampum beads.

In 1609, Henry Hudson sailed into their territory, and, soon afterward, Dutch traders and settlers arrived. The western Wappinger fought the Dutch from 1640 to 1645, losing some 1,600 people in the war. Further reduced by disease, most of the Wappinger joined the Nanticoke at Otsiningo (Chenango), New York, under the protection of the Seneca. They later merged with the Delaware and fought on the American side in the Revolution.

Some of the eastern Wappinger joined the Stockbridge and Scaticook Indians, while others moved to Canada. The Wappinger then ceased to exist as a separate tribe.

BIBLIOGRAPHY: Ruttenber, E.M. *History of the Indian Tribes of Hudson's River.* Albany: Munsell, 1872.

WAPPO: a northwest California group located, in the early 19th century, in the Napa Valley and along the southern shore of Clear Lake, numbering perhaps 2,000 at that time. In the late 1970s, there remained only about 50 Wappo descendants, living in California, and the tribal language was nearly extinct.

The Wappo language belonged to the small Yukian language family, which also included the three dialects of the Yuki language (which was spoken by the Yuki, Huchnom and Coast Yuki). The Wappo were entirely cut off from the other Yukian speakers by intervening Pomo territory. The tribal name may have been derived from the Spanish term *guapo,* meaning "harsh," "brave," or "handsome."

Wappo villages were led by a chief, male or female, who was chosen for life. The villages were usually located along creeks, and were composed of oval grass-thatched houses. When a Wappo died, his body was placed on three sticks and carried by six men to a place a mile or so from the village, where it was burned, along with his personal effects. Female mourners cut their hair and covered their heads with clay.

The Wappo diet included acorns, shellfish, salmon, deer, rabbit, ducks, geese, honey and various roots. Animal skins were made into clothing, and excellent basketwork was produced. The Wappo made frequent trips to the coast to gather shellfish and seaweed for flavoring their food. Clamshells were used for spoons and as money.

The origin of the Wappo and their relationship to the Yuki, whom they resemble linguistically but not physically or culturally, are still unknown. The Wappo were generally very peaceful, except for occasional warfare with the Pomo and struggles against Spanish incursions in the Napa Valley. Some Wappo were kept at the Sonoma mission between 1823 and 1824. In 1860, about 240 Wappo, along with other Indians, were moved to a reservation at Mendocino, which was closed in 1867. By 1910, the Wappo population had dwindled to about 70, and, by the late 1970s, to about 50.

BIBLIOGRAPHY: Driver, Harold E. "Wappo Ethnography." *University of California Publications in American Archeology and Ethnology*. vol. 36, 1936.

WASCO: *See* WISHRAM.

A Wasco Indian, Oscar Mark, or Little Vessel, (about 1876).
Smithsonian Institution
National
Anthropological
Archives

WASHO: a small tribe located on the Nevada-California border, in the area around Lake Tahoe, in the early 19th century, numbering about 1,500 at that time. In the late 1970s, there were perhaps 900 Washo living in Nevada and California. Washo was derived from Washiu, a term meaning "person" in their language, which belongs to the Hokan language family.

The Washo lived in tiny autonomous settlements, with leadership provided by chiefs, hunt leaders and shamans. Shamans cured the sick, using supernatural powers acquired through dreams and apprenticeships of several years. In a four-night ceremony, the shaman prayed, smoked, sang and finally sucked out the disease-causing object.

The most important ceremony, the Pine Nut Dance, was a four-day celebration, which included dances, games, gambling, feasting and prayers for a good harvest. The girls' four-day puberty rite was the most important personal ceremony. Marriage was accomplished by an exchange of gifts between the two families. The Washo cremated their dead and placed the unburned bones in a creek. Mourners cut their hair, and the horse of the deceased was burned or abandoned.

In the winters, the Washo lived in the Pine Nut mountains, where they built conical bark-slab houses. In spring, they moved to the shores of Lake Tahoe and adjacent valleys for fishing and gathering of wild plants, where they camped in the open or constructed brush shelters.

Fishing was the main source of summer food. The Washo used three-pronged harpoons, nets, dams and conical basketry traps to fish Lake Tahoe and its feeder streams. Deer, antelope and rabbit were hunted in communal drives, organized by hunt leaders.

During spring and summer, they gathered a wide variety of roots, grass seeds, berries, chokecherries and bird's eggs. In fall they went to the California oak groves for acorns, which were shelled and ground into flour on bedrock mortars. Before the flour was used to make soup or mush, the bitter taste was leached out with hot water. In late fall, the Washo returned to the mountains to gather pine nuts, the single most important food source. These too were cooked and ground into flour for soup. Washo material culture included an assortment of both twined and coiled baskets for gathering and storing wild plants, sifting flour, etc.

The Washo remained fairly secluded from the pressure of white civilization until 1848, when the discovering of gold in California brought miners flocking through their territory. In the 1850s, trading posts and settlements began springing up. The real blow came, however, with the discovery of the Comstock silver lode in 1858, which attracted more than 20,000 fortune-hunters to the Virginia City area. Washo pine nut forests were cut to provide timbers for the mines and lumber for settlements. Ranchers soon followed, their cattle scaring off the game and destroying the seed bearing grasses the Washo used for food. By the 1870s, commercial fishermen were fishing the waters of Lake Tahoe. The Washo, with nowhere to go and no reservation provided for them, eked out an existence on the fringes of white settlements. Some small plots of

8

508 INDIAN TRIBES OF NORTH AMERICA

land were eventually purchased by or for the Washo, becoming the nucleus of several colonies.

In the late 1970s, there were about 900 Washo in the California-Nevada area, with the largest concentrations in colonies near Carson City, Dresslerville and Reno-Sparks, Nevada and in the Woodsford Colony in Alpine County, California. The Washo had managed to preserve a surprising amount of their culture. The Washo language was still spoken, and women still made basketry as well as rabbitskin blankets. The Washo enjoyed trips to California and the mountains to gather acorns and pine nuts and to hunt deer and rabbit. The girls' puberty rites were still a vital tradition, and, for special occasions, acorns were ground in the old way with stone mortars.

BIBLIOGRAPHY: Downs, James F. *The Two Worlds of the Washo.* New York: Holt, Rinehart and Winston, 1966; Freed, Stanley A. "Changing Washo Kinship." *Anthropological Records.* vol. 36, 1939.

WEA: See MIAMI.

WENROHRONON: an extinct New York state tribe who occupied lands south of Lake Ontario, in the area of the present counties of Niagara, Orleans, Genesee, Wyoming and Allegany. They were bordered on the west by the Erie and Neutral tribes, and on the east by the Iroquois Confederacy. They may have numbered as many as 2,000 in 1600.

The Wenrohronon spoke an Iroquoian language and were also referred to as Wenroes or Ouenrionons. The tribe name, meaning "people of the place of the floating scum," probably referred to an oil spring in their territory.

Very little is known of Wenrohronon culture, except that they built earthworks and fortified their villages. According to some reports, they traded with the Dutch along the Delaware River.

In the early 17th century they were engaged in an alliance with the Neutral Indian nation against the Iroquois Confederacy. When the alliance fell apart, in about 1639, the Wenrohronon sought protection Huron. About 600 of the tribe set out for Huron territory but many died along the way due to disease and the hardships of the journey. The Wenrohronon who remained in New York shared the fate of the Neutrals, while those who settled with the Huron along the east bank of the Detroit River shared the fate of that tribe. All three tribes were destroyed by the Iroquois in the mid-17th century, their members killed, dispersed or forced into captivity.

BIBLIOGRAPHY: Silver, Dilworth M. *The Location of the Nations of Indians Called the Wenroes or Wenrohronons and the Eries.* Buffalo: 1923.

WEST ALASKA INUIT: a number of Inuit (Eskimo) groups located along the Alaska coastal area from Point Hope southward to Kodiak Island, numbering about 11,000 in the late 19th century. In the late 1970s, there were about 22,000 Inuit occupying the same general region. Those living north of Norton Sound spoke dialects of the Inuk (or Inupik) branch of the Inuit (Eskimo) language, whereas those to the south spoke dialects of the Yuk (or Yupik branch). The name Eskimo was derived from an Abnaki Indian term meaning "raw meat eaters," whereas the term Inuit, meaning "people," is their own name for themselves.

The West Alaska Inuit were divided into about 16 groups, each located in a specific geographic region and usually referred to by the name of the region plus the suffix *miut*. These were further subdivided into local groups and settlements, often named in the same manner. The family was the most important economic and political unit. In some groups, this meant the nuclear family, and in other groups, the bilaterally extended family, in which all the males cooperated in hunting activities. In some groups, there was a tendency toward patrilineages, in which secret hunting songs, amulets, ceremonies and property marks were passed down through the male line.

Families tended to live in larger settlements during the winter, splitting into smaller groups for summer hunting or fishing. Partly because of the fluidity of both winter villages and summer camps, leadership was mainly advisory. A hunting leader inspired cooperation because of his personal prestige and respect for his ability as a hunter. Non-related men sometimes formed hunting, food-sharing, trading or other types of partnerships. Wife exchange was sometimes practiced between such partners.

Shamans both men and older women, provided religious leadership through their power to deal with various spirits. Shamans cured the sick, controlled the weather, and assured successful hunting by means of trances, songs and masked dances, performed to the accompaniment of a drum. Individuals also performed certain ceremonies, recited prayers, observed taboos and used amulets, usually in connection with hunting or death. Important group ceremonies included the Messenger Feast, a social gathering involving gift exchange, and the Spring Whaling Ceremony, a religious thanksgiving for bountiful whale hunting. Some groups held memorial feasts honoring the dead.

Burial customs varied according to region, but usually included removing the body through the window or skylight and placing it either in a shallow grave or on the ground, along with broken weapons, tools or other grave goods. The Kovagmiut of the Kobuk River area, however, buried their dead in canoes or on platforms. In the Bering Sea area, the dead were placed in painted wooden coffins, and wooden posts, carved

**A West Alaska
Inuit man
and boy,
Nunivak Island,
1929.**

The National Archives

with animal figures, were erected. During a four or five day mourning period, there were many taboos and restrictions on hunting and other activities.

House styles among the Western Alaska Inuit varied somewhat according to the materials available. The basic winter house, usually located in a small village or settlement, was semisubterranean, of sod or earth with wood posts and beams, with entrance by way of a shallow tunnel. Inside was a single room with sleeping benches around the outside and a central fireplace with an overhead smokehole. On Kotebue Sound, a more elaborate multifamily dwelling was built in the same style,

**A West Alaska
Inuit
spearing seal
near Nome,
Alaska.**

The National Archives

but in the shape of a cross with a central main room and separate family sleeping quarters in each of the arms of the cross.

At the caribou hunting camps along the Kobuk and Noatak rivers, multifamily dwellings were constructed, of willow framework covered with sod and moss. Each family had its own section, complete with ice-slab window, fireplace and smokehole. They also built a wide variety of temporary dwellings, including willow frame domes covered with caribou skins, spruce bark, moss, brush, grass, earth and combinations thereof. On King Island, there were rectangular walrus skin tents with wood plank floors, all having a round door which faced the sea. Along the lower Kuskokwim River, sod block houses were used, and along the Yukon, there were summer dwellings housing one to three families, with two plank walls, two log walls and a gabled board roof. Most villages had one or more men's houses, or *kazigi,* where the men gathered to work on equipment, perform ceremonies, take meals and sometimes sleep. Women were allowed in the *kazigi* for certain ceremonies and gatherings.

Economic activities and subsistence varied from area to area, depending mostly on the available game. Fishing was important to the Kovagmiut along the Kobuk River, with dog salmon predominant in summer and whitefish caught year around. Salmon was also a staple along Bristol Bay and the Yukon and Kuskokwim rivers. In fall, caribou hunting was important along the upper Kobuk and Noatak rivers, Seward Peninsula and Cape Newenham.

West Alaska Inuit in kayaks, Nunivak Island, 1936.   The National Archives

The people along the Bering Sea hunted seals, walrus, and caribou and fished for whitefish and salmon. The Nuniwagamiut on Nunivak Island harpooned seals both on the ice and in open water from kayaks. Whales were hunted off the Seward Peninsula from the village of Wales. Other animals hunted or trapped by various groups included mountain sheep, black bear, moose, muskox, fox, wolf, marmot, mink and muskrat. Ptarmigan, ducks and geese were taken with snares and lake trout, grayling and herring were caught with gill nets, traps and leisters, or three-pronged spears. Berries, roots and other plant food were a minor addition to the diet. Most groups lived in established winter villages and ranged in the summer to hunt caribou, seals, or fish.

Transportation included kayaks, *umiaks* (larger open boats), dog sleds, hand-pulled sleds and snowshoes. They made stone and pottery lamps for heat and light, and produced numerous types of containers, including skin bags, pottery bowls, twined and coiled baskets, wooden boxes, buckets and dishes.

Clothing varied in style and material, with caribou skins most prized for their warmth, light weight and durability. Marmot, mink, muskrat and bird skins were also used, and fish skin clothing was used for summer in some areas. The basic items were a hooded parka, trousers, boots and mittens. Undergarments included long skin or woven grass socks, inner shirts, short pants and aprons.

In the late 18th and early 19th century, there was some Russian influence on the Yukon and Kuskokwim river areas. By the mid-19th century, life in the villages along the Bering and Beaufort seas was totally disrupted by the whiskey, disease and depletion of game brought by the whaling crews and traders of various nations. In the 1890s, reindeer herds were imported from Asia, along with Chukchi and Lapp herders, in an experiment that eventually failed. Whaling declined in the 1890s. Missions and schools were established, with most villages with more than 100 population having a school by 1914.

Fox hunting for the fur trade reached its peak in the 1920s. About that time, Inuit whaling crews began motorizing their previously-adopted wood whaling boats. After World War II, contact with the outside world increased, along with wage-earning opportunities, as the reindeer herds and sea mammal populations declined. Village councils were established in some areas after the 1930s. The last major caribou herd was located on Nunivak Island, along with a muskox herd begun in the 1930s.

In recent decades, the poor health conditions have gradually improved, and tuberculosis, in particular, has declined.

In the 1970s, about 22,000 Inuit lived in Western Alaska. For the purpose of the Alaska Natives Claims Settlement Act, they were organized into Bering Straits Regional Corporation, Bristol Bay Native Corporation, Calista Corporation and Nana Regional Corporation. Muskrat and mink trapping were still important in the Kuskokwim delta. Ivory carving and other crafts were important in some areas. Hunting and fishing were still important, although wage work was increasing.

BIBLIOGRAPHY: Hughes, Charles Campbell. "Under Four Flags: Recent Culture Change Among the Eskimos." *Current Anthropology*. vol. 6. 1965; Oswalt, Wendell H. *Alaskan Eskimos*. San Francisco: Chandler Publishing Company, 1967.

WEST GREENLAND INUIT: a large Inuit (Eskimo) group located on the western coast of Greenland, numbering about 6,000 in the early 19th century. In the 1970s, there were about 38,000 West Greenland Inuit, largely mixed with an immigrant European population. They spoke a dialect of the Inuit (Eskimo) language, which was spoken, with minor variations, from Alaska to Greenland. The name Eskimo was derived from an Abnaki Indian term meaning "raw meat eaters." The term Inuit, meaning "people," is their own name for themselves.

The West Greenland Inuit had no real political organization. The main social and economic unit was the nuclear family, plus usually one or more other relatives. Religious leadership was provided by an *angakok*, or shaman, whose powers derived from "assisting spirits" acquired through trances. The *angakok* conducted seances, in which he entered an ecstatic state and called upon his assisting spirits to help him cure the sick, find lost souls or bring an abundance of game.

The West Greenland Inuit had a rich mythology, which included many spirits and deities. Among the most important were: the Old Woman of the Sea, who controlled all the marine animals; the Sun woman and her brother the Moon, whose whittling on walrus tusks caused snow; giant kayaks; an animal with an iron tail; a giant worm, and a giant bear. They had many taboos and ceremonies connected with hunting, the activity on which their lives depended. Breaking of any taboos would result in illness and possibly death.

For seven to nine months the West Greenland Inuit lived in small semi-permanent winter settlements, consisting of communal dwellings of stone and sod and housing several families. In spring, they broke up into small hunting groups of one or two families, living in sealskin tents anchored by rocks or sod.

The marine mammals—seals, walrus and whales—were of prime importance, providing the Inuit with food, skins for clothing, boats and tents, blubber and oil for lamps, sinews for thread, and bone and ivory for needles and tools. In summer, seals, walrus, narwhal and white whale were harpooned from kayaks and open boats called *umiaks*. Seals were also trapped with nets placed under the ice. In winter, seals and walrus were hunted at their breathing holes out on the sea ice. They also hunted caribou, as well as ptarmigan and other birds. Trout, cod and other fish were caught using nets, hooks and three-pronged spears, and mussels, seaweed and crowberries were gathered to supplement the diet. Meat and fish were eaten raw, dried or boiled. Cooking pots and blubber lamps for heat and light were carved from soapstone, and boxes were made from coiled grass.

For winter transportation, the West Greenland Inuit made excellent sleds with wood runners shod with bone or ivory. Wood was also used to make snow goggles, eye shades and buckets. Clothing was of caribou skin and sealskin, fit loosely to provide for evaporation of perspiration. For maximum insulation, inner garments were worn with the hair side in, and outer garments with the hair side out. Special waterproof sealskin kayak suits and mittens were made, as well as gut-skin jackets for wet weather. Boots were all important, and were put on over inner stockings, which were worn with the hair side in.

Greenland was probably first settled more than 4,000 years ago, by successive groups from the south and west. Caribou hunters, now known as the Dorset culture, probably entered Greenland by the first century AD. Around 500, a seafaring people arrived, probably originally from northeastern Asia. Known as the Thule culture, they hunted marine life in kayaks and *umiaks*. As the Thule people moved down the west coast, their culture was modified and became known as the Inugsuk culture.

Around 982, a new immigration began from the east. Icelanders, led by Erik the Red, settled West Greenland, referring to the earlier inhabitants as Skraelings. These European settlements died out in about 1500. Successive waves of people continued to enter Greenland from North America as late as 1865, and European whalers made visits in the 17th and 18th century. Danish colonization began about 1721. In the 19th century, a mixture of Danish, Norwegian and Dutch continued to immigrate to the more inhabitable west coast.

In the 20th century, the Danish government established fisheries, introduced cattle and sheep to replace the dwindling caribou and established schools, churches, trading posts and medical facilities. In 1950, Greenland became a province of Denmark.

In the late 1970s, there were about 38,000 West Greenland Inuit, living in more than 100 coastal settlements. There was a considerable mixture of European blood and continuing intermarriage with the 8,000 or so Danish population. The schools were bilingual, with children learning both Inuit and Danish. Although the Inuit engaged in other economic activities, the old seasonal hunting life was still important, modified in some areas by such modern adaptions as rifles and motorboats.

BIBLIOGRAPHY: Persson, Ib. *Anthropological Investigations of the Population of Greenland.* Copenhagen: C.A. Reitzels Forlag, 1970.

WICHITA: a confederacy of the Caddoan language family, whose villages were probably the fabled land of Quivira, visited in 1541 by the Spanish explorer Coronado. Located in the area of the great bend of the Arkansas River in south central Kansas, the confederacy may have numbered 15,000 or more at that time. By the late 18th century, they totaled about 4,000. In the late 1970s, there were about 800 Wichita descendants, mostly living in Oklahoma.

The language of the Wichita, closely related to that of the Pawnee, was still spoken in the late 1970s. The Wichita called themselves Kitikiti'sh, meaning "men," or "pre-eminent men." They were also known as the Black Pawnee, possibly from their heavy use of tattooing.

The Wichita confederacy was composed of six or seven sub-tribes, each occupying independent villages. The main sub-tribes included the Wichita proper (Ousita), Tayovaya (Toayas) and Yscani. Tribes which later were grouped with the Wichita included the separate but related Tawakoni, Waco and Kichai. Each village was ruled by a chief and sub-chief, who were elected by a council of warriors. The smallest unit was the matriarchal family, consisting of a woman, her husband, their daughters, and their daughters' families. Polygamy was practiced, usually with men marrying sisters or their brother's widow.

The Wichita worshipped a number of deities and spirits, headed by Kinnikasus, the creator of all. Others included the Sun, Moon, Morning Star and Earth Mother. Two important ceremonies were the Deer Dance, held three times a year, and the Calumet Ceremony. Each village had numerous secret societies, for both men and women, each with its own dances and ceremonies. The Wichita believed in an afterlife and buried their dead in shallow graves on a hill near the village, accompanied by

A Wichita village on Rush Creek, from the U.S. War Department's *Exploration of the Red River of Louisiana,* **1853.**

goods the dead person's spirit would need. Men were buried with weapons and tools, and women with their household and gardening implements. Mourners cut their hair and gave away some of their possessions.

Wichita villages were usually located overlooking rivers and reportedly sometimes had as many as 1,000 grass lodges. The lodges, 15 to 30 feet in diameter, were constructed of a heavy pole framework thatched with coarse grass. Each lodge had two doors and a smoke hole above the cooking fire in the center. Sleeping platforms were along the interior walls.

The Wichita were both hunters and agriculturalists. Spring and summer found them in their grass lodge villages growing corn, beans, squash, pumpkins and tobacco. They often grew a surplus, which they traded to the more nomadic tribes. Corn was dried and stored in underground caches; tobacco was pressed into flat loaves, and pumpkins were cut into long thin strips, which were dried, flattened and woven into mats for easy storage and carrying. Wild plums, grapes, nuts and acorns were gathered to supplement the diet. After the fall harvest, the Wichita became roving hunters, in search of the buffalo, deer, bear and antelope, living in portable skin tipis.

After the 1541 Coronado expedition, the Wichita were visited by other Spanish explorers. By 1700, they acquired horses, which greatly increased their mobility as buffalo hunters and warriors. They made a leather armor to protect their horses in combat. The Wichita, however, were essentially peaceful people, living in unfortified villages. Therefore, when they began to be pressed by the Osage to the northeast who had acquired firearms from the French and the Comanche to the northwest, they began moving south to Oklahoma and Texas.

By about 1720, the Wichita had begun trading with the French, who helped negotiate a peace treaty between the Wichita and Comanche in 1746. Thereafter, these two tribes carried on extensive trade and allied themselves against the Apache.

By 1757, several of the Wichita sub-tribes were living in villages along the Red River. Between 1758 and 1778, they were periodically at war with the Spanish. A smallpox epidemic in 1801 swept the Wichita and neighboring Oklahoma and Texas tribes. Their population was further reduced in the following years by Osage raids and conflict with American settlers. In 1835 and 1837, the various bands made treaties with the United States, as well as with the Osage and the eastern tribes that were being moved into their area.

In 1859, the Wichita were moved to lands south of the Canadian River in Oklahoma, but during the Civil War, most of them fled to Kansas, at the site of present day Wichita. In 1867, they were assigned land on the Washita River in Caddo County, Oklahoma along with other Caddoan tribes. Their lands were allotted to them in severalty in 1901.

In the late 1970s, there were about 800 Wichita descendants, including Kichai, Tawakoni and Waco, most of them living in Caddo County, Oklahoma. Interest in their tribal heritage was growing, with tribal songs and stories being recorded and groups gathering to improve their tribal language proficiency. A traditional dance was held annually in August, and the Wichita and Pawnee took turns hosting an annual celebration.

BIBLIOGRAPHY: Newcomb, W.W. *The People Called Wichita.* Phoenix: Indian Tribal Series, 1976.

WINNEBAGO: a Siouan tribe living in the predominantly Algonquian area of Green Bay, Wisconsin, in 1650, numbering about 3,800 at that time. In the late 1970s, about 3,500 descendants of Winnebago occupied reservations in Nebraska and Wisconsin.

The Winnebago called themselves Hotcangara, or "people of the real speech," while Winnebago is a Sauk term meaning "people of the dirty water." The Winnebago shared many aspects of culture both with their Algonquian neighbors, the Menominee, Sauk, Fox and Ojibwa, and with their Siouan linguistic kin further west, the Iowa, Oto and Missouri.

The Winnebago were divided into two phratries, or tribal divisions. The *wangeregi*, or air phratry, was composed of four clans, while the *manegi*, or earth phratry, had eight. Each person inherited the clan of his father and was required to marry outside his clan and phratry. Winnenbago clans built small effigy mounds over large parts of Wisconsin representing the totemic animal of their clan.

Young Eagle,
a Winnebago,
(1904).

Library of Congress

Winnebago deities included Earthmaker, Sun, Moon, Earth, Morningstar, Diseasegiver, Thunderbird and Water Spirit. Important festivals included clan feasts, the Winter Feast and the Summer Medicine Dance, performed by members of a secret medicine society. In early times, scaffold burials were common; mourners blackened their faces with charcoal and observed a four-day wake.

Winnebago villages often contained a long, bark-covered council lodge, used for meetings and ceremonies. Sometimes there was a bark-covered sweathouse, used for curing and ritual purification. Houses were either round or long, of pole framework covered with bark or woven mats.

The Winnebago had a mixed economy, based on agriculture, fishing, hunting and gathering. They grew corn, beans, squash and tobacco, used in ceremonies. Fruit, berries, wild potatoes and wild rice were gathered, the latter harvested from canoes. Fish were taken with weirs and spears, especially at night by the light of pine pitch torches. Communal buffalo hunts were held on the prairies, while deer, bear and small game were taken in the woods with bows and arrows, traps, and, later, firearms.

Birchbark canoes and dugouts were used for transportation, and snowshoes for winter travel. Women made pottery cooking vessels, wove bags with intricate designs, and did fancy beadwork. Men wore headdresses of red-dyed deer hair, often adding an eagle feather.

When the Winnebago were visited by the French explorer Jean Nicolet in 1634, they occupied territory from the southern shore of Green Bay south to Lake Winnebago, with the Menominee living to the north.

Shortly thereafter, these two tribes were nearly inundated by Michigan and eastern tribes, driven into the area by the Iroquois Confederacy. The Siouan Winnebago were soon surrounded by Algonquian tribes: the Sauk, Fox, Potawatomi and Ojibwa, with whom they got along fairly well.

By the early 19th century, the Winnebago had expanded into southwestern Wisconsin and northwestern Illinois, living in as many as 40 small bands. They fought on both sides in Black Hawk's War in 1831-32.

Between 1825 and 1837, they ceded their Wisconsin lands for reservations west of the Mississippi. Between 1840 and 1865, most of the Winnebago were moved from Wisconsin, to Iowa, to three different locations in Minnesota, to South Dakota and finally to Nebraska. Some returned to Wisconsin in about 1874 and were given 40-acre homesteads. Most of this land was poor, however, and was subsequently sold. In the 1930s, the U.S. government began purchasing homesites for the Winnebago which, by 1963, when the tribe voted to reorganize, were scattered over ten counties and several hundred miles.

In the late 1970s, about 1,000 Winnebago descendants lived on or near the Nebraska reservation in Thurston County, while another 2,500 lived on the widely scattered homesites of the Wisconsin reservation.

BIBLIOGRAPHY: Radin, Paul. *The Winnebago Tribe,* 1923. Reprint. New York: Johnson Reprint Corp., 1970.

WINTU: a northwestern California group numbering about 14,000 in the early 19th century. By the late 1970s, there were perhaps 900 Wintu, living mostly in California. Their tribal name means "person" in the Wintu language, which belongs to the Wintuan (or Wintun) division of the Penutian language family. Other members of the division are the Nomlaki and Patwin languages.

The Wintu were divided into nine major groups by location, but the only political unit was the village. Each village was led by a chief, usually hereditary, whose duties included arbitrating disputes, hosting ceremonies and gatherings, and dealing with chiefs of other villages.

Religious leadership was provided by shamans, who received their power during a five-day initiation period, during which the candidates fasted, danced and received instructions from the incumbent shaman. Curing techniques of the shaman included massage, soul capture and sucking out the disease-causing object. The Wintu worshipped a supreme being whom they referred to as "the one who is above." They also prayed and talked to the sun each morning and recognized numerous other deities and spirits.

The Wintu also had a rich collection of mythology. They believed that when a person died his soul traveled along the Milky Way. His body was

A Wintun chief
on the McCloud
River,
California,
in about 1882.
Smithsonian Institution
National
Anthropological
Archives

dressed in good clothes and wrapped in a deer or bear skin in a crouched position. It was then removed through a special opening made in the rear of the house, and buried in a graveyard along with acorn meal, water and personal items. Widows cut their hair and rubbed a mixture of pitch and charcoal on their faces.

The Wintu built conical houses using a pole framework covered with bark. A semisubterranean earth lodge, 20 feet in diameter, was used as a sweat lodge and gathering place for the men.

Hunting, fishing and gathering were all important in securing the food supply. Deer and rabbits were hunted communally in drives, and bear were sometimes smoked out of their dens. Communal fish drives were held to catch salmon and trout. Surplus fish were dried and stored. Families gathered acorns, the men climbing the trees to shake them down for the women to gather. The acorns were dried and pounded into meal, and the bitter taste leached out by placing the meal in a sand pit and pouring water over it. The diet was supplemented by gathering seeds, pine nuts, grapes, berries, greens, roots and grasshoppers.

Wintu craftsmen specialized in producing arrows, arrowheads, bows and fishing equipment. They also made tools of bone, horn or stone, as well as burden baskets, sifters and containers of twined basketry. Deer and rabbit skins were made into blankets and capes. Clothing was minimal, women wearing a shredded maple bark apron, and men doing without.

Between 1830 and 1833, an estimated 75 percent of the Indians of the Wintu region were wiped out by epidemics. In the mid-19th century, their lands were stolen and their food sources destroyed by ranchers' cattle and sheep. Their fishing streams were polluted by miners. The Wintu were massacred by the hundreds and forced onto reservations. In the late 1930s dam construction was begun, flooding large areas of Wintu territory. In the late 1970s, there remained about 900 Wintu descendants, but their tribal life was essentially disrupted, and most of their cultural traditions and language were lost.

BIBLIOGRAPHY: Du Bois, Cora. *"Wintu Ethnography." University of California Publications in American Archaeology and Ethnology.* vol. 36, 1935.

WISHRAM: a Chinookan tribe occupying the north bank of the Columbia River in Washington, for five miles above and below the Dalles, numbering about 1,500 in the 18th century. In the late 1970s, some Wishram descendants were mixed with other tribes on the Yakima Reservation, and others lived in their traditional territory.

The Wishram spoke the same Chinookan family language as the culturally similar Wasco, their neighbors directly across the river at the Dalles. Also known as Five Mile Rapids, the Dalles was the most important trading spot in the region, attracting several thousand Indians during the trading season. The Wishram and Wasco acted as the middlemen in the Dalles trade.

The Wishram, who called themselves the Tlakluit, were composed of a number of villages, each led by an hereditary chief. Socially they were divided into four classes: nobles, middle-class, commoners, and slaves, acquired in trade or warfare.

The nobility often intermarried with the nobility of neighboring tribes, the couple usually residing with the man's family. Marriage was formalized by the exchange of gifts and visits between the two families, and infant betrothal was sometimes practiced. Adolescent boys sought guardian spirits by fasting in lonely places or performing feats of endurance or daring, such as diving into underwater caves. Shamans usually had several animal guardian spirits which aided them in curing the sick.

Important Wishram ceremonies included First Salmon rites and guardian spirit dances. When a person died, his body was wrapped in buckskin and placed in plank family burial houses, containing carved and painted wood images of men and animals. An important Wishram burial ground was located on Memaloose Island in the Columbia River. Widows often married their husband's brother, and widowers their wife's sister.

Winter houses were semisubterranean earth lodges housing from one to six families. Built over a circular pit six feet deep, the lodges were constructed of a pole framework covered with tule mats and layers of grass and dirt or cedar bark. Entrance was through a hole in the roof, and bed platforms were placed around the walls. In summer, the Wishram lived in gable-roofed mat lodges of varying lengths, with from one to four fireplaces according to the number of families housed. They also had sweat lodges, which were used by the sick, by hunters before the hunt and by mourners, for purification after a death.

The Wishram and Wasco were primarily fishermen, catching salmon, trout, pike, sturgeon, smelt and eels with nets, spears, weirs and traps. Fishing stations were owned and inherited by groups of related families. The fish was dried or smoked and pulverized, in which condition it would keep for several years. Lewis and Clark, on their visit to the Dalles, observed some 10,000 pounds of dried salmon packed for storage or trade. Salmon eggs were also dried and used as a light-weight, high-nourishment trail food by hunters.

Gathered foods, including camas, wild onions, wild potatoes, huckleberries, hazel nuts and acorns, were next in importance. Of less importance was game, which included deer, elk, bear, cougar, wolf, and fox. Snowshoes were used for stalking deer and elk in winter, while shovel-nosed cedar dugouts were the main means of transportation.

Material culture included carved wood mortars, bowls, ladles and spoons and twined baskets and bags with geometric designs, made from various grasses and bark. Early clothing consisted of breechclouts or aprons and fur robes or rabbit skin blankets, although Plains style clothing was adopted in later times. Women wore basketry caps, and face paint and dentalium shell ear pendants were worn for adornment.

In the late 18th century, the Wishram and Wasco occupied what was probably the most important trading place on the Northwest Coast. Both interior and coast tribes, including the Yakima, Spokan, Columbia, Klikitat, Wallawalla, Umatilla, Cayuse, Palouse, Nez Perce, Klamath and Kalapuya, met there to exchange goods and ideas. The Wishram and Wasco often acted as middlemen, buying and reselling blankets, robes, shells, horses, slaves, canoes, dried salmon, skins, furs, dried roots and numerous other items.

They bitterly resented the white traders who moved into their territory in the early 19th century, when, along with the other Columbia River tribes, they were decimated by epidemics. Also, during this time, the Wasco and Wishram were allied against the Northern Paiute, Bannock and Northern Shoshoni in warfare which lasted until mid-century. In

1855, both the Wishram and Wasco were forced to cede their lands in treaties.

In the late 1970s, some Wishram descendants were mixed with the other tribes on the Yakima Reservation, while others continued to live in their traditional territory. The Wasco were mixed with Paiute and other tribes among the more than 2,000 population of the 564,000-acre Warm Springs Reservation in Oregon. Tribally-owned enterprises included Kah-Nee-Ta resort, with its mineral hot springs and recreation facilities.

BIBLIOGRAPHY: Spier, Leslie and Sapir, Edward. "Wishram Ethnography." *University of Washington Publications in Anthropology.* vol. 3, 1930.

WYANDOT: *See* HURON and TIONONTATI.

YAKIMA: a Sahaptian tribe located along the Columbia, Yakima and Wenatchee rivers in Washington in the late 18th century, numbering about 3,000 at that time. In the late 1970s, Yakima descendants were among the 10,000 population of the Yakima Reservation in Washington.

The Yakima, whose name means "run-away," called themselves Waptailmim, meaning "people of the narrow river." They spoke a language of the Sahaptian division of the Penutian language family.

The Yakima were composed of a number of autonomous bands. Band leaders were selected for their wisdom and generosity, although leadership often tended to be hereditary. Shamans provided religious leadership and cured the sick through the aid of powerful guardian spirits.

Adolescent boys sought guardian spirits through fasting and solitary vigils in lonely places. Important ceremonies included first food feasts, celebrating such events as the first salmon or the first roots or berries of the season. Yakima mythology centered on tales of Speelyi (the Coyote trickster-transformer character) and the Grandfather Day stories.

Aboriginal Yakima dwellings included semisubterranean lodges of mats and earth on a pole framework. A later style was the long, tent-shaped mat lodge, with an extra layer of mats added in winter. Skin-covered tipis were adopted when the Yakima acquired horses and began to hunt buffalo.

Fishing was the mainstay of the Yakima economy, with five kinds of salmon, steelhead trout, sturgeon and eel being caught with dip nets from platforms, weirs, traps, two-prong spears and harpoons. Salmon was dried, pulverized and stored in baskets. Second in importance was the gathering of camas, wild onions, wild potatoes, wild carrots, acorns, hazel nuts and huckleberries. Deer, elk, and mountain sheep were hunted with bows and arrows, and bear, wolf, fox and cougar were taken with deadfalls.

U.S. Travel Service
Yakima Indians travelling to a celebration on horseback.

Yakima crafts included skin bags, carved wooden bowls, water-tight basketry cooking vessels and woven bags. Clothing was of skins, including breechclouts, aprons, vests, moccasins, fur robes and, later, Plains-style leggings and dresses.

Before acquiring horses, the shovel-nose dugout canoe was the main means of transportation, with snowshoes being used in winter. By the early 18th century, the Yakima had acquired horses and began crossing the Rocky Mountains to hunt buffalo.

In 1805, they were visited by Lewis and Clark, who were followed by a throng of fur trappers, traders, missionaries and settlers. In the early 19th century, their population was reduced by epidemics of smallpox and measles and by warfare with the Shoshoni.

In 1855, the Yakima and 13 other tribes and bands, including the Wishram, Klikitat, Wenatchee and Palouse, were induced to sign a treaty ceding their lands in exchange for a reservation. War broke out later that year, led by Yakima chief Kamaiakan, when the government failed to keep miners and settlers off Indian lands. The war was ended in 1858, and 24 Indian leaders were executed.

The Confederated Yakima tribes were settled on the Yakima Reservation in 1859, although the Palouse and other groups refused to recognize the treaty or move to the reservation. In 1891, lands were

Yakima girls dancing.   U.S. Department of Commerce

allotted to individuals, resulting in the eventual sale of much of the best lands to non-Indians.

In 1972, some 22,000 acres of Yakima land, including their sacred mountain, Pahto (Mt. Adams), was restored to them. In the late 1970s, about 80 percent of the residents of the 1,367,000-acre reservation were non-Indian. The Indian population of about 10,000 on or near the reservation was a mixture of the descendants of the Confederated Yakima tribes. Longhouses on the reservation were used as social and ceremonial centers, where first food feasts, dances, marriages, funerals, tribal business meetings and other gatherings were held. Yakima language classes were taught for both adults and children.

BIBLIOGRAPHY: Daugherty, Richard D. *The Yakima People.* Phoenix: Indian Tribal Series, 1973; Relander, Click (Now-Tow-Look). *Strangers on the Land.* Yakima, Washington: Franklin Press, 1962.

YAMASEE: an extinct Muskogean tribe that led an uprising against the South Carolina colonists in the early 18th century. The Yamasee, who numbered about 2,000 in 1650, lived at various times in northern Florida, southern Georgia, and South Carolina.

Living in Florida in about 1570, the Yamasee came under Spanish influence and were Christianized. In 1687, angry over some of their number being sent by the Spanish as slaves to the West Indies, the

Smithsonian Institution National Anthropological Archives

Tomo Chachi Mico, king of Yamacraw, and his nephew Toonahowi, who were painted by the Flemish painter Willem Verelst during their visit to London in 1734. Yamacraw, a town of the Creek confederacy, was settled in 1730 by Creek and Yamasee.

Yamasee moved to South Carolina.

In the early 18th century, the South Carolina Indians were outraged by abuses being committed by English traders and colonists, particularly the selling of Indians into plantation slavery, cheating them in the fur trade and stealing of their land. Led by the Yamasee and Catawba, most of the coast Indians took part in an uprising in 1715-16 in which about 200 traders and settlers and over 1,000 Indians were killed. The rebellion was put down with the aid of the surrounding colonies.

**Ishi, the last
Yana Indian,
chipping a flint
implement.**

Smithsonian Institution
National
Anthropological
Archives

Having lost about half of their tribe, the Yamasee fled to Florida. There they were the target of continual raids by the English and their Indian allies between 1725-28. The Yamasee fled inland and became dispersed among the Lower Creek and later the Seminole.

BIBLIOGRAPHY: Fairbanks, Charles H. *Ethnohistorical Report on the Florida Indians.* New York: Garland Publishing, Inc., 1974.

YANA: a northern California group living in the upper Sacramento River Valley and the adjacent eastern foothills in the early 19th century, when they numbered less than 2,000. By the early 20th century, the Yana were extinct as a group.

The word "Yana" meant "people." The Yana language was a member of the Hokan language family, and had four divisions: Northern, Central, Southern and Yahi. Politically, they were divided into tribelets, usually consisting of a main village with several smaller satellite villages. Each village probably had a hereditary chief or head-man, with the tribelet chief located at the main village, which contained the assembly house. Shamans, who received their power by fasting in remote places or swimming in certain pools, cured the sick by singing, dancing and sucking out the offending object.

When a Yahi Yana died, he was usually cremated. The other three groups buried their dead. The body was wrapped in a deerskin blanket in a flexed position and buried after four days along with personal items such as bow and arrows, baskets and blankets. Mourners cut their hair, covered their head with pitch and ashes and burned the house and possessions of the deceased.

The Yana groups varied in their house styles, with earth-covered multifamily houses being built by the Northern and Central Yana and conical bark-covered houses being used by the Southern and Yahi Yana. All of the groups made temporary brush shelters while hunting or gathering.

Acorns, fish and venison were the main elements of the Yana diet. The men climbed the trees to shake the acorns down, which the women gathered, shelled and dried. Acorn meal was used to make soup, mush or bread. The women also gathered roots, bulbs, berries, pine nuts and grasshoppers.

The men stalked deer with bow and arrow, wearing a deer-head disguise. They used pits, deadfalls and snares to take rabbit, quail and other small game. Salmon and trout were taken with spears, nets, traps and poison. Some fish were dried and stored for later use.

The Yana made basketry by twining, using hazel, willow, pine roots and sedge. Women's aprons or skirts were made of shredded bark or tule, and other clothing was made from deerskin.

Yana relations with their neighbors vacillated between trade and warfare. Exports included deer hides, salt, baskets and fire-making drills, while imports included obsidian arrow points, wildcat skin quivers, clam disc beads, and woodpecker scalps.

In the mid-19th century, white settlers and ranchers began moving into Yana territory, endangering their food supply. In the 1860s, the settlers set out to exterminate the Yana, and, through massacres, disease and starvation, the Yana population was reduced from about 1,900 to less than 100 in about 20 years. The surviving Yana fled into the foothills.

In 1911, the last surviving Yahi Yana, Ishi, was discovered. He lived, until his death in 1916, at the University of California Museum of Anthropology, where he taught anthropologists a great deal about Yana culture.

BIBLIOGRAPHY: Kroeber, Theodora. *Ishi in Two Worlds,* Berkeley: University of California Press, 1961; Sapir, Edward and Spier, Leslie. "Notes on the Culture of the Yana." *University of California Anthropological Records.* vol. 3, 1943; Waterman, T.T. "The Yana Indians." *University of California Publications in American Anthropology and Ethnology.* vol. 13, 1918.

Yankton Sioux: Two Man's children.

YANKTON: one of the seven main divisions of the Dakota, located in northern Minnesota in the early 17th century and moving gradually south and west to the Plains by the early 18th century. The Yankton had a population of about 3,000 by the mid-19th century. In the late 1970s, most Yankton lived on or near reservations in North and South Dakota, numbering perhaps several thousand.

The Yankton and Yanktonai spoke the Nakota dialect, which composed the middle or Wiciyela division of the Dakota language, a member of the Siouan linguistic family. Their tribal name meant "end village." They were organized into eight bands, which were subdivided into patrilineal clans. The chief governing body of the band, the band council, was composed of the hereditary band chief and leaders of the various clans.

Yankton material culture changed dramatically as the tribe changed their location from the woodlands of northern Minnesota to the prairies of southwestern Minnesota and finally to the plains of Iowa and the Dakotas. In northern Minnesota, they hunted deer and moose, grew corn, beans, squash, pumpkins and tobacco, and gathered wild rice and maple sugar. They lived in bark-covered summer houses and small, snug, mat-covered winter houses. They navigated the many lakes and streams of northern Minnesota with birchbark canoes and dugouts.

With the move to the Plains, hunting of buffalo became all important, though the Yankton also hunted deer, elk and antelope. They also grew some corn, squash and beans in the bottom lands along the rivers and gathered fruits and berries. With the acquisition of horses, they ranged far and wide in search of the buffalo. They adopted many cultural aspects from the older Plains dwellers, including translucent skin tipis, round bullboats and dog travois.

The Yankton worshipped Wakan Tanka, the Great Spirit, and celebrated the Sun Dance. As Plains dwellers, they placed their dead wrapped in skins on high scaffolds along with their weapons and personal effects. Sometimes they used ground burials, surrounding the grave with a thick hedge of stakes and brushwood. Mourners daubed white clay on their faces, cut their hair and affected a disheveled appearance.

The Yankton and Yanktonai were originally one tribe, living in northern Minnesota in the early 17th century. In the 1680s, they were located near Leech Lake. About this time, the two tribes separated. By the early 1700s, the Yankton were living near the pipestone quarries of southwestern Minnesota. Shortly thereafter, they moved south to the east bank of the Missouri River, in northwestern Iowa.

In the early 19th century, they occupied this same area, while roving west to the James River in South Dakota and north into Minnesota. Between 1816 and 1825, they ranged up the Missouri, trading with the Americans at Fort Lookout, South Dakota.

In the 1830s, a decline began for the Yankton, as smallpox, the growing scarcity of game, and war with the Pawnee, Oto and Omaha took their toll. In treaties of 1830 and 1837, they ceded their Iowa lands to the United States. By 1860, the Yankton had ceded all their remaining lands, and most had moved to the Yankton Reservation on the Missouri River in southern South Dakota. Other Yankton were removed to the Crow Creek and Lower Brulé reservations in South Dakota and to Fort Totten in North Dakota.

In the late 1970s, Yankton and Yanktonai were intermingled with other Dakota, with the Yankton population being estimated at several thousand.

BIBLIOGRAPHY: Woolworth, Alan R. *Ethnohistorical Report on the Yankton Sioux.* New York: Garland Publishing, Inc. 1974.

YANKTONAI: one of the seven main divisions of the Dakota. In the early 17th century, they lived in northern Minnesota, and then migrated south and west, reaching the Plains by the early 18th century. The Yanktonai population was about 6,000 by the mid-19th century. In the late 1970s, most Yantonai lived on or near reservations in North and South Dakota and Montana, and numbered about 5,000.

The Yanktonai, like the Yankton, spoke the Nakota dialect, which formed the Wiciyela or middle division of the Dakota language, a member of the Siouan language family. Their tribal name meant "little end village." They were composed of two divisions, the Upper Yanktonai, consisting of six bands, and the Lower Yanktonai, or Hunkpatina, consisting of seven bands. Bands were subdivided into patrilineal clans. The chief governing body of the band was the band council, consisting of the hereditary band chief and leaders of the various clans.

Yanktonai material culture underwent drastic change as the tribe moved from the woodlands of northern Minnesota to the prairies of southwestern Minnesota, and from there to the Plains of Iowa and the Dakotas. In northern Minnesota, like the Yankton, they hunted deer and moose, grew corn, beans, squash, pumpkins and tobacco, and gathered wild rice and maple sugar. They lived in bark-covered summer dwellings and small mat-covered winter houses. They travelled the waterways of northern Minnesota in birchbark canoes and dugouts.

Once on the Plains, hunting buffalo became of prime importance, though deer, elk and antelope were also hunted. With the acquisition of horses, the hunters were able to range far afield. Agriculture was also practiced, with corn, beans, and squash being grown in the bottomlands along the rivers. Fruits and berries were also gathered.

They adopted many of the ways of the older Plains tribes, including the building of earth lodges, which they copied from the Arikara. The Yanktonai also made ceremonial lodges for special occasions by combining several skin tipis. They also adopted the use of bull boats and dog travois, as well as scaffold burial.

The Yankton and Yanktonai were originally one tribe, living in northern Minnesota in the early 17th century. The Assiniboin, who were originally part of the Yanktonai, probably separated from them in the early 1600s. The Yankton and the Yanktonai (the latter probably being the parent tribe) separated in about the 1680s.

As the various Dakota tribes moved westward from their Minnesota homes, the Yanktonai and Yankton occupied territory between the Teton Dakota, who ranged furthest west, and the Santee Dakota, who remained in Minnesota until the 1860s. Probably by the early 18th cent-

**Mad Bear,
a Yankton
Sioux.**
The National Archives

ury, the Yanktonai left their Mille Lacs, Minnesota, homes and followed the Teton tribes west. By the early 19th century, the Yanktonai were ranging in their buffalo hunts from the Red River, west to the Missouri River, and north to Devil's Lake in the Dakotas. Their trading ground was along the Jones River, where they obtained British trade goods from the Sisseton and Wahpekute Dakota, to trade with the Teton tribes further west.

In 1856-57, the Yanktonai experienced a severe smallpox epidemic. By an 1865 treaty, the Yanktonai ceded their lands to the United States and were sent to a number of reservations. The Upper Yanktonai went to Standing Rock and Devil's Lake reservations in the Dakotas, while the Lower Yanktonai were divided among Standing Rock, Crow Creek (South Dakota), and Fort Peck (Montana) reservations.

In the late 1970s, Yanktonai and Yankton were intermingled with other Dakota. The Yanktonai population was estimated to number about 5,000.

BIBLIOGRAPHY: Hodge, Frederick Webb. "Handbook of American Indians North of Mexico." *Bureau of American Ethnology Bulletin.* no. 30, 1907-12.

YAQUINA: *See* ALSEA.

YAVAPAI: a nomadic hunting and gathering tribe ranging over a vast area of western Arizona in the late 17th century, numbering about 1,200 at that time. In the late 1970s, there were an unknown number of Yavapai mixed with other tribes on four Arizona reservations.

The name Yavapai has been variously translated as "people of the sun" or "crooked mouth people." They were also known as the Mohave Apache, or Apache Mohave, because they occasionally raided with Western Apache groups. The Yavapai spoke a Yuman language of the Hokan language family, closely related to that of their close cultural relatives, the Walapai and Havasupai.

The Yavapai were divided into three subtribes—Southeastern, Northeastern and Western—each of which were further subdivided into local bands. There were no tribal, subtribal or band chiefs, although each band recognized a head man who had distinguished himself in war. The head man did not rule, but rather, advised and exhorted his people. The Southeastern Yavapai differed from the other two subtribes in certain customs adopted from the Western Apache, including matrilineal clans, masked dances and the mother-in-law taboo.

Religious leadership was provided by shamans, who were initiated in ceremonies which included the making of sand paintings. They specialized in feats such as curing, caring for snake bite or arrow wounds, controlling weather or assuring a successful hunt. Curing techniques included singing, smoking tobacco and sucking out bad blood from an incision made with a sharp stone. The Yavapai cremated their dead and burned the house and possessions of the deceased. The Southeastern Yavapai cremated their dead inside their houses. Widows and widowers cut their hair, and the name of the deceased was never spoken again.

The Yavapai lived in caves, rock shelters and domed pole-frame huts covered with thatch or juniper bark and a layer of earth. Sunshades and earth-covered sweat lodges were also constructed.

The Yavapai relied mainly on hunting and gathering, although the Western band grew a little corn along the lower Colorado river. All three bands migrated seasonally, following the ripening of the various wild plant foods. Mescal, a sweet, nutritious food made by roasting agave hearts in underground pits for two days, was the staple. The women also gathered saguaro fruit, acorns, sunflower seeds, mesquite, manzanita berries, juniper berries, lemon berries, hackberries, elderberries, wild grapes, pine nuts, walnuts and camas. The available food supply varied with the season and the location. The men hunted deer using deerhead masks and rabbits in communal drives, as well as antelope, mountain

Yavapai Indians, a photograph taken possibly at Fort Apache, in about 1880-1900.

Smithsonian Institution National Anthropological Archives

lion and turkeys. Meat was dried and stored in skin bags.

The Yavapai women made a plain pottery and an assortment of basketry items, including seed beaters, winnowing and parching trays, burden baskets, cradle board hoods and pitch-coated water jars. The men dressed skins and made garments, including two-piece aprons for women and breechclouts, leggings and tunics for men. Moccasin boots and mittens were also made. For adornment, men and women used face painting and tattooing, and warriors had their noses pierced.

The Yavapai were inveterate warriors, making regular raids on the Walapai, Havasupai, Pima and Maricopa. For weapons the Yavapai used clubs, hide shields, mulberry bows and cane arrows with obsidian points.

In the late 16th century, Spanish expeditions began venturing into Yavapai territory, but contact was minimal until the mid-19th century. At that time, the Yavapai ranged the Rio Verde valley and the Black Mesa from Salt River to Bill Williams Mountain in western Arizona. In 1873, about 1,000 Yavapai were removed to the Rio Verde Agency, only to be moved again in 1875 to San Carlos Agency. By 1900, most of the tribe had drifted back to the Rio Verde area, and in 1901, Camp McDowell was assigned to their use. They suffered through a serious tuberculosis epidemic in 1905.

In the late 1970s, there were Yavapai mixed with Mohave and Apache on Camp Verde, Fort McDowell, Payson and Yavapai reservations. Farming, livestock raising and wage work were the main sources of income.

BIBLIOGRAPHY: Gifford, E.W. "The Southeastern Yavapai." *University of California Publications in American Archeology and Ethnology.* vol. 29, 1932; Gifford, E.W. "Northeastern and Western Yavapai." *University of California Publications in American Archaeology and Ethnology.* vol. 34, 1936.

YAZOO: *See* TUNICA.

YELLOWKNIFE: *See* CHIPEWYAN.

YOKUTS: a large California group occupying the San Joaquin Valley and the western foothills of the Sierra Nevada, between the Fresno and Kern rivers. Estimates of the total population of the 50 or so Yokuts tribes prior to European contact range from 18,000 to nearly 50,000. In the late 1970s, probably less than 1,000 Yokuts descendants remained, some living on reservations, but most scattered among the central California population.

The numerous dialects of the Yokuts language belong to the California Penutian language family. The three geographical divisions of the Yokuts included the Northern Valley Yokuts, the Southern Valley Yokuts and the Foothill Yokuts. The 50 Yokuts tribes each had its own name, dialect and territory, thus distinguishing the Yokuts from other California Indian groups. The name Yokuts is from a term in several of the Yokuts dialects meaning "people".

The various Yokuts tribes were usually led by one or more hereditary chiefs. The chief, who was usually wealthy, was obligated to sponsor ceremonies, host guests and aid the poor.

Shamans were important in all three Yokuts regions, their powers either derived from vision quests or unsolicited dreams. Besides using their supernatural powers to cure the sick, they presided at most public rituals and ceremonies.

Both cremation and burial were practiced by the Yokuts, with the latter more common in later times. Both private and public mourning ceremonies were held. At a public mourning ceremony, held at the end of the mourning period, the mourners were washed and given new clothes, and a feast was held.

Types of houses varied with the region. The Southern Valley Yokuts made both single-family oval-shaped houses and large ten-family dwellings, in which each family had its own door and fireplace. Both styles were of a pole framework covered with tule mats. Northern Valley Yokuts made a similar single-family dwelling, while the Foothill Yokuts used a conical hut thatched with grass or bark slabs. Other structures in a typical village included granaries, sweathouses and sunshades.

The economy of the Yokuts varied somewhat according to the region, with fishing, plant gathering and hunting important in all three regions. The Southern Valley Yokuts fished for lake trout, salmon, perch and other fish, using nets, basket traps or spears, from scaffolds built out from the river banks. Wild fowl, mussels, seeds and tule roots were also important. The Northern Valley Yokuts were better supplied with salmon and acorns and these were their staples, supplemented by pine nuts, manzanita berries, tule roots, perch and sturgeon. They also hunted deer, rabbits, quail, ducks and squirrels.

In all three areas, the Yokuts made a wide assortment of basketry, both by twining and coiling, including waterbottles, seedbeaters, conical burden baskets,cooking vessels, flat winnowing trays, cradles and caps. Canoes were made of tule rushes lashed together, and cordage was made from milkweed fiber.

Clothing was minimal for the Yokuts, the men wearing skin breechclouts and the women aprons of skin, grass or tule. In cold weather, rabbitskin blankets were used for clothing as well as for bedding. Chin tattooing was common among the women, and ears and noses were frequently pierced for attaching ornaments.

In the early 19th century, many Northern Valley Yokuts were drawn into the Spanish mission system, but the Southern Valley Yokuts and Foothill Yokuts were protected by their relative inaccessibility. In 1833, an epidemic killed 75 percent of the Indians in the valley. During the gold rush after 1849, the Indians were forcibly moved from their lands and murdered by the hundreds. In 1873, the Tule River Reservation was established, and in 1921 the Santa Rosa Rancheria.

In the late 1970s, there were about 325 Yokuts descendants living on or near the Tule River Reservation in Tuolumne County. The men were mainly employed in lumbering, ranch work or farm work. Some Yokuts dialects were spoken, and an Acorn Festival was held each September.

More than 100 Tachi Yokuts were located on the Santa Rosa Rancheria in Kings County, where a few of the older people still spoke Yokuts dialects. Several hundred other Yokuts descendants were scattered among the central California populace.

BIBLIOGRAPHY: Latta, F.F. *Handbook of the Yokuts Indians.* Bakersfield, California: Kern County Museum, 1949.

YUCHI: an extinct agricultural and hunting tribe living in eastern Tennessee and northern Georgia at the time of the 1539 DeSoto expedition to this region. They consisted of a number of distinct bands,

Timpooche
Barnard,
a Yuchi Indian:
from a lithograph
in McKenny
and Hall's
*Indian Tribes
of North
America,*
(1836-44).
Smithsonian Institution
National
Anthropological
Archives

each with its own name. There were probably about 2,500 Yuchi by the mid-17th century, speaking a Siouan language, sometimes referred to as Uchean. Their name may have meant "from far away".

They reportedly described themselves as "children of the sun from far away" when some of them moved southward through Georgia to live among the Creek Indians in the 17th and 18th centuries. Others remained in the Appalachian area and settled among the Cherokee.

As with many tribes of this area, they worshipped the sun as the chief source of life and power. The corn harvest festival, a religious occasion lasting three days and two nights, included dancing, offerings, the ceremony of the new fire and scarification of males. Marked by a ceremonial stickball game, the partaking of the first green corn was another religious festival, during which young males were admitted to the ranks of manhood.

The creation myth of the Yuchi tells of a giant crawfish who brought up mud from below a watery world to form the earth. They felt a newborn infant was still connected with the spirit world from whence he came. Therefore, not until the fourth day would a baby be named, usually for a grand-uncle or grand-aunt.

Disease was said to be caused by an evil spirit sent by some offended animal spirit. The usual cure was for a shaman to brew a mixture of herbs for the sick person to drink, accompanied by prescribed songs and chants by the shaman. The Yuchi believed a person had four souls, only one of which would pass to a future life. It was necessary for this soul to pass an obstacle at the entrance to the sky; if not it would return to earth to harass the living.

The men hunted using blow guns, clubs, bow and arrow and dogs. Fishing was sometimes done by poisoning a stream to stun the fish. Although hunting was important to the Yuchi, corn was the favorite staple food. A soup was made of ground corn meal boiled with powdered hickory nuts, meat or marrow and a little wood ash for flavor. A milky beverage was made by boiling ground-up hickory nuts.

The Yuchi settled near streams, grouping their houses around a central square where religious and social occasions were celebrated. The houses were covered with bark or woven mats or sometimes clay. Their highly developed pottery included animal effigy pipes as well as incised and decorated bowls. They made wooden ware as well as fine basketry of cane and split hickory.

The Yuchi bands were essentially dispersed by the mid-19th century, some settling with the Cherokee, some among the Upper Creek and others joining the Seminole in Florida. Many of these, following the removal of the Indians to the West, settled in Indian Territory (now Oklahoma) along with their adopted tribes. In the late 1970s, the Yuchi were extinct as a tribe.

BIBLIOGRAPHY: Speck, Frank G. *Ethnology of the Yuchi Indians,* University of Pennsylvania Museum *Anthropological Publications.* vol. 1, 1909.

YUKI: a northwestern California group located in the upper Eel River valley in the mid-19th century, when they numbered about 6,800. In the late 1970s, Yuki descendants were mixed with other California tribes on the Round Valley Reservation in Mendocino County, California.

The tribal name was a Wintu term meaning "enemy". The Yuki and Wappo languages composed the Yukian language family. Yuki dialects were also spoken by two closely related groups, the Huchnom and Coast Yuki. The Yuki language was nearly extinct in the late 1970s.

The Yuki had six main divisions, each subdivided into tribelets. Tribelets, composed of several small villages, were each led by an elected chief and a war chief. Religious leadership and health care were provided by two types of doctors: shamans, who cured through powers received through a vision or other supernatural happening, and other doctors, who learned the trade as apprentices to older healers.

The Yuki believed in a supreme creator god, Taikomol ("he who walks alone"), as well as numerous other spirits. Their principal religious ceremonies were related to the training of young men for adult life. The Yuki buried their dead wrapped in skins, in a flexed position with head pointing east. Female mourners cut their hair and covered their head and face with pitch. As the soul of the deceased departed for the hereafter,

A Yuki woman pounding fish, (about 1889-95).

Smithsonian Institution
National
Anthropological
Archives

his property was buried or burned, and his name never spoken again.

The Yuki built conical winter houses, about ten feet in diameter, of pole framework covered with bark. Summer houses were made of brush. They also constructed a combination dance house and sweathouse, similar to the winter dwelling.

Staple foods included acorns, salmon and venison. Deer were stalked, usually by a hunter wearing a deerhead costume. The men took salmon and trout with nets, traps and spears, while women gathered acorns, seeds, nuts, roots, berries, grasshoppers, mushrooms, honey and birds' eggs.

Before the mid-19th century, the Yuki, allied with the Wailaki, engaged in warfare against the Pomo and Nomlaki. The arrival of white settlers in their territory was a disaster to the Yuki, whose population reportedly dropped from 6,800 to 300 between 1850 and 1864. Those who were not exterminated by white ranchers moved to the Round Valley Reservation, where they subsisted by hunting, gathering and some farming. In the late 1970s, the population of the reservation included about 350 Yuki, Wailaki, Nomlaki and Pomo Indians.

BIBLIOGRAPHY: Foster, George M. "A Summary of Yuki Culture." *Universtiy of California Anthropological Records.* vol. 5, 1944.

YUMA: a Yuman tribe located on both banks of the Colorado River, near its junction with the Gila River, in the early 17th century, numbering about 4,000 at that time. In the late 1970s, there were more than 2,000 Yuma, of which about 1,300 lived on the Fort Yuma

Reservation in Arizona and California. They were also known as Quechan, from Kwatcan, their name for themselves. They spoke a language of the Yuman division of the Hokan linguistic family. The tribal leader of the Yuma was the *kwoxot,* a man recognized for his ability, personal appeal and generosity. The position was not hereditary, although leaders tended to come from certain more powerful families. The *kwoxot* gave feasts, took care of the poor, safeguarded captives and served as rainmaker and scalp custodian. There was also a war leader, or *kwanami,* and a funeral orator. All of these officials, as well as shamans, achieved their power through dreaming.

The Yuma were geographically divided into a number of distinct bands. Each band had a number of villages, each governed by its own leading men. Socially, the Yuma were divided into clans, with each person inheriting the clan of his father. Marriage was forbidden within one's own clan.

Shamans specialized in certain supernatural powers, such as curing illness, treating snakebite, arrow wounds or fractures, dealing with witchcraft or ghosts, or controlling weather. Important ceremonies included the four-day girl's puberty rites, after which the girl's chin was tattooed. At about age seven, boys endured a nose-piercing ceremony, which also included fasting and footracing. The mesquite harvest feast in June and the crop harvest feast in autumn were also important ceremonies. Both celebrations included games, contests, gambling and songs accompanied by flutes and gourd and deer hoof rattles.

An annual four-day mourning ceremony, the *keruk,* honored those who had died during the year. The Yuma cremated their dead after a day of mourning. The house and possessions, of the deceased were burned and his horse killed. Souls of the deceased were believed to pass through four levels, finally arriving at the land of the dead, where food was plentiful and everyone was happy.

The Yuma formed scattered settlements near arable land. In summer, they lived in rectangular, open shelters of pole framework covered with arrow weed. In cold weather, everyone crowded into a few enclosed semisubterranean houses covered over with a layer of sand. They also built semi-circular roofless sunshades for work or cooking areas. A woven cylindrical granary, several feet high, was used for storage.

Agriculture was the mainstay of the economy. The Yuma used the natural flooding of the river to irrigate their fields, planting seed with a dibble stick when the waters receded. They used their knowledge of the position of certain stars and constellations to predict the river's flooding. They planted a fast-maturing corn, as well as squash, beans, pumpkins and, later, melons.

Second in importance to the economy was the gathering of wild foods, especially mesquite beans, screw beans, ironwood nuts and sage brush

A Yuma Indian decorates pottery: Colorado Indian Agency, Parker, Arizona, (1940).

seeds. Seeds and corn were parched in trays with hot coals before being ground to meal or flour on stone metates. Squash and pumpkins were cut in strips to dry. Game was scarce, but the men occasionally took deer, rabbits or wild fowl. More important than hunting was fishing, with nets, traps, and bows and arrows.

The women made pottery bowls, dippers and cooking pots, as well as coiled basketry trays and storage containers. They also used nets attached to headbands to carry things on their backs. Women wore a two-piece willow bark skirt complete with bustle, whereas men wore buckskin or bark breechclouts or less. Sandals were made of deerskin, and robes were of rabbitskin.

The Yuma used rafts of cottonwood logs or tule reeds for river travel. They were excellent swimmers, and often swam across rivers, floating babies and other valuables in large pottery jars. By the late 18th century, the Yuma had acquired a few horses, but they considered it unsportsmanlike to use them in warfare.

They were inveterate warriors, usually fighting the Maricopa and Pima. Yuma weapons included mesquite bows, clubs, stone knives, circular hide shields and spears made by sharpening and fire-hardening long sticks.

By the early 18th century, the Yuma began coming into contact with Spanish expeditions, but with little impact on their culture or way of life. The California gold rush of 1849, however, brought fortune-seekers streaming through Yuma lands. The Yuma resistance to this incursion was ended by U.S. troops in 1852. In the last big fight between the various Colorado River tribes, the Yuma and Mohave were defeated by the Pima and Maricopa in 1857. The Fort Yuma Reservation was established in the center of the traditional territory in about 1883.

By the late 1970s, most of the remaining 9,000 acres of their reservation were located in California. Materially the Yuma (or Quechan) were largely acculturated, but they retained a surprising amount of their traditional ceremonial and religious life. Farming was still the basis of the tribal economy.

BIBLIOGRAPHY: Forbes, Jack D. *Warriors of the Colorado.* Norman: University of Oklahoma Press, 1965. Forde, C. Daryll. "Ethnography of the Yuma Indians." *University of California Publications in American Archaeology and Anthropology.* vol. 28, 1931.

YUROK: a northwest California group living along the Pacific coast and lower Klamath River in the early 19th century, numbering about 3,000 at that time. In the late 1970s, there were between 3,000 and 4,000 Yurok descendants, living mostly in California. Yurok was a term in the Karok language meaning "down river," but they referred to themselves as Olekwo'l, or "persons." Their language probably belongs to the Algonquian language family.

The Yurok lived in villages, usually under the leadership of the wealthiest man. About ten percent of the male population made up the aristocratic class of individuals known as *peyerk*, or "real men." The *peyerk* underwent special training and sought a vision either on a mountain retreat or while accomplishing a swimming feat. The aristocracy (*peyerk* and their wives and children) spoke in a more elaborate style than commoners, lived at higher elevations and acquired treasured heirlooms such as albino deerskins, large obsidian knives and costumes heavily decorated with shells and seeds. The *peyerk* of a district occasionally gathered in council to arbitrate disputes, which were usually settled by a payment of compensation to an injured party.

The Yurok believed in a creator known as Wohpekumeu and in the trickster hero Coyote. Ceremonies and dances were numerous and included the Jumping Dance, Deerskin Dance and Brush Dance.

A Yurok in a canoe on the Trinity River, northern California.

Ceremonial regalia for the Jumping Dance included headdresses containing some 70 redheaded woodpecker scalps. Curing was usually performed by women doctors, by the use of prayer and by eliciting confessions of wrongdoing by the sick person or his relatives.

When a Yurok died, his body was removed from his house through the roof and buried in a family plot. The spouse of the deceased guarded the grave against sorcerers for several nights, until the person's soul had departed for the afterlife. The family of the deceased wore necklaces of braided grass until they fell off.

The Yurok lived in houses of redwood planks with gabled roofs, except when away gathering acorns or drying salmon, when they used temporary brush shelters. Salmon and acorns were the staple foods of the Yurok living along the river while the coastal group depended more on fish and shellfish. To supplement the diet, sea lions, elk, deer and small game were hunted, and various roots and seeds were gathered. Rights to certain acorn groves, fishing places, hunting grounds, stands of redwood, tobacco plots and other resources could be owned by individuals, families or villages.

Yurok crafts included the weaving of basketry bowls, hats and storage containers as well as the making of clothing of dressed skins and furs. They also made square-ended redwood canoes, which were used on both the swift-flowing river and the ocean. These they traded to the Karok and other neighboring tribes.

The Yurok were peaceful people, engaging only occasionally in feuds among themselves or with neighboring tribes. They remained virtually isolated from European contact until the California gold rush era, when some Yurok were employed as laborers at the mining camps that sprang up in the area.

In the late 1970s, the Yurok language was still spoken, and some of the traditional ceremonies were still performed. There was a revival of interest in tribal culture and crafts, such as basketweaving and wood-working. Less than 200 of the several thousand Yurok descendants lived on the Trinidad Rancheria and Hoopa Extension Reservation, both in Humboldt County, California. Most of the other Yurok lived in the surrounding area which was part of their traditional territory.

BIBLIOGRAPHY: Kroeber, A.L. Handbook of the Indians of California. *Bureau of American Ethnology Bulletin,* no. 78, 1925.

ZIA: a small Keresan tribe and pueblo on the north bank of the Jemez River, 16 miles northwest of Bernadillo, New Mexico. In 1970, the population of the tribe was about 600. The Zia, also spelled Sia, spoke a dialect of the Keresan language family. Their tribal name derives from *tsia,* a native game. The tribe was organized into 36 clans and culturally resembled the other Keresan tribes, which included Acoma, Laguna, Cochiti, Santo Domingo, San Felipe and Santa Ana (*q.q.v.*).

The pueblo was established in about 1300, when the tribe migrated from a site further up the Jemez River. First contact with Europeans was probably with the Spanish explorer Castañeda in 1541, followed by Espejo in 1583. They participated in the Pueblo Revolt against the Spanish in 1680, and in 1687, the village was the scene of the most bloody battle in that revolt. The town was destroyed; 600 Zia were killed, and 70 were taken into slavery. In 1689, they were granted the right to their land by Spain, and in 1692, they allied with the Spanish to rebuild the pueblo, incurring the wrath of the other pueblos. In the same year, a Spanish Catholic mission was established.

In 1858, the United States confirmed their original land grant from Spain. In 1863, President Lincoln presented them with a pair of ebony canes, which were subsequently used by chiefs as symbols of authority.

In the 1970s, about 600 Zia lived on the 112,500-acre reservation, governed by a tribal council. Many traditional activities were still practiced, and an annual festival was celebrated each August 15th. Both the old religion and Catholicism were important in the life of the pueblo.

ZUÑI: the largest Pueblo tribe, located 40 miles southwest of Gallup, New Mexico, with a population of more than 6,000 in the late 1970s. The Zuñi occupied six pueblos in the same area when visited in 1540 by a Spanish expedition led by Coronado, who gave an exaggerated population estimate of 10,000. The Zuñi, who called themselves Ashiwi, or "the flesh," spoke the Zuñi language, which comprises its own Zuñian language family.

The Zuñi were organized into clans, with each person inheriting the clan of his mother and forbidden to marry within the clan. There was also condemnation of marriage within one's father's clan. Residence was matrilocal, a newly-married couple going to live with the woman's family. Each clan was made up of one or more extended families, consisting of a woman and her husband, their daughters and daughters' husbands and unmarried children or grandchildren. Houses, and often fields, were owned by the women, and inherited through the female line.

Zuñi was a theocracy, ruled by a council made up of the heads of the various priesthoods and societies, who governed the pueblo in all traditional and religious matters. Mundane problems were handled by a secular government—a tribal council composed of a governor, lieutenant governor and eight assistants—who were appointed by the religious leaders and were responsible to them. These secular officials acted as a liaison between the pueblo and the outside world, and also kept order and arbitrated disputes within the pueblo.

The Zuñi developed a complex social structure intertwined with a rich ceremonial life. Each clan had certain annual ceremonies for which it was responsible, and acted as guardian of sacred fetishes and ceremonial paraphernalia. There were also a number of secret cults and societies, each with responsibility for particular ceremonies. Some cults were extremely complex, such as the Uwanami, or "rainmakers," which had 12 priesthoods.

All adult Zuñi males belonged to the *katcina* cult, into which they were initiated between the ages of 11 and 14. The cult was divided into six *kivas*, or ceremonial centers, representing the six directions: above, below, north, south, east, and west. A boy joined the *kiva* of his ceremonial father, who sponsored and attended him through the initiation. Members of the *katcina* society performed masked rain dances, in which they impersonated the *katcina*, spirits associated with rain gods and Zuñi ancestors. One of the most important Zuñi ceremonies was the Winter Solstice, or Shalako, a rite performed by the priests of the *katcina* society in November or December. The Shalako, couriers of the rain gods, wearing fantastic 12-foot high masks, came to bless the pueblo for the coming year.

The Zuñi formerly cremated their dead, but later changed to burials. After four days, the possessions of the deceased were burned or buried,

Zuñi dwellings, (1879).

The National Archives

prayersticks and sacred corn meal were offered, and purification rites were performed by the family.

The Zuñi, when first visited by the Spanish, occupied six pueblos in the Zuñi River valley. By the end of the 17th century, they were consolidated into one town, Halona, composed of five-story, terraced apartment buildings of stone and adobe. Ladders, which could be pulled up in time of danger, led to the upper stories, and the ground floor was entered through a hatchway in the roof. The buildings were plastered with adobe inside and out and whitewashed inside. Roofs were made of willow boughs and brush packed with earth, and floors were of packed adobe. Men built the houses, and women did the plastering and other finishing touches. Tiny windows of translucent selenite, as well as dome-shaped beehive ovens for baking bread were introduced during Spanish times.

The Zuñi men grew at least six varieties of corn, as well as beans, squash and cotton, using diversion dams for irrigation and sagebrush windbreaks around the fields. Women tended small garden plots and gathered wild fruits, seeds and roots. Chilies, peaches and other foods were introduced by the Spanish. Corn was dried on the rooftops and ground into meal or flour, to be served as mush or baked into a variety of breads. To supplement the diet, the men hunted deer and antelope with bow and arrow, as well as rabbits, in communal drives, with throwing sticks.

The women made baskets of willow and yucca leaves as well as fine pottery. The men gathered water and wood, and wove cotton into

A plate decorated with the traditional Zuñi serpent pattern.

ceremonial costumes and kilts, as well as dresses and belts for the women. Women wore one-piece black dresses, belted at the waist with the left shoulder bare. Moccasins and knee-length deerskin leggings completed the costume.

The ancestors of the Zuñi probably came into the valley from both the north and south, bringing the attributes of both the ancient Mogollon and Anasazi cultures. By the early 11th century, the Village of the Great Kivas, 16 miles north of Zuñi, had been built. Drought in the late 13th century probably brought immigrants from the Chaco Canyon area. In the 14th and 15th century, there were a large number of villages in the Zuñi valley. By the mid-16th century, these had been reduced to six.

In 1539, part of a Spanish expedition in search of the fabled Seven Cities of Cibola reached Zuñi territory, where they were driven off. The Coronado expedition attacked the Zuñi town of Hawikuh the following year, but most of the Zuñi had fled to a nearby mesa top called Corn Mountain, or Thunder Mountain. Several more Spanish expeditions followed, and a mission was established at Hawikuh in 1629. The missionary was killed by the Zuñi in 1632, but a new mission was established at the Zuñi pueblo of Halona in 1643.

By 1680, the Zuñi, reduced to three villages, were tired of supplying the Spanish with corn, women and labor and of enduring harsh treatment for continuing to practice their traditional religion. They therefore joined in the general Pueblo Revolt of that year, burning the missions and driving out the Spanish. The Zuñi retreated to their Corn Mountain stronghold until the Spanish reconquest in 1693. At that time, the Zuñi consolidated themselves in one village built at Halona, where the Spanish reestablished a mission in 1699. After a Zuñi uprising in 1703, they retired once again to Corn Mountain until 1705. In 1877, a reservation was established on the original Spanish land grant of 1689.

In the late 1970s, more than 6,000 Zuñi occupied the 405,000-acre pueblo. Many of the people spent the summer months at the outlying farming settlements of Nutria, Pescado, Tekapo and Ojo Caliente, returning to the main pueblo after the harvest. Sheep-raising, farming, wage work and crafts were the major economic activities. The Zuñi were famous for their beautiful silver and turquoise jewelry, as well as pottery and beadwork. The ancient religion, so important in Zuñi life, was still practiced. A few of the ceremonies, such as the Shalako, were open to the public.

BIBLIOGRAPHY: Stevenson, Matilda Coxe. "The Zuñi Indians." *Bureau of American Ethnology Annual Report.* no. 23, 1901-02.

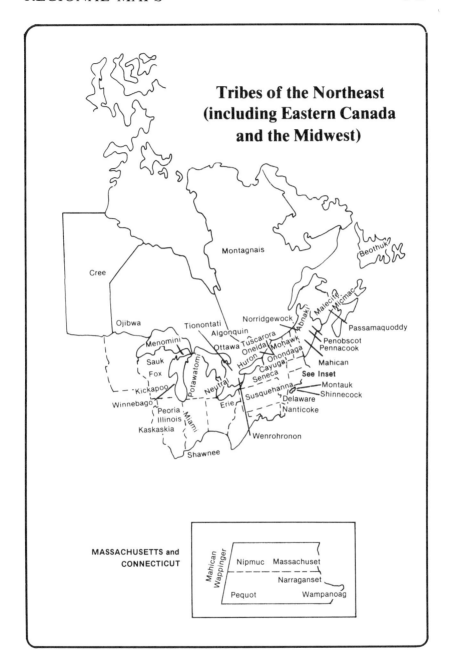

Tribes of the Northeast
(including Eastern Canada
and the Midwest)

Montagnais

Beothuk

Cree

Ojibwa

Tionontati

Norridgewock

Malecite

Micmac

Passamaquoddy

Algonquin

Menomini

Ottawa

Tuscarora

Oneida

Mohawk

Abnaki

Penobscot
Pennacook

Sauk

Huron

Onondaga

Mahican

Fox

Potawatomi

Cayuga

Seneca

See Inset

Kickapoo

Neutral

Susquehanna

Montauk
Shinnecock

Winnebago

Erie

Delaware

Peoria

Miami

Nanticoke

Illinois

Kaskaskia

Wenrohronon

Shawnee

MASSACHUSETTS and
CONNECTICUT

Mahican

Wappinger

Nipmuc   Massachuset

Narraganset

Pequot   Wampanoag

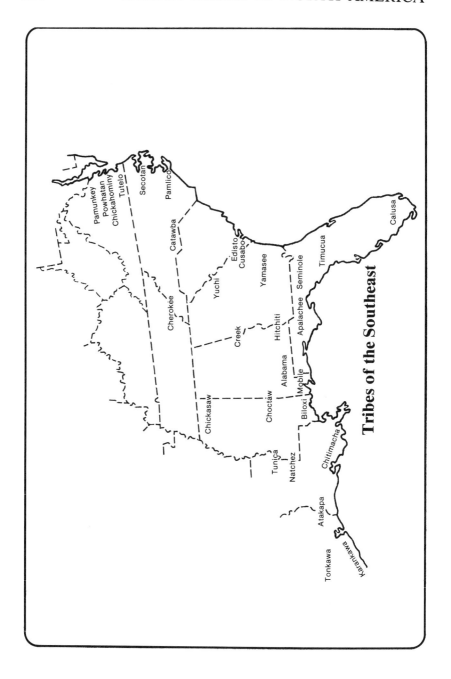

Tribes of the Southeast

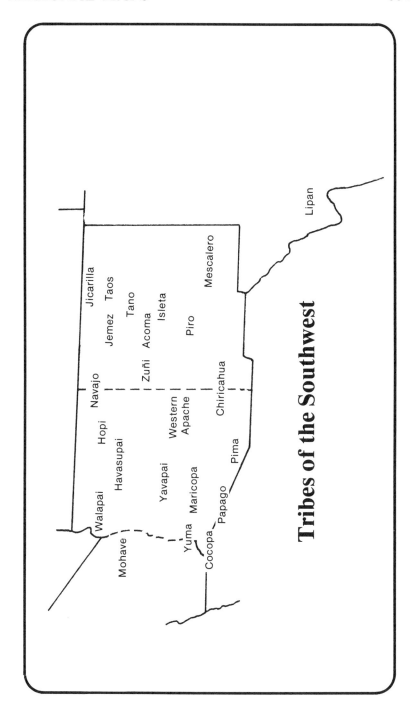

Tribes of the Southwest

Tribes of the Plateau, the Basin, and the Plains

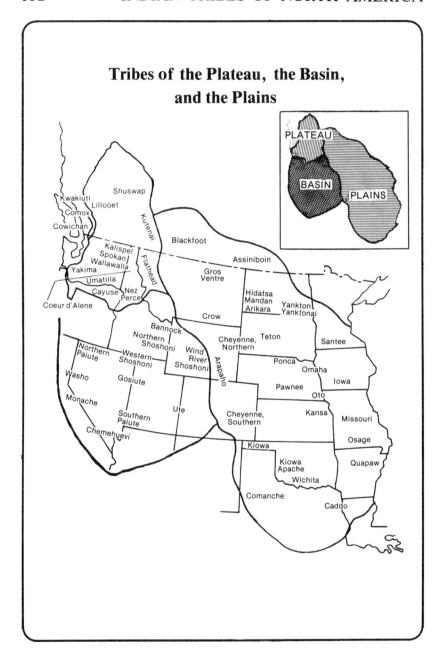

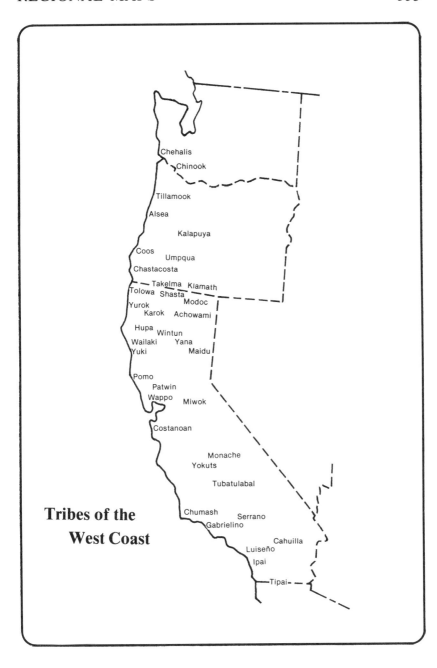

Tribes of the West Coast

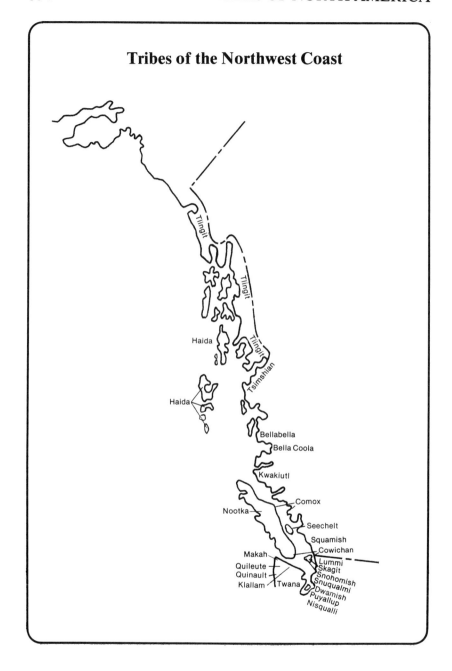

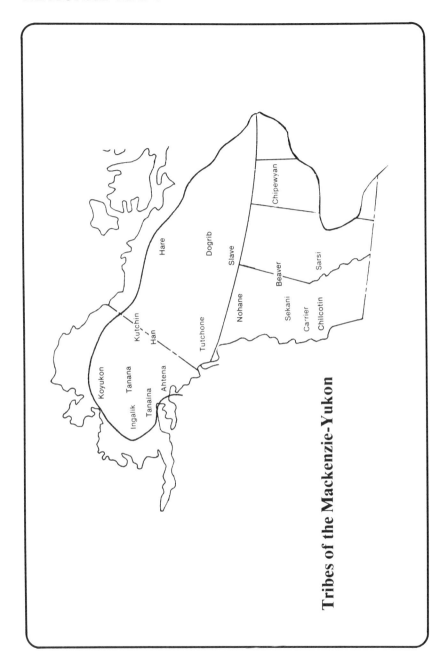

Tribes of the Mackenzie-Yukon

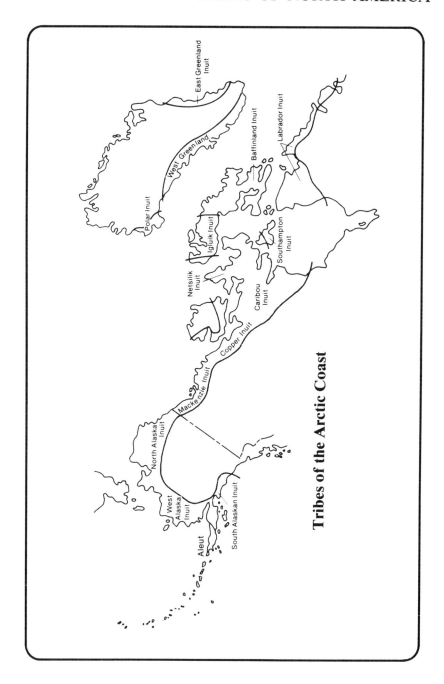

Tribes of the Arctic Coast

Glossary

AGAVE: a family of flowering plants with fleshy spiky leaves clustered at the base. One species, the Century plant, (*Agave americana*), is found in the southwest United States. Mescal (*see below*) is made from it, and its leaf fibers provide sisal.

BABICHE: a thong or thread, made from rawhide, sinew, or gut.

BULLBOAT: a shield-shaped receptacle, usually hide-covered, used to float babies, possessions, etc., across rivers or streams.

CAMAS: also called the wild hyacinth. Any plant of the *Quamasia* genus. The name especially refers to the bulbs, a standard food of some North West Coast tribes. The bulbs are steamed before being eaten.

CALUMET: a reed pipe or flute of particular symbolic or sacred significance, the smoking of which was a means of communicating with the spirit world.

CAYUSE: an Indian pony. It was given this name because many ponies were bred by the Cayuse tribe, who were renowned horse dealers.

CHUNKEY: a game played with stone discs and wooden poles, in the Southern region of the United States. Of ancient origin, it was played by tribes belonging to the Temple Mound culture.

DEADFALL: a trap so designed that a log or other heavy weight falls on the prey, killing or disabling it.

HOGAN: a Navajo dwelling, traditionally facing east, and built of logs and boughs, covered with earth, stones, and/or sod.

KATCINA: also "Kachina." A deified ancestral spirit of the Hopi.

KIVA: the Hopi name for the sacred ceremonial and assembly chamber among the Pueblo tribes. Situated underground, the *kiva*, which may be either round or square, is entered from the roof by means of a ladder.

MESCAL: a food made from the roasted leaf base and trunk of the agave.

MESQUITE: a spiny tree or shrub whose pods yield the mesquite bean.

OLLA: a large globular earthenware jar, having a wide mouth and looped handles. Its is found in use in the Southwestern United States area.

PEMMICAN: a concentrated food made from dried and pounded meat.

POTLATCH: a ceremonial feast of the North West Coast tribes, characterized by the distribution of gifts or the destruction of possessions for the purpose of enhancing status by a display of wealth.

SACHEM: originally the supreme chief of an Algonquin confederation, but later, by extension, a title given to the chiefs of certain neighboring tribes.

SAGAMORE: the Abnaki name for an elected chief. The name was later applied to lesser sachems among the Massachuset Indians.

SOFKEE: a thin sour gruel, prepared from corn by Creek and other tribes.

SUCCOTASH: a dish made of green corn, and string or lima beans, boiled with milk, butter, etc. The name derives from the Narraganset word for an ear of corn.

TULE: either of two species of large bullrushes, found in California, the southwest United States, and Mexico.

WICKIUP: a temporary shelter made from a rough frame covered with reed mats, grasses, or brushwood.

Index

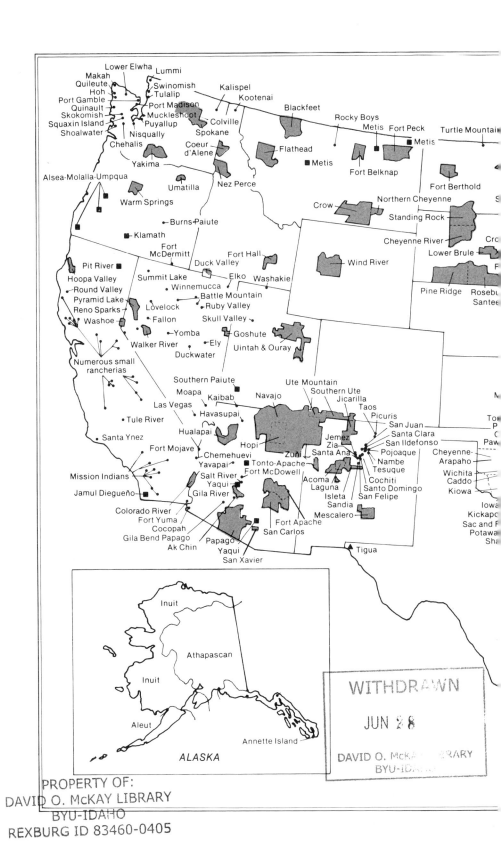

Lower Elwha
Makah
Quileute
Hoh
Port Gamble
Quinault
Skokomish
Squaxin Island
Shoalwater
Chehalis
Lummi
Swinomish
Tulalip
Port Madison
Muckleshoot
Puyallup
Nisqually
Kalispel
Kootenai
Colville
Spokane
Coeur d'Alene
Yakima
Blackfeet
Rocky Boys
Metis
Fort Peck
Metis
Turtle Mountain
Flathead
Metis
Fort Belknap
Fort Berthold
Alsea-Molalla-Umpqua
Umatilla
Nez Perce
Warm Springs
Crow
Northern Cheyenne
Standing Rock
Cheyenne River
Burns-Paiute
Klamath
Fort McDermitt
Fort Hall
Duck Valley
Elko
Washakie
Wind River
Lower Brule
Pit River
Hoopa Valley
Round Valley
Pyramid Lake
Reno Sparks
Washoe
Summit Lake
Winnemucca
Battle Mountain
Ruby Valley
Lovelock
Fallon
Yomba
Walker River
Ely
Duckwater
Skull Valley
Goshute
Uintah & Ouray
Pine Ridge
Rosebud
Santee
Numerous small rancherias
Southern Paiute
Moapa
Las Vegas
Kaibab
Havasupai
Tule River
Santa Ynez
Hualapai
Fort Mojave
Chemehuevi
Yavapai
Mission Indians
Jamul Diegueño
Salt River
Yaqui
Gila River
Hopi
Navajo
Ute Mountain
Southern Ute
Jicarilla
Taos
Picuris
San Juan
Santa Clara
San Ildefonso
Pojoaque
Nambe
Tesuque
Cochiti
Santo Domingo
San Felipe
Zuñi
Jemez
Zia
Santa Ana
Acoma
Laguna
Isleta
Sandia
Mescalero
Tonto-Apache
Fort McDowell
Colorado River
Fort Yuma
Cocopah
Gila Bend Papago
Ak Chin
Papago
Yaqui
San Xavier
Fort Apache
San Carlos
Tigua
Cheyenne-Arapaho
Wichita
Caddo
Kiowa
Iowa
Kickapo
Sac and F
Potawa
Sha

Inuit
Athapascan
Inuit
Aleut
Annette Island
ALASKA